PENGUIN BOOKS

TOMBSTONE

'The fullest and most authoritative account ever published of the
Great Leap Forward . . . It is safe to say that you will never have read
a book like it . . . the author's personal and professional credentials
could not be bettered . . . Wise words from a courageous man'
George Walden, *Standpoint*

'Though a sense of deep anger imbues Yang Jisheng's book, it is all the more
powerful for its restraint . . . *Tombstone* meticulously demonstrates that
the famine was not only vast, but manmade; and not only manmade but
political, born of totalitarianism' Tania Branigan, *Guardian*

'*Tombstone* combines telling details with a rigorous historical
reconstruction from oral and written sources, all assembled to allow us
to understand how and why the famine occurred. The product
of a lifetime of devoted research, *Tombstone* is a monument'
James C. Scott, *London Review of Books*

'Casts new light on one of the darkest episodes in China's recent past'
Robert Bickers, *BBC History*

'A monumental account . . . the details are often new and fascinating
and will shock many contemporary Chinese readers who remain
largely ignorant of just how brutal and insane it was . . . Again and
again Yang records how officials feasted on the food they had
confiscated while peasants dropped dead from starvation outside
full granaries' Jasper Becker, *Spectator*

'A compelling account of the 40 million lives lost to Mao's regime
is a long overdue addition to the history books'
Gavin Bowd, *Scotland on Sunday*

Tombstone

The Untold Story of Mao's Great Famine

YANG JISHENG

Translated from the Chinese by Stacy Mosher and Guo Jian
Edited by Edward Friedman, Guo Jian and Stacy Mosher
Introduction by Edward Friedman and Roderick MacFarquhar

PENGUIN BOOKS

PENGUIN BOOKS

Published by the Penguin Group
Penguin Books Ltd, 80 Strand, London WC2R ORL, England
Penguin Group (USA) Inc., 375 Hudson Street, New York, New York 10014, USA
Penguin Group (Canada), 90 Eglinton Avenue East, Suite 700, Toronto, Ontario, Canada M4P 2Y3
(a division of Pearson Penguin Canada Inc.)
Penguin Ireland, 25 St Stephen's Green, Dublin 2, Ireland (a division of Penguin Books Ltd)
Penguin Group (Australia), 707 Collins Street, Melbourne, Victoria 3008, Australia
(a division of Pearson Australia Group Pty Ltd)
Penguin Books India Pvt Ltd, 11 Community Centre, Panchsheel Park, New Delhi – 110 017, India
Penguin Group (NZ), 67 Apollo Drive, Rosedale, Auckland 0632, New Zealand
(a division of Pearson New Zealand Ltd)
Penguin Books (South Africa) (Pty) Ltd, Block D, Rosebank Office Park,
181 Jan Smuts Avenue, Parktown North, Gauteng 2193, South Africa

Penguin Books Ltd, Registered Offices: 80 Strand, London WC2R ORL, England

www.penguin.com

Originally published in Chinese in a different format by Cosmos Books, Hong Kong 2008
English translation first published in the United States of America by Farrar, Straus and Giroux 2012
First published in Great Britain by Allen Lane 2012
Published in Penguin Books 2013

002

Copyright © Yang Jisheng, 2008
Translation copyright © Yang Jisheng, 2012
Introduction copyright © Edward Friedman and Roderick MacFarquhar, 2012
Map copyright © Jeffrey L. Ward, 2012

Printed in Great Britain by Clays Ltd, St Ives plc

ISBN: 978-0-241-95698-4

www.greenpenguin.co.uk

CONTENTS

	Map	*vii*
	Introduction by Edward Friedman and Roderick MacFarquhar	*ix*
	Translators' Note	*xiii*
	A Chronology of the Great Famine	*xv*
	An Everlasting Tombstone	3
1.	The Epicenter of the Disaster	23
2.	The Three Red Banners: Source of the Famine	87
3.	Hard Times in Gansu	112
4.	The People's Commune: Foundation of the Totalitarian System	156
5.	The Communal Kitchens	174
6.	Hungry Ghosts in Heaven's Pantry	197
7.	The Ravages of the Five Winds	248
8.	Anxious in Anhui	269
9.	The Food Crisis	320
10.	Turnaround in Lushan	350
11.	China's Population Loss in the Great Leap Forward	394
12.	The Official Response to the Crisis	431
13.	Social Stability During the Great Famine	465
14.	The Systemic Causes of the Great Famine	483
15.	The Great Famine's Impact on Chinese Politics	499
	Notes	*523*
	Bibliography	*577*
	Index	*611*

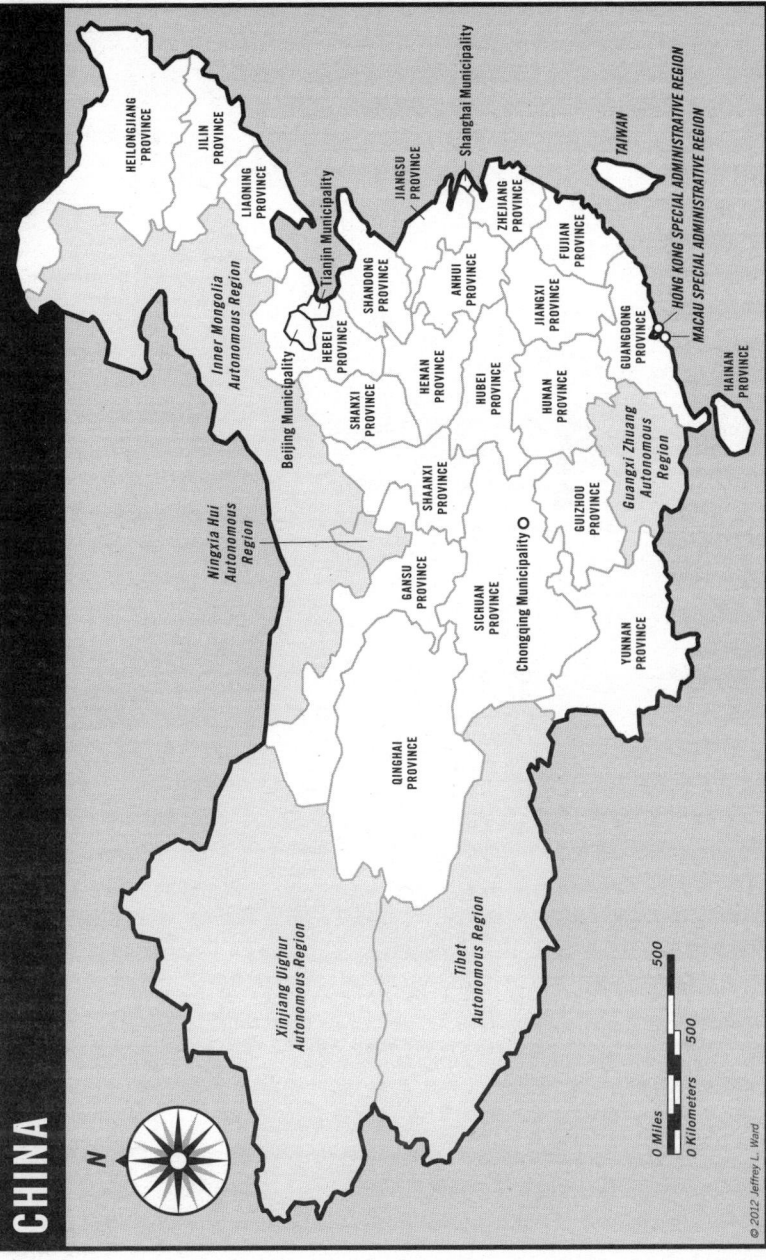

INTRODUCTION
by EDWARD FRIEDMAN and RODERICK MacFARQUHAR

Tombstone describes and analyzes the worst famine in human history, the disaster inflicted upon the Chinese people between 1958 and 1962. Author Yang Jisheng, a distinguished journalist by profession and an inspired investigator by avocation, wrote this book in part to expiate his shame for watching his father die of starvation in 1959 and not understanding the cause. At the time, Yang was loyally supporting the policies of the Great Leap Forward. Only thirty years later did he accept that the state system and Chinese Communist Party (CCP) policies were the direct cause of his father's death.

This book is about the murderous impact of the Great Leap policies and the CCP leaders who conceived them. Author Yang shows that the supreme leader, Mao Zedong, soon knew that his economically irrational policies were deadly. But Mao protected his power by reaffirming them against the few brave colleagues who questioned them. Had Mao continued to heed those criticisms, which he did briefly, the death toll would have been massively reduced.

Tombstone is about a hierarchical authoritarian system of concentrated power in which every official is, as Yang puts it, a slave facing upward and a dictator facing downward. At the bottom of the system were the Chinese people, mostly farm households, who suffered under the murderous brutality of the lower-level officials, proving an iron law of bureaucracy: the pettier the bureaucrat, the harsher his rule.

During the Great Leap Forward and its aftermath, CCP system harshness became murderousness: an incalculable number of Chinese chose to kill other Chinese. There *were* exceptions to that rule in famine-struck China, and Yang gives them their heroic due. For those officials, however, trying to save lives usually brought the end of their careers, often the loss of their freedom, and even the end of their lives.

Most of this book depicts the fate of the tens of millions of people like Yang's father who died during the famine. Yang's estimate is at least 36 million, somewhere between the 28 to 30 million estimated early on by demographers, the 42 to 43 million arrived at by an official fact-finding mission in the early 1980s, and the 45 million plus in one recent scholarly analysis.

All the estimates of the innocent dead are mind-boggling. It is the strength of Yang's investigation that makes the statistics come alive as people confront death by a system and its policies. He also exposes horrific survival choices: to keep one child alive by starving the others; to eat a recently dead relative or even to dig up a corpse from a grave; to desert one's family and flee to another province knowing this could lead the local CCP to kill one's family members; to protect oneself by informing on one's neighbors; to sell oneself to an official for a few scraps from his table (because, for officialdom, there was always plenty to eat). Yang helps us feel the anguish of immoral options.

What is extraordinary about the famine figures is not just their size but that, whichever figure is correct, this system, its leader, and his policies killed even more Chinese than did the brutal Imperial Japanese Army during the Sino-Japanese War of 1937–45. This is not an easy fact for patriotic Chinese to swallow.

The pathbreaking work of Nobel Prize–winning economist Amartya Sen has shown that famines are not necessarily the result of lack of food. But the argument that lack of information about shortages is often a cause does not apply in this case. While junior officials did falsify data to benefit their own careers, Mao had enough reports from senior colleagues to know that his policy of extracting an increasing percentage of grain from the countryside was causing millions of deaths. The lives of Chinese villagers in the tens of millions were sacrificed in the interest of other policy objectives, including Mao's own retention of power.

Yang's history builds on solid recent Chinese scholarship that has been published in China. *Tombstone*, however, is banned in China, perhaps because Yang's material makes clear the culpability of the Chairman, his colleagues, his party, and their system that caused tens of millions of deaths. Perhaps also the authorities were appalled at the extent of Yang's vivid documentation of the killing. This was not just one man's history. Yang got people who experienced the famine to describe it in their own words. He found local journalists who'd witnessed and reported on murders and starvation and got them to write their memoirs. He located and interviewed local implementers of the fatal policies. He got surviving re-sisters to recount their experiences.

Using his privileged status as a high-ranking journalist, Yang culled dozens of archives throughout the country that contained contemporary secret party reports of the impact of the famine and the summary man-ner in which officials had ordered the killing of resisters. This English version highlights the voices that Yang alone sought out and captured so that the murderous impact of the Great Leap Forward could be experi-enced in the words and feelings of the survivors.

Yang's two-volume masterpiece was originally published in 2008 in Hong Kong, running to 1,200 pages in Chinese and reprinted eight times in two years. The highly qualified Stacy Mosher translated the whole work. Guo Jian, wonderfully comfortable in the argot of both Chinese and American cultures, then polished the translation. Finally, Edward Friedman, a specialist on the politics of rural China, assisted the transla-tors in condensing and editing the manuscript. Yang invited Friedman and Harvard's specialist on Chinese elite politics, Roderick MacFarquhar, to write this preface to introduce the book to an English-reading audience.

TRANSLATORS' NOTE

As translators, we faced two major and interrelated challenges: the length of Yang Jisheng's monumental work and the ordering of its chapters.

The original Chinese version of *Tombstone* totaled more than 800,000 Chinese characters and was published in two volumes totaling more than 1,200 pages. Recognizing that in today's media environment no one would publish a translated work of that length, Mr. Yang reduced the Chinese version to something over 500,000 characters. We initially translated this version, but were advised that it was still an impractical length. With the assistance of our colleague Edward Friedman, and with Mr. Yang's permission, we edited the book down to the version presented here. Our primary goal was to preserve the essence of Mr. Yang's work in all respects—a representative sampling of his comprehensive coverage and the bulk of his analysis and reflections on this epic tragedy. We hope we've produced an edition of *Tombstone* that is accessible to a general reader while also enlightening to scholars and specialists.

In the initial process of reducing the length of *Tombstone*, Mr. Yang proposed reordering the chapters for a non-Chinese audience. In the original two-volume work, the first volume is largely microscopic, examining the calamity as it affected individual provinces all the way down to the grassroots level, while the second volume, macroscopic in design, covers the nationwide agricultural collectivization movement and analyzes the political system that was ultimately responsible for the disaster. Since the early chapters in the second volume could serve as an introduction to the overall situation of the famine, Mr. Yang considered starting the book with these chapters to better prepare Western readers for the provincial chapters.

In discussions among ourselves and with others, however, we found that placing the macroscopic "policy" chapters first reduced the drama and impact of the human stories that consequently followed much later in the book. The consensus we reached was that Mr. Yang's initial instinct as a veteran journalist had been the best: that is, first to present the tragedy in all its horror so the reader comprehended the need to explore how the system and its practitioners brought about the disaster. We therefore arrived at a compromise: we have begun the book, as in Mr. Yang's original Chinese version, with the chapter on Henan and the Xinyang tragedy, but rather than presenting the rest of the provincial chapters together in a block, we have alternated them with policy chapters that are particularly relevant to the conditions of each province. The book presented here consists of four of the original fourteen "provincial" chapters, the six "central," or "policy," chapters, and five (instead of eight) "analysis" chapters.

In addition to Edward Friedman's invaluable and multipronged effort to ensure the publication of Mr. Yang's book in English, we are indebted to a number of other people whose assistance was essential. We would particularly like to thank the Keck Center for International and Strategic Studies at Claremont McKenna College and its director, Minxin Pei, for their vital support as the host institution for this project. We are grateful to the National Endowment for the Humanities and a generous anonymous donor who funded the lengthy translation process. We thank the translator of *Tombstone*'s French edition, Louis Vincenolles, for collegial and helpful exchanges, and Nancy Hearst, librarian for the Fairbank Center Collection of Harvard University's H. C. Fung Library, for an expert reading that saved us from many lapses. Most of all, we thank Mr. Yang Jisheng for the honor of allowing us to translate his great work and for his patient replies to our many queries.

Stacy Mosher and Guo Jian

A CHRONOLOGY OF THE GREAT FAMINE

1949

October 1: The People's Republic of China (PRC) is established.

1951

April 17: The Shanxi provincial party committee submits a report advocating a cooperative "more advanced than the current mutual aid team" in the countryside, which Liu Shaoqi considers "an erroneous, dangerous, fantastical example of agricultural socialist thought." Mao Zedong supports the Shanxi provincial party committee's views and Gao Gang's agricultural collective economy methods in the Northeast.

1953

March 26: The Central Committee issues a resolution promoting mutual aid teams and the pooling of land for agricultural cooperatives.
October 16: An enlarged meeting of the CCP Central Committee passes the "Resolution Regarding the State Monopoly for Purchasing and Marketing."
December: Centralized purchasing and marketing of grain commence nationwide.

1954

December 27: The Xinhua News Agency reports that more than four hundred thousand agricultural cooperatives have been established throughout the country. Some peasants resist the new system.

1955

March: Deng Zihui arrives in Zhejiang to rectify and consolidate the cooperatives.
July 31: Mao Zedong delivers his report "On the Question of Agricultural

Cooperation," criticizing the effort to shrink agricultural cooperatives and dismissing the concept of "rash advance."

August 25: The State Council issues provisional measures for purchasing and marketing of grain in the countryside and setting grain supply quotas and a food ration system for urban residents.

September: Mao Zedong compiles *Socialist Upsurge in China's Countryside*, published in December. His preface expresses pointed criticism of "right opportunism" and predicts doubled or tripled grain yields by 1967.

1956

January: The Supreme State Conference passes "The Program for Agricultural Development from 1956 to 1967." Agricultural minister Liao Luyan projects a total grain yield of 500 billion kilos in 1967. Mao says China will overtake the United States in steel production. State Council ministries hurriedly revise their targets for the Third Five-Year Plan (ending in 1967).

February 6: Zhou Enlai feels pressured by excessively high targets and points to the emergence of "rash advance."

June 20: *People's Daily* publishes an editorial revised and finalized by Liu Shaoqi, Lu Dingyi, and Hu Qiaomu entitled "It Is Necessary to Oppose Conservatism and Also Impetuousness."

September 5–27: The political report of the Eighth National Party Congress states: "Our country's main domestic contradiction is the contradiction between the people's demands to establish an advanced industrial nation and the reality of a backward agricultural nation; it is the contradiction between the needs of the people for the rapid development of the economy and culture, and the present conditions under which the economy and culture cannot satisfy the people's needs."

December: By the end of 1956, 96.3 percent of the peasant population has joined cooperatives, and the socialist transformation of industry and business is completed. The abolition of private ownership and the establishment of a comprehensive planned economic system allow the state to monopolize all means of production and all means of livelihood.

1957

During this year, the Anti-Rightist Movement proceeds in the cities, while the Socialist Education Movement proceeds in the countryside. Ultimately more than six hundred thousand intellectuals are persecuted, and dissenting views are effectively eliminated.

Mid-April to late May: Peasants in twenty-nine of the thirty-three towns and villages in Zhejiang Province's Xianju County demand to withdraw from or disband their cooperatives.

June 14: The CCP Central Committee and State Council handle mass starvation in Guangxi by disciplining and discharging twelve senior provincial leaders. Some replacement cadres are subsequently disciplined for blaming starving deaths on the Central Committee's policies of collectivization and the state monopoly for grain purchasing and marketing.

October 9: During the enlarged Third Plenum of the Eighth CCP Central Committee, Mao Zedong criticizes those who oppose "rash advance" and overturns the resolution of the Eighth National Party Congress by declaring that the country's main domestic contradiction is "between the proletariat and the bourgeoisie, and between the socialist road and the capitalist road."

November: Mao Zedong leads a delegation to the International Congress of Communist and Workers' Parties in Moscow, where he says that China will catch up with or surpass the United Kingdom in fifteen years.

Winter 1957 to spring 1958

A labor force of tens of millions is deployed to irrigation projects across the country. Small cooperatives are merged in line with Mao's repeated endorsement of the "superiority of large cooperatives."

1958

January 11–22: The Nanning Conference continues criticism of opponents of "rash advance," and Zhou Enlai undergoes self-criticism. The conference is followed by a new upsurge in "criticizing right deviation and struggling to leap forward."

March–September: Luliang County, Yunnan Province, records 33,319 cases of edema, affecting 13 percent of the county's residents and causing the deaths of 2.04 percent of the population.

March 9–26: At the Chengdu Conference, Mao Zedong is described as "in an invincibly advantageous position." Zhou Enlai once again undergoes self-criticism and pronounces Mao "the representative of truth."

April 7: The Central Committee issues "Opinions Regarding the Problem of Developing Local Industry," leading to an upsurge of chaotic and unfocused industrial projects.

April 20: Chayashan Collective is formally established and on May 5 changes its name to become China's first people's commune.

May 5–23: The Second Session of the Eighth National Congress of the CCP passes a resolution to "unanimously endorse the CCP Central Committee's General Line of 'Go all out, aim high, and build socialism with greater, faster, better, and more economical results' as proposed and recommended by Comrade Mao Zedong."

May 29: *People's Daily* publishes an editorial emphasizing speed as the "soul of the General Line."

June 8: *People's Daily* reports a per-*mu* yield of 1,007.5 kilograms of wheat at Sputnik Commune of Henan's Suiping County, setting off waves of exaggerated reporting.

June 14: During a talk to the leading party group of the All-China Women's Federation, Liu Shaoqi speaks of eliminating the family and establishing communal kitchens.

June 16: Missile scientist Qian Xuesen publishes "How High Will Grain Yields Be?" in *China Youth Daily*, convincing many who were previously skeptical of "Sputnik" grain yield reports.

June 17: In a report to the Central Committee, Bo Yibo says, "Apart from electrical power, all of our main industrial output will exceed that of the United Kingdom." On June 22, Mao comments, "Surpassing the United Kingdom will not take fifteen years or seven years, but will only need two or three years, especially in steel production."

June 19: A meeting of central leaders at the swimming pool of Mao's Beijing residence leads to the launching of the great iron- and steel-forging campaign, which doubles the annual steel production target to 11 million tons.

June and July: A "purge of counterrevolutionary remnants" and a "counterattack against well-to-do middle peasants" in Shanghai's Fengxian County is accompanied by arbitrary detentions and "struggle sessions." Deep-plowing and irrigation campaigns involve around-the-clock labor, driven by verbal and physical abuse, resulting in 960 deaths.

July 1: Chen Boda introduces the concept of the people's commune in an article in *Red Flag* magazine.

July 14–18: While on an inspection visit of Shouzhang County, Shandong Province, Liu Shaoqi accepts exaggerated crop-yield claims and praises the communes for "overpowering the scientists, who never dared to dream of what you have accomplished. This is revolution."

July 19–August 6: Zhou Enlai makes inspection visits to Henan Province's "wheat bumper harvest exhibitions," where he endorses the claims of the Sputnik harvests and warmly praises Henan's communal kitchens.

August: Liu Shaoqi sends people to Shouzhang County to gain a better understanding of high production levels there, and the investigation report proposes the slogan "Greater daring brings greater bearing."

August 4: Mao makes an inspection visit of Xushui County and asks, "What will you do with so much extra food?"

August 6: A "Communist pilot project" is launched at Xushui under orders from the Central Committee, drawing 320,000 visitors from across the country and effectively launching the Communist Wind.

August 9: While inspecting Shandong Province, Mao says, "The people's commune is good. Its advantage is in combining industry, agriculture, commerce, education, and the military for more convenient management."

August 29: The enlarged Politburo meeting at Beidaihe passes the "Resolution Regarding the Establishment of People's Communes in the Countryside" as a viable and quick transition to communism. By the end of October the number of rural communes has grown to 26,576, with an overall household participation rate of 99.1 percent.

September 10–29: Mao Zedong carries out inspection visits in several provinces. He endorses the practice of an Anhui commune that provides free meals to its members.

September 27: Liu Shaoqi promotes Jiangsu Province's deployment of more than three million people in steelmaking: "They've put up shacks and gotten to work; their morale is high, and they don't argue over trifles or wrangle over wages."

September 30: During a visit to a Jiangsu commune, Liu Shaoqi endorses the grain supply system (as opposed to a wage system) and observes, "Not only have [the peasants] not become slackers, but they have experienced a boost to their morale and are even more passionate about production."

October 25: A *People's Daily* editorial promotes communal kitchens. Mao Zedong repeatedly endorses communal kitchens, which are established throughout the cities and countryside.

October 26: A "counterrevolutionary insurrection" arises at the Dasongshu New Village colliery in Yunnan's Luquan County, followed by the arrest of 117 individuals, with 31 beaten to death and 50 sentenced to imprisonment.

November 2–10: The First Zhengzhou Conference affirms the current stage of socialism and collective ownership as the basis for the people's communes.

November 21–27: The Wuchang Conference calls for suppression of unrealistic production targets, criticizes the trend toward wild exaggeration, acknowledges the need for pay according to work done, and proposes a pragmatic approach to economic matters.

November 25: Public security forces quell a "bandit rebellion" in Yunnan's Zhaotong Prefecture that opposed communal kitchens and nurseries and around-the-clock hard labor.

November 28–December 10: The Sixth Plenum of the Eighth CCP Central Committee criticizes the Exaggeration Wind and utopian attempts to surpass the socialist phase, and calls for developing practical and realistic work styles.

December 6: A report by Yunnan's Dehong prefectural party committee states that 14 percent of the population fled the prefecture's border counties from January to November 20.

1959

In the course of the year, China's grain exports reach an all-time high, equivalent to 5 million tons of unprocessed grain, as compared to 200,000 tons of unprocessed grain imported. Large quantities of oil products, fresh eggs, meat, and fruit are also exported.

January: The "Guantao Incident" comes to light. Communal kitchens throughout Shandong's Guantao County shut down or suspend operations as commune members forage for food or flee. Production grinds to a halt, mass starvation ensues, and many die.

January 27: The Guangdong provincial party committee submits a report stating that food shortages result from "false reporting of output and private withholding by the production teams and units."

February: The State Planning Commission's internal publication *Jingji xiaoxi* (*Economic News*) publishes an investigative report entitled "Is It a Food Shortage Problem or an Ideological Problem?," which calls on all localities to criticize "right-deviating conservatives and apply themselves wholeheartedly to the current grain supply work." Mao Zedong writes lengthy memos that give rise to a nationwide campaign against "false reporting of output and private withholding."

February 27–March 5: At the Second Zhengzhou Conference, Mao Zedong proposes fourteen phrases for people's commune ownership, which uphold production teams as the basic accounting unit and distribution according to work done, rectify indiscriminate distribution and excessive collectivization, and reaffirm the law of value and equal value exchange.

March: In Jining, Shandong Province, peasants eat wheat sprouts, tree bark, and chaff. Reports find 670,000 people suffering from edema, and many deaths.

March 25–April 5: An enlarged Politburo meeting and the Seventh Plenum of the Eighth Central Committee, both held in Shanghai, resolve to pay restitution on property affected by equal and indiscriminate transfer of resources. Steel output and other economic indicators are adjusted.

April 6: The State Council secretariat submits a report on food shortages in Shandong, Jiangsu, Henan, Hebei, and Anhui provinces, followed on April 9 by a statistical table on the spring famine in fifteen provinces, which states that more than twenty-five million people are without food. Mao and the Central Committee continue to consider the food shortages a localized and "temporary crisis," and offer no letup on grain procurement.

April 18–25: The First Session of the Second National People's Congress approves the 1959 National Economic Plan and formally announces the elevated economic targets.

April 29: Mao Zedong issues an "internal party memo" to all cadres from the provincial to production team level rectifying extremist views on output quota assignments, close-planting, economizing on food supplies, the size of cultivated areas, mechanization, and the need for truthful reporting.

May 7: The CCP Central Committee issues its "Urgent Directives on Agriculture," addressing the sharp decrease in livestock with calls to combine individual rearing with collective rearing.

May 11: The Politburo approves Chen Yun's proposal that 1959 steel production targets be lowered to 13 million tons.

June 11: The Central Committee issues a directive allowing commune households to resume raising livestock and fowl.

July 2–August 16: The Lushan Conference includes an enlarged Politburo meeting and the Eighth Plenum of the Eighth CCP Central Committee. The early phase of the enlarged Politburo meeting counters leftism; on July 14, Peng Dehuai writes a letter to Mao Zedong pointing out serious problems with the Great Leap Forward. On July 23, Mao delivers a speech attacking Peng. The Eighth Plenum passes a resolution against the "errors of the anti-party clique led by Comrade Peng Dehuai," and another to "defend the party's General Line and oppose right opportunism."

August 30: The Central Committee transmits the Guizhou provincial party committee's report on food supply and market conditions, which falsely claims that the food shortage has been completely resolved. Mao Zedong writes a lengthy memo linking the struggle against right deviation with the food supply issue.

October: A three-month campaign to "dig up grain and collect funds" is launched in Shanxi's Shouyang County, during which 11,159 homes are ransacked and 3,116 people are subjected to physical abuse, resulting in at least 349 deaths.

October–April 1960: The "Xinyang Incident": More than one million people starve to death in Henan's Xinyang Prefecture.

Winter 1959 to spring 1960: The "Tongwei Incident": Gansu's Tongwei County loses a third of its population to starvation.

1960

The number of starvation deaths in the Great Famine reaches its peak in spring during the gap in food supply between the planting and harvest seasons. Known cases of the disaster include the "Zunyi Incident" (in Guizhou Province), involving massive deaths and cannibalism, and the "Luoding Incident" (in Guangdong Province), during which more than seventeen thousand people die within a few months.

China exports more than 2.72 million tons of grain in the course of the year, along with large quantities of oil products, fresh eggs, meat, and fruit. Only 66,300 tons of grain are imported.

January 7–17: An enlarged Politburo meeting is held in Shanghai, during which 1960 is pronounced a Great Leap Forward year. The meeting proposes a three-year deadline for fulfilling the Forty-Point Program for Agricultural Development, and five years to surpass the United Kingdom, while at the same time organizing people's communes in the urban areas and launching massive industrialization and irrigation projects. The Five Winds resume.

March 4: Mao Zedong and the Central Committee distribute a report by the Guizhou provincial party committee that extols communal kitchens and advocates eliminating plots of land for household cultivation.

March 18: The Central Committee recommends three reports with a memo from Mao Zedong calling for a focus on effective organization of communal kitchens.

March 24–25: Mao presides over an enlarged meeting of the Politburo standing committee in Tianjin, which discusses extending communal kitchens and people's communes throughout the cities and countryside, making the iron and steel campaign more reliant on small enterprises, and bringing forward completion of the Forty-Point Program for Agricultural Development. The Tianjin Conference upholds the Three Red Banners while opposing the Communist Wind.

March 25: Massive starvation deaths in Ningxia Hui Autonomous Region, known as the "Zhongning Incident," come to light, and an autonomous region party committee work group carries out a massive purge in the Zhongning County party committee.

March 30–April 10: The Second Session of the Second National People's Congress passes the "National Program for Agricultural Development 1956–1967" and the "Resolution to Strive to Bring About the National Program for Agricultural Development Ahead of Schedule." *People's Daily* publishes an editorial entitled "We Must and Can Continue Leaping Forward."

May 28: A riot known as the Wanquantang Rebellion occurs in Sichuan's Kai County. More than three hundred people are involved in looting shops, killing or wounding four party cadres and abducting sixteen others.

June: Rebellion, led in part by commune party secretaries, occurs in Jiangkou County, Guizhou Province. Following a military crackdown, the county head who opened the state granary for starving peasants commits suicide.

June 10–18: An enlarged Politburo meeting is held in Shanghai, during which Mao Zedong recommends lowering projected targets and stressing quality over quantity in iron and steel production. He writes a "Ten-Year Summary" in which he begins to reflect on the error of elevated production targets.

July 5–August 10: The Central Committee convenes a working conference at Beidaihe during which Sino-Soviet relations and domestic economic issues are discussed. The conference proposes adjustments to the national economy focusing on grain and steel production. It also calls for economizing and increasing exports.

July 6: The Central Committee advocates the development of food substitutes, and *People's Daily* publishes an editorial entitled "Produce Large Quantities of Chlorella."

July 16: The government of the Soviet Union tears up six hundred agreements with China and announces the withdrawal of its experts from the country. These agreements are not related to agriculture.

August: Li Fuchun, in charge of planning, proposes a policy of "rectification, consolidation, and enhancement" in response to the difficulties caused by the Great Leap Forward. His proposal is revised and formalized by Zhou Enlai into "adjustment, consolidation, replenishment, and enhancement."

August 15: The Central Committee issues the "Directive on Ensuring the Fulfillment of the Grain Allocation and Transport Plan."

September 7: The Central Committee issues the "Directive on Reducing Grain Ration Standards in the Countryside and Cities."

October 23–26: Mao Zedong calls in regional leaders to hear their reports on agriculture. The discussion centers on how to rectify the Communist Wind. Wu Zhipu reports on the Xinyang Incident, which Mao attributes to "the inadequate thoroughness of the democratic revolution" at the local level.

November 3: The Central Committee issues the "Urgent Directive Regarding

Current Policy Issues in the Rural People's Communes" (also known as the "Twelve Agricultural Provisions"). This document rectifies leftist tendencies by emphasizing "three-level ownership, with production teams as the basic accounting unit," but retains the communal kitchens.

November 10: The Central Committee convenes a national conference on food substitutes, followed by the launch of a nationwide campaign on November 14. Some peasants die from food poisoning and other effects of eating food substitutes.

November 15: After reading a report on the deployment of thousands of cadres to the countryside, Mao claims that scoundrels hold power in one-third of the regions, where incomplete revolution has resulted in starvation and cadre abuses.

November 16: The Central Committee endorses and transmits the "Summary of the Discussion on Resolutely Carrying out Autumn and Winter Food Supply Work at the National Conference on Financial and Economic Work."

November 17: The Central Committee issues "Notice Regarding Immediately Focusing on Grain Allocation and Transport."

December 24: A riot occurs at Adu Commune in Yunnan's Xuanwei County and then spreads to other communes with calls for a "second land reform" that will return land to individual owners, the disbanding of communal kitchens, and resumption of free markets.

December 24–January 13, 1961: A Central Committee work conference discusses issues relating to the International Communist Movement and emphasizes rectification of the Five Winds and problems with the 1961 National Economic Plan.

1961

Following the mass starvation deaths in 1960, grain imports are increased to nearly 5.81 million tons in 1961, while grain exports drop to 1.355 million tons.

January 14–18: The Ninth Plenum of the Eighth CCP Central Committee is held in Beijing, deciding on a national economic policy of "adjustment, consolidation, replenishment, and enhancement."

January 18: Mao suggests making 1961 a year for investigating operational problems. On January 20 he sends out working groups headed by Chen Boda and others to carry out investigation and research in Zhejiang, Guangdong, and Hunan.

March: While in Guangzhou, Mao presides over the drafting of the "Work Regulations for Rural People's Communes" (known as the Sixty Agricultural Provisions).

March 28: Anhui's first party secretary, Zeng Xisheng, convenes a meeting of the provincial party standing committee to decide on implementing "responsibility fields." The practice is to spread throughout the country and become the most effective means of saving peasant lives at the time.

April 19: With Mao's permission, a Central Committee investigation group convenes a mass rally in Shaoshan (Mao's hometown in Hunan Province) to announce the disbanding of the communal kitchens. Commune members rejoice.

April 26: The Central Committee transmits a letter by Hu Qiaomu and four related documents that formally advocate disbanding the communal kitchens.

May 21–June 12: The Central Committee convenes a working conference in Beijing to discuss questions raised by Mao on investigation and research, the mass line, restitution, and rehabilitation. The conference discusses and approves the revised Sixty Agricultural Provisions, effectively terminating the system of communal kitchens.

August 23–September 16: The Second Lushan Conference discusses food supply issues, market issues, the Two-Year Plan and industrial issues, and the management of industrial enterprises. Mao estimates that the economy reached its lowest point in 1961 and that the situation will improve from this point on.

November 10: At a conference of regional bureaus, the Central Committee ascertains grain procurement issues. Deng Xiaoping emphasizes the importance of ideology in the rectification of work styles, and the conference decides that procurement targets must be fulfilled without haggling.

1962

January 11–February 7: At the Seven Thousand Cadres Conference, Liu Shaoqi sums up the party's shortcomings and errors in economic construction since 1958 and proposes the formulation of "three parts natural disaster and seven parts man-made disaster." Mao Zedong engages in self-criticism.

February 21–23: An enlarged Politburo standing committee meeting (the "Xilou Conference") is convened in the Zhongnanhai compound. Chen Yun delivers a grim prognosis of the economic situation. Subsequent enlarged State Council and Politburo standing committee meetings propose measures to further adjust the economy and surmount existing difficulties. Mao Zedong, absent from all these meetings, agrees with the majority views and endorses Liu Shaoqi's recommendation to appoint Chen Yun head of the Central Committee Finance Committee but believes it is wrong to paint a "uniformly bleak" picture of the situation.

April–May: In Guangdong Province, more than 110,000 people attempt to steal across the border to Hong Kong. Of the 60,000 who reach Hong Kong, 40,000 are deported back to mainland China.

Spring and summer: More than sixty thousand residents of the border areas of Xinjiang's Ili Kazakh Autonomous Prefecture flee to the Soviet Union with their families, livestock, farming implements, and vehicles.

May 7–11: Liu Shaoqi presides over a Central Committee work conference, subsequently referred to as the "May Conference." Discussion focuses on documents arising out of the Xilou Conference and subsequent meetings, and a plan is drawn up to restructure the economy along the lines of "emergency measures for times of emergency."

July: Tian Jiaying, Chen Yun, Deng Zihui, and others discuss assignment of production to households with Mao; Mao insists on maintaining a collective economy. Afterward, at his swimming pool, Mao asks Liu Shaoqi, "Why can't you keep things under control?" Liu retorts, "History will record the role you and I played in the starvation of so many people, and the cannibalism will also be memorialized!"

July 25–August 24: The Central Committee holds a work conference at Beidaihe. On August 6, Mao Zedong delivers a speech on class, criticizing the "wind of gloom," the "individual-farming wind," and the "verdict-reversing wind," and calling for maintaining the Marxist-Leninist course through daily discussion of class struggle.

September 24–27: The Tenth Plenum of the Eighth CCP Central Committee is held in Beijing. The report of the plenum announces, "Throughout the entire history of proletarian revolution and dictatorship of the proletariat, and throughout the entire transition from capitalism to communism (this period requires several decades or even longer) there exists a class struggle between the proletariat and the bourgeoisie, and a struggle between the two roads of socialism and capitalism."

1963–1965

The "Four Clean-ups" (*siqing*) Movement, focusing on purging capitalist roaders within the party, takes place.

1966–1976

The Great Proletarian Cultural Revolution results from intensified internal divisions and struggles between the government's "pragmatists" and "idealists." The Cultural Revolution takes the standpoints of the idealists to a destructive extreme. The failure of the Cultural Revolution leads to a reversal that engenders the economic reforms launched at the end of 1978.

TOMBSTONE

AN EVERLASTING TOMBSTONE

I originally intended to title this book *The Road to Paradise*, but eventually changed it to *Tombstone*. I had four reasons for choosing this title: the first is to erect a tombstone for my father, who died of starvation in 1959; the second is to erect a tombstone for the thirty-six million Chinese who died of starvation; and the third is to erect a tombstone for the system that brought about the Great Famine. The fourth came to me while I was halfway through writing this book, when a temporary health scare spurred me to complete the book as a tombstone for myself. Although my health concerns were subsequently put to rest, the risk involved in undertaking this project might yet justify its serving as my own tombstone. But, of course, my main intentions are the first three.

A tombstone is memory made concrete. Human memory is the ladder on which a country and a people advance. We must remember not only the good things, but also the bad; the bright spots, but also the darkness. The authorities in a totalitarian system strive to conceal their faults and extol their merits, gloss over their errors and forcibly eradicate all memory of man-made calamity, darkness, and evil. For that reason, the Chinese are prone to historical amnesia imposed by those in power. I erect this tombstone so that people will remember and henceforth renounce man-made calamity, darkness, and evil.

1.

At the end of April 1959, I was spending my after-school hours assembling a May Fourth Youth Day wall newspaper[1] for my school's Communist Youth League. My childhood friend Zhang Zhibai suddenly arrived from our home village of Wanli and told me, "Your father is starving to death!

Hurry back, and take some rice if you can." He said, "Your father doesn't even have the strength to strip bark from the trees—he's starved beyond helping himself. He was headed to Jiangjiayan to buy salt to make salt-water, but he collapsed on the way, and some people from Wanli carried him home."

I dropped what I was doing and requested leave from our league sec-retary and head teacher. Then I collected a three-day meal ration of 1.5 kilos of rice from the school canteen and rushed home. Upon reaching Wanli, I found things radically changed. The elm tree in front of our house had been reduced to a barkless trunk, and even its roots had been dug up and stripped, leaving only a ragged hole in the earth. The pond was dry; neighbors said it had been drained to dredge for rank-tasting mollusks that had never been eaten in the past. There was no sound of dogs bark-ing, no chickens running about; even the children who used to scamper through the lanes remained at home. Wanli was like a ghost town.

Upon entering our home, I found utter destitution; there was not a grain of rice, nothing edible whatsoever, and not even water in the vat. Immobilized by starvation, how would my father have had the strength to fetch water?

My father was half-reclined on his bed, his eyes sunken and lifeless, his face gaunt, the skin creased and flaccid. He tried to extend his hand to greet me, but couldn't lift it, just moving it a little. That hand re-minded me of the human skeleton in my anatomy class; although it was covered with a layer of withered skin, nothing concealed the protrusions and hollows of the bone structure. I was shocked with the realization that the term *skin and bones* referred to something so horrible and cruel. A murmur escaped from his lips, his voice faint as he told me to go quickly, go quickly back to school.

My father had seemed fine just two months earlier—in fact, his legs had already shown signs of edema at the time, but I didn't know it was from malnutrition. He had been in charge of grazing his production team's buf-falo. That buffalo was a lovely beast, robust and clean under my father's painstaking care. Although this little buffalo could not speak, its eyes were expressive, by turns intimate, worried, longing, or angry. It was able to communicate with my father through those eyes, and even I understood some of its expressions. Whenever I came back from school, I would ride the buffalo up the hill. Two months earlier my father had sent for me to come home. The production team had secretly slaughtered the buffalo and given our family half a kilo of the meat. Knowing my life was hard at school, my father had called me home to eat the buffalo meat. As soon as I entered the house, I smelled an alluring odor. But my father ate none of the meat. He said he had been too close to the buffalo, there had been an understanding between them, and he couldn't eat the meat. In fact, he was just making an excuse to let me eat all of it. I wolfed it down as he watched, his eyes glowing with kindness. Now I wondered had he eaten that buffalo meat whether his condition might not be so desperate.

I kneaded my father's hand, then hurried off with buckets on a shoulder pole to fill the water vat. Then I grabbed a hoe and went to dig up sprouts from where we had planted peanuts the year before. (The peanut sprouts from the year before had, during the spring, pushed out shoots that were much coarser than bean sprouts. It was said that they contained toxins and were inedible, but even so, they had been almost completely dug up by others.) I dug and dug some more, my heart full of remorse and guilt. Why had I not come back earlier and harvested some wild herbs? Why hadn't I come back earlier with some rice?

But all my self-blame was useless. I boiled congee from the rice I'd brought and took it to my father's bed, but he was no longer able to swallow. Three days later he departed this world.

With the help of other villagers, I hastily buried him. While he was still alive I had hardly taken notice of him, but now that he lay at rest in the earth, instances from the past vividly replayed themselves in my mind.

My father's name was Yang Xiushen; he was also known by the names Yufu and Hongyuan. He was born on the sixth day of the sixth month of the lunar calendar in the year 1889. He was in fact my uncle and foster father, raising me from the time I was three months old. He and my foster mother had treated me better than if I had been their own son, and the extraordinary love they showed me was known throughout our home village. I later learned from fellow villagers that even in the worst weather my father would carry me through every lane and path seeking milk, so that I had wet nurses scattered throughout the area. One time I became ill and fell into a coma, and my father knelt and prayed unceasingly before the ancestral shrine until I regained consciousness. Once, I developed an abscess on my head, and my mother sucked the pus out of it with her own lips until it was cured. Although they were extremely poor, they used every means to ensure that I obtained schooling. They had extremely strict expectations regarding my conduct.

In 1950 the government of our township, Mayuanxiang,[2] regularly convened public "struggle sessions" against "landlords" and "local despots." Once, my father took me to a large-scale struggle session held at Zaociling. A temporary platform had been built at the foot of a hill, and the hilltop was packed with villagers. Voices shouting slogans thundered, and armed militia flaunted their prowess. The people being "struggled" were trussed up on the platform, and when people had finished venting their grievances against each one, others would rush up and beat them. They beat each of these people unconscious, then took them to the hillside and shot them. At this session, fourteen people were executed. I noticed that my father said nothing from beginning to end. After we went home, several other village boys and I played at struggling landlords. Quite to my surprise, my father pulled me into the house and gave me a thrashing. Later he told me that not all of those killed were bad men, and not all of those who beat them had any cause for grievance. He never took me to a struggle session again.

When my foster mother died in 1951, my father and I became entirely dependent upon each other. After my mother's death, I dropped out of school for a time. My father didn't let me work in the fields, but cleared the only table in the house and supervised my studies. One time, however, when he had to pay his agricultural tax, he allowed me to come along, carrying two little satchels of unhusked rice.[3] He said he'd had no land in the past, but now he had a field, and paying the agricultural tax was an important event that he wanted me to experience. However, halfway there, I became too tired to continue. He hoisted me and the two satchels on his shoulder pole and carried me to the grain distribution center. At the time of the Land Reform,[4] my family was allocated about three mu[5] of land, enough for twenty-four buckets of grain.[6] My father was ecstatic at being given land to farm, and small as I was, I shared his joy. But two or three years later, the land was reclaimed for collectivization.

In 1954, I passed the entrance exam for Xishui Junior Middle School. I was only a day school student, because we lacked the funds for me to board. It was 10 kilometers[7] from our home to the school. In order to shorten the journey, my father found an old house in Maqiao, about 5 kilometers from the county seat, and opened a tea shop there. That 5 kilometers of road was a major thoroughfare, providing me with better access to the school. Every day before dawn, my father would awaken me so I could reach school in time for the seven o'clock study session.

One day a rainstorm caused the gable of that old house to collapse, nearly crushing him. Eventually, the school provided me with a scholarship that allowed me to board, greatly alleviating my father's hardship.

I grieved deeply over my father's death, but never thought to blame the government. I harbored no doubts regarding the party's propaganda about the accomplishments of the "Great Leap Forward" or the advantages of the people's communes. I believed that what was happening in my home village was isolated, and that my father's death was merely one family's tragedy. Compared with the advent of the great Communist society, what was my family's petty misfortune? The party had taught me to sacrifice the self for the greater good when encountering difficulty, and I was completely obedient. I maintained this frame of mind right up until the Cultural Revolution.

At that time, I felt no suspicion and completely accepted what had been instilled in me by the Communist Party and the Communist Youth League. I excelled academically, and joined the Young Pioneers in primary school and the Communist Youth League in junior middle school. During the Anti-Rightist Campaign in 1957, I believed the party when it declared rightists to be bad elements. I was a student activist in 1958, and a poem I wrote eulogizing the Great Leap Forward was sent to the Huanggang Regional Education Exhibition Center. At that time, I was the propaganda head of the Youth League committee and chief editor of my school's mimeographed tabloid, Young Communist. During the day, I took part in physical labor, and at night, I edited the newspaper. At the beginning of 1959, I composed a "New Year's Message" for the newspaper in which I passionately extolled the Great Leap Forward. During the school's New Year assembly, the principal read out my essay as his congratulatory message to the school's teachers and students without changing a single word.

I did all this with complete sincerity and without a shred of self-interest. My sadness at my father's death did not weaken my confidence in the Chinese Communist Party. Like me, many young people who enthusiastically participated in the Great Leap Forward were suffering from hunger along with their family members, but they never complained. Communism inspired them, and many of them would gladly have sacrificed their lives for this great ideal.

My support for the Great Leap Forward was due not only to the inspiration of Communist ideals, but also to ignorance. I came from a remote village whose residents knew virtually nothing about matters beyond the hills. One time I heard an old villager tell my father that someone had seen Xuantong,[8] and that it was possible that he would regain the throne. They did not know that Emperor P'u Yi, as he was also known, had already been convicted of treason and imprisoned. They cherished the memory of the emperor. They did not know of the great event that occurred in Beijing on October 1, 1949. The village cadre Huang Yuanzhong knew, and he held a meeting in the village on that day. The next day, his son (nicknamed Laizi, or "Scamp") told me, "Chairman Mao has been enthroned." I asked, "What do you mean?" He replied, "He's the emperor." He said that was what his father had told him.

The vast majority of us never circulated beyond a 50-kilometer radius of our village. Although we were situated only a little more than 100 kilometers from Hankou,[9] that great city seemed impossibly remote to us. Our wistful regard for the city was expressed in lines from a children's song: "Moonlight, moonlight, go with me, all the way to the Hankou sea; Moonlight, let me run with you, all the way to Yuanjiaqiao." The county seat, Xishui, was much closer, but even going there took one full day, with half of the roadway consisting of rugged mountain paths. Many villagers went to the county seat only once or twice a year.

A summer night after one's bath was the time of greatest contentment for villagers. Whole households would sit together outside their homes, drinking tea brewed from the coarse plants they'd cultivated and waving fans they'd woven from straw as they chatted about household matters. Those who preferred more varied company would gather in a cool place to gossip. Someone might retell the story of the "Peach Garden Pledge" from *The Romance of the Three Kingdoms*, or recount Sun Yatsen's attempts to unseat the Qing dynasty, passed along from Wuhan decades earlier. But these stories had become old hat. If anyone mentioned some recent incident occurring in the county seat, everyone's ears would prick up, and the storyteller would be accorded great respect.

Although the closed-off nature of the village kept its residents in ignorance, it also preserved a kind of innocence. My father's disgust with the struggle session in 1950 arose not from rational judgment, but from human instinct. When I left the village in 1954 to attend school at the county seat, I brought a mind devoid of guile.

After the CCP gained power, it sealed China off from information beyond its borders, and imposed a wholesale negation of China's traditional moral standards. The government's monopoly on information gave it a monopoly on truth. As the center of power, the party Center was also the heart of truth and information. All social science research organs endorsed the validity of the Communist regime; every cultural and arts group lavished praise on the CCP, while news organs daily verified its wisdom and might. From nursery school to university, the chief mission was to inculcate a Communist worldview in the minds of all students. The social science research institutes, cultural groups, news organs, and schools all became tools for the party's monopoly on thought, spirit, and opinion, and were continuously engaged in molding China's youth. People employed in this work were proud to be considered "engineers of the human soul."

In this thought and information vacuum, the central government used its monopoly apparatus to instill Communist values while criticizing and eradicating all other values. In this way, young people developed distinct and intense feelings of right and wrong, love and hate, which took the shape of a violent longing to realize Communist ideals. Any words or deeds that diverged from these ideals would be met with a concerted attack.

The party organization was even more effective at instilling values than the social science research institutes, news and cultural organs, and schools. Each level of the party had a core surrounded by a group of stalwarts, with each layer controlling the one below it and loyal to the one above. Successive political movements, hundreds and thousands of large and small group meetings, commendation ceremonies and struggle sessions, rewards and penalties, all served to draw young people onto a single trajectory. All views diverging from those of the party were nipped in the bud.

At that time, I sincerely believed that a weak and impoverished China that had been bullied by imperialism for nearly one hundred years could embark on socialism through the Three Red Banners, and go on to implement the highest ideal of mankind: communism. Compared with this sublime ideal, what were the petty problems I faced?

I believed in the Three Red Banners not only out of ignorance, but also because of the formidable political pressure imposed by society as a whole, which allowed for no doubt. I personally witnessed many cruel incidents. Wan Shangjun, a schoolmate in the class above mine, lost his chance to take the university entrance exam because he praised a speech by Tito[10] that criticized the "socialist camp." He had placed first in the county's junior middle school entrance exam the year before I had, so I knew him well. An outstanding and thoughtful student, he lost his future at the age of seventeen because he thought too independently. In another case, in the spring of 1959, someone found the words "Down with Mao" scribbled on a toilet stall partition, and in a panic, reported it to the school leadership. The school hastily reported it to the public security bureau, which quickly cracked the case. The words turned out to have been written by a student in the class above mine, who had vented frustration at his hunger. I saw him thrown into jail in manacles.

The ceaseless mass criticisms and harsh punishments one witnessed instilled a feeling of dread. This dread was not the sudden fear experienced by the appearance of poisonous snakes and ferocious beasts, but the kind that seeped into the nerves and blood, becoming part of each person's instinct for survival. People learned to avoid political peril as they would a raging fire.

In a country in which an imperial mentality was deeply entrenched, people from the outset regarded the central government as the voice of authority, and the party used the "magical power" of the central government to instill its values in the entire populace. Inexperienced youth sincerely believed in these teachings, and their parents, out of either blind faith or fear of the regime, did their best to prevent their children from revealing any line of thought diverging from that of the government, requiring their children to be submissive and obedient.

In 1960, I passed the entrance exam for Tsinghua University in Beijing.[11] As soon as I entered the campus, I toured the university's anti-rightist exhibition, embarking on an education in loyalty. This was followed by more than fifty days in the countryside to learn through labor and to develop the defense of policies under the Three Red Banners. Although our stomachs rumbled with hunger, we never doubted these ideals.

The university, which had enjoyed a reputation for intellectual openness, turned out to be extremely insular. Tsinghua University had had many famous professors, but I only knew of Wen Yiduo and Zhu Ziqing, from Mao Zedong's writings, and had never heard of Chen Yinque or Wu Mi.[12] The university's library had an impressive collection of books, but the only ones I could borrow, apart from those on engineering and technology, were related to communism. Two of the university's alumni, Yang Zhenning and Li Zhengdao, had won the Nobel Prize for Physics in 1957,[13] but the university kept this fact under wraps, and even warned, during Youth League cadre meetings, that these two men were intellectual reactionaries and that we should not follow their "elitist" road.

While at university, I served as the Youth League's branch secretary and joined the Communist Party in May 1964. At that time young people like me were considered very naïve and simple, and it was true: our minds contained only the beliefs imbued by the public opinion apparatus, and nothing else. In this way the party molded the generation growing up under the new regime into its loyal disciples. If no major events had occurred during these decades, our generation would have retained those beliefs for our entire lives.

My thinking began to change when the Cultural Revolution[14] began in 1966, and I was astonished by the emergence of thousands of big-character posters[15] at Tsinghua University, which exposed the corrupt lives and debased mentalities of old revolutionaries whom I had long revered. From August to December, several classmates and I went to more than twenty cities to "establish ties." In these places we likewise found big-character posters revealing corruption and privilege among senior officials. I began to lose my faith in authority and officialdom, and I no longer believed everything I read. I began to doubt the myths the party had inculcated in me, and it was opposition to official privilege that led me, like most ordinary people, to take part in the Cultural Revolution. It was also during the Cultural Revolution that the governor of Hubei Province, Zhang Tixue, said something that shocked me: during the three years of hardship in that province, some three hundred thousand people had starved to death. Only then did I realize that my family's tragedy was not unique.

Upon graduating, I was assigned to the Xinhua News Agency, where reporters encountered aspects of society that others never saw. I learned many facts that contradicted what was written in party history texts, and observed the hard life of urban workers. As a Xinhua reporter, I learned how "news" was manufactured, and how news organs served as the mouthpieces of political power.

"Reform and opening," in the late 1970s, brought considerable relaxation of intellectual strictures, and some historical truth began to come out. In the past, the party had taught us that only the Communists had fought Japan, while the Kuomintang had capitulated and collaborated. Now we learned that more than two hundred Kuomintang generals had given up their lives in the resistance effort. In the past, the party had taught us that natural calamity had caused famine in limited areas of the country. Now we knew that it was a man-made disaster that had caused tens of millions of people to starve to death. I began to understand how history had been distorted and edited to suit the needs of the party.

The realization that I had been deceived for so long engendered a will to shake off this deception. The more the authorities concealed the truth, the more I felt compelled to pursue it, and I began reading volumes of newly published material. The turmoil in Beijing in 1989 led me to a profound awakening; the blood of those young students cleansed my brain of all the lies I had accepted over the previous decades. As a journalist, I strove to report the truth. As a scholar, I felt a responsibility to restore historical truth for others who had been deceived.

In my effort to shake off deception, I came to understand the social background of my father's death and to reflect more profoundly on his life. In the 1980s a trend arose in my home village to erect gravestones for those who had passed on. High officials elsewhere erected particularly imposing tombstones. Friends and relatives encouraged me to erect a gravestone for my father. I thought that even though I was not a high official, I would erect for my father a tombstone grander than any of those others. Then I recalled that in 1958, many of the village's tombstones had been dismantled for use in irrigation projects or as bases for smelting ovens in the steelmaking campaign during the Great Leap Forward; some had been laid out on roadways. The more impressive the monument, the greater the likelihood of it being demolished. My father's tombstone had to be erected not on the ground, but in my heart. A tombstone in the heart could never be demolished or trampled underfoot.

I did erect a tombstone for my father, in my heart, and this book is made up of the words I carved into that tombstone. Even after I leave this life, these heartfelt words will remain behind in libraries throughout the world.

2.

My family tragedy was repeated in some ten million families throughout China.

In chapter 11, on population loss, readers will see that multiple sources indicate around 36 million starvation deaths in China from 1958 to 1962.

Because starvation also caused a drop in the birth rate, there was also an estimated shortfall of 40 million births in China during those years.

In some regions, nearly every family experienced at least one death from starvation, and some families were completely wiped out. Entire villages were left without a single living inhabitant. It was as Mao Zedong wrote in one of his poems: "A thousand villages overgrown with weeds, men wasted away; Ten thousand homes where only ghosts sing."[16]

How can we conceptualize the 36 million people who starved to death? This number is equivalent to 450 times the number of people killed by the atomic bomb dropped on Nagasaki on August 9, 1945.[17] It is 150 times the number of people killed in the Tangshan earthquake on July 28, 1976.[18] It is greater than the number of people killed in World War I. The Great Famine even outstripped the ravages of World War II; the war caused 40 to 50 million deaths throughout Europe, Asia, and Africa over the course of seven or eight years,[19] but the Great Famine's 36 million victims died within three or four years, with most deaths concentrated in a six-month period.

The Great Famine makes all of China's other famines pale in comparison. The most severe famine previously recorded occurred in 1928–30 and affected twenty-two provinces. That famine broke all previous records, but still killed only 10 million people. In the seventeen years from 1920 through 1936, crop failures took the lives of 18.36 million people.[20] Li Wenhai and others, in the books *China's Recent Famines* and *China's Ten Greatest Recent Famines*,[21] believe that number is exaggerated, and that the number of people who died during the most severe famine in 1928–30 did not exceed 6 million. The number of people who starved to death from 1958 to 1962 was many times greater than the number who died in any previous disaster in China.

There were no anguished appeals to heaven, no hemp-robed funerals, no firecrackers and hell money to see the departed to their final destination, no sympathy, no grief, no tears, no shock, no dread. Tens of millions departed this world in an atmosphere of mute apathy.

Some villages transported corpses by the truckload for burial in common graves. In villages where survivors lacked the strength for proper interment, the limbs of the dead protruded from the ground. In some places, the dead remained along the roadsides where they had dropped in their futile search for food. More than a few were simply left in their homes, where rats gnawed at their noses and eyes.

In the autumn of 1999, I went to a Henan village that the famine had struck with particular severity. A villager in his seventies, Yu Wenhai, pointed to several trees growing in a wheat field and said, "Where those trees are standing was once a pit in which at least a hundred corpses were buried." If Yu, a witness to the events, had not pointed this out, no outsider would have known of the horrendous tragedy that lay buried beneath the fresh green seedlings and stately trees.

Starvation was a prolonged agony. The grain was gone, the wild herbs had all been eaten, even the bark had been stripped from the trees, and bird droppings, rats, and cotton batting were used to fill stomachs. In the kaolin clay fields,[22] starving people chewed on the clay as they dug it. The corpses of the dead, famine victims seeking refuge from other villages, even one's own family members, became food for the desperate.

Cannibalism was no longer exceptional. Ancient annals report cases of families exchanging children to consume during severe famines, but during the Great Famine, some families resorted to eating their own children. I met people who had eaten human flesh, and heard them describe its taste. Reliable evidence indicates there were thousands of cases of cannibalism throughout China at that time.[23] Some are described in the chapters that follow. It is a tragedy unprecedented in world history for tens of millions of people to starve to death and to resort to cannibalism during a period of normal climate patterns with no wars or epidemics.

At that time and in the decades to follow, China's books, newspapers, and official documents assiduously covered up this massive human tragedy. Officials sealed their lips and falsified statistics, and the authorities ordered the destruction of all data reporting the depletion of China's population by tens of millions.

Refugees who escaped to Hong Kong and family members of Chinese living overseas managed to spread some news of the calamity, and based on this information, some Western media published reports on the famine. The Chinese government categorically labeled these piecemeal reports as "vicious attacks" and "slanderous rumors."

To shape international public opinion, the Chinese government invited "friends of China" to visit and see for themselves, in the hope that they would write reports that "clarified the facts and truth." The government meticulously planned every step of a visitor's itinerary, including which places he would visit, the people with whom he could come into contact, and the lines people should recite when receiving the guests. Foreign guests were kept segregated from ordinary people, and well-fed and well-clothed individuals were sometimes put on display.

Fang Shi, at that time deputy director of Xinhua's domestic news service, was tasked with accompanying foreign guests on tours of An-hui Province. He later told me how the Anhui provincial party committee deceived foreign visitors, who then published "eyewitness" reports prais-ing China's "great accomplishments" and saying people were well fed and well clothed.

British journalist Felix Greene[24] wrote in his 1964 work *A Curtain of Ignorance* that he had traveled throughout China in 1960 without see-ing any signs of mass starvation. The American journalist Edgar Snow was another who passed his deception on to others.[25] The Xinhua News Agency translated all of those overseas articles into Chinese as "export products sold in the home market" for dissemination in *Cankao xiaoxi* (*Reference News*) and *Cankao ziliao* (*Reference Material*), to serve as tools for unifying public opinion and suppressing alternative views within China.

Some twenty years after these events, foreign scholars and Chinese liv-ing outside the mainland began researching this tragedy. These studies were of great value, but suffered from the authors' lack of access to inter-nal materials in official archives.

Beginning in the early 1990s, I took advantage of my reporting trips to consult relevant materials and interview people who had survived the famine. I traveled from the northwest to the southwest, from North China to East China, from Northeast China to South China, consulting archives in more than a dozen provinces and interviewing more than a hundred eyewitnesses. In ten years I accumulated documents totaling millions of words and ten notebooks full of notes, which helped me gain a relatively comprehensive and in-depth understanding of the Great Famine.

Confronted by the severe consequences of the Great Famine, Presi-dent Liu Shaoqi once said to Mao Zedong, "History will record the role you and I played in the starvation of so many people, and the cannibalism will also be memorialized!"[26] In the spring of 1962, Liu once again noted that "Deaths by starvation will be recorded in the history books."[27] Yet after more than forty years, no full account of the Great Famine has been published in mainland China. More than regrettable from a historical standpoint, it is an offense to the memories of the tens of millions of innocent victims. I have spent several years bringing this book to completion in the hope that it may serve as a tombstone and perhaps a consolation to those tens of millions of hungry spirits.

Liu Shaoqi also once said that this disaster should be engraved on a memorial tablet as a record "to be passed down to our children and grandchildren so that such an error will never be committed again." I believe that my book alone will be inadequate to keep this historical lesson firmly in mind. There are memorials to the Tangshan earthquake, to Hiroshima and Nagasaki, and to the victims of World War II in Europe. China should also erect memorials to the victims of the Great Famine in the places where the deaths were most concentrated, such as Xinyang, Tongwei, Luoding, Bozhou, Fengyang, Zunyi, Jinsha, Pi County, Yingjing, Rong County, Fengdu, Dayi, Guantao, and Jining, and in the provincial capitals of the most heavily affected provinces, namely Sichuan, Anhui, Guizhou, Henan, Shandong, Gansu, and Qinghai, as well as at Tiananmen Square in Beijing. These memorials would not only commemorate the dead, but also serve as a permanent reminder of the importance of preventing such a tragedy from ever happening again.

3.

Even with the reduction in cultivated land and massive population growth of the reform era that began in 1976, China's grain is more abundant than ever, and its young people are ignorant of hunger. This came about after the people's communes were replaced by remuneration linked to output, demonstrating the critical influence a system can have on famine.

The Nobel Prize–winning economist Amartya Sen wrote:

> In the terrible history of famines in the world, no substantial famine has ever occurred in any independent and democratic country with a relatively free press. We cannot find exceptions to this rule, no matter where we look: the recent famines of Ethiopia, Somalia, or other dictatorial regimes; famines in the Soviet Union in the 1930s; China's 1958–61 famine with the failure of the Great Leap Forward; or earlier still, the famines in Ireland or India under alien rule. China, although it was in many ways doing much better economically than India, still managed (unlike India) to have a famine, indeed the largest recorded famine in world history: Nearly 30 million people died in the famine of 1958–

61, while faulty governmental policies remained uncorrected for three full years. The policies went uncriticized because there were no opposition parties in parliament, no free press, and no multiparty elections. Indeed, it is precisely this lack of challenge that allowed the deeply defective policies to continue even though they were killing millions each year.[28]

The basic reason why tens of millions of people in China starved to death was totalitarianism. While totalitarianism does not inevitably result in disasters on such a massive scale, it facilitates the development of extremely flawed policies and impedes their correction. Even more important is that in this kind of system, the government monopolizes all production and life-sustaining resources, so that once a calamity occurs, ordinary people have no means of saving themselves.

In the chapters that follow, I will relate how the People's Republic of China combined a ruthless suppression of political dissent with a highly centralized planned economy to produce a system that Mao Zedong himself characterized as "Marx plus Qin Shihuang." This combination of Soviet-style autocracy and ancient Chinese despotism resulted in an abuse of executive power exceeding that of the Soviet Union or of any of China's emperors, controlling politics, the economy, culture and ideology, and every aspect of daily life. The dictatorship's coercive power penetrated every corner of even the most remote village, to every member of every family, into the minds and entrails of every individual. Referring to this system as "totalitarianism" denotes the expansion of executive power to its ultimate extent and extreme.

Mao occupied the core position among the handful of people who controlled the PRC: the standing committee of the Politburo of the CCP Central Committee. Apart from his position as leader of the party and state, Mao was chairman of the Military Commission, which gave him control over the armed forces. The others at the top of the pyramid stood in awe and terror before Mao, and were constantly preoccupied with maintaining their own positions. In this way, the CCP's dictatorship of the proletariat made Mao the most powerful emperor who had ever ruled China.

In the totalitarian administrative process, the will of the senior leadership was magnified at each successive level, while the voices at the lower levels were suppressed by increasing degrees. In this way, erroneous policies were intensified by both positive and negative feedback, until disaster resulted. Remedies could never reflect ill on the supreme leader, so redress never went quite far enough. In their blind worship of power, officials conformed to the prevailing trends and focused their efforts on self-preservation. The more ruthless their infighting, the more threatened Mao felt by those around him, and the more vicious his purges. In the midst of these intense power struggles, people would not hesitate to lie or sell out their friends for the sake of self-preservation and promotion.

In 1955, in accordance with Mao's wishes, economic policy took on a "rash advance," marked by high production targets at high speed that burdened the national economy. When high grain-procurement demands caused starvation in the countryside in 1956, Zhou Enlai, Chen Yun, and other senior officials tried to rein in the ruinous policies, only to suffer Mao's wrath; Zhou was nearly dismissed from his position. Learning from this episode, Mao's subordinates yielded to his fanaticism in 1958, and adopted corrective measures only after the grave consequences became clear. Even so, when defense minister Peng Dehuai criticized the erroneous policies, Mao immediately turned against him and abandoned the corrective measures. As a result, people continued to starve for three more years. The peasants, positioned at the bottom of the pyramid, bore the brunt of the famine, while the homogenization of Chinese society under totalitarianism meant that no part of China escaped its disastrous effects.

With Mao as China's sole theoretical authority, as well as the ultimate wielder of political and military power, China's government became a secular theocracy that united the center of power with the center of truth. Divergence from Mao's views was heresy, and since the government had the power to penalize and deprive an individual of everything, the merest thought of discontent prompted an overwhelming dread that in turn gave rise to lies. Dread and falsehood were thus both the result and the lifeblood of totalitarianism: the more a person possessed, the more he stood to lose. Possessing more than the average person, officials and intellectuals lived in that much greater fear, and demonstrated their "loyalty" to the system through virtuoso pandering and deceit. The lies they spun in official life, academia, and the arts and media enslaved China's people in falsehood and illusion.

Under the imperial system of earlier eras, people had the right to silence. The totalitarian system deprived people of even that right. In one political movement after another, each person was forced to "declare his stand," "expose his thoughts," and "bare his heart to the party." Repeated self-abasement led people continuously to trample upon those things they most cherished and flatter those things they had always most despised. In this way the totalitarian system caused the degeneration of the national character of the Chinese people. The insanity and ruthlessness of the Great Leap Forward and the Great Cultural Revolution were the result of that degeneration and the great "achievement" of the totalitarian system.

The regime considered no cost or coercion too great in making the realization of Communist ideals the supreme goal of the entire populace. The peasants bore the chief burden of realizing these ideals; they shouldered the cost of industrialization, of collectivization, of subsidizing the cities, and of the extravagant habits of officials at every level. Most of this cost was imposed through the state monopoly for purchasing and marketing. Peasants were obliged to sell their produce to the government at prices that did not cover their costs. With official priority placed on feeding the burgeoning urban population and importing machinery in exchange for grain exports, grain was all but snatched from peasant mouths. President Liu Shaoqi at one point frankly acknowledged this:

> At present there is a conflict between the amount of grain the government needs and the amount that the peasants are willing to sell, and this conflict is quite severe. The peasants' preference is to sell the government whatever is left over after they've eaten their fill. If the government only took its procurement after the peasants had eaten their fill, the rest of us would not have enough to eat: the workers, teachers, scientists, and others living in the cities. If these people don't get enough to eat, industrialization cannot be carried out and the armed forces will also have to be reduced, making our national defense construction impossible to implement.[29]

The inadequacy of the grain left after the peasants sold their "surplus" to the government was one of the reasons so many starved to death.

At the time when the cities were implementing nationalization, the villages were implementing collectivization, both of which processes served totalitarianism by stripping individuals of their rights and interests. Agricultural collectivization deprived peasants and cadres of the power to decide what would be planted, over how large an area and by what means. Peasants were initially allowed to retain a small amount of land, enough to raise vegetables for their own consumption, but in 1958 even that bit of land was collectivized and villagers were all deployed to collective labor in production teams.

All agricultural products, including foodstuffs, cotton, and cooking oil, were procured for marketing by the state, and all goods needed for daily life were supplied to urban and rural residents through a system of state-issued ration coupons. These coupons could be exchanged for goods only in the locality where one was registered under the household registration system (*hukou*). Likewise, under the *hukou* system, peasants were allowed to engage only in agricultural labor, and could leave their villages only with permission from production team heads. The labor and lives of peasants were thus tightly restricted within the confines of political authority. If an error in policy prevented the collective from supplying daily necessities, peasants had no other recourse.

The people's communes went further by integrating government administration with enterprise management, and making all economic activity subservient to political goals. All assets came under the control of government officials, and the government's organizational structure replaced the family, religion, and all other forms of social organization. In 1958, labor in the people's communes was organized along military lines for massive steel, irrigation, and agriculture projects. Communal kitchens and nurseries further eroded the family's function as an economic and social unit.

The communal kitchens were a major reason why so many people starved to death. Home stoves were dismantled, and cooking implements, tables and chairs, foodstuffs, and firewood were handed over to the communal kitchen, as were livestock, poultry, and any edible plants harvested by commune members. In some places, no chimneys were allowed to be lit outside the communal kitchen.

The first damage inflicted by the communal kitchens was the waste of food. During the first two months of operation, commune members gorged themselves under the influence of Mao's pronouncements that there might be "too much food." Believing the government would come up with more food when current supplies were exhausted, some communes consumed all their grain by the end of 1958 and were left to wait for government replenishment that never arrived.

As the quality and quantity of food declined, the communal kitchens became bastions of privilege for cadres, who always managed to eat their fill. By controlling the communal kitchens, cadres were able to impose the "dictatorship of the proletariat" on every individual stomach, as anyone who proved disobedient could be deprived of food. In effect, the communal kitchens forced villagers to hand their food ladles over to their leaders, thereby transferring their survival to the hands of these leaders; losing possession of their ladles, the villagers lost control over their very survival.

Cadres inflicted brutal punishment on villagers, who had mixed feelings about the communization process, who furtively consumed the collectives' seedlings out of hunger, or who had no strength for the massive irrigation projects, and on some conscientious cadres. Punishments included being beaten while suspended in midair, forced into protracted kneeling, paraded through the streets, deprived of food, exposed to the cold or the sun, and having one's ears or fingers cut off. In the villages, the so-called dictatorship of the proletariat was in fact the dictatorship of the cadres, and those with the greatest power were able to inflict the greatest amount of arbitrary abuse. As detailed in the following chapters, many deaths resulted from such beatings, even though they did not occur in every production team. Usually when famine strikes, people appeal for outside aid or flee. Under the system in China at that time, however, villagers had no power to seek aid or escape. Officials at all levels used all means at their disposal to prevent news of the famine from leaking. Public security bureaus controlled all postal communications and held all letters being mailed outside the locality. Entire villages were placed under lockdown, and refugees who were caught attempting to escape were paraded through the streets, flogged, or otherwise punished as "vagrants."

For the most part, people submitted; the exceptional people who opposed the system were usually crushed by it. In the face of a rigid political system, individual power was all but nonexistent. The system was like a casting mold; no matter how hard the metal, once it was melted and poured into that mold, it came out the same shape as everything else. Regardless of what kind of person went into the totalitarian system, all came out as conjoined twins facing in opposite directions: either despot or slave, depending on their position respective to those above or below them. Mao Zedong was the creator of this mold (strictly speaking, he was the successor and developer of the autocratic model), and he himself was to some extent a creature of this same mold. Within the framework of this system, Mao's own actions were to a certain extent also beyond his control. No one had the power to resist such a system, not even Mao.

Totalitarianism is the most backward, barbaric, and inhumane of all systems existing in the modern world. The death of tens of millions of innocent people during the three-year famine rang the death knell for this system, as the Socialist Education Movement and Cultural Revolution that rose in response to it only managed to push it beyond all possibility of redemption.

After more than twenty years of economic reform, the totalitarian system has become more flexible; the people's communes have long been dismantled, the state monopoly for purchasing and marketing has been abolished, and the people are able to seek and develop their own livelihood through the marketplace. China has undergone an enormous transformation. But because the political system remains unchanged, the great changes in the economic and social sphere have resulted in an unequal allocation of the fruits and costs of economic reform. The combined abuses under the exclusive profit orientation of a market economy and the untrammeled power of totalitarianism have created an endless supply of injustice, exacerbating discontent among the lower-class majority.

In this new century, I believe that rulers and ordinary citizens alike know in their hearts that the totalitarian system has reached its end. The question now is how to minimize social upheaval and damage as the system changes. I believe that if everyone approaches the problem not from the perspective of personal interest or group interest, but for the sake of the wider social interest, and makes a conscious choice to undertake political reform, we can find the means to minimize the shock and damage that result. The establishment of a market economy has already formed a firm economic base for a democratic political system, and totalitarian society has already eased into a post-totalitarian society. I firmly believe that China will one day see totalitarianism replaced by democracy. And this day will not be long in coming.

With this book I erect a tombstone anticipating the ultimate demise of the totalitarian system. Through it, later generations will know that there was once a system established at a certain juncture of history in the name of "liberating mankind" that in reality enslaved humanity. This system promoted itself as the "Road to Paradise," but in fact it was the road to perdition.

1 THE EPICENTER OF THE DISASTER

Henan is a rural province north of Shanghai and south of Beijing. The Chinese Communist Party's "Three Red Banners" waved highest here, and the famine likewise hit hardest. Political movements set off the famine in Henan. Some seventy thousand Henan residents were labeled "rightists" in 1957—nearly 13 percent of those targeted in the Anti-Rightist Movement nationwide, and 15 percent of the province's cadres.[1] In 1958 a new campaign was launched against the "Pan, Yang, Wang rightist antiparty clique" within the party, which will be detailed later in this chapter.[2] These two campaigns combined to create dread and fanaticism that led to wild exaggeration and horrendous brutality that in turn brought about a series of catastrophes—among which the "Xinyang Incident" is the most notable.

PART I: THE XINYANG INCIDENT

Xinyang Prefecture lies in the southeast of Henan, bordering the provinces of Hubei and Anhui. In 1958 the prefecture administered eighteen counties, the city of Xinyang, and the town of Zhumadian. It was home to 8.5 million people. Most of the prefecture consisted of mountain ranges that had served as bases for China's revolutionary forces, and where hundreds of thousands of lives had been sacrificed in the civil war with the Kuomintang. Elderly residents say, "Even the trees and grasses of the Dabie Mountains served the Communist Party." This lush region was the province's main producer of grain and cotton and an abundant source of tea leaves, timber, bamboo, tung oil, and medicinal herbs. Scenic Jigong Shan (Rooster Mountain) is located here. In short, Xinyang, along with nearby Nanyang and Luoyang, was the economic engine of the province. Yet from the winter of 1959 to the spring of 1960, at least one million people starved to death here—one out of every eight residents.

Li Jian, an official of the CCP Central Control Commission (the precursor of the Discipline and Inspection Commission) sent to Henan in the wake of the famine, found that the largest number of starvation deaths occurred in Xinyang and two other prefectures: Nanyang and Xuchang. The most horrific situation became known as the "Xinyang Incident."[3]

In September 1999, I went to Xinyang, accompanied by a senior reporter from Xinhua's Henan branch, Gu Yuezhong, and a former Xinhua reporter who had been stationed in Xinyang during the famine, Lu Baoguo. Gu had excellent relations with local officials, but the Xinyang municipal party committee was clearly disconcerted by the purpose of our visit, and arranged a scenic tour of Rooster Mountain. Nonetheless, we managed to interview a number of cadres and villagers who had lived through the famine, and gained access to a number of documents that shed light on the Xinyang Incident.

POLITICAL PRESSURE BREEDS EXAGGERATION

In a political system such as China's, those below imitate those above, and political struggles at the higher levels are replicated at the lower levels in an expanded and even more ruthless form. This is what happened in Xinyang.

Following the provincial-level campaign against the "Pan, Yang, Wang" clique and the campaign against right deviation, Xinyang's Guangshan County on November 11, 1959, conducted a criticism, or "struggle," session against the secretary of the CCP county secretariat, Zhang Fuhong, who was labeled a "right deviationist" and a "degenerate element." During the struggle session, county party secretary Ma Longshan took the lead by kicking Zhang, after which others set upon him with fists and feet. Other struggle sessions were conducted by county-level cadres on November 13 and 14, during which Zhang was beaten bloody, his hair ripped out in patches, and his uniform torn to shreds, leaving him barely able to walk.

On November 15, Zhang was handed over to commune cadres, by which time he could only lie on the floor while he was kicked and punched and had what remained of his hair torn out. Another struggle session by commune cadres on November 16 left Zhang near death; by the time he was dragged home that day, he had lost control of his bodily functions and could no longer eat or drink. On November 17 he was accused of malingering and attacked again. On November 18 he was accused of pining for the return of Kuomintang leader Chiang Kai-shek and was dragged from his bed for more struggle. When he asked for water, he was refused. Around noon on November 19, Zhang Fuhong died.[4]

Xinyang's deputy party secretary and prefectural commissioner, Zhang Shufan, subsequently related in his memoirs why Zhang Fuhong was targeted. In the spring of 1959, in order to alleviate famine conditions among the peasants, Ma Longshan sent Zhang Fuhong to a production team to launch a pilot project in which output quotas were assigned to each household. Other localities were doing the same, but following the political reversals of the Central Committee's Lushan Conference,[5] household output quotas were labeled right opportunism. Ma denied responsibility, saying Zhang Fuhong had initiated the use of quotas. Although Zhang insisted that Ma had assigned him to carry out the system,[6] an official one level higher can crush his subordinate, and that is what happened here.

Campaigns against right deviation in other counties were similarly brutal. In Xi County, party secretary Xu Xilan directed a struggle session against deputy secretary Feng Peiran. Xu sat above Feng with a handgun at his side while someone held Feng by the neck as others beat and kicked him. According to Zhang Shufan's memoirs, some twelve thousand struggle sessions were held in the prefecture,[7] and all kinds of ridiculous statements were made under political pressure.

In 1958, Xinyang's Suiping County was given nationwide publicity for Great Leap production successes referred to as Sputniks, or "satellites." These "grand achievements" were attributed to the "struggle against right-deviating conservatism." In an atmosphere of extreme political pressure, anyone who dared question the accuracy of these reported crop yields risked being labeled a "doubter" or "denier" engaged in "casting aspersions on the excellent situation," and anyone who exposed the fraudulence of the high-yield model was subjected to struggle.

A drought in 1959 drove down Xinyang's crop yields, but prefectural party cadres, overcome by fanaticism, proposed the slogan of "Big drought, big harvest" and claimed higher yields than the year before. Commissioner Zhang Shufan, who was directly responsible for agriculture, in early August convened a meeting of leading county cadres to provide "practical and realistic" appraisals of the disaster and to adopt advanced measures such as varied crop plantings to prevent a famine.

Following the Lushan Conference, the prefectural party committee had each county report its projected yields. Under the political pressure of the times, each county's estimate was exceeded by that of the next, as all feared being criticized for reporting the lowest projection. Yu Dehong, a staff member at the prefectural party committee meeting, later recalled that the first projection totaled 15 billion kilos. Zhang Shufan and others thought this excessively optimistic and asked everyone to submit new figures, which subsequently totaled 7.5 billion kilos and finally 3.6 billion kilos. During a meeting of the prefectural party committee's standing committee, eight of the nine standing committee members believed that the 1959 crop yield would exceed that of 1958, and that given the 1958 yield of 2.8 billion kilos, a 3.6 billion kilo yield for 1959 was very reasonable. Zhang Shufan, however, expected a yield of only 1.5 to 2.0 billion kilos.

In late August and early September, the Henan provincial party committee convened an enlarged meeting to implement the spirit of the Lushan Conference. Each prefecture was asked to report projected crop yields. Zhang Shufan led off for Xinyang by reporting that his standing committee projected a crop yield of 3.6 billion kilos, but that his more modest personal projection was 1.5 to 2 billion kilos. The provincial party committee was dissatisfied with Zhang's report and subsequently asked prefectural party secretary Lu Xianwen, "What's going on in Xinyang?" Under pressure, Lu convened another meeting of county party secretaries requesting new projections. At first no one spoke, but finally someone asked, "Isn't it what we already reported in our meeting?" Lu Xianwen replied, "Someone took exception to those projections." By "someone," Lu was referring to Zhang Shufan. Soon afterward, right-deviating elements were sought out and subjected to struggle, and this county head who had dared to speak the truth was stripped of his official position.[8]

PROCUREMENT BASED ON ABSURD PROJECTIONS

Exaggerated yield projections meant high state procurement quotas. In Henan, every county was forced to hand over every available kernel of grain. Zhang Shufan recalls:

Following the expanded meeting, I returned to the prefecture to head up the autumn harvest procurement. The provincial party committee based its procurement on the big 1958 harvest, and our prefecture met our quota of 800 million kilos by taking every kernel of grain ration and seed grain from the peasants. Immediately after the harvest, many localities were left with nothing to eat, and people began to leave the prefecture in search of food. Many communal kitchens had no food to serve their members, and the helpless villagers staved their hunger at home as best they could with sweet potatoes and wild herbs.

Higher levels reported a somewhat smaller procurement quota, but agreed that excessive procurement had serious repercussions:

In 1959, Xinyang suffered a drought. The total grain yield of the prefecture was less than 1.63 billion kilos, a decrease of 46.1 percent from 1958, but the prefectural party committee projected a grain yield of more than 3.21 billion kilos. On that basis, the province set Xinyang's procurement quota at 480 million kilos, which was 21.5 million kilos more than in 1958. The prefectural party committee added 5 percent to the procurement quota for each county, raising the total procurement quota to 502.45 million kilos. After the prefecture met its quota, the food ration left after seed grain and fodder were excluded was only 82.25 kilos of unprocessed grain per person for the year. Based on typical consumption of 17.5 kilos per person per month, that was enough to feed the population for four months. With no supplementary foodstuffs or oil, the 17.5 kilos of unprocessed grain amounted to 12.5 kilos of edible grain, barely enough to prevent starvation. In addition, some 1.8 million people were engaged in irrigation projects in the prefecture, and they alone consumed a large share of the available grain.[9]

The Henan provincial party committee subsequently found,

Last year the autumn yield of the entire prefecture of Xinyang was estimated at only a little more than 1 billion kilos, but was exaggerated to 3.2 billion kilos, and the province set the prefecture's procurement quota at 480 million kilos, with additional procurements at the prefecture, county, and commune levels increasing the procurement quota by more than 20 percent. After the prefecture met its mid-October procurement quota of more than 350 million kilos, 3,751 communal kitchens (370,000 people) were left without food. Even under those conditions, the campaign against false underreporting of output and of widespread private withholding of foodstuffs continued in all communes and production teams.[10]

As this campaign gained force, it exacerbated the famine.

In 1958, Xinyang Prefecture organized about 30 percent of the prefecture's working population for the great iron and steel production campaign.[11] The steel furnaces didn't actually smelt any iron; rather, the woks and cooking utensils of the peasants, the door knockers from their homes, and the bells from temples were all melted down in order to report success. In addition to the 1.2 million laborers used for this campaign, more than half a million were engaged in ball bearing production, and another 2.0 million in irrigation projects.[12] Feeding these laborers left that much less grain for the farm production teams.

THE VIOLENT CAMPAIGN AGAINST FALSE REPORTING OF OUTPUT

Excessively high requisition quotas made procurement difficult. If farmers were unable to hand over the required amount, the government would accuse production teams of concealing grain. A "struggle between the two roads" (of socialism and capitalism) was launched to counteract the alleged withholding of grain. This campaign used political pressure, mental torture, and ruthless violence to extort every last kernel of grain or seed from the peasants. Anyone who uttered the slightest protest was beaten, sometimes fatally.

A meeting at Rooster Mountain pushed the campaign against grain hoarding to a climax. Li Ruiying, the wife of Zhang Shufan, was chair of Xinyang Prefecture's Federation of Women. In June 1959 the prefectural party committee had her lead a work group to Rooster Mountain Commune to report on a pilot project to produce 5,000 kilos of paddy per *mu* of land, the brainchild of the county party secretary. Li Ruiying's team stayed at Rooster Mountain for a month, during which they learned that this model commune was a fraud and that the peasants there were starving. Li wrote to prefectural party secretary Lu Xianwen requesting

105,000 kilos of grain, but Lu refused and labeled Li Ruiying a right deviationist. A cadre sent to Rooster Mountain to replace Li also truthfully reported the hunger of commune members, only to be labeled a "vacillator."

Li's replacement, Wang Binglin, tried to appease party secretary Lu Xianwen by organizing an on-the-spot meeting to oppose "false reporting of output and private withholding," the arcane official formulation for hoarding. All that was produced were rice husks covered by a thin layer of grain. The prefectural party committee ordered local cadres to stifle the public outcry, stop villagers from fleeing in search of food, and halt the closure of communal kitchens. After that, anyone who claimed to have no grain was labeled a "negator of the Three Red Banners," a "negator of the Great Harvest," or a "right deviationist," and was subjected to struggle. If communal kitchens closed due to lack of food, this was labeled "the masses threatening the cadres," and abandoning starving children along the roadsides was labeled "an assault against the party."[13]

Punishments were inflicted on cadres and villagers alike. In Guangshan County, 2,241 people were beaten, 105 fatally, and 526 cadres were stripped of their official positions. The number of deaths from physical abuse rose even higher toward the end of the campaign. In *The Xinyang Incident*, Qiao Peihua describes the situation in one village:

At the end of September 1959, Wang Pinggui, a member of the Wangxiaowan production team, was forced to hand over grain kept in his home, and was beaten with a shoulder pole, dying of his injuries five days later. Not long after Wang's death, the rest of his four-member household died of starvation.

In October 1959, Luo Mingzhu of the Luowan production team, upon failing to hand over any grain, was bound and suspended in midair and beaten, then doused with ice-cold water. He died the next day.

On October 13, 1959, Wang Taishu of the Chenwan production team, upon failing to hand over any grain, was bound and beaten with shoulder poles and rods, dying four days later. His fourteen-year-old daughter, Wang Pingrong, subsequently died of starvation.

On October 15, 1959, Zhang Zhirong of the Xiongwan production team, upon failing to hand over any grain, was bound and beaten to death with kindling and poles. The brigade's cadre used tongs to insert rice and soya beans into the deceased's anus while shouting, "Now you can grow grain out of your corpse!" Zhang left behind children aged eight and ten who subsequently died of starvation.

On October 19, 1959, Chenwan production team member Chen Xiaojia and his son Chen Guihou were hung from the beam of the communal dining hall when they failed to hand over any grain. They were beaten and doused with cold water, both dying within seven days. Two small children who survived them eventually died of starvation.

On October 24, 1959, the married couple Zheng Jinhou and Luo Mingying of the Yanwan production team had 28 silver coins seized from their home during the campaign and were beaten to death. Their three children, left without anyone to care for them, starved to death.

On November 8, 1959, Xu Chuanzheng of the Xiongwan production team was falsely accused of withholding grain. He was hung from the beam of the communal dining hall and brutally beaten, dying six days later. The six family members who survived him subsequently starved to death.

On November 8, 1959, Zhong Xingjian of the Yanwan production team was accused of "defying the leadership," and a cadre hacked him to death with an ax.[14]

These are only a portion of the incidents Qiao recounts.

Liu Wencai, secretary of Guangshan County party secretariat, was in charge of the anti-hoarding campaign at Huaidian People's Commune, during which he flogged more than forty peasants, four of whom died. Some 93 percent of commune-level cadres in Guangshan County led such campaigns and personally took part in beatings. On November 28, 1960, a report was sent to Henan party secretary Wu Zhipu.

In the calamity at Guangshan County's Huaidian people's commune in the autumn of 1959, the commune's average yield per *mu* was 86 kilos, for a total of 5.955 million kilos. The commune's party committee reported a yield of 313 kilos per *mu*, for a total of 23.05 million kilos. The procurement quota set by the county was 6 million kilos, which exceeded the commune's total grain yield. In order to achieve the procurement quota, every means had to be taken to oppose false reporting and private withholding, and every scrap of food had to be seized from the masses. The final procurement was 5.185 million kilos. All of the communal kitchens were closed down, and deaths followed. Liu Wencai and the commune party committee attributed the kitchen closures and deaths to attacks by well-to-do middle peasants and sabotage by class enemies, and to the struggle between the two paths of socialism and capitalism. They continued the campaign against false reporting and private withholding for eight months. Within sixty or seventy days not a kernel of grain could be found anywhere, and mass starvation followed.

The commune originally numbered 36,691 members in 8,027 households. Between September 1959 and June 1960, 12,134 people died (among them, 7,013 males and 5,121 females), constituting 33 percent of the total population. There were 780 households completely extinguished, making up 9.7 percent of all households. The village of Jiangwan originally had 45 inhabitants, but 44 of them died, leaving behind only one woman in her sixties, who went insane.

There was a total of 1,510 cadres at the commune, brigade, and production team level, and 628, or 45.1 percent, took part in beatings. The number beaten totaled 3,528 (among them 231 cadres), with 558 dying while being beaten, 636 dying subsequently, another 141 left permanently disabled, 14 driven to commit suicide, and 43 driven away.

Apart from the standard abuse of beating, kicking, exposure, and starvation, there were dozens of other extremely cruel forms of torture, including dousing the head with cold water, tearing out hair, cutting off ears, driving bamboo strips into the palms, driving pine needles into the gums, "lighting the celestial lantern,"[15] forcing lit embers into the mouth, branding the nipples, tearing out pubic hair, penetrating the genitals, and being buried alive.

When thirteen children arrived at the commune begging for food, the commune's party secretary, surnamed Jiang, along with others incited kitchen staff to drag them deep into the mountains, where they were left to die of hunger and exposure.

The official communal dining hall was divided into three types: a special dining room for party secretaries, a slightly larger room for party committee members, and a large mess hall for ordinary cadres. The special dining room served meat, fish, eggs, and fried peanuts.

This was not the first time people had been beaten here. During the Anti-Rightist Movement in 1957, not a single rightist escaped beating. They originated the practice of shaving the character for "right" into a person's hair and herding miscreants in front of pig troughs, where they were forced to scoop out congee with their hands and eat it.

With no means of escaping a hopeless situation, ordinary people could not adequately look after their own. Families were scattered to the winds, children abandoned, and corpses left along the roadside to rot. As a result of the extreme deprivations of starvation, 381 commune members desecrated 134 corpses.[16]

Lying became a means of survival. A Huangchuan County party committee member and the director of agriculture and labor carried out socialist education sessions at Sanpisi Commune. There was not a bite for them to eat in the production teams during the day, so they had to return to the commune at night to eat, but dared not report that the production team had no food.

After the Xinyang Incident, the commune's first secretary, Jia Xinyuan, told a provincial party committee work group, "It wasn't that I didn't know anything at the time; of the 200 people who reported for military service last year, only 40 percent met the minimum weight requirement. I also knew about 100 or 200 people dying in one day. Struggling with myself, I went to the county three times to report what was happening, but turned back each time out of fear of being labeled a right deviationist. After returning, I then had to carry out campaigns against false reporting and private withholding."

During procurement, the leader of the Sanpisi production brigade told his commune party secretary, "People actually have no food to eat down there." The commune secretary criticized him: "That's right-deviationist thinking—you're viewing the problem in an overly simplistic manner!" That brigade held four meetings to counter hoarding and to search out hidden caches, and local leaders became struggle targets. The brigade was compelled to report 120,000 kilos of concealed grain, but not a single kernel was discovered.[17]

An accountant for one production team recalled, "The production team cadres gathered at Zhangli for a meeting. Everyone had to report grain, and those who failed had to go through group training, criticism, struggle, and beating. So it was reported that there was a storehouse here holding millet and another there holding soybeans, and so on. Once reported, the grain had to be delivered at a certain time the next day. In order to pass muster, our team lied like the others. The next day I was sitting next to the production team's telephone. At ten o'clock it rang and someone asked, 'Has the grain been sent over?' I said, 'It's being packed.'

Another telephone call came at noon: 'Why hasn't the grain arrived yet?' I said, 'It's on the way!' Another phone call came later, and I said, 'I'm the accountant, I don't know anything!' There was another assembly that night, and anyone who didn't lie would be beaten. Afraid of being beaten, most people lied."[18]

As people starved, cadres focused on meeting procurement quotas. When Huangchuan County failed to meet its quota, it sent a report on October 30, 1959, attributing the problems to the ideological shortcomings of the county party committee and commune party committee leadership, to their failure to anticipate the arduousness, complexity, and protractedness of the struggle between the two paths in relation to the issue of grain, and to their lack of vigilance and in-depth understanding of the grain issue as the focus of the struggle between socialism and capitalism. The right-deviationist thinking of some cadres within and outside the party had also become a threat to grain production, manifested in a failure to acknowledge the Great Harvest. The report recommended meeting the procurement quota through a socialist education campaign and mass debates. While the report was being written, people starved to death.[19]

The Henan provincial party committee thoroughly endorsed this false report, and on November 17 sent it throughout the province with calls for a new upsurge in grain procurement.

At Huangchuan County's Taolin Commune, the communal kitchen had closed down and commune members were starving, but procurement was intensified all the same. The county claimed there was plenty of grain and had its cadres search every nook and cranny and deliver every kernel of grain that was discovered. The county and the commune held telephone conferences nearly every day, during which cadres were ordered to report progress, and underperforming production brigades were ordered to conduct self-criticisms. Some production brigade secretaries trembled at the news of a telephone conference. If no grain was recovered, there would be another round of mobilization, debate, and reports. At the Hepi production brigade, combing every haystack recovered just 1,500 kilos of grain.[20]

The Huangchuan County party committee subsequently reported, "Our thinking was to achieve the procurement quota by any means available . . . [U]pon reaching 60 percent of the quota, the prefectural party committee convened a telephone meeting, and we ranked third from last, with provincial party secretary Song Zhihe specifically mentioning

Huangchuan County . . . We feared that reporting low yields would be interpreted as negating the Great Leap Forward and the Great Harvest, and we feared being criticized and labeled right-deviating opportunists."[21] Officials pandered to their superiors at the expense of the lives of ordinary people, and each level of officials put pressure on the next level down. The most common form of pressure was physical violence.

The procurement effort in Xi County was brutal. In early November, with the communal kitchens shut and people starving, the campaign to extort grain and oppose false reporting of output continued. The commune's acting first secretary, Qian Qinghuai, held reporting meetings for ten production brigades at midnight every night, and the three brigades trailing farthest on their procurement quotas were struggled. Eight production brigades reported twenty-two brigade cadres struggled, along with twenty-nine production team cadres and forty-four production group heads. One person was beaten to death during a struggle session, and another seven died subsequently. Cadres who spoke the truth were labeled "deniers of achievement" and "right deviationists," and were subjected to merciless struggle. When Liu Bingzhi, party secretary of the Yezhuang production brigade, said that there was no food and that the procurement quota could not be met, he was lifted by his arms and legs and hurled like a battering ram against the floor.[22]

Forty years later, elderly peasants still remembered how Secretary Qian and ten lieutenants (commune militia leaders and other toughs) grabbed every kernel of grain, 5,000 kilos in total, and that Qian was promoted as a result. The brutal campaign involved tortures such as "stir-fried beans" (referred to in Sichuan as "scrubbing the taro"), in which a person was pushed around a ring of people until he collapsed. Some victims with heart problems died during this ordeal. Although the statistics are incomplete, available evidence indicates that 1,065 people were beaten or persecuted to death during the campaign against false reporting in Xi County.[23]

In the winter of 1959, China's very first commune, Chayashan People's Commune, in Suiping County (originally called the Satellite People's Commune), had a new head, Guo Shuzhi, replacing the original head, who led a delegation to India to describe how China used socialism to end rural poverty. By then all of the commune's grain had been seized to meet its procurement quota, and Guo was anxiously considering how he would feed the commune members, when he received a phone call from prefectural party secretary Lu Xianwen. Lu bellowed,

> The struggle between the two paths regarding the issue of food is now intense and has reached a fight to the death. The Great Harvest is an objective reality—it's a fact that cannot be denied. Chayashan People's Commune is famous throughout China and the world, so how can there be any problems with food supply? This is the struggle between the two paths, and unlawful elements must be attacked. False reporting of output and private withholding are widespread, and most is perpetrated and led by cadres. They conceal grain in every available place, from heaven to earth and from mountain to stream, inside and outside the villages, and that is the main reason why grain supplies are so tight. It's necessary to launch struggles against wave-gazers, autumn reckoners, and extreme rightists. We cannot be lenient, but must ruthlessly struggle and criticize until every kernel of grain is unearthed. Tomorrow Suiping County must organize an upsurge in uncovering grain, and failure to report success to the prefectural party committee will be punished.

Guo quickly assembled the commune's production brigade and production team cadres and told them, "We must resolutely and ruthlessly find every kernel of grain in every corner. We must struggle all those who deserve it, and arrest all those who should be arrested. We cannot be lenient or indulge the whims of others. Anyone who tries to protect the guilty will be punished with them."

Gao De, the party secretary of the Shengqiao production brigade, had collapsed from stress during the county's anti-hoarding campaign, and had just begun to recover after spending several days at home on medication. When he was called to the meeting and told to discuss ways of finding more grain, he collapsed after a seizure, muttering, "There is no grain . . . really, there is . . . no grain."

A production team accountant named Bao Gen was targeted for struggle and criticism. Unable to withstand the kicks and blows, Bao said that he and the production team head, Zhu Suiping, had concealed 250 kilos of grain. The attacks then turned to Zhu Suiping. He initially derided Bao Gen's weakness and squared his shoulders against the mass attack, but eventually collapsed under the beating and kicking and was dragged upright by his hair. Someone grabbed a stool and made Zhu stand on it on one leg like a stork, after which someone else kicked the stool out from under him, sending him tumbling to the ground. The group then descended upon him with feet and fists, after which he was made to stand on one leg again. Beaten bloody, Zhu still refused to acknowledge hiding any grain. He was then bound hand and foot so tightly that the rope dug into his flesh. The other end of the rope was carried up into a tree, and the others used their combined strength to suspend Zhu in midair. Drained of strength and streaming with sweat, Zhu Suiping begged for mercy: "Please let me go, I'll tell you everything."

Seeing this, the other production team cadres reported grain and soybeans stored here and there, and the Suiping County party committee told the Xinyang prefectural committee that it would be able to recover nearly 23,000 kilos of grain in three days. In the end, however, not a single bean or kernel of grain was found.[24]

With starvation deaths at their peak in December 1959, deputy party secretary Song Zhihe, of the Henan provincial party committee, nonetheless reported that production was very good, and that "with gradual comprehension of the situation of class struggle, and by emphasizing reliance on the poor and lower-middle peasants and mobilizing the concentrated effort of the masses, some counties (Xincai, Shangcai, and Ru'nan) have made relatively swift progress on procurement and have met their quotas, while some have advanced more slowly and have performed poorly." He cited "three main reasons for the failure to meet quotas": the first was ideological shortcomings among the grassroots cadres; the second was cases in which ideological problems coexisted with work problems; and the third was cases in which an appropriate effort was made, but yield was poor. He believed that "whenever the poor and lower-middle peasants gained the upper hand and took leadership of production brigades and production teams, the procurement quotas were successfully met and the lives of commune members were well arranged. But where the leadership of production brigades and production teams was usurped by the well-to-do middle peasants with excessively capitalistic thinking, there were serious problems of false reporting of yield and private withholding, with the result that procurement quotas were not met and the life of commune members was badly managed; there the actual objective of false reporting of yield and private withholding was to undermine the communal kitchens." At the same time, the report acknowledged:

"In these districts it is not desirable at present to simply requisition grain; redistribution must be carried out as well as requisition, and proper arrangements must be made for the livelihood of commune members . . . If grain procurement continues in an unyielding fashion, there is a danger of alienating the masses."[25]

At a production brigade in Guangshan County, all food grain, seed, and livestock feed had been requisitioned. Although the communal dining hall was closed due to lack of food, the production team leader still stipulated "three major rules": no fires should be lit in the homes of commune members, no wild herbs should be gathered, and no one should leave the commune to escape starvation. The brigade then organized a twelve-man inspection team that searched homes every three days. Of the brigade's 25 party members, 21 took part in beatings. Commune members referred to the production brigade office as "the palace of Yama" (King of Hell). Of the production brigade's 346 households, 39 were completely wiped out. Out of an original population of 1,496 people, 555 died—490 by starvation, 55 by beatings, and 10 by suicide. Another 438 were severely beaten.[26]

The Henan provincial party committee subsequently reported, "There was a total of 50,000 cadres at the production brigade level or above, and it is estimated that at least 50 percent engaged in violations of law and discipline. Once beatings became routine, thousands of people were beaten to death, driven to commit suicide, or permanently crippled. The vast majority of communes and production teams established prisons and labor reform teams, and arbitrary detention was common."[27]

HORRIFIC STARVATION AND DEATH

As grain supplies dwindled, most communal kitchens had shut down by October and November 1959. In mid-November, Huangchuan County's Taolin Commune, which consisted of 122 production teams under 12 production brigades, experienced grain shortages at all its 291 communal kitchens, with no grain available for more than eighty days. In mid-September (just before the Mid-Autumn Festival), the Wuji production brigade stopped providing grain to the communal kitchens, and by mid-October, all of the brigade's communal kitchens had closed. The commune had not a single living elm tree; all had been stripped of their leaves and bark by starving peasants.

As of September 1959, Taolin Commune had 7,645 households totaling 34,897 individuals. By 1960, 15.64 percent of the population had died, with 692 households wiped out entirely. The death rate in the Hepi production brigade was 24.9 percent, with a 49 percent death rate among the labor force. When grain supplies had been cut off for more than eighty days, commune members first lost weight, then swelled with edema, then wasted away until they vomited fluid and died. Yang Chunshan, a member of the Malu production team of the Wuji brigade, was afraid that his sons, ages three and four, would be left with no one to care for them, so he drowned them in a pit just before he died.[28]

Lacking grain, the leaders of communal dining halls devised food substitutes:

> *Rice straw*: Rice straw was normally used to feed livestock, cover roofs, or twist into twine. Now it was chopped into small pieces and cooked in woks, after which it was ground into a fine meal and then sifted into flour that could be mixed with sweet potato flour and steamed into bread.
>
> *Corn stalks*: Peasants normally burned corn stalks to heat their cooking pots, and in normal years such stuff was not fed even to animals. Now it was eaten by humans. It was made edible by stripping away the outer husk, cooking it in woks, and then cutting it into small pieces, grinding it into meal, and mixing it with sweet potato flour to make steamed bread.
>
> *Egret droppings*: A species of waterfowl, egrets ate fish. Their droppings were pale-colored and had no foul odor. Starving people collected the droppings, rinsed them in water, then steamed them to eat.

Other food substitutes included wild herbs, peanut sprouts, rats, sparrows, roots, tree bark, clam shells, and cotton batting.[29]

Journalist Lu Baoguo recalled,

> In the last half of 1959, I took a long-distance bus from Xinyang through Luoshan to Gushi. Looking out the window, I could see one corpse after another in the ditches along the roadway, but no one on the bus dared to talk about the starvation. I saw a corpse outside the western gate of Luoshan County and telephoned the Luoshan party committee to tell

them. Guangshan County had the largest number of starvation deaths—a third of the population, with entire households wiped out. Even with people starving all around them, the leading cadres continued to stuff themselves. While I was staying at the Gushi County party committee guesthouse, party secretary Yang Shouji was treating guests to *pisi* soup [a local delicacy].

Lu Baoguo did not write about what he saw, however, even to inform the central government: "After I personally witnessed how people who spoke the truth were brought to ruin, how could I dare to write an internal reference report?"

Yu Dehong, former secretary to Xinyang commissioner Zhang Shufan, recalled:

After the grain was requisitioned and taken away, the peasants found themselves with no grain right after the harvest. On our way to inspect agricultural production at Shizhaipu in Suiping County, we passed through the Qingshiqiao brigade and thought to stay there for the night. The brigade leader was extremely flustered, and we told him, "Don't go to any trouble, just cook up something simple for us." Finally around 9:30 that night he brought us porridge made with a few chunks of pumpkin. The brigade leader said, "There's no way I can hide the truth any more: if you hadn't come, we wouldn't have prepared even pumpkin porridge. The communal kitchen has been closed for days, and we had to search all through the village just to find a couple of little pumpkins."

When we went to the Wangmiao brigade of Xi County's Dongyuemiao Commune, no one had gone down to work the fields by 5:30 that evening. When we asked why, the peasants said, "We haven't had anything to eat today!" We saw two elm trees that had been chopped down and stripped of their bark, and some people were still there chewing on bark as they peeled it away. The next day we went to Tangpo and found people eating sorghum stalks even before they had a chance to form ears.

This was the situation less than one month after the autumn harvest. It became even worse later on. Not long afterward, all the communal kitchens were shut down. By the tenth lunar month, all the roots and tree bark had been consumed. After that, massive starvation deaths occurred. I went back twice to my home village in Fanghu, Huaibin County. Just before the Lunar New Year, I saw six corpses along several kilometers of roadway . . . five kilometers from my home, there were dead bodies everywhere, at least 100 corpses lying out in the open with no one burying them. Among the reed ponds along the river embankments I saw another 100 or so corpses. Outside it was said that dogs had eaten so many corpses that their eyes glowed with bloodlust. But this was inconsistent with the facts: people had already eaten all the dogs, so where would there be dogs to eat the corpses?

When people first began to die, they were carried out and placed on planks and hauled off by oxen. Later no one bothered. In the Yang household at Liuchangying Village west of Fanghu, the adults weren't taken away when they died, and three surviving children, ages eight to twelve, stayed alive by eating the corpses over a period of several months. Eventually a pile of human bones was cleared out of the house. The children said the heels and palms tasted the best.

How many people actually died in Xinyang? The Xinyang prefectural party committee reported to the provincial party committee that more than 380,000 people died.[30] According to the report sent to the central government by Li Jian and Li Zhenghai of the central government's investigation team sent here to carry out inquiries, 1.05 million people died. I believe that figure is not excessive. I myself am from Huaibin, and in that county alone, 180,000 of the original population of more than 400,000 died. At Fanghu Commune (my native place), more than 20,000 of the 50,000 inhabitants died, or 42 percent, and the Wuzhai production brigade where my home was located suffered a fatality rate of 52 percent. My home production team totaled 75 people, of whom 38 people died in two or three months during the winter of 1959, including six members of my own family: my father, my second uncle and his wife, my third uncle and his wife, and my third uncle's adopted son.

In a memoir, Yu Dehong wrote:

Although circumstances varied among the prefecture's eighteen counties, and the disaster hit some areas harder than others, with starvation more severe in some places than others, the disparities were not great, and there were no localities that did not experience a substantial percentage of deaths by starvation . . . In all the villages of which I have direct knowledge, the death rate was close to half.

Among the corpses I saw on the road from Baoxin to Fanghu on my way home in December 1959, I saw flesh cut from the buttocks and thighs of some, possibly for others to eat. It made me extremely sad . . . There were cases of cannibalism in nearly every village, and many incidents so tragic that I cannot bear to speak of them.[31]

Yu Wenhai, a production team accountant in Huaibin County's Fanghu Township, told me his vivid memories of the crisis:

My father, mother, my uncle and his wife, my paternal grandmother, my two younger sisters, and one of my children starved to death . . . It was not unusual for people to eat corpses. I myself did so at Yaozhuang. I had gone to see the production team head Yao Dengju, and in the production team office I smelled the fragrance of cooked meat. He said, "Have some meat." I asked, "What kind of meat?" He said, "Meat from a dead pig." I opened the pot and took out a piece. It was tender in my mouth. I said, "This isn't pork." He said it was the flesh of a dead person that someone else had cut away, that it had been cut from a buried corpse, and that he had taken a piece and cooked it. (At this point, my driver, Xiao Chen, asked, "Did the human flesh taste good?" Yu Wenhai answered, "It was pretty good! Just a bit spongy.")

Gao Hongwen of the Gaozhuang production team had three children. When he went to build the railway at Guangminggang, his wife cooked up all three children and ate them . . . At that time it was mostly dead people who were eaten; it was rare to eat the living. It was winter then, and the corpses could be left outside without decaying.

Yu Wenhai said that after the winter passed, the corpses were buried in a large pit near the village. He led me to the location and pointed to a large field planted with crops. No one would have guessed that hundreds of starved corpses lay under that verdant plain. Near that mass grave, someone had planted several trees. Nourished on the remains of the dead, they provided the only memorial to this sad history.

At least twenty cases of eating human flesh were recorded in Xinyang's Luyi, Xiayi, Yucheng, and Yongcheng counties. In Pangwang Village, an eighteen-year-old girl, Wang Yu'e, drowned her five-year-old cousin, Wang Huailang, and ate him. Huailang's elder sister Wang

Xiaopeng, aged fourteen, was also driven by hunger to eat her brother's flesh.[32]

The official files of Henan Province contain many records of starvation deaths. The central work group's report of June 18, 1960,[33] quotes prefectural party committee statistics declaring that from October 1959 to April 1960, 436,882 people died in Xinyang Prefecture—5.92 percent of the total population; natural deaths comprised 1.96 percent. The work group's inquiries indicated that the actual number of deaths might be higher.

Male deaths exceeded female deaths, and the death rate was higher among laborers in the prime of life, resulting in many orphaned children. July 1 Commune in Gushi County had more than 370 orphans, and Sanpisi Commune in Huangchuan had more than 200.

Every locality had families extinguished by starvation. According to figures provided by five production brigades under Huangchuan County's Renhe Commune, 10 percent of the commune's households were wiped out. The Chenwan brigade was hit particularly hard, and its original fifty-one villages were consolidated into forty-one.

The death rate among ordinary commune members exceeded that among grassroots cadres and their families. According to figures from Huaibin County's Qiaogou Commune, the death rate among cadres of the Wanwei brigade and its production teams was 8.8 percent; 26.7 percent of ordinary commune members died. In Zuowei, the death rate among cadres was 11.8 percent, while among ordinary commune members it was 15.24 percent. The Yangbo brigade of that county's Chengjiao Commune had 156 households, among which only 31 experienced no deaths, and of those, 13 were cadre households, 4 were the households of kitchen staff, and 1 was the family of the miller. Yangbo brigade's Qiandian production team had 31 households, among which only 6 had no deaths. Five of those 6 were cadre households, and the other was that of a communal kitchen worker.

Deaths were even higher among the "Five-Category Elements" (those designated in various political movements as landlords, rich peasants, counterrevolutionaries, bad elements, and rightists). In the Zuowei brigade, the death rate among poor peasants was 13 percent, while among landlords and rich peasants it was 31 percent.

The largest number of deaths in Xinyang occurred from October 1959 to January 1960. The Sanpisi Commune work group reported on June 3, 1960:

From October 1959 to April 1960, the commune had a total of 6,668 deaths, comprising 14.5 percent of the commune's total population. The Xiaohuangying communal kitchen under the Huangying production team of the Tandian brigade covered four villages comprised of 21 households totaling 96 people. Of these, 50 died, comprising 53 percent of the population, and two households were entirely extinguished. The four villages have now been consolidated into one village. In the four-member family of Xu Yingzi, the parents died first, and lacking their care, the two small children also died. The four corpses lay exposed for more than ten days. The Yangdaweizi squad under the Sanpisi brigade's Chenzhai production team originally had 23 households comprising 119 people. Of these, 51 died, including three entire households. Because the dead were too many, and the living lacked strength, the dead were not buried. A child named Yang Youlan died in the communal canteen and was left there for more than ten days. Finally party secretary Cheng Linde found someone to bury 36 corpses in a common grave.

The commune began winding down operations in mid-October, and by December 7 it had been shut down for 53 days. County-level cadres were all aware of this but dared not say anything.

The Zhugang communal kitchen covered 37 households of 138 people, among whom 47 died, including five entire households. The surviving households were largely those of cadres, accountants, and laborers (who were able to forage for wild herbs), while the households in which everyone died had relatively few laborers or none to forage for wild herbs.[34]

Former Xinyang commissioner Zhang Shufan wrote:

In Xinyang's Wulidian Village, a teenage girl killed her four-year-old brother and ate him. Their parents had both died, leaving the two children behind. Overcome with hunger, the girl ate her brother. When this case was brought to my attention, I found it hard to deal with. I had little choice but to handle it according to the law. I thought about it overnight, and the next day I had the girl arrested. My thinking was that if she weren't arrested, the girl would simply starve to death anyway. If we put her into detention, at least she'd be given something to eat.[35]

The greatest number of deaths in Xinyang occurred in Guangshan County, while the proportion of deaths was highest in Huaibin County. An old cadre from Xinyang told me that the car carrying provincial control commission secretary Liu Mingbang and prefectural party secretary Lu Xianwen drove right past the corpses, but they didn't tell the higher levels. In his investigation report, Yang Weiping, a member of the provincial party committee secretariat, wrote, "The deaths in Guangshan County comprised at least 20 percent of its total population. The death rate at Huaidian Commune's Dalishu brigade was at least 60 percent, and at the Xinhua brigade of Huangchuan County's Shuangliu Commune it was at least 65 percent, with no signs of life in thirteen villages."[36]

No one mourned publicly, and corpses lay out in the open. When grain was distributed in the spring, commune members were given gloves and dragged the corpses into dry wells. By then the corpses were unidentifiable. Typically each well held more than one hundred bodies.

An investigation group reported on Xi County in October 1960:

According to incomplete statistics from the county party committee, a total of 104,523 people died in Xi County from October 1959 until April 1960, making up 14 percent of the county's population. In fact, the number of dead was greater than that. This is because (1) the time period was truncated at the beginning and the end, while quite a few people died before October and well into the third quarter of 1960; (2) the threshold for natural deaths was too high, and many people who died unnatural deaths were included among the natural deaths. We estimate the number of deaths in Xi County at 120,000 to 140,000. The county public security bureau's tally is 130,000. After the deaths, villages were consolidated. In the first half of 1959 there were 5,489 villages, but now there are 4,805 . . .

Zhang Wenru, a member of Zhangtao Commune's Wenquanzi production brigade, last November went out selling flesh cut from human corpses at a price of 30 cents per half kilo, claiming it was beef. When he was discovered, he was beaten to death. A poor peasant named Li Shiping and his son Li Xinquan and daughter Li Xiaoni went at night to the graveyard and dug up corpses; they argued with a middle peasant named Wang Zhenyu, who was there for the same purpose. Li and his son beat Wang to death and took his corpse home, where they cooked it and ate it. A cadre discovered them and struck Li in the head with the back of his knife. Li died at the scene . . . Chen Dengchang, age thirty-eight, was a middle peasant from Xi County's Xiangdian Commune. On November 29 of last year, he strangled his gravely ill six-year-old daughter and cooked her to eat. On May 2 he ate the corpse of a two-year-old male child from his production team. He was arrested and sentenced to twenty years in prison, and died in custody.[37]

Cadres continued routinely to eat more than their share while people starved around them. A member of the Qiandian production team of Huaibin County's Tangbo brigade said, "We were swollen with starvation, while the cadres were swollen with overeating." In this brigade in early October 1959, each person was allotted 250 grams of sweet potato per day, along with a bowl of potato leaves for each adult and half a bowl for each child. From October 21 to November 25, each person received a daily ration of 200 grams of sweet potato and a small amount of potato leaves. From November 26 to the first half of December, all there was to eat were green vegetables, a bowlful for adults and half a bowl for children. In mid-December, each person was provided with one meal of vegetables every five days, after which the communal kitchen was closed for five days. Under these conditions, drought-combating work was carried out for twenty days, with only two to three hours of sleep allowed each day.[38]

The "Investigation Report on Deaths Due to the Inadequate Living Arrangements by Huangchuan County's Taolin Commune" found that the death rate at the Hepi production brigade was 24.9 percent, and reached 49 percent among laborers. Among sixty production team cadres, only two died—villagers rated these two as good cadres who didn't eat more than their fair share. None of the brigade's twenty-three cadres died, nor did any of them even suffer symptoms such as edema. A subsequent investigation found that following the autumn harvest until May 13, 1960, brigade cadres ate extra allotments of food and took food home as well, including 1,500 kilos of beef and pork, more than 300 ducklings, 75 kilos of fish, 15 sheep, 285 kilos of cooking oil, and more than 2,500 kilos of grain.

Li Wenyao was party secretary of Xinyang's prefectural commissioner's office. His wife, during a visit to her home village, saw human flesh being cooked, and although she didn't eat any, she brought back some to her child. Li Wenyao's own father dropped dead in the street from hunger. Even so, Li Wenyao continued to claim that the situation was excellent, and vigorously criticized Zhang Shufan and Yu Dehong. Yu Dehong said to him, "Your wife has eaten human flesh and your father starved to death, and still you criticize me. Have you lost all human feeling?"

Wang Dafu, the deputy secretary of Xinyang's prefectural party committee, was in charge of the campaign against right deviation, an assignment he carried out with great dedication. He was a native of Xincai County, where quite a few people had died. Members of his family had visited him and he knew the true situation, yet he persisted with his campaign. Subsequently Yu Dehong and others reported him to the provincial party committee, saying he bore responsibility for the Xinyang Incident. Only then was Wang disciplined and transferred to another post.

Despite death and cannibalism in Xinyang, the party's *Henan Daily* continued to report on the excellent situation in a series of seven essays entitled, "Onward Toward Communism."

Yu Dehong says that during the famine, Xinyang had more than 500 million kilos of grain stored in its silos; added to that year's harvest of 1.45 billion kilos, some 2 billion kilos were available. If the reserve grain had been distributed, no one would have starved. Subsequently, Xinyang was able to provide its own reserves and didn't need supplements from outside. The starving people saw storage silos full of grain, but no one attempted to steal it. People sat alongside storage depots waiting for the government to release grain and crying out, "Communist Party, Chairman Mao, save us!" Some people starved to death sitting next to the grain depots.

General You Taizhong was a native of Guangshan County, where the largest number of people starved to death. After going home for a visit, he returned to headquarters and told the truth, only to come under attack. Hubei's provincial governor, Zhang Tixue, was a native of Balifan in Xin County. One of his family members starved to death, and after going home, he relayed what was happening, but no one took heed.

How many starved to death in Xinyang? The June 8 figure from the prefectural party committee cited earlier gave the death toll from October 1959 to April 1960 as 5.92 percent of the prefecture's total population, including 1.96 percent attributed to natural causes.

The Henan provincial party committee's self-criticism in November 1960 states: "In the entire prefecture 549,171 people died between the winter of last year and the spring of this year, or 6.54 percent of the total population of 8.4 million . . . Among the prefecture's 4,473 production brigades, the death rate in 520 of them was upwards of 20 percent, and in some brigades the death rate exceeded 50 percent. In Guangshan County, the death toll was 97,151—19.87 percent of the population—and 5,639 households were completely wiped out."[39]

A senior public security official reported on December 6, 1960, "The total mortality figure continues to rise, and the damage is really serious, something like one-eighth of the population of 8 million."[40] That is, a million deaths.

People whom I interviewed who had personally experienced the Xinyang Incident were virtually unanimous in the assertion that at least 1 million people died of unnatural causes, including starvation and physical abuse.

THOUSANDS OF PEOPLE BEATEN TO DEATH

Many were beaten to death in the anti-hoarding campaign, including those who stole out of desperate hunger, those who spoke the truth, and those who did not blindly obey. Yang Weiping, a member of the Henan provincial party committee secretariat, found that 2,104 were beaten to death in Guangshan and Huangchuan counties, and another 254 were permanently crippled by beatings in Huangchuan. Among the 1,008 people beaten to death in Guangshan, 1 was a member of the county party committee secretariat, 4 were production brigade cadres, 47 were production team cadres, 11 were party members, 61 were Youth League members, 848 were ordinary people, and 87 were "bad elements."[41]

Yang reported that from October 1959 to June 1960, 404 people were beaten to death in Guangshan County, including one who was buried alive. Cadres at the production team level or above comprised 199 of the victims, but it was more common for cadres to beat ordinary commune members. At the Taowan production brigade, 27 cadres took part in beating commune members. A branch party secretary surnamed Huang beat 47 commune members on the fifteenth day of the Lunar New Year, with one fatality. A Youth League branch secretary at Hushan Commune personally beat 92 people, and killed 2 by the cruel torture of "lighting the celestial lantern." My interviewees believed that Yang Weiping's figures were low.

At Xi County's Xiazhuang Commune in November 1959, two brigade officials strung wire through the ears of seven commune members who had stolen a plow ox, after which they were paraded through the streets while being beaten. Two other brigade members were beaten to death for killing an ox.[42]

In Chayashan Commune's Liubaohe production team, Zhao Qiang, enfeebled with edema, fainted near a corn stack. Upon regaining consciousness, he discovered an ear of corn and stuffed it into his shirt to take home to his starving children. Brigade leader Yan, witnessing the "theft," beat Zhao savagely with a shoulder pole and sent him back to work. Zhao staggered to the edge of the field and died.

One night, an old sow died in Chayashan Commune. Pig keeper Song He furtively hauled the carcass home, and upon butchering the sow, he found twelve tender fetal piglets. Just then, brigade leader Zhai burst in with a group of others and gave Song He a blow that set blood flowing down his face. Song was trussed up, dragged to the brigade office, and suspended from the roof beam. Members of the brigade party committee feasted on the sow's meat while Song He hung in the cold, crying for mercy. The next day the sow's head and the piglets were hung around Song He's neck and the brigade cadres marched him through the streets and forced him to shout, "I'm a thief. I killed a pig in secret." After being paraded all day, Song He dropped dead.[43]

At Chayashan Commune's Hanlou brigade, a starving elderly man who slaughtered a sheep was paraded in the streets, then bound and suspended from a tree until he died, after which the local militia commander dragged his corpse up a hill, covered it with wheat stalks, and burned it.[44]

Chayashan Commune members Liu Zhilan and Yuan Zhihong were struggled and beaten to death for killing a piglet.[45] A brigade leader at Guangshan County's Chengguan Commune had seventeen villagers strung up after they decided to slaughter an ox. Six of them died—Liu Taiguo, Huang Lanyou, Huang Guofu, Wang Shenxi, Wang Shengzhao, and Wang Yuanfu.[46]

Qiao Peihua reports regarding Huaidian Commune:

On November 8, 1959, a cadre discovered a small piece of beef in the home of Fang Zhengyi of the Xuwan production team. Fang was harshly beaten on the spot and died six days later.

On November 25, Hu Dehou of the Yanwan production team did not pull up vegetables as ordered by a cadre, and he was harshly beaten, dying two days later.

Also in November, Yan Jiaxin of the Yanwan production team was beaten for failing to repay funds owed to the production team, and he died five days later. Yan's wife, Huang Xiuyin, was discovered by a cadre cooking some wheat at home and was subjected to group struggle for stealing grain. She was then bound and doused with cold water, dying soon afterwards. Of the couple's five surviving children, the eldest daughter, age fourteen, managed to flee to a relative's home. The other four starved to death.

On November 20, Ruan Xianghai of the Hanwan production team, upon failing to gather cow dung in accordance with a cadre's orders, was bound and beaten and deprived of food. When in desperation he took some peanuts from the communal kitchen, he was beaten to death on the spot.[47]

As early as October 1958, a letter from members of Changge County's Pohu Commune reached Mao Zedong's hands. It described brigade cadres inflicting brutal torments, including on party members, Youth League members, and other cadres.[48] Cadres who refused to take part in beatings were accused of lacking a fighting spirit. On November 29, 1958, Mao passed this letter on to Henan party secretary Wu Zhipu, with the comments, "The cause must be analyzed and the reasoning explained. Don't publicize or handle it in a way that will intimidate people. It should be handled carefully; otherwise it might cause panic, in particular among comrades who committed relatively minor errors."[49] Mao worried more about the abusers than the victims.

Old cadres from Xinyang told me, "If you didn't beat others, you would be beaten. The more harshly you beat someone, the more firmly you established your position and your loyalty to the Communist Party. If you didn't beat others, you were a right deviationist and would soon be beaten by others."

PARTY COMMITTEES CONCEAL THE DEATH TOLL

As peasants starved, public security bureaus took control of post offices to keep the news from spreading. Post offices in Xinyang confiscated more than twelve thousand letters appealing for help. In one village, a party branch lost twenty of its twenty-three members to starvation. The surviving three wrote a letter in blood to the provincial party committee, pleading for aid. This letter was suppressed like all the rest, and its writers were hunted down and punished. In Guangshan County, a doctor was arrested for telling a sick peasant that two bowls of congee would cure him.[50]

To prevent starving people from fleeing and spreading news of the disaster, county party committees deployed armed guards to patrol borders and access roads. Sentry posts were set up on roadways, and checkpoints at every village. Bus stops were manned by police officers, and long-distance buses could be driven only by party members. Anyone discovered trying to leave had all his belongings confiscated and was beaten. Xinyang's rail depots were monitored by the railway public security bureau. The peasants could only stay home and await death.

Escapees were treated as "criminal fugitives" and sent to labor reform camps. Xinyang City established hundreds of detention centers that processed 190,000 attempted runaways. Detainees were deprived of food, and many died from hunger and physical abuse.

The Yangzhai production brigade organized a ten-member core militia to intercept people attempting to flee. From November 1959 to the Spring Festival of 1960, they beat more than 40 people—12 fatally—and stripped 195 of their clothes. Huangchuan County set up 67 detention centers, where detainees were interrogated, searched, and beaten before being sent to forced labor and deprived of food. These detention centers processed 9,330 refugees, of whom 2,195 were beaten to death or permanently crippled. A man nicknamed Blind Li at Chengguan Commune said he knew of more than 300 people who had died at the Chengguan detention center, with 3 to 10 dead bodies dragged out every day. Some were tossed out while still taking their last breath. A Chengguan Commune member recalled 87 bodies being dragged out of a detention center prior to a visit by provincial officials.[51]

The CCP Central Committee supported these suppressive tactics. In March 1959 the Central Committee and the State Council jointly issued an "urgent communiqué" designating those who fled the countryside as "vagrants" and ordering the detention and repatriation of all rural dwellers who attempted to enter cities or industrial or mining regions. Local officials, who feared word getting out about starvation in their jurisdictions, vigorously enforced these prohibitions against famine refugees.

No effort was spared in blocking attempts to reveal the truth. Prior to August 1960 there were fifty-eight letters from residents of Xi County attempting to disclose the lack of food. Six anonymous letters were treated as "reactionary" and handed over to the public security bureau. Handwriting analysis on an anonymous letter sent to the Supreme People's Procuratorate determined that it had been sent by Zheng Lianbang, a cadre at Ru'nan Bank, and he was immediately arrested. On March 12, 1960, a public health clinic cadre, Wang Qiyun, wrote to the CCP Central Committee requesting distribution of grain reserves. The public security bureau located and arrested Wang, and he was subjected to brutal struggle.[52]

The chair of the Xinyang Prefecture's Federation of Women, Li Ruiying (the wife of commissioner Zhang Shufan), went to Xiping County, where she saw people starving and learned that some were eating the flesh of the dead. She wanted to relay the situation to her old comrade, Li Xuefeng, an official in the party's North China bureau. To avoid discovery, she first sent a note to Li's wife, Zhai Ying: "Are you at home? If so, please reply to this letter, as I have something important to tell both of you." That letter was returned to her the next day.[53] The fact that even an official of Li Xuefeng's rank could not communicate freely indicates the extent of controls on information at that time.

When the Guangshan County post office discovered an anonymous letter to Beijing disclosing starvation deaths, the public security bureau began hunting down the writer. One of the post office's counter staff recalled that a pockmarked woman had mailed the letter. The local public security bureau rounded up and interrogated every pockmarked woman without identifying the culprit. It was subsequently determined that the writer worked in Zhengzhou and had written the letter upon returning to her home village and seeing people starving to death.[54]

Elderly people told me of a man known as "Smithy" (Tiejiang) Zhang, who risked his life to petition the authorities. Official archives verified the details. Smithy Zhang was Zhang Fu, deputy director of the Henan provincial department of civil affairs, who had originally worked as a blacksmith. In December 1959 he went to Xinyang to look into disaster relief. He twice reported what he learned to provincial leaders. Zhang Fu had learned that more than 300 of the 1,900-odd members of a Renhe brigade had died, and 2,363 people had died at Shuangliu Commune between October 1 and December 26, 1959. Zhang compiled the data and sent copies to the county and provincial leaders, as well as making verbal reports.

He took a further opportunity to report on the deaths in Xinyang while paying New Year's respects at the home of a provincial leader, Liu Mingbang, but Liu pretended to doze off. Zhang then informed the provincial deputy procurator, Xiao Jianbo, that he intended to report the matter to the CCP Central Committee. Xiao snapped, "Who's trying to deceive superiors and defraud subordinates? Whom do you intend to report to the CCP Central Committee?" The next day, Liu Mingbang asked Zhang, "Why are you planning to report your superiors to the Central Committee? What business is it of yours?" Zhang Fu prepared to go to Beijing, but he was threatened and intimidated by civil affairs department officials, one of whom said, "The provincial control commission called and isn't allowing you to go to the Central Committee. They've already notified the public security bureau. You can't go." When Zhang Fu went to the train station to buy a ticket, he was obstructed again.[55]

In early April 1960, Liu Mingbang finally realized it was impossible to keep the matter under wraps and reported the starvation deaths in Gushi County to the party's Central Control Commission.

Even with officials concealing signs of starvation—for example, by prohibiting the infirm from walking along the roads with canes—word got out, and some letters made their way to the Central Committee, which sent people to Xinyang to investigate.

THE COVER-UP PERSISTS AFTER DEATHS ARE REVEALED

Huangchuan County's Sanpisi Commune received notice of an imminent visit by a provincial party committee work group in May 1960. Since the commune had reported only 500-odd deaths, it sent personnel to each brigade to arrange a cover-up. The Tuanjie brigade, for example, followed up with an urgent communiqué: "To all production team leaders and accountants: The commune has allocated thirty-four deaths to our brigade. We have therefore decided to allocate the number of deaths . . . to each production team as follows: Team 1, four people; Team 2, five people; Team 3, five people; Team 4, five people; Team 5, two people; Team 6, seven people; Team 7, four people; Team 8, two people." Any children under twelve were excluded from the statistics. Sanpisi Commune first reported 523 deaths, then 3,889 deaths, and finally 2,907. The provincial party committee work group ultimately concluded that 6,668 had died.[56]

Reporting deaths followed a rule of "Seven 'don't includes' and one 'doesn't count.'" Not included were local people expiring outside of the locality, nonlocals who died in the locality, very young children, those who died outside the statistical time frame, those who had fled the locality, those whose whereabouts were unknown, and duplicate names; in addition, any instance where questions arose regarding inclusion didn't count.[57] Follow-up inquiries raised the death toll, however. "Zhengyang County originally reported 18,000-plus deaths from winter of last year to spring of this year; now preliminary inquiries have confirmed 80,000 deaths; Xincai County originally reported 30,000 deaths, and that has now been increased to nearly 100,000. Chayashan Commune previously reported 600-plus deaths, but now more than 4,000 deaths have been confirmed, comprising 10 percent of the population."[58]

Provincial officials were often complicit in the deception, as indicated in a report by Wang Binglin, deputy head of the Xinyang prefectural party committee secretariat:

> In May 1960, Yang Weiping [a member of the Henan provincial party committee secretariat] went to Xinyang to conduct inquiries. He was received and accompanied by the deputy head of the Xinyang prefectural party committee secretariat, Wang Binglin. Wang Binglin was surprised that Secretary Yang at no time mentioned the matters occurring from the winter of last year to the spring of this year. Wang Binglin took the initiative to report the problem of the deaths in Xinyang to him, but Yang took no stand on the issue. The party secretary of Guangshan County's Qinhe Commune spoke of the deaths there, and Secretary Yang still made no comment. Guangshan County party secretary Ma Longshan told Secretary Yang that 38,800 people had died in the county, and Secretary Yang instructed him: "It's enough that you're clear on the number of dead. The reason for the deaths is a natural disaster. There's no need to follow up or make further inquiries into the deaths . . ."

Wang Binglin recalls that during Secretary Yang's ten days in Xinyang, he took only one meal at Chayashan Commune. All his other meals were taken with organizations at or above the county level, and included five or six dishes and one soup, with meat, eggs, and alcoholic beverages. Yang also watched one stage production and three films.

Wang Binglin found that when the prefecture reported deaths to the province in May 1960, the province inserted the phrase "(including natural deaths)" before passing the report to the CCP Central Committee and disseminating it to the counties. Yang Weiping also altered the self-examination report by the Xinyang prefectural party committee to play down the errors in Xinyang.[59]

The enlarged meeting of the prefectural party committee in July 1960 (also known as the Rooster Mountain Conference) served as a cover-up that reaffirmed the "excellent situation" and obscured the prefectural party committee's responsibility. Located at the border between Hubei and Henan, Rooster Mountain was a famous summer resort. At the end of the Qing dynasty, foreign missionaries built holiday villas there, and during the Republican era it was a popular vacation spot for notables. That summer, the white villas peeking out from the vast expanse of green hills were mirrored on the plains by the corpses of the starved, and ruddy-cheeked cadres ascended the bucolic slopes in sedan chairs borne by peasants pale with hunger. Insulated from the scene of their crimes, officials punctuated a leisurely meeting schedule with feasting and napping. At the meeting, Yang Weiping said, "The work in Xinyang is generally good." "Regarding the death figures, it doesn't matter whether it's 480,000 or 450,000." "Regarding the problems in Xinyang Prefecture . . . Chairman Mao Zedong gave us a one-finger opportunity."[60] He was referring to Mao's saying that problems arising with the Three Red Banners would constitute "one finger," while the other nine fingers were accomplishments.

This "one-finger" formula discouraged thorough disclosure, and many participants had no opportunity to speak at the conference. Criticisms directed at the prefectural party committee were deflected to county officials. When the deputy director of the prefectural party school, Yan Zhongru, criticized the errors of the prefectural party committee, Yang Weiping told prefectural deputy party secretary Wang Dafu, "This person [referring to Yan Zhongru] has an incorrect point of view; you need to speak with him." The next day, Yang Weiping criticized Yan Zhongru during his comments without mentioning him by name. Li Li, a member of the provincial party committee secretariat, said, "How could your party school have such a person as deputy director?" When Gushi County party secretary Yang Shouji also criticized the prefectural party committee, Yang Weiping said, "Gushi has such serious problems . . . he should be required to undergo self-criticism."

During the Rooster Mountain Conference, Wang Guohua, a Long March veteran and the province's vice-governor, spoke up for Zhang Shufan and Li Ruiying. Zhang recalls, "Wang Guohua's statement at the conference had enormous reverberations. He was the first to criticize Lu Xianwen by name and the first to speak up for me." The conference resolved to arrest Guangshan County party secretary Ma Longshan and sentence him to death, in that way showing that the party was dealing with the Xinyang Incident while downplaying its own blame.

Zhang Shufan's secretary, Yu Dehong, recalled:

There was no longer any way to cover up the starvation deaths in Xinyang. The investigation report that Li Jian, Li Zhenhai, and the others spent three months compiling gave a death toll of 1.05 million. Under these conditions, the leaders of the provincial and prefectural party committees were in a state of high anxiety. Starting on July 20, the Xinyang prefectural party committee convened an enlarged standing committee meeting at Rooster Mountain. The provincial party committee sent Yang Weiping, Li Li, and Liu Mingbang to attend. Cadres who had been labeled right deviationists held out high hopes that this meeting would bring everything out into the open. But in fact, it was just another cover-up. Facing this situation, Comrade Zhang Shufan made statements three times (totaling 14,000 words), disclosing the essential problems in Xinyang and thereby throwing the meeting into confusion. Lu Xianwen, Wang Dafu, Yan Bingyu, Wu Jianhua, and others held a secret meeting behind Zhang Shufan's back, during which they decided that Zhang Shufan was persisting with right-opportunistic revisionism, and that the meeting should be turned into a criticism session against Zhang. It was only after Yang Weiping and others intervened that this plan was abandoned . . . The meeting concluded on August 15, and Guangshan County party secretary Ma Longshan was ultimately arrested.[61]

At the end of September 1960, Henan party secretary Wu Zhipu sent out a directive stating, "Xinyang Prefecture's performance was very good in the past, and it achieved many accomplishments in implementing the general and specific policies of the CCP Central Committee. The problem that has just occurred is a one-finger problem, or at most a matter of 70 percent achievement and 30 percent error during this particular period . . . bad cadres make up only 4 to 5 percent, and no more than 10 to 20 percent even in the few areas where the situation is particularly serious." By then Lu Xianwen had been dismissed from his position as first secretary of the prefectural party committee, an act that Yang Weiping claimed followed the spirit of the Central Committee's directives.[62]

In November 1960 the CCP Central Committee sent Li Xiannian, Tao Zhu, Wang Renzhong, and others to Xinyang, accompanied by Wu Zhipu. Zhang Shufan received them at the Xinyang Infantry Academy. While they were drinking tea, Wu Zhipu said to Zhang Shufan, "Comrade Shufan, the provincial party committee was initially completely unaware of the problems in Xinyang Prefecture; we were kept completely in the dark. I understand you and Lu Xianwen saw things differently; why didn't you come to speak with me? If you'd come to see me earlier, might we not have avoided such a serious problem?"

Zhang bluntly retorted,

Comrade Zhipu, did you really know absolutely nothing? Didn't the provincial party committee authorize the criticism and struggle that I was subjected to for . . . the remarks I made at the production disaster relief meeting and the low grain yields I projected? Wasn't it because during the campaign against false reporting of output, I did not hand over more grain, but took more than 3.5 million kilos of grain out of storage to feed the masses? It was because I accused the cadres of Kuomintang methods in their coercion and killing that I was labeled a right deviationist and subjected to struggle and criticism . . . Comrade Zhipu, how can you say you knew nothing of this? Wasn't it you who arranged my denunciation? And yet I should have gone to you to discuss these matters?

Wu Zhipu's face turned scarlet with humiliation. Tao Zhu quickly interrupted Zhang: "There's no need to go on; we've got the picture. It was wrong to criticize you back then. We've rehabilitated you, and there's no need to mention it further."[63]

THE CENTRAL COMMITTEE'S INVESTIGATION

In February 1960 a section director under the CCP Central Committee's Internal Affairs Department went to Xinyang. When he heard that two hundred thousand to three hundred thousand people had starved to death, he immediately reported it to Beijing. According to Zhang Shufan, the matter was referred to the secretary-general of the State Council, Xi Zhongxun, who told the secretary of the Central Control Commission, Dong Biwu. Dong then sent Li Jian and Li Zhenhai to Xinyang.[64]

Li Jian confirmed this to me, and recalled how his team came to be dispatched to Xinyang:

Before then, Qian Ying of the Internal Affairs Department had reported on people dying from edema, but Tan Zhenlin had criticized the department, saying, "It has not yet been proven that edema is caused by nutritional problems." . . . Therefore all five of us had misgivings: "Even Peng Dehuai was victimized, so how will we be able to say anything!" Once we reached Xinyang, the prefectural party committee added two people to our group, making seven in all. We left the city and passed through Luoshan to Huangchuan, and on the hillsides and in the ditches we saw unburied bodies.

We arrived in Gushi, where more than 30,000 people were said to have died . . . On the streets of Gushi Town we saw a dozen or so people bound hand and foot being led through the streets by a rope . . . they were peasants who had tried to flee the famine.

When we reached Shangcheng, we saw irrigation works still underway. The county's deputy party secretary told us that tens of thousands had died in Shangcheng. On the road from Shangcheng to Xin County (also called Jiangjun County) we saw a woman lying along the road. We looked closer and saw she was near death, but we could still feel breath coming from her nostrils. We took her to the commune and had the communal kitchen provide her with some food, and she revived. At Guangshan County's Pohe Commune, people working at an irrigation project told us how many of their family members had died, and how many people at the commune had died. But Guangshan County's party secretary Ma Longshan . . . gave a lower death toll. On the road back to Xinyang, we saw a teenage boy dead along the roadside covered with flies. The weather was hot, and the corpse had started to smell.

We told the Xinyang prefectural party secretary Lu Xianwen that we hoped he would strengthen relief measures. We said to Lu Xianwen, "So many have died. Was sabotage involved?" He answered, "There is no possibility of sabotage." He said people had starved because of the exaggerated crop-yield claims and because of the communal kitchens. If people had been allowed to gather wild herbs, fewer would have died. When Commissioner Zhang Shufan saw me, he wept. I asked how many people had died, and Zhang said 400,000. That number came from the public security bureau. I was afraid the number wouldn't stand up, so I had the two men with me obtain the death toll for each county from the secretary of each county's control commission (they subsequently told me the total was 1.05 million) . . . We verified the figures in Zhengzhou, where we were again told that 400,000 died in Xinyang.

. . . Chairman Mao was also in Zhengzhou, and I felt that the starvation deaths of 400,000 people was the weightiest matter to have arisen since the founding of the People's Republic. I wanted to report it to Chairman Mao, but after thinking it over, I didn't go. The province's cadres were received by Chairman Mao in Zhengzhou, and I also took part.

Wu Zhipu had the agriculture secretary come to see me. I said, there are still people lying dead along the roadsides; you need to strengthen relief efforts and ease up on the irrigation projects.

We continued our inquiries elsewhere in Henan . . . then returned to Beijing and wrote a report. The Central Control Commission did not pass it on to the Central Committee, because Tan Zhenlin did not agree with it. He was a member of the Central Committee secretariat and vice-premier in charge of agriculture; if he didn't agree with the report, there was no way for it to be passed upward. The secretary of the standing committee of the Central Control Commission, Liu Lantao, sent Yu Sang and others from the public security bureau to investigate. Yu Sang's inquiries came up with the figure of 600,000. That report . . . was sent to Liu Shaoqi, who directed in a memo: "Mobilize the masses and turn the situation around." Liu's instructions were delivered to Henan, and the Henan provincial party committee set about to resolve the leadership of Xinyang.

In October 1960, we made a second trip to Xinyang . . . This time the death toll our inquiries arrived at was 1 million . . . I saw people still starving in Yuanyang. With my own eyes I saw a man in a leather cap die along the roadside. In Yuanyang I received a telephone call from the

Central Committee asking me to report back. After I returned to Beijing, An Ziwen heard my report, then wrote a report to Premier Zhou Enlai.

Mao Zedong also sent people to make inquiries. On November 15, he wrote the following memo on an investigation report: "In the context of the excellent situation and the policy of emulation, it is necessary to solve the problems of one-third of the regions . . ." The memo designated the Xinyang Incident as a case of democratic revolution not being thoroughly accomplished. As a result, many grassroots cadres were rounded up and provided with "group training."

In January 1961 . . . I went again to Henan to investigate. I found many people dead of starvation in Xinxiang and Kaifeng. It was also said that people were rioting. In the countryside I learned that a woman . . . was telling people, "Liberate the pigs, liberate the sheep, liberate the grain, disband the communal dining halls." She was arrested.

On October 21, 1960, the data from the inquiries reached Li Fuchun, a member of the CCP Central Committee Politburo and secretariat. On October 24, Li sent this report to Mao. On the morning of October 26, Mao wrote in a memo, "Request that Liu [Shaoqi] and Zhou [Enlai] read this immediately today and in the afternoon discuss how to deal with it."[65]

According to Wang Congwu,

The comrades from the Central Control Commission overcame considerable difficulties to gain direct access to the peasant masses and obtain an understanding of the situation. It was only then that they understood the gravity of the problem and the enormous number of deaths. They then continued their inquiries in several other counties, where they found the situation equally serious. Their preliminary inquiries established that more than 700,000 had died.

They immediately reported this situation to the main leaders of the Central Control Commission and the Central Committee's Organization Department, who saw that the problem was even more serious than originally perceived and decided that same night that the Organization Department's deputy director, An Ziwen, would report the situation in Xinyang to Premier Zhou Enlai. Immediately after that, the Control Commission's deputy secretary, Wang Congwu, also wrote a report on the Xinyang Incident and sent it to Zhou Enlai. After reading Wang's report, Zhou Enlai perceived the seriousness of the situation and went to speak with Chairman Mao Zedong about it. In accordance with Mao's opinion, the next day Zhou Enlai convened an urgent meeting of the State Council to report on the Xinyang Incident. During the meeting, Zhou said with great emotion, "I am responsible for such a serious incident occurring in Xinyang. Not a single person reported it to us, and the central government knew nothing about it." At the meeting, Zhou decided to immediately form a central work group to carry out an in-depth investigation in Xinyang . . .

The head of the work group was the deputy secretary of the Central Control Commission, Wang Congwu, and the deputy heads were the vice-minister of public security, Xu Zirong, and the deputy director of the CCP Central Committee's Organization Department, An Ziwen. They led dozens of officials from their three departments to Xinyang Prefecture. The central work group carried out inquiries in Xinyang for more than a month, covering the counties where the situation was most serious. After the work group returned to Beijing, it drafted a formal report for the CCP Central Committee and the State Council, appending some fragmentary and ad hoc reports. Finally, in accordance with Mao Zedong's directives and Zhou Enlai's arrangements, a large quantity of grain was sent to Xinyang to meet the urgent need, while at the same time a number of cadres from units directly subordinate to Henan Province were transferred to Xinyang to help local officials carry out supplementary training in democratic revolution and rectification campaigns.[66]

Various official inquiries allowed Mao to arrive at a basic view of the matter by October 1960, as quoted in an official report: "Villains held power, beating and killing people; grain yields dropped and people went hungry. The democratic revolution has not yet succeeded, and feudalistic influences created great mischief and increased antagonism toward socialism, destroying socialism's production relations and productive capacity." "The Xinyang Incident is a restoration of the landlord class and counterrevolutionary class retaliation." "It is necessary to carry out thorough supplementary training in democratic revolution, and as during the Land Reform movement, to thoroughly overthrow the enemy, to completely expose all wrongdoing, to seize leadership, and to achieve a complete reversal of the situation."[67]

The report by the Central Committee's investigation group parroted Mao: "The facts revealed by the accusations of the masses completely verify the Chairman's directive: The nature of the Xinyang problem is absolutely a matter of counterrevolutionary restoration, and a ruthless class retaliation against the working people by landlords and by Kuomintang in the garb of the Communist Party."[68]

On another occasion, Mao said that many landlords, rich peasants, counterrevolutionaries, and bad elements had seized political power and committed evil acts in Xinyang. Two-thirds of the region was in an excellent condition, and only one-third was in a bad condition. The areas in a bad condition fell under three categories: places where remnants of the feudalistic landlord class had infiltrated the party's ranks; places where the quality of party members had degenerated, as in the case of the first secretaries of Xinyang Prefecture's nine counties, most of whom had married the daughters of landlords and had become spokesmen for the landlord class; and places where bureaucratism was a serious problem and where officials were prone to beating and killing.[69]

Liu Shaoqi concurred that the landlord class of Xinyang had been restored to power, that the Xinyang Incident was a counterrevolutionary incident, and that the people of Xinyang needed to be liberated a second time.[70] Although Xinyang was one of the earliest CCP-liberated areas, its grassroots cadres became targets of a mass movement for "supplementary training in democratic revolution."

GRASSROOTS CADRES TAKE THE BLAME

In November 1960 the CCP Central Committee sent Li Xiannian and others to Xinyang to launch the movement. When he learned how many had died, Li wept. He said, "In all my life I've shed tears only twice; the first time was during the Long March, when the army broke through to northern Shaanxi, and this is the second time."

Li's sorrow was no impediment to the reorganization of the prefectural and county leadership, however. The Xinyang cadres were all deemed inadequate, and the Central Committee transferred 4,779 officials. The leadership of the prefecture, counties, communes, and brigades changed virtually overnight, and more than 10,000 cadres were subjected to struggle.[71] Li Xiannian said, "Those people will be dealt with by killing some, imprisoning some, and managing others."

In Gushi County, Wu Zhipu personally led a mass rally at which Yang Shouji was denounced as a counterrevolutionary and arrested. When edema had begun to appear in 1959, Yang had submitted a report to the provincial party committee relating the true situation and requesting grain. Wu Zhipu targeted Yang Shouji to cover up the truth and his own responsibility.

In Huangchuan County, the rectification committee held that the enemy had usurped control in half the communes, and that the other half had become morally degenerate. According to the Huangchuan County rectification committee, among 15,156 cadres at the production team level or above, 2,144 were "bad elements" who had managed to infiltrate the revolutionary ranks.

The Central Committee Special Investigation Group on November 20, 1960, reported:

> In Xinyang Prefecture during the winter of last year and the spring of this year, Lu Xianwen and other counterrevolutionaries and bad elements usurped party and administrative leadership, and using the campaign against right deviation as a cover, they . . . adopted the tactics of landlords and the Kuomintang, such as arbitrary beatings, arrests, and killings to implement wide-scale class retaliation . . .
>
> Leaders and cadres at all levels became organizers and leaders in the domination and oppression of the people, and cold-blooded killers as well.[72]

An investigation targeting thirty-nine people divided them into three categories: The first was "individuals from an alien class seizing power," which included twelve people. The second category, comprising Ma Longshan and three others, included those who had been "dragged into collusion with counterrevolutionaries and bad elements." The third category, of twenty-one people, was "degenerate elements."

As with the struggle sessions against landlords during the Land Reform era, rallies for the venting of grievances were convened. Grassroots cadres were denounced, and 80 percent or even all cadres were penalized in some communes. Violence was common. In Shangcai County, thousands of people were beaten and cadres suffered the punishments imposed on commune members over the past two years.

As many as ten thousand people were investigated in each county, and offices and schoolrooms were packed with detainees. Yu Dehong estimated that four hundred thousand people were rounded up, while Zhang Shufan put the number at two hundred thousand. The detainees were divided up according to the gravity of their wrongdoings. Those who had serious problems were sent to special training classes, where their personal freedom was limited and sentries armed with machine guns were posted outside the door. Those with less serious problems were sent to group training, where restrictions on personal freedom were left to uniformed overseers.

Some rural cadres had genuinely committed a great deal of mischief, and the worst of them certainly deserved to shoulder responsibility for their acts. Even so, placing all the blame on grassroots cadres and turning them into scapegoats was manifestly unjust. The central government that formulated and promoted the fatal policies remained "correct and glorious," while the engenderer of the policies, Mao, was still "sagacious and great," and the system that had produced the famine was "incomparably superior."

When the Henan provincial party committee convened a meeting of its standing committee on December 6, 1960, the second secretary of the South Central bureau, Wang Renzhong, observed:

> What is at issue is our inadequate understanding of the very evident contradictions between the enemy and us, and our inability to clearly perceive the Kuomintang implementing a bourgeois class retaliation in the guise of Communist Party members . . .
>
> To see the masses dying, yet keep the grain locked in storerooms and refuse to distribute it; to watch the communal kitchens close down and yet not allow the masses to light stoves in their own homes; to refuse to let the masses harvest wild herbs or flee the famine; to deny canes to those crippled with starvation; to treat people worse than oxen or horses, arbitrarily beating and even killing them, lacking even a shred of human feeling—if these were not the enemy, what were they?
>
> . . . These people, for the sake of their own self-preservation, slaughtered our class brothers, and we must kill them with equal ruthlessness.[73]

Public security bureau deputy director Xu Zirong said:

The total death toll continues to rise, and the damage is truly enormous, on the order of one-eighth of the population of 8 million. This is in truth a massacre by the enemy . . . In Shangcheng's Zhongpu Commune, more than 8,000 out of some 88,000 people have died, and more than 500 villages have been obliterated. Apart from cadres and their families, not a single household among the masses was unaffected. The fortunate households lost only one or two members, while more than 1,900 households were completely wiped out.[74]

The mass deaths were blamed on those with bad class backgrounds, but in fact people with bad backgrounds suffered the most. Even so, Xu Zirong, as a public security official, continued to target three thousand to five thousand people so identified in Xinyang:

Many counties and communes have been infiltrated by the five bad elements, landlords and local despots, henchmen of feudalism, bandits, reactionary secret societies, and secret agents. It is certain that some have already formed counterrevolutionary cliques. Shi Shaoju has a group of people who are always getting together and drinking and running wild, and promotes bad people by recategorizing landlords as rich peasants. Xu Xilan also assisted a group of bad elements in committing evil acts. Ma Longshan's problem is even greater, collaborating with secret agents from Hong Kong.

The deputy secretary of the Central Control Commission, Wang Congwu, remarked:

The large amount of information revealed in Xinyang and other regions bears out Chairman Mao Zedong's directive. The nature of the Xinyang problem is class enemies usurping power and carrying out frenzied class retaliation . . . wearing the cloak of the Communist Party to carry out the work of the Kuomintang.[75]

Because the Xinyang Incident was determined to be a counterrevolutionary restoration, the main leaders of the Central Control Commission and the South Central bureau devised a formula for dealing with those held most culpable in the matter: in each large county of Xinyang, eight hundred people were to be killed, and four hundred in each small county, with three to five people killed in each production brigade, totaling upwards of ten thousand people throughout the prefecture. The central government did not approve this plan. Finally it was decided to execute Guangshan County party secretary Ma Longshan and Gushi County party secretary Yang Shouji. When Mao Zedong was consulted, he said, "I've never killed a county party secretary. How about death sentences with a two-year reprieve?"

Prefectural party committee secretary Lu Xianwen was ultimately sentenced to three years in prison, and among eight county party secretaries, Guangshan's Ma Longshan received a suspended death sentence, while several years' imprisonment was imposed on other county leaders.

Family members were also persecuted. Xi County leader Xu Xilan's wife was detained and the family's home searched, after which the rest of the family was thrown into the street. The couple's two-month-old infant, separated from its mother, died of starvation. Three other children ages three to seven spent three years foraging for food in the street. Ma Longshan's wife and children became vagrants, living off roots and rubbish, begging and selling scrap. Ru'nan County leader Fu Liangtai's wife was detained, leaving the couple's children home alone to suffer the insults and taunts of neighbors and schoolmates.

Guangshan party secretary Ma Longshan, in his self-examination of October 21, 1960, managed to speak some truth that others dared not express: "This kind of serious incident did not take place in one county or one commune, but rather was endemic and serious throughout the prefecture. This suffices to demonstrate that the prefecture's thinking and work methods were not correct." The reason this occurred was that "over the past few years, especially last year and this spring, the emphasis was placed exclusively on the so-called state view, and the struggle between the two paths of socialism and capitalism was magnified, and within this context, a great campaign against right deviation was launched using erroneous thinking and methods."[76]

Most of those hapless county party secretaries have since passed away. In the autumn of 1999, in a retirement compound for Xinyang's elderly cadres, we found former Huaibin County leader Shi Shaoju, feeble as a guttering candle, sunning himself on a rock. Shi recalled watching a performance of *Mu Guiying Takes Command*[77] in Zhengzhou in

1958. "Chairman Mao Zedong sat in the seventh row, accompanied by Wu Zhipu. I was in the same row, but off to the side." Shi still considered watching this performance with Mao to be the greatest honor of his entire life.

Shi's wife, Zhang Shengzhi, had served as chair of the Gushi County Women's Federation. She recalled:

Around ten o'clock on the night of the seventh day of the eleventh month of the lunar calendar in 1960, arrests were made throughout the prefecture . . . More than thirty thousand people were detained in Gushi. First they held them at gunpoint and led them away in handcuffs. Then they searched their homes and sealed them off. Some who were taken away were arrested, others were sent to group training. [Shi Shaoju] was arrested, and I was sent to training. Our training session was guarded by militia armed with machine guns. I performed well and was released very quickly. If I'd had the misfortune of landlord origins, it would have been worse. Yang Shouji's wife had a landlord background, and husband and wife were both arrested. Their four children were very small at the time, the oldest only seven or eight and the youngest only three or four. Their children wept and cried out for their father and mother as they were taken off. There was a mass public criticism session for Yang Shouji in Gushi.

Shi Shaoju added:

I was dismissed and prosecuted and subjected to discipline and self-examination, spending a year in prison. But I was still treated like a cadre. I don't dare talk about what happened back then—it leaves me sleepless. The problem wasn't a lack of grain, but rather an unwillingness to act. When I saw the peasants had nothing to eat, I went to the deputy secretary of the grain bureau, Zhou Yiyuan, thinking I would borrow around two million kilos of grain and replace it when the harvest came in. Zhou Yiyuan said, "There's grain, but Secretary Wu Zhipu said that the grain in the state silos can't be touched. Anything that's added or taken out has to be reported to the prefecture, so how is it possible to take out two million kilos at once?" In fact, if we had distributed grain just two months earlier, fewer people would have starved.

Shi's wife continued:

My grandmother and my elder sister starved to death. My sister was in Xi County and died in November. She was left in her home and not buried. The reason was so her family could continue collecting her ration of food, but the communal kitchen had closed down in any case. She was buried the following February. After being left out for several months, her face had been gnawed at by rats and was unrecognizable. People from my home village who were starving to death came to me, but I didn't dare to let them stay. At that time peasants weren't allowed to leave their villages, and if discovered there would be criticism. I gave them some food and hurried them on their way.

As the chair of the Women's Federation, I knew very well what women were suffering. At that time, 60 percent of the women stopped menstruating, and some 20 to 30 percent suffered uterine prolapse. There were no more births until 1961.

Given that every part of China suffered events similar to those in Xinyang, the treatment of Xinyang County's party secretaries was gradually relaxed. In September and October of 1963, they were released from prison and sent to the countryside to work for around 50 yuan per month. Decades later, realizing that Xinyang's situation had been far from unique, these cadres began sending letters demanding complete rehabilitation. They felt that lower-level cadres should not have had to shoulder the blame when responsibility extended all the way to the CCP Central Committee.

Lu Xianwen was a revolutionary veteran who had joined the party in 1937. He lived a simple life as a loyal subordinate to Wu Zhipu, who passed the blame for the Xinyang tragedy completely on to Lu. During the struggle against Lu, Wu said, "We should always be on guard against others. In the past I didn't know you, Lu Xianwen, but now I do!" Lower-level cadres proved themselves to the provincial party committee by brutally beating Lu Xianwen. Provincial party secretariat member Yang Weiping declared that Lu was a counterrevolutionary and should be summarily executed.

In his appeal, Lu emphasized that people had starved to death throughout the province. In 1993, retired and ill with cancer, he dictated an essay titled "The History, Social Origins and Lessons of the Xinyang Incident," in which he pinpointed the causes of the Xinyang Incident as "erroneously launching a political movement and utilizing methods of political struggle to promote one voice and suppress all dissenting views, thus making it impossible to address the errors." He went on:

> In 1958, after the Second Session of the Eighth Party Congress, Xinyang Prefecture took the lead in implementing the people's communes. Because the party constantly promoted the people's communes as the Golden Bridge, and communism as paradise, the masses were inspired by the empty propaganda and wanted to immediately plunge into life under communism. The production and living conditions of the people's communes were under the control of cadres at all levels, with a view to implementing the planned economy. The masses had no control over production or initiative in their own lives. The masses no longer cared about production, and became entirely dependent on the party organization. Grain was taken straight from the fields to the state storehouses, leaving nothing for the masses. As soon as the harvest was taken in, they were left in hunger. The masses firmly believed that the party would not allow them to starve, and they hoped the higher leadership would deliver grain to them. But it was easier for the grain to leave than to return! In a sense, therefore, the organization of the people's communes was the social factor leading to the Xinyang Incident.

PART II: HENAN PROVINCE BECOMES THE STANDARD-BEARER OF THE GREAT LEAP FORWARD

The problems in Henan were not isolated; they were provincewide. Some suggest that without the "Pan, Yang, Wang Incident," the Xinyang Incident would never have occurred.[78]

THE PAN, YANG, WANG INCIDENT

In 1958, Henan Province experienced a major political incident involving what came to be known as the "Pan, Yang, Wang right-deviating anti-party clique." At issue were three leaders of the provincial party committee. Pan Fusheng was the committee's first secretary and the political commissar of the Henan military district, Yang Jue was secretary of the party committee secretariat, and Wang Tingdong was the committee's deputy secretary-general. Their nemesis was Wu Zhipu, Henan's second party secretary and provincial governor.

Wu was born in March 1906 to a peasant family in Qi County. In 1920 he entered the county agricultural school, followed by Kaifeng No. 2 Provincial High School in 1924. In March 1925 he joined the Chinese Communist Youth League, and that December he became a member of the Chinese Communist Party.

In February 1926 the party sent Wu to study at the Guangzhou Peasant Movement Training Institute, where he heard Mao lecture on the peasant movement. Before graduating, Wu followed Mao to Haifeng and other places to observe the peasant movements led by Peng Pai and others.[79]

Wu was a fervent admirer of Mao and shared Mao's love of classical literature; when he went to the countryside, he brought along a bamboo suitcase full of books. Yang Jue said that while in Beijing for a meeting, Wu Zhipu went to the Liulichang secondhand-book district and spent more than 300 yuan on an old volume, from which he read aloud with gusto.

The "right-opportunistic errors" of Pan, Yang, and Wang were laid out at the ninth plenum of Henan's provincial party congress, held from June 6 to July 1, 1958:

1. Denying class struggle, denying the struggle between the two paths, manufacturing a theory of "the extinction of class struggle";
2. Attacking the cooperative movement and denying its superiority, promoting the superiority of a "small-farm economy";
3. Attacking and scheming to abolish the policy of state monopoly for purchasing and marketing grain, opposing efforts to criticize spontaneous power;
4. Working in concert with bourgeois rightists within and without to launch fierce attacks on the party;
5. Pretending to lead the Anti-Rightist Campaign while doing their utmost to obstruct and sabotage the campaign;
6. Persistently disseminating documents promoting capitalism;
7. Deceiving the CCP Central Committee and resisting the Central Committee's correct line (mainly referring to the Qingdao Conference in July 1957, when Pan Fusheng told Mao of the situation in Henan);
8. Forming an anti-party faction and engaging in a conspiracy to split the party.

The Central Committee had approved the campaign against Pan, Yang, and Wang, along with other literary and political figures, during the Second Session of the Eighth National Congress of the CCP just one month earlier. Wu had described "right opportunism as the main danger currently facing the party," particularly blaming Pan Fusheng, who was absent from the meeting due to illness. Outside the meeting hall, Deng Xiaoping assured Wu, "The truth is on your side." Pan was dragged from the hospital to be criticized three days in a row, and on May 18 the CCP Central Committee dismissed Pan and replaced him with Wu.

Deng Xiaoping directed that criticism of Pan Fusheng be confined within the party. Wu, however, launched a mass campaign in every city and village to criticize "Pan, Yang, and Wang" and to "plant red flags and supplant white flags." The movement took over society. *Henan Daily* and the newly created party organ *Central Plains Commentary* devoted pages to criticism of "Pan, Yang, and Wang." The three surnames were repeated endlessly on the radio, and trains broadcasted criticism of the trio while passing through Henan Province. The province was festooned with banners and caricatures denouncing Pan, Yang, and Wang. Plays impugned them. Party organs at every level convened meetings and expanded public participation through symposia, denunciation meetings, and lectures. The party calculated in October 1958 that there were some 1.6 billion big-character posters denouncing Pan, Yang, and Wang. Anyone who failed to put up a poster risked being labeled a "little Pan Fusheng." Anyone expressing an alternative viewpoint or who had previously expressed agreement with Pan's "propaganda points" was labeled a "white flag" to be "supplanted," and was criticized as a "little Pan, Yang, Wang." The movement's zealots gained promotion as "red flags."

Pan, Yang, and Wang were subjected to brutal struggle. Even while confined to his home with a high fever, Pan was hauled to a meeting to be criticized. He was not allowed to sit or drink, and as his persecutors jabbed their fingers in his face and screamed imprecations, all he could do was hang his head and admit his guilt.

Three straw men representing Pan, Yang, and Wang were set up in front of Pan Fusheng's home and throughout the province. The doors of the three men's homes were hung with posters enumerating their crimes, and children were encouraged to urinate through their doorways and throw stones through their windows. Not a single window was left intact, and posters hung on every wall, while their beds and floors were covered with stones and tiles that had been thrown through the windows. The three were obliged to write self-criticisms and were often forced to read out loud what was written on the big-character posters. They had to attend struggle sessions every afternoon, standing in the middle of the room with their heads bowed as they were abused and insulted. Some of their attackers struck or kicked them, or spat at them until their faces streamed. All three were ultimately assigned menial labor in the countryside.

On July 15, 1958, the State Council vice-premier Tan Zhenlin told a conference of Henan cadres, "I must first congratulate Henan comrades on this happy occasion. I congratulate Henan Province for its great summer harvest, and for its victory over the right opportunists led by Pan Fusheng and the supplanting of the white flag. I also congratulate you for consolidating the red flag leadership under Comrade Wu Zhipu."

Nearly every county ferreted out "little Pan Fushengs," whose treatment was even more devastating. An estimated one hundred thousand people and their families were persecuted, with more than one hundred dying.

Intellectuals had been intimidated into silence since the unearthing of seventy thousand "rightists" in Henan in 1957. In the even more charged political atmosphere of the 1958 campaign against the "Pan, Yang, Wang" clique, even fewer people were willing to speak the truth. As Henan's first in command, Wu Zhipu devoted himself to anti-rightism, and his zealous implementation of the Three Red Banners made Henan a focal point and disastrous example for the entire nation.

High-yield "satellite" farms were a Henan innovation,[80] and Henan was a pioneer in developing the people's communes[81]; likewise, it was Henan that first promoted irrigation projects, deep-plowing methods, and close-planting that had little scientific basis. As *People's Daily* reported on the Henan experience, Henan became the national standard-bearer for the Great Leap Forward.

WASTEFUL IRRIGATION PROJECTS

Henan's Great Leap Forward began with agriculture, and agriculture's Great Leap Forward began with irrigation.[82] In October 1957, Henan convened a conference on water conservancy projects, after which Wu Zhipu convened a symposium that called for an immediate irrigation Great Leap Forward. The CCP's top agriculture spokesman, Tan Zhenlin, came to lend his support. From November to early December, the CCP's provincial congress held its second session, during which Wu Zhipu analyzed the situation of class struggle and criticized the "grievous rightist errors" of the provincial party committee. He urged a "Great Leap Forward in agricultural production" to implement the National Program for Agricultural Development ahead of schedule. Tan Zhenlin addressed this meeting as well. On December 7 the CCP Central Committee disseminated the Henan provincial party committee's "Situational Report," which described the province's efforts at combating drought, planting wheat, and collecting manure, and its irrigation and winter production campaigns.

Henan's leaders met with officials in charge of agriculture, forestry, and water resources at the beginning of 1958. Wu Zhipu organized a discussion of the 1958 agricultural Great Leap Forward, recommending massive increases in paddy fields and irrigated areas. At the end of January, Wu followed the lead of the Central Committee's Nanning Conference by setting targets for irrigation, grain production, and the elimination of illiteracy and the "four harmful creatures."[83]

According to Wu, Henan had "moved 8.8 billion cubic meters of earth and stone and created 26 billion cubic meters of water storage . . . achieving an irrigated area totaling 125.46 million *mu*." The amount of earth and stone excavated was "equivalent to forty-eight Panama Canals." For all the investment of money and manpower, however, actual excavation was much less than Wu stated. Even by the end of the 1980s, Henan's water storage capacity had reached only 15 billion cubic meters, with an irrigated land surface totaling only 50 million *mu*.

The year 1958 saw the simultaneous construction of nine large-scale reservoir projects, with a total storage capacity of 60 billion cubic meters. The Danjiangkou Reservoir alone required the labor of thirty thousand Henan workers. In 1959 the number of major reservoir projects simultaneously under construction reached eleven, with dozens more medium-size projects. The capital and labor involved vastly exceeded what Henan could afford at the time.

A scientific approach was replaced with a "can-do" spirit. The Zhaopingtai and Yahekou projects were scheduled to be finished within a year but were not completed until the late 1960s or 1970s. Work was also undertaken from November 1957 to July 1958 on the Communist Canal, which was publicized as irrigating 100 million *mu* of cropland but in fact irrigated only 120,000 *mu*. The canal was ultimately abandoned. Likewise failing to reach its target was the Lankao-Shangqiu Sanyizhai People's Great Leap Canal (constructed from March to August 1958), which was to use an old course of the Yellow River to hold 4 billion cubic meters of water. In November 1959, 130,000 laborers embarked on the Huayuankou turnkey project on the Yellow River at Zhengzhou, and although it was completed in the early 1960s, the dam had to be blown up because of design flaws. Many other canal projects also failed to achieve the desired results, while impractical irrigation targets drew large amounts of water from the Yellow River, resulting in serious secondary salinization of cropland.

In 1958–59, a large-scale canal excavation project on the Henan Plains attempted to connect the Hai, Huai, Han, and Yellow rivers. There was also a big "long vines bear fruit" irrigation system, in which soil was piled up on flat land to create irrigation ponds under a system known as "one piece of land to one piece of sky." However, chaotic directives typically replaced technical blueprints; the Tiefosi and Baiguochong reservoirs were built without the use of water diversion, and on May 17, 1960, heavy rains burst their walls, drowning nearly two thousand people.

Villagers deployed to irrigation projects labored on full stomachs for the first two months, but from October 1958 on into 1960 they went hungry. Cadres resorted to violence, threats, and humiliation, and countless irrigation workers died of starvation or physical abuse. In Gushi County alone, more than seventeen thousand people starved to death on three major irrigation projects. Many laborers also died of starvation or physical abuse while working on the Communist Canal in northern Henan.[84]

LAUNCHING "SATELLITES" WHILE PEASANTS STARVE

At the Chengdu Conference on March 8–26, 1958, Wu Zhipu proposed achieving production targets well in advance of the timetable decided by the provincial party committee in January. He promised Mao that Henan would achieve full state ownership within four years.

On March 20, Mao said, "Henan proposes implementing 4-5-8 within one year,[85] and possibly also the goals of bringing all farmland under irrigation, the elimination of the four pests, and the abolition of illiteracy . . . We can allow Henan to experiment for one year. If Henan proves itself, all the other provinces can launch new movements next year, and the Great Leap Forward is sure to progress even further." He also said that Wu's goal of implementing militarization of operations and mass line leadership methods within one year "might encounter some major shortcomings; at the very least, the implementation will be very crude, and the masses will be too keyed up." During the conference, Mao said, "Henan's irrigation projects are a struggle between the two lines." The figures endorsed by Mao exceeded those for 1957 by a factor of 2.4. While Mao repeatedly questioned Henan Province's elevated targets, he encouraged Wu more than he criticized him.[86]

In April, Wu projected a total grain output of 27.5 to 30.0 billion kilos, and all farmland under irrigation within three years. The result was a rapid upsurge in exaggerated crop-yield claims.

The exaggeration frenzy began in the summer of 1958. At Suiping County's Chayashan Satellite Commune, the leader of the Hanlou production brigade and the head of the women's brigade cultivated an experimental field of 2.9 *mu*, and the wheat crop was quite good. Just as they were preparing to gather in the crop, the commune head called an urgent meeting and told them, "The upper levels have instructed us to create a high-yield satellite. We're the country's first people's commune, and we have great influence in and outside of China. How can we not launch a high-yield satellite to demonstrate the superiority of the people's communes?"

The desired yield was at least 1,500 kilos per *mu*, while in the past an average yield had been just over 50 kilos per *mu*. This dramatic increase seemed beyond reach, but the commune head urged, "Put your heads together and think of a solution—you can't disappoint the party!" The solution was to combine the wheat from all 10 *mu* of land. After removing some seed grain, they reported a yield of 1,765 kilos.[87]

People's Daily reported the phenomenal yield the next day (June 12, 1958):

Satellite Commune Launches Second Sputnik: A 2.9-*Mu* Field Produces Yield of 1,765 Kilos per *Mu*.

Following reports of an average yield of 1,052.5 kilos of wheat per *mu* from 5 *mu* of land at the No. 2 production brigade of Satellite Agricultural Commune . . . on June 10 the No. 2 production team of the No. 1 production brigade reported 5,119 kilos of wheat from 2.9 *mu* of land, for an average yield of 1,765 kilos per *mu*. This is . . . more than four times the yield . . . from this plot of land last year. This miraculous bumper crop was raised in a high-yield experimental field . . .

On June 10, when the wheat from this 2.9-*mu* field was threshed, the threshing, winnowing, and weighing was overseen on the threshing floor by a Suiping county party committee member . . . as well as dozens of commune members. After the threshing, the yield was assessed several times. The plot of land was remeasured several times, so the bumper yield is completely reliable.

The writer of this article, Fang Huang, recalled: "I was ordered to go to the countryside and look for satellites, and when I heard some county leaders say the Hanlou brigade had launched a satellite of 1,791.5 kilos, I was skeptical. When I arrived, I saw there really was a very large hoard, and it had been weighed in the presence of county and commune leaders, so even though I had my doubts, I didn't dare express them; I just reported as fact what I was told. Then it turned out to be false! To have been a journalist in this system leaves one feeling nothing but shame and regret." Fang repeatedly told me that she had wronged the people, but anyone sent to report at that time would have written the same, unless he or she wanted to stop working.

A *People's Daily* editorial added color to the narrative, starting out, "In previous years we sold grain with a basket; last year with a boat; this year even a truck cannot contain it; next year a train will be scorned as too small." It went on:

What for centuries has been regarded as a beautiful dream and a thing of myth has today become solid reality! . . . The ultimate record for wheat yield was set at Satellite Agricultural Commune in Henan Province's Suiping County. A field of 2.9 *mu* produced 1,765.375 kilos per *mu*. This would seem to be an ideal, but it is the reality; it is already within our grasp![88]

The 3,660-kilo-per-*mu* yield claimed by Xiping County's Chengguan Commune was an even more blatant exaggeration. So much grain would have risen half a meter deep on the threshing floor; it was simply impossible. Doubts circulated, and the prefectural party committee sent deputy secretary-general Wang Binglin to verify the matter. Wang came back reporting it was true. Decades later, he told me, "The yield was not reported until one month after the harvest. We viewed the packaged grain and measured the surface area of the field. At the time I suspected that the grain had not been harvested from one *mu* of land, but in that political climate, who would dare say anything? It was better to say it was true."[89] Anyone who expressed doubts would become the target of "debate," that is, criticism and struggle involving physical torture.

Zhou Enlai attended two bumper crop exhibitions in the summer of 1958. When he saw the average wheat yield of 3,660 kilos per *mu* for a 2-*mu* field at Xiping County's Heping Commune, and the 3,600.5-kilo-per-*mu* yield at a 1.7-*mu* field at Mengjin Commune, he said, "Your Xiping County is the leader, the top-ranker."[90]

During the autumn harvest, the Henan provincial party committee announced that Henan was China's second province to achieve paddy yields of 500 kilos per *mu*. Local cadres coerced farmers into cutting the crops from several or even dozens of fields and stacking them upright in one field for others to view. By October, Wu Zhipu was claiming wheat yields of 3,650 kilos per *mu* and sesame seed yields of 2,800 kilos, with per-unit-area yields increased seventyfold. Corn, sorghum, and millet yields "were 100 times the average yields of the past," and the "annual total grain output would reach at least 35 billion kilos." Quoting Mao's 1955 prediction that production would increase on such a scale, Wu observed, "It has been brought to living fruition."

In 1958, Henan's grain yield was actually 14.05 billion kilos, but inflated claims turned it into 35.1 billion kilos. In 1959, Henan suffered a drought, and the grain yield dropped to 10.88 billion kilos, but it was inflated to 22.5 billion kilos. The result of elevated estimates was high procurement quotas; the national quota for 1958 exceeded that of 1957 by 22.23 percent, and Henan's procurement was boosted by 56 percent to nearly 41 percent of the actual yield.

Peasants were forced to hand over seed grain, animal feed, and food grain to meet the procurement quota. As a result, soon after the autumn harvest, they suffered food shortages. Yet Wu Zhipu denied that rural households lacked grain, and insisted that local cadres had been influenced by well-to-do middle peasants to conceal the actual yield and hold back grain for private use. This required a "struggle between the two roads of socialism and capitalism" in the form of a provincewide campaign against "false reporting and private withholding." Homes were dismantled and floors dug up, and countless cadres and peasants were killed or brought to ruin.

THE SHIFTING FORM OF THE GREAT LEAP FORWARD

Irrigation projects required "cartification"—replacing traditional shoulder poles with wheelbarrows and handcarts. Enabling carts to move faster required installing ball bearings on their axles. Ball bearings are a machinery component requiring a very hard alloy created with a high degree of precision, and the average workshop is not capable of producing them. Henan Province nevertheless required peasants to produce their own ball bearings. Shangqiu Prefecture alone employed around a million workers in home workshops under the slogan "Every household a factory, every home ringing with a ding-dong sound." The ball bearings thus produced were naturally unusable. Even so, this "bearingification" experience, publicized by *People's Daily*, quickly spread throughout China.[91]

Other enthusiasms included planting sweet potatoes and deepplowing. Henan provincial authorities ordered farmers to plant 25 million *mu* of sweet potatoes, to plow fields to a depth of half a meter, and to apply 15,000 to 25,000 kilos of fertilizer to each *mu* of land. At a national agriculture meeting on July 27, Wu Zhipu boasted that Henan had carried out deep plowing on 80 million *mu* of land, with 25,000 kilos of fertilizer applied to each *mu*.

Henan became the vanguard for Great Leap policies, and its pioneering Chayashan Commune received some 3,000 visitors a day in the summer of 1958. The province's 38,473 collectives had been converted into 1,355 people's communes, with an average of 7,200 households each and incorporating about 95 percent of all peasant households. The founding meeting of Shangcheng County people's commune attracted some 100,000 attendees, including domestic and foreign journalists and an official from the Soviet embassy. The State Council awarded the province a certificate of merit.

Wu Zhipu extolled this "Great Leap Forward of the superstructure," but the capital and materials for grand projects in irrigation, pig farming, industry, and communal living depended on wholesale expropriation from the peasants. Those who objected to the pillage and chaotic implementation were subjected to the usual roster of grisly torments.

Henan also led in steelmaking. On March 18, 1958, peasants were mobilized for the production of steel in "every county, village, and commune." By summer they were ordered to produce "300,000 tons of steel per year, and 1.509 million tons of iron." The party Center's September Beidaihe Conference decided to "exceed the iron and steel production quotas ahead of schedule by three months of hard struggle."

On September 12, *Henan Daily* appealed for "hard effort around the clock for four days to produce 10,000 tons of iron per day." On September 15, *Henan Daily* announced that eight counties were producing more than 1,000 tons of iron per day, with Yu County reaching 4,396 tons. On September 17, *People's Daily* published an editorial entitled "Congratulating Henan's Smashing Victory" at "launching a satellite" in the form of 18,000 tons of iron produced by its backyard blast furnaces.

In early October, Wu Zhipu announced that the province had 5.77 million people toiling at more than 220,000 smelting furnaces. Henan became the Great Leap mecca visited by throngs of pilgrims from every corner of China.[92]

With so many engaged in steelmaking, irrigation, and industry, half the autumn harvest was left in the fields. Women were deployed to farming, and communal kitchens and nurseries were established for "socialization of home duties." The September issue of *China Youth* included an article by Wu Zhipu equating Henan with the Paris Commune[93] in its combining of economic organizations with government.

As Henan became the "advanced province" of the nation, some of its officials became arrogant. When the deputy minister of industry, Gao Yang, visited Henan's Yu County and expressed opinions on the quality of the iron and steel produced in the little backyard furnaces, the county party secretary complained to the provincial party committee that Gao Yang had dashed cold water on the mass movement. Wu Zhipu allowed county officials to criticize Gao Yang on the spot and sent the report on to Beijing, where Gao Yang was criticized once again upon his return. When Yang Xianzhen, deputy director of the Central Party School, visited Henan and expressed some alternative views to the "Great Daring Brings Great Bearing" banners he saw, he met with criticism there and upon his return to Beijing. Peking University and People's University organized a joint investigation group of teachers leading 150 students to Henan. When they saw the actual situation, they drew up a "Compilation of Questions." This material was later described as a "heavy-duty artillery shell" lobbed by Peng Dehuai against the party and socialism. Because of this incident, the vice president of People's University, Zou Lufeng, was driven to commit suicide.[94]

Henan's political activism stirred up a powerful "Communist Wind." The provincial party committee's report proudly detailed how some communes had already "proclaimed the transfer of all means of production to state ownership, the unified allocation and transfer of all products by the state, profits turned over to the higher authority, and production costs and commune member consumption unified and fixed by the state." Wu Zhipu said that the communes "universally implemented not only militarization of operations, but also partial rationing and the voluntary transfer of all personal means of production or other assets to the state." Pigs, sheep, chickens, and ducks all became the property of the commune, along with garlic, turnips, and cabbage. The Communist Wind resulted in the authorities expropriating all remaining life support. The people's communes were presented as a paradise of cost-free eating as peasants were stripped of the right to provide their own meals.

The Communist Wind blew from the villages to the cities, where grand construction and industrial projects were launched. In 1958 the province allocated 1.604 billion yuan to construction projects (while revenues that year totaled only 1.416 billion yuan). Wu Zhipu crowed, "By the end of August, the province will have built or expanded 378,000 factories and mines of all kinds." Workers employed in the province's state-owned enterprises more than doubled in number from 1957. This intensified pressure on food supplies and led to expropriation of personal property.

In April 1959, during a brief nationwide reconsideration of the fanaticism of 1958, Henan readjusted its 1959 planning targets, with steel production reduced from 800,000 tons to 220,000 tons, pig iron production reduced from 1.5 million tons to 800,000 tons, grain production from 50.0 billion kilos to 32.5 billion kilos, and investment in capital construction from 1.86 billion yuan to 1.36 billion yuan. The targets nevertheless remained unrealistic, and by the end of the year, production of steel came in at only 51,400 tons, pig iron at 690,000 tons, and grain at only 9.7 billion kilos. Investment in capital construction, on the other hand, was pushed close to its original target at 1.8 billion yuan.

Wu Zhipu stubbornly pressed ahead with new goals in heavy industry and agriculture, intensifying the chaos brought about by years of rash efforts. During the fifteenth plenum of the provincial party committee and the accompanying conference of all the province's cadres in February 1960, Wu insisted on continuing the campaign against right deviation, and promoted communal industry, irrigation projects, and collective pig farms to realize Henan's Great Leap Forward.[95]

Henan had been commended by Mao as the first to organize a people's commune and the first to establish a communal kitchen. Now Wu Zhipu and his colleagues wracked their brains to go further. In February 1959 the province embarked on a campaign to mechanize the communal cooking process. It was claimed that thirty-two cooking tools had been adapted for this purpose, including "Great Leap" stoves, vegetable washing and cutting machines, "Great Leap" millstones, and noodle cutters. These were wooden implements suitable for nothing but display.

Before the Lushan Conference in 1959, the secretary of the Henan provincial party committee secretariat, Shi Xiangsheng, reported these developments to Mao, who invited Shi to bring the modified utensils to Lushan. The machines remained in their crates during the initial criticism of the "Five Winds," but after Mao attacked Peng Dehuai on July 23, they were brought out and put on display. Mao then learned that the machines were useless and that the mechanization of the communal kitchens was a fiction.[96]

As the situation in the countryside deteriorated, some villagers and cadres began fixing output quotas for households. These lifesaving measures were supported by Xinxiang prefectural party secretary Geng Qichang, Luoyang prefectural party secretary Wang Huizhi, and Kaifeng prefectural party secretary Zhang Shen. In the subsequent struggle against right deviation, however, these measures were regarded as opposing the socialist road. Geng Qichang and Wang Huizhi were labeled right opportunists, and many cadres were persecuted. Driven insane, Wang Huizhi roamed the streets like a wild man, attempting to jump in the river. When people chased him, he ran off shouting, "Wu Zhipu is here!"[97]

PART III: AT LEAST THREE MILLION STARVED TO DEATH

The Great Leap Forward and the commune movement devastated agriculture. Official figures valued Henan's agricultural output in 1959 at 3.555 billion yuan, a decrease of 8.9 percent from 1958. Total grain output was 9.745 billion kilos, a decrease of 22.9 percent from the previous year.

Agricultural output decreased another 11 percent in 1960. State procurement and enormous waste depleted grain reserves. Edema and gynecological disorders were rampant in the human population, and an estimated 740,000 head of livestock died.[98] Yet Wu Zhipu reported that only 5 percent of the people suffered inadequate living standards, and he denied the need for emergency food supplies or a reduction in the state grain procurement.

In January and February 1959, the Central Committee and the State Council received numerous letters reporting that many in Henan were stricken with edema or had died of starvation. A January 20, 1959, letter to the Central Committee and State Council, signed by "the masses north and south of the Liudiquan train station," stated, "On the day of the Spring Festival, people covered the grasslands of Xiayi and Yucheng searching for wild plants to eat, but there was nothing left. People have died of starvation in all of the villages on the border between the two counties. Some dropped dead while waiting in line to buy food; others perished while seeking wild herbs in the fields."

A February 25 letter signed by "All officers and soldiers of Troop Unit No. 0220 at Jimo County, Shandong Province" reported that peasants in Henan's Yucheng and Xiayi counties were receiving a grain ration of only 150 grams per day, and that any who said he had not eaten his fill was denounced and beaten as a rightist. The masses were like sheep, the letter said, and dared not speak.[99]

As starvation spread, the 1960 New Year's Day issue of *Henan Daily* published an editorial calling for "Getting Off to a Good Start with Spring in the Air." After presenting a February report on "The Struggle for Implementing Continuation of the Great Leap Forward in 1960," Wu Zhipu in March claimed that 99 percent of Henan's population had joined communal kitchens and that two-thirds of these kitchens were well organized.[100] When elevated production targets were criticized during the two Zhengzhou conferences, Tan Zhenlin and Wu Zhipu continued to push for 1,000-kilo-per-*mu* crop yields. When Mao inspected Henan, Wu Zhipu covered up the starvation in Xinyang.

By spring 1960, one communal kitchen after another had run out of food. In January 1962, Wu Zhipu admitted, "On Henan's grain yield in 1958 and 1959, I made rough estimates that far surpassed the reality . . . I delivered false reports to the Chairman on Henan's grain yield more than once . . . At the time that I said only 5 percent of the masses were experiencing substandard livelihoods, many people in Xinyang Prefecture were already suffering from edema or had died."

Xinyang prefectural party secretary Lu Xianwen had informed Wu Zhipu of the starvation deaths in February, but Wu ignored the problem and on April 15 led a CCP delegation to a Communist Party congress in Finland. While Lu faced opposition from his cadres and the public, Wu told him to buck up and maintain Xinyang's "advanced position" in grain and steel production and as the home of the first people's commune. As a result, hunger and disease spread through the Yellow River Basin. Apart from Xinyang, the prefectures of Nanyang and Xuchang also experienced high levels of starvation. In Nanyang's Xichuan County, the population was reduced by one-fifth over two years, a mortality rate matching that in Xinyang.

In Nanyang Prefecture's Tanghe County, party secretary Bi Kedan was an enthusiast of the Great Leap Forward. In the autumn of 1958, Tanghe County set up 4,617 steel furnaces, and hoes, shovels, and other farming implements were sent to the smelters. *Henan Daily* touted the usual incredible crop yields, which resulted in high procurement quotas, and most of Tanghe's grain was transferred out of the county. In September 1959 the communal kitchen was shut down, and by the spring of 1960, tens of thousands of villagers had starved to death. Awakened from his delusion, Bi Kedan made five requests to the upper levels to buy back grain, but was refused. Prefectural officials criticized Tanghe County for its feeble effort against "private withholding of grain," and the province and prefecture sent a work team to Tanghe to conduct "supplementary lessons in democratic revolution." The work team concluded that Tanghe County's leadership had "rotted away," and Bi Kedan was removed from his position and placed under investigation. Nanyang Prefecture arrested four other leaders in Xichuan, Deng, and Xinye counties, urging the province to have them summarily executed. Although permission for the executions was ultimately withheld, the leadership of all Nanyang's counties was shaken to its core.

On November 21 the Tanghe County party committee convened an exposure meeting. Bi Kedan stood at the door of the conference room and shook hands with attendees, who assumed that Bi was bidding farewell before going to prison. Early the next morning, Bi Kedan and his wife, Liu Guixiang, lined up with their four children in front of a well

THE EPICENTER OF THE DISASTER ■ 83

and jumped in. Bystanders managed to save Bi's wife and son, but Bi and his three daughters died.[101]

The exact number of people who died in Henan during the famine remains a mystery. During the Cultural Revolution, critics of Wu Zhipu claimed that three million people died. Since Mao's death, estimates have risen to five million. However, neither of these claims was based on solid figures.

I have calculated a rough estimate based on figures in the *Henan Statistical Yearbook*.

TABLE 1.1: NATURAL FLUCTUATIONS IN HENAN'S ANNUAL POPULATION FIGURES

Year	Avg. population (millions)	Birth rate (%)	Death rate (%)	Natural increase (%)
1955	46.06	3.079	1.175	1.904
1956	46.93	3.585	1.400	2.185
1957	47.87	3.367	1.180	2.187
1958	48.91	3.315	1.269	2.046
1959	49.61	2.806	1.410	1.395
1960	48.98	1.398	3.956	−2.558
1961	48.11	1.525	1.020	0.505
1962	48.72	3.750	0.804	2.946
1963	49.70	4.508	0.943	3.565
1964	50.89	3.584	1.061	2.523
1965	51.70	3.610	0.845	2.765
1966		3.604	0.824	2.780

Source: Henan Statistical Yearbook (2000), *p. 103.*

The famine increased unnatural deaths and lowered the birth rate. My calculations (explained in chapter 11 on population loss) show that unnatural deaths in 1958–60 numbered 101,700, 173,100, and 1,418,000, for a total of 1,692,800. Shortfalls in births for the years 1958–61 were respectively 76,300, 329,900, 1,015,400, and 936,200, for a total of 2,357,800. This is in line with statistics provided in *China Population: Henan*, which indicate 1,664,500 unnatural deaths in Henan during the famine years, and a shortfall in births of 2,350,000.

Official statistics tend to be lower than the reality, but it is safe to assume that at least one million people starved to death in Xinyang, and that the number of starvation deaths in Nanyang, Xuchang, and Shangqiu prefectures totaled at least two million. Many people also starved to death in eastern Henan and other regions.

Wu Zhipu estimated that from October 1959 to November 1960 at least two million people died. His estimate did not include the period from the end of 1958 to October 1959 and the year 1961. If these two periods are included, Wu's total would also reach around three million dead. Cao Shuji[102] arrived at a figure of 2,939,000 starvation victims in 1959–61, a figure very close to my own calculations.

Wu Zhipu was not disciplined for these deaths, but cadres lower down were less fortunate. From January 30 to February 12, 1961, the Henan provincial party committee held a "discovery meeting" to unmask the problems from 1958 onward. The meeting discussed the famine in Xinyang, eastern Henan, Mi County, Changge County, and Pohu. There were many tearful speeches and blood-soaked narratives indicting prefectural and county-level leaders. Following the new Central Committee line, they referred to Wu Zhipu as an alien-class element, an incorrigible bureaucrat, and an enemy wearing the cloak of the Communist Party, and described the provincial party committee as a power base seized by villains. Demands for Wu to be brought to justice were brushed aside, however, and representatives of the Central Committee guided the conference to designate the error as "not the erroneous line of left adventurism, but rather the committing of left adventurist errors in executing the line of the Central Committee." This substantially mitigated the offense.[103] The Center's representatives, Tao Zhu and Wang Renzhong, treated prefectural leaders as alien-class elements and counterrevolutionary restorationists, but provincial leaders could not even be accused of "line errors." Thus lower officials were sacrificed to save those higher up.

In the Center's cover-up, Wu Zhipu had resolutely executed the Center's line from the time he became acting secretary of the Henan provincial party committee during Pan Fusheng's illness in 1955. He had executed this line during the 1957 Anti-Rightist Movement, during the struggle against Pan Fusheng's right opportunism, in the steel campaign, and in establishing the people's communes, although he had, of course, committed some errors.

Wang Renzhong asked, "How should the Henan provincial party committee's errors be weighed against its accomplishments? They should be assigned the proportion of three against seven, with the accomplishments assigned seven parts and the errors assigned three parts." He then asked, "Who should ultimately bear the blame for the deaths in Xinyang Prefecture? Against whose account should this blood debt be laid? Who bears the primary responsibility? Obviously it is the counterrevolutionaries Lu Xianwen and Ma Longshan who are the criminal ringleaders."[104]

Wu Zhipu eventually conceded that he had "committed left adventurist errors in executing the policies of the Central Committee, with the result that enemies had seized the opportunity, and defeat in the class struggle had led to disastrous results in which deeply painful lessons had been learned." In this way he still placed the blame on "class enemies" in line with Mao's claim that "one-third of the political power is not in our hands." Wu Zhipu went on to claim that class enemies had seized control over at least 40 percent of Henan's counties, communes, and production brigades, and had "used our operational errors and natural disaster to create opportunity out of hardship and to carry out relentlessly brutal class retaliation against the poor and lower-middle peasants in the villages." Wu compared the deprivation and brutality to the "dark pre-Liberation days of the Kuomintang, landlords, local despots, bandits, and hooligans" and estimated that "from October 1959 to November 1960, at least two million people died in the province."

Tao Zhu reported back to Zhou Enlai, and the Central Committee secretariat decided how to handle the Henan provincial party committee leaders: as long as they thoroughly revealed and corrected their errors, they would not be punished, but a partial reorganization should be carried out in the provincial party committee. Wu Zhipu was not punished in any way, for which Tao Zhu offered the following explanation: "Wu Zhipu's and Pan Fusheng's circumstances were different. Pan Fusheng committed line errors and was defiant and unwilling to correct his errors. The Henan provincial party committee headed by Wu Zhipu did not commit line errors. Over the past years, their work has consisted largely of achievements; there were only a few months in which they committed errors, and as soon as the Center exposed these errors, they resolutely conceded and resolutely corrected the errors." The Central Committee transferred Guangdong provincial party secretary Wen Minsheng to serve as the executive secretary of the Henan party committee, and transferred Hubei provincial party secretary Liu Yangqiao to serve as the Henan party committee's secretary and secretary-general. In July, Guangxi's first party secretary, Liu Jianxun, was appointed first party secretary of Henan. In April 1962, Wu Zhipu was transferred to the South Central bureau to serve as secretary for culture and education.

In January 1962, Wu Zhipu submitted a self-examination report in which he acknowledged falsely reporting high grain yields while people were dying of starvation. Deeply grieved, he said, "The provincial party committee and I committed very serious errors, and our crime is enormous . . . no matter how severely the party deals with me, I can offer no objection. If it's decided that I should be executed, I can only extend my neck to receive the blow." Wu expressed his sorrow on several occasions: "I can never repay my debt to the fifty million people of Henan as long as I live."[105]

Upon being transferred to the South Central bureau, Wu Zhipu took along more than one hundred crates of his beloved thread-bound classics. An elderly Guangdong cadre, Jin Ming, said that on one occasion, Chairman Mao visited the South Central bureau, and when Tao Zhu introduced him to the members of the secretariat, Mao saw Wu and said, "Ah, you've come here!" Wu wept. On another occasion, when officials of the provinces under the South Central bureau held a meeting, Wu went to the rooms where the Henan provincial cadres were staying and begged their forgiveness, saying, "I'm guilty, I've sinned against the people of Henan."[106]

2 THE THREE RED BANNERS: SOURCE OF THE FAMINE

In order to understand how China descended into catastrophic famine and starvation, it is necessary to understand the "Three Red Banners" of the Chinese Communist Party—the General Line, the Great Leap Forward, and the people's communes. Serving as the political banners that were to lead the Chinese into communism, they sparked the fanaticism of 1958, and as such can also be considered the direct cause of the Great Famine.

Yet China's rulers regarded this source of calamity as a precious treasure. From 1958 until just before the launch of reform in 1978, one's attitude toward the Three Red Banners was a major criterion for determining loyalty—or lack of same—to the party.

The "General Line" was shorthand for the "General Line for socialist construction." It referred to the directive to "go all out, aim high, and build socialism with greater, faster, better, and more economical results."[1] The news media spread the message that "speed is the soul of the General Line," and the Great Leap Forward was the embodiment of that ideal. Conceptually, therefore, the General Line and the Great Leap Forward were one and the same, with the General Line emphasizing guiding ideology and the Great Leap Forward emphasizing action; the Great Leap Forward was action guided by the General Line.

The General Line for socialist construction was formulated during the Second Session of the Eighth National Congress of the CCP in May 1958, but it had been taking shape since the founding of the People's Republic in 1949, and already served an important function at the Chengdu Conference of March 9–25, 1958.

PUSHING REVOLUTION AND CONSTRUCTION
"A LITTLE FASTER"

Marx, Lenin, Stalin, and Mao all anticipated that the Communist revolution would come sooner rather than later. The writings of Marx and Engels described the revolutionary crisis in Europe as imminent. Lenin expounded on the final phase of capitalism, and intended that Russia should make a direct transition to communism. It was only after this proved impossible that he turned to implementation of a new market-oriented economic policy. Lenin predicted that "the generation of those who are now fifteen will see a Communist society, and will itself build this society."[2] Lenin's and Stalin's impetuosity arose from their inability to perceive the ability of the market economy under democratic systems to redress constantly and automatically the so-called "maladies inherent in capitalism." This blind spot led them to develop a system flawed by hostility to the market and disdain for democracy.

Given the poverty and backwardness of China, its Communist leadership harbored an even more pressing desire for change. Speed took precedence over practicality, with a particularly heavy reliance on mass movements.[3] The leaders responsible for economic work were more practical, but any attempt to express their ideas risked accusations of "right-deviationist thinking." As soon as Mao began criticizing right deviation, the majority joined in, creating enormous political pressure. Leaders who persisted faced criticism not only from Mao but also from their peers. Mao emphasized "going all out and aiming high," along with "eliminating superstition and liberating the mind" and "daring to think, daring to speak, daring to act," believing that only through this outlook could a matter be swiftly accomplished. This guiding ideology served as Mao's departure point in criticizing "right-deviating conservatism" in economic construction.

At an assembly of more than 120 Beijing-based members of the CCP Central Committee and leaders of all party, government, and military organs in the conference room of Zhongnanhai's Western Pavilion on the afternoon of December 5, 1955, Liu Shaoqi transmitted Mao's directives on criticizing right-deviating conservatism and striving to achieve the transition ahead of schedule:[4] "If we proceed along a conventional route, the time required will be longer and the results less impressive. This is the conservative route. At present our work in all areas is lagging behind the evolving situation; many of our comrades are proceeding along this conservative route."[5] The CCP leadership was aiming for "surpassing development" (*chaoyue fazhan*), a goal to which anyone might have aspired, given China's impoverished and backward conditions.

The December 27, 1955, version of Mao Zedong's preface to *The Socialist Upsurge in China's Countryside* projected, "When the Third Five-Year Plan is completed, that is, in 1967, the yields for grain and many other agricultural products should be double or triple the highest yields obtained before the founding of the People's Republic."[6]

The eventual reality was that in 1967, China's total grain yield was 218.7 billion kilos, less than half of Mao's target. Not until 1993 did China achieve a total grain yield of 450 billion kilos.

Once it became clear that all sectors could come under criticism if perceived as lagging, every ministry under the State Council pushed aside practical concerns and hastily revised the harvest targets proposed in the summer of 1955 for the Third Five-Year Plan. Grain production targets were raised from 300 billion kilos to 425 billion (or 500 billion kilos with soybeans included). Some cadres even moved the deadline from 1967 to 1962. The State Planning Commission, likewise fearing accusations of right-deviating conservatism, on January 14, 1956, rubber-stamped a plan with these unrealistic production targets.[7]

In January 1956, Mao repeatedly observed that the Americans produced a mere 100 million tons of steel and a few hundred hydrogen bombs and that China would catch up with them as a first step before ultimately overtaking them. Beginning on February 14, 1956, a total of thirty-four ministries and commissions reported back to the CCP Central Committee. As each report was read out, Mao would become very excited, interposing encouraging remarks such as "China's industrial development can proceed more swiftly than the Soviet Union's," and "China has two advantages: one is emptiness, the other is blankness, with no encumbrances of any kind. The United States in George Washington's era was blank, so it could develop very rapidly. The Soviet Union was also blank at the outset." (Subsequently, the published version was changed to "poor and blank.")[8] These remarks led ministries, commissions, provinces, and cities to raise their targets.[9]

One reason behind Mao's desire to build socialism was his rivalry with Soviet leader Nikita Khrushchev for the leadership of the International Communist Movement. After Stalin's death in 1953, Mao looked down on Khrushchev. The Korean War had raised Mao's own status and had given him a feeling of invincibility within the Comintern. Although he continued to pay lip service to the Soviet Union as the leader of the socialist camp, in his heart he had already usurped this position. In order for Mao to take over actual leadership, however, China's socialism had to overtake other socialist countries. Mao spoke of surpassing the United Kingdom and the United States, but his greatest wish was to overtake the Soviet Union.

ZHOU ENLAI INITIATES THE CAMPAIGN AGAINST "RASH ADVANCE"

The term "rash advance" (*maojin*) that became current at this time referred to proceeding too rapidly without due consideration of actual circumstances and likely consequences. Opposition to rash advance in economic construction first arose in early 1956 and continued until early 1957. The main opponents to rash advance were senior officials in charge of economic affairs in the State Council, including Zhou Enlai, Chen Yun, Li Xiannian, and Bo Yibo. They later formed the backbone of China's "pragmatic faction," and, following the deaths of Mao and Zhou, they became a major force shaping China's economic policies in the reformist 1980s.

Fearing attack for right deviationism, all levels of government elevated economic targets from 1955 onward. Capital construction rose precipitously, and the number of projects proliferated, putting enormous pressure on steel and cement production. Provinces and cities added their own projects. Zhou Enlai, who was in charge of State Council work, was sure the plans were impossible, and pointed out the emergence of a "phenomenon of impetuous and rash advance."[10]

After careful consideration, Zhou Enlai, Li Fuchun, and Li Xiannian, at a planning and finance meeting on February 6, 1956, reduced the capital construction investment for 1957 from 18 billion to 14.7 billion yuan. Even so, the capital construction budget was 68 percent higher than for the year before.[11]

During the State Council's Twenty-fourth Plenum, on February 8 [1956], Zhou said, "It would be very dangerous to rush into projects that . . .

have no basis in reality." "If the leader becomes too hot-headed, a splash of cold water might clear his mind . . . Please, everyone, be practical and realistic."[12]

In late April, however, during a Politburo meeting Mao proposed increasing the capital construction budget by 2 billion yuan. Zhou disagreed, but Mao persisted with his own view and adjourned the meeting. Afterward, Zhou went to Mao and said, "As premier, I cannot in good conscience agree with this decision." This infuriated Mao.

Starting in May, Zhou began correcting the rash advance. During a full meeting of the State Council on May 11, for example, he suddenly said, "The campaign against conservatism and right deviation . . . can't go on forever!"[13]

Then, in May 1956, the CCP Central Committee decided that economic development required opposing both conservatism and rash advance. The draft budget that the Ministry of Finance submitted to the Politburo for discussion on June 3 echoed the preference for balance. Presided over by Liu Shaoqi, the Politburo on June 10 approved in principle the draft budget and assigned Mao's secretary, Hu Qiaomu, to amend it in accordance with the views expressed. The capital construction budget for 1957 was reduced again from 14.7 billion yuan to 14 billion yuan.[14]

The CCP Central Committee's Propaganda Department took charge of drafting a *People's Daily* editorial stating that "Impetuous emotion has become a serious problem at present, because it exists . . . first and foremost among the upper ranks of the leading cadres . . . no departments wanted to be accused of right-deviating conservatism, and they vied to assign the most aggressive targets to the lower levels, with each level passing an even heavier burden on to the level below, ultimately resulting in an intolerable situation." Before it was published, the editorial was sent to Mao for approval. He annotated it with four words: "I'm not reading it."[15]

While working out the Second Five-Year Plan and the 1957 economic plan, Zhou and others continued to counter rash advance and reduced some excessively high economic targets.[16] These moves were reflected upon during the Eighth National Congress of the CCP, convened September 5–27, 1956. Liu Shaoqi's political report contained two assessments. First, "Our country's contradiction between the proletariat and the capitalist class has been basically resolved. The millennia-long history of the system of class exploitation has been basically brought to a close, and socialism has been basically established as the social system of our country."

The implication that class struggle had been concluded formed the basis for a new assessment of what constituted China's main domestic contradiction: "Our country's main domestic contradiction is the contradiction between the people's demands to establish an advanced industrial nation and the reality of a backward agricultural nation; it is the contradiction between the needs of the people for the rapid development of the economy and culture, and the present conditions under which the economy and culture cannot satisfy the people's needs." In short, economic construction was now the crux of the matter.

Zhou Enlai's report on the Second Five-Year Plan, approved by the Eighth National Party Congress in September, stressed that "the party's responsibility is to take pains at all times to prevent and correct any tendency toward right-deviating conservatism or left-leaning risk-taking." The real target was rash advance.

In a parliamentary system, Mao might have been obliged to resign. In China, however, his paramount position was extremely stable. He was not about to let his subordinates violate his wishes; he would retaliate against the opposition to rash advance when he found the right opportunity.

MAO CRITICIZES THE OPPOSITION TO RASH ADVANCE

A year later, by the second half of 1957, anti-Soviet uprisings in Poland and Hungary had been quelled, and China's Anti-Rightist Campaign had concluded; the First Five-Year Plan had been completed; and an upsurge in irrigation and water conservancy projects had begun. Mao decided that circumstances were favorable for his counterattack.

At the Third Enlarged Plenum of the Eighth CCP Central Committee on October 9, 1957, Mao declared:

> Last year several things were swept out. One of the things swept out was "greater, faster, better, and more economical" . . . everyone was opposed to greater and faster, which some comrades called "rash" . . . We always need to strive to achieve as much and as quickly as possible, and only oppose the subjective sense of "greater" and "faster." In the second half of last year, a gust of wind swept out that slogan, and I want to restore it. I want all of you to look into this.
>
> Also swept out was the Forty-Point Program for Agricultural Devel-

opment. That forty-point program fell into bad odor last year, and now it will be restored.

Also swept out were the committees for promoting progress. I have asked in the past whether the nature of the Communist Party . . . at all levels . . . is that of promoting or of hindering progress. They should be promoting progress. I see the Kuomintang as a committee for hindering progress and the Communist Party as a committee for promoting progress. The wind that blew up last year swept out the committees for promoting progress, so can we restore them now? If you all disagree with restoring them and insist on organizing a committee for hindering progress, with so many of you preferring hindrance there's nothing I can do . . . Those who wish to hinder us are members of that rightist Zhang-Luo Alliance.[17]

For Mao to equate those who opposed rash advance with a "committee for hindering progress" and to group them with the Kuomintang and the freshly denounced "rightist Zhang-Luo Alliance" was extremely damaging. Now opposition was tantamount to being a counterrevolutionary. Mao also cavalierly overturned the Eighth National Party Congress resolution on China's principal domestic contradictions, saying:

There can be no doubt that the contradiction between the proletarian class and the bourgeois class, and between the socialist road and the capitalist road, is the principal contradiction our country now faces . . . We are in the midst of a socialist revolution, and the spearhead of revolution is aimed at the bourgeoisie . . . It is the contradiction between the socialist road and the capitalist road. The resolution of the Eighth National Party Congress did not raise this issue. The resolution has one section about the principal contradiction being between an advanced social system and a backward productive force. This formulation is incorrect.[18]

No one resisted. Before Mao spoke, Zhou Enlai had persisted with his position of "opposing conservatism and also opposing rash advance." Once Mao made his pronouncement, however, all those opposing rash advance held their tongues. Mao's "comrades-in-arms" were now his submissive subordinates, and his every opinion would be parroted as a golden rule by all those beneath him. In addition, most party cadres were experts in class struggle, and were galvanized by its very mention, spoiling for a fight to prove themselves by targeting dissenters.

In November 1957, Mao led a delegation to the International Congress of Communist and Workers' Parties in Moscow. Inspired by Soviet general secretary Nikita Khrushchev, Mao raised the question of surpassing the United Kingdom and catching up with the United States. During a meeting of the Supreme Soviet on November 6, Khrushchev announced that within the next fifteen years, the Soviet Union would not only catch up with the United States but would be able to surpass its current main production capacity. During the Moscow meeting, on November 18 Mao commented, "Comrade Khrushchev tells us that in fifteen years the Soviet Union can surpass the United States. We can also say that after fifteen years we can catch up with or surpass the United Kingdom. I spoke twice with comrades Pollitt and Gollan[19] and asked them about their country's situation. They said that the United Kingdom current annual steel production is 20 million tons, and that in fifteen years it may climb to 30 million tons. As for China, in fifteen years, our steel production may be 40 million tons, so why should we not surpass the United Kingdom?"[20] Mao imagined that China could produce 40 million tons of steel by 1973, a target met only in the post-Mao reform era. Mao's grand plan had not been discussed or analyzed at any stage by the CCP Central Committee or the State Council, nor was there any examination by experts. At the Eighth National Congress of the All-China Federation of Trade Unions on December 2, 1957, President Liu Shaoqi represented the CCP Central Committee with a speech endorsing Mao's vision, which then became the guiding ideology of the party and the country.

Mao left Beijing on December 8, 1957, and stayed in eastern China for one month. He publicized his thoughts through articles in *People's Daily* by the like-minded Zhejiang provincial first secretary Jiang Hua and Shanghai municipal first secretary Ke Qingshi. At a conference in Hangzhou on January 3 and 4, 1958, Mao claimed that Anhui Province had excavated 1.6 billion cubic meters of earth over the winter, exceeding the total excavated over the preceding seven years. This fake statistic, in Mao's view, demonstrated that the original plan was too modest and that right-deviating conservatism should be criticized. "Criticizing right-deviating conservatism feels good," he said. "The more you criticize it, the happier you feel." He said that the third, fourth, and fifth years of the Second Five-

Year Plan must be revised and that right deviation should be criticized with gusto. Industry had grown by 31 percent in 1956, and without this advance by leaps and bounds in 1956, the First Five-Year Plan could not have been accomplished. He called on all localities to engage in competitions, province against province, county against county, cooperative against cooperative. He had *People's Daily* reprint the *Zhejiang Daily* editorial entitled "Are We in the Promoting Camp or the Hindering Camp?" and called for "striking while the iron is hot," claiming that attempts to establish a "new democratic order" were a waste of effort.[21]

THE NANNING CONFERENCE: MAO ATTACKS ZHOU ENLAI

On January 11–12, 1958, Mao presided over the Nanning Conference. In a large, single-story villa where Vietnamese leader Ho Chi-minh often stayed, criticism of efforts against rash advance surged anew.

Zhou Enlai's and Li Xiannian's speeches against rash advance in 1956 were distributed along with a *People's Daily* editorial with a similar tone as reference materials for criticizing the campaign against rash advance. Before the editorial was printed for the meeting, Mao scribbled in many critical remarks: "philistine dialectics," "pointedly directed at me," "since cadres have gone to the extreme, isn't this an error of guiding principle?," "does this criticize rightism?," "vulgarized Marxism," and so on.[22] In his speech at the Nanning Conference, he dismissed the article's ostensibly "balanced" criticism as sophistry, and said the real target was rash advance. "I noted on this editorial that I would not read it. Why should I read something that's attacking me? Who is the editorial aimed at? Its criticism is aimed at my 'Preface'"[23] (to *The Socialist Upsurge in China's Countryside*). The other reference material presented for criticism consisted of excerpts from a talk by Zhou Enlai.[24]

On January 11, Mao said, "Don't use the phrase 'opposing rash advance' . . . it's terrible for 600 million people to become deflated. Of course we should oppose empty storehouses and market tension, and wasted manpower and funding . . . This wind blew away three things: One was 'greater, faster, better, and more economical,' another was the Forty-Point Program for Agricultural Development, and the third was the committees for promoting progress . . . Should we preserve enthusiasm and encourage drive, vigor, and ambition, or discourage and deflate enthusiasm?"

Mao liked to use "The relationship of ten fingers to one finger" as a formulation to play down errors and shortcomings. Whenever problems were exposed, the critic was accused of ignoring the majority of positive factors and "attacking one point without taking the remainder into account."

Mao then went on to reply to his critics:

> Chen Mingshu criticizes me for "delusions of grandeur, listening only to what he wants to hear, moody and changeable, and with no love for antiquities." Zhang Xiruo criticizes me for "delusions of grandeur, eager for quick success and instant benefit, disparaging the past and having blind faith in the future."[25] In the past, northern crop yields stood at a little more than 50 kilos per *mu*, and southern crop yields at 100 to 150 kilos. Generalissimo Chiang [Kai-shek] accumulated twenty years of experience and left us with only 40,000 tons of steel. If we don't despise the past and believe in the future, what hope can we have? As for listening to only one side, that is inevitable; the question is whether the view we're favoring is that of the bourgeoisie or of the proletariat. Some comrades are not biased enough and need to show more favoritism. As for having no love for antiquities, this is a question of favoring advancement or backwardness. Antiquities are somewhat backward, aren't they? What comes later typically supersedes what came before, rather than the other way around. It's not that antiquities can't be appreciated, just not too much. When Beijing dismantled its decorative archways and knocked holes in the city walls, Zhang Xiruo bawled his head off—this is a political issue.

Mao mocked those who would preserve China's ancient glories. As for the accusation of "delusions of grandeur," he replied, "What's wrong with bragging about the greatness of 600 million people, and showing off the accomplishments of socialism?"

In a speech the next day, January 12, he said, "Because of the ups and downs over the last three years, the attacks by the rightists have sent some comrades to the brink of rightism, only 50 meters away from it."[26] This referred to Zhou, who at that time was in Beijing receiving foreign guests. Upon arriving in Nanning on January 13, Zhou sensed a change in the atmosphere.

On the evening of January 13, Mao called Zhou and Liu Shaoqi in for talks that continued into the early morning hours. At the meeting on January 16, Mao singled out an article by Ke Qingshi for extravagant praise. This was Ke's December 25 report on the Shanghai Party Congress meeting, which Mao had revised and wanted *People's Daily* to publish in full. Mao said, "This article dwarfs all of us. Shanghai's gross industrial output value comprises one-fifth of the national total; the city has one million proletarians, even though it was a center and birthplace of capitalism, which had a long history there, and class struggle was intense. Only a place like this could inspire such an article." He asked, "Comrade Enlai, you're the premier, would you be capable of writing this article?" Noting the expression in Mao's eyes, Zhou said, "I couldn't write it." Mao said, "Aren't you opposed to rash advance? I'm opposed to opposing rash advance!"[27]

Ke Qingshi, Kang Sheng, and Li Jingquan all supported Mao and criticized efforts against rash advance, while Tao Zhu expressed the wish to "catch up with the venerable Mr. Ke." Tension grew, and an anxious Li Xiannian resorted to sleeping pills. Who exactly was being criticized? Liu Shaoqi said, "The Chairman is criticizing the people in charge of economic work." On the evening of January 17, Mao had Li Fuchun, Li Xiannian, and Bo Yibo come in to talk, and he insisted that his criticism was aimed primarily at Chen Yun, who did not attend the Nanning Conference. On January 19, Mao spoke privately with Zhou Enlai, and then called a full meeting that lasted until 1:00 a.m. Zhou undertook self-criticism, saying, "Opposing rash advance is a problem that for a period of time [summer to winter of 1956] caused directional vacillation and error . . . It's a type of right-deviating conservative mentality. It's a policy of hindrance contrary to the Chairman's policy of promotion. I take the chief responsibility for this erroneous opposition to rash advance."[28]

On January 21, Mao delivered the final report at the Nanning Conference, focusing on the need for what ultimately took shape as the "Sixty Work Methods." It required leaders at all levels to implement a "double accounting" system: "Of the Central Committee's two account books, one is for plans that must be accomplished, and it is public; the other is for plans where completion is hoped for, and this book is not public. The localities also have two account books, the first being the same as the Central Committee's first book, which must be completed, and the second for local projects where completion is hoped for. Comparisons and assessments should use the Central Committee's second book as the standard."

It then became common practice for each level to assign responsibility to the next level down, thereby ratcheting up targets at each consecutive level. Under this system, even if the Central Committee set relatively modest targets, they would become progressively harder to meet at each successive level—not to mention if the Central Committee itself set excessively high targets. This put enormous pressure on grassroots cadres, and made "elevated targets" and the Exaggeration Wind all but inevitable.

Since the founding of the PRC, the relationship between Mao and Zhou had become one of a monarch and his minister, and Zhou routinely abandoned his own views in submission to Mao's. After the Nanning Conference, Mao put Zhou under such pressure that he resigned. Six months later, however, on June 9, 1958, Mao called a meeting of the Politburo standing committee at the Zhongnanhai swimming pool to discuss "the suitability of [Zhou] continuing to serve as prime minister," as well as Peng Dehuai's request to resign from his position as defense minister.[29] Attending the meeting were Mao, Liu Shaoqi, Zhou, Zhu De, Chen Yun, Lin Biao, Deng Xiaoping, Peng Zhen, Peng Dehuai, He Long, Luo Ronghuan, Chen Yi, Li Xiannian, Chen Boda, Ye Jianying, and Huang Kecheng. The unanimous decision was that Zhou and Peng "should continue to serve in their current positions."[30]

THE CHENGDU CONFERENCE: THE GENERAL LINE TAKES SHAPE

The Chengdu Conference that convened on March 9, 1958, was an enlarged meeting of the Politburo standing committee, but not all provincial party secretaries were invited. Mao was in a state of excitement, continually interposing remarks while listening to reports. He delivered six lengthy speeches during the eighteen-day meeting, and Wu Lengxi described him as "brimming with ideas, radiating vital energy, and in an invincibly advantageous position."[31]

Since the Nanning Conference in January, every province and central government ministry had been increasing production targets and endorsing Mao's position. Henan provincial party secretary Wu Zhipu said: "Chairman Mao's directive on uninterrupted revolution has provided the theoretical and ideological answer to the question of whether we can and dare to leap forward. It demolishes the vulgar 'theory of balance' and shatters the opposition to rash advance (which is opposition to leaping forward)."[32]

The central theme of the Chengdu Conference was again to criticize opposition to rash advance and unify thinking around the "General Line of going all out, aiming high, and achieving greater, faster, better, and more economical results." While Mao said targets should not be excessively high and should allow for unforeseen circumstances, his overall tone was one of rousing enthusiasm, and his caveats were taken as tactical.

He said, "In comparing the two methods, one a Marxist 'rash advance' and one a non-Marxist opposition to rash advance, which should we adopt? I believe we should adopt the rash advance." He called for daring thought and action, and particularly encouraged young people: "Ever since ancient times, innovative thinking has always originated with under-educated young people." "History shows that those with little education overturn those who are well-educated."[33] Once these words were transmitted to the grass roots, many ignorant youth took the opportunity to do as they pleased, and heedless of all but their political mission, they became an enormous force of destruction.

Mao said that leaping forward had to be accompanied by methods and measures; otherwise, the elevated targets could not be met. He said, "Having high targets that can't be achieved is subjectivism, but there's no great harm in it, and it doesn't call for a hard spanking. This is not the time to dash cold water on the proceedings, but to encourage truthfulness." He went on to say, "We must go all out, aim high, and achieve greater, faster, better, and more economical results—but don't force what cannot actually be done. Right now a wind is blowing, a storm-force gale, but don't block it openly; reduce it through internal clarification. In eradicating false reports and exaggeration, we should not strive for fame but for practical results." He called for publicizing dozens or even a hundred bumper harvests,[34] and as a result, "satellites" of exaggerated achievement were launched throughout China. Once these exaggerations became models for emulation, no one dared to "dash cold water" or deliver "spankings," and they grew into a devastatingly treacherous "Exaggeration Wind."

Faced with a Mao "radiating vital energy and invincibility," Liu Shaoqi conceded:

The Chairman is wiser than any of us; whether in terms of thinking, viewpoints, impact, or methods, none of us can come close to matching him. It's our duty to genuinely learn from him, or it should be said that we must learn to the best of our capabilities. Of course there are some areas where we can't hope to match the Chairman; with his rich historical and theoretical knowledge, his wealth of revolutionary experience, and his prodigious memory, none of us can hope to absorb all there is to learn from him . . . Ultimately, how fast should China's socialist construction proceed? . . . at present right-deviating conservatism seems to be holding sway.[35]

Then, on March 25, Zhou Enlai again criticized himself for opposing rash advance:

I take the main responsibility for submitting the report opposing rash advance, in effect dashing cold water on the upsurge among the masses. The result was not to promote but to hinder; not greater, faster, better, and more economical, but less, slower, shoddier, and more wasteful . . . that is the essence of the problem.

The error of opposing rash advance was in taking one finger for many fingers, and imposing restrictions and fetters instead of bolstering the mass upsurge and coming up with solutions. At that time I lacked perception, and it was only later that I gradually came to understand that this was a directional error on the issue of socialist construction.[36]

Once Mao's most powerful lieutenants debased themselves, no one else would dare challenge his views. Officials subordinate to Liu and Zhou also carried out self-criticism. On March 21, Chen Yun delivered a relatively long speech examining his error of opposing rash advance. Mao's secretary Chen Boda proposed the slogan "One day as twenty years," which gained Mao's endorsement.

Tao Zhu's speech on March 18 recommended solving "problems of standpoint in carrying out socialism." He gave an example where some 80 percent of cadres from the county level down had difficulty carrying out socialism. Mao interjected: "That problem remains to be solved throughout the country." Tao Zhu vindicated himself by saying, "Two years ago when there was opposition to rash advance, I didn't oppose it; rather, I was opposed [for supporting it]." On March 19, Hubei provincial party secretary Wang Renzhong was entrusted with speaking for Henan and Hunan, two provinces that were not represented at the meeting. He asked, "How fast are we actually moving? In my view, whether we're talking of agriculture or industry, the speed of development is extremely fast, faster than we could estimate under normal conditions." "Whether we're talking of Henan or Hubei, production is actually increasing at an extraordinary pace. Hubei's wheat harvest this year is 50 to 70 percent higher than last year." "Each week another county is becoming mechanized; reform of mass access to implements is bearing enormous results." Wang also vindicated himself: "We never opposed rash advance . . . the overall direction of the provincial party committee for the year has been to oppose conservatism."[37]

During the Chengdu Conference, everyone surrendered to Mao; whoever had not opposed rash advance or had been criticized for rashness made sure everyone knew about it. Participants pandered and toadied, carrying Mao's viewpoints to the extreme.

Mao repeatedly referred to "going all out" and "aiming high," and linked these slogans with "achieving greater, faster, better, and more economical results" to form the "General Line." On March 25 the CCP Central Committee presented conference participants with a "Draft Report" that the Central Committee intended to submit to the Second Session of the Eighth National Party Congress. Mao revised one paragraph to state, "Our task from now on is to implement and execute the proposal by the CCP Central Committee and Comrade Mao Zedong to muster all positive factors, correctly handle the people's internal contradictions, go all out, aim high, and achieve greater, faster, better, and more economical results in socialist construction, and strive for technological revolution and cultural revolution." In an attached memo, Mao noted, "This is usable. Slightly amended. Further amendments may be needed, at the discretion of Comrade Shaoqi and Comrade Xiaoping."[38]

Among the thirty-seven documents passed was "Views on the Appropriate Amalgamation of Small-scale Agricultural Cooperatives into Large Collectives," which played a crucial role in the emergence of the people's communes.

The Chengdu Conference also confronted the topic of the cult of personality. On March 10, Mao noted, "Some people are very interested in opposing the cult of personality." He continued:

There are two kinds of personality cult. One involves appropriate worship of proper objects such as Marx, Engels, Lenin, and Stalin's correct aspects; these we must worship, eternally worship, and it's terrible not to worship them. The truth lies in their hands, so why shouldn't we worship them? We believe in truth; truth is a reflection of objective existence. A team must worship its team leader; failing to do so is wrong. The other kind is inappropriate worship, a blind worship lacking analysis . . .[39]

Mao created what amounted to a secular theocracy under which the supreme leader was the embodiment of truth. When Mao said it was necessary to worship truth, what he meant was that others should worship him. In this speech, Mao quoted Lenin: "Better that I should be a dictator than you." Dictatorship, in other words, was reasonable.

Others then leaped to pledge their fervent support. In a speech on March 18, Chen Boda raised the cult of personality to its theoretical apogee, saying, "A distinction should be made between necessary authority and the cult of personality." Quoting Engels's "On Authority," Chen said, "For Marxists . . . without authority the revolution cannot move forward, just as a boat cannot move forward without a helmsman. Every social class at every stage of history has had a central individual and central ideology representing the masses. It was the case with Marx and Lenin, and in China it is the case with Comrade Mao Zedong. He is the central personality in China's proletarian thought . . . this is not a cult of personality."

Mao interjected, "How is this not a cult of personality? How can you not have a personality cult? You endorse Engels but oppose the cult of personality. I advocate the cult of personality: that is, I advocate and agree with what's correct, but oppose what's wrong."[40] Tao Zhu said, "We must have blind faith in the Chairman." Ke Qingshi said, "Our faith in Chairman Mao must be blind faith, and our submission to him must be blind submission."[41]

Others in the central leadership chimed in. Some said, "Chairman Mao is on a higher level than we are; we should believe that the Chairman is much wiser than we and make a conscious effort to emulate him." Others said, "We must publicize Chairman Mao's leadership role, and publicize and study Chairman Mao's thought." Still others said, "Chairman Mao's thought has significance as an international universal truth."[42]

In early April, Mao held a report meeting in Wuhan, which his secretary Tian Jiaying subsequently described as a supplement to the Chengdu Conference. Mao continued his criticism of the opposition to rash advance.

During a speech by Hunan provincial party secretary Zhou Xiaozhou on April 5, Mao interjected, "From the second half of 1956 until 1957 there was talk of opposing rash advance, which caused a lot of discomfort. This setback had some benefit as a form of negative education of the cadres and masses. The losses that resulted led to a saddle shape [in production]. The opposition to rash advance marked the low tide between two crests." He made another interjection during a report by Fujian's provincial first secretary Ye Fei: "In a big country like ours, always taking the slow and steady route will lead to disaster. It's better to move faster. At some point we need to come up with a new slogan to destabilize the 'old reliable faction.' 'Rash advance' was the slogan the reliable faction used to oppose 'leaping forward,' so let's use 'leap forward' to replace 'rash advance' so they can no longer so easily oppose it." Mao went on to say, "Some people might belong to a 'wave-gazing faction' or an 'autumn reckoning faction'; if we don't have a bumper harvest this year, someone will come out and say, 'I predicted this from the outset, and I was right,' and will launch a vigorous attack. Those with rightist inclinations within the party are the 'wave-gazing faction'; they sit at the window and gaze out at the sea and the moon."[43] During the Great Leap Forward it was common to hear people labeled as members of the "wave-gazing" or "autumn reckoning" faction because of this comment of Mao's.

Mao was not completely out of touch with reality; at the Wuhan Conference, he noted that "it is necessary to allow for unforeseen circumstances."[44] In a system lacking checks and balances, however, there was no negative feedback, and Mao's more prudent statements were interpreted as applying to methods and tactics.

After the leader put forward a guiding ideology, the entire party joined in lockstep, and the mass media propelled it with tremendous momentum. As the ancient philosopher Mencius once put it, "Subordinates magnify the actions of their superiors."[45] Leaders' ideas were taken to extremes by subordinates. When the leader came out to correct the situation, he looked wiser and more aware than others, but those below continued following the established trend. The leader favored those who took his ideas to an extreme over those who didn't follow him closely: "The Right is a problem of standpoint, the Left is a problem of methods," while extremists had "naïve class sentiment." Those below were very clear on this point, so any corrective comments by the leader served little purpose.

THE SECOND SESSION OF THE EIGHTH PARTY CONGRESS: THE GENERAL LINE IS BORN

In a single-party autocracy, anyone who has a different opinion must relinquish his own view in favor of the leader's. If anyone in a leadership position openly opposes the supreme leader, this is "splitting the party," an unforgivable crime. Hence, Liu Shaoqi and Zhou Enlai were compelled to demonstrate docile subservience to Mao.

The Second Session of the Eighth National Congress of the CCP was convened in Beijing on May 5–23, 1958. The assembly heard and discussed the work report Liu presented as a representative of the Central Committee, Deng Xiaoping's report on the International Congress of Communist and Workers' Parties in Moscow, and Tan Zhenlin's explanation of the "The Program for Agricultural Development (Second Revised Draft)," and also elected new members to the Central Committee.

Liu Shaoqi's report harshly criticized opposition to rash advance and blamed that opposition for causing a "saddle shape" in production (the end of 1957 dipping in comparison with 1956 and 1958). Then, he elaborated on the General Line of "going all out, aiming high, and achieving greater, faster, better, and more economical results in building socialism," and emphasized "speeding up construction as much as possible." He sharply criticized those who said that "speeding up construction will cause too much tension," those who suspected that "the policy of greater, faster, better, and more economical will lead to waste or loss of economic equilibrium," and those who doubted the possibility of increasing economic production so rapidly. Liu Shaoqi went on to echo Mao: "Some people criticize us for delusions of grandeur, and for being eager for quick success and instant benefit. They're right! How could we not desire greatness for our 600 million people, and boast of the accomplishments of socialism? Are we supposed to prefer smallness and failure, labor for no reward, be content with backwardness, and govern by inaction?"[46] Liu called on leaders at all levels to "utterly cherish" the enthusiasm of the masses.

Mao spoke four times at the congress. In his first speech on May 8, he described how young people surpassed the old and how those with little education excelled over the educated: "The lowly are the cleverest and the noble are the stupidest." During the meeting, he wrote in a directive, "Dispelling feelings of inferiority . . . and stimulating a dauntless creative spirit of daring to think, daring to speak, and daring to act will definitely be an enormous help in achieving our goal of surpassing England in seven years and overtaking the United States in another eight or ten years."[47] Through his praise of the uneducated, Mao encouraged the public's rejection of science and its attacks on experts and scholars.

Also in his speech on May 8, Mao promoted emulating Emperor Qin Shihuang, who "advocated wiping out those who use history to criticize the present." When Marshal Lin Biao interjected, "Qin Shihuang burned books and buried scholars," Mao responded:

> What was Qin Shihuang? He only buried 460 scholars, but we buried 46,000 scholars. During the suppression of counterrevolutionaries, didn't we kill some counterrevolutionary intellectuals? I've discussed this with advocates of democracy: "You call us Qin Shihuang as an insult, but we've surpassed Qin Shihuang a hundredfold." Some people curse us as dictators like Qin Shihuang. We must categorically accept this as factually accurate. Unfortunately, you haven't said enough and leave it to us to say the rest for you.[48]

In his speech on May 17, Mao focused on both the domestic and international situations. Discussing villagers crying out that they lacked food, oil, and cloth, Mao said:

> You have to analyze this further—there's really no food, oil, or cloth at all? Comrade Ke Qingshi told me that Jiangsu did some calculations for 1955 among cadres at the county, district, and township levels. Thirty percent of them raised a terrible fuss on behalf of the peasants, saying the state monopoly for purchasing and marketing "monopolized" too much. And what was the background of these cadres? They were well-to-do middle peasants, or else they had started out as poor peasants and then became well-to-do middle peasants. The discomfort they complained of was the discomfort of well-to-do middle peasants. Well-to-do middle peasants like to hoard grain but don't like to surrender it; they want capitalism, so yowl about the hardship of the peasants. When they yowl down there, some people at the prefectural, provincial, municipal,

and central levels yowl, too, don't they? . . . Whose standpoint is it? Is it the standpoint of the worker class or the poor and lower-middle peasants, or the standpoint of the well-to-do middle peasants?

Mao's words sealed the lips of the cadres; whoever claimed that the peasants lacked food was taking the wrong standpoint, and if a cadre committed a standpoint error, his political future was finished. During the three-year famine following the winter of 1958, therefore, many cadres not only failed to plead on behalf of starving peasants, but even said they had plenty of food.

Mao went on: "A split in the party would lead to a period of chaos . . . pay particular attention to the overall situation; whoever fails to do so will end up the worse for it . . . No one should cause divisions—it's not right."[49] He was warning those with doubts about the General Line to step carefully, intimating that those who disagreed with him would come to a bad end.

During the Second Session of the Eighth Party Congress, Zhou Enlai and Chen Yun were obliged to perform self-criticism once again. Chen Yun said, "The error in opposing rash advance lay in failing to perceive, or underestimating, the mighty accomplishments of the upsurge in production by the masses at the time, and in exaggerating the pressure that would be placed on the economy and the market . . . Had we not benefited from Mao Zedong's timely correction and allowed the error to develop further, it would have inevitably led to our cause suffering grievous loss."[50] On May 17, Zhou Enlai declared:

The speeches at this conference . . . reflect the miraculous construction and revolutionary mettle of the people during the Great Leap Forward in production and the great liberation of consciousness. Truly, one day is as twenty years, and half a year exceeds several millennia. Positioned in this great era, any true revolutionary will be stirred by these magnificent feats of communism and must to the depths of his being acknowledge the correctness of the course constructed by the party Central Committee and Chairman Mao, as well as the serious errors of the opposition to rash advance. I am one of the people most responsible for the opposition to rash advance and should therefore learn even more from this incident.[51]

He went on:

> The historical experience of China's decades of revolution and construction prove that Chairman Mao is the representative of truth. Departing from or violating his leadership and directives results in error and loss of bearings, and damages the interests of the party and the people, as the errors I have repeatedly committed have amply proven. Conversely, doing things correctly and at the correct time are inseparable from Chairman Mao's correct leadership and leading ideology.[52]

Zhou's affirmation of Mao was echoed in the speeches of others. Tao Zhu called for the entire party to study Mao's writings:

> In order to eradicate superstition and liberate thinking, it is essential for the entire party to study Chairman Mao's writings extensively and deeply. In the last few years, our studies have . . . placed excessive emphasis on the study of foreign classics . . . This is wrong. Chairman Mao is the greatest Marxist of our time; Chairman Mao's writings are a glorious example of the integration of theory and practice, which through a series of basic tenets have defended and developed Marxist-Leninism. For that reason, Chairman Mao's writings are the best textbook of Marxist-Leninism available to us members of the Chinese Communist Party . . . Chairman Mao's works are not only a mighty weapon for us to achieve revolutionary victory but also a mighty weapon for us to achieve successful construction.[53]

Higher-ups vied to ingratiate themselves with Mao. The title of Wang Renzhong's speech was "How to Lead Large-scale Mass Movements." Debate meetings became struggle and criticism sessions. Mao's advocacy of "planting the red flag" and "supplanting the white flag"[54] at this meeting immediately spread throughout the country. The number of people whose honest words brought them to ruin through "mass debate" and "supplanting the white flag" can scarcely be imagined.

The subject of Ke Qingshi's speech was cultural revolution, projecting fifteen years into the future: "Everyone is literate and well-informed, everyone can read *Das Kapital* and is proficient in calculus. Flies, mosquitoes, bedbugs, rats, sparrows, and other pests are all long extinct, and every work team is blessed with its own Li Bai, Lu Xun, and Nie Er.[55] This ultimate construction of communism is not far off."

All endorsed the General Line and raised already elevated targets. On May 23 a resolution passed unanimously to endorse the General Line of "go all out, aim high, and build socialism with greater, faster, better, and more economical results."

The Great Leap Forward commenced, and officials hurried to implement the General Line through specific targets. State Planning Commission head Li Fuchun declared, "The Second Five-Year Plan will bring an enormous leap forward."

Fearing the appearance of backwardness, departments set Leap Forward targets far exceeding those of the State Planning Commission. Metallurgy Ministry head Wang Heshou set steel production goals that reached 120 million tons by 1972. General Wang Zhen, who was in charge of agricultural reclamation, proclaimed that 300 million mu[56] of virgin land would be cultivated within ten years.[57]

Provincial party secretaries, competing with one another to show their fealty to Mao, set targets even higher than those of the central departments and ministries. Only Mao could express reservations as to whether these targets were realistic.

Mao's ambitions knew no bounds during the Eighth National Party Congress, and he savored the phrase "leap forward." On May 25, he was presented with a copy of the editorial in the November 13, 1957, edition of *People's Daily* and was told that the phrase "leap forward" had been used there for the first time. He immediately set pen to paper:

Comrades of the Politburo and Secretariat, Party Secretaries of all Provinces, Cities, and Autonomous Regions:

Rereading the People's Daily editorial from November 13, 1957, I find it delightful, its theme unequivocal, its tone calm, its analysis correct, and its mission unambiguous. The substitution of "rash advance" with "leap forward" commenced in this article. The two phrases are opposite. After the introduction of the phrase "leap forward," those who opposed rash advance had nothing more to say. It's acceptable to oppose "rash advance" (a synonym for left opportunism) and to be plausible and voluble about it. But it's different with "leap forward"—that's not easy to oppose. Opposing it places one in an invidious position. When that editorial was published, some of us were in Moscow. It was handled by comrades here in China whose achievement is equal to that of Yu the Great.[58] If we are to grant any Ph.D.s, I recommend that the first should be given to the scientist (or scientists) who invented this powerful slogan (that is, "leap forward").

Mao Zedong, 7:00 a.m., May 26[59]

In fact, Zhou Enlai had used the phrase "leap forward" 140 days earlier in his "government work report." Feeling robbed of his due credit, Zhou delivered a copy of the government work report to Mao that very night, indicating where the phrase had been used. He also defended his opposition to rash advance, albeit with caution and courtesy:

Chairman:

I deliver to you herewith a copy of the government work report. Pages 9 and 14 refer to the 1956 construction as a "leap forward" in development.

I read this report once again and feel that my gist at the time was to defend socialism and deliver a counterattack against the rightists by affirming the actual achievements of the 1956 construction as a leap forward in development, and abandoning the appraisal of the 1956 construction as a "rash advance." But at the time I did not realize that opposing "rash advance" was an error of guiding principle. Consequently I did not realize that the guiding principle of "greater, faster, better, and more economical" and the Forty-Point Program for Agricultural Development could promote socialist construction and make it leap forward from quantitative to qualitative change. In this speech I delivered to the party congress . . . a truth becomes evident, which is that using the same phraseology is a question of form, and the main point is what flag is planted and what curse is broken. The two editorials raised the great flags of "greater, faster, better, and more economical" and the Forty-Point Program for Agricultural Development, while crushing the evil influence of opposing "rash advance" and promoting regression. For that reason the editorials were able to concentrate on the main points and promote the construction of socialism with irresistible force. I therefore feel that the two People's Daily *editorials share the same value and merit.*

Zhou Enlai, evening, May 26, 1958[60]

To ensure that Zhou was properly credited for his earliest use of the phrase "leap forward," Mao distributed the "government work report" Zhou had sent to him, along with his letter, to those attending the meeting.

> Comrade Xiaoping: Make copies of this document and immediately distribute them to all comrades attending the meeting.
>   Mao Zedong, 11:00 a.m., May 27, 1958

The General Line was firmly established, and propaganda touting it flooded the country. A May 29 *People's Daily* editorial entitled "Plant the Flag of the General Line Throughout the Land" emphasized that "speed is the soul of the General Line" and that it was necessary to "use the greatest speed to develop China's social productivity and implement industrialization and agricultural modernization." China's literary and artistic circles also lent their effort to ensuring that every corner of the country rang with songs extolling the General Line: "Leap forward, leap forward, leap forward again!"

At that time, Deng Xiaoping was a member of the standing committee of the CCP Central Committee Politburo, and general secretary of the Central Committee. With Zhou Enlai under criticism for opposing rash advance, and Chen Yun likewise sidelined, much of the work of the State Council fell to the Central Committee secretariat, giving it a pivotal position of power in 1958. In regard to the Three Red Banners, Deng was an enthusiastic supporter of Mao, and many Great Leap policies originated with the secretariat under his direction. After the problems of the Great Leap Forward were revealed, however, Deng was able to deal with them in a relatively pragmatic manner, while maintaining his support for the Three Red Banners. Publications after the 1980s reforms avoid reference to Deng's activities during the Great Leap Forward.

Between the First Session of the Eighth National Congress of the CCP in September 1956 and the Second Session in May 1958, CCP ideology was dramatically transformed under Mao. The CCP system not only lacked a mechanism to rectify the errors of its top leader, but also pushed its leader toward even greater error. Mao was excessively hotheaded, and leaders in charge of economic matters, having discovered errors in his thinking in the course of their work, had attempted practical corrections (for instance, by opposing rash advance). Confronted with the dire consequences of disagreeing with Mao, however, other leaders abandoned their efforts to correct these errors. The flaws in the guiding ideology of 1958 were therefore attributable not only to the supreme leader and leadership group, but also to flaws in the system as a whole.

3 HARD TIMES IN GANSU*

Located in China's far west, Gansu Province is rife with poverty in its parched eastern section. Its west has enjoyed relative prosperity, but after 1958 it suffered the same severe famine as many other parts of China.

USING POLITICAL PRESSURE TO CREATE LIES

Provincial first party secretary Zhang Zhongliang had served as political commissar for the Gansu Military Region, and he retained his military work style. On February 9, 1958, he noted in a report[1] that the Anti-Rightist Campaign begun in June 1957 and the mass debates initiated in August had developed into a rectification campaign. More than 9,700 rightists had been unearthed, along with counterrevolutionaries and other bad elements.

Behind these figures lay broken families and destroyed lives, but Zhang prided himself on using rectification methods to focus on a "Great Leap Forward." He touted the "exposure of the anti-party clique led by Sun Diancai, Chen Chengyi, and Liang Dajun as well as other anti-party and antisocialist elements, and the drawing of a clear line delineating the fundamental issues separating the two roads."

Ferreting out anti-party cliques was common in 1958: Henan rooted out its "Pan, Yang, Wang" anti-party clique; Shandong, its Li Guangwen, Zhao Jianmin, Wang Zhuoru anti-party clique; Fujian, its Jiang Yizhen and Wei Jinshui–led clique (in 1959); Qinghai, its Zhang Guosheng clique (in 1959); Zhejiang, its "Sha, Yang, Peng" (Sha Wenhan, Yang Siyi, and

*The translators gratefully acknowledge reference to an initial translation of this chapter by Ms. Yang Zhang.

Peng Ruilin) anti-party clique; and Anhui, its Li Shinong, Zhang Kaifan, and Liu Xiushan anti-party clique.

For Zhang Zhongliang, the "crimes" of the "Sun, Chen, Liang" anti-party clique boiled down to failure to promote socialism. These men considered the "present inferior to the past," failed to acknowledge the huge reported crop yield of 1.3 billion kilos following collectivization, disagreed with the view that sheep should be incorporated into collectives, compared forced corvée labor for collective irrigation works with the "Qin Emperor's oppression of the people," and made excuses for capitalism. Because of the "crimes" of these officials, many farmers were cultivating private fields and engaging in capitalistic sidelines.

To Zhang, opposing the Sun, Chen, Liang anti-party clique reflected "class struggle within the party and the struggle between the two roads within the party." Zhang put a strong emphasis on class struggle: "The greatest domestic contradiction remained that between the proletarian and bourgeois classes." He criticized "comrades inside the party with seriously right-deviating thinking" for handling many "contradictions between the enemy and us" as if they were "contradictions among the people."

Zhang criticized the view that "anything that seems to transcend reality is subjectivism," observing, "This argument has now become the main ideological hindrance to the advancement of our socialist revolution. It not only causes setbacks to the revolutionary zeal of the mass of cadres and people and affects the leaping development of our work in all areas, but also provides a theoretical basis for right-deviationist thinking." This was in fact the ideological foundation for the Great Leap Forward. Zhang promoted the "the revolutionary cause," meaning Mao's Three Red Banners.

To bring about another production upsurge, Zhang argued for ending "the tenacious obstruction of right-deviationist thinking." He advocated "uninterrupted revolution," that is, "revolution undertaken as one struggle after another, one movement after another."

Under Zhang's leadership, seven topics became taboo: the actual circumstances, the deaths by starvation, the elevated procurement quotas, the inability to accomplish tasks, the weakness of Gansu compared with neighboring provinces, the objective conditions, and work reassignments.[2] It was in this atmosphere that the Great Leap Forward proceeded in Gansu Province.

Zhang attended the Lushan Conference from July 1 to August 16, 1959. While he was away, the provincial party committee wrote to the CCP Central Committee reporting that food scarcity was "very serious . . . grain shortages are severe in the six counties of Wuwei, Minqin, Tongwei, Longxi, Min, and Jingning, and the city of Zhangye." The report went on to say that inhabitants of the regions experiencing the worst food shortages typically consumed less than a quarter of a kilo of grain per day, and that the incidence of death from starvation and edema and of residents fleeing the province had become severe. The Lushan Conference declared that this report "provided ammunition to right-opportunistic anti-party elements."[3] After Zhang returned from the Lushan Conference, he designated the leaders behind the famine report, including deputy provincial committee secretary Huo Weide, as part of a right-deviating anti-party clique. Tongwei county party secretary Xi Daolong, who had provided data on deaths, was said to have "fired bullets and shot poison arrows at Lushan."

During the campaign against right deviation following the Lushan Conference, anyone who spoke the truth was subjected to ruthless struggle and merciless attacks. In the three years from the latter half of 1957 through 1960, more than 190,000 people were criticized, including more than 40,000 cadres who were not engaged in production. During the campaign against right deviation in 1959, more than 11,000 cadres not engaged in production were harshly criticized, among them 151 high-ranking officials. Eleven of the 47 committee members and alternate members of the second provincial party congress were criticized and disciplined. Within the provincial party committee's standing committee, only a minority escaped reproach.[4]

Zhang reported to the party Central Committee on September 11: "We're currently experiencing bumper summer harvests . . . the autumn crops are growing well, and bumper harvests are anticipated. Speedy progress is being made on the summer grain procurement, with a view to meeting our quota by the end of September." Mao had the Central Committee reply with its endorsement.[5] Meanwhile, people were dying of starvation. Zhang pushed for political struggles that resulted in one case of injustice after another. Years later the charges against these victims were declared bogus.

Not all of Zhang Zhongliang's suggestions were his original ideas. From 1959 onward, Zhu De, Chen Yun, Deng Xiaoping, Tan Zhenlin, and other members of the central leadership visited Gansu and expressed their approval. It was probably Deng who praised Gansu's campaign against right deviation by saying, "Why is struggle within the party in Gansu so frequent and intense? It's because the scope of its leap forward is great, and the lagging forces are great."[6] The denunciation of Huo Weide, likewise, was approved by the CCP Central Committee.

THE XU GUOHE, ZHANG WANSHOU
COUNTERREVOLUTIONARY CLIQUE

The typical case of this alleged counterrevolutionary clique in Zhenyuan County was recounted in a report published in 1999.[7] A revolutionary base in the Shaan-Gan-Ning Border Region,[8] Zhenyuan County became part of Pingliang Prefecture after 1949. Following implementation of the state monopoly for purchasing and marketing of grain, the county always exceeded its procurement quotas. In 1954 the actual grain requisition totaled 30.5 percent of production, with 27.1 percent of the procurement sold back to the county.

When famine struck in 1955, the county met a procurement quota of 22.9 percent, but then bought 106.3 percent of that amount back from the state. The 1956 harvest was better, but after meeting procurement targets, the county bought back 43.6 percent of that grain. In 1957 the county experienced long drought, early frost, and insect infestation. Crop yields plummeted by nearly half, with an average yield of only 41 kilos per *mu*.

Fearful of reporting poor yields, officials revised the yield upward to 57.5 kilos per *mu*, and the county's procurement quota was set on that basis. The county was obliged to buy back more than 130 percent of its procurement quota. In 1958, with most of the county's manpower deployed to steel and irrigation projects, a bumper crop was not fully harvested, and the county was obliged to repurchase 75.6 percent of its procurement quota.

The county had never laid up reserves, and now was constantly short of food. Villagers turned to food substitutes, including alfalfa stalks, potato vines, cotton seeds, and the hulls of millet and buckwheat. Deaths from edema and food poisoning became common. The county government sent cadres to the villages and reported the dire situation to the upper levels, and county head Xu Guohe and deputy head Zhang Wanshou also sent reports under their own names to the provincial and prefectural leadership. Provincial and prefectural organs sent officials to Zhenyuan County to investigate. In January 1958 the deputy commissioner of Pingliang Prefecture, He Yuqing, tried to put villagers' minds to rest by ordering a halt to procurement. His criticism of the rashly exaggerated output figures also had a salutary effect.

On May 14, 1958, more than twenty leading cadres investigated the food shortages in Zhenyuan County. They then asked the provincial party committee to send 9 million kilos of grain. The county immediately convened a three-level cadre meeting. However, the prefectural leadership insisted that the main cause of the food crisis was manipulation by counterrevolutionary elements, and demanded a thorough investigation. As a result, the food crisis turned into a campaign against "counterrevolutionary cliques."

In July 1958, Pingliang Prefecture sent a work group to Zhenyuan County to launch a "political revolution" and "organizational revolution." Taking over the county leadership, the work group encouraged the masses to speak out, "pull down white flags," "oppose right deviation," counter "false reporting of output and private withholding," attack "sabotage by class enemies," and root out the source of the county's backwardness. County leaders who had sought food to feed the hungry were sent to toil in the countryside, while the county's public security, procuratorial, and law organs were ordered to combine their offices. The work group leader criticized county head Xu Guohe, saying that all political movements in the county since 1949 had been "extremely superficial." Supposedly "many politically impure elements and counterrevolutionaries had infiltrated the party and climbed to various levels of the leadership structure," and the work group leader declared Zhenyuan County "a base camp of counter-revolution."

After being charged with crimes such as "right conservatism" and "localism," Xu Guohe and Zhang Wanshou were struggled and stripped of their official positions. Nine days were spent criticizing more than thirty county- and village-level cadres, and more than four hundred cadres of agricultural cooperatives were dismissed. The prefectural work team leader said, "Xu Guohe's problems are very serious. His claims that the procurement was too burdensome and the provisions inadequate are a political issue." He labeled Xu, Zhang, and the others as "right opportunists" and members of a "right-deviating anti-party clique." He dismissed other party leaders, including one who had joined the party in 1937.

The work group leaders concluded that the county's procuratorial cadres and police officers were also unreliable. All of them therefore had to step aside, along with their family members. Xu Guohe's wife, Wang Long, was Zhenyuan's deputy party secretary and was studying at the provincial party school at the time. She was ordered back to the county, where she was subjected to criticism for several months and forced to divorce Xu. Xu's father-in-law, Wang Zihou, was a veteran cadre who had joined the party in 1936. He was the founder of Zhenyuan's party organization and a hero in the establishment of the party's base in the Shaan-Gan-Ning Border Region. At the time, he was studying at the Central Party School in Beijing, but was recalled for criticism and stripped of his position as administrative commissioner of Wudu Prefecture. Xu's brothers, Xu Guofu, Xu Guocai (a peasant), and Xu Guozhi (a party cadre), and sister-in-law Li Ximei were criticized and imprisoned. Xu Guocai died in custody. Even Xu's seventy-year-old mother was attacked and suffered temporary mental derangement. Xu's six-year-old son was expelled from the family's official living quarters and forced to roam the streets in the dead of winter. He survived only through the kindness of an elderly resident surnamed He, who took him into his home.

In the villages, the work group used accusations of "right conservatism," "thought failure," "denial of the Great Leap Forward," "serving as a mouthpiece for well-to-do middle peasants," "opposing food supply policies," and "inciting disturbances" to publicly denounce large numbers of grassroots cadres and farmers. Many peasants were labeled "conspicuous capitalists." Their homes were ransacked, and they were tied up and beaten. Chaos and terror pervaded the county.

The work group leaders would not let the matter rest: "We must put up millions of big-character posters, conduct mass debates involving all the people, expose all wrongdoing, and launch a campaign to pull down the white flags." Party cadres and enterprise staff were each required to write a hundred big-character posters per day, while middle-school students were to produce fifty per day, and the content could not be repeated. People spent their waking hours producing big-character posters, racking their brains for something new to say. Opportunists trumped up accusations against the innocent.

In September the new county party committee convened rallies to publicize the "counterrevolutionary crimes" of Xu, Zhang, and others. Mass arrests followed. The prefectural party committee work group's

October 2 "Situational Report on Two Months' Work in Zhenyuan County" stated that more than 5 million big-character posters had been put up, more than 20,000 "red flags" had been "planted," more than 870 "white flags" had been "pulled down" (people dismissed), and more than 2,000 "class enemies" had been attacked. The number arrested reached 1,096 by October 20.

During the mass arrests, the county was divided into five sections, each of which appointed one work team member or county party committee standing committee member to serve as team head. The team head carried a stamped arrest warrant at all times, which could be filled in to arrest a person on the spot. One time a team head heard members of one cooperative say they had nothing to eat and request that the state sell some grain back. He had their names taken down, then called a rally and arrested forty-eight people. On another occasion, a work team leader and a county party committee deputy secretary went to the countryside and arrested more than two hundred people, who were bound with hempen rope and hauled en masse to the county seat.

On October 22, provincial first secretary Zhang Zhongliang arrived in Zhenyuan County. After receiving an oral report from the work team leader, Zhang ordered, "Quickly round up the whole gang!" On October 24 martial law was declared, and machine guns were set up as if to confront a formidable enemy. Xu Guohe, Zhang Wanshou, and 167 other cadres were arrested. On October 31 the county party committee designated the case as the Xu Guohe, Zhang Wanshou counterrevolutionary clique.

Of the 1,503 who were eventually arrested, 333 died in prison. All suffered cruel physical abuse. At the time of arrest they were hurled to the floor and bound hand and foot in such a way that any movement constricted them even further. Some were bundled so tightly that they fainted, while others were crippled for life. Xu Guohe and Zhang Wanshou had to wear fetters and handcuffs weighing more than 10 kilos. Because he had a "poor attitude toward his guilt," Zhang Wanshou also had to wear "riding fetters" that shackled his hands through his crotch. This made it impossible for him either to stand or to squat, and his cries of agony assaulted the ear day and night.

The accusers also targeted provincial and prefectural cadres who had been responsive to Zhenyuan County's food crisis, such as prefectural first secretary Xue Cheng and commissioner Cui Shijun, provincial party committee deputy secretary Huo Weide and finance and trade department head Zhang Tian, and the head judge of the provincial people's high court, Wu Sihong. Others who had previously served as Zhenyuan County's party committee secretary or county head were also rounded up, including Zhou Jiemin, who as county head in the 1930s had assisted senior Red Army officers when they were garrisoned in Zhenyuan during the Long March. Although having no relationship with Xu Guohe or Zhang Wanshou, Zhou was designated a member of the Xu, Zhang counterrevolutionary clique. He was sentenced to death, but died in custody before the execution was formally authorized.

In the politically charged atmosphere, those above had only to say the word and those below would follow. No one dared to speak the truth. After a rapid process of communization, the county deployed seventy thousand workers (72.5 percent of its total manpower) to forge steel. A campaign to collect scrap metal was carried out under the slogan "Handing in a hoe eliminates one imperialist; concealing one nail conceals a counterrevolutionary." Next came irrigation projects, for which the county rounded up more than eighty thousand laborers (83 percent of its workforce). Here the slogan was, "Dam three rivers to send water up to five plateaus; battle hard for 100 days to complete five canals, three reservoirs, and one dam; dig 100,000 wells and 8,600 pits until they outnumber the stars." A number of other big projects were announced—making Zhenyuan a "10,000-factory county," "eliminating illiteracy in seven days," creating 700 universities, and so on.

Localities competed to "launch satellites." Everywhere there were "500-kilo villages," "500-kilo communes," "5,000-kilo plateaus," "plowing to 5 meters" "for every *mu,* 1 million kilos of fertilizer, 90 kilos of seed, and 200,000 kilos of grain produced," and "cultivating for one year to eat for fourteen." The county's food grain yield for 1958 was projected at double the entire grain yield for the year before. The Communist Wind blew in with the slogan "Where there is food, everyone eats; where there are clothes, everyone has something to wear; where there is money, everyone spends it; where there are debts, everyone repays them; no points recorded for labor, equal distribution for all." Labor, land, livestock, poultry, farming implements, living quarters, trees, and other elements of livelihood were allotted arbitrarily; in some villages, caskets prepared for the aged were assigned to others. The Great Leap Forward became a source of unspeakable misery.

Wanton pillage led to severely depressed production levels. According to statistics from 1961, the county's population shrank by 6,708. According to a survey of three production brigades, the mortality rate reached 12 percent. The county's workforce dropped 18.8 percent from 1957 to 1961, and the number of livestock was reduced by 4,346 head.

On December 4, 1961, the Pingliang prefectural party committee proposed rehabilitating Xu Guohe and his colleagues, and on July 17, 1962, the provincial party committee concurred. However, the rehabilitation screening work was implemented by people who had created the injustice, and most of the redress was carried out internally. Although many of those unjustly accused were reassigned, the work was seldom commensurate with what they had done before, and they continued to suffer unfair treatment.

It was only after Deng Xiaoping came to power in 1977 that the prefectural party committee worked with the county party committee for a thorough rehabilitation. On March 19, 1981, Gansu Province acknowledged that "the so-called 'Xu Guohe, Zhang Wanshou counterrevolutionary clique' never existed, and the case was an utter and major injustice."

THE COMMUNIST WIND BLOWS UP BIGGER STORMS

During the Great Leap Forward, a second Communist Wind was stirred up in September 1959 under the influence of the Lushan Conference. During the campaign against right deviation following the Lushan Conference, the Gansu provincial party committee put forward the goal of a three-year transition to communization, with communal assets making up at least half of the rural economy. This blew the Communist Wind into a veritable cyclone.

The impact can be seen by what happened in Dingxi Prefecture:

- Communization of farming and grazing land brought uncompensated redistribution of land, labor, and livestock. The Beizhai communal farm took 2,700 *mu* of land from the production teams, along with 132 head of cattle, more than 2,000 sheep, and 150 pigs.
- In the name of putting the food supply under the party organization, local organizations and schools took over agricultural land without compensation. The Dongjia production team in Lintao

County's Chengguan Commune lost 311 out of its 426 *mu* of paddy fields.

- "Thousand-cattle ranches" and "ten-thousand-pig farms" collectivized all pigs and cattle without compensating the owners. A large number of livestock ended up dead; the mortality rate in Longxi County's communal pig farm was upwards of 80 percent.
- The designation of land for "capital works projects" allowed the seizure of prime farm land. Nine county-level government agencies in Lintao County took 92.5 *mu* of land from Chengguan Commune without a penny's compensation.
- Work was assigned randomly and without allocation of work points.
- "Adjustment of crop areas" allowed land to be transferred from one production team to another without compensation.
- "Helping the commune with office repairs" facilitated using manpower and material from the production teams without compensation.
- Communes "storing up grain for times of need" took grain from production teams without compensation.

The Communist Wind sapped enthusiasm for labor. Vast stretches of land lay fallow, and grain yields plummeted. In the spring of 1960, when members of the Dongguanlin production team heard that their camels would be reallocated, they killed all forty and ate them. When the Dongguan production team learned that the commune was setting up a collective pig farm, team members slaughtered more than forty pigs and piglets and ate them.[9]

The Central Committee's Zhengzhou Conference clarified once again the issues of ownership, and in an effort to rein in the Communist Wind stressed a "three-level ownership system with the production team as the basic unit" (the three levels being the commune, the production brigade, and the production team). In Gansu Province, however, the 1959 campaign against right deviation had criticized the "four-level accounting system" (the commune, the production brigade, the production team, and the work group) and brought many cadres under discipline. Combined with years of Communist education, which had taught cadres that the transition to communism should be made as quickly as possible and that complete public ownership should develop as rapidly as possible, the overall result was a deep distrust of the "three-level ownership" concept. The upper leadership was urging communes to undertake major public enterprises, but where were the capital and material resources to come from? The only apparent source was uncompensated transfer of resources from individual commune members and production teams.

The Shenyu production brigade of Wuwei County's Yongchang Commune enjoyed natural advantages that brought it initial prosperity, but it was fiercely lashed by the Communist Wind in 1958 through the indiscriminate and uncompensated transfer of resources. The county and commune capriciously reallocated manpower and livestock from the production teams and used their bricks and lime to repair a power station, while the production brigade gathered up all the production teams' livestock for centralized feeding and grazing. There was no consistent recording of work points, as labor was transferred among the production teams for a massive project to repair residential areas, generate methane, and dismantle some five hundred residence structures at a cost of more than twenty-five thousand manpower days and 15,000 yuan. Commune members' sheep were seized, and their privately cultivated trees were felled. The results were devastating: of more than sixty small livestock gathered for collective feeding, only three survived, and the production brigade's total livestock numbered less than half the level in the autumn of 1958. With human enthusiasm sapped and animal power depleted, production plummeted from an average of 125.0 kilos of grain per *mu* in 1958 to 78.5 kilos per *mu* in 1959 and only 31.5 kilos per *mu* in 1960. In the half year from January to July 1960, 141 people died.[10]

The Xihu production team was similarly despoiled, with all property seized and redistributed without compensation. From the autumn of 1958 to the end of 1960, large livestock decreased from 208 head to 160, sheep from 463 to 75, and pigs from 78 to none. Grain production dropped from 270,000 kilos in 1958 to only 95,000 kilos in 1960, and the average per capita annual income of commune members fell from 32 yuan in 1958 to 10 yuan in 1960.[11]

THE YINTAO FOLLY

Gansu's Yintao Project was a key factor in the acceleration of the province's famine conditions. The project's impetus arose from the severe water shortage in the central and eastern regions, known as Longzhong and Longdong. The Qing dynasty's General Zuo Zongtang[12] once observed, "The barrenness of Longzhong is unequaled on earth." Typical annual rainfall is a scant 400 millimeters, the dryness exacerbated by an evaporation rate of up to 1,400 milliliters. More than 70 percent of the region's precipitation is concentrated in the monsoons of July, August, and September. With no water available in the spring, wheat won't sprout. Eastern and central Gansu are part of China's fabled "yellow earth"; the topsoil would be exceedingly fertile if not for the lack of water.

The region's groundwater is scarce, ruling out well-digging, and most of its rivers run dry outside the brief monsoon season. The one exception is the Tao River, but only residents of nearby Lintao and Min counties enjoy its benefits.

During the Great Leap Forward, Gansu's provincial party decided to divert the Tao River up to the loess plateau. This was the Yintao Project.[13] The plan involved irrigation works extending east to west by 320 kilometers and south to north by 200 kilometers. The canal would run 1,150 kilometers, with a width of 40 meters and water 6 meters deep allowing the passage of ships weighing 50 to 100 tons. There would be another fifteen canals with a total length of 3,500 kilometers. In addition, the project incorporated two reservoirs involving displacement of 2.0 billion cubic meters of earth and stone and using 2.73 million cubic meters of mortared stone and concrete, and allowing for the construction of dozens of hydroelectric stations. The vision was of "a desert turned into paddy fields, mountaintops fragrant with flowers, warehouses overflowing with grain, tree-shaded mountain ridges, vast herds of sheep and cattle, ponds full of fish and ducks, forests of power stations lighting up every home, the rumble of machinery, and the tooting of steam whistles from convoys of ships."

Once the Yintao Project was launched on June 12, 1958, it involved more than 3,000 full-time staff and a civilian workforce of more than 100,000 that increased to 160,000 at the height of the effort. The project was to be completed in four and a half years. The average daily manpower employed was 106,000 in 1958, 112,000 in 1959, and 80,000 in 1960. By the end of 1960, some 60 million manpower days had been devoted to the project.

The vision stirred excitement throughout China. In September 1958 all 447 representatives attending the Third National Water and Soil Conservation Work Conference went to view the project. In the autumn of

1958, State Council general secretary Xi Zhongxun visited the project and said, "This project has . . . international significance . . . It demonstrates that we are not only the masters of society, but also the masters of nature. The crucial factor here is daring . . . This is the spirit of communism . . . Gansu has let us see the future of communism." On the cliffs at the command post were words carved in the calligraphy of National People's Congress standing committee chairman Zhu De: "The uphill water diversion is a great pioneering work through which the people of Gansu have transformed nature." Whoever expressed an alternative view risked being labeled a right opportunist.

Despite its enormous complexity, the project was carried out piecemeal in the form of "simultaneously surveying, designing, working, and revising," and "surveying, designing, and constructing in segments." In the initial plan, the main canal would include fifty-three tunnels with a total length of 64 kilometers. These were later eliminated, and the entire canal was constructed as an open ditch. Where a hill presented an obstacle, the solution was either deep-cutting or lengthy diversion. Deep-cutting could involve depths of up to 219 meters and excavation of 23 million cubic meters of soil. Thousands of workers might labor for months with no end in sight, only to have the deep-cutting abandoned and a tunnel dug instead.

The Gucheng Reservoir section was to have a capacity of more than 300 million cubic meters and a dam 42 meters high. The initial attempt using indigenous methods at a dam in May 1958 failed because of a breach. A second attempt was made in July, but heavy rains in August swelled the upper reaches of the Tao River and clogged the drainage ditches with timber and plants. With the integrity of the dam and the lives of its twenty thousand workers threatened, the dam was intentionally breached to drain off the excess water. This breaching was deemed an "incident of sabotage," and those responsible were severely punished.

On October 21, amid heavy snow, tens of thousands of workers began a third attempt to construct a dam. After less than two years of effort, the project encountered unanticipated difficulties. Zhang Zhongliang proclaimed the Yintao Project "a great and pioneering work of the heroic people of this province, and a result of the Great Leap Forward . . . It can only be done well and not badly; it must be done quickly and not delayed."

In December 1960 the Gansu provincial party committee was reorganized, and Zhang stepped down. The new provincial party committee terminated the Yintao Project after deciding it was overly optimistic. Under a best-case scenario, the project would have required 1.2 billion manpower days to complete, and many technical issues had not been addressed. These included the stabilization of steep slopes against landslides, the prevention of seepage, and damage from slurry areas, loess siltage, and cave-ins.

The Yintao Project's massive manpower requirements affected agricultural production. In addition, according to official sources, the project "consumed 60 million yuan in three years, and represented a national investment of 160 million yuan. It accomplished the displacement of 160 million cubic meters of earth and stone, merely 8 percent of the original plan, and did not result in the irrigation of a single *mu* of land. Some portions of the project were washed away by mountain torrents as soon as they were completed."

The quoted investment of 160 million yuan is a drastic understatement. At a time when the Communist Wind was sweeping through the land, the value of rural manpower and resources reallocated arbitrarily and without compensation for this project was actually much greater.

Someone said, "The Yintao Project started with fireworks and ended in blood." The blood referred mainly to human deaths. The end stage of the project corresponded with China's "time of hardship," and countless workers starved to death at the project sites. Another considerable number died from on-site injuries.

There was nothing essentially wrong with irrigation projects; many were both necessary and successful. The "East-West Canal" in my native county of Xishui, Hubei Province, brought benefit to local people through the 1990s. The Red Flag Canal in Henan is still regarded as a success. Why did the Yintao Project go down in infamy while the Red Flag Canal continues to garner praise? The virtue of the projects is not necessarily reflected in their success or failure; in all fairness, the people's genuine aspirations lay behind much of the folly of the Great Leap Forward. The problem lay in arbitrary and dictatorial decision making at the expense of good practice, and coercive implementation that deprived people of their rights and property. Both flaws were rooted in the political system.

FAMINE THROUGHOUT THE PROVINCE

The Gansu provincial party committee projected the province's grain output for 1958 at 11 billion kilos. This was later reduced to 6.25 billion, and the provincial party committee ultimately acknowledged taking in 5.5 billion kilos. The actual harvest, however, did not reach even 4 billion kilos.

The 1959 projection for grain yield was 13.5 billion kilos, but the actual harvest came in even lower than in 1958. Procurement was nevertheless carried out with great success. In 1958, Gansu gained a sterling reputation within the CCP Central Committee as a "province that had progressed from shortage to overflow," and provincial first secretary Zhang Zhongliang was convinced that the food shortage issue had been resolved. Once the procurement was completed, however, no grain was left for human or animal consumption or for seed grain for the next crop.

TABLE 3.1: GRAIN SUPPLIES IN GANSU, 1957–61

Year	1957	1958	1959	1960	1961
GRAIN YIELD (BILLION KILO):					
Unprocessed	3.725	3.83	3.245	2.0695	2.25
Processed (trade)	3.239	3.3305	2.8215	1.7995	1.9565
Procured	0.8455	1.11	1.2545	0.617	0.4825
Sold	0.654	1.019	0.9635	0.897	0.5375
In hand	3.0475	3.2395	2.5305	2.0795	2.0115
Population (million)	12.5506	12.8148	12.9312	12.4404	12.1082
Per capita allotment (kilo)	242.815	252.755	195.73	167.155	166.125

Data source: Crop yield, procurement, and sales figures come from the August 25, 1962, issue of the "Food Ministry Planning Department Grain Data Summary." Total population data come from China Population: Gansu. *Other figures were calculated from the aforementioned data.*[14]

Famine struck in spring 1958, and as starvation deaths mounted, residents began to flee. Zhang nevertheless continued to imagine Gansu as having a surplus of food. Reports of food shortages were considered a political problem, and those who spoke the truth were accused of false reporting of output and private withholding, and subjected to public censure. In the winter of 1959 and spring of 1960, Zhang and his allies still attributed the crisis to the political attitudes of grassroots cadres and continued the elevated procurement targets. In July 1960, with thirteen counties suffering serious hardship, Gansu told the Central Committee of problems in only nine counties, and claimed that most of the province's famine refugees had returned. While painting this rosy picture, the provincial party committee forced peasants to get by on less than 200 grams of grain per day and insisted on meeting procurement quotas.[15]

In early 1960, while communal kitchens in Qingshui County had exhausted their food supplies, campaigns against private withholding continued. Zhangshuyi Commune sent deputy party secretary Xu Xiaorui to the Songhe production brigade to "mobilize the masses in ruthless struggle." Xu searched every home for food, then reported that he had unearthed nearly 60,000 kilos of grain, or 11 kilos per person, enough to cover the brigade's consumption until the end of June while also meeting the procurement quota of more than 25,000 kilos. To convince the commune of the veracity of his report, Xu forced the brigade's leader, Mao Wenqing, to draw up a register of names and affix his fingerprints to a statement that the brigade's food supply was adequate. By the end of January, forty-four had starved to death, and Mao Wenqing had committed suicide.[16]

Throughout the county, cadres imposed scores of physical torments and withheld meal rations.[17] The province followed the spirit of the Central Committee by designating the cruelties a matter of "the failure to complete the democratic revolution," and launched "supplementary training in democratic revolution" in Qingshui County. It promoted this effort as a model throughout the province—"the Qingshui experience."

While people were starving in the countryside in 1959, Zhang Zhongliang and provincial party committee secretary-general He Chenghua went on an inspection of Hexi Prefecture with Zhangye prefectural party committee secretary An Zhen and proposed reducing the rural grain provision from 80 or 90 percent to 20 percent. As a means of documenting the adequacy of food supplies in the villages, He Chenghua had someone write up a report entitled "A Glimpse of the Countryside," which greatly glossed over the reality.[18] In 1958 the provincial health bureau reported that edema was caused by "malnourishment and excessive labor." The standing committee of the provincial party committee criticized this viewpoint as "an attack on the great production campaign." When residents of some localities tried to alert the upper levels to the spread of starvation, they were attacked. First secretary Yang of Gaotai County party committee sent cadres to the post offices to confiscate and censor more than ten thousand letters in which residents described their living conditions. When this action was brought to the attention of the provincial party committee, it did nothing.

According to an official report, from the spring of 1958 to the end of 1960, "Three-quarters of the province's prefectures experienced severe food shortages. Among the province's population of more than 13 million, some 7 million were limited to only about 200 grams of grain per day. Lacking oil, vegetables, and meat, this small amount of grain is their only sustenance under heavy physical labor . . . Many people have fled the region as edema becomes increasingly pervasive, disease spreads, humans and animals perish in droves, and vast tracts of land lie fallow."[19]

While it was mainly the "Tongwei problem" (described on page 137) and the "Qingshui experience" that became known to the outside world, the province's other prefectures were also not spared the ravages of the Great Famine. The following tables were created by departments of the Gansu provincial party committee on December 23, 1960. There are slight discrepancies between these figures and those provided in the 1988 edition of *China Population: Gansu*.[20]

These official statistics indicate that from 1958 to 1960, more than 400,000 died from unnatural causes. This number underrepresents the actual situation. Table 3.2 shows deaths in Linxia Hui Autonomous Prefecture as 46,376 in 1959 and 1960. The Linxia City work group, however, found that 41,381 died during those two years in the city alone.[21] Linxia City was just one of eight county-level units in the prefecture and experienced far from the greatest number of deaths. In another example, the death rate for Tongwei County revealed in 1965 was more than 30 percent in 1960, but Table 3.3 indicates only 18.4 percent. A 1998 article by the provincial deputy governor Yun Xiaosu acknowledged that during the years of hardship in the 1960s, "More than a million people starved to death because of the food shortage in Gansu."[22] In 1980, Xinhua journalists Fu Shanglun, Hu Guohua, and Dai Guoqiang went on a news-gathering

TABLE 3.2: MORTALITY RATES IN GANSU PROVINCE, 1958–60, COMPILED ON DECEMBER 23, 1960

Prefecture	1958			1959			1960		
	TOTAL POP.	DEATHS	MORTALITY RATE	TOTAL POP.	DEATHS	MORTALITY RATE	TOTAL POP.	DEATHS	MORTALITY RATE
Lanzhou	1,172,840	9,166	0.78	1,236,065	14,586	1.18	1,261,521	7,045	0.56
Pingliang	2,226,510	19,317	2.20	2,248,230	42,134	1.67	2,303,158	38,856	1.69
Tianshui	3,230,337	114,331	3.50	3,172,816	46,610	1.47	3,033,746	81,607	2.69
Dingxi	2,480,864	26,483	1.07	2,548,531	55,993	2.20	2,392,720	107,972	4.51
Zhangye	2,756,347	59,707	2.17	2,800,203	46,982	1.68	2,787,016	73,102	2.62
Gannan	340,206			377,016	6,687	1.77	351,614	10,384	2.95
Linxia	874,353	18,511	1.55	898,359	17,384	1.94	882,060	28,992	3.27
Total	13,081,457	272,465	2.10	13,281,225	228,385	1.70	13,011,835	348,388	2.68

Note: The total population of the province in 1957 was 12,726,493. The 142,044 recorded deaths represent 1.12 percent of this total.

TABLE 3.3: DEATHS IN GANSU'S FOURTEEN COUNTIES AND CITIES, 1958–60, COMPILED ON DECEMBER 23, 1960

City/County	1958			1959			1960		
	TOTAL POP.	DEATHS	MORTALITY RATE	TOTAL POP.	DEATHS	MORTALITY RATE	TOTAL POP.	DEATHS	MORTALITY RATE
Baiyin	223,612	1,519	0.68	239,512	2,150	0.9	252,818	1,191	0.47
Yumen	170,050	1,262	0.74	182,372	1,384	0.76	186,891	2,524	1.35
Jiuquan	336,317	9,072	2.7	365,291	5,962	1.63	389,643	11,458	2.94
Zhangye	359,440	9,848	2.74	343,285	6,787	1.98	386,512	16,380	4.87
Dingxi	230,902	2,882	1.25	239,181	6,098	2.55	220,713	10,561	4.78
Tongwei	281,091	4,155	1.48	270,494	10,229	3.78	213,992	39,473	18.4
Longxi	367,641	4,553	1.24	360,434	16,249	4.51	336,367	17,454	5.19
Min	386,228	4,249	1.1	398,279	6,389	1.59	360,146	23,649	6.57
Jingning	489,633	6,823	1.39	485,070	11,421	2.35	455,070	12,560	2.67
Wushan	573,751	11,374	1.98	578,306	9,420	1.63	542,217	28,253	5.21
Qingshui	335,357	13,566	4.04	340,000	8,041	2.37	283,472	16,425	5.79
Gaotai	168,456	5,222	3.1	167,788	2,282	1.36	151,131	10,635	7.04
Minqin	230,036	6,574	2.75	242,183	3,740	1.55	204,576	5,012	2.89
Hezheng	276,661	6,500	2.36	277,368	5,128	1.85	265,588	13,361	5.03

mission to parts of Gansu Province, including Tongwei, Huining, Dingxi, Ningjing, and Xihaigu, where they learned that during the three years of hardship, starvation deaths occurred in all the counties of this region, with the lowest estimate of total deaths nearing one million.[23]

Although these figures actually underrepresent the reality, they still indicate the reach and severity of the famine, with deaths in 1960 exceeding 5 percent of the population in six counties and cities. The figures also show that after the Lushan Conference, the number of deaths rose further because of the campaign against right deviation; the number of deaths in 1960, and the percentage of the population they represented, greatly exceeded those in 1959.

China Population: Gansu provides the figures in Table 3.4. These official figures also understate the effect of the famine, but come closer to reality than other official statistics.

TABLE 3.4: POPULATION FIGURES FOR GANSU PROVINCE, 1955–66

Year	Population (millions)	Birth rate (%)	Death rate (%)	Natural growth rate (%)
1955	11.5504	2.88	1.19	1.69
1956	12.187	2.82	1.08	1.74
1957	12.5506	3.0	1.13	2.17
1958	12.8148	3.15	2.11	1.04
1959	12.9312	1.93	1.74	.19
1960	12.4404	1.55	4.13	−2.58
1961	12.1082	1.48	1.15	.33
1962	12.401	4.14	.82	3.29
1963	12.4917	4.21	1.04	3.17
1964	12.9003	4.72	1.56	3.16
1965	13.4544	4.53	1.23	3.3
1966	13.9297	4.25	1.149	3.11

Source: China Population: Gansu.

According to the figures in Table 3.4, and using my calculation methods, 666,700 people starved to death in Gansu Province from 1958 to 1961, and there were 800,000 fewer births than under normal conditions. Given that these are official figures, the estimate of nearly 700,000 unnatural deaths is a bare minimum. Cao Shuji arrived at a total of 1.023 million unnatural deaths in Gansu Province from 1959 to 1961.[24]

Information reported in bulletins from those years that are preserved in the provincial archives provides a piecemeal impression of the famine conditions.

Tianshui: A report by the Tianshui prefectural party committee on December 24, 1960, states that 24.2 percent of the members of Mapaoquan Commune's Xiakou production team were suffering from edema, emaciation, or uterine prolapse brought on by malnourishment. Food supplies, calculated at 6 kilos per person per month, would last only until February. This report noted that there were 1,800 production teams in similar circumstances in the prefecture, affecting around 40 percent of all production teams.[25]

Min County: A report by the provincial rural work department on August 19, 1960, states that problems in Min County were severe.[26] More than 50,000 suffered from edema, and more than 21,900 people died, comprising 3.16 percent of the population.

Wuwei: Data on the worst year, 1960, are unavailable, but at the beginning of 1962 the famine was still severe. On January 15, 1962, the Wuwei prefectural party committee reported, "1,876 households totaling 8,782 people have run out of food, making up 11.9 percent of the total population."[27] The wording of the report regarding efforts to meet procurement quotas indicates an attempt to gloss over the famine situation.

Gannan: Famine conditions continued up until April 1962. On April 8, 1962, the Gannan prefectural party committee reported, "The incidence of outward migration and disease continues to increase, and livestock are being slaughtered throughout the area. Because of a shortage of seed grain, there is a danger that not all available grain fields will be cultivated. Lintan County is short 1.845 million kilos of grain, but the prefecture sent only 550,000 kilos. The county's Changchuan Commune is short 71,370 kilos of seed grain and 99,478 kilos of food grain for a total shortage of

170,848 kilos, but the county sent only 57,000 kilos with no food grain . . . Due to the lack of seed grain, many communes and work teams have discontinued sowing crops . . . Many households have been forced to sell off household goods or engage in barter. Edema, disease, and child malnutrition are rampant."[28]

Linxia: The Linxia prefectural party committee reported on the Bonan ethnic minority: "Members of this minority have suffered even greater deprivation . . . In an effort to preserve their lives, they have dismantled and sold off their homes, sold off furnishings and clothing and even their children. Their homes have been stripped bare and they are utterly destitute . . . Unnatural deaths continue, and people are abandoning the area to go begging for food."[29]

Behind the bare bones of these figures lie blood-drenched human dramas. Li Lei, who served for many years as chairman of the Gansu Province Women's Federation, was a veteran cadre from the Yan'an era. From 1956 to 1961 she served as secretary of Linxia Hui Autonomous Prefecture's party committee secretariat. She was labeled a right opportunist for speaking the truth, but was ultimately rehabilitated in December 1960. In 1999 she published a memoir describing conditions in Linxia during the famine:

On December 9, 1959, I was assigned to Hezheng County's Suji Commune. The people there had no food and were emaciated and swollen from edema, with some dying of starvation or exposure. All the bark had been stripped from the trees and eaten. One day there was a telephone call from the county saying that provincial vice-governor Zhang Pengtu was coming on an inspection tour and ordering us that very night to organize a work party to cut down the stripped trees that lined the highway and move them to a concealed area. With everyone at death's door, who had the strength to chop down trees and carry them off? We couldn't do it, and we left the trees standing for vice-governor Zhang Pengtu to see. But he never arrived. The first party secretary of Hezheng County at that time was Comrade Xue Zhentian, and he would rather ignore the loss of human life than put his official career at risk.

One time I went to Linxia to tell Ge Man [first party secretary of the prefectural party committee] about the starvation and eating of tree bark. Ge Man simply didn't believe me and said that it was just trouble being stirred up by landlords and rich peasants intending to create a false impression, and we had been hoodwinked. I told him that the people who were begging, eating tree bark, and starving to death were poor and lower-middle peasants. He said, "The well-to-do middle peasants don't dare show themselves, and are purposely making the poor and lower-middle peasants do this. The people you say are starving to death are just ill people dying of natural causes." He then told me to launch a drive against false reporting and private withholding and to uncover hidden food, saying that a certain other commune had searched out millions of kilos of grain. Ge Man spent all day in the prefectural party committee offices; he never went to the countryside to see what the masses were eating or how they were struggling on the verge of death, but focused on large-scale construction projects in Linxia, such as the creation of four major public parks . . .

He Chenghua came to Hexi for an inspection, and his vehicle became stuck in the mud. When the masses saw a provincial official's vehicle, many disregarded their own safety to dash into the freezing mud and pull the car out. All this did was convince him that if the people were able to move a car, they must be getting enough to eat. He then had *Peasant Daily* chief editor Huang Wenqing write an article entitled "A Glimpse of the Countryside." It can only be wondered how many deaths this glimpse caused, because the officials believed the villages had enough food and didn't provide them with any more . . .

According to a March 18, 1961, report by a work group that the party Central Committee sent to Linxia City, 41,381 people, or 8.7 percent of the population, died in Linxia City in 1959 and 1960. The mortality rate exceeded 15 percent in Maji, Hanji, Hongtai, and Qiezang communes. Some production teams and squads lost a third of their populations. The nine squads under Qiezang Commune's Jinguang production team lost 67 of their 106 members, or 63 percent. In the city overall, 388 households were wiped out and more than 100 orphans left behind. Some infants were found trying to suckle milk from the breasts of their dead mothers.

Cannibalism occurred in many places. Among 41 production brigades in ten communes of Linxia City, 588 people ate the remains of 337 others. In Hongtai Commune alone there were 170 people who ate 125 corpses as well as killing and eating five other people. Cannibalism occurred in six of the eight production teams of the Xiaogoumen production brigade, with 23 households eating 57 people. In some cases individuals barbarously consumed their own parents, children, spouses, and siblings. Some ate corpses of people who had just died, while others dug up bodies that had been dead for a week or even a month. In Qiezang Commune's Jinguang production brigade, Ma Xishun ate the corpse of a diseased person and then died himself, along with the rest of his eleven-member family. A commune member named Bai Yinu ate a total of eight dead bodies, including his father, wife, and daughter. A poor peasant from Qiezang Commune, Ma Abudu, near death, enjoined his daughter Ma Hasufei, "There's no meat left on my body, but after I die, cut out my heart and eat it." His daughter followed his instructions. In Qiezang Commune's Tuanjie production brigade, a poor peasant couple, Ma Yibula and his wife, killed and ate their fourteen-year-old daughter, and after Ma died, his wife ate him. Li Galiu of Hongtai Commune's Xiao-goumen production brigade ate his two dead children. After Li died, he was eaten by a fellow commune member, Hu Ba, who in his turn was eaten by Xiao Zhengzhi.[30]

Although urban dwellers suffered much less, they felt the effects of the famine. On December 9, 1960, Gansu's provincial industry and communications department reported that its ranks had been hit hard by edema. Some 60 percent of the seven thousand workers at the Yongchang nickel mine in Baijiaju were found to have abdomens so swollen that they looked pregnant. Three had already died. Out of ninety-four female staff in the geology and construction bureaus, fifty-five were suffering from amenorrhea, and eight hadn't menstruated for half a year or more.[31]

On December 18, 1960, the Baiyin municipal party committee reported, "Edema has become an extremely serious problem in the city's factories and mines, enterprises, party schools, and among a portion of commune members and staff. The problem arose in November . . . The main cause is malnutrition and excessive labor."[32]

On December 11, 1960, the Yumen municipal party committee reported:

Among only fourteen work units, including the Yumen petroleum management bureau, the Yumen railway office, the Xibei mining machinery factory, the municipal commerce bureau, and the municipal party school, 3,132 persons are suffering from edema, which afflicts 25 percent of the staff in the most seriously affected units . . . The illness has struck workers more than cadres, those employed in heavy physical labor more than those in light work, and those eating at communal kitchens more than those taking their meals at home.[33]

A report by the party committee of the Jiuquan Iron and Steel Company on December 30, 1960, described edema, amenorrhea, and impotence among its staff. Apart from a decrease in grain rations, there had been several months with no oil ration. "An increasing number have expressed a fear of dying in the Gobi Desert and have requested to return home; some have sold off their belongings, while others have disappeared without notice."

A provincial capital was usually better off, but the Lanzhou municipal party committee raised a starvation alert: "Since November . . . we've found 3,346 cases of edema among 68,096 staff and workers in 51 industrial work units . . . Among 3,313 staff and workers in the municipal finance and trade sector, 401 have been stricken . . . Among 1,882 staff and workers in the 21 work units of the propaganda and education system . . . 12 percent have fallen ill. Among 5,900 staff and workers in the municipal party political organs . . . 9 percent have fallen ill . . . 31 of the 145 children in Lanzhou Municipal Nursery School are suffering from edema." The main cause was malnutrition.[34]

People undergoing forced labor in reeducation (*laojiao*) or reform (*laogai*) camps were even worse off. A report by the Yumen prefectural reform through labor department stated, "Disease and death . . . have become extremely serious and are increasing rapidly." Since November 1960, 265 have died at the Yinma and Mogutan labor farms. At the Yinma Labor Farm, 34 people died on November 21 alone, with a total of 395 dying from 1960 onward. The cause of most deaths was starvation, with excessive labor and exposure as contributing factors. The food ration for inmates was meager, and part of it was confiscated for use in the cadre canteens.

Gansu Daily reporter Wang Jinghe and his wife He Fengming were labeled rightists and banished to the labor camps at Jiabiangou and Anxi. Wang Jinghe died at Jiabiangou and his body was never recovered. He Fengming, who narrowly escaped death at Anxi Labor Farm, wrote a memoir recording the misery of that time. Jiabiangou originally had more than 2,800 inmates, but only 600 or 700 survived. Many corpses were eaten by inmates. Most of those who starved to death were outspoken intellectuals.[35] Only cursory burials were carried out, and bleached bones littered the ground. One story related in her book concerns Dong Jianyi, an American-educated doctor who was sent to Jiabiangou as a rightist in 1957:

His wife, Gu Xiaoying, had also studied in the United States. During the two or three years that Dong Jianyi was in the labor camp, Gu Xiaoying traveled all the way from Shanghai every two or three months to visit him . . . In 1960, many inmates starved to death at Jiabiangou. One day in early November, Dong Jianyi, as a doctor, realized that he was near death . . . Because so many corpses were left exposed to the elements, Dong taught his section head, Liu Wenhan, how to shroud his corpse in a woolen blanket. Three days later he died at the age of thirty-five. Liu Wenhan bound him up in the blanket and placed him in a pit that had been eroded into the earth by a heavy rainfall. About a week after Dong Jianyi died, his wife Gu Xiaoying arrived from Shanghai . . . Liu Wenhan could only tell her, "Lao Dong passed away just over a week ago." He had no sooner finished saying these words when Gu Xiaoying burst out with a heartrending wail . . . After two or three hours she composed herself and asked the other inmates to take her to Lao Dong's body. But when they reached the pit, the inmates were horrified to see that the body had disappeared. After much searching, they finally found the corpse discarded in a gulley . . . and portions of his flesh had been cut away and eaten . . . Gu Xiaoying knelt beside the skeleton, weeping and embracing it endlessly. As night fell, the others urged Gu Xiaoying to go back and get some rest, but she cried out, "I won't go back, I want to die here with him!" Several people physically removed Gu Xiaoying back to the cave [where they were living]. Later inmates gathered up some tree branches and kerosene and cremated the remains.[36]

THE TONGWEI PROBLEM

Tongwei County's catastrophe exceeded even the Xinyang Incident, with nearly a third of the population lost to unnatural death. The party referred to this horror as the "Tongwei Problem."

Tongwei, in Gansu's southeast, is part of Dingxi Prefecture. Established as a county in 114 B.C.E., Tongwei is one of China's most ancient counties, and marked a key stage in the Red Army's Long March.

While retreating from its Jiangxi base, the army stopped in southern Gansu, and at a meeting in Ejie in September 1935, the CCP Central Committee decided to head toward northeastern Gansu. On September 21, 1935, the Red Army arrived in Hadapu (now part of Dangchang County in Gannan Tibetan Autonomous Prefecture), where Mao and the others learned from a report in *Dagong News* that there was a Red Army battalion in northern Shaanxi, and a revolutionary base. Ecstatic at the news, they held a meeting in Tongwei County's Bangluo Town on September 28 and decided that northern Shaanxi would be the target destination of the Long March. On September 29, Mao, Peng Dehuai, and the others with the first column arrived at Tongwei's county seat. Central Committee and Military Commission leaders, including Zhou Enlai and Ye Jianying, arrived in due course with the second column. A party was held at Wenmiao Street Primary School, during which Mao for the first time read out a poem he had composed along the Long March:

> The Red Army fears neither the length nor hardship of the March,
> Brushing aside a thousand mountains and rivers:
> The endlessly rippling Five Ridges,
> The majestic clay orbs of the Wumeng Range,
> The Yangtze lapping cloud-capped cliffs,
> The frigid chain links of the Dadu River Bridge.
> Delighting in Min Mountain's vast snowscape,
> The three armies march on with beaming faces.[37]

Nine years after the Chinese Communist Party came to power, this very place, Tongwei, suffered catastrophe.

In August 2000, I met with veteran cadres and other people to discuss the "Tongwei Problem." "Directives from above" blocked my access to files relating to it in the local archive, but I eventually consulted those records through a different archive.

According to the *Tongwei County Annals*, the population fell by 78,462 from 1958 to 1961, a loss of 28.1 percent. In the years from 1956 to 1958, the population increased at an average rate of 2.67 percent. Without the famine, Tongwei should have had 299,506 people in 1961, but the actual population was 201,255. That means a shortfall of 32.8 percent, including people who starved to death, those who would have been born under normal circumstances, and those who fled. Official records showed only 3,892 had fled and had failed to return by February 1960.[38]

A medical team reported:

The food shortage . . . resulted in frailty among those who were formally robust, death among the elderly, amenorrhea among women, stunted growth among children, and a general loss of body mass . . .

Emaciation in itself is simply a lack of nutrition and doesn't display symptoms; its dangers are therefore easily overlooked compared with the alarm raised by edema . . . The most notable example is Zhangjiacha Village under . . . Chengguan Commune's Dongfanghong [East is Red] production brigade. In 1958 the village had 204 residents, but the population was reduced by one-third from November 1959 until the end of 1960. Among the surviving 128, 65 are ill and 13 recently died, mostly elderly or children who died suddenly.

. . . Apart from malnutrition, emaciation is also associated with intestinal and stomach disorders, indigestion leading to diarrhea, and intestinal parasites. This is caused by a lack of sustenance, indiscriminate eating, or impurities in food or drink. Among 119 members of the 23 households of Qiaodiwan Village under Chengguan Commune's Shuangbao production brigade, 70 have fallen ill, all but 12 from intestinal or stomach disorders and roundworm. In the production brigade's Chenjiacha production team of 130 individuals in 35 households, 97 are ill, all of them with intestinal or stomach disorders and 93 of them with roundworm.

Based on the conditions in Tongwei, an incomplete analysis has been carried out on the causes of emaciation:

1. Poor living conditions and food shortages leading to a high incidence of illness from consuming food substitutes;
2. Infirmity brought on by illness, leading to failure to recover for extended periods;
3. An unsuitable choice of food substitutes. At Xinjing Commune, some people ate buckwheat husks, and upon being exposed to wind, experienced numbness all over their bodies, a tingling sensation to the skin, and a darkening of the face quickly followed by swelling. At Jichuan and Yigang communes, some people ate wild castor-oil plants, as a result of which they suffered dizziness

and abdominal distension, followed by death in the most serious cases;

4. Consuming unboiled water and uncooked grain and vegetables is the cause of intestinal parasites and digestive disorders;

5. The shortage of food has led to an upsurge in domestic abuse. Adults abuse children, young men abuse the elderly, healthy people abuse those who are seriously ill, and bias in favor of men leads parents to abuse their daughters and daughters-in-law. Those suffering abuse tend to also suffer more from emaciation;

6. It is said that those who eat the flesh of dead humans are unwilling to eat grain, and that they become reduced to skin and bones. Before such people become emaciated, their eyes tend to become severely bloodshot.[39]

In the ancient county of Tongwei, once a model of decorum, starvation caused people to lose their rationality and all sense of human dignity. When the communal dining halls began serving soup, they started out with one jar or one basin of soup per family. As the soup became thinner and the people more anxious, those sent to fetch the soup for their families became increasingly inclined to consume every drop of it themselves. Homes became battlegrounds for the last scrap of food. Eventually it became every man for himself, with individual family members all joining the throng at the door of the communal kitchens. Even after the communal kitchens closed, desperate conflict continued, with each family member cooking up whatever he could find. When the communal dining halls were operating, the favored practice was for families to use washbasins or earthenware crocks to collect the soup ration, and when the soup was finished, the container was licked down to the last drop. With jars, only a child might be small enough to lick up most of it, and then use a little finger to get the rest. One day at the communal dining hall, a slice of potato dropped from the bowl of a cadre, and a child of seven or eight darted out to scoop it off the floor. The cadre slammed his foot down on the little hand, turning a deaf ear to the child's howls of pain.[40]

People who starved to death had to be referred to as "ill," and the county ordered that all the "ill" must be buried. The county party committee directed that this process be referred to as "sanitation work," not burial of the dead.

A 1965 county report stated that in 1959 and 1960, "the county suffered a population loss of 60,210; 2,168 households were completely wiped out, 1,221 children were left as orphans, 11,940 people fled the county, more than 360,000 *mu* of fields were left fallow, more than 33,000 head of livestock perished, more than 40,000 sheep were slaughtered, pigs, chickens, and cats and dogs were virtually wiped out, more than 50,000 homes were demolished, more than 270,000 trees were felled, agricultural production ground to a halt, schools and factories were shut down, and society roiled with unrest."[41]

At our August 2000 meeting, veteran cadres in Tongwei told me that the statistics in the *Tongwei County Annals* understate the disaster and that in fact a third of the population starved to death. At that time, more than 70 percent of all households experienced at least one death. Many corpses went unburied. Among the seven hundred members of three Jiudianzi production teams under the Wuxing production brigade of Chengguan Commune, more than thirty people died of starvation each day in the early winter of 1959. The living piled the corpses onto a wagon and hauled them off to a nearby drainage ditch. At Jichuan Commune, the seven family members of Ma Qingfeng (later headmistress and star teacher of the local nursery) all starved to death; she escaped starvation because she was studying at Longxi Normal College. Later the county authorities ordered a "sanitation drive" in which all burial pits were stomped flat so that no trace could be found.

Jing Gennian had been chairman of the county people's congress before retirement. During the famine, he was a cadre in the provincial metallurgy office, and was sent to Tongwei as part of a work team. When the work team arrived in the autumn of 1959, countless bodies lay on beds and in roads and fields, the living indistinguishable from the dead. The work team immediately fed soup to the living. They didn't concern themselves with the dead, however numerous—the real worry was the living, many of whom had turned to cannibalism. In February 1960 the team went to Chengguan Commune's Zhonglin production brigade. The brigade leader, Liu Tingjie, led them to Wangjiazhuang Village, where they saw smoke rising from a chimney—the only evidence of a lit fireplace for miles around. When they went inside they saw something being cooked in a wok, and when they raised the lid they saw human flesh. The woman cooking it had "sesame eyes" (a local term referring to blindness or defective eyesight). Jing Gennian recalled, "The wok contained an arm that still had a hand attached, from which I could see that it had come from a child." Later, at Xiangnan Commune, production brigade leader Dong Xiaoyuan told them that a woman named Cai Donghua had eaten human flesh. By chance they encountered the woman; her eyes were deeply bloodshot, and her hair was falling out in clumps, leaving only stubble behind. She had eaten her own four-year-old daughter. When asked why, she replied, "I was mad with hunger."

Cannibalism was not exceptional. In 1980, Xinhua reporters went to Tongwei and were told by the party secretary of Longyang Commune, "During the three-year hardship, in my home village a woman in her twenties cooked and ate her own daughter. When her man came back from Xinjiang and asked after his daughter, the other villagers covered up the matter, because many of them had also eaten human flesh. People were driven mad by hunger. They'd go out with a basket, and if they saw a corpse along the side of the road, they'd cut off any edible flesh to cook at home." This party secretary had come home from working on the Yintao Project to find that his entire family—his wife, younger sister, and three children—had all starved to death.[42]

Veteran cadre Zhang Dafa was one of the editors of the *Tongwei County Annals* and had access to the county's historical archives. I suggested that he salvage the data. He subsequently wrote a book, *On the Golden Bridge*. Following are some extracts:

> In one four-member family, the son had died, leaving behind his mother, wife, and daughter. One day the little girl died, and the young mother stood over her daughter's body in the courtyard, too dazed and feeble to weep. The grandmother dragged herself out of the house and pulled the girl's bony corpse into the backyard. After a while, the mother went back and discovered that the grandmother had chopped the girl into pieces and cooked her. The grandmother died nonetheless, perhaps overwhelmed by the gravity of her crime.
>
> The late Lu Nianzu, once a doctor of traditional medicine in Tongwei County, recalled that at the end of the lunar year in 1959, his aunt took her daughter down by the brook in search of human flesh . . . She cooked a human leg for her dying husband, but he couldn't bear to eat it and waved her away. The moment she brought it out of the living room, several starving people who had been drawn by the aroma of cooked meat snatched it right from her hands. A few days later, Lu's aunt dis-

appeared, and eventually a pair of bound human feet, in shoes recognized as hers, were found on a ridge behind the village.

... A man from Jichuan Commune who had been sent away to work heard of the famine back home and sent his family ration coupons for more than five kilos of grain. After buying some flour, his wife returned home and locked the door. When several days passed without anyone leaving or entering the house, some villagers jumped over the wall and found the starved corpses of several children inside. The woman, however, had disappeared, and no one could learn what had become of her. In the early 1970s the facts came to light. The woman had abandoned her children and run off, but before she left the village boundary, someone had killed and eaten her. An investigation was carried out, but the suspected murderer had died by then.

In the Dawan production team of Longyang Commune's Zhoudian production brigade, Zhang Siwa clubbed his own twelve-year-old daughter to death and cooked her. Even so, no one from the four-member family survived the famine. A middle-aged woman surnamed Niu in Shenjiashan likewise killed and cooked her four-year-old daughter, with no better results.

A cadre told us a story about his family of six: "My father had gone to work at the Tao River irrigation project, and my mother was looking after my younger brother and sisters and me. My mother was a very calculating woman, and somehow she'd managed to find and hide away a small amount of food. Late every night, after my younger brother and sisters were asleep, my mother would quietly wake me up and stuff some cooked meal into my mouth, then cover my head with a quilt until I'd swallowed it, after which she would go to sleep ... One time I saw my mother gazing at my sisters and brother, who were reduced to skin and bones, and her face was full of anguish. I asked her why she was sad, but she just shook her head and didn't answer. Soon after that, my brother and sisters all died. A year later, sometime in the spring of 1961, my father returned from Tao River. My mother handed me over to him and said, 'This was the best I could do. I could only keep one alive for you, only ... only one.' Before she could finish speaking, she fell to the floor weeping. My father picked her up and carried her to the bed and wept along with her ... Soon after that, my mother became blind from her ceaseless weeping. She was only in her early thirties.

Eventually I understood that my mother was preserving one child to carry on the ancestral duties."

In a remote mountain village in Disanpu, there was a family with five or six children, and the parents were at a loss over how they could all survive. When the situation became desperate, the mother tossed one six- or seven-year-old girl into the underbrush ... It seemed that fate had something else in store for her, however, for the girl managed to scavenge enough to eat from the wild plants around her, and she survived. Now she herself is a mother, and you have to wonder how she feels when she looks back on that time! There was another mother who cooked and ate her own younger daughter. When the elder daughter realized what was going on, she pulled at her mother's jacket and begged her, "Mama, please don't eat me! When I grow up I'll look after you!"

Bai Shangwen, who had served as Tongwei County's deputy county head, lost his mother to starvation, and Yan Yuxiang, who had served as chairman of the county people's congress, lost six family members. An elderly man in Zhaojiashan who was a production brigade cadre at that time recalls, "More than half of the people in the village had died, but the production team storehouse still held a few dozen kilos of oil dregs and a few dozen kilos of grain, and none of it was distributed to the commune members. When the head of the provincial party committee work group, Wang Bingxiang, came to the village to investigate the situation, he asked, 'The people were starving to death; why not distribute this food to the commune members?' There was nothing we could say in reply, but in our hearts we understood: Who would dare to eat it? In any case there wasn't enough to save us all."[43]

In 1958, Tongwei's county party secretary was Xi Daolong, a thirty-five-year-old native of Shanxi Province who had been imprisoned by the Kuomintang for taking part in the Communist revolution. The county head was Tian Buxiao, a native of Shaanxi Province. He was known as an honest man who was practical and realistic.

The provincial party committee was very satisfied with operations in Tongwei County. On May 5–23, 1958, Xi attended the Second Plenum of the Eighth CCP Central Committee as "representative of an advanced county." Xi became a model for cadres throughout the province. It was at this plenum that the decision was made to launch the Great Leap Forward. Xi Daolong "received the Gospel" at that meeting, and upon his return home, his work was even more energetic.

In response to Mao's slogan of "The people's communes are good!" Tongwei's party officials in 1958 united all 169 of the county's high-level cooperatives into fourteen individual people's communes, with the county serving as one united commune. In one month, 2,759 communal kitchens were organized, and every man, woman, and child ate in the canteens. Village leaders implemented militarization of organization, combativeness of operations, and collectivization of daily life. A people's militia was organized for the county, and each commune became a combat unit. "Report for work lined up like a dragon, attack your work like a swarm of bees." The dominant production slogans were "500-kilo (grain yields) marshals summon the troops; 5,000-kilo (potato yields) satellites fly into the heavens." Most people supported the communization movement, but some hurriedly harvested the crops on their plots of land and slaughtered their sheep and pigs.

To eliminate these impediments, the county launched mass debates. The topic was: What is communism? How do we construct communism? Villagers had little light to shed on these questions, but one thing was made clear: communism was "paradise," and the people's communes were the "golden bridge" leading to this paradise. Whoever opposed the people's communes also opposed communism and must be subjected to struggle. Those with alternative views were "white flags" that had to be "pulled down." In 1958, 565 "white flags" were pulled down (including 3 cadres of county organs, 11 commune cadres, 66 production brigade cadres, and 485 production team cadres).[44] These were the figures reported by the Dingxi Prefecture Organization Department, but the actual number was much greater. Communes handed down "white flag" quotas, and work teams that reached them "pulled down" even anyone who arrived late for a meeting. While some pulled down "white flags," others energetically "planted red flags" that stoked the fanaticism of some young people. In a July 5, 1965, report, the Tongwei County party committee noted that the during the pulling down of white flags and criticism of well-to-do middle peasants from 1957 to 1959, more than 10,360 people had been wrongfully denounced.[45]

Ushering in communism threw the county into disarray. The uncompensated collectivization and redistribution of land, labor, work animals, farming implements, trees, buildings, domestic fowl, and livestock, and even humble household necessities reached an estimated value of more than 9.9 million yuan.

What crops should be planted was no longer a choice for farmers, but was predicated on the planting patterns of "Four Don't Plants," "Five Eliminates," and "Eight Essential Crops." Much of the agricultural workforce was diverted. In the spring of 1958 more than 17,900 workers (19.7 percent of the county workforce) were sent to industrial production. In May, another 18,000-plus workers were deployed to the Yintao irrigation project. In August, just as the crops were turning golden, the harvest was ignored in order for workers to prepare for an inspection by the central government's soil and water conservation inspection team. Some fifty thousand workers (51.4 percent of the county workforce) embellished 60 kilometers of roadway with festive bunting, fluttering red flags, and oceans of big-character posters, filling the streets with a deafening clamor of gongs and drums and carrying out some last-minute soil and water conservation work. In October more than twenty-five thousand people were deployed to big campaigns in Huajialing and Shijiashan. In 1959, more than fifty thousand laborers were sent to irrigation projects. Large tracts of land went uncultivated: the crop yield for 1957 was 82,115,000 kilos, decreasing to 57,880,000 kilos in 1958, 41,930,000 kilos in 1959, and 18,160,000 kilos in 1960.[46]

During this dramatic decrease in crop yields, the county reported bumper harvests. Total output for 1958 was first estimated at 190 million kilos and then reported as over 130 million kilos, which was more than double the actual yield. The procurement quota was set on that basis at 21.8 million kilos, and 20.77 million kilos were delivered to the storehouses, which was 36 percent of the total yield. Output for 1959 was projected at 120 million kilos, and a yield of 90 million kilos was reported following the autumn harvest, again more than double the actual yield. The procurement quota was set at 27.0 million kilos, with 47.2 percent of the total yield actually delivered. Of course, it was the upper levels that coerced the county into making these unrealized projections and exaggerated production reports.[47]

The annual procurement quotas recorded in the *Tongwei County Annals* are slightly lower than those just cited, but still indicate how heavy a burden was borne by the people of Tongwei from 1953 to 1959. By 1960, deaths and decreased productivity led to reduced procurement quotas, which didn't return to the 1959 level until the 1990s.

By 1957 many localities experienced food shortages as soon as the harvest was shipped to the storehouses. Local governments purchased stale grain, and members of the collectives were paid in cash rather than grain. By the spring of 1958, people were starving. The situation became even more desperate in 1959. During the winter, 102 of the county's 162 production brigades failed to distribute grain for three months. In some communes, members went forty days with no grain and resorted to eating roots, husks, and tree bark, and to cannibalism.[48]

By the spring of 1959, the grain situation was dire throughout Dingxi Prefecture. Since 1958 had been reported as a bumper harvest, many officials believed that the villages had plenty of food and that the demand for food was a manifestation of class struggle. The provincial party committee recommended that "need is subordinate to what is feasible; sales are subordinate to quotas; arrangements are subordinate to allocation; the countryside is subordinate to the cities." The provincial authorities called for class struggle to facilitate grain procurement. Dingxi Prefecture then imposed restrictions on food supplies while demanding more grain from the villages.

Even with people starving in large numbers, the Tongwei County party committee maintained that "the lack of food is an ideological problem, not an actual problem." The county party committee demanded that the communes convene "10,000-person mass criticism sessions" and that the production brigades hold "1,000-person mass criticism sessions" to denounce peasants who requested food from the government and the grassroots cadres who spoke for them. The party committee also proposed attacking well-to-do middle peasants and crushing the "shirking of labor, sabotage of production, and illegal income."[49]

The high procurement levels were set by the state, and provincial party secretary Zhang was accountable only to his superiors. Under his pressure, cadres dared not raise the subject of starving villagers or excessive production targets, or suggest that procurement quotas could not be met. Dingxi prefectural party secretary Dou Minghai said, "The party's victory in previous struggles has always been a victory against right deviation" and "In the struggle against right deviation, don't fear the left but the Center."

Production levels in Dingxi Prefecture dropped steadily from 1958, yet procurement levels continued to rise. In spring 1960, when the villages had run out of grain, Dou Minghai said, "Better that people starve to death than that we should request grain from the state."[50] Zhang Zhongliang held Dou in high regard as a model cadre.

During the food supply crisis, the provincial party committee offered Tongwei County party secretary Xi Daolong an advantageous transfer to Min County as first secretary—but only after Xi had met the grain procurement quota in Tongwei. Xi then imposed even harsher methods on procurement.

Starting in August 1958, Tongwei County's campaign against right deviation resulted in the labeling of 1,169 cadres at the production team level or above. When county head Tian Buxiao reported the truth, Xi labeled him an "anti-party element." On October 29, 1959, the thirty-five-year-old Tian killed himself. After his death, the county party committee stripped his party membership for the crime of "utter and incorrigible right opportunism," and a criticism meeting was held over his corpse.[51]

Xi turned a blind eye to the starving. When more than fifty people had died and production had halted in Biyu Commune's Zhaohe production brigade, Xi reported, "Morale is high, the work animals are strong, and production is progressing well."

In his speech at a rectification and procurement "thousand-person on-site meeting" at Longchuan Commune, Xi emphasized, "We must continue opposing right deviation and encourage enthusiasm . . . We absolutely must meet our procurement quotas. As for those who stubbornly refuse to hand over their grain, we must think of every means to force them . . . Politics is revolution, and revolution is not a dinner party;[52] it does not allow for refined behavior, but requires the iron fist and iron action of revolution." The county told the communes: "Anyone who doesn't meet the procurement quotas should report back with their heads on a platter."

When Changhe Commune party secretary Zhao Dianjing finished listening to the countywide telephone conference, he sat beside his bed in silence. County Youth League committee secretary Sun Yuye asked, "What do you think?" Zhao replied, "If we don't meet the quota tomorrow, I'll have to turn up with two heads on a platter. Since I only have one head, where will I get the other?" That night, the two of them went to collect grain.[53]

The county dispatched "commune rectification groups" to every production team and home to confiscate grain, rummaging through chests and cupboards and grabbing whatever they found. In some places they dug up the ground a meter deep. A search of 637 homes in Longyang Commune seized 21,916 kilos of coarse cereal grain, 1,617 kilos of flour, 15,545 kilos of potatoes, and 75 kilos of vegetables, as well as 272 silver coins, 202 kilos of copper, and 30 bolts of cloth. Villagers referred to the groups as "ten-thousand-member grain-searching teams" or "ten-thousand-member robbery gangs."

Brutal punishment was inflicted under slogans such as "Better to owe a blood debt than a grain debt: Fulfilling the grain procurement quota is a fight to the death." Grain coercion meetings became wars against the enemy, complete with machine guns, rifles, and sabers. Maying Commune party secretary Zhang Xuesheng assaulted more than 160 people, with 66 sent to reeducation through labor. Struggle sessions employed more than 120 types of torture, and more than 1,300 people were beaten to death or driven to suicide. Villagers referred to the perpetrators as "Qin Shihuang," "the King of Hell," "Huang Shiren,"[54] and "wolfhounds."[55]

On November 3, 1959, Tongwei County first secretary Xi proclaimed, "No one under criticism can return home; they must be reeducated through labor under the armed supervision of cadres and militia." Fourteen camps were then formed to hold 1,637 people.[56]

Statistics collected in the spring of 1960 by a provincial and prefectural party committee work group indicate that eleven commune party secretaries were responsible for the deaths of seventy-nine people who were beaten to death or driven to suicide. Their mottos were "firm stand," "merciless," "deft of hand," and "sharp of blade." The party secretary of Longyang Commune, Li Shengrong, assaulted fifty-three people, among whom twelve died from beating or suicide. Maying Commune party secretary Zhang Xuesheng managed a "1,000-person mass criticism session" with militia bearing twelve machine guns and more than fifty rifles and other firearms. He directed the denunciation and flogging of more than 160 commune members. Among 66 sent to reeducation, 4 died of abuse.[57]

Meanwhile, cadres enjoyed privileges. The bulletin of an enlarged meeting of the Dingxi prefectural party committee on January 13, 1961, reported that when provincial leader Zhang Zhongliang went to Lintao County to lead a pilot project, he refused to eat the local alfalfa rice, but had his meals delivered from the luxurious Lanzhou Hotel. In 1960,

Dingxi prefectural party secretary Dou Minghai requisitioned 169.85 kilos of meat, 11.5 kilos of oil, more than 260 eggs, 236.5 kilos of grain, 31 kilos of sugar and pastry, and 160 kilos of red dates, as well as various quantities of ham, chicken, canned goods, noodles, tea leaves, and fruit from the commerce and grain bureaus.

The truth was that Xi Daolong was not thoroughly heartless, and when he saw so many people starving, he provided them with a chance for survival. In the spring of 1959 he took advantage of some policy compromises to allocate land for household cultivation. He also assigned the upkeep of draft animals to households. In the first half of January 1960, upon learning of an upsurge in starvation deaths, Xi rushed to the prefecture seat at night to report on the seriousness of the situation, only to meet with criticism. These displays of conscience eventually brought Xi personal misfortune.

The provincial party committee work group continued its campaign against right deviation.

Some people took great personal risk to reveal Tongwei's situation in letters to the CCP Central Committee. Veteran cadres told me that a student wrote to Vice-Premier Tan Zhenlin, who then directed Wang Bingxiang, secretary of the provincial party secretariat and vice-governor of Gansu Province, to meet with that student. When Wang led a work group to Tongwei with foodstuffs on February 8, 1960, however, their objective was not to fight the leftism that had caused the famine but to counter right deviation in the wake of the Lushan Conference. On March 1, 1960, in accordance with a resolution by the provincial party committee, the work group had first party secretary Xi Daolong and sixteen other county party committee and government leaders arrested as "active counterrevolutionaries." Wang reported that "the severity of the Tongwei problem is rooted in the collusion of right opportunists with counter-revolutionaries."

Wang's report stated that the chief crimes of Xi Daolong and the others included "allocating a great deal of land to 'crops harvested by those who sowed them, and retained by those who harvested them,' and dividing up livestock to be reared by individual households," "masquerading as ultraleftists and using 'rectification of the cooperatives' and 'meeting procurement targets' to rob the masses of their foodstuffs and property," as well as "setting up labor reform camps and detaining and flogging the masses" and "starting up capitalist free markets and carrying out smuggling operations." Making production contracts and allowing peasants to cultivate fallow ground were important measures for avoiding the worst of the famine, yet the work group criticized these actions as capitalism.

The Tongwei County party committee mobilized the masses to carry out criticism against seventy-eight individuals with "serious problems." Allegedly headed up by Xi Daolong, these people had responded to the famine by reducing the size of accounting units, disbanding the communal kitchens, and appointing officials with undesirable family backgrounds. The Gansu provincial party committee cited Xi for assigning livestock rearing and planting to households, and for allowing commune members to reap what they sowed, deemed "a series of bourgeois restorationist policies."[58]

The provincial party committee work group did curb beatings and released some food, but that wasn't enough. The "Tongwei Problem" was essentially a leftist problem, and the provincial party committee's designation of it as a problem brought about by right deviation only exacerbated the death toll, which in 1960 was nearly quadruple that in 1959.

In the 1990s, Wang Bingxiang retired in honor, depicted as a virtuous official committed to rescuing the starving multitudes. When the *Tongwei County Annals* was being finalized, Wang ordered the deletion of the section on his errors and had the following paragraph added: "On February 9, 1960, the secretary of the Gansu provincial party committee secretariat and vice-governor of Gansu Province, Wang Bingxiang, led a joint provincial-prefectural work group of more than 100 people to Tongwei. After gaining an understanding of the situation, he truthfully reported to the CCP Central Committee and the provincial party committee that many people had died in Tongwei, and immediately provided grain and organized cadres and teachers to go to the countryside to save lives."

From this it can be seen that in cases where cadres who had been in charge during the Great Famine continued to hold office or served in important positions in the 1980s, it is very possible that population statistics and historical records regarding that particular region were falsified.

THE CAMPAIGN TO GET TO THE BOTTOM OF THE MATTER

Following the meeting of the Northwest bureau in Lanzhou in December 1960, the CCP Central Committee and provincial and prefectural party committees sent a task force and medical team to Tongwei. They distributed more than 16.85 million kilos of grain, 3.3 million yuan in relief funds, 136 tons of medical supplies, nearly 400,000 meters of cotton cloth, and 30,000 kilos of cotton batting, along with sugar, honey, red dates, and other foodstuffs, reclaiming more than eighty thousand souls from the brink of death. The relief effort cost the lives of two members of the medical team, Wang Jun and Liu Chunhua.

Production was also regenerated through state loans and subsidies totaling 1.42 million yuan, investment totaling more than 2.7 million yuan, the purchase of more than 4,700 head of livestock, and the replacement or repair of more than 40,000 farming implements.[59] Relief aid was refused, however, to nine classes of people: landlords, rich peasants, counterrevolutionaries, bad elements, rightists, degenerate elements, alien-class elements, conspicuous well-to-do middle peasants, and right opportunists.

The last vestiges of famine were eliminated in 1962. The *Tongwei County Annals* records, "The weather this year was good for crops, and there were bumper harvests in both summer and autumn, alleviating the food supply problem throughout the county." In that year, commune members were allotted more land for cultivating their own crops, as well as being allowed to take leases on fallow wasteland. Draft animals and sheep were allocated to individual households for raising.

Documents indicate that the turning point for Tongwei was the Lanzhou Conference, which was held following Mao's memo on the Xinyang Incident, and after the Central Committee began acknowledging serious problems in other parts of the country. The Northwest bureau chose to address the Tongwei Problem through "supplementary instruction in democratic revolution" and class struggle. The Gansu provincial party committee subsequently characterized the causes of the Tongwei Problem as follows: "Control over many departments and communes fell into the hands of bad elements. In 152 communes, there were 24 leading cadres at the level of commune head or above who were secret agents, Yiguandao adherents, and hostile counterfeits within the party, Youth League, army, police, and militia, making up 15.2 percent of the total. Eight out of 30 members and alternate members of the county party committee, or 22.6 percent of the total, had various problems in their political history."[60] This was cited as evidence that the democratic revolution had been insufficiently thorough, and resulted in many grassroots cadres being forced to undergo supplemental lessons in democratic revolution.

Tongwei's supplemental instruction in democratic revolution was carried out under the name of rectification, a process that unleashed full-fledged power struggles. In January 1961 the county party committee proposed, "Proceed further in lifting the lid off the 'Tongwei Problem'; pull it out by the taproots, lateral roots, and tiny rootlets." Apart from the county-level cadres who had been detained earlier on, more than 360 cadres below the county level underwent various forms of group training.

Because Mao and other senior cadres accepted responsibility during the Seven Thousand Cadres Conference in February 1962, the provincial and prefectural party committees decided on May 13 to release Xi Daolong and the sixteen other county-level cadres. Xi became deputy director of Dingxi Prefecture's water control bureau before retiring with honor.

THE HANDLING AND REPERCUSSIONS OF THE GANSU PROBLEM

In December 1960 the CCP Northwest bureau's Lanzhou Conference exposed the errors of Zhang Zhongliang, He Chenghua, Ruan Dimin, Wang Bingxiang, and others. A reorganized Gansu provincial party committee criticized Dou Minghai and others and reorganized the prefectural party committee. Yet, following the example of Xinyang, supplementary training in democratic revolution was also carried out, and tens of thousands were subjected to criticism and denunciation. On February 27, 1961, the new provincial party committee ordered that "all entrenched alien-class elements and plucked-out degenerate elements who have carried out class retaliation on the working people or otherwise harmed the people must be punished in order to appease the wrath of the people, and should undergo special training as a matter of priority."[61] More than ten thousand "group training" inmates were denounced at gunpoint. According to veteran cadres, the number criticized was actually much larger.

At the end of 1962, Wang Bingxiang and Ruan Dimin tried to restore their reputations by criticizing the Northwest bureau's Lanzhou Conference: "Instead of affirming and taking account of achievements before exposing and criticizing shortcomings and errors, and drawing lessons on that basis, they instead denied all achievements and exposed and criticized across the board." In their view, "Gansu's errors were . . . a matter of executing central policies."

Many other cadres likewise demanded a reversal of their verdicts on the grounds that Gansu was similar to other provinces. Since the central leadership had supported them at the time, they now felt greatly wronged. This feeling was even stronger at the lower levels. The Dingxi prefectural party committee collected views such as these from grassroots cadres in a report to the provincial party committee in November 1961:

- When problems developed in Gansu, some comrades from the Central Committee leadership personally carried out inspections and also sent a task force to work in Gansu. They gave a very high assessment of operations in Gansu and did not raise any problems.
- The Central Committee knew about the Yintao Project. When the project was launched, they sent a congratulatory telegram, and Zhu De and Xi Zhongxun came to inspect it without discovering any problems or correcting any errors.
- Comrade Tan Zhenlin was responsible for agriculture . . . He said, "We've already resolved the food supply issue," and, "Rope-drawn plowing is the direction of agricultural development."[62] He also said, "Currency is currency and also not currency, and merchandise is merchandise and also not merchandise; this is primary distribution according to work done." These sayings increased the confusion of lower-level cadres.
- The Communist Wind, the communal kitchen movement, and free meals were the Central Committee's ideas, and it should be held responsible.
- When President Liu said during a work inspection in Henan that there should be only one commune under each county, this had a huge influence on the cadres below.
- The "Five Winds" were stirred up by those above. Coercive commandism at the lower levels was imposed by inspection groups from above.
- The provincial party committee said it would not assign blame for past errors, but Zhang Zhongliang and Dou Minghai remained party secretaries, while lower-level cadres were subjected to group training, special training, dismissal, or legal measures. Although the provincial and prefectural party secretaries did not personally cause injury or loss of life, they forced their subordinates to commit violations of law and discipline. The main reason for the errors of the last

few years is: "The agenda is set by those above and executed by those below; when those below mess things up, those above support them." It is unfair to place all the blame on those below.[63]

On December 3, 1962, the Gansu provincial party committee criticized the grassroots cadres "attempting to push the blame on the Central Committee and Chairman Mao." "The errors that were particular to Gansu arose largely from the individual thinking and character of Zhang Zhongliang and other comrades."[64]

Judging from available historical materials, it is manifestly unjust to attribute all the problems in Gansu Province to the thinking and character of Zhang Zhongliang. The famine struck the entire country, but different regions suffered in different degrees, depending on how subordinate cadres magnified the actions of those above. Zhang was faulted for applying all of the state's investment in the communes for irrigation projects and commune-managed enterprises, instead of applying 70 percent to assist the poor in accordance with the Central Committee's stipulations. In addition, he was blamed for putting a disproportionate emphasis on large-scale irrigation projects and for expanding the campaign against right deviation outside the party.[65] Viewed from the present, these incidents do not appear so egregious; much greater "magnification" took place in Henan, Sichuan, and Anhui.

Zhang Zhongliang was subsequently demoted with a transfer to serve as a secretary in the Jiangsu provincial party committee secretariat.

4 THE PEOPLE'S COMMUNE: FOUNDATION OF THE TOTALITARIAN SYSTEM

The ruthless controls and abuses imposed during the famine would have been unthinkable without the people's communes. The communes did not develop from China's cooperative movement; the government referred to collectivization as a cooperative movement, and as a result, the two terms are confusingly applied, but they are conceptually distinct. The cooperatives were based on household interests, while collectivization expropriated household interests. Cooperatives provided mutual benefit based on private ownership, while collectivization replaced private ownership with a system of state ownership.

Negating household ownership and interest facilitates an extraordinary concentration of state power, without which China's totalitarian system could not have come into being. Collectivization ruthlessly expropriated peasant property, and the process was inevitably brutal and coercive. The people's communes intensified the logic of collectivization, taking the negation of household interests a step further. This baseline structure of the totalitarian system formed the organizational foundation for the Great Famine.

MAO CALLS FOR A SURGE IN AGRICULTURAL COLLECTIVIZATION

After China carried out Land Reform, some people had the wherewithal to buy large-scale farming implements, while others made use of draft animals, and yet others employed hired hands. Peasants in difficulty began to sell off or rent their land allotments, as a result of which some became landless while others accumulated land. In 1950, the leader of the Northeast bureau, Gao Gang, proposed a shift from household farms to collectives. Liu Shaoqi argued that a lack of farm machinery made collectively owned farms counterproductive. Mao admired Gao Gang's idea and disapproved of Liu Shaoqi's view.[1]

Income differentiation was not actually proof of class polarization, however. Some researchers believe that the main trend was toward middle-income households. According to a survey in 1954 of 14,334 rural households in twenty-one provinces, at the conclusion of Land Reform, poor peasants and farm laborers made up 57.1 percent of all households, a figure that dropped to 29.0 percent by the end of 1954, while the percentage of middle peasants rose from 35.8 percent to 62.2 percent, and the percentage of rich peasants decreased from 3.6 percent to 2.1 percent.[2]

To slow polarization, the party divided middle peasants into subclasses. The resulting lower-middle peasants, when grouped with poor peasants, comprised 60 to 70 percent of the rural population. This artificially created rural majority was to propel villages down the socialist road. Well-to-do middle peasants, on the other hand, were treated as a force against socialism.

The requirements of a planned economy provided an even more important impetus to collectivization. In order to implement a state-run economy, all grain had to be held by the state. No government was capable of controlling 110 million peasant-run farms scattered throughout China. Without collectivization, it would be impossible to implement the state monopoly for purchasing and marketing. A government could not deal with individual units as numerous as hairs on a head, but combining them into one long braid would allow the government to bring them within grasp. In order to concentrate power in the center, production, livelihood, and thinking all had to be brought under state control, and this could be accomplished through collectivization.

Peasants had little choice in the matter. In Daming County, Hebei Province, when Dishang Village began organizing two cooperatives, the village cadres set up two tables on the street and told the villagers, "Now we'll see whether you follow the socialist road or the capitalist road. If you follow the socialist road, sign your name here to join a cooperative." "Our village has two cooperatives; you have to join one or the other." Cadres in Wenji Village said at a village meeting, "Anyone who refuses to join is taking the road of the landlords, rich peasants, capitalists, and Americans." In Jinnan Village, at least half of the 127 households in the Yehongshan Cooperative joined against their will.[3] The Hebei provincial party committee sent people to Daming County three times to correct this tendency and to disband some substandard cooperatives, only to have Mao subsequently criticize the committee for the error of "opposing rash advance." In Wuxing County, Zhejiang Province, a mass struggle session was held against rich peasants in Shanlian District, during which the propaganda head of the county party committee said, "Following the socialist road means joining the cooperative; if you don't join, you're the same as them!"[4]

Under the recommendation of the State Council vice-premier Deng Zihui, an agrarian policy leader, Zhejiang Province reduced the size of more than fifteen thousand substandard agricultural cooperatives in 1955. This was harshly criticized by Mao, and Deng Zihui was forced to undergo self-criticism.

On September 26, 1955, Mao wrote the following comments on the text of the self-criticism Deng Zihui had prepared for the Sixth Plenum of the Seventh CCP Central Committee:

> Why take such delight in frustrating the factors of socialism and not those of capitalism? None of you have answered this question. The answer should be: your brains still harbor a serious capitalistic mentality, so you feel the factors of socialism are not so desirable, and you mercilessly frustrate them . . . You've been influenced by the spontaneous capitalistic tendencies of the 20 to 30 percent of well-to-do middle peasants, while ignoring the enthusiasm of the 60 to 70 percent of poor and lower-middle peasants—this you're happy to write off, and instead of cherishing it you frustrate it. Can this be pure coincidence?[5]

Following agricultural collectivization, the party organization at the agricultural cooperative level took over organizing the rural economy, and also gained effective political control over the rural areas from the township level downward. The agricultural cooperatives became the effective organizations through which the central government controlled rural towns and villages. The state apparatus gained control of the basic means of production and livelihood in the rural areas, thus facilitating the comprehensive control of rural residents.

In September 1955, Mao Zedong personally took charge of explaining "the superiority of large cooperatives," as he referred to the collectives. He wrote:

Under the current semi-socialist cooperatives, in order to facilitate the process and allow cadres and the masses to gain experience more quickly, small cooperatives of twenty to thirty households are relatively prevalent . . . we should start moving toward amalgamation. In some places it will be possible to have one cooperative for each township; in a minority of places one cooperative can serve several townships, while in many there will naturally be several cooperatives under each township. Large cooperatives need not be restricted to the flatlands, but can also be organized in the hill country.[6]

Among the thirty-seven documents adopted during the Chengdu Conference in March 1958 was "Views Regarding the Appropriate Amalgamation of Small-scale Agricultural Cooperatives into Large Cooperatives," which made the people's communes all but inevitable.

FROM THE XIANJU INCIDENT TO THE SOCIALIST EDUCATION MOVEMENT

Agricultural collectivization encroached on the interests of peasant households. Conflicts arose when families sought to withdraw from the collectives. Efforts to prevent their withdrawal involved considerable coercion and persecution.

In December 1955, Xianju County, Zhejiang Province, had only four advanced agricultural cooperatives, or collectives. By June 1956, coercion had resulted in 88.15 percent of households joining collectives, with the percentage reaching 91.0 percent by the spring of 1957. Scale was excessive, and accounting chaotic. Disregarding the views of members, the collectives changed from two crops a year to three. As a result, annual production decreased by 22 percent. Pay for a day's labor averaged thirty-three cents. Village cadres accused people of undesirable political tendencies, then docked their work points, ransacked their homes, and abused them physically. Cadres took no part in physical labor, yet were awarded extra work points. When villagers responded by withdrawing from the collectives, instead of addressing the source of the problem, local party officials targeted them for mass criticism against their "well-to-do peasant mentality."

From April to May of 1957, 29 of the county's 33 towns and villages were hit by public disturbances. More than 100 cadres who tried to prevent withdrawals or the splitting up of collectives were beaten, and 430 homes of cadres and collective members were ransacked. Membership plunged, and 116 of the county's 302 cooperatives were completely disbanded, while another 55 were in a state of partial collapse. The state's coercive forces responded by arresting nine people and detaining forty-two.[7] Reports on the Xianju turmoil went up the party chain of command, and the Central Committee called on local officials throughout China to strengthen ideological education and forcefully retaliate against the opponents of collectives, designated as landlords, rich peasants, and counterrevolutionaries.

By then, similar events had transpired from January to April 1957 in Zhejiang's Shangyu County, and food supply became an issue. In July more than two thousand villagers rose up in Baiguan Town and Yongxuxiang's Majia Village, led by the Daqihui (a Buddhist organization).[8] After firing shots into the air, police opened fire on the protesters, killing two and wounding twelve before the crowd dispersed. Police subsequently arrested fourteen villagers as key instigators and detained another twenty-three.[9]

Demands to withdraw from collectives occurred in other provinces as well. Starting in the winter of 1956, several counties of Henan Province were hit by uprisings and withdrawals from collectives. Some members took complaints and petitions higher up, while others removed livestock from the collectives, divided up grain, seeds, oil, tools, and fodder, or assaulted cadres. Available statistics show a total of at least 66 cadres beaten, 4,946 head of livestock taken, and 62,500 kilos of grain divided up, along with some 12,000 kilos of seed grain, more than 195 kilos of oil, 200 farming implements, and more than 26,000 kilos of firewood. The events initially occurred mainly under cover of darkness, but eventually emerged into broad daylight. Covert ferment developed into public meetings, and actions by women and the elderly were followed up with those by sturdy young men. Discontent among a few individuals or households gradually spread to entire production teams, then to entire cooperatives or towns. The disturbances and withdrawals disrupted wheat planting in Linru County, and in Yu County's Yuxian Town only 18.6 percent of the winter plowing was completed. Production in Minquan County's Hunzi Town halted for a month because of conflicts. At Zhengyoumo Village in Zhongmou County's Liuzhuang Cooperative, eleven head of livestock died in one week after conflicts disrupted feeding.[10]

According to incomplete statistics, some 70,000 rural households, or 1 percent of the total, withdrew from Guangdong Province collectives by August 1957; 102 collapsed, and 127,000 households, or about 2 percent of the membership, were in the process of withdrawing. In Foshan Prefecture's industrialized cash crop counties of Shunde, Nanhai, and Zhongshan, the mass withdrawals affected 65 towns and more than 210 collectives. Villagers appealed to the provincial party committee for permission to withdraw and demanded the return of their original land-holdings and plow oxen. Some villagers locked up boats so the collective couldn't use them. Some people netted fish and plucked mulberry leaves at collective ponds and plantations, or tilled the collective fields for their own winter plantings. In many instances, cadres and collective leaders were surrounded and beaten by members attempting to withdraw.[11] Available statistics, albeit incomplete, from nine counties in Liaoning show that more than four thousand households had pulled out of collectives, taking their horses with them.[12]

Starting in spring 1957, disturbances occurred throughout Jiangsu Province. Some 60 to 70 percent of collective members who wanted to withdraw were classified as middle peasants. Most complained about loss of income, while others cited unreasonable compensation for their plow oxen, farming tools, and orchards; the lack of freedom within the collectives; or discriminatory treatment by cadres.[13]

Central party officials insisted that withdrawals were few, and that bad class background was the cause. A report by the CCP Central Committee's Rural Work Department cited complaints relating to lost income and excessive control over working hours, quoting peasant comments that the collectives were "exhausting and too restrictive, and the bullying is intolerable"; "Joining the cooperative is worse than being sent to a labor reform camp [*laogai*]; at least in the *laogai* camp you have Sunday off." Other sources of discontent were the insufferably dictatorial attitudes of the cadres, the irrational collectivization of every tree and shrub, and the inability to garner extra income from free markets.[14]

In response, the CCP Central Committee required all localities to persuade villagers of the superiority of the collectives and of the state monopoly for purchasing and marketing. Villagers were to be taught to comply and to see complainers as counterrevolutionaries. Mass debates were to be held on these topics to clarify basic questions of right and wrong. The Central Committee required party organs to send work groups to "criticize the capitalistic thinking of well-to-do middle peasants and oppose individualism and selfish interests that disregard the national interest and collective interest."[15]

This so-called socialist education was meant to single out political targets for struggle in the countryside in concert with the Anti-Rightist Campaign in the urban areas. The campaigns targeted those who criticized "foul-ups in collectivization" and "foul-ups in the state monopoly for purchasing and marketing," and who "opposed the CCP leadership." Villagers who resisted collectivization and the state monopoly were attacked for "having capitalist leanings." In Guangdong Province alone, more than 16,000 people were struggled against as "landlords, rich peasants, counterrevolutionaries, and other criminal elements." More than 2,000 were arrested, more than 1,100 had new political labels imposed on them, and 135 were put under surveillance. In Xianyang County, Shaanxi Province, 158 people were struggled against and 79 strung up and beaten. In Yiliang County, Yunnan Province, 643 people were struggled, with 102 beaten, 15 committing suicide, and 8 fleeing the county. Among the people struggled in Huilai County, Guangdong Province, one-third were beaten. In Shandong more than ten people were beaten or persecuted to death. Among the four-hundred-plus households in Wangkuai Village in Hebei's Xingtai County, sixty-five were labeled as rightists.[16]

The formula for treating poor peasants who opposed collectivization was to show them the advantages of acknowledging the errors of their ways. The case of "Liu Jiemei repents forgetting his origins" became a model for the whole nation. An impoverished resident of Huanggang County, Hubei Province, Liu became chairman of his local peasant association in 1950, joined the party, and headed a work team. During Land Reform he was allocated some land and assets (the confiscated property of wealthier villagers), and he dreamed of cultivating his field, engaging in business, and building a family fortune. When collectivization and the state monopoly dashed these hopes, he resisted. After being "taught" to see the error of his ways, Liu admitted to "forgetting his origins" and expressed his determination to return to the fold of socialism.[17] Newspapers trumpeted this official tale of the return of the prodigal son, and the Museum of the Chinese Revolution organized an exhibition that toured the country.

"THE PEOPLE'S COMMUNES ARE GOOD"

Villagers gradually resigned themselves to collectivization, and most young people actually favored it, galvanized by working with other young people instead of laboring under the stern discipline of their fathers. As rectification addressed some abuses, resisters became increasingly isolated and submitted to the inevitable.

The people's commune movement was launched from the top, in line with the central leadership's obsession with communism and with imposing totalitarian control. A massive irrigation campaign was critical in pushing the movement forward.

From the winter of 1957 to the spring of 1958, tens of millions were mobilized to engage in the construction of irrigation and water conservancy projects all over the country. Massive engineering projects required extensive labor and capital, which in turn required larger administrative jurisdictions. Mao therefore emphasized "the superiority of large collectives."

The lead story in *People's Daily* on April 12 promoted Mao's ideas on the conversion of small cooperatives into large collectives, turning small villages into large ones, and combining several into one large commune.

The leaders of Henan's Suiping County had moved toward giantism in attempting large-scale irrigation works and slope development that required coordinating the highlands and the flatlands. How could conflicts be resolved? Suiping County party secretary Lou Benyao and the deputy director of the county party committee's rural work department, Chen Bingyin, decided to follow the spirit of the Chengdu Conference and consolidate the towns of Baozhuang, Yangdian, Huaishu, and Tushan into a large collective, and requested advice from the prefecture.

Unwilling to wait, Lou and Chen convened a meeting of party secretaries and town heads, who agreed to the consolidation. A Chayashan collective was formally established on April 20, 1958, and prefectural party secretary Lu Xianwen approved the appointment of Chen Bingyin as party secretary and of Zhong Deqing, a national model worker and member of the county party committee, as the collective's head. The collective, which included 30,113 individuals in 5,566 households, was organized into eight departments: agriculture, industry, irrigation, forestry, livestock, culture, health, and communication and transportation. The county party committee named the collective the Chayashan Sputnik Agricultural Collective, inspired by the Soviet Union's 1957 *Sputnik* launch.

On May 5, 1958, Tan Zhenlin, secretary of the CCP Central Committee secretariat and vice-premier of the State Council, was visiting Henan and received Suiping County party secretary Lou Benyao. Tan asked, "Why are you calling it an agricultural collective? The type of management and distribution you're carrying out at this farm is actually of a higher level than that of the Soviet Union's agricultural collectives. I feel this is more akin to the situation at the Paris Commune, so it should be called a commune." The unit's name was changed accordingly to Chayashan Sputnik People's Commune.[18]

The term *commune* was actually coined by several central government leaders. In a speech at the first Zhengzhou Conference, Liu Shaoqi recalled, "I remember discussing the term 'commune' here with Comrade [Wu] Zhipu. On the train to the Guangzhou Conference [on April 25 or 26], [Zhou] Enlai, [Lu] Dingyi, Deng Liqun, and I were boasting about work-study programs, universal education, and also communes, utopia, and the transition to communism. We felt that the current socialist construction is preparing the conditions for communism."[19]

During this train ride, Liu Shaoqi talked about how socialism paved the way to communism, saying, "We have to make the first stage prepare the way for the second stage. That's how we accomplish revolution; before we take a new step, we have to think of the next step and create the conditions for it." They boasted about utopian socialism, nurseries, collectives, the collective lifestyle, about organizing schools inside factories, and factories inside schools. Liu Shaoqi asked Deng Liqun to edit a book on utopian socialism, and Lu Dingyi to compile a collection of quotes on communism by Marx, Engels, Lenin, and Stalin.[20]

When they reached Zhengzhou, Henan provincial party secretary Wu Zhipu met them. Liu told Wu what they had been discussing and asked Wu to experiment a bit. Wu was enthusiastic, and promoted self-contained experimental units integrating farming, manufacturing, social services, and commerce. The consolidation of towns and collectives had taken place some time earlier, without the use of the term *commune*, for work-study and collectivized living. The large units functioned before the term *commune* was adopted.

On May 19, Lu Dingyi told the National Party Congress,

> Speaking of the situation of our country a few decades from now, Chairman Mao and Comrade [Liu] Shaoqi have said that at that time our countryside will have many Communist communes, and that every commune will have its own agriculture, industry, universities, middle schools and primary schools, its own hospitals and scientific research institutes, its own shops and service industries, transportation, nurseries and communal kitchens, and its own clubs and police for maintaining public order. Several rural communes encircling a city can form an even larger Communist commune. The dream of utopia of our predecessors will come to fruition and will be surpassed.

This portion of Lu Dingyi's speech was added the night before he delivered it,[21] and reflected Mao's vision and expectations.

Lu Dingyi swiftly assembled the staff of the Central Committee's Propaganda Department to compile materials on communes and communism, completing a first draft in June. The first quote was from Engels's February 8, 1845, "Speech at Elberfeld," in which he described communism and referred twice to communes as the basic organization of Communist society. This spurred Mao's resolve to give the name "people's commune" to the new giant collectives. At the subsequent Beidaihe Conference, Mao recommended the book, *Marx, Engels, Lenin, and Stalin on Communism*, to all in attendance.

The people's communes were put on the agenda of the enlarged meeting of the CCP Central Committee Politburo on August 17, 1958, after which they spread like wildfire throughout the country.[22] Politburo member and deputy Propaganda Department chief Chen Boda sent the editor of *Red Flag* magazine to Chayashan, where he spent a month helping draft the "Charter of Chayashan Sputnik People's Commune." Chen Boda then passed the draft on to Mao, who regarded it as a treasure. He amended it and added a memo to his subordinates: "All comrades please discuss [this document]. This seems suitable for distribution to all provinces and counties as a reference document." *People's Daily* published the charter on September 24, 1958, under the title "The Trial Draft Plan of Chayashan People's Commune," and it became the blueprint for establishing communes throughout China.

The concept of the people's commune was formally introduced at the national level in *Red Flag* magazine on July 1, 1958. Chen Boda communicated Mao's vision in *Red Flag* on July 16: "Comrade Mao Zedong says that our direction should be the progressive and orderly integration of industry, agriculture, commerce, education, and the armed forces (militia; that is, all citizens in arms) into one large commune that constitutes the basic unit of our society."

Henan Province took the lead. Its communes averaged 7,000 households each, or 10,000 households in flatland areas. Xiuwu County tried to organize its entire population of 130,000 into one people's commune.[23]

On August 6, 1958, while inspecting Henan's Qiliying People's Commune, Mao said, "It looks like people's commune is a good name, encompassing industry, agriculture, commerce, education, and the military, and the management of production, livelihood, and political power. The masses can put whatever name they like at the beginning of people's commune." While inspecting Shandong Province on August 9, he said, "The people's communes are good. Their advantage is in combining industry, agriculture, commerce, education, and the military for more convenient management."[24] People's communes would comprehensively manage life.

The "CCP Central Committee Resolution Regarding the Establishment of People's Communes in the Countryside" was passed on August 29, 1958. It described the people's commune as leading peasants to achieve socialism ahead of schedule and progressively transition into communism: "The transition from collective ownership to full state ownership is a process. Some localities may proceed faster and complete it in three or four years, while others may proceed more slowly and require five or six years or even longer." The resolution ended with a bold declaration: "The realization of communism in our country is no longer an event for the distant future. We should actively employ the people's commune as a means of forging a concrete path for the transition to communism."

The entire countryside was then organized into communes; apart from Tibet and some other areas, China's 27 provinces and autonomous regions were organized into 23,384 people's communes comprising 90.4 percent of all rural households. In 12 provinces, every rural household joined a commune.[25] By the end of October, there were reportedly 26,576 people's communes incorporating 99.1 percent of households.[26] These were soon broken down into 52,781 smaller communes.

The people's communes were characterized by the phrase "big and collective" (*yida ergong*). Using size to achieve economies of scale requires effective management. The average commune contained five thousand households, which gave rise to serious problems of chaotic management and coercive commandism. In some mountain areas, the large scale brought even greater problems. At Heping Commune in Pu'er County, Yunnan Province, the Yalu production brigade included seven different ethnic groups in its 552 households, and covered an area spanning forty kilometers from east to west and thirty kilometers from north to south. Apart from a significant number of stand-alone households, there were thirty-nine natural villages comprised of as few as three households. Most of the production teams were located five to ten kilometers apart, and one team included villages that were seventeen kilometers apart. Consolidation into one brigade in 1958, and the implementation of unified distribution and income leveling, caused a steady decrease in production. This was a typical example.[27]

Collective referred to the system of ownership. Land, livestock, farming implements, and all other means of production and commonly held assets were transferred to the commune under a centralized accounting system. Land that had been cultivated for household use, along with privately owned assets such as woodland and livestock, were also claimed by the communes, eliminating all "remnants of private ownership of the means of production." The transfer of basic-level state management of grain supplies, commerce, finance, and banking from village-level economic units to the people's communes added a state ownership component. Likewise, eradicating the "remnants of private ownership of the means of production" allowed the collective to "collect" private assets.

Maintaining the requisite scale and countering resistance to collectivization required a highly concentrated power structure—economic organization, production plans, labor deployment, allocation of resources, distribution of produce, and even what should be planted on a particular piece of land and under what standards. Production teams merely organized the manpower. As an administrative unit, the commune supervised construction, finance, trade, civil administration, education and culture, health and sanitation, public security, the military, and all other matters in its geographical jurisdiction. At the outset, communes also organized military affairs. All assets came under the control of government officials, and the government took on the roles previously played by family, religion, and other social organizations.

The commune's party committee provided the core leadership. Each production brigade had its own party branch, the secretary of which was appointed by the commune party committee. The production brigade party branch implemented the decisions of the commune party committee, and the brigade's party secretary was in charge of all of the brigade's operations. Since the brigade party secretary was typically reappointed for several terms, his power increased over time, and some party secretaries became tyrants.

The number of officials soared. The commune level had at least thirty cadres, and a production brigade usually had around ten, while a production team typically had five. The system of 52,781 communes, 690,000 brigades, and 4,810,000 teams involved upwards of 60 million cadres of various ranks, making up 7 percent of the rural population and consuming 10 to 30 percent of rural incomes. Villagers commented, "In the past, several villages provided for the upkeep of one cadre; now one village has to provide for the upkeep of a team of cadres."[28] Imposing central decrees on every rural family routinely involved bursting into homes with knife, gun, or cudgel. Every peasant was fettered to the administrative system; there was no more civil society, only the state.

The "free-supply" system of rationing that replaced distribution based on labor made wartime "military communism" part of daily economic life. In theory, free-supply rationing covered grain, food, and daily necessities. The most widely implemented was meal rations, provided to peasants without charge. The bulk of communes implemented a "seven guarantees" or "ten guarantees" rationing system. The "seven guarantees" included meals, clothing, childbirth, housing, education, medical treatment, and marriage and funeral services. The "ten guarantees" included all of these plus heating, haircuts, and movies.

In practice, the government lacked the capacity to provide these things. The system was short-lived and enormously wasteful, especially in regard to food supplies. As the "providers" of all basic necessities, officials could enrich themselves while increasing control over the daily lives of villagers on a most basic level. Recalcitrant commune members could be barred from the canteens where meals were provided.

Life was organized as for a military campaign, including collective living arrangements for men and women alike. The steel-forging, irrigation, and agriculture campaigns, communal kitchens, and nurseries imposed a communal system that replaced the family unit.

Chayashan People's Commune in Henan Province established twenty-seven production corps and one steel production corps. One production team formed a regiment, one sub-team formed a battalion, and under the battalions, villages and project teams were organized into companies, platoons, and squads. Members were expected to adhere to the following rules: obey the leader and follow orders; take an active role in production, don't arrive late or leave early; put collective interests before individual interests; wage a constant struggle against capitalist thinking; take care of public property; and cooperate. Members were to work at least twenty-eight days each month. Applications for leave could be made to the platoon commander for half a day, to the company commander for one day, and to the battalion commander for more than one day. Everyone was to respond to bugle calls to rise in the morning, take their meals, begin and finish work, and finally go to sleep in unison. Village housing was replaced by a barracks system, with men living in the eastern barracks, women in the western barracks, and children and the elderly housed in the "rear" barracks. A young couple seeking time alone, when discovered by a military patrol, would be brought back for mass criticism, the man admitting his error with hanging head, the woman helpless with weeping.[29]

Control was virtually total. Political power extended into the most remote corners of China's map and allowed the dictatorship of the proletariat to invade every family, every brain, and every stomach.

The supremacy of power and worship of the leader initially sapped resistance to the expropriation of assets, but resistance increased as hardships intensified and villagers chafed under their enslavement. The rulers resorted to constant political movements and ideological indoctrination, while expanding the scope of so-called class struggle to impose harsh punishment on all dissent. As the CCP Central Committee promoted the people's communes, it also ordered a "Socialist and Communist Education Movement" as a major sweep against non-Communist ideology. The effectiveness of their tactics made those in power even more enamored of their might and even less likely to seek alternatives to coercion.

The multitudes of rural cadres were the key to the totalitarian system's penetration of every corner of the countryside. China's rural cadres had come of age through the Land Reform movement, and Land Reform veterans were the most ardent promoters of collectivization. Even so, not every Land Reform cadre was retained as a rural commune cadre. One official in Jiangsu noted that "village cadres were put through something like a sifting process," and that during a movement, "a certain number of cadres were sifted out." The sifting standard was obedience to the party. For most villagers during the Imperial era, the sovereign was as remote as the heavens above. Under the people's communes, however, government and management integrated under a phalanx of cadres tested for subservience ensured that the party's voice would be heard and obeyed by every individual. Control was thus imposed with unprecedented thoroughness.

THE RETREAT FROM COMMUNISM TO SOCIALISM

The pervasive control under the people's communes was presented as an ultimate good. One slogan, attributed to Mao's ally Kang Sheng, stated that "communism is paradise, and the people's commune is the golden bridge."

Mao's fascination with the people's communes can be traced back to his youthful passion for the New Village Movement. In December 1919 he wrote:

> The basic ideal is connecting the New Family, New School, and the New Society into one unit.
>
> Each student in the New School creates a member of the New Family. The more students there are in the New School, the more New Families will be created. Combining several New Families can create a New Society. The New Society is inexhaustible in its variety, including public nurseries, public nursing homes, public schools, public libraries, public banks, public farms, public factories, public stores, public theaters, public hospitals, parks, museums, and autonomous regions.[30]

The young Mao was influenced by Kang Youwei's *The Great Harmony* and the Japanese warrior Mushanokoji Saneatsu's New Village (*Atarashiki-mura*) Movement.[31] Mao had joined with others to plan a "New Village" in Yuelushan where thinkers could work and study together and share their assets and the fruits of their labor. He had never had the opportunity to put that plan into practice.

In 1958, Mao believed the time had finally come. He had written, "When Kang Youwei wrote *The Great Harmony*, he had not and could not have found a road to that Great Harmony."[32] Mao believed he had found that road in the communes.

Many central leaders likewise propagated the benefits of communism. They passed a resolution at the Beidaihe Conference to achieve full state ownership in "a minimum of three to five years and a maximum of five to six years." During discussions on the communes, Mao said, "In about ten years, more or less, our produce may be extremely plentiful, our ethics impeccable; we will be able to practice communism in the food we eat, the clothes we wear, and the homes we live in. Free food in communal canteens—that's communism." He added, "Comrade Liu Zihou in Hebei Province brought in ten or so people to talk about Communist thinking and work styles . . . you should also boast like that."[33]

Devastation spread within two or three months as the Communist Wind raised by the people's commune movement swept across China. Peasants began to grumble, and Mao and other leaders were compelled to make adjustments. Even so, response to the crisis could not transcend the confines of ideology and system. Specific errors could be corrected, but only superficial changes were allowed, and the Three Red Banners could not be challenged.

On October 13, Mao left Beijing to journey south, and he did not return to Zhongnanhai until the last day of the year. During his October inspection trip, his mood and tone were considerably more subdued than on previous tours.

CCP Central Committee meetings in late 1958 in Zhengzhou and Wuchang produced a resolution that gave high marks to the communes but reined in the popular fervor for communism. The leaders decided that: (1) the present stage was still socialism, not communism; (2) the communes still employed collective ownership, not public ownership; (3) the production of commodities still required considerable development; and (4) it was necessary to continue maintaining distribution according to work done. At the same time, the resolution tried to keep to the course of action of the previous several months, finding that distribution combining wages with rationing was "a pioneering undertaking in the mode of socialist distribution" and that it "possessed the sprouts of communism." Mao continued to praise free meals, however, indicating that his retreat to socialism was ambivalent at best.

The CCP Central Committee Politburo held an enlarged meeting in Zhengzhou from February 27 to March 5, 1959 (subsequently referred to as the Second Zhengzhou Conference). Mao put forward fourteen paired phrases to serve as the guiding principles for the communes:

1. unified leadership with the production team as the basic accounting unit;
2. tiered management delegating power downward;
3. three-tiered accounting, with profits and losses calculated for each unit;
4. distribution determined by the communes;
5. appropriate accrual and reasonable transfer;
6. equal value exchange of goods, capital, and labor;
7. and distribution according to work done, with acknowledgment of differences.[34]

This constituted a retreat from communal ownership. A subsequent Politburo meeting in Shanghai in March and April took the retreat to "ownership by the production brigades" a step further through a three-tiered accounting system with "production teams as the basic accounting unit."

The Lushan Conference from July 2 to August 16, 1959, brought this retreat to a grinding halt, however, and put the cadres responsible for restricting communism under severe political attack. A campaign against right deviation accelerated the transition to communal ownership with even greater urgency.

As famine intensified in 1960 and the number of deaths rose, Mao Zedong finally began to revise his policy in the second half of the year. During the Beidaihe Conference in July and August, he acknowledged that there were problems with his March 4 memo on communal kitchens and that it should be amended. Then, in a November 28 report, he noted, "I have also made mistakes and must correct them."[35] As a result, policies in effect prior to the Lushan Conference were allowed to resume, as long as they did not injure the Three Red Banners. Class struggle methods were also used against cadres accused of the "five unhealthy tendencies," or Five Winds. In effect, local officials were scapegoated in a way that consolidated the government's power and intensified its extralegal behavior.

It was not until September 27, 1962, that the basic accounting unit of the people's communes changed back to small production teams. Then commune members were once again remunerated based on labor, with a welfare fund meeting the needs of hard-up households, and each unit was once again responsible for its own profits and losses. Ownership reverted to the conditions under the collectives. This economic retreat came about, however, only after the devastating cost of the three-year Great Famine. The political system of total control was still in place, though, and remained unchanged.

5 THE COMMUNAL KITCHENS

The communal kitchens, although a component of the people's communes, deserve separate attention because of their direct relevance to the Great Famine. Communal kitchens opened in the summer and autumn of 1958 and closed in the summer of 1961, but their disastrous consequences far surpassed that brief time frame.

ELIMINATING THE FAMILY UNIT

Seeing the family as the social foundation of the private ownership system and a major impediment to communism, some reformers advocated eliminating the family, a notion that appealed to Mao and other leaders of China's Communist Party in their youth.

In a speech on March 22, 1958, Mao said:

> In socialism, private property still exists, factions still exist, families still exist. Families are the product of the last stage of primitive communism, and every last trace of them will be eliminated in the future. Kang You-wei perceived this in his *Great Harmony*. Historically, the family has been a production unit, a consumption unit, and a unit for giving birth to the next generation of the labor force and educating children. Now worker families are no longer production units . . . This is even more the case for families involved in the bureaucracy and the army . . . it is possible that in the future, the family will no longer be beneficial to the development of productivity . . . Many of our comrades don't dare to consider problems of this nature because their thinking is too narrow.[1]

Once Mao gave voice to these thoughts, his followers took action. Some localities had organized canteens for the busy farming seasons.

After the upper leadership praised this as the apogee of communism, the practice of communal mess halls spread.

Mao and the other leaders were ecstatic at the emergence of a means of implementing their Communist ideals, and Mao repeatedly praised the communal kitchens. On December 10 he touted the actions of the late Han warlord Zhang Lu,[2] in particular the provision of lodging and food at no cost. Mao wrote, "The most interesting part is eating at road-houses along the way without having to pay, which is a precedent for our people's commune canteens . . . The 'Biography of Zhang Lu' is worth reading."[3]

During two visits to Henan Province's "bumper wheat harvest exhibitions" on July 19 and August 6, 1958, Zhou Enlai commended the communal kitchens. When he heard that Henan's communal canteens didn't charge for their meals, he said, "Shanghai's communal canteens only sell meals—they're not as good as those here." He said thorough liberation required liberating women from their household duties, and he promoted communal kitchens and communal nurseries as the sprouts of communism.[4]

Some of Liu Shaoqi's encouraging words for communal mess halls are quite revealing. Speaking to the leading party group of the All-China Women's Federation on June 14, 1958, he noted:

Chairman Mao speaks of "three no's": no government, no country, no family. This will be implemented everywhere in the future. Chairman Mao has said twice that the family must be eliminated. I wonder how well you understand this concept. You need to sit down and talk about it. Of course the elimination of the family won't happen tomorrow, but sometime in the future. In China, Kang Youwei was the first to talk of eliminating the family. He advocated men and women marrying for no more than a year, and said that this would eliminate families in sixty years. He was thinking in terms of eliminating private property; he believed that families held private property and that by eliminating families it would be possible to eliminate private property. He said that if a wife and children were considered to be one's personal property, it would be impossible to achieve the common good for all [*tianxia weigong*]. For that reason, he advocated eliminating the family.

Chairman Mao says the family is a historically produced phenomenon and will be eliminated . . .

At present there is a great deal of wasted manpower in society . . . Household duties are performed by each family; every family makes meals, every family washes clothes, every family raises children, every family mends clothes and makes shoes . . . Embarking on Communist society should liberate women from all household labor. For that reason, this is my vision: we need to establish many nurseries and communal kitchens, and run many service-type industries. Henan has an agricultural cooperative with more than 500 households, among which more than 200 households run a communal kitchen and no longer cook meals at home. After the communal kitchen was organized, the workforce increased by 30 percent. Previously 200 people were cooking meals, and now only 40 people cook—and people are eating more and better, while saving grain. The biggest advantage is the reduction from 200 people cooking to 40 people cooking. Making cooking a collective undertaking has brought greater productivity and economy.[5]

After foreign publications criticized the CCP for wanting to eliminate the family, China's newspapers stopped referring to this goal in order to prevent "giving the reactionaries a pretext for gossip." The slogan of eliminating private ownership was retained, however, and propaganda encouraging the implementation of communism continued unabated. From then on, communal kitchens proliferated rapidly. In some places, communal canteens gained the participation of every peasant family within ten days.[6]

By the end of 1958 more than 3.4 million communal kitchens had been set up, with an estimated 90 percent of the country's rural population taking their meals in them.[7] The communal kitchen movement reached its apogee in October 1958.

Eliminating the family unit gave officials greater control. A July 1959 survey[8] found that "People eat together in the canteens and go out to work together . . . Before the canteens, commune members could only work for seven to eight hours a day; now they work an average of ten hours a day . . . At breakfast, as soon as the bowls are pushed away, the section heads lead people out to work . . . Before and after meals, commune members read newspapers and listen to radio broadcasts together, improving their education in communism." The alleged advantages of communal kitchens, such as saving labor and giving commune members more and better food to eat, all proved to be false, but the increased control over commune members was genuine.

Eliminating the family as a basic living unit reduced its capacity to combat famine. Without pots and pans, it was impossible even to boil water at home, let alone prepare food substitutes to stave off hunger.

COMMUNAL KITCHENS DRIVE RURAL FAMILIES TO DESTITUTION

In setting up the mess halls, homes were dismantled and woks, basins, bowls, cups, and other cooking utensils, plus chairs and tables, were requisitioned. Grain supplies were centralized at the communal kitchen, along with firewood, livestock, and poultry. Even wild herbs were handed over to the canteen. In some villages, cadres allowed commune members to retain a few pots and pans to reheat food brought home from the mess hall.

Kindergartens, nurseries, and facilities for the elderly were established with resources seized from families without compensation, and homes were vacated to house the facilities. In Mao's home village, "Upwards of 30 percent of the residential area was affected by the chaotic organization of communal dining and living quarters. Original owners could not return to their own homes, and people who had lived in their own homes were unable to preserve their property rights, leaving every family in a state of uncertainty."[9] In some localities, widely dispersed residences were demolished, and "Communist New Villages" were built in centralized locations. If a home was torn down before a new village was built, families had to be split up, with males and females quartered separately.

When Liu Shaoqi visited his home county in 1961, officials told him that Ningxiang County had a population of 840,000, but that its original 700,000 dwellings had been reduced to 450,000. Of those, more than 30,000 had been occupied by the state and the collective without compensating the owners, leaving only 420,000 dwellings for commune members.[10] Buildings were also demolished to use old brick for a great "fertilizer collection campaign."

Cadres and militia ransacked homes and sometimes beat and detained occupants. When villagers handed over their assets, it was in an atmosphere of extreme political pressure. The campaign against private property rendered many families destitute and homeless.

Mess hall facilities had been constructed in April and May of 1959 in Wanle and Wannian in Sichuan Province. More than 1,000 yuan was spent on the Wannian communal kitchen for paint, whitewash, plaster, doors, and windows at a time when pay for one day's labor was only about 0.20 yuan. Around the same amount of money was spent on the Wanle mess hall, which could seat 700 to 800 people at a time. The dining hall of the Wannian communal kitchen seated around 500 to 600. Apart from their red-and-green-painted main dining halls, both canteens had several side rooms with colorful signs designating them as "Club Room," "Library," "Storeroom," "Male Visitors," "Female Visitors," "Tailor," "Barber," "Clinic," "Nursery," and so on. The gaily decorated walls were festooned with bulletin boards for ideological writings. Walking into the canteen parlor, one was greeted by a long table covered with a colorful tapestry and flower vases, thermos flasks full of hot water, and reading materials. In the entryway was a flower bed with calla lilies, garden balsam, and orchids. A dozen flagpoles protruded above the main entrance, with China's national flag hanging from the central and highest position.

Each household contributed four to five yuan toward the cost of the canteens. The premises had been obtained through "persuasion," with dozens of households required to leave their homes. The hundred tables and four-hundred-odd benches in each dining hall had been similarly commandeered; all items were painted a uniform color to prevent recognition by their erstwhile owners. Once completed, the facilities received an endless stream of visitors and raised a buzz of excitement. The dining hall servers and kitchen staff all wore white uniforms and aprons decorated with a lotus leaf motif. Visitors helped themselves to white rice, steamed rolls, stuffed buns, steamed buns, and meat and vegetable dishes, while ordinary commune members ate watery gruel.[11]

In theory, households were still allocated private plots, known as *ziliudi*, but they were not to exceed 5 percent of the village's average per capita land allocation.[12] However, a CCP Central Committee resolution promulgated on August 29, 1958, stipulated that "plots of land for personal use may become collectively run in the process of merging the commune."[13] Since families no longer cooked at home, it was supposedly unnecessary to grow one's own vegetables, and with no livestock of one's own, it was unnecessary to produce animal feed. The CCP Central Committee recommended that "land allocated for personal use of commune members must be transferred to the communal kitchen." Sichuan was the first province to do this, and as provincial party secretary Li Jingquan subsequently observed, "It's a good thing we insisted on taking back land allocated for private use in Luzhou Prefecture last year;

otherwise we'd have had to fight hard to set up communal kitchens this year."[14]

With the confiscation of livestock, poultry, and household plots, only collective production was left. When the famine struck, families had no means of saving themselves and could only await death. This situation continued until November 1960, when the CCP Central Committee surrendered to reason and stipulated, "Commune members should be allowed to farm small amounts of land allocated for private use." This stipulation still maintained that only a maximum of 5 percent of the average per capita landholding could be allocated for household use,[15] and as it was winter by then, villagers could not immediately solve their food shortage problems.

THE RISE AND FALL OF THE COMMUNAL KITCHENS

With free mess halls, commune members gorged themselves for two months until food supplies ran out, at which time many communal kitchens closed, while a large portion operated only intermittently. In the Hongliugou production brigade of Jinya Commune in Gansu's Yuzhong County, all 308 members of the brigade's 54 households joined the communal kitchen within ten days in August 1958. At the outset, every individual received a grain ration of half a kilo a day (in actuality, slightly more), and once their appetites were whetted, they went on to steamed buns, noodles, and cooked rice, with additional offerings of stuffed buns and steamed twisted rolls on holidays. With everyone eating their fill, little notice was taken of cadres and kitchen staff helping themselves to a little extra. In April 1959 the grain ration was lowered, first to 375 grams, then to 250 grams, and the extra food taken by cadres and kitchen staff was now greatly resented. After nine months, the communal kitchen closed. In November 1959 an order came down to reopen the kitchen, but the commune members were unwilling, precipitating a "struggle between the two roads." A dozen or so households were coerced into rejoining the communal kitchen, while the rest didn't join until April 1960, when the grain allocation from the production team and the remaining food from the prior household plots was gone. At that time, the per capita grain ration was only 250 grams per day. Villagers ate coarse gruel, and sometimes not even that. There were many complaints. After the Central Committee reversed itself, commune members started eating at home again in December 1960, and the communal kitchens were effectively dismantled. They were revived again about nine months later. These two stages totaled about eighteen months.[16] My investigations indicate that the experience of Yuzhong County was typical.

Mao remained optimistic as the communal kitchens opened and closed. At the end of November 1958 he said:

> If communal kitchens serve cold rice or only rice and no vegetables, some of them are bound to close down. It would be unrealistic to expect otherwise. It's only reasonable for those that are poorly run to be closed. Generally speaking, the collapse is partial and temporary, and those not collapsing will keep running forever; the overall trend is toward development and consolidation.
>
> I go around talking about unfortunate matters, whether it's the collapse of communal kitchens or communes or splits in the party . . . guerrilla warfare. We have Marxism to guide us. No matter what, these unfortunate matters are temporary and localized.[17]

By the summer of 1959, the famine was intense, and popular criticism of the communal kitchens grew bolder. The CCP Central Committee's Propaganda Department found local officials unhappy with the mess halls, with some recommending "overthrowing the communal kitchens" or "disbanding the communal kitchens" and others noting many shortcomings.[18]

In the face of famine, the Central Committee on May 26, 1959, put forward the idea of "genuinely rectifying the communal kitchens," and stipulated, "Grain rations are to be distributed to households and individuals. Those who eat at the communal kitchens are to hand over their rations to the communal kitchens, and any savings are to be passed back to the individual. Those who don't eat at the communal kitchens are to take care of and use the rations themselves."[19] In May and June, the Central Committee restored allocating plots of land for household use and allowed commune members to raise their own livestock and poultry. The communal kitchens changed in the first half of 1959. The main measures included implementing the principles of "allocation of grain rations to households, voluntary participation, grain rations set on an individual basis, surplus all returned to the individual"; adjusting the scale of the communal kitchens in line with production and the convenience of commune members, with most using production teams as the basic unit; in accordance with the principle of freedom, decreasing with greater collectivization, adopting more flexible methods and stressing the convenience of commune members; and establishing the necessary democratic management system and financial management system. These emergency measures led to some improvement.

Nonetheless, grain seldom left the grasp of the production team. In the course of my inquiries in twelve provinces, I found that the practice of designating rations to households while the actual grain remained in the possession of the work team was universal. Cadres were unwilling to distribute grain to households because then commune members would not take their meals at the communal kitchens, and the kitchens would have to close down. In the winter of 1960, when 396 communal kitchens closed down in Zhejiang's Ningbo Prefecture, in 176 cases it was because grain had been distributed to households.[20]

Villages in some areas abolished the ration system and disbanded the communal kitchens. In the first half of May 1959, Sichuan's Luzhou prefectural party committee convened a meeting of county party secretaries at which agreement was reached to suspend operation of communal kitchens. Longchang County disbanded 98.72 percent of its communal kitchens (including some that had already closed down); Fushun County, 75.5 percent (in addition to those already closed); Hejiang County, 63 percent (including those already closed); Xuyong County, 75 percent (including a small number of those already closed); and Lu County and Gulin County also disbanded most of their communal kitchens.[21] Zhang Kaifan, a member of Anhui's provincial party secretariat, on a temporary oversight mission in Wuwei County, observed villagers struggling at the brink of starvation and he chose to disband more than four thousand communal kitchens.[22] Hebei Province had more than 99 percent of the rural population taking meals at canteens after the autumn harvest of 1958. By the end of June 1959, only 19.65 percent continued to take their meals communally.[23]

Mao Zedong was extremely displeased with the collapse of the communal kitchens. On June 22, 1959, while on a VIP train taking him to the Lushan Conference, he told Henan's leaders, "We have to carry on with the communal kitchens, and we can carry on with them. I don't want your communal kitchens to close down; I hope they can keep running."[24] On the boat to Lushan on June 29, Mao convened an enlarged meeting of the Politburo standing committee, during which he reaffirmed the need for communal kitchens while proposing some modifications: allocation based on individuals, distribution to households, voluntary participation, and surplus returned to the individual. If necessary, locales could charge for meals, with only a minority eating for free. In Sichuan, for example, children and the elderly were not charged, and Hubei used a partial rationing system. Rationing could make up the smaller proportion—say, 30 percent or 40 percent, with room for flexibility—but the rationing system should not be abandoned.[25]

While speaking on communal kitchens during the Lushan Conference in July and August, Peng Dehuai cited "prematurely offering free meals" and "advocating eating to one's heart's content" as "a kind of leftist inclination."[26] Zhou Xiaozhou found that the communal kitchens "paid no regard to conserving grain, raising pigs, renewing timberland, or collecting manure, and wasted manpower while failing to provide satisfactory meals."[27] Zhang Wentian pointed out, "Some people equate the rationing system and communal kitchens with socialism and communism, and fear that abolishing the rationing system is insufficiently progressive and that withdrawing from the communal kitchens is nonsocialist. In fact, these are different matters altogether and fall into different categories. Socialism does not necessarily employ methods such as rationing and communal kitchens."[28] These senior officials who dared to speak the truth were labeled as members of a right-deviating anti-party clique, and their correct views were regarded as evidence of their crimes of right opportunism.

In his lengthy speech to the Lushan Conference on July 23, Mao Zedong countered, "The communal kitchens are a good thing and cannot be greatly faulted. I endorse operating them with vigor and enthusiasm." He added, "Some that have been disbanded must be resumed." He said that places that persisted in operating communal kitchens, "Henan, Sichuan, Hubei, and so on are leftist. But the right has emerged: a science academy survey group went to Hebei's Changli County and came out with a lot of rubbish about the communal kitchens, finding nothing at all good about them, attacking one aspect and ignoring all the rest."[29]

On August 5, Mao commented:

Dozens of communal kitchens in one production brigade all closed at once. Then after a while they reopened. The lesson is: we should not bow our heads in the face of difficulty. Matters such as the people's communes and communal kitchens have a deep social and economic basis . . .

Perhaps in a few days, or in a few weeks or months, or after an even longer time, sooner or later they will be revived. Mr. Sun Yatsen said, "All matters must take place in their due time, in accordance with nature, human feeling, world trends, and the needs of the mass of people, and what those with foresight carry out with determination cannot but succeed."[30] This is a true saying. Our Great Leap Forward and people's communes belong in this category. There will always be difficulties, and people will invariably make mistakes, but these can be surmounted and rectified. The trend toward pessimism is an extremely evil trend that corrupts the party and the people; it violates the will of the proletariat and the impoverished peasants, and also violates Marxism-Leninism.[31]

Mao applied political labels such as "right-opportunistic element" to those who disbanded communal kitchens. Particularly enraged by the actions of Secretary Zhang Kaifan of Anhui's provincial party secretariat, Mao accused him of "deliberately sabotaging the dictatorship of the proletariat and splitting the Communist Party." The propaganda apparatus followed Mao's lead, singing the praises of the communal kitchens and castigating critical viewpoints. On September 20, 1959, *People's Daily* reprinted an article from *Women of China* (*Zhongguo funü*) entitled "Done Correctly, Done Well, and Done at the Right Time," which rebutted the view that the communal kitchens had been organized too early, too quickly, and too haphazardly.

On September 22, 1959, *People's Daily* editorialized on "The Boundless Prospects of the Communal Kitchens": "At a time when most peasants enthusiastically support the communal kitchens, we not only have a few distant imperialists kick up a great fuss about it, but even some individuals in our very midst incorrigibly cling to their accustomed power and take advantage of the temporary shortcomings of a few communal kitchens to engage in indiscreet debate." The editorial ended by saying, "The calumny and slander leveled at our communal kitchens by the imperialists have only served once again to expose their shamelessness and ignorance . . . Is their greatest anxiety and fear not precisely what our country's working people most enjoy and love?" "As for those right-opportunistic elements, if they persist in views that distance them from the masses and school themselves in the tune of the imperialists . . . sooner or later they will discover that it is they themselves that the people will forsake, and not the people's communes or the communal kitchens."

In implementing the spirit of the Lushan Conference, each province found a "rightist" to attack, its own "Zhang Kaifan." The situation was most intense in Sichuan Province. Before the Lushan Conference, on May 22, 1959, on learning of the disbanding of communal kitchens in one prefecture, the provincial party committee immediately declared the action right-deviating and ordered the prefecture to resume the communal kitchens. A few days later, provincial party secretary Li Jingquan telephoned the prefectural party committee to demand that the canteens resume within seven days. He accused well-to-do peasant cadres of undermining the mess halls with the intention of undermining the people's communes and opposing socialism. He demanded harsh criticism of any cadres who resisted resumption of the communal kitchens and the immediate arrest of those who had undermined the communal kitchens and initiated a run on foodstuffs. Most of the communal kitchens then resumed despite a lack of food. Following the Lushan Conference, the Sichuan provincial party committee labeled as right-opportunistic elements those prefectural party committee members who permitted canteens to close.[32] The provincial party committee directed, "[R]ectify the grassroots organization, dismiss and replace those right deviationists, and consolidate the leadership dominance of enthusiastic supporters of the General Line, Great Leap Forward, and communization movement."[33]

Communal kitchens that had been closed down reopened under the enormous political pressure of the campaign against right deviation. According to January 1960 figures from the State Statistical Bureau, up to the end of 1959, four hundred million people were taking their meals in the canteens, comprising 72.6 percent of the population of the communes.

Provinces or major cities in which at least 90 percent of the population joined communal kitchens included Henan (97.8 percent), Hunan (97.6 percent), Sichuan (96.7 percent), Yunnan (96.5 percent), Guizhou (92.6 percent), Shanghai (94.5 percent), and Anhui (90.5 percent); 70 to 90 percent of the population joined in Beijing (87.4 percent), Xinjiang (85.1 percent), Zhejiang (81.6 percent), Guangxi (81.0 percent), Guangdong (77.6 percent), Hebei (74.4 percent), and Shanxi (70.6 percent); 50 to 70 percent of the population joined in Hubei (68.2 percent), Fujian (67.2 percent), Jiangxi (61 percent), Shaanxi (60.8 percent), Jiangsu (56 percent), and Ningxia (52.9 percent); less than 50 percent of the population joined in Gansu (47.7 percent), Shandong (35.5 percent), Qinghai (29.9 percent),

Jilin (29.4 percent), Heilongjiang (26.5 percent), Liaoning (23 percent), and Inner Mongolia (16.7 percent).[34]

Statistics for the end of February 1960 showed that the percentage of the rural population taking their meals at mess halls comprised 99.0 percent in Henan, 86.1 in Hebei, 81.0 in Shanxi, 63.3 in Gansu, 55.4 in Shandong, 40.0 in Heilongjiang, 33.0 in Liaoning, and 29.4 in Jilin.[35]

As food ran out over the winter, however, the passing of the 1960 Spring Festival brought a rash of closures. The Central Committee responded with classic methods, for example, describing the experience of a model from which the entire nation could learn. The point was that "elements among the well-to-do middle peasant class who opposed the people's communes sabotaged the communal kitchens as a first step in sabotaging the people's communes." On March 4, Mao wrote and distributed to every province a memo on a report about such a model. He wrote:

The Guizhou provincial party committee's report on the current situation of the rural communal kitchens is very good and is hereby distributed to all of you to emulate and implement, without exception. The Central Committee has passed this judgment because this report on the communal kitchens in Guizhou is a scientific summing up that will help us make a great leap forward in the transition from socialism to communism in the next five to ten years. For that reason, the whole country must follow this example, without exception. Following this example will require taking measures, will require strong leadership . . . If all of China's communal kitchens can reach the standard of Guizhou in 1960, that will be very good. In places where leadership is weaker, more time may be needed, and they can be given until 1961. It may even be possible to allow a little more time . . . I request that you convene large-scale meetings in the spring regarding communal kitchens—this is a priority.[36]

Model Guizhou Province was among the provinces that eventually suffered the largest percentage of starvation deaths relative to its total population, officially 5.3 percent of the province's population of 17 million. The province also experienced a reduction of 1.2 million births from 1958 to 1961. The famine hit most severely in 1960, and as villagers struggled on the brink of death, policy pushed them over the edge. It was at this time that the provincial report Mao praised claimed that the masses extolled the communal kitchens: "The communal kitchens are really great! With communal kitchens we have something to rely on, and we eat our fill of soft rice and fragrant dishes, going from strength to strength!" The report claimed that because some communal kitchens were operating so effectively, members had surrendered their plots of land to the communal kitchens. Supposedly, communal kitchens provided the atmosphere of a big family, and consolidation of residential areas was creating the conditions for building New Villages.

The report went on to say, "The greatest source of conflict between us and the well-to-do middle peasants has been opposition to the communal kitchens." "It is essential to stabilize the communal kitchens as bases of socialism."[37]

After the Center endorsed the Guizhou model, it promoted the Hebei provincial party committee's requirement that all rural branch secretaries and production team cadres take their meals at communal kitchens, except in cases of illness or other special circumstances. Cadres had to accept the same rations as ordinary commune members and not help themselves to larger rations or better fare. In addition, all cadres who visited the countryside were required to take their meals in the canteens.[38] These provisions came with no oversight or penalties, and were therefore all but impossible to implement.

On March 18, 1960, the CCP Central Committee issued a document to all localities recommending more model experiences. A report on Henan Province stated that 99 percent of the rural population took their meals at mess halls. About 66 percent of the canteens were well run, another 31.2 percent were second class, and only 2.8 percent were categorized as third class. Mao believed this report and wrote:

> Regarding this extremely important matter of the communal kitchens, I ask all of you to focus on it twice this year, once in the first half of the year and once in the second half, studying the scientific summing up carried out in Guizhou, Henan, and other provinces and applying it universally. At each of the four levels from the province to the commune, welfare committees should be organized and should delegate as leader a party secretary who understands politics, is enthusiastic and diligent, good at analyzing problems, conscientious in carrying out inspections at

the communal kitchens, and free from a bureaucratic work style. Each communal kitchen should organize a communal kitchen management committee.

With the entire country mobilized to criticize Peng Dehuai for his frank comments at the Lushan Conference, and with the campaign against right deviation reaching a climax, no province dared to report anything derogatory about the communal kitchens.

A Central Committee document stated, "At present, most communal kitchens are well run." The five criteria for effective operation were: growing vegetables and rearing pigs, eating enough and eating well, establishing a management system incorporating commune members, improving kitchen facilities, and meeting sanitation standards. The report also said, "Rectification and consolidation of communes is being undertaken everywhere, with purges and restructuring among communal kitchen staff . . . and training of supervisors, cooks, and custodians." "Many communal kitchens are improving their kitchen facilities; in Henan Province, half of the communal kitchens have undergone mechanization." "There has been great improvement in the management of the communal kitchens . . . Shandong has established a welfare committee . . . Henan has established a canteen management committee . . . Many places have established livelihood committees."[39]

The report called for focusing on several issues: First, the grain ration distribution policy comprised "quotas allocated to households, grain distributed to the communal kitchen." In other words, commune members received only a quota, and the actual grain remained in the possession of the canteens. This was a move leftward from the pre-Lushan 1959 policy of "grain distributed to the households." In addition, household garden plots were to be gradually eliminated, and grain was to be mixed with other food to economize on supplies. The report cited the negative example of Gansu's Tongwei County, which supposedly, due to the extreme right deviation of its leadership, had closed down all but a dozen of its 2,800 communal kitchens. At this time, in fact, Tongwei County had exhausted its food supplies, and the corpses of the starved littered the countryside as the county lost one-third of its population in 1960.

In accordance with the spirit of this Central Committee report, communal kitchens underwent reorganization in the spring of 1960. Kitchens replaced so-called antisocialist, well-to-do middle peasants among their staff, with more than twenty-eight thousand such "impure elements" or "unqualified" individuals purged or reassigned in the Henan prefectures of Xinyang, Luoyang, and Xuchang.[40] Plots of land for household use were once again confiscated. Goods were distributed to and through communal kitchens, which experienced a wide-scale revival. As of April 1960, the participation rate in Henan Province reached 99 percent. On June 21, *People's Daily* claimed, "The communal kitchens throughout our country's rural areas have been universally reorganized since this spring and are being run more effectively than ever."[41]

In fact, operating the canteens was increasingly difficult. Nonetheless, the CCP Central Committee in November 1960 required that the commune members' livelihood be organized around the kitchens, and drawing on the slogan "Party secretaries to the kitchens, politics to the canteens." In December the Central Committee argued that "the communal kitchens are currently the spearhead of class struggle in the villages," and insisted that "operating the communal kitchens be raised to the status of class struggle." In Hebei, some 140,000 provincial cadres were transferred to the countryside to carry out rectification at 180,000 communal kitchens, purging "bad elements" and dismissing and replacing "kitchen managers who engaged in favoritism and irregular behavior," while also attacking many village cadres and well-to-do middle peasants. This coercively imposed communization brought disaster to the villages.

IMPOSING DICTATORSHIP ON EVERY STOMACH

The communal kitchens were most damaging in their waste. During the first two or three months that the canteens operated in the autumn of 1958, members feasted. Believing that food supply problems had been completely resolved, Mao and other central leaders worried about "what to do with the extra food," which in turn led villagers to believe that the state had access to vast stores of food to supplement local supplies when they ran out.

The slogan was, "With meals supplied communally, there is never any fear of eating too much." By the end of 1958, however, some communes experienced food shortages, and by the spring of 1959, villagers were confronted with famine.

Jiangxi's Xiaogang Commune imposed no restrictions on consumption of rice, which was accompanied by three or four dishes of meat or vegetables and a soup. Some commune members, fearing that they might lose out on their fair share, gorged themselves, or even took an extra bowl of rice home with them, feeding leftovers to their pigs and chickens. Production teams that worried about this overindulgence and imposed fixed rations had their cautionary practice curtailed by leaders. In the spring of 1959, villagers found they had consumed seven or eight months' provisions in five months.[42]

A Henan County leader recalls, "When the communal kitchens first opened, there really was a wide variety of food. Sweet potatoes alone were prepared in a dozen different ways—deep fried, sautéed, steamed in broth . . . All we thought about all day was the next meal." A Liuzhuang kitchen served fried dough strips, glutinous cakes, dumplings, fish, and meat to its delighted members.[43] In Hebei's Huailai County, teams competed to make the largest food-steaming basket and appoint the most expert cooks to their communal kitchens. At mealtime, each commune member grabbed a tea mug and bowl and went for food, to all appearances engaging in genuine communism. Every meal included freshly prepared green vegetables, corn bread, and steamed buns. Previously enjoyed only at holidays or when entertaining special guests, these became part of the daily fare. So it was that the villages feasted themselves to ruin.[44]

After two or three months, the grain was largely consumed. Instead of providing more grain, the state launched drives against private withholding. Food shortages spread at the end of 1958, and communal kitchens began closing. Among the tens of millions of people who would die during the Great Famine, about 7.72 percent died in 1958, most of them in the last two months of that year.

In the villages, the so-called dictatorship of the proletariat was actually the dictatorship of the cadres. Anyone who disobeyed them could be deprived of food, and villagers were forced to surrender their very survival to these cadres.

In Liu Shaoqi's home county, a local leader said, "In order to build socialism, everyone has to leap forward, and leaping forward means treating every day as if it were twenty years. In order to attain this rate of speed, the entire populace must be mobilized; even the old and feeble cannot be allowed to eat for free, but must contribute their effort. If they can't carry a double load, they can share a load with someone else, and if they can't use their shoulders, they can use their hands; even crawling to the field with a bowl of dirt in one hand contributes more than lying in bed." Those who refused to work, or who worked halfheartedly, were penalized with the withholding of meals. Soon tight food supplies, coupled with food penalties, drove commune members to eat tree bark and grass roots. A man in his seventies named Xiao Xingjie had been a mainstay of his local peasant association in 1927, but because of his diminished work capacity, he was deprived of meals. Before dying, he told his children and grandchildren, "On the anniversary of my death, please place a bowl of white rice on the threshold and call out my name so that as long as my spirit exists, it can come back and eat its fill."[45]

In addition to the dictatorship they imposed on peasant stomachs, cadres took more than their fair share, and communal kitchens became bases of cadre privilege throughout the countryside. Any grade of cadre, down to the lowliest work team branch secretary, needed only to gain the confidence of his direct superior to become a "local despot" with utter impunity. Corruption eroded already inadequate food supplies and intensified the famine.

At the communal kitchens, members had to line up for their rations, and if they were late, they got nothing. Some people had to walk long distances to their mess halls, and food was often cold by the time they arrived home. Because it took so long to fetch the food, children were left weeping with hunger. In the mountain regions, people had to tramp over hill and dale for a bowl of gruel. In the spring of 1960 the newly appointed first secretary of Yunnan Province went to the countryside for an inspection. In the hill country he saw an old woman, covered from head to toe in mud, lugging a basket up a slope during a rainstorm on her way to the kitchen. Some villagers told him that this elderly woman had to cover only two hills and seven-plus kilometers, which was not so bad; some had to travel fifteen kilometers on their donkeys to reach the communal kitchen, spending a good part of a day fetching two meals. The leader suggested to the county party committee that if the communal kitchen was not operating effectively, it should be disbanded, but the committee, afraid to defy the Central Committee's directive, continued imposing arduous journeys on members for their daily bowls of congee.

The quality of the canteen food was often execrable. Boiling cauldrons of congee might contain rat droppings and sheep dung, and the vegetables fried up in the mammoth woks were all but inedible. As supplies ran out, members gathered wild herbs and handed them over to the communal kitchens for even less palatable meals. Since commune members had no choice, it was hard to motivate the production of better food. Figures from 19 provinces and cities reported at least 785 incidents of food poisoning in January and February 1959, affecting 8,042 people, many of whom died. The situation worsened in March.[46]

Another problem was waste of manpower and reduction of work points. In one Hunan commune, preparing the food and tending the vegetables and pigs to feed seventy-two members required the labor of seven men and two women. In other words, 12.5 percent of the labor force was devoted full time to the kitchen.[47] The Gansu provincial first secretary concluded that in Linxia, a kitchen consumed 13.16 percent of a team's collective workday.[48] An investigation of Mao's birthplace concluded, "Operating the communal kitchen has taken up labor to cut firewood, grow vegetables, and cook food, and the number of workers deployed to livelihood tasks takes up one-third to one-half of the production team's total workforce. This has caused a great reduction in work points for agricultural labor and has directly affected enthusiasm for work." In one production team, a day's labor was worth 0.94 yuan in 1957. In 1961 there were 1,466 agricultural laborers earning work points worth 0.69 yuan per day, but because 1,812 communal kitchen workers had to be added in, the work point value dropped to 0.32 yuan.[49] In that same production team, every household had reared its own pigs and chickens in 1957. After the communal kitchen started operating, however, the team's fifty-four pigs and more than one hundred chickens were reduced to four pigs and eleven chickens.[50]

My research suggests that without the communal kitchens, the number of starvation deaths during the famine might have been reduced by a third or more.

THE DISBANDING OF THE COMMUNAL KITCHENS

Through all this, cadres held their tongues for self-preservation. Especially following the campaign against right deviation, no one dared speak the truth. It is said that Mao finally learned the truth from relatives in his home village.

In September 1960 a cousin of Mao's named Mao Zerong said, "These days the cadres and the masses are all afraid to speak, and we're the only ones who can directly approach our Chairman brother to report this matter." Another cousin, named Wen Dongxian, said, "In January 1954, I saw the Chairman in Beijing, and he asked me about the situation in the countryside, repeatedly urging me to tell the truth. Now that the problem is so serious, we have to report it directly to him."

With the 1960 National Day fast approaching, Mao had no time to receive them, so they stayed with another of Mao's cousins, Wang Jifan, who was then serving as an adviser to the State Council. Wang organized their observations and prepared for a face-to-face report to Mao.

After National Day, the cousins were granted an interview with Mao and reported on the diminishing quality and quantity of food, and the number of people surviving on rice husks and rotten cabbage. They told the Chairman that commune members had no will or strength for labor and that malnutrition was causing edema.

Mao Zerong raised his voice and said, "Chairman Brother, no cadres dare report any of these matters to you. You live in Beijing, as remote as the emperors of old, and you don't know what's happening. Now all is in chaos, and people are starving to death; you need to do something!" Wen Dongxian added, "Chairman, you know our Shaoshan is at the junction of Xiangtan, Xiangxiang, and Ningxiang counties—the situation is the same in these three counties! You could send someone down to investigate."[51]

Mao Zedong concluded from this that the communal kitchens were being badly run, and in December he called for rectification of the kitchens and the purging of all "scoundrels" within them. Regarding the communal kitchens in general, he sought more views.

In the winter of 1960, while taking a train to Hangzhou, Mao had party secretaries and other officials from six regions join him. Those endorsing the communal kitchens still made up the majority. The Jiangsu first party secretary, Jiang Weiqing, initially held his peace. When Mao asked him to express his views, Jiang blanched, but Mao encouraged him, promising, "We won't attack you or label you for what you say."

Jiang then pointed out three problems with the communal kitchens: "First, we can't afford to eat up a year's worth of food in half a year! Second, the communal kitchens can't raise enough pigs. If each household raises a pig, that's 300 million pigs. Now there are few pigs and few chickens. Third, the losses caused by the communal kitchens are incalculable. Dishes are broken and chopsticks discarded on a daily basis. We've cleared our woodlands to stoke the ovens. In the past, when meals were cooked at home, children could go out and gather kindling and leaves. Now we're burning lumber! What a pity!"

Mao said to Zhou Enlai, "Premier, what he says is right!" Zhou nodded in agreement.[52]

During the Ninth Plenary Session of the Eighth CCP Central Committee in January 1961, Mao appealed to the party to carry out investigations to clarify the actual situation. He appointed Tian Jiaying, Hu Qiaomu, and Chen Boda to be heads of three separate investigation groups to carry out inquiries.

Upon arrival in Shaoshan in March, the investigation groups were told, "The people need food above all else; if we can't eat our fill, how can we develop production?" "At the communal kitchens we get no fats, no vegetables, just a bowl of rice and some broth flavored with chilies and salt, and our stomachs rumble with hunger as soon as we finish." "The communal kitchens are nothing more than a means for cadres to grab commune members' grain. Next they'll take our bowls of rice as well. The hunger is worse than being scolded and beaten!" They requested disbanding the communal kitchens, distribution according to work done, and rewarding and punishing all alike.

A nearby investigation subgroup was told, "If a communal kitchen can't be run well, it's better just to shut it down and allocate plots of land for private use. Everyone can grow vegetables in front or in back of their homes, and when people have plenty to eat, production will increase. If we don't shut down the communal kitchens, we're wasting our breath discussing any other issues." Some said, "What they call edema or wasting disease is really just illness caused by not getting enough to eat." Others said, "Only by closing the communal kitchens can we root out cadres' special privileges; only by closing the communal kitchens can commune members hope to survive." The sentiment in favor of closing down the kitchens was overwhelming.

The investigation subgroup dared not take a stand, however. Some members said the communal kitchens were the sprouts of communism; this was written in central government documents, so who dared deny it? Someone said, "Provincial party secretary Zhou Xiaozhou was dismissed for criticizing the communal kitchens. If we come out and say the communal kitchens should be disbanded, what crime will we be accused of?" The investigation subgroup consensus was to deliver a factual report.

Neighbors of Mao's home village went to Shaoshan to relate the harsh reality of food shortages, reduced production, and increasing edema, malnutrition, and death. The provincial party committee investigation group wired the county party committee to look into these matters and report their findings to the Central Committee investigation groups.

On the basis of these reports, Hu Qiaomu drafted four documents reflecting life in the villages: the communal kitchens were harmful, and most villagers did not want them. On April 14, Hu Qiaomu had the four documents sent to Mao Zedong, then in Changsha. An accompanying letter mentioned massive starvation deaths in the county. Mao read the letter and documents that night. On the morning of April 15, he wrote a memo inviting provincial leaders to discuss them.

At 4:00 p.m. on April 15, Mao received one of the investigators, Mao Huachu, who told him, "Wherever we went, the masses surrounded us and expressed their views to us. It appears that edema is currently a serious problem in the villages, and unnatural deaths have increased, affecting the enthusiasm of the masses in production. The masses have urgently requested that the communal kitchens be closed, and say that the communal kitchens are intolerable."

Mao Zedong asked, "Why are the masses unwilling and unable to operate communal kitchens?"

Mao Huachu replied, "The main reason is that there's not enough food, and there's no freedom."

Mao Zedong pursued the point: "When there's still so much grain, why can't people get enough to eat at the communal kitchens?"

Mao Huachu replied, "The main reason is that [in a household setting] not everyone eats the same; older and younger members of the family eat different amounts, and with the food they raise in their household garden plots, they can eat less rice. In a family of several people, old and young, it doesn't matter much whether one person eats a little more or less."

Mao Zedong nodded and then asked, "Why does operating communal kitchens cause so much damage to the hillside forests?"

Mao Huachu replied, "A lot of people eat at the communal kitchens; they have to use huge woks and big stoves to prepare the food. Grass doesn't provide a strong enough flame, so trees have to be cut down for wood to burn."

Mao Zedong asked, "Do you all agree that it's best not to run communal kitchens?"

Mao Huachu replied, "Yes."

Finally Mao Zedong said, "You have spoken well and truthfully. Cadres should always report the truth. Some people report only good things to the leadership and make no mention of any worries, and the people suffer harm as a result . . . Regarding the closure of the communal kitchens, this is not a decision I can make alone. This has to be discussed and decided by the Central Committee because it concerns the whole nation."[53]

Mao Huachu returned to Shaoshan from Changsha on April 17 and reported Mao Zedong's instructions to Hu Qiaomu. Hu immediately convened a meeting of the investigation groups and commune cadres to make the necessary arrangements for a trial closure of the communal kitchens.

On the evening of April 19 the investigation groups went back and held a meeting of commune members to announce that the communal kitchen would be closed. A plan had to be drawn up for allocating cooking utensils and land for household gardening and residential quarters. The commune members rejoiced, proclaiming the Central Committee investigation groups the embodiment of the legendary Judge Bao "Qingtian," releasing the peasants from their bondage. In fact, preparations had already been made for closing the communal kitchens. Commune members met until late that night working out the details. After breakfast the next morning, cooking utensils, grain, oil, salt, firewood, and vegetables were distributed, and everyone cooked their own noon meal at home. By April 25 all of the commune's production brigades had closed their communal kitchens.

On April 26, 1961, Hu Qiaomu's letter and four attached documents were circulated throughout the country with an editorial comment by the Central Committee:

> In accordance with directives from Comrade Mao Zedong, this letter from Comrade Hu Qiaomu and four appended documents are transmitted to all of you. You are requested to study them closely as references in studying and resolving the communal kitchen issue and related problems. It will be left to your discretion whether or not to transmit these documents to the lower levels.[54]

This document did not order the closing of communal kitchens, however, nor did it dictate whether it should be transmitted down the bureaucratic ladder.

Other leaders organized rural investigation groups and went to the villages. They also concluded that the communal kitchens should be disbanded. On May 9, 1961, Gansu's provincial first secretary, Wang Feng, wrote:

> The masses deeply detest and loathe the communal kitchens. The masses say, "Make friends with a canteen manager and you'll never want for buns and soup." The masses say, "There are no limits on the stomachs of the kitchen staff, the warmed brick beds of the livestock keepers, and the rations of the team leaders and managers." The masses say, "A knife hangs over the rice ladle." The masses say, "The communal canteen is a dining hall (a place for getting food), a tribunal (a place where kitchen staff and managers beat and scold people), and a bordello (where team leaders and managers hire the prettiest girls as kitchen staff and mess around with them)." For example, the leader and manager of Team 6 . . . took more than their share out of commune members' grain rations and used these rations to seduce and rape thirteen women. In 1960, thirty-nine people who ate at this communal kitchen died.[55]

During a CCP Central Committee work conference held in Beijing in May and June of 1961, the Central Committee revised the requirement that every production team must operate a communal kitchen and the rigid rule that commune members' grain rations had to be distributed to the communal kitchen. It declared that commune members themselves would decide whether to operate a communal kitchen, and that grain rations were to be distributed directly to households, after which members would themselves decide what to do with them.[56] With this, China's communal kitchens vanished.

Wang Feng's subsequent report quoted the joyous responses of commune members to the closing of the kitchens: "Now I can grip the handle of the rice ladle with my own hand, and they can no longer grip me by the neck." "Going home to cook dinner, our wok is warmed, our brick bed is warmed, and our hearts are warmed."

6 HUNGRY GHOSTS IN HEAVEN'S PANTRY*

Sichuan is known as Heaven's Pantry, its superior natural conditions making it a breadbasket of China. Yet more than ten million people starved to death here during the Great Famine.[1]

In March 1958 the Central Committee convened a conference in Sichuan's capital, Chengdu, during which it promoted the core concept of the Three Red Banners: the General Line for socialist construction. The conference was held at the Jinniuba Guesthouse, where provincial first secretary Li Jingquan, a Mao loyalist, ensured that the facilities conformed to Mao's living habits and security.

The day after Mao arrived, a provincial leader took him on a tour. Chengdu's city walls, constructed during the reign of Emperor Kangxi (1662–1722), were well preserved, but Mao was unimpressed: "We've knocked down Beijing's city walls. These walls are unsightly and obstruct traffic . . . City walls are backward; dismantling them is progressive." The city walls of Chengdu were dismantled that same year.

From his car window, Mao took note of Sichuan's distinctive teahouses and commented that such venues occasioned excessive expenditure. Every teahouse was then closed.

During the Chengdu Conference, Mao took his meals at the Yaohua Restaurant. From then on, the section of the restaurant where he had eaten was made into a memorial site where visitors could pay their respects.

On March 21, Mao went to Guan County to view the Dujiang Dam. Pointing at the rocky Lidui Hill beneath his feet, he asked, "Will this ever be destroyed by flooding?" The answer: "No, this is granulite, it's very strong." He asked further, "How about a million years from now?" No

*The translators gratefully acknowledge reference to an initial translation of this chapter by Lu Yong.

one offered a reply, but soon thereafter, reinforced concrete was added to strengthen the rock structure.

On March 16, following a nap, Mao visited the countryside, and first secretary Li accompanied him to Hongguang Collective in Pi County. Local leaders had received advance notice of the visit. On entering the collective, Mao strode into a nearby courtyard, entourage in tow, ducking his head under the doorway of a thatched cottage. The dim-sighted sixty-year-old woman of the house, Wen Yaoniang, blinked in confusion and alarm at the tall, sturdy fellow pushing his way in with a crowd of cadres in his wake. Mao questioned her about her life in the collective, but all the responses were handled by the collective's deputy director, who had planted himself at Madame Wen's side.

A report on Mao's visit concluded:

After the Chairman left, there was a great rainfall that night, and the work point recorder of the No. 24 work team said it was genuinely a case of "Flowers blooming where the dragon has trod." When asked his meaning, he said, "Spring rain is as precious as oil; the Chairman came to us in the afternoon, and that evening our Hongguang Collective had rain, ensuring increased production for us this year. Have we not enjoyed special favor?"[2]

Dong Fu later reported:

From the evening of Mao's visit, all of Hongguang Collective was immersed in joy and excitement. Those fortunate enough to have encountered the Great Leader proudly recounted every detail to everyone around them, while the less fortunate could only sigh with regret. Everyone vied to shake the hand that had shaken Chairman Mao's hand in hopes of sharing in that happiness. Long afterward, the villagers recounted and relived the Great Leader's every movement, every expression on his face, every single word he uttered, while retracing his every step and footprint. Preparations were made to erect a "Happiness Gate" at the spot where Mao Zedong had alighted from his vehicle, while the tractor path he had walked down would be made into a "Happiness Road" lined with cypress trees. There would be a memorial hall and a "Happiness Pavilion." The field Mao Zedong had inspected would be named "Happiness Field," and the gully he crossed would be spanned with a "Happiness

Bridge." In accordance with Mao's instructions, a newly built primary school was named "Happiness School," and the eighteen children graced with his presence were to be known as the "Happy Tots." (Subsequent inquiries determined that only one of the eighteen had the appropriate "good family background" to enjoy this title.) The supremely honored Wen Yaoniang gave the name "Happiness Tree" to the tangerine sapling Mao had inspected in her courtyard, and the vegetable patch in which Mao had roamed she converted into a floral "Happiness Garden." A tobacco pipe and bamboo basket that Mao had touched were judged unworthy of the "Happiness" name, but Wen Yaoniang set them aside as treasured objects all the same.[3]

What the Chengdu Conference brought to Heaven's Pantry was not happiness, however, but a calamity shared by all of China.

THE THREE RED BANNERS RAISE A HURRICANE

As the Three Red Banners and their evil winds swept through Sichuan, Hongguang Commune released a 1,876-kilo-per-*mu* "Sputnik" with its early rice harvest at the end of July. On the night of August 5 the head of Pi County, Gao Yilu, announced that the county's average yield for the early harvest had hit 515 kilos per *mu*, double that of the previous year and the highest in the province. All of the province's high-yield "satellites" exceeding 1,500 kilos per *mu* were launched from Pi County. Gao said, "This is the red glow (*hongguang*) shining from Pi County since Chairman Mao's visit! It's the fresh bouquet produced by the boundless enthusiasm of our people!" This was followed by an intensely publicized competition among communes for ever-increasing crop yields.

On the morning of August 27, prefectural first secretary Song Wenbin led a delegation to Xipu, where the reaping began that afternoon. More than one hundred peasants swarmed a plot of land measuring just over one *mu* as the Sputnik was prepared for launch. However, rice experts from the provincial Institute of Agricultural Science said the claimed crop yield was bogus, and that it had resulted from the transplanting of mature rice plants into that field. The provincial party committee secretary-general in charge of propaganda work, Yan Xiufeng, then announced, "Newspapers should not publish reports on this satellite."

Sichuan Daily nevertheless splashed a report on Xipu's bumper crop on the front page of its August 28 edition. The banner headline led throngs of people to Xipu to view the miraculous field. Ultimately the yield was announced at 22,608.75 kilos per *mu*.

Upon learning the truth, prefectural first secretary Song Wenbin ordered that the error be acknowledged, but before the county party committee could submit its self-criticism, a September 2 *People's Daily* article affirmed the bogus Sputnik as genuine. The September 12 edition of *Sichuan Daily* then reported that a field in Pi County's You'ai Town had yielded 40,000 kilos per *mu*, the highest yield to date nationwide. This *Sichuan Daily* report was the result of provincial first party secretary Li Jingquan's return from a national leadership meeting at Beidaihe; *Sichuan Daily* was Li's mouthpiece.

Li Jingquan, born in 1909 in Jiangxi, enlisted when the Red Army troops went south after the Nanchang Uprising in 1927. He was appointed political commissar of the Thirty-fifth Regiment in the Soviet region in 1931, and served as director of political affairs of the CCP central troop unit during the Long March. During the Japanese occupation, Li served as a political commissar in the Eighth Route Army, and during the Civil War of 1945–49 he was secretary of the Central Committee's Jin-Sui regional bureau. In 1952 he became Sichuan's provincial party secretary and governor, but cadres still addressed him as Commissar Li.

Li was displeased with the delay to the "satellite" launch, and told prefectural first secretary Song Wenbin, "If the 20,000-kilo yield at Pi County was fake, why didn't you arrange for a real one?" Li ordered the prefectural party committee to acknowledge the accomplishment of the satellite and restore the reputation of Pi County. The prefectural party committee quickly admitted failure to hold steadfast to the goal of "small plantings, high yields, big harvests," and inadequate encouragement to Pi County.

A subsequent report from Pi County stated that the Exaggeration Wind began with crop yields, then expanded to production, from planting to harvest, and every stage was plagued with "celestial statistics" and "Great Leap statistics." Reports of hundreds of thousands of kilos of fertilizer applied to a *mu* of land, or exponential increases in planted surface area, were all products of the Exaggeration Wind.[4]

Pi County combined the already sizeable Hongguang and Chenguang communes with others. Larger communes meant larger and more widely dispersed communal kitchens, and some peasants had to walk four kilometers for a meal. Cadres were seldom acquainted with the individuals under their governance, and even many commune members did not know one another.[5]

During the steel-forging campaign, hundreds of thousands of smelting ovens were erected in a matter of days, and smelting went on around the clock. Wenjiang Prefecture, which had neither coal nor iron-ore mines, rounded up more than half a million of its strongest workers and sent them out in smelting corps to the western hills. Where coal was lacking, trees were cut down to stoke the fires. The smelting corps ate and slept in the mountains. When the smelting corps of Chongqing County needed brick kilns, it commandeered the labor of tens of thousands of students, workers, cadres, and local residents to dismantle the city walls and move bricks up the mountain around the clock. Every work unit in every town and city had stoves burning, and the metal implements of every household, right down to family heirlooms and Grandma's hairpins, were cast into the ovens to be turned into useless lumps of pig iron. Sichuan created a technology known as "big kiln steel-forging," in which a valley or ravine was selected and all of its surrounding trees chopped down. The ravine was then filled with a layer of timber and topped with a layer of ore, after which the wood was set afire and kept burning for days. The result was neither ore nor steel ingot, but it was presented to the authorities with a fanfare of gongs and drums.

Sichuan was also struck with the gale force of the deep-plowing campaign. Wenjiang Prefecture established a set procedure for deep-plowing and improving the soil: (1) use a plow or hoe to dig up the first layer of topsoil; (2) move the topsoil aside; (3) turn over the second layer of "immature soil"; (4) form the immature soil into hollowed-out mounds; (5) burn kindling in the mounds to "smoke" the soil; (6) sprinkle the smoked soil with manure and water; (7) break up the smoked soil and spread it evenly over the ground; (8) cover the smoked soil layer with fertilizer, compost, broken-up bricks, and so forth; (9) replace the topsoil, smooth it out, and rake it . . . Similar measures were carried out for "deep-plowing satellites" that turned the soil to a depth of several feet, in some cases interring soil that had been maturing for thousands of years.

In an instant, the plains of western Sichuan were transformed into the appearance of a graveyard, clustered with mounds of poisoned earth, while the highlands were likewise pimpled with "hills atop hills." Firelight glowed everywhere, day and night, shrouding the land in smoke. Under fluttering red flags, tens of thousands of deep-plowing troops toiled in military fashion, battling around the clock and in all weather. Since half of the manpower of Dayi County had been sent to the hills for the steel campaign, the deep-plowing involved teenagers and the elderly. Organized into "field armies," they pitched their camps everywhere in non-stop assaults on the earth.

Throughout the prefecture, the steel campaign, water conservancy, and other projects drew most of the men from the fields. Two projects alone, the ultimately abandoned Min River electrical plant and Chengguan Railway (from Chengdu to Dujiangyan), sapped Wenjiang of a hundred thousand laborers. Military organization, collective living, and combat operations in labor expanded cadres' power. Chaotic directives and abusive treatment of villagers became routine, along with special privileges for cadres.

Redevelopment entailed the mass destruction of homes and relocation of families. Rong County was struck by the Communist Wind in 1958, again during the 1959 autumn wheat planting season, and yet again in the spring of 1960. A vanity project called Bumper Harvest Roads concentrated vast quantities of labor and material resources on planting fields along roadsides for viewing by visiting dignitaries. The main requirement of the "bumper harvest roads" was that they should be "pleasing to the eye," that their plantings should be orderly, and in ladder step or "pagoda" formations, and that they should be assigned serial numbers. Sowing just one *mu* of land required dozens of farmers working an entire day. At Changshan Commune, more than one hundred people worked day and night without finishing the planting of even a tenth of a *mu*. Since attention was focused on roadside fields, more remote areas were often left fallow, and a quarter of the county's arable land went uncultivated. As production teams were consolidated, 1,133 of Changshan Commune's 2,870 households were forced to relocate. Collective living quarters put several families in a single house. Women and men lived separately, and some slept in pigsties and cattle pens.

Commune members lost household implements, poultry, and livestock. After large communal kitchens were set up, vegetables, fuel, and cooking utensils from smaller mess halls were combined. People said, "All we've been allowed to keep is one pair of chopsticks and one bowl," and, "All we own is the clothes on our backs and the food that remains in our stomachs," while others went so far as to say, "We don't even own ourselves." The cadres responded, "Communism means eliminating all private property."[6]

At Hongguang Commune, a roadside area of more than 2,000 *mu* was cleared of more than 180 dwellings. At least 12,000 homes were dismantled throughout the county. Unrelated families were obliged to share quarters, sometimes with domestic fowl. Cadres burst into homes without notice, tossed out belongings, and reduced a house to rubble in an instant. Commune members returning from deployment elsewhere wept upon finding their homes, wives, and children gone. Some families relocated seven times in a year. Cadres ransacked homes, often snatching desirable goods. Some commune members retaliated by hiding snakes in their rice jars.[7]

In a district of Leshan County's Tongjiang Commune, the number of farming tools was reduced from 2,686 in 1958 to only 515 by 1961, crippling production. The district's No. 4 production team lost 93 of its original 110 drying mats, with the result that more than 10,000 kilos of rice, amounting to more than 18 percent of the 1960 harvest, developed sprouts and had to be discarded. The No. 1 production team originally had 106 plows and rakes, but 96 were lost, and the consequent delay to the transplanting of mid-season rice seedlings left 30 *mu* of land fallow. The grain yield dropped by more than 15,000 kilos.[8] In the No. 2 administrative district of Mianzhu Commune, the grain yield dropped by 25.7 percent in 1960, in spite of ideal weather conditions.

Excessive requirements for uniformity reduced production further. Upper-level cadres required that rice seedling beds be planted in a "tiled roof" formation, and that all pathways run straight. Paddy fields that didn't meet these conditions had to be replanted. Potatoes were to be planted in a banded formation, and when this condition wasn't met in one 43-*mu* field, the potato seedlings had to be pulled out and replanted. The transplanting of seedlings along roadways required the use of rulers and string to guarantee straight, parallel rows, and substandard plantings had to be redone.

The rules took no account of season or weather. Even in hot weather, cadres demanded that commune members use hotbeds to produce sweet potato seedlings, with the result that 5,500 kilos of sweet potatoes were spoiled by overheating. Cadres also stipulated that sweet potatoes could not be harvested before the first frost, and earlier harvesting brought accusations of sabotaging production or intending to falsely report output.

When the temperature dropped suddenly after the first frost, the sweet potatoes could not be dug out quickly enough, and many rotted in the fields. In the busy spring plowing season, manpower was deployed to cosmetic landscaping, and plantings missed the critical "grain rain" and "summer onset" periods.

Geography was routinely ignored. More than 170 *mu* of marshy, low-lying fields best suited for mid-season rice were planted with early rice on orders from upper-level cadres, while peasants were forced to plant corn in more than 100 *mu* of land better suited to sweet potatoes. These two measures reduced yield by at least 20,000 kilos.[9]

In 1958 a district of Chengxi Commune employed "large-scale warfare" tactics during a deep-plowing campaign in which 180 people spent an entire day and night digging up a field of just over 1 *mu*, followed by the planting of 30 kilos of wheat. The resulting yield was less than the seed that was planted.

Four production teams had a total of 129 *mu* of fields and 172 *mu* of other land that went unused in 1959, and the wheat yield dropped 63.14 percent.[10] In some communes, the unified deployment of manpower resulted in people from one production team going to another team to transplant seedlings, while members of that team went to the first team to pull weeds. As large groups of farmers were dispatched hither and yon, vast tracts of land lay fallow.[11]

LI JINGQUAN TRIMS HIS SAILS AGAINST THE WIND

Disasters caused by the policies of the Great Leap Forward and the people's communes at the end of 1958 and into 1959 led the Central Committee to adopt a series of rectification measures. But Sichuan's provincial first secretary, Li Jingquan, trimmed his sails against the wind and spurned these measures. In Sichuan, Li's word was law, his status derived from his ties to Mao. In a photo of the Chengdu Conference attendees, Mao had Li seated next to him; a month or so later, Li was made a member of the Central Committee Politburo, along with Ke Qingshi and Tan Zhenlin.

Mao's trust in Li Jingquan arose from Li's ability to comprehend Mao's thinking at the most fundamental level. When Mao was compelled in late 1958 and early 1959 to adopt some "cooling" measures to correct "leftist" errors, Li completely ignored these measures without any criticism from Mao. When the Lushan Conference changed direction on July 23,

Li was among the staunchest defenders of Mao's leftist policies. Li continued to embrace the Great Leap Forward even after the cooling measures were put in place following the Sixth Plenum of the Eighth CCP Central Committee in Wuchang. The meeting of Sichuan's prefectural party committee secretaries at Jinniuba in December 1958 prepared for the task of an even greater leap forward in 1959.

To Li, the locality represented peasant particularism, while administration of large entities by higher-ups represented the proletariat. Bemoaning the downward delegation of authority during the cooling period, Li asked, "Should production be left entirely to the peasants or to the proletariat?" Although the Second Zhengzhou Conference clearly stipulated that production teams should become the basic accounting unit of the communes, Li Jingquan announced to a mass meeting, "The basic unit for us is the administrative district."[12]

Li continued to push high production targets. On April 19, 1959, the provincial party committee issued "Eight Stipulations" on agricultural production, which strictly regulated seeding areas, fertilizer, the depth of plowing, and the density of planting. They required all regions to "firmly grasp ideology, models, and small movements from beginning to end" and raise yields to a new high. Production figures relating to pigs, steel, and irrigation were expected to soar.[13]

The Central Committee endorsed Sichuan's Eight Stipulations and, on April 26, distributed them to every province, city, and autonomous region with a memo attached: "On the issue of agricultural production, a tendency toward slacking off has emerged in some localities, along with the setting of excessively low targets to counter the tendency toward exaggeration and false reporting. You should take note of and surmount these tendencies, and, as Sichuan Province has done, produce regulations as necessary and initiate production campaigns."[14]

While other provinces began curbing the Exaggeration Wind after the Second Zhengzhou Conference, Li's unyielding stance was exemplified in his refusal to pass a letter from Mao to production team cadres. On April 29, 1959, Mao wrote an "internal party communiqué" on agricultural production that was practical and realistic:

> In setting production quotas, state only how much you can actually produce, and don't make false claims that exceed what you can realistically produce through hard effort. On harvests, state how much you have

actually harvested instead of falsely claiming a figure inconsistent with reality. Measures to increase production . . . cannot employ false claims. Those who are honest and who dare to speak the truth are ultimately serving the best interests of the people and will not come to grief for it. Those who like to make false claims do harm to the people and to themselves and ultimately will suffer the consequences. It should be said that much of the falsehood has been prompted by the upper levels through boasting, pressure, and reward, leaving little alternative to those below. For that reason, we must have enthusiasm and drive, but lying is not allowed.[15]

After hearing Mao's letter over the telephone, Li directed, "Send it to the county party committees, and verbally relay it to the communes, but let it stew for a while before transmitting it to the production teams. Changing direction too dramatically could have a negative effect on morale." He told prefectural and municipal party secretaries that Mao's letter had to be "understood from a positive angle." High production targets and close-planting requirements persisted, with a warning that "conservatism and tailism[16] must be opposed." There was to be no vacillation on grain production quotas. Li suggested that transmitting the "internal party communiqué" to the grass roots would result in letting things slide, and all should be on guard against such a development.

On May 7, 1959, the Central Committee repeated the order to transmit Mao's memo to the production teams immediately. Li ignored it. The memo did reach some local leaders, but before their pleasant surprise could sink in, Li ordered the internal memo recalled. On May 14 the provincial party committee transmitted an "urgent directive" from Li to promote close-planting.

During a study session for Sichuan's northwestern region, the convener, Liao Zhigao, rationalized that "someone in Beijing was dashing cold water on the proceedings, and the Chairman was under pressure." After Wenjiang Prefecture's first party secretary Song Wenbin stated at the meeting that he was a "moderate," Li Jingquan telephoned Song several times, berating him for "pushing the cold front" and insisting that close-planting be maintained.

Li explained away Mao's memo by saying that falsehood could take two forms: "underreporting," as with false reporting and private withholding, and "overreporting" through exaggeration. Li defended the second type as arising from ignorance rather than vanity, and said it was chiefly a matter of "the conflict between the state wanting to take a little more and the peasants wanting to eat a little more . . . Speaking truthfully, we all want the state to take a bit more. Don't you?"

Was Li Jingquan intentionally resisting Mao by airing views so flagrantly contrary to his directives? There is not a shred of evidence to suggest that Li's loyalty to Mao ever wavered. His "alternative views" arose from his abiding confidence that he understood Mao better than anyone else, and that his actions conformed to Mao's consistent standpoint.

And in fact, Li was right. Cadres who took the Central Committee's rectification measures at face value subsequently suffered for their naïveté, and some were labeled right opportunists. The fact was that Mao never vacillated on the principles at the root of the great errors of 1958. All he wanted rectified was a handful of measures and work styles, and once these were dealt with, he wanted the Great Leap Forward to proceed.

At a time when Mao was adopting a moderate tone, Li Jingquan repeatedly emphasized the need to affirm the accomplishments of the Great Leap Forward and to maintain its momentum. The superiority of the people's communes "is altogether beyond doubt and utterly certain. If doubts can arise on such a fundamental issue, that is a great error—it's right opportunism." Li criticized the Exaggeration Wind and the Communist Wind but praised the cadres who engendered the Five Winds: "They display the enormous zeal of a Communist," and this extremely precious enthusiasm "should be resolutely protected."

Li knew that in his heart of hearts, Mao preferred high production targets. While Mao's memo said, "Inflexible commands from above on close-planting are not only useless, but have caused considerable harm to the people," Li surmised that, deep down, Mao actually favored close-planting. When Mao's secretary Tian Jiaying carried out a survey of Sichuan in the spring of 1959, he found commune members objecting to the province's dense-planting practices, and called for adherence to Mao's memo. The provincial party committee nevertheless continued close-planting, simply relaxing the requirement at communes where Tian Jiaying was assigned.[17]

A Central Committee directive on May 7, 1959, stipulated cultivation of all arable land, allowing production teams and individuals to rear at least 80 percent of all pigs and resuming the allotment of plots of land for household cultivation, with a minimum of 5 percent of a commune's total farmland allocated for this purpose. Allowing households to raise pigs necessitated households planting forage for the pigs. Avoiding that slippery slope, the Sichuan provincial party committee ordered that pigs be given to the production teams, which would be provided with a certain amount of land for producing pig feed, effectively ruling out household cultivation and pig rearing.

A Central Committee directive on May 26, 1959, allowed for communal kitchens to be set up for only a portion of commune members, and to be operated only when agricultural activity was at its busiest. Communal kitchens could also be reduced to a more appropriate scale. Grain rations were to be distributed to households on a per capita basis, and commune members who chose not to eat at communal mess halls could take charge of their own grain rations. Where this directive was implemented, communal kitchens were disbanded.

The Sichuan provincial party committee, however, insisted that the communal kitchens keep operating and prohibited distribution of grain rations to individuals, effectively nullifying the Central Committee's provisions.

On June 11, 1959, the Central Committee directive went further in rectifying Great Leap excesses:

1. Commune members could raise pigs, sheep, and poultry as their personal property;
2. Plots of land would be reallocated for household cultivation, whether or not commune members raised pigs or ate at collective canteens;
3. Commune members could freely dispose of produce from their plots of land;
4. Commune members were encouraged to cultivate extra land and retain what they grew; and
5. Commune members could once again grow trees around their homes.[18]

The Sichuan provincial party committee refused to issue this directive to the production team level as instructed; nor did it allow commune members to raise pigs or allocate land for household cultivation. Sichuan simply boycotted every rectification directive issued by the Central Committee right up until the Lushan Conference.

During the early stage of the 1959 Lushan Conference, anti-leftists criticized Great Leap problems but not Sichuan's Li Jingquan.[19] Li's persistence paid off on July 23, when Mao attacked Great Leap critics and reversed the direction of the conference. Mao made a point of praising Sichuan:

> Participation in communal kitchens remains above 90 percent in Sichuan, Yunnan, Guizhou, Hubei, and Shanghai (Shanghai has eleven counties). Keep trying, don't give up on them. Aren't there four steps in dancing? "Stand off to the side, give it a try, throw yourself into it, defy death." Isn't that how it goes? I'm a bumpkin and completely uncivilized. I want to give it a try. What is one-third of the rural population of 500 million? It's 150 million, and if they persevere, that's already a world-changing development . . . If more places follow the example of Henan, Sichuan, Hubei, Yunnan, and Shanghai, it will be possible to involve half of the rural population . . . some that have been disbanded must resume operations.[20]

After Lushan, the vindicated Li Jingquan boasted, "We did the right thing when we took back plots of land for private use last year." "Last year we achieved a relatively high level of communization. The Chairman said that some of the things the Central Committee issued last May and June had negative items that required examination, and afterward another directive had to be issued on agricultural work."[21] Mao's confidence in Li grew, and Li's position became more secure. In autumn 1959, Li reaped his political reward, but the ordinary people of Sichuan paid the price as Sichuan suffered the most sustained effects of the Great Famine.

THE FAMINE LASTED LONGEST IN SICHUAN PROVINCE

The famine struck in the winter of 1958 and lasted in Sichuan until the autumn of 1962. Starvation deaths persisted longer than in any other part of China.

In Mianzhu County's Hongqi (Red Flag) Commune, 115 communal kitchens, serving a total of 26,498 people, ran out of food by the end of February 1959. These communal kitchens then used feed grain reserved for livestock, and some used seed grain as well. Fewer people had the strength for labor, and the workday was shortened.[22] The situation was similar in other localities. As food supplies ran out, livestock died off. Li responded to the problem by covering it up, and rejected claims that there was no food. During a meeting of prefectural party secretaries on February 27, 1959, he said, "Some comrades believe the high-yield satellites are fake . . . What kind of problem is this lack of faith in other people's experience?" At another meeting on March 19, Li explained away the mass die-off of pigs:

> If 3 or 4 million pigs died . . . that's a small proportion since we had a total of 37 million pigs in the province before December. Probably half were slaughtered to eat . . . and some died of illness. Fewer pigs died in the poor production teams, and more in the wealthier teams. The well-to-do middle peasants didn't take good care of the pigs, and some landlords and rich peasants might even have killed some . . . I would say there were 1 million pigs that shouldn't have died. It belongs to the category of nine fingers versus one finger.[23]

By applying Mao's "one finger" standard to minimize problems, Li allowed the famine to worsen. Any resistance to state requisition resulted in anti-hoarding campaigns.

In Changning County's Taoping Commune, where most communal kitchens had closed down by May 25, commune members had to fend for themselves, resorting to wild herbs and Guanyin clay. In the Dahe administrative district, 219 people starved to death in April, and by June another 218 had died. By July 6, 560 people had died, 6.64 percent of the local population.[24]

On July 23 a provincial deputy party secretary reported to the province that food shortages had led to the closure of 1,918 communal kitchens in Renshou County, affecting 150,000 people. Five percent of the total population was afflicted with edema, with the percentage reaching 30 to 50 percent in some production teams. Nearly 200 deaths from edema had been recorded as of July 20.[25] These figures were probably an underreporting.

More people died from the winter of 1959 until the summer harvest of 1960. At Mianyang County's Shima Commune, 946 out of 7,531 died.[26] In the Chunhua administrative district of Dianjiang County's Chengxi Commune, after the Mid-Autumn Festival people had nothing to eat but vegetables and sweet potato leaves. When sweet potatoes were harvested in November, farmers ate the potatoes as they dug. Cadres continued to use the pretext of "false reporting and private withholding" to penalize commune members through physical assaults, withholding of meals, and seizure of property. The result was death on a massive scale. This administrative district had 420 households in 1958, but by 1961 that figure had been reduced to 344. One communal kitchen lost more than half of its 141 members by January 1961. The Citangwan communal kitchen was reduced from 135 members to 65, with eight entire households wiped out. Guo Shiyi's family in the No. 4 production team originally had eleven members, but was reduced to just one child, and the dead went unburied. Forty-seven natural villages became virtual ghost towns.[27]

Reports reached Li Jingquan, but he was unmoved. At a symposium on February 14, he said:

The Chairman has raised the point that the whole country needs to get communal kitchens going in March, April, and May, and that the communal kitchens have to take control of food supply, with all the provinces following the example of Hunan, Henan, and Sichuan in pledging to keep the communal kitchens going. I said the vast majority in Sichuan are persevering, and some are operating like military mess halls. The Chairman said, wherever there are difficulties, they should be operated like military mess halls . . . If food is distributed to individuals, that causes problems . . . We have to be resolute in getting the communal kitchens running properly in March, April, and May. We did the right thing when we took back the plots of land for household use . . . Cadres all have to eat at the communal kitchens, and any ration coupons in their possession have to be taken back.[28]

The points on which Li Jingquan was most complacent (household plots of land recalled, a high level of communization, food rations not controlled by individuals, communal kitchens continued) were exactly what caused Sichuan Province to suffer such protracted effects of the famine. In the meantime, Li made light of reports of serious problems. During a meeting on March 26, he said:

Our province has a few counties . . . where the problems are reportedly somewhat exceptional and need to be resolved and in fact have already been resolved. Leaders have been transferred, food supply is not being delegated downward, and productivity is up again. In any case, this problem has to be solved . . . The Huayang county party secretary didn't go down to the countryside for three months, and many pigs died in the commune where he lived. Then there's an administrative district where people have died and where edema is serious—that's a result of bureaucratism.[29]

The most serious bureaucratism was by senior officials such as Li who were unwilling to face the truth and allowed the situation to go from bad to worse.

In February 1960, the Food Ministry convened a national conference in Nanchong, Sichuan, to discuss livelihood. Vice-minister Zhao Fasheng said on February 9, "Every year, Sichuan transfers large amounts of foodstuffs to support the rest of China. Yet Sichuan's urban residents eat only ten kilos or less per month, and the rural communal kitchens serve only two congees and one rice a day, for a total of 200 grams. The people of Sichuan have sacrificed for others." The conference proposed the slogan "Learn from Sichuan, learn from Nanchong." According to the materials Sichuan Province submitted to the conference, the livelihood of Sichuan residents was well arranged.[30]

While Sichuan officials were puffing up their own reputations, the province's ordinary residents were wasting away in misery. Fan Sui, a reporter for Xinhua's Sichuan branch, recalls:

During the 1950s, the province shipped out an average of 1.612 billion kilos of grain every year. During the three years of the Great Leap Forward, the launching of "satellites," artificial production targets, and excessive exaggeration led to three successive years of reduced production. Annual output in 1960 was 1.5 billion kilos less than in 1949, but there was no reduction in the amount of grain the province shipped out. It reached 3.42 billion kilos in 1960—double the previous level. In the three years starting from 1959, the amount of grain the province was allowed to retain, including grain rations, seed grain, and animal feed, plummeted from 256 kilos to 130 kilos per capita. Because too much grain was coercively requisitioned, the grain stores were empty. With no grain sellbacks after the spring famine, the peasants could only await slow death by starvation. More than 10 million people died just this way in Sichuan Province during the three years of the Great Famine.[31]

The figures in the memoirs of the provincial party secretary in charge of agriculture, Liao Zhigao, are consistent with Fan Sui's. Liao wrote:

> During the First Five-Year Plan, Sichuan transferred . . . an average of 1.627 billion kilos per year. Starting in 1958, the province's grain production levels decreased significantly for three years in succession, but its procurement quotas increased. Sichuan supplied 1.98 billion kilos of grain to the state in 1958, 2.45 billion in 1959, and 3.42 billion in 1960. The amount of grain retained by the province (including seed grain, feed grain, and grain rations) dropped from 256 kilos per capita in 1958 to 139 kilos in 1959 and 130 kilos in 1960 . . . The central leadership explained that the political, economic, and other ramifications of the problems in Sichuan were less significant than those in Beijing, Tianjin, and Shanghai. This policy was subsequently known as "Better that people should starve to death in Sichuan than in Beijing, Tianjin, and Shanghai."[32]

In Kai County, the No. 3 production team of Zhaojia Commune's Renhe administrative district lost 91 out of 207 people to edema. The county cadres insisted that grain was being concealed, and mounted "grain donation" campaigns under the slogan, "Everyone must come clean, everyone must pass the test; examine yourselves and give your opinions."[33]

On October 22, 1960, the Bishan County party committee reported that the county's death toll from January comprised 4.5 percent of the rural population.[34] According to a report made on January 19, 1962, by the provincial party committee's Bishan work group, in 1961 Daxing Commune lost 839 members to starvation, 10 percent of its population and 67.9 percent of its full-time and part-time labor force. Bishan County's party committee reported on January 2, 1962, that in 1960 the death toll rose steadily to 20,000 people, or 5.9 percent of the population, and in 1961, to 21,685 people. Of the latter figure, 20,987 were rural inhabitants and comprised 6.2 percent of the rural population. All in all, 55,000 people, or 15 percent of the county's population, died in those three years,[35] without taking into account deaths at the end of 1958 and in 1962. Mianyang County's Songya Commune had excellent growing conditions in 1959 and 1960, yet lost 13.2 percent of its 1958 population.[36]

Starvation released primitive brutality, and many cases of cannibalism were recorded in Sichuan. For example, in Dayi Commune's Anrenjiu administrative district, a thirty-year-old woman named Liu Yuanfang on April 23, 1960, bound her eight-year-old daughter, Li Suiqing, and nine-year-old son, Li Yongan, dragged them to a river, and drowned them, after being brutalized and deprived of food rations when her hungry children stole grain.[37] In the No. 3 production team of the No. 9 administrative district of Guan County's Puyang Commune, a forty-one-year-old woman, Pan Suhua, in March 1960 dug up the body of her husband after he committed suicide and, apart from cooking and eating the flesh, sold 5.875 kilos of his bones as bear bones at 75 *fen* per kilo.[38] Following the 1961 autumn harvest, many provinces began to emerge from the famine, but starvation continued in Sichuan. An August 31, 1961, inspection report on Guanyin clay consumption in Qu County noted:

> In late June, fifteen of the twenty households of the Wenxing production brigade of Daxia Commune were found to be digging up and eating Guanyin clay from Pujiashan. As more people began digging clay, the supply ran out in mid-July, and the commune members moved on to Taigongshi and Hedizi to find more. By late July and early August, the practice of digging and eating clay had spread to eighteen communes in those three districts.
>
> . . . An estimated 400-plus cubic meters of clay weighing about 250,000 kilos was dug up in approximately 10,000 individual diggings. The limited number of pits necessitated people to line up for their turn in the hot sun. Those who had traveled great distances and could not scale the mountain that same day to dig clay stayed overnight . . . then rose early the next day to go out digging . . . Because of hunger, many people ate the clay as they dug it up . . .
>
> After bringing the clay home, people would process it by dilution, grinding, or other methods and then mix it with pumpkin blossoms, gourd blossoms, or other vegetation and form it into cakes. These cakes were even sold in some places. Among the 262 households of the Qing-feng production brigade, clay was eaten by 214 households . . . The consumption of clay was generally reflected in stomach aches and constipation, and it caused many illnesses, with six people dying. Pre-

liminary inquiries at three production teams found that thirteen people had died from eating clay.[39]

Guanyin clay (more properly known as kaolin clay, and containing high levels of aluminum oxide) had a fine texture that reminded people of flour, but it had absolutely no nutritional value, and even animals wouldn't eat it.

By 1962, when most of China had recovered from the famine, people in Sichuan continued to starve. A report on edema by the Jiangjin prefectural party committee on January 21, 1962, stated that as of January 20 the number of edema cases was more than double that of the previous year. A report by the Jiangjin prefectural party committee on January 29 stated that Jiangbei County had 22 percent of its population suffering illness, and that 84 percent of the infirm were suffering from edema or emaciation.[40] On January 25, 1962, Ma Jiliang of the Changshou County party committee work group said 36,000 people were suffering from edema as of January 15, a 157 percent increase since the latter half of December; by January 22, 9.2 percent of the population was affected. Edema hit 25.5 percent of the population in Jiangnan District, and 1,700 of the county's residents died in the first half of January. Lack of food led wives to kill husbands, fathers to kill sons, and brothers to kill brothers. At Yunji Commune, 1,513 households, or 37.8 percent of the total, were eating Guanyin clay.[41] A bulletin on edema by the Wanxian prefectural party committee on January 26, 1962, found that the number of edema and emaciation cases had increased by 17.87 percent over the previous week, and mortalities had increased by 25.3 percent.[42]

On March 17, 1962, food minister Chen Guodong wrote a report to Vice-Premier Li Xiannian based on a report by the deputy director of Sichuan's grain bureau, Guan Xuesi. The report found that in the eleven hardest-hit counties, 145,800 people had died from July 1961 to March 1962. As of the end of January, Jiangbei County had 147,000 cases of edema, affecting 24.6 percent of the population. In December 1961 alone, 7,225 people had died in that county, and as of early March an average of 100 people were dying each day. Corpses could be seen along the roadsides and floating in the rivers. At Bishan County's Daxing Commune, 12 percent of the population had died in the previous three months, and in the Xinglong production brigade, 13.8 percent of the population had died.[43]

In a report on May 27, 1962, Sichuan's deputy secretary-general, Zhou Yi, wrote:

> Tracts of fallow fields can be seen along the Xichang, Dechang, and Miyi highways. This is reportedly not because of drought, but because too many people have died during the previous years, and there is no one left to till the fields . . . While we were passing through the No. 6 and No. 7 production brigades of Ya'an's Zishi Commune, a woman was found beaten senseless along the road, and people said she had been severely beaten for stealing food . . . in the wheat fields, the weeds grew as tall as the wheat, while huge paddy fields lay fallow. Disease is still a serious problem, and people continue to die. Members of the commune say a third of their people have died, and there's no sign of any letup.[44]

During the 1962 autumn harvest, there were still reports of starvation deaths in Ya'an County. Lushan County had at least a thousand orphans. In production teams with a higher incidence of mortality, orphans made up 20 percent of the population. The Guangming production team of Qingyuan Commune was reduced by nearly half to fifty-five members, including thirteen orphans.[45]

CALLING IT AN "EPIDEMIC," NOT STARVATION

Amid the massive population loss, throughout China reference was made only to "epidemics," and no mention of starvation was allowed. The May 23, 1959, edition of the Central Committee Propaganda Department's *Propaganda and Education Trends* cited Health Ministry reports of 6,700 edema deaths. Shandong had 779,000 edema cases and 618 deaths in the first quarter of the year, and Henan had 153,000 cases of edema and more than 2,000 deaths. This report contained no information on Sichuan and Anhui, because the situation in those two provinces was still being kept tightly under wraps.

This report analyzed the causes of edema as: (1) due to tight food supplies, people were eating salt to build up their stamina, consuming more than 50 grams per day (as opposed to the normal daily intake of 15 grams), and the salt was causing metabolic obstructions that brought about edema; (2) food supplies lacked variety, with a severe shortage or imbalance of fats and protein; (3) edema cases from the previous year had not been completely cured; and (4) the disease accompanied chronic illness, anemia, physical frailty, old age, and poor digestion.[46]

As peasants starved in the millions in the spring of 1960, Mao drafted directives on health work: "Health work has slacked off . . . The Central Committee reminds all comrades to take this matter seriously, and to relaunch the patriotic health campaigns that were allowed to slide over the past two years."[47]

On February 1, 1961, the Central Committee endorsed a Health Ministry report that classified conditions associated with starvation, such as edema, emaciation, amenorrhea, and uterine prolapse, as routine illnesses. The report demanded that all localities reinforce their "treatment of disease."[48] The Sichuan provincial party committee responded by issuing a notice that used the term *disease* to disguise starvation and advocated "health work" in place of "famine relief." The notice proposed: (1) launching a crash campaign to prevent and treat edema; (2) further strengthening collectivized hygiene work centered around the communal kitchens and ensuring that the communal kitchens were operating effectively; and (3) using prevention and treatment of edema as the core of integrated efforts to prevent and treat hookworm, schistosomiasis (snail fever), malaria, filariasis, and seasonal contagions. These measures ignored the fundamental lack of food. From this time on, reports used the terms *disease*, *infectious disease*, or *epidemic* when referring to infirmity and death caused by starvation.

On the morning of August 9, 1959, a Sichuan provincial party committee member reported that edema and diarrhea were rampant in Changning County, and that 13 percent of the population had been stricken since June. One production team had suffered a mortality rate of 17 percent since spring. Doctors attributed the "epidemic" to unsanitary conditions in the communal kitchens and a lack of vitamin B, while practitioners of traditional Chinese medicine blamed humidity and digestive imbalances.[49] The report dared not attribute the deaths to starvation.

Soon after the 1959 autumn harvest, Gulin County suffered a high rate of starvation deaths, which official reports attributed to an "epidemic." A December 7 prefectural party committee report shrank the number of "epidemic" patients to 403 and implied that the locality's real problem was hookworm disease. "Edema is a latter-stage manifestation of hookworm disease," the report said, and insisted that it was "not caused by consuming food substitutes."[50]

This report met with Li Jingquan's approval, and he wrote a memo on it the next day: "This report brings out a problem, which is that edema and hookworm disease often coincide . . . we should focus on curing hookworm disease."[51]

On December 12 the Luzhou prefectural investigation group on the Gulin epidemic found no trace of malnourishment or starvation, but focused on hookworm disease, influenza, and gastrointestinal illness: "Immediate action is needed . . . against diseases and pests, with a major focus on the prevention and treatment of hookworm disease, as well as propaganda and education work aimed at improving hygiene in the communal kitchens and taking vigorous preventive measures against various common winter illnesses and infectious diseases."[52] This cover-up was called a "patriotic health campaign."

Since the patriotic health campaign did nothing to alleviate hunger, the "epidemic" progressed. The mortality rate in Lu County reached 7 percent, and during five days in January 1961, 218 people died.[53]

While all localities were ordered to organize medical treatment, the government refused to relax its hold on the one effective cure: grain. Anyone calling on the state to supply food was accused of being a right opportunist. Each locality then developed its own prescription for edema.

In April 1960, Zizhong County's prescription was one egg, 50 grams of sorghum spirits (100 proof or higher), and 10 grams of realgar (an arsenic sulfide). The ingredients were blended and consumed in one dose. It was claimed that this treatment prevented recurrence of the condition while producing no side effects.[54] All localities reported their prescriptions to the provincial party committee, which passed them on to other localities. These prescriptions involved brown sugar, soybeans, and medicinal herbs, with some also adding eggs—all rare and precious commodities to which only cadres, and not the average peasant, had access.

The Sichuan provincial party committee called on all localities to round up stricken individuals for treatment. School buildings, ancestral halls, and cowsheds were used as medical wards. A March 1961 report stated that 27,005 provisional edema hospitals had been set up and that more than 952,000 people were under treatment.[55]

Conditions at these sites were abysmal, lacking doctors, medicine, and financial resources. No one was in charge of managing care, and mishaps were frequent. Hechuan County's Yongxing Commune recorded six injuries from burns or falls within half a month, with three people dying of burns.[56]

A hospital at the Zhongjian production brigade of Jiangbei County's Renmu Commune had 158 patients and only one doctor, who himself was bedridden. The three nursing attendants had no professional training. The hospital had no vegetables, no boiled or hot water, no heat, and no medicine.

At the hospital in the Liu'er production brigade of Jiangbei County's Shiba Commune, 172 patients shared 30-odd beds. Dozens of people lay packed together on thin layers of straw and without basic sanitation. Nearly a third were stricken with influenza.

The hospital at Fuling County's Mingjia Commune was managed by a production brigade cadre with no medical training. One of the hospital's so-called doctors was an accountant, and one of the two nursing attendants was an eleven-year-old orphan. The smell of the wards was so horrendous that the nursing attendants couldn't bear to enter them.[57]

At the hospital in Fuling County's Wuma Commune, patients never knew when they would get their next meal, and saltwater replaced vegetables. Patients died every day. Since admission to the hospital meant a reduction of work points and food rations, many discharged patients succumbed to starvation.[58]

At the provisional hospital in the Luxi production brigade of Lushan County's Qingyuan Commune, patients cooked their own meals. Lacking cooking implements and fuel, more than twenty took turns cooking in a single washbasin. Tianquan County's Daping Commune admitted 88 people to its hospital, of whom 33 were dead within two months.[59] During an inspection visit to Ya'an, a provincial deputy secretary-general asked why edema sufferers weren't in a hospital. They said the hospitals were so bad that people died faster there.[60] The edema hospital in Jintang County's Wuxing administrative district had been converted from a cowshed, and 90 percent of the patients lay on the floor on thin straw mattresses. Some patients had no blankets, though the weather was cold even during daylight. At Guanghan County's Jinyu Commune, the hospital director loaded moribund patients into coffins and buried them alive.

The edema hospital in the No. 2 administrative district of Jintang County's Qixian Commune was a shack made of cornstalks. Patients slept on straw, with men and women sharing the same quarters. At Zhongxing Hospital, patients died without anyone disposing of the corpses. Patients in the same room who could still walk moved to another room, but those too weak to move "shared the ward with the dead for three days and nights."[61]

The hospital at Guanghan's Songlin Commune took in 250 patients in half a year's time. When prefectural party cadre Wang Shuben looked into the situation, he learned that 97 had died. Two more died on the day of his visit and three the day after. Few were expected to survive another two weeks.[62]

Gynecological disorders were rampant, especially amenorrhea and the excrutiatingly painful uterine prolapse. The sudden termination of menstruation was accompanied by dizziness, weakness of the limbs, abdominal bloating and cramping, and an emaciated appearance that rural people referred to as the "parching illness." A Wenjiang County survey in June 1960 of more than fifty thousand women between the ages of eighteen and forty-five found that more than twenty thousand had stopped menstruating, with more than two thousand suffering from uterine prolapse. The report noted that these figures were "probably an understatement." A survey of Jinma and Yongxing communes found that half of the women at Jinma had stopped menstruating, and 60 percent at Yongxing. Among the 896 women at Jinma Commune who were no longer menstruating, 334 were ages eighteen to twenty-five. A survey from the Huafeng administrative district of Wenjiang's Yongquan Commune stated that among 124 women ages fifteen to fifty, 90 had stopped menstruating, comprising more than 70 percent of the total.[63]

These illnesses were caused by malnutrition, but no supplementary nourishment was provided. Ineffective treatment was compounded by incompetence. Struggling desperately to treat more patients than they could manage, doctors frequently overmedicated, with disastrous results. Li Mingzheng, a doctor at a "convalescent hospital" in Qionglai's Shuangjiang Commune, mixed toxic herbs into a prescription that attendants gave to patients without regard to appropriate preparation or dosage. Two hours later, all twenty-nine patients who had taken the medication began crying out in anguish, but the attendants had gone off-site to rest. By the time Dr. Li rushed back at 5:00 a.m., he found four of the patients already in rigor mortis and others gasping on the verge of death. He ran from the hospital and drowned himself.[64]

"Medical treatments" could not cure starvation, so the "epidemic" spread. A production team in Yibin County lost about a quarter of its population in seven months.[65] The high number of deaths left many fields uncultivated. At Yibin County's Anbian Commune, 2,506 *mu* out of 13,171 *mu* of arable land lay fallow.[66] The Yibin prefectural party committee reported in February 1962 that its remedies were ineffective and that deaths continued to rise.[67]

COMMUNE MEMBERS STARVE WHILE CADRES FEAST

The assignment of all food supply to the communal kitchens and the prohibition against cooking at home put life-and-death power in the hands of cadres, enabling them to seize public property and enforce official privilege. While peasants ate gruel, cadres ate rice; while peasants ate vegetables, cadres ate meat; and while peasants ate only a mouthful of meat, cadres ate several days' worth.

The staff of the communal kitchens held the ladles, and therefore enjoyed the greatest power in distributing food. They could dredge a richer stew from the bottom of a pot or merely skim a few vegetable slices from the thin broth near the surface. Staff could also creep back to cook something for themselves in the dead of night and carry food home for family members. These key postings typically went to relatives or trusted confederates of cadres.

In Sichuan as elsewhere, cadres routinely took more than their share of scarce food supplies during the famine. A report by provincial inspectors found that at Changning County's Taoping Commune, nine out of twelve party branch members had corruptly diverted resources. At least 60 percent of the commune's cadres had corruptly diverted or divided up resources for personal use. In the commune's Shizi administrative district, Yan Haichen and four others privately divided up 7,000 kilos of millet, while the head of the Zhongba administrative district, Zhang Jichen, corruptly made off with more than 1,500 kilos of grain. Commune members said, "All of the food we've worked so hard to grow has been gobbled up by the crows."[68]

At the Xiaohe production brigade, branch party secretary Jiang threw a birthday feast for his father in 1961, at which 160 guests consumed more than 50 kilos of grain. Jiang was dismissed but then reinstated in 1962, at which time he operated a cadre mess hall that used up more than 400 kilos of the grain retained by the production brigade and another 200 kilos provided by the state for commune members, while taking more than 150 kilos home for himself. At the Nianpan production brigade, fifty-three cadres made their way through 830.5 kilos of grain between January and August of 1962. Commune members said, "We starve until our skulls shine through our scalps, while the cadres glisten with fat." "Commune members are wan and emaciated, while cadres are fat and flush."[69]

As the communal kitchen of the Chunhua administrative district of Dianjiang County's Chengxi Commune ran out of food, cadres helped themselves to scarce supplies and feasted as if nothing were amiss. In the latter half of 1959, several of the district's cadres divided up the seed grain that remained after the late autumn planting, taking some home and squandering the rest. Following the Mid-Autumn Festival, they commandeered dozens of ducks from the sideline occupation team and divided them up.[70]

At Dianjiang County's Jiefeng Commune, 177 people were discovered to have committed thefts, including 137 cadres at the level of production team leader or above. This larcenous majority made up 77 percent of the commune's thieves. Apart from stealing grain and other property, these cadres engaged in a variety of abuses against commune members. A production brigade leader in the Shihua administrative district used "confiscating the assets of rich peasants" as a pretext for raiding the home of an old upper-middle peasant named Xia Bingcheng and taking away two bedspreads, three mosquito nets, 55 kilos of tung oil seed, 10 kilos of sesame seeds, half a kilo of lacquer, a kilo of chili peppers, and 0.75 kilos of tobacco leaves, not even sparing the straw mats on the beds.[71]

Hongguang Commune had two notorious couples; one consisted of the head of the county party committee's rural work department, Pan Zhaoqing, and commune party secretary Zheng Gongyao, and the other was made up of Hexing Commune party secretary, Liu Shaoyuan, and the Hedubai administrative district party secretary, You Fuqun. The cadre canteen they operated used up all the sugar and eggs set aside for the sick and for the kindergarten. On New Year's Day 1960, the commune slaughtered a 65-kilo pig, of which Liu and You took away 30 kilos. At that time, six of Hedubai District's communal kitchens had closed due to lack of food, and commune members were given only a small amount of boiled sweet potato leaves, but Liu and You held a sumptuous feast in honor of their son's first birthday. In order to serve silver carp at dinner, during the depths of winter they forced a dozen commune members to go out and catch 30 kilos of fish, of which Liu, You, Pan, and Zheng ate more than 15 kilos. Once when Liu Shaoyuan encountered a commune member carrying a chicken, he claimed the chicken was stolen and grabbed it. When the commune member objected, Liu went to the local administrative office and pretended to call the police. At that, the peasant ran off, and Liu and his friends ate the chicken. In 1960, Pan Zhaoqing and Zheng Gongyao had much to celebrate: Pan was promoted to Huayang County party secretary, and Zheng to the standing committee of the Pi County party committee.[72]

Sichuan Province's files have retained only the records of misconduct by grassroots cadres, and nothing on the special privileges enjoyed by cadres above the county level; this is the result of the tight control of information imposed by the Sichuan provincial party committee. An official of Chongqing's municipal party secretariat later described Li Jingquan's living conditions at the time. While Li stayed at Chongqing's Panjiaping Guesthouse, he watched a movie after nearly every evening meal, followed by a game of bridge, or else he enjoyed a play followed by dancing. The movies and plays were always special presentations, and the dancing or card games were followed by a midnight snack.[73] While grassroots cadres focused on getting enough to eat, a minority of high-level cadres pursued pleasure as the bodies of the starved littered the countryside.

FOOD PENALTIES

In the throes of starvation, peasants ate anything they could find, including unripened wheat, rice, and corn. If caught in the act, they were fined or had meals withheld, or suffered corporal punishment that sometimes proved fatal. Peasants were often accused and punished even when they had not stolen food.

On a spring day in 1961, Zhu Yufa, a member of Wuyi Commune, dug up 1.25 kilos of sown lima beans, for which he was fined 120 yuan (equivalent to four months' pay for a departmental-grade cadre). All of the clothing, mats, and foodstuffs in his home were seized, and the clothes on his back, after which he was struggled and required to give up grain and work points every day.

The prefectural party committee had assigned counties the duty of extracting 1.2 million yuan, and the county level passed this duty down to the districts, which passed it on down to the communes. In each commune, the production brigades adopted merciless measures to meet their extraction targets, even if it meant the ruination and dissolution of families. In the villages of Chengjia, Ledao, Longtan, and Tangshan districts, cadres on "extraction" duty seized chickens, ducks, and other property on sight, grabbing even clothing and quilts. Some turned the extraction process to their personal benefit. When commune member Tong Guangqian took advantage of his wood-chopping duties to take a few sticks of firewood home from the communal kitchen, he was fined 270 yuan. Since Tong didn't have the money, the commune took away the two lacquered coffins his elderly parents had prepared, while the production team took a ewe, a chicken, and a duck. Using debate rather than evidence, all but one of the 255 households in Funan Commune's three production brigades were judged to have engaged in theft.[74]

Apart from stiff fines, penalties included withholding meals, corporal punishment, detention, ransacking homes, and seizing property. In a work team in Changjiang Commune, sixty-four out of seventy households had meals withheld. This penalty could be imposed for not arriving at the communal kitchen on time, missing work due to illness, and failing to provide the communal kitchen with wild herbs. Three types of people were exempted from this penalty: cadres, the family members of cadres, and relatives of cadres.

A survey of twenty-two communes in Gulin County for January to June 1960 found seventy-six cases of serious injury from cadres beating commune members. Sixteen died, six were crippled, and seven severely injured, while seven starved to death after being deprived of meals and many committed suicide. The head of the No. 5 production team of Shengdeng Commune's No. 9 administrative district, a man surnamed Zhang, routinely took a double ration of rice. When commune member Huang Wenxian failed to turn up for work one morning, Zhang docked his morning meal. Huang demanded, "Why are you docking my meal? Is someone going to eat a double share?" Considering this a personal affront, Zhang ordered commune member Mao Xueyou to pick up some dung and shove it into Huang's mouth.[75]

The provincial party committee's Wenjiang rectification work group reported:

From the end of 1959 to early 1960, in the course of taking a firm grasp of production and livelihood and further developing the struggle against right deviation, there was a widespread tendency to engage in violations of law and discipline, such as fines, withholding of meals, and penalties based on unreasonable assessments of losses. In February, March, and April of 1960, the entire county engaged in an "assault on backwardness," which included the merging of administrative districts and communal kitchens, and during which practices such as fines, withholding of meals, and trussing up, hanging, and beating commune members, as well as "scrubbing the taro," "overseas study," and "symposia for well-to-do middle peasants" [referring to penal labor under surveillance during the day, and multiple struggle sessions at night], arbitrary detention and arrest, and arbitrary dismissal of cadres became increasingly serious and widespread . . . Corporal punishments have not stopped as of the time of this meeting.[76]

The report further stated that in Zhugao District from February to November 1960, cadres were responsible for the beating deaths of six commune members, the suicide of eighty-three members subjected to "taro scrubbing" or being hung and beaten, and the starvation death of one commune member deprived of meals. Preliminary figures from Zhugao Commune from January to December 1960 showed that cadres punished 241 commune members through "taro scrubbing" or hanging and beating, deprived 265 of meals, ransacked 230 homes, docked the work points of 99 members, fined 68, and sent 27 to "reform through labor." Seventeen of those penalized died, and 3 were permanently crippled.

The reader will recall that "scrubbing the taro" consisted of surrounding the victim and thrusting him from one tormenter to the next. The report found that in Longwang Commune, three people died from "taro scrubbing," and two were permanently crippled. A poor peasant named Gong Mingtong who stole some sweet potatoes after having his meals withheld for fifteen days was put through a "taro scrubbing" that left him severely injured, and upon returning home he killed himself. In the Daming administrative district, a sick commune member, Xiao Yougen, was accused of "malingering" when he took too long carrying a load of rice, and was subjected to three rounds of taro scrubbing. On the second day, he hanged himself. Xiao's father dropped dead upon learning of his son's death, while Xiao's wife became mentally deranged and his young son soon died of neglect.

In August 1960, cadres at Shuangliu Commune persecuted five commune members to death. The commune's party secretary caused the deaths of two commune members in 1960, while penalizing more than ten people with "taro scrubbing," withholding meals from more than three hundred, and imposing fines or hard labor on more than twenty. According to incomplete figures, eight people starved to death in Tuqiao District from January to November after cadres withheld their meals. Another twenty-six people committed suicide after accusations of "taking petty advantages" resulted in their being struggled or subjected to "taro scrubbing," while two others were literally beaten to death by cadres.

Incomplete statistics from Taoping Commune showed that of 441 cadres at the rank of mess leader or above, 212 had deprived commune members of meals, 19 had taken part in beatings, 48 had engaged in trussing up commune members, and 31 had engaged in physical abuse resulting in death. The cadres set up unauthorized labor reform teams and prisons, deprived the sick of food, and forced ill people to work. In the Niankan production team, a woman and her three children were deprived of food for ten days while bedridden with illness, and three died. The labor reform team of the Zhongba administrative district included an eleven-year-old girl named Chen Yuxiu, who was forced to work for five straight days and nights. She collapsed, bleeding from the nose and mouth, and ultimately died. In the Datong administrative district, commune member Li Youcheng was so afraid of having his meals withheld that he went to work while ill and collapsed in the field. After he was carried home, the production team leader accused him of malingering and kicked him several times. Li died.[77]

In spring 1960, party secretary Tan of Nanping Commune declared that anyone stealing food would be hung, beaten, and fined, and he personally oversaw the beating of six people to set an example. He said, "We have plenty of workers, so if a few are beaten to death it doesn't matter; beating ten to death makes five pairs, and they can be cut up and made into nice fat pumpkin buns." "A militant approach has to be taken toward these people, and anyone who refuses to take part is a right deviationist." Theft of one lima bean or an ear of corn brought a fine of one yuan, while stealing a sweet potato resulted in a fine of five yuan. Beatings, fines, ransackings, and the withholding of meals became routine. According to available statistics, 89 out of 159 cadres at the rank of production team leader or above took part in trussing up and beating commune members. A total of 565 commune members were beaten, while 478 were fined and 588 had their homes ransacked. Corporal punishments included tortures known as "hanging a side of pork," "ducklings floating in the pond," "monkey squeezing a pimple," and so on.[78] An inspection team found that

44 people died after being beaten or deprived of food, and 19 were permanently crippled, while 378 households were fined a total of 12,400 yuan. In at least one case, cadres strung up a man, then used part of his fine to buy food and liquor for a private feast.[79]

During an "assault on backwardness" in February and March of 1960, the deputy party secretary of Taiping District, known to local residents as "Tang the King of Hell," engaged in what he termed "breaking up nests of backwardness," during which he forced the relocation of 178 households in "backward" compounds and harshly penalized the recalcitrant. A commune member named Zhong Xiangcheng drowned himself.[80]

When peasants fled Jintang County to escape the famine in January 1960, the county party committee stipulated, "The families of out-flowing laborers should write letters telling them to return; otherwise they will be responsible for supplying their own food, and the commune will categorically refuse assistance."[81] Longsheng Commune went a step further, requiring family members to write daily letters to the refugees; failure to produce a letter meant the withholding of that day's meals. Through these and other conditions, the managers of communal canteens held life and death in their hands.

The campaign against "false reporting of output and private withholding" provided an additional pretext for persecuting commune members. In October 1959, Rong County had reached only 70 percent of its autumn procurement quota. The county party committee launched a panicked campaign of beatings and arrests to ensure that the quota was met. County party secretary Xu launched the struggle by saying, "The masses are truly rising up to beat people, and we shouldn't discourage them." The attack on right deviation in Changshan District led to more than thirty commune and production team cadres being strung up and beaten, with more than ten crippled and three arrested.

On October 25 a cadre meeting at Zhonggulou focused on fighting right deviation and rooting out concealed foodstuffs. Beatings were even harsher and more widespread than at Changshan. Four of Lede Commune's fourteen commune-level cadres were beaten, another eight were dismissed, and two more were disciplined. A total of 142 cadres of various ranks from that commune were beaten, with one production team head dying and a production brigade leader crippled. Party secretary Xu and others raised slogans such as "grain before people," "socialism before people," and "hand over grain or be beaten." Units set up their own "police forces," "prisons," and "labor reform teams." The practice spread to the urban areas, and to party organs, factories, and schools. At least seven cadres were beaten to death at Changshan, Renhe, and Liujia communes, and three commune members were beaten to death in the No. 3 production brigade of Fuxing Commune.[82]

In September 1960, Shuinian Commune's party secretary Ye declared that any cadres involved in false reporting and private withholding would be transferred, and any commune members involved in theft would also be transferred. After the meeting, a plan was drawn up for the relocation of sixty households. Under party secretary Ye, 60 percent of the commune's households were ransacked, forty-eight individuals were trussed up, hung, and beaten, and seventy-six households had meal rations withheld. In a fifteen-member county party committee working group, thirteen members had participated in beating, penalizing, and ransacking. Ye himself trussed up and beat seven people.[83]

Fuling County's Ma'an Commune officially provided commune members with a food ration of 187.5 grams per day, but cadres routinely skimmed off a portion of this ration. In the Taiyi production brigade Xia Daozhen took corn from the brigade during an interruption to food supplies and was docked 850 kilos of grain, levied in a 20 percent deduction from his ration. Someone objected that Xia would starve to death at that rate, but the brigade leader retorted, "If he can't pay it off in one year, we'll keep up the deduction for two or three years! If someone starves to death, we'll haul him out, and if two starve, we'll carry them out, too!" Whenever crops were stolen from the fields, the watchmen had to make up for the loss. In the Dashi production brigade, Zheng Derong was guarding a corn field when more than a hundred ears were stolen and he was forced to surrender 48 kilos of his grain ration. Penalties compounded starvation and edema. The Dashi production brigade lost fifty-one of its members from January to September, and more than 90 percent of its women suffered from amenorrhea. Only two children were born that year, both to cadre families.[84]

Jiangjin County's Shanglong Commune imposed fines for infractions that included eating unripe lima beans, missing meetings, overstaying a leave, the death of a pig, failing to report the death of a pig, failing to meet a production quota, catching eels during the midday nap, transplanting seedlings too far apart, and damage of crops by children (when starving children stole unripened grain). In one district of Tongliang County's Xijiao Commune, plucking a single lima bean brought a fine of 10 fen, more than a day's pay at the time.[85]

On the road from Bishan to Yongchuan, two cadres from the province and prefecture, Liu Wenzhen and Zhang Fengwu, saw three commune members carrying household goods and stopped their car to inquire. Zhou Jingming from Mafang Commune explained that her husband had fallen ill and she had no food for him, so she had asked for food at the communal kitchen. One of the kitchen staff gave Zhou permission to pull some turnips, but the work group leader accused her of stealing. Zhou had to surrender the turnips and was fined 37 yuan, more than a month's pay for a departmental-level cadre. His starvation unrelieved, Zhou's husband died. With no way to pay the fine, Zhou married Ding Shulin of Yongchuan County and took her children with her. Ding invited the work group leader to a meal and requested that Zhou's fine be withdrawn. The work group leader refused, but accepted some of Zhou's household effects in compensation. That left 19 yuan for Zhou to repay before being allowed to move. Liu Wenzhen and Zhang Fengwu were astonished that a lowly work group leader could impose such tyrannical control over commune members.[86]

By putting every aspect of life under the control of cadres, the system of communes and communal kitchens served as the foundation for appalling large-scale persecution of peasants throughout China. Of course, conditions were stricter in some areas and more relaxed in others. The deciding factor was the character and capabilities of the cadres. Most were of poor quality, and pressure from above ensured that persecution was the rule. Mao attributed this outrage to the "democratic revolution not being thoroughly accomplished," and blamed atrocities on Kuomintang influence. This was clearly inconsistent with reality and was merely a means of shifting blame. During the rectification of communes and incorrect work styles, abusive cadres were punished and many were dismissed. In Xinfan County's Hetun Commune, for example, some 66 percent of the cadres were dismissed or demoted. However, the mass dismissals caused so much disruption that many dismissals were rescinded after 1962.

A COUNTERCURRENT OF RELIEF

Even as Li Jingquan promoted communization and communal kitchens, a grassroots countercurrent led to the allocation of land to households and the disbanding of communal kitchens. These moves were crucial in reducing starvation deaths, but suffered ruthless suppression.

An inspection report on August 4, 1959, found several production teams at Xuyong County's Tiantang Commune assigning sweet potato output quotas to households and allotting work points based on production. Supporters said the method provided motivation for production while reducing the burden on cadres. Households with a greater labor capacity particularly endorsed it, while those with a weaker labor capacity lost out. Li Jingquan weighed in with a memo on August 31 labeling the report "a classic case of right-deviating material."[87] On September 1, 1959, the inspection group described methods employed in Luzhou Prefecture:

> . . . Following a meeting of county party secretaries, each county drew up its own plans for disbanding the communal kitchens. It was said that there were shortages of grain rations and firewood, that the communal kitchens caused wastage of food and provided "loopholes for graft and embezzlement," and that "although the communal kitchens have advantages, we can't afford these advantages at present." . . . The majority of communal kitchens were closed down in many counties . . . On May 22, after the provincial party committee learned of this, it immediately issued a stern accusation of right deviation and ordered the prefectural first secretary to resume operation of the communal kitchens within a set time. There was also a stern accusation of rich peasant cadres undermining the communal kitchens with the intention of undermining the people's communes and opposing socialism.
>
> . . . In Longchang County and other localities, land was divided up and allocated to peasants on two occasions in January and May . . . The amount of land so allocated exceeded the amount provided for under the advanced agricultural cooperatives; commune members showed increasing enthusiasm for the operation and management of the land they cultivated themselves, and decreasing concern for collective production. It affected the stability of the communal kitchens; it affected the commune's ability to meet its grain quotas.
>
> . . . In early May, at the same time that the prefectural party committee arranged for the disbanding of communal kitchens and delegated the rearing of pigs to the production teams, it also arranged for a portion of the collectively owned pigs to be returned to individual commune members.

This report concluded by saying:

> All of the above reflect right-deviationist thinking . . . A portion of well-to-do middle peasants and cadres with a well-to-do middle peasant background have advocated going off on their own and opposing collectivization, exaggerating the extent of the food supply problem, opposing the communal kitchens, and calling for pigs to be returned to individuals. The leadership considered this an evil trend and voiced its criticism, while at the same time coming under the influence of this thinking and making concessions. Some leading cadres passed down the message that "it doesn't matter if a cat is yellow or black, as long as it catches mice," which suggested that collective production and individual production are of equal value.

(It appears that Deng Xiaoping some twenty years later borrowed his famous maxim on economic reform from his home province.)

On September 2, Li Jingquan responded:

> It would appear that Luzhou Prefecture's right-opportunistic errors relating to communal kitchens, plots of land allocated for private use, and private rearing of pigs is a prefecture-wide phenomenon . . . This greatly warrants further discussion and the continued adoption of all necessary means to bring about rectification.[88]

Many cadres in Luzhou were replaced, and some were subjected to criticism. In the ensuing campaign against right deviation, prefectural party secretary Deng Zili and deputy party secretary Chen Huaitong were cited as the prime examples of right deviation in Sichuan Province. Harsh political suppression failed to stem the reformist countercurrent, however, and while the Sichuan provincial party committee continued to issue "directives on rectifying the assignment of output quotas to households," the practice was never abandoned.

A September 19, 1961, report by a Sichuan provincial party committee work group found that the rectification of the right-deviating error of assigning output quotas to households was not thorough enough, however, and a certain number of cadres were unwilling to give up the practice. An ever-increasing surface area was being devoted to household output quotas for spring grain crops and the cultivation of autumn vegetables on collective land. "Among the masses, the erroneous right-regressionist thinking favoring the assignment of output quotas to households has become quite serious." "Among ten communal party secretaries in Xinglong District, not one resolutely opposes the assignment of output quotas to households." The report went on to say that right-regressionist error had already become a tenacious force, and, if not addressed, would cause a relapse into old malpractices. For that reason, "[i]t is necessary to extensively and penetratingly carry out rectification of the right-regressionist error of assigning output quotas to households through a mass movement centered on socialist education."[89]

On September 25, 1961, Li Jingquan issued a lengthy memo agreeing with the report's recommendation of a Socialist Education Movement, but the campaign failed to stem the flow of the salutary countercurrent. A year later, it was reported that in Jiangbei County "assignment of output quotas to households is common and serious. Among the district's 591 production teams, almost all of last year's sweet potatoes were produced under allocation of quotas to households, along with 60 percent of this year's late autumn harvest." The county's rationale was that only household output quotas could increase enthusiasm for production, as opposed to the careless and haphazard effort devoted to collective production; quotas to households rewarded effort with more to eat; household quotas made individuals responsible for their losses so that they took precautions against theft, while no one felt the immediate effects of losses to collective food resources; output quotas to households relieved cadres from assigning work and reduced friction over work points. In summation, after output quotas were assigned to households, the food supply increased and starvation was eliminated. "When you let fields lie fallow and don't allow us to cultivate them, how will people not starve?"[90]

Other localities also allocated large amounts of land to households. At the Wuyi production brigade of Pingshan County's Qingliang Commune, 70.1 percent of the arable land and 44.0 percent of the plow oxen had been allocated to households by August 1961. Provincial party committee leader Mou Haixiu said, "At first only a few percent were involved, but . . . it now involves 26 percent of the production teams. I think it could well spread to all of them."[91]

The Sichuan provincial party committee tried to reverse the trend by awarding more work points for higher grain output. Peasants still couldn't control grain allocation, however, and the unpopular initiative was abandoned before being fully implemented.

No action at the upper levels could eliminate the practice of assigning output quotas to families, which had served as China's primary economic unit for thousands of years. Nevertheless, many grassroots cadres and peasants paid the price of harsh political oppression for the preservation of this countercurrent. To this day it is unknown how many families and lives were destroyed in the repeated campaigns against this lifesaving reform.

THE CAMPAIGN AGAINST RIGHT DEVIATION
EXACERBATES THE FAMINE

Sichuan's prolonged famine was directly related to the repeated campaigns against right deviation. The 1959 Lushan Conference was followed by a nationwide campaign to "defend the General Line and oppose right opportunism." Sichuan leader Li Jingquan had been ahead of the game, and with Mao's endorsement, he proceeded with even greater vigor.

On August 30, Li told provincial cadres to "smash one" and "defend four": "resolutely smash the activities of the right-opportunistic anti-party clique led by Comrade Peng Dehuai, defend the party's General Line, defend the central party leadership headed by Comrade Mao Zedong, defend party unity, and defend the socialist cause." He also reaffirmed the people's commune movement: "Failing to lead this movement will cause problems. If you don't believe me, see what happens if you disband it."[92]

At a meeting on September 7, 1959, Li insisted that "countering rightism is class struggle." Sichuan's governor, Li Dazhang, likewise concluded his report by emphasizing, "We are currently focused on countering rightism, which is an issue of standpoint and an issue of class."[93]

From August to September of 1959, Sichuan's provincial party committee convened an enlarged session during which it tasked more than 1,300 municipal and prefectural cadres with reading and taking a position on three controversial documents from the Lushan Conference. Political insiders had been tipped off and knew what to say, while other astute cadres took equivocal stands. Only a small minority of honest and uninformed cadres expressed support for all three documents. Once everyone had taken a stand, a recording of Mao's speech was played and the Central Committee's resolution was distributed. Through this process, sixty-one of the meeting's attendees were dubbed right opportunists, seriously right-deviating vacillators, class enemies who had infiltrated the party, and other bad elements (of whom the right opportunists and vacillators made up forty-nine). Eight of the right opportunists were selected for focused criticism at the conference.[94]

Among the eight primary targets was Zhang Jiayi, political commissar of the Eleventh Regiment of the Chengdu Military Region. His trouble was rooted in a single trip he had made back to his home village in Jiangsu the preceding July and August. Li Jingquan distributed a background document on this trip, including two letters Zhang wrote to the cadre department of the military region. On July 19, Zhang wrote:

> . . . upon arriving home I found many difficulties, including a lack of food, even if one has the money to buy it. Eating a few mouthfuls of grass and leaves has been a real education, and makes it difficult for me to think of staying home for long.
>
> The morale of the ordinary people is very poor; they have no confidence in production and are in great conflict with the leadership (saying Chairman Mao and the Communist Party are good, but the lower-level cadres are bad). Apart from a few people who are living somewhat better and are getting enough to eat, everyone else is suffering from hunger. This is the busy farming season, but adults are fed only 313 grams per day, and children 188 grams. The vast majority has been starved to an emaciated state of skin and bones and can hardly move. In our village of 700, in the two months of May and June (when people were being fed only 125 grams per day) more than 30 people died of illnesses related to malnutrition, starvation, or killing themselves by hanging or drowning. When doctors examine patients, they write on their prescriptions that the patients should have their food ration increased by 100 grams, and in that way they have managed to save a dozen or so people.
>
> My family is quite large, including my mother and father and six siblings. Apart from an estranged uncle who died of starvation, overall my twenty-member family is managing well. When I arrived home, everyone wept and wailed, especially my parents, and they begged me to take them away. They have money, but are unable to buy anything; they've been unable to use up the 30 or 40 yuan I send them every

month, and have considered suicide many times. If I don't take them away, it's quite possible that they'll starve to death or kill themselves. This situation weighs mightily on me, but I've been keeping it to myself.

Because of the above conditions, I'd like to bring my parents and fourth younger brother to Chengdu for a time (my brother has been too good—he eats nothing, but gives all of his food to our parents, and as a result he's all but unrecognizable). This is because the money I send home serves no purpose, given that there is no food to buy.

Please notify me as soon as possible regarding whether this request can be granted . . . If it's not possible, please also notify me. I won't raise a fuss over it, because I know this is not only my family's hardship . . .

Everything I have written above is true, and there is no exaggeration in it.

I've looked into production in my home village, and it's really horrifying. Very few people are in a condition to work, and more than twenty buffaloes have died, leaving only one calf. A great portion of the fields are lying fallow, and the situation is perilous.

Respectfully yours,
Zhang Jiayi, July 19

On August 6, Zhang responded to the reply he'd received:

. . . I have complied with the instructions in the department's letter regarding my parents, please don't worry.

From your letter I felt that my understanding of the current problems in the countryside is insufficient, and is even extremely problematic. I am deeply indebted to your timely expression of concern and criticism. But the problems in my home village should be considered serious; otherwise it will be difficult for me to blame this extremely grave problem on my thinking alone, and I will find it difficult to acknowledge my wrongdoing . . . these conditions actually exist. Compared with the political mood, living conditions, production, drive, and cadre-mass relations in Sichuan, Shaanxi, Henan, and other provinces, the situation in my home village is much worse. Why this is, I'm at a loss to say.

I believe that the region will quickly experience improvement, because it has attracted the attention of the upper levels, and rectification is now being carried out, along with the disciplining of a *number of cadres and the dismissal of quite a few (at the township level and below). Reportedly some will be brought to justice, along with mobilization of the masses (the masses are extremely backward here).*

. . . Because participating in some activities was very educational for me, I gained the following impressions: When studying documents relating to the people's communes, I gained a relatively firm grasp of their advantages, but had an insufficient understanding of the serious difficulties existing within the communes (in my home village, not in the entire country) and the complexity of building the communes due to objective issues (cadre work styles, poor living standards, not being rewarded for more effort, insufficient comprehension by the masses of the party's general and specific policies), and this home visit has resolved this; regarding reduction of expenses and practicing strict economy, this has resolved more than listening to several reports; the danger brought about when the masses don't firmly grasp the party's policies, and cadres alienate themselves from the masses; the importance of socialist education here, where the party's political ideological work is needed; a much greater understanding of the previously unanticipated virulence of the struggle between individual ownership and collective ownership, and the deep-rooted capitalist spontaneous power among the masses. I consider these my very fundamental points. There's more yet, which we can discuss when we meet. Please criticize me where I'm wrong.

These two letters transformed this political commissar into one of Sichuan's eight major right opportunists.

The Central Committee attached great importance to the report of the enlarged session of the Sichuan provincial party committee and distributed it throughout China on October 13, 1959,[95] with the following editorial remarks:

Right opportunists and people with seriously right-deviating thinking comprise only a minority of our ranks, but they obstruct execution of the General Line . . . their thinking will expand outward and spread its contagion like bacteria . . . It is necessary to thoroughly expose and criticize all right opportunists, all right-deviationist thinking, and all right-deviating actions, and eradicate them from every nook and cranny in the same way that we handle infectious germs.

Comparing right deviationists to germs and emphasizing the elimination of all such thinking set the tone for the campaign against right deviation as it escalated throughout the country. The Sichuan provincial party committee defined right deviationists as people who lowered production targets, underreported production, withheld grain while complaining of food shortages, and did not support communal kitchens.[96] The officials who drafted the provincial directives favored high production targets and procurement quotas and preservation of the large and collective people's communes, along with their communal kitchens, all of which epitomized the "struggle between the two roads." It was precisely these elements that created the Great Famine, and preserving them only prolonged it. Yet that was the goal of the campaign against right deviation.

According to a September 20 report from Wan County, Longbao Commune's campaign against right deviation required everyone to take a stand. Among 234 communal and production team cadres, 42.3 percent endorsed the General Line, while 44.9 percent displayed right deviation on particular issues. Another 10.3 percent were found to be seriously right-deviating, while incorrigible right opportunists made up the remaining 2.5 percent. A backbone contingent was trained to ensure that in mass debate, the seriously right-deviating individuals had "no leg to stand on and could only acknowledge the superiority of the communes and the communal kitchens." One hundred cadres and commune members were criticized, and organizational rectification was carried out to "ensure that poor peasants and farm laborers and promoters of progress dominated the leadership."

During the campaign against right deviation, all localities reported unearthing falsely reported output and private withholding. A December 18, 1959, report to the Central Committee secretariat by the Sichuan provincial party committee secretariat showed Wan County finding more than 3.7 million kilos of unreported grain. Shuangtang Commune and eight others in Zigong City admitted to more than 3.1 million kilos of unreported grain, comprising 8 percent of their total output. Qionglai County used large-scale warfare tactics to transform 400,000 *mu* of winter paddy fields. The figures on underreported and withheld grain were pure fiction that only resulted in higher procurement quotas.

Campaigns against right deviation were also carried out in factories and schools. Li Jingquan expanded the scope of the struggle at a meeting on November 7, 1959. He said,

Should non-party masses in government agencies be included in the campaign? In a word, yes. Should workers and staff members be included? New workers bring peasant viewpoints into the factories and the worker ranks are impure, so they need the struggle between the two roads to serve as a guiding principle for reform. Schools also need a campaign against rightism, but the Central Committee says we shouldn't pull out the white flags or engage in large-scale anti-rightist struggle. Some people are in fact rightists but aren't to be labeled as such. They should just have their thinking criticized.

Those in charge of the campaigns mobilized everyone to "air their views" as a means of "drawing the snake from its den." Pi County reported dividing its campaign into four stages: (1) calling for everyone to speak out; (2) organizing rallies and speeches to affirm achievements and establish positive models; (3) carrying out targeted criticism and voluntary self-examination, during which those with serious right-deviating thinking would be disciplined; and (4) "resolutely opposing right-deviationist thinking, and increasing production while economizing on food supplies so as to successfully emerge from the famine," arranging to collect grain for storage, establishing production plans, and getting a firm handle on late-autumn crops.[97] The campaign in Sichuan continued until 1962.

Incomplete statistics indicate that as of November 20, 1959, Sichuan had 197,015 cadres at the provincial, prefectural, and county levels, of whom 9,425 became key targets of criticism. Among these, 2,973 were labeled right opportunists, and 6,452 were found to have seriously right-deviationist thinking.[98] Other reports give somewhat higher numbers for political targets.[99]

There are no provincewide figures for the number of cadres at the commune level or below who were criticized, but case studies suggest there were many. In Hechuan County in 1959, 1960, and 1961, the extension of the campaign against right deviation to the grassroots level, combined with rectification of the communes and anti-hoarding campaigns, resulted in the disciplining of 5,184 cadres, one out of every five of the county's total. Among the 17,716 cadres at the commune level or below, 26.5 percent were disciplined, distributed among the ranks as follows:

At the commune level: party secretary, 60 percent; deputy party secretary, 35.7 percent; commune director and vice-director, 36.7 percent; ordinary cadre, 28.6 percent. At the production brigade level: party secretary and deputy party secretary, 57.2 percent; brigade head and deputy head, 38.7 percent; ordinary cadre, 31.6 percent. At the production team level: team head and deputy head, 24.8 percent; ordinary cadre, 11.8 percent.[100]

In Jiangbei County's Xinglong district from 1958 to 1962, among 328 cadres at the production brigade level, 40 percent were disciplined, and among 454 cadres at the production team level, 51 percent. Each number represents bloody torment and merciless attack, and the destruction of thousands of families through political persecution.[101]

In September 1961 the Sichuan provincial party committee responded to the CCP Central Committee call to "reexamine" the cases of those wrongly persecuted during the 1959 campaign against right deviation. Financial compensation was paid where people had died, become disabled, or committed suicide. However, party or Youth League membership was not posthumously restored in cases of suicide, which was considered a crime against the party.[102]

Following the Central Committee's "Seven Thousand Cadres Conference," a discussion by some cadres in Chongqing touched on how many people had starved to death in the province. This raised the question of how much the Central Committee knew. Liao Bokang, vice-chairman of Chongqing's municipal party committee secretariat and the Communist Youth League municipal party committee secretary, suggested that the Central Committee might have been kept in the dark. Yu Keshu, a deputy secretary of the Youth League's municipal party committee, suggested writing a letter to the Central Committee describing the actual situation in Sichuan, and the other deputy secretaries agreed. Yu had an anonymous letter from "a Communist party member" typed up.

In June 1961, Liao Bokang and Yu Keshu went to Beijing to attend the third plenum of the Youth League's seventh central committee, during which they reported the situation in Sichuan to Hu Yaobang. A brief report of their discussion was sent to the Central Committee secretariat, after which Yang Shangkun met with Liao and Yu for three and a half hours. Yang then reported to the Central Committee secretariat. After Deng Xiaoping learned of the situation, he had a group appointed to investigate. Once Li Jingquan learned of this, he wreaked his revenge.

From April 23 to May 8, 1962, Chongqing Municipality convened an enlarged party committee meeting during which an "anti-party clique" led by Liao and others was uncovered. The provincial party committee designated members of this clique as representatives of elements stirring up ill winds of wrongdoing, reversal of verdicts, and individualism in Sichuan Province.[103]

HOW MANY PEOPLE STARVED TO DEATH IN SICHUAN PROVINCE?

Figures from the Sichuan Province statistics bureau show that in 1961 the province's grain yield was 44.1 percent lower than in 1957, accompanied by a 56 percent reduction in live pigs, a 5.7 percent reduction in plow oxen, and a 51 percent reduction in edible oil. Former Xinhua Sichuan branch journalist Liu Zongtang believes these figures greatly understate the actual loss, as the statistics bureau provided figures it believed the leadership could accept. In Liu's view, oil production dropped at least 70 percent during that period, and any head count of pigs was meaningless, because surviving pigs had been reduced to skin and bones. (Sichuan was China's key pork producer.)

TABLE 6.1: SUPPLY OF GRAIN, LIVE PIGS, PLOW OXEN, AND OIL PRODUCTS IN SICHUAN PROVINCE, 1955–61

Year	1955	1956	1957	1958	1959	1960	1961
Grain (billion kilos)	20.23	22.25	23.25	24.6	18.4	16.15	13.0
Live pigs (millions)	19.073	20.0	25.0	26.0	20.0	12.0	11.0
Plow oxen (millions)	4.926	5.097	5.155	5.253	5.563	5.161	4.965
Oil (million kilos)	421.3	407.2	407.3	421.9	500.0	250.0	200.0

Sichuan's provincial planning commission found the statistics bureau's figures on grain yield too high, and in July 1962 it carried out a retrospective analysis of Sichuan's grain yield for the years 1957–61. The result was a revised grain yield of 21.5 billion kilos for 1957; 23.5 billion kilos for 1958; 19.5 billion kilos for 1959; 16.15 billion kilos for 1960 (the commission felt that even this figure might be too high); and 13.0 billion kilos for 1961.[104] The 1961 grain yield was 40 percent lower than in 1957.

Most pig deaths were concentrated in 1960. In October 1960, Neijiang had only 52,892 pigs, a decrease of 43.6 percent from 1959 and a decrease of 37.2 percent from June 1960. From January to October 1960, the county lost 47,298 pigs, comprising 58.5 percent of the pig stock at the end of 1959 and equivalent to 89.4 percent of the existing pig stock. Swine mortality was attributed 61.2 percent to starvation and 27.2 percent to disease.[105]

The population of Xinfan County's Hetun Commune stood at 10,650 when the commune was formed, but by March 1962 it had dropped to 8,500. Plow oxen decreased from 400 head to 343, and pigs from 4,700 head to 1,684. The commune's supply of buckets dropped from 1,576 to 750, and its drying mats from 5,340 to 785. Large farming implements were reduced by 70 to 80 percent. One thirty-household production team had only three winnowing baskets, two worn-out bamboo baskets, and one pouch for storing dried manure.[106] Hetun Commune was on the Chengdu Plains, benefiting from the Dujiang Dam and proximity to the provincial capital of Chengdu. In 1959 the rice yield was 228.5 kilos per *mu*, but it dropped to 190 kilos per *mu* in 1960 and 138.5 kilos in 1961. The distribution of profits in 1961 came out as negative 68 percent—peasants labored under starvation conditions for a year, only to end up indebted to the collective.

When Daozuo Commune was established in Qionglai County in November 1958, its No. 3 administrative district had a population of 840. With births as well as new residents moving in, the population should have reached 870 by the end of 1960, but instead, the district was hit by a wave of deaths in February and March of that year. All the communal kitchens ran out of food, and survivors were too weak to bury the dead. An elderly buffalo herder named Wang Qimao and his wife died in their bed and lay there several days before commune members, ordered to dispose of the bodies, simply dragged them to an open manure pit. When

Wang Qihong, Liao Wenlan, and four others died, their bodies remained on a slope a few meters from the roadway, clearly visible to passersby as crows pecked their flesh away. By year's end a work group calculated that 262 people in the district had died, while several dozen others had fled to parts unknown. The population had been reduced by 40 percent.[107]

In Wenjiang County's Qingping Commune, Li Fangping was on the verge of death when a county inspection team arrived. Fearful that Li would reveal the dire situation, a cadre locked him in a storeroom, where he died. Commune member Zhang Shaochun fainted with hunger while weeding a rapeseed field, and the production team leader quickly dug a hole and began to bury him. Suddenly Zhang revived and cried out, "You're burying me alive!" sending the team leader racing off in a fright.[108]

The party secretary of Xingjing County said half of the residents of his county died. "Some villages were left without a single living inhabitant, and residents of other villages had to be sent over to bury the dead. The villagers so assigned had to perform this arduous labor on empty stomachs, and some died in the process, requiring peasants from yet another village to come over and bury them."[109]

A deputy head of education in Wenjiang Prefecture's propaganda bureau, Liang Jinxue, recorded the horror he witnessed as a cadre work group member at Xindu County's Majia Commune:

> I went to the No. 2 production brigade first, and upon emerging from the back of Majia Middle School, I saw the late spring crops growing very poorly, especially the rapeseed crop, some of which was reduced to yellow stalks topped with a few flower buds. I saw no one working in the fields, just a few women washing some wild herbs. I walked over and asked, "Where are your men? Why isn't anyone working?" They replied, "The men are at the residential quarters, and just us few women have been left here to work." I was surprised and said, "You've built residential quarters? Where are they?" They pointed and said, "Along the river, go take a look." I walked in the direction they had pointed, and after walking about half a kilometer I reached the river bank. There I saw to my horror that the collective cemetery was full of graves, almost all of them fresh, numbering more than a hundred. Thunderstruck, I walked back to the

communal kitchen used by the production brigade's three production teams, and by the sweet potato cellar near the kitchen door I saw a dead child. I went to the production team leader and said, "Find someone to bury that dead child." He found several commune members and had them carry the dead child into the potato cellar, where an old woman had already been placed. Embarrassed, the team leader said to me, "We're so hungry, that's the best we can do. We simply can't tend to the dead anymore."[110]

Veteran Xinhua reporter Liu Zongtang recalls that the greatest number of deaths occurred in the winter of 1961.

At that time I was assigned to western Sichuan. The western Sichuan plains had a fertilizer called *tiaozi* (a plant called "trumpet creeper," also known as green manure), which was routinely also used as pig feed. Some peasants were so hungry that they also ate *tiaozi*. Once when I was reporting in Pi County, I rose in the morning to find the ground covered with hoarfrost. In a *tiaozi* field I saw someone lying there, and as I drew closer, I found he was dead, with some half-chewed *tiaozi* still in his mouth; apparently he'd been gnawing at it as he crawled. I went with a local reporter named Li Shiyi to another place, where we saw an old peasant cursing the Communist Party. We learned that this was the father of the party branch secretary—who else would dare express himself so freely? When someone asked him about it, he said, "I'm cursing my son!"

Chongqing cadre Liao Bokang wrote in his memoirs:

The deputy director of the provincial party committee's organization department, Miao Qianming, called an organization work symposium for eastern Sichuan in Fuling, then went on to Chongqing, where the director of Chongqing's municipal party committee organization department, Xiao Zekuan, invited him to dinner. During the meal, Xiao asked Miao about the situation in Fuling. Miao Qianming replied, "Adding up all of the prefecture's counties, a total of 3.5 million people have died . . . Among the places in Sichuan where the most people died, one was Ya'an Prefecture's Xinjing County, and the other was Fuling Prefecture's Fengdu County. In Fengdu County, more than 100,000 people died of "edema" within three years, rightly earning the county a reputation as a ghost town.[111]

In Rong County in 1960, food ran out before the harvest, resulting in sixty thousand deaths—more than 10 percent of the population. This is without taking account of the deaths in 1959, 1961, and 1962.[112]

According to the 1989 *Pi County Annals*, the county's population plummeted from 280,000 in 1958 to 230,000 in 1961. The county's labor force decreased 20 percent from 1958, and in seven communes, the decrease reached 30 percent. The No. 1 administrative district of You'ai Commune had a labor force of 855 in the first half of 1958, but at the end of 1961 it stood at 500. In Yongding Commune's No. 1 administrative district, each member of the workforce covered 3.9 *mu* of land in 1958, but each had to cover 13.0 *mu* of land by the end of 1961 because the labor force had decreased by 60 percent.[113] The total population of Wenjiang Prefecture stood at 4.94 million in 1957. By 1961 it had dropped to 4.33 million.[114]

China Population: Sichuan[115] provides population, birth, and death rate figures for each year.

It is possible to calculate unnatural deaths and shortfall in births based on these figures (using the method described in this book's chapter on population loss):

A fair estimate is that Sichuan lost eight million people to unnatural deaths and experienced a shortfall of six million births that would have occurred under normal circumstances. The statistics are all from official sources, however, so the results are very likely significantly lower than the actual number of deaths.

It is impossible to obtain reliable figures on the number of starvation deaths because the Sichuan provincial party committee "strengthened population statistical work" during the Great Famine. In early 1960, Sichuan required using the campaign against right deviation and the principle of "going all out" as the foundation for population census work. For example, when Jintang County reported few births and many deaths at each of its communes, the prefectural party committee demanded a new calculation based on the principle that "births must outnumber deaths, and deaths cannot outnumber births." The Jintang County party committee convened a meeting stressing that "population statistical

TABLE 6.2: POPULATION FIGURES FOR SICHUAN PROVINCE, 1955–66

Year	1955	1956	1957	1958	1959	1960	1961	1962	1963	1964	1965	1966
Population (year end, millions)	67.906	67.906	69.452	70.81	70.779	68.973	64.592	64.856	66.958	68.983	71.368	73.863
Birth rate (%)	2.893	2.85	2.922	2.403	1.671	1.173	1.181	2.801	5.011	4.694	4.241	3.995
Mortality rate (%)	0.918	1.041	1.207	2.517	4.691	5.397	2.942	1.462	1.282	1.387	1.146	1.076
Natural population growth (%)	1.921	1.809	1.715	-0.113	-3.026	-4.223	-1.76	1.339	3.728	3.307	3.095	2.92

Source: Liu Hong Kang, ed., China Population: Sichuan, *Beijing: Zhongguo caizheng jingji chubanshe, 1988.*

**TABLE 6.3: UNNATURAL DEATHS AND SHORTFALL IN BIRTHS IN SICHUAN
PROVINCE (MILLIONS)**

Year	1958	1959	1960	1961	1962	Total
Unnatural deaths	.9853	2.5337	2.9942	1.2304	.2265	7.9701
Shortfall in births	.8696	1.3961	1.7259	1.6553	.545	6.1919

Source: Calculations based on figures in Table 6.2.

work has great political significance," and criticized districts and communes reporting high death figures as having an "inadequate understanding of the significance of population statistical work." To avoid
being labeled right deviationists, cadres quickly carried out new "surveys." The six communes of Tuqiao District originally reported 1,800-
odd births and more than 3,800 deaths, but the new "survey" found a
substantial decrease in the number of deaths. Statistics from some communes were sent back time and again for revision until the eleventh
"reexamination" attained the goal of "the number of births exceeding
the number of deaths."[116]

During the Cultural Revolution, the number of starvation deaths in
Sichuan was stated as 8 million. In his memoirs, Liao Bokang states
the number of starvation deaths as 12.5 million.[117] Dong Fu's manuscript puts the figure at more than 10 million. Former Sichuan provincial party committee propaganda bureau head Ming Lang says, "In some
counties, the number of deaths approached 20 percent of the population, and it exceeded 10 percent in many others."[118] In July 1962 a survey
by *People's Daily* deputy editor-in-chief Xiao Feng stated, "The population in 1957 was 73 million, or an alternative figure of 71.75 million. In
1960 the provincial party committee organization department transmitted a combined figure from all localities of 62 million. Adding in the
starvation deaths from the 1961 and 1962 spring and summer famines,
and taking into account the offsetting of deaths with births, the province lost more than 12 million people, or around 17 percent of its population."[119] According to Cao Shuji[120] from 1959 to 1961, the number of
unnatural deaths in Sichuan Province totaled 9.402 million. If the deaths
at the end of 1958 and in 1962 are added in, unnatural deaths totaled more

than 10 million. I estimate a shortfall of 4 to 8 million births, while 10 to 12 million people starved to death in Sichuan Province during the Great Famine.

According to a 1961 survey, when Mao visited Hongguang Commune, the commune had 4,020 people. By the third anniversary of his visit, the population had dropped to 2,750.[121]

7 THE RAVAGES OF THE FIVE WINDS

The "Five Winds" referred to "unhealthy tendencies" that arose during the commune movement. Known as the Communist Wind, Exaggeration Wind, Coercive Commandism Wind, Cadre Privilege Wind, and the Chaotic Directives Wind relating to production, they all contributed directly to the Great Famine.

THE LUDICROUS HISTORICAL LEGACY OF THE COMMUNIST WIND

Summing up the CCP Central Committee Politburo meeting convened at Beidaihe from August 16 to 30, 1958, Mao said, "Some people say that equal distribution produces slackers. But how many slackers have we seen in the last twenty-two years? I haven't seen more than a handful. Why is this? The main reasons are politics in command, class struggle, common goals, and hard effort on behalf of the majority."[1] This "directive from the highest reaches" advocating egalitarianism—equal distribution regardless of effort—helped unleash the Communist Wind.

The conference was followed by articles pandering to Mao. Zhang Chunqiao[2] criticized the wage system and touted the free-supply rationing system. Mao recommended his article to People's Daily with an editorial note, and in August, People's Daily used this article to launch a series on "The Legal Rights of the Bourgeoisie." Guan Feng[3] argued that "a partial rationing system is the best form of distribution in the transition to communism," while Hu Sheng[4] criticized the wage system and praised rationing. People's Daily published many other articles praising communism that appealed to the average cadre.

The replacement of capitalism by socialism and the ultimate progression to communism was presented as objective law. For many years,

China's intellectuals had embraced this theory and instilled it in their students from elementary school to university. This historical determinism became a "manifest destiny" impossible to resist. Any means employed in removing obstacles to communism were considered a service to heaven's decree.

The message was that full state ownership was communism and paradise. As the media spurred every locality to strive for an earlier entry to paradise, Hebei's Xushui County became China's model for embracing communism.

On July 1, 1958, county party secretary Zhang Guozhong appealed to cadres to launch a great revolution. His specific demands were for militarization of operations, employing factory methods in field management, the ideological dominance of communism, and leadership methods in compliance with the mass line. The cornerstone of this "fourfold revolution" was militarization. Zhang called for all people to be armed and united around the party. Party members, Youth League members, and militia were to lead a military-like structure. The townships were to establish a "socialist leap forward militia corps," with commanders, political commissars, logistics heads, and other such positions held by party secretaries and township heads. The communes were to organize in battalions, companies, and platoons. Every village would be a battalion or a company, with branch secretaries and production team heads serving as political instructors, commanders, and logistics heads. The logistics heads were responsible for communal operations such as kitchens, nurseries, kindergartens, clothing factories, laundries, and grain processing. Townships were to be divided into several military theaters in which tasks would be divided.

On August 6 a pilot project in communism was launched in Xushui County. Hebei's provincial party committee was told, "Socialism will be more or less completed in the Second Five-Year Plan. During the Third Five-Year Plan, we'll make the transition to communism . . . Comrade Liu Shaoqi has directed us to launch a pilot project in communism in Xushui that will integrate industry, agriculture, the military, education, and commerce, and that will be carried out in the villages, schools, and party organization." The county party committee was urged to study *The Communist Manifesto* and Marx's *Critique of the Gotha Program* to gain a deeper understanding of communism. Copies of Kang Youwei's *The Great Harmony* were presented to each leader of the county party committee.

On August 22, Xushui County proposed that "The goal of the struggle is: the essential completion of the construction of socialism in 1960 and beginning the transition to communism, and embarking onto the great Communist society in 1963."[5] Xushui's residents were then told, "Communism is handing over all vehicles and livestock to public ownership . . . Apart from private ownership of articles for daily use and bank savings, all else will be publicly owned. That is what is known as communism." "The more that is publicly owned, the better—we will all prosper collectively." Some cadres went on to say, "When that day comes, we'll have all the food, clothing, and everything else that we want."

On September 15, Xushui County established Xushui County People's Central Commune (later renamed Xushui People's Commune) and gave it control over distribution. On September 20 the county party committee decreed that beginning in September, salaries would be abolished for cadres and state workers, and commune members would no longer be paid according to work done. All county residents would be guaranteed fifteen items, including food, clothing, living quarters, medical care, and burial services, the costs of which would be borne by the county people's commune. An additional allowance of 8 yuan would be provided for county-level cadres, 5 yuan for department-level cadres, 3 yuan for the rank and file, and 2 yuan for subsidiary staff members. Rationing would be accompanied by accounting handled at the commune level. Property would be held in common, including the materials for daily living. Collective and individual ownership were to be replaced by public ownership.

On September 1, *People's Daily* reported, "In the near future, Xushui People's Commune will take its members to the ultimate paradise of human history. That will be the era of the realm of freedom under 'from each according to his ability, and to each according to his need.'"

Mao referred to Xushui several times during the enlarged Politburo meeting convened at Beidaihe on August 17–30. He and Liu Shaoqi both paid visits and praised Xushui's communism. This praise was given prominent coverage to inspire the rest of the country. Under the influence of Mao and Liu, most central government officials also toured Xushui, along with 930 prominent individuals from more than forty foreign countries. More than 3,000 work units made similar pilgrimages, with some 320,000 people touring the county from March to October. Not everyone was impressed, however; the party's leading rural specialist, Deng Zihui, observed, "Xushui is a classic case of the 'Exaggeration Wind' and 'Communist Wind.'"[6]

The county's revenues, however, were inadequate to provide what was promised. In November and December, Xushui County used its commercial revolving fund to meet necessities. With all financial sources exhausted, the rationing system could not be sustained.

By mid-October 1958 the fraud had been exposed, and on November 9, Mao stated that Xushui should no longer be promoted. By then, however, its Communist Wind had already spread throughout the country, and rash ventures proliferated. Shandong's Shouzhang County drew up a plan for "essentially constructing a presentable version of communism" within two years. Shandong's Ju'nan County formulated a plan for a two-hundred-day all-out effort for transition to communism. Henan's Wuxiu County, which was the first to implement one commune for the whole county, promised "communism within five years."

Shandong's Fan County proposed that within two years it would implement full industrialization and electrification, achieve grain yields of 10,000 kilos per *mu*, build four to six universities and one academy of science, and realize the ideal of "from each according to his ability and to each according to his need." "For anyone who enters a new paradise, there is no need to pay for food, drink, or clothing. There will be all kinds of fresh meat, four dishes per meal, fruit every day, and all kinds of clothes. Everyone says heaven is good, but it's nothing compared with the New Paradise."

On November 6, during the Central Committee meeting in Zhengzhou, Mao read about Fan County and wrote a memo: "This is very interesting; it's poetic, but it also seems feasible. The timetable seems too rushed, only three years. There's no need to hurry; if it can't be done in three years, a delay is acceptable." He had the article about Fan County distributed to central government leaders, heads of major regions, and provincial party secretaries at the Zhengzhou Conference.[7]

Paoma Commune in Hubei's Dangyang County was another model of communism. The commune's first party secretary "assumed command" and led most workers into the hills to participate in the great iron and steel campaign, while second party secretary Zhang Tiangao remained behind to direct the commune's operations.

In October, Paoma Commune implemented a distribution system combining rations with the wage system, and organized welfare services around the communal kitchens. On November 17, Zhang said, "I hereby proclaim that today is the end of socialism and tomorrow is the beginning of communism." "Communism must abolish private ownership and eliminate the family, apart from spouses—that's my opinion, nothing can be privately owned." Posters declared, "Humanity's Most Glorious Society—Communist Society—Has Arrived," and "No Distinction Between Individuals; Each Takes What He Needs."

Zhang told teachers, "This is communism now; whatever stationery supplies you need, just take them from the stationery stores." He led the supply clerk of Banyue Middle School to the stationery shop to take 115 items of musical and sporting equipment valued at 1,436 yuan. The other schools followed suit, quickly emptying the store. Zhang also led a group that took fertilizer and pesticide for the commune party committee's experimental field. The store was soon plundered of the remainder of its supplies. When commune members said they needed clothing, Zhang said, "Those who need clothes should take them," and the commune shops were soon stripped bare. With property rights eliminated, production teams dragged off one another's livestock and ate one another's poultry and vegetables. The commune consumed more than 2,800 chickens and more than 34,300 kilos of vegetables belonging to its members, and collectivized 12,753 pigs and 36,251 chickens. Eventually, 6,164 of the pigs and 3,691 of the chickens died.

Paoma Commune created collective living quarters, boarding schools, full-time nurseries, and homes for the elderly. The collective living quarters were tiny, squeezing three generations, male and female, into a single room. In the schools, four children shared a quilt. With children taking the family quilts, adults slept under straw raincoats.

Complainers were penalized with hard labor, criticism, beatings, and food deprivation. Twenty-eight cadres punished sixty-eight commune members.

Paoma Commune's Communist Wind quickly spread. Fearing that their belongings would be "communized," villagers cut down their bamboo groves and sold the floorboards of their homes. The rationing system led some to say, "Whether I work or not, there's an iron rice bowl, and even if I do nothing I will get to eat for free." Productivity plummeted as commune members waited for cadres to call them to work, waited for all to assemble before going to the fields, and waited for the team leader to assign tasks before working.[8]

Liaoning's Fanhe Commune reported at the end of 1960:

The "Communist Wind" began blowing in this commune at the beginning of the communization campaign. Following corrections made last spring, the wind blew up again. Every movement, every "upsurge," every "big development" required another gust of the "Communist Wind." Big campaigns brought big gusts, little campaigns brought little gusts, and when there were no campaigns, the blowing was sporadic. The "Communist Wind" blew through units from the provincial level down ... The scope of the "Communist Wind" encompassed not only land, labor, and vehicles, but also bricks and tiles, scrap metal, cooking and eating utensils, hemp and leather rope, even curtain rods and incense burners for ancestor worship. The masses said, "It has taken away everything but our wives and children" ... In general, the "Communist Wind" ... blew most harshly in key work sites, well-off production units, cities and suburbs, communes and keynote projects—in short, any place in proximity to officialdom.[9]

The Communist Wind blew to every corner of the country and stripped peasants of all they owned. Low production led to insistence that communism had arrived; deplorable conditions prompted insistence that all was well; and where the most basic requirements for rationing were absent, the system was all the more rigorously applied.

Given that the Communist paradise was propped up with lies, the Exaggeration Wind was inevitable. Since the average commune cadre could not manage the oversize communes, the Chaotic Directives Wind likewise followed as a matter of course. Power was concentrated with no checks, breeding cadre privilege. Coercive commandism was the only means of imposing this setup on the peasants whose rights and interests it violated. So it was that the Communist Wind gave rise to the other "unhealthy tendencies."

Mao mulled over the time required for the transition to communism. In August 1958 he suggested three to four, or possibly five to six years.[10] On November 6 he considered "a minimum of three to four years, or a maximum of five to six years" to be on the fast side, but he also said, "Struggle hard for three years, then keep at it for twelve years so we can complete the transition to communism in fifteen years; there's no need to publish this, but it's not good if we don't do it."[11] On November 21 he said again, "Generally speaking, the Soviet Union definitely has to be allowed to reach the Communist stage first, and then we'll follow. And what if we actually reach it first? We can simply hang the shingle of socialism while actually practicing communism."[12] On March 23, 1959, he wrote, "Don't talk about a transition from socialism to communism for at least twenty years; it can't possibly go that quickly."[13]

The proportion of rationing differed by location. It was half rationing and half wages in Hebei, Zhejiang, Fujian, and Heilongjiang; 60 percent rationing in Hubei, Shanxi, Henan, Shaanxi, Sichuan, Guangdong, Jiangsu, Jiangxi, and Inner Mongolia; and 65–70 percent rationing in Anhui, Hunan, Liaoning, Jilin, Guizhou, Gansu, and Ningxia.[14]

According to statistics for 21,176 communes in 23 provinces and autonomous regions, 78 percent had implemented meal rationing; 14 percent had implemented food rationing; 5 percent had implemented rationing of all basic living necessities; 1 percent supplied half of their food through rations; 0.6 percent implemented a full wage system; and 1.5 percent implemented a workday system. Cash wages averaged 3–5 yuan per laborer per month, only pennies a day.

According to statistics from Henan, Shanxi, Shandong, Anhui, Fujian, Hunan, Guangxi, and Heilongjiang, in two or three months there was no money to pay wages. People became totally dependent on government rations, and if the government gave them nothing, people had nothing to eat.[15]

THE CONTAGIOUS INSANITY OF THE EXAGGERATION WIND

The Exaggeration Wind was manifested in the launching of production Sputniks and also the great iron- and steel-forging campaign. Some parts of Yunnan claimed that a new factory opened every 1.05 minutes and that each factory cost only 2 yuan to establish.[16] In 1958, Gansu's Jingning County reported erecting more than ten thousand factories in fifteen days.[17] Guizhou Province's Zhenning County, a Miao ethnic minority area, claimed in 1958 to have built 494 factories and 1,205 blast furnaces, 1 for every 250 people.[18]

The Exaggeration Wind also took over the sciences. In the Biology Institute of the Chinese Academy of Sciences (CAS), a Propaganda Department spokesman proposed that research units should compete with peasants over high-yield fields. "If the research unit did not win, it should be stripped of its label as a research institution." This official was reportedly Yu Guangyuan,[19] head of the Propaganda Department's science division at the time.

One time, Marshal Nie Rongzhen (responsible for military science) brought Yu Guangyuan along with Zhang Jinfu (then secretary of the leading party group of CAS) to the swimming pool at Zhongnanhai to see Mao Zedong. Nie wanted Zhang to report on the situation at CAS and Yu Guangyuan to report on science and technology. Yu reported that Shandong farmers had successfully grafted apple twigs onto pumpkin vines. Yu's view at the time was that one must believe the party and the masses, but he ultimately learned his lesson and became a steadfast opponent of pseudoscience.[20]

The Exaggeration Wind also influenced education. Newspapers announced that as of the end of July, 28.1 percent of China's counties had basically eliminated illiteracy.[21] New colleges sprang up everywhere. In Henan's Zhuping County at the end of August, 10 communes had established more than 570 "red and expert" (hong zhuan) comprehensive universities, water conservancy and mining institutes, and spare-time agricultural colleges,[22] and Henan's Dengfeng County set up 44 "red and expert" universities in two days.[23] A village party secretary could appoint a professor.[24] The middle school where I studied, Xishui No. 1 Middle School, cleared out a few classrooms to set up "Xishui College," and some of our teachers became college professors overnight. Within a few months, "Xishui College" shut down.

A Great Leap Forward was launched in cultural work. Jiangxi Province organized more than five thousand folk song clubs, Sichuan Province set up more than twenty-two thousand rural artistic creation committees, and every production team in Anhui Province had a creative work committee. To launch artistic "Sputniks," all levels of government assigned projects such as "surpass Lu Xun in two years," "write sixty plays in one night," or "every county must produce a Guo Moruo."[25] Many of the "new folk songs" had a distinct Paul Bunyan flavor: "Rice grains the size of soya beans, soya beans like potatoes / Sesame seeds rivaling corn kernels, corn cobs big as a man / Peanuts like sweet potatoes, sweet potatoes big as winter melons / A picture of a bumper harvest, a painting of peasants leaping forward." And another: "This year we'll have a bumper harvest / Autumn grain piled high as a hill. / I wonder how much grain it will take / To slow the earth to a standstill."[26]

Everywhere people were urged to write poems celebrating the Great Leap. Most were jingles such as "Years of hoping, decades of dreams / Now the commune is built. / Six townships, now a family / And socialism's lily is gilt." Poems were collected and published, and poetry and song campaigns snowballed. Every train passenger was required to hand in a poem. One commune bragged, "We'll produce ten thousand poems in a year," while another vowed, "We'll compose five novels and five plays." Zhangjiakou Prefecture produced a "poetic pacesetter" who composed ten thousand poems in one month.[27]

Many famous writers, poets, and artists joined in. Guo Moruo, the literary lion of that era, wrote many poems along these lines:

Peasant:
Sun, oh Sun, please tell me true,
Who works harder, us or you?
We've been out working half the day;
We wait for you, but you delay.
Going home, we'll need your light,
But you'll have turned in for the night.
Sun, oh Sun, please tell me true,
Who works harder, us or you?

Sun:
Comrade, you are right to ask;
My absence here I cannot mask.
I go out west for half the day
And leave you, I regret to say.
Things out west give you a shock—
Lazy people run amok.
Pass the United Kingdom in fifteen years?
Comrade, you need have no fears.

The poem built up to a crescendo of hyperbole in this chorus of the peasant, sun, moon, and stars:

Chorus:
Thank you, party, from our hearts,
Our bright Red Sun that's never dark.

The east wind wins against the west,
Socialism shines the best.
Going all out, aiming high,
More, fast, good, cheap—paradise!
The red flag rises 'round the world,
On every hilltop waves, unfurled![28]

The Exaggeration Wind influenced statistics most of all, and the dire lack of accurate information contributed to policy error. The Beidaihe Conference resolution on the steel campaign presumed that the "agricultural problem had already been solved," an impression created by faked statistics on the 1958 summer harvest.

The "leaping" statistical system was formed under criteria meant to verify the correctness of the Great Leap Forward road. Statistics bureaus were under constant pressure to reflect success by concocting one high-yield satellite after another.[29] Statisticians received orders from above that "whatever statistical data the party leadership needs, we will provide it; our statistical work will follow in whatever direction the political campaigns and production campaigns lead."[30] "We must operate according to the direction of the party and actual work requirements; whatever the party tells us to do, we will do it."[31] These are the words of Xue Muqiao and Jia Qiyun, the central government's chief statisticians at that time.

In a speech in June, Xue argued that "the main thing is the direction and the path, and professional duties are secondary." "Our statistical work is carried out in service to others, not to ourselves. Whether something is wanted or not, or what is wanted, is up to others. The calculation methods and specifications are likewise applied according to the requirements of whomever we serve."[32]

A National Statistical Work Conference convened in Baoding, Hebei Province, in June 1958 concluded, "Whatever statistical data the party leadership needs, we will provide it, and whatever direction the political and production movements take, statistical work will follow."[33] This was meant to show the power of the mass movement for a bottom-up "statistical leap forward."

Statisticians who exaggerated achievement and concealed error were commended and promoted. All statistics had to be approved by the local party committee. In August 1958 the heads of five or six provincial statistical bureaus vented their grievances to chief statistician, Xue Muqiao:

"The provincial party committee wants the statistics bureau to report false numbers, and if we don't, we'll be disciplined." They asked Xue what to do. Xue replied, "The Great Leap Forward is an irresistible trend; all you can do is obey the provincial party committee. Some day the central government will ask you for the actual figures, so you must make sure to have all the real numbers ready to present to them at any time."[34]

In the spring of 1959 the CCP Central Committee conceded to demands to allow households to raise their own pigs and to expand household garden plots. A symposium of statistical bureau heads took the opportunity in April to propose improving the accuracy of statistical data. The State Bureau of Statistics also submitted reports reflecting actual problems in steel production and relating to female workers. These statistical reports played a genuine and active role in resisting the Five Winds, but they were soon criticized as "blowing cold wind on the Great Leap Forward."

After the Lushan Plenum revived the Exaggeration Wind, the State Bureau of Statistics was compelled to submit self-criticism acknowledging that "inadequate political consciousness" had caused it to "blow cold wind on the Great Leap Forward." The bureau was required to "resolutely defend the party's General Line and launch a counterattack in the struggle against right opportunism."[35]

Mao summed up the process at an enlarged meeting of the Politburo on March 5, 1961: "We always demanded statistics on how much of what had been planted, how much was produced, how much fertilizer had been spread today, what would be done tomorrow. With all that reporting and calculating, it was impossible for statistics to keep up. That's how things go: you issue chaotic directives and I give a nonsense report, and the result is exaggeration that makes no sense at all."[36]

CHAOTIC DIRECTIVES WREAK ECONOMIC HAVOC

Many "great campaigns" were launched involving "large-scale warfare tactics" that deployed "casts of thousands" at a moment's notice to ensure "a tide of red flags flapping during the day, and an ocean of torches glowing at night." Some county leaders would stand on a hilltop to view the glowing torches and then broadcast the great effort the next morning. The result was chaos that wasted effort and pushed cadres to extremes. What crop a production team should plant, how much and when, and what cultivation method should be used—all were decided at an upper level and based on the intentions of officials at an even higher level. The prime examples were close-planting and deep-plowing. Mao had made pronouncements on both, and those below took his words as divine decrees to be imposed on the peasants.

Mao made only a single fleeting mention of close-planting, but at each level of leadership its significance was magnified. In many places, county officials stipulated how far apart grain seedlings were to be planted. Pulling out and replanting seedlings that failed to conform to directives was legitimized as "removing the white flag" and "planting the red flag." The "white flags" were those who protested that close-planting reduced production. Cadres who enforced the planting of hundreds of kilos of seed on 1 *mu* of land were lauded as "red flags" and were promoted.

In Sichuan's Qingxia Commune, corn was planted in accordance with "gathering earth, setting direction, double rows, cross-nesting, and close-planting." The distance between rows was measured with a ruler, and direction was set with a compass. The Shou'an Commune in Pujiang County had during 1958 incurred huge losses on an experimental close-planted field. Commune party secretaries concluded that repeating the process on a large piece of land would result in unmitigated disaster, but the prefectural party committee refused to let up: "You're an organization of the CCP, and this was stipulated by the Central Committee, so you should implement it."

With excessively close-planting, rice seedlings did not get adequate ventilation or sunlight, and the grain produced did not even replace the seed grain that was planted. Nevertheless, since the directive came from the highest level, no one dared object until Mao's April 29, 1959, "internal party communiqué" rescinded the close-planting policy.

On deep-plowing, Mao made several pronouncements. As a result, fields were plowed to a depth of 1 meter or more, bringing immature soil to the surface and pushing rich, loamy soil below ground. This wasted labor and was detrimental to the soil, resulting in greatly reduced grain output.

In Paoziyan Village in Jilin, the commune in October 1958 implemented a military structure of regiment, battalions, and companies and launched "large-scale military campaigns" for the Great Leap Forward, the first of which was deep-plowing. Even tottering elders and small children joined the battle to plow the entire planting area to a depth of 1 meter. Because the No. 10 production team advanced slowly, its team leader was labeled a "white flag" and was plucked out on the spot. The campaign left only the elderly and women to take in the autumn harvest, 10 percent of which remained in the fields.[37]

At Fanhe Commune in Liaoning, upper-level officials ordered close-planting regardless of the quality of the soil, using rulers to ensure the specified distance between seeds. One farmer who spaced his rows slightly farther apart than stipulated was hauled off for "debate" until he admitted to "sabotaging production." Members of the Yangweilou production team composed a jingle: "Farming isn't left to the people, manpower is carelessly deployed, the grass is taller than the rice stalks, but we still claim 5,000 kilos." Chaotic directives persisted until 1960, when a commune member said, "In 1958 you gave your chaotic directives and we gave our views. In 1959 you gave your chaotic directives and we did what we could clandestinely. This year we've thrown it in: if you tell us to plant rocks, we'll do it. At any rate, we're starving, and even you are hungry."[38]

On November 16, 1960, a provincial party committee work group in Jiangsu submitted this report:[39]

In production, as regards the cultivated area, crop arrangements, planting specifications, technical measures, choice of seeds, and so on, all was decided on orders from the upper level; the production teams and commune members had no say in the matter and were not allowed to adapt measures to local conditions. This spring, the municipal party committee convened an on-site meeting attended by commune party secretaries and production brigade party secretaries, at which the emphasis was placed on cultivating large tracts of land, with corn rows to be spaced six, seven, or eight inches apart and seeds to be planted four, five, or six inches apart in each row. At the meeting, municipal party secretary Liu Rugao yelled out, "You all have to do it this way; if there's a problem, it's my head on the line, but if you don't follow the instructions, I'll have your heads!"

When Wuli Commune's No. 2 production brigade didn't follow these instructions, the commune held a debate at which the production brigade secretary was struggled. Following directives from above, the No. 8 production brigade designated the No. 1, 3, and 4 production teams as the "sweet potato area," and the No. 6 production team as the "animal feed area." With a total of 470 *mu* of land, the No. 1 production team was forced to plant 250 *mu* of sweet potatoes, with the result that output of both sweet potatoes and corn was greatly reduced. The sweet potato fields produced only 45 kilos per *mu*, not even enough to replace the seeds. The No. 3 production team had more than 20 *mu* of sorghum that was already more than a foot tall, but in order to fulfill the upper level's stipulations on continuous field area for cotton, all the sorghum had to be pulled out and replaced with cotton at great loss. On the other hand, this same production team had another field of more than 80 *mu* that was suitable for growing cotton, but the upper level insisted that they grow sugar beets there, and the seeds never even sprouted. The No. 5 production team had more than 30 *mu* suitable for growing sorghum, but in order to meet the requirement of continuous growing area, they were forced to plant corn, and each *mu* produced only 15 kilos.

The chaotic directives led to greatly reduced yields. Commune members angrily commented, "If even half the fields had been left to us, the yields wouldn't have been this bad!"

COERCIVE COMMANDISM AND CADRE PRIVILEGE

Under the political system of the time, cadres regarded peasants as expendable. Cadres became overbearing and vicious in imposing one campaign after another, subjecting disobedient or intractable individuals to beatings, detention, and torture. An unknown but not insignificant number died from flogging and other forms of physical abuse.

Because political and economic power was highly concentrated, all resources within the iron grasp of cadres, who often wielded their power to personal benefit, especially with regard to access to food. Cadres and their families typically took more than their fair share, and the feasting of the cadres rose in stark contrast to the starvation of the peasants.

THE SOURCE OF THE FIVE WINDS

Some regard Mao as the source of the Five Winds, and he also described himself as the "originator of bad precedent." Others saw Liu Shaoqi as the source through his many fanatical pronouncements in the summer and autumn of 1958. In any event, nationwide agitation was typically stirred up by the senior leadership. If a campaign had local origins (typically local officials anticipating the intentions of the central government), it gained nationwide influence only through the affirmation and encouragement of the senior leadership.

In June 1958, Liu elaborated on Kang Youwei's vision of utopian socialism: "Kang Youwei wanted to break nine boundaries, that is, the boundaries of the nation-state, male versus female, the family, private property, and so on. Conditions weren't ripe for implementation of utopian socialist ideas at that time. Now Marxists have seized hold of class struggle and have already abolished class or are in the process of doing so, and are thereby implementing the utopia that utopian socialists were unable to implement."[40]

Liu told editors at *Beijing Daily* on June 30, "I believe we'll be able to achieve Communist society in thirty or forty years." "We're already beginning to experiment with the basic organization of Communist society . . . We need to make everyone equally competent as workers, farmers, businessmen, scholars, and soldiers."[41] On July 1, Liu said, "Anything that doesn't conform to the General Line must be done away with."[42]

Liu told workers in Beijing on July 5, "We don't need ten or more years to overtake the United Kingdom; two or three years will be enough . . . Our steel and coal can overtake the United Kingdom next year." He also said, "On the question of overtaking America in fifteen years, we won't actually need fifteen years—seven or eight years will do it . . . It won't take long for China to embark on communism—all of you will live to see communism."[43]

On July 19, Liu said, "By jumbling cooperatives together into one and reallocating the resources, things can be smoothed out, and no one will feel they're losing out or that someone else is enjoying an advantage."[44] On September 10 and 11, Liu visited the model Xushui Commune, where he was told that irrigating yam fields with a dog meat broth produced yields of 600,000 kilos per *mu*. He responded, "Have you really achieved this result? Ha ha! You should start raising dogs, then! Dogs are very easy to breed!" Liu Shaoqi was an enthusiastic proponent of close-planting, and during an inspection of a close-planted field, he suggested, "When it's time for weeding and thinning out the seedlings, you can make tiny inch-wide hoes and use tweezers."[45]

Liu accepted without question reports that peasants jumped for joy in response to the communal kitchens, and used these reports to discredit concerns over a negative effect on production.[46] He was equally credulous regarding false reports of high-yield satellites,[47] and touted the alleged successes of the steel drive to urge on the cotton mills, endorsing the mass deployment of workers wherever needed.[48]

Of course, Liu was not exceptional; most members of the central leadership expressed solidarity with Mao. More than twenty years later, the architect of China's economic reforms, Deng Xiaoping, observed, "During the Great Leap Forward, was it only Comrade Mao Zedong who was so fanatical and none of the rest of us? Neither Comrade Liu Shaoqi, Comrade Zhou Enlai, nor I opposed him, and Comrade Chen Yun said nothing."[49] Indeed, they added fuel to the fire. If responsibility is sought for the Five Winds, it must be laid at the feet of the entire central leadership. Under that political system, all supported the Great Leader who could—and did—humiliate opponents of rash advance.

In a system of highly concentrated power, once there was movement from the Center, collaborators at the lower levels joined in, building up the breeze until it became a gale-force wind. This "brotherhood of the wind" arose through a variety of circumstances: some joined through their own conscious initiative and agreement; others, through force of self-preservation; a third group, through opportunism; a fourth, through blind ignorance; and a fifth, through a desire to use chaos to their personal advantage.

Among those who followed through conscious agreement were intellectuals and senior cadres who cherished Communist ideals. A goodly portion of the blindly ignorant consisted of "hot-blooded youth" who believed unwaveringly all they had learned in the course of Communist education, and everything published in the newspapers about the Great Leap Forward. These two groups represented intellectual polar extremes, but greatly resembled each other in their contribution to the Five Winds. Both groups could be considered "true believers" who felt a sense of sacred duty in fulfilling their ideals.

At the same time, the "depths" and "heights" of these two groups were noticeably different. The consciously endorsing intellectuals and high-level cadres had the ability to appeal for support and mobilize the masses, and at key junctures they could propose new slogans and new expressions to push the movement to a higher level. The ignorant "hot-blooded youth," on the other hand, were the most radical and the most prone to extremism— and the most potentially destructive. These two groups formed the nucleus of support for the Five Winds.

The hot-blooded youth had nothing on their minds but the faith in communism instilled in them by propaganda. The upper leadership could easily mobilize them to sacrifice all in defense of their values. Their dauntlessness was built on a foundation of ignorance. Hot-blooded youth formed the vanguard of every political movement under the Chinese Communist Party and provided Mao with his most destructive source of power. They were easily excited and inclined to an extremism that could be tolerated and even cherished as long as it didn't interfere with the government's objectives.

Those who joined in out of self-preservation felt they had no alternative; failing to follow along would have been regarded as having "attitude" or "standpoint" problems, and could have been considered committing "orientation" or "line" error. The "right-deviation" label was under the control of the upper levels and could be applied at will, with unbearable results. Most members of this group were not radical, but there were some unscrupulous individuals among them who sought to build themselves up through radical language or extremist action. At the outset, when some localities launched "high-yield satellites," not all cadres believed their claims, and many local leaders initially maintained a wait-and-see attitude. When those who engaged in blatant exaggeration were endorsed by the central government, however, those on the sidelines worried that if they didn't go along, they would be targeted, and proceeded to launch their own "satellites." Likewise, as will be seen later in this book, those who negated and criticized Peng Dehuai's opinions at the Lushan Conference were initially a minority, but after watching what others were doing, and in particular after observing the attitude of the central leadership, the majority joined forces against the "common enemy," which led to a surge in the campaign against right deviation. Those who followed along knew their actions went against the facts and their own consciences, but they felt they had no choice. Among them, some with a deep sense of conscience suffered great anguish over their acts, accompanied by deep apprehension regarding the consequences.

Some opportunists joined in out of hope that pandering to the leadership would advance their own interests. This was largely a matter of personal character, which at its most basic level was a product of China's cadre system. The promotion of cadres and the appointment and dismissal of personnel were not carried out through a merit-based process, but purely through the pronouncements of the leaders. The approval of a key leader was all a cadre required for his career to advance unimpeded. In such a system, a cadre who saw that the upper ranks wanted yields of 500 kilos per *mu* would ensure that his fields reported 1,000 kilos per *mu*. The words and deeds of such cadres were aimed at creating a favorable impression among the upper ranks, and the cadres would assiduously follow the prevailing wind.

The villages had cohorts of individuals of extremely bad character who inevitably took the lead in any political movement. In his 1927 "Report on an Investigation of the Peasant Movement in Hunan," Mao referred to these people as "ruffians." Without these ruffians, a movement could not gain headway, and for that reason, Mao maintained an approving attitude toward "ruffian movements." During Land Reform and the subsequent "Four Clean-Ups Movement," these individuals were referred to as "valiant." The ranks of rural cadres at the commune level and below included some of these toughs, who in previous political movements had used radicalism to derive personal advantage from chaos. It was these people who were most likely to engage in brutal behavior that violated official policy, such as flogging, trussing up, and beating peasants.

The key sources of the Five Winds and the multitudes who abetted them were able to join forces through the CCP structure, which provided organizational backing for the spread of the Five Winds. Each level included core individuals surrounded by another layer of individuals, with each layer controlling or loyal to another. Every movement relied on the power of these layered cores and various conferences to instigate nationwide mobilization and to launch mass movements. The CCP emphasized mass movements, considering them a means of promoting its work—not only political work, but also industrial construction with a strong scientific element. The 1960 "Angang Constitution" (in which Mao expounded the principles for managing socialist enterprises) included a provision on mass movements. Behind any mass movement lay the will of the supreme leader, who could "move" the masses to strike blindly out in any direction. As long as extremism could be confined within certain limits, the supreme leader would regard it positively. Led by the notion that "correction requires overcompensation," ignorant people could be mobilized as tools of destruction against any opposition.

Even the "wind sources" and their collaborating brotherhood would have been unable to stir up the Five Winds to sustained nationwide effect without the propaganda machine inciting emotions to gale-force levels.

All of the followers just described acted under the encouragement of propaganda instruments. Indeed, even the key personalities who served as the sources of the wind were influenced by propaganda. Propaganda instruments included not only mass media such as newspapers and radio, but also literature and art, education, and the social sciences. All were under the CCP's control for use in mobilizing the masses, instilling a Communist worldview among them, and criticizing all non-Communist ideologies. Education impressed this message on children's minds. Artists and writers created stories that would move the people and influence their feelings. Sociological research used Communist theory to "arm" the masses by altering people's basic sense of right and wrong, while the omnipresent news media used "facts" in major education offensives.

Everyone who worked in these organizations was well educated. Nearly every political movement since the founding of the People's Republic had targeted intellectuals, and the minority who survived were submissive, unscrupulous, or too young to know any reality but communism. They provided propaganda for communism and the Three Red Banners, sometimes even demonstrating genuine creativity.

Public discourse was unanimous, theory was unanimous, culture and education were unanimous. Only one voice was heard, and this provided the "perfect storm" conditions for the Five Winds.

In a situation of complete control of ideology and public discourse and information blackout, the deployment of propaganda instruments to promote a policy and criticize its detractors created in the minds of ignorant youths a distinct and intense demarcation between right and wrong and love and hate that took the form of a desperate longing to put lofty ideals into practice. Any views opposed to or divergent from the object of this longing came under fierce mass attack.

THE IRREPRESSIBLE FORCE OF THE FIVE WINDS

By late 1958, Mao had developed reservations about the Communist Wind. In a speech given during the Second Zhengzhou Conference, from February 27 to March 5, 1959, he observed that the Five Winds had "raised an enormous panic among the peasants." This spurred efforts to purge the Communist Wind and rein in the Five Winds, but they soon blew up again, following Mao's criticism of Peng Dehuai and the campaign against right deviation launched at the Lushan Conference.

On November 3, 1960, Hubei's Mianyang County party committee reported that since the second half of 1958, in spite of constant efforts to bring the Communist Wind under control, it continued with growing intensity, smashing all in its path. As commune members phrased it, "Every coin must be taken, every belonging reallocated, every home dismantled, every bucket of grain carried away"; "from the treetops to the dust," everything was caught up in the whirling wind, and production teams were reduced to "broken pots" and "battered stalls."[50]

On November 15, 1960, Mao returned to the topic:

> In the next few months we must resolutely and thoroughly correct the extreme errors of the Communist Wind, the Exaggeration Wind, Coercive Commandism, Cadre Privilege, and Chaotic Directives regarding production, and with an emphasis on redressing the Communist Wind, also correct the other four unhealthy tendencies. One good method is for each provincial party committee to carry out a comprehensive and thorough investigation of one commune (one with serious errors) to gain a clear idea of the situation. Following this experiment, the method can be applied more broadly . . . It is essential to follow the mass line and fully mobilize the masses themselves to correct Five Wind errors among the cadres and to oppose leniency.[51]

Mao later focused on the muddled thinking of the Central Committee:

> We launched several major campaigns such as the iron- and steel-forging campaign, the rural industry campaign, the road-building campaign, and the literacy campaign, and these all stirred up the Communist Wind. These actions were mutually counterproductive. Although we didn't tell people to engage in wholesale reallocation of property, we also failed to put an effective stop to it . . . In the future we cannot have mutually contradictory policies; we can't oppose on the one hand and stir up or encourage on the other. One question worth noting at present is that following the Lushan Conference, it was projected that this year's harvest would be good. It was believed that . . . the Communist Wind would be dampened . . . and that the campaign against right deviation would spur enthusiasm . . . Against expectation, the natural disaster was even greater in 1960, and accompanied by man-made disaster. This man-made

disaster was not created by our enemies; we created it ourselves. This year, the campaign for equal and indiscriminate transfer of resources was even worse than in 1958; in 1958 it only went on for four or five months, but this year it lasted the entire year.[52]

Mao then blamed a resurgence of the Communist Wind for the devastating waves of mass mobilization. In his analysis, he correctly traced the resurgence of the Five Winds back to the central leadership and identified the crisis as a "man-made disaster." What he failed to do, however, was acknowledge the disastrous effect of the campaign against right deviation that he launched during the Lushan Conference.

Thirty years later, Bo Yibo wrote in his memoirs, "The continuity of the 'Communist Wind,' and its recurrence after being stilled, its cycle of being purged and stirred up again, is undoubtedly closely related to inadequate thoroughness in purging and restitution, and especially to the campaign against right deviation at the 1959 Lushan Conference. But from a fundamental standpoint, it stemmed from the inherent problems of the people's communes themselves and the influence of a utopianism that exceeded the actual stage of development."[53]

Bo listed the systemic maladies of the people's communes: (1) the "large and collective" system of public ownership; (2) the distribution system of rations combined with wages; (3) the military organization, combat operations, and collective living arrangements; and (4) the integration of governmental administration with commune management.

Bo was right to blame the Five Winds on the system of the people's communes and the unrealistic ideals that had become systemic or were in the process of becoming so. The more fundamental source of the Five Winds, however, was the totalitarian system as a whole. Without addressing the leader and his political system, any attempt to tame the Five Winds was doomed to failure. Indeed, while the Communist Wind was ultimately stilled, the other four winds continued to blow right through the beginning of the twenty-first century.

8 ANXIOUS IN ANHUI

Fengyang is in Anhui's northeast, along the south bank of the middle reaches of the Huai River. The Ming dynasty's ruthless founding emperor, Zhu Yuanzhang, was a native of Fengyang. His imperial city and mausoleum are found here, as is the Longxing Temple where Zhu was once a Buddhist monk.

The well-known "Fengyang Flower Drum Song" describes peasants fleeing famine in search of food:

> Talking about Fengyang,
> Once a good place, Fengyang.
> Then Emperor Zhu appeared,
> With famine nearly every year.
> Well-off families sell their sheep,
> Humble families sell their sons;
> The poor with neither sheep nor child
> Set off with their begging drums.

Under "Emperor Mao," the starving peasants of Fengyang County did not even have the freedom to "set off with their begging drums."

The eight-hundred-page *Fengyang County Annals* published in 1999 describes the glories of Fengyang's history but devotes only this brief passage to the calamity of 1959–61:

> February 15, 1960: The entire county collected 4,534,399 kilos of food substitutes, including potato roots, bracken, cogon grass roots, and *qiabuqi*.[1]
>
> February 15, 1960: According to statistics, from 1959 to 1960, the county experienced an outward migration of 11,196 people from

the countryside, or 3.3 percent of the rural population of 335,698, along with 102,994 people falling ill, or 30.7 percent of the rural population, leaving 1,580 unaccompanied elderly and 2,280 orphans. The grain yield for 1960 was 47,535,000 kilos, a reduction of 66,265,000 kilos from the 1957 grain yield of 113,800,000 kilos.

On August 4, 1961, the Fengyang county party committee . . . summarized the errors and lessons of the previous two years of "Five Winds" in Fengyang: (1) high production targets, high production estimates, and high procurement targets leading to the selling of too much grain; (2) closing off information and covering up the actual number of deaths; (3) failing to discriminate between right and wrong and targeting good people with bad during the campaign against right deviation; (4) failing to set boundaries and allowing the Communist Wind to be stirred up time and time again; (5) imposing too heavily on the rural labor force and crippling the agricultural front line; (6) maintaining inconsistent stands and issuing chaotic directives on production; and (7) demanding excessively high targets with excessive haste and inadequate allowance for rest.

Glossing over such an unprecedented tragedy is in itself a tragedy.

PART 1: THE GREAT LEAP FORWARD IN FENGYANG

In Fengyang, the Great Leap Forward was in fact the Great Catastrophe, and local records provide a historical account of the disaster.

High production targets, high production estimates, and high procurement targets. Fengyang enjoyed bumper harvests in 1957 of 103.12 million kilos. For 1958 the county party committee set a target of 400 million kilos. The actual grain yield for 1958 was 75 million kilos, but the county party committee estimated the yield as 200 million kilos. In 1959 a grain yield of 53.45 million kilos (as recorded in the *Fengyang Annals*) was reported as 202.5 million kilos.[2] While yields dropped, local officials reported increases.

High production targets and high production estimates resulted in high procurement targets. In 1958 the state requisitioned 35.51 million kilos, or 43.28 percent of the yield. Since a good portion of the retained grain was for industrial use, urban consumption, seed grain, and animal feed, a state procurement quota of even 30 percent left only a bare minimum for the county's rural inhabitants. The situation was even worse in 1959, when the state requisitioned 29.87 million kilos, or 54.49 percent of the yield.[3] According to county party secretary Zhao Yushu, "From the winter of 1959 to the spring of 1960, 30,000 were stricken with edema, and unnatural death was both widespread and grave. Xiaoxihe Commune's Shanhe brigade lost 30 percent of its population."[4]

Under conditions that left peasants hungry, high procurement targets still had to be met and were imposed through political pressure. Meetings were held through the winter of 1959 and spring of 1960 to force peasants to meet procurement quotas. The county party committee demanded that communes provide three reports every day: their plans for bringing grain to the warehouses, to be reported in the morning; the amount of grain actually brought to storage, at noon; and the day's final procurement amount, in the evening. Every evening, county cadres lavished praise on communes and brigades that had managed to stock their warehouses well, while those reporting scant returns were criticized. Political pressure was heavy. During the 1960 wheat harvest season, the party committee of Xiaoxihe Commune ransacked 8,046 homes, 73.4 percent of the commune's households. Only one home in the Changtang production brigade escaped the search party's attention.[5]

The "Communist Wind" blew up again and again.[6] As elsewhere, the Communist Wind hit Anhui in the autumn of 1958, then died down somewhat in the spring of 1959, only to return with renewed vigor in the spring of 1960. Anhui likewise joined the other "great campaigns" devoted to hastening the arrival of communism.

On the generally held belief that collective ownership by the communes was closer to true communism than ownership by the production teams, the Shanhe production brigade collectivized not only pigs and poultry, but also all of the sweet potato seeds held by commune members. Even household toilets were eradicated in favor of newly constructed public toilets. Most of the collectivized pigs and fowl died, and the sweet potato seeds rotted in storage. Yams, taros, and ginger were the special products of Fengyang's Xiaoxihe District and a major source of local income for households. The cadres, however, felt this was inconsistent with Communist principles. Commune members were forbidden to make their own plantings, and errant shoots were instantly eliminated. In some localities it was said that "any sight of seedlings within three years was illegal."[7]

As a means of lending momentum to the Communist Wind, memorial archways and "Great Leap Gates" were erected, and rooftops, field ridges, roadways, and hillsides were emblazoned with posters and banners fervently anticipating the arrival of communism. The construction of Communist-style "New Villages" made ghost towns out of twenty-five hamlets in Xiaoxihe Commune's seven production brigades. In the Daying production team of the Shima production brigade, five villages were combined into one, with segregated quarters for men, women, the elderly, and children. The Qiaoshan production brigade originally included thirty-one villages, but in June 1960, branch party secretary Mei forcibly consolidated them into six in half a day, with more than three hundred homes destroyed. Party and Youth League members who balked were stripped of membership, while ordinary commune members who refused to cooperate had their meal rations withheld. Commune members were promised a new village, but no new homes replaced those that were destroyed, and more than one hundred people were forced into collective living quarters. Fourteen households totaling forty people had to share three interconnected quarters, with the main door locked at night and guarded by militia and everyone forced to share a common toilet.[8]

At the end of 1958 the county had 224,143 homes, but over the next two years, 39,555 disappeared, of which 13,400 were purposely demolished. Twenty-nine of the county's villages had all their homes razed. Commune members became refugees, their land lying fallow amid the weeds and multiple generations sharing a room under conditions that precluded even the most basic level of dignity. The mere mention of an impending consolidation reduced some women to hysterical weeping.[9]

Absurd and chaotic production directives were issued. Peasants were required to plant "red flags" throughout the countryside and to till the fields while singing patriotic songs and shouting slogans. In order to pass inspection by the upper levels, cadres deployed the greatest labor of man and beast and the largest quantities of fertilizer to the fields adjoining the railroad tracks and the border areas of communes and counties, while vast stretches inland lay fallow. The entire county had only 1,412,000 *mu* of cultivated land, but during the spring and summer planting seasons of 1960, county cadres reported to the upper levels that 1,848,000 *mu* had been planted.[10]

Peasants woke each morning with no idea what task they would be assigned. Even production team leaders often didn't know. Directives and deployment were centralized under commune and county leaders who acted as if preparing for battle. Among the 13 production brigades of Xiaoxihe Commune, 86 production teams, 284 work teams, and 3,395 individual laborers engaged in such large-scale warfare tactics starting in the spring of 1960, with some operations continuing for forty days or even three months straight. Distribution was not based on work done, resulting in a great deal of pointless display. One day, cadres from the Daiwei production team sent more than one hundred commune members with more than two thousand bunches of seedlings to transplant in Dahan Village, but because the fields hadn't been prepared in advance, they were sent on to Liu Yuan, where again no fields were ready to take them, and they were sent on to Qianmiao. It was evening when they arrived, so no transplanting could be done, and all the seedlings died unplanted. Such chaotic directives sapped enthusiasm and sabotaged production.[11]

In Fengyang, this chaos attained an almost sublime absurdity. Ignoring agricultural seasons, some localities planted corn during the Spring Festival (early February), paddy rice during the Qing Ming Festival (early April), and tobacco at the onset of autumn. Directives from above had to be obeyed. To meet a task for 700,000 *mu* of rice paddy, some localities put dry land to use as paddy fields, or even plowed under existing dry land crops to turn those fields into rice paddies. The Hongguang production brigade of Mentai Commune lacked the appropriate conditions for rice paddy fields, but orders came from above to convert the fields to paddies all the same. In 1958 the brigade converted 1,600 *mu* of dry land to paddy, which resulted in an average yield of only 25 kilos per *mu*. In 1959 the brigade converted another 850 *mu* of land, and the average yield fell to 15.5 kilos per *mu*. Conversion of 900 more *mu* in 1960 brought the average yield down to less than 1.5 kilos per *mu*. Lacking the wherewithal to irrigate this dry land, the brigade deployed forty-eight people and twenty-five plow oxen to carry 15,000 kilos of rice seeds to a commune thirty kilometers away for soaking and raising seedlings. After twenty-nine days the seeds had to be discarded.

The No. 4 production team had 500 *mu* of soybean plants already 16 centimeters tall, but the production brigade ordered them plowed under to make way for sweet potatoes. The commune members objected, but 480 *mu* of fields were plowed under all the same. The resulting yield came to only 150 kilos of sweet potatoes, while the 20 *mu* of soybeans left undisturbed produced more than 100 kilos.[12]

At Mentai Commune's Hongguang production brigade, the wheat was golden, almost ready for harvest, in 1960 when more than five hundred brigade members were sent to Huangwan. After a two-day journey, the workers rested for one day, spent another day rummaging up tools, took another day's rest when no food arrived, then spent two more days trudging back to their home brigade. Having spent eight days to do half a day's work, they arrived home to learn that a downpour had spoiled much of their unharvested grain.[13]

Waste was pervasive. At Xiaoxihe Commune's Qiaoshan production brigade, 8 *mu* of barley had already sent out roots when cadres ordered the fields plowed under to be replaced with peas. Not a single pea was harvested. The Jianxi production team under this brigade sowed 600 kilos of peanuts in 80 *mu* of land in the spring, only to harvest less than 2 kilos in the autumn. In March 1960 the Xintian production brigade's Qintang production team planted 7 *mu* of wheat, but overzealously applied 50 kilos of fertilizer per *mu*, burning up the wheat and making the soil inhospitable even for weeds. A cadre on temporary work assignment at the Guangming production brigade insisted on harvesting wheat during rain and transplanting seedlings on sunny days. At the Changtang production brigade, commune members were forced to plant tobacco in 250 *mu* of paddy field, and not a single tobacco leaf was harvested.[14]

The county party committee required crops to be planted with unreasonable density, dictating the way seeds were sown, the amount of seed and fertilizer to be applied, and the ridging of fields for irrigation purposes. Innovations such as water wheels, small transport vehicles, and ball bearings were employed even when their cost exceeded their benefit.

Liufu Commune banned the preparation of dry nurseries for rice seedlings, but the leader of the Liufu production brigade, Wang Guizhen, planted one and a half *mu* of rice seeds in a dry nursery as appropriate to local conditions. When the commune's party secretary learned of it, he had Wang publicly criticized. Defending himself, Wang said, "I only did it to bring in more grain." But the party secretary retorted, "Obeying the party means planting rice in a wet nursery, even if that produces not a kernel of grain. A cadre who disobeys the party is a bad cadre, no matter how much grain he produces." Wang was then stripped of his position.[15]

The arrival of a new key task brought deployments to around-the-clock "crash operations" at pitched camps that took minimal notice of weather or rest. Many women became afflicted with amenorrhea or uterine prolapse due to hunger and exhaustion. Long-term exposure to these conditions resulted in death on a massive scale.

At the height of the iron and steel campaign, more than 63,000 workers were sent to the production front line, which slashed Fengyang's agricultural productivity. From November 10, 1959, to May 8, 1960, the county had 30,000 to 50,000 laborers deployed to irrigation projects every day, at one point reaching a level of 70,000 laborers, or 63 percent of the county's workforce. Another 3,700-odd workers were routinely assigned to railroad work, and more than 2,000 to highway construction. The county party committee ordered a gross industrial output value for 1959 that was fourteen times the output value for 1958. Industrial workers increased from 924 in 1957 to 8,724 in 1961. More than 25,000 peasants were also transferred to industrial work. Peasants had to leave the fields before the autumn planting was completed and were not allowed to return home for the spring plowing season. Almost all those left behind to handle the farm work were women and children.[16]

NINETY THOUSAND STARVATION DEATHS IN THREE YEARS

Fengyang County lost ninety thousand people to starvation in the Great Famine—nearly one-fourth of its population. In some communes, one out of three people died.[17] Xinhua journalist Zhang Wanshu observed, "Although weather conditions in 1960 were highly conducive to good harvests, the destruction of rural productivity left many fields fallow, and many people fled their homes in search of food, or died of starvation. Statistics from Dingyuan, Fengyang, and Jiashan indicate that those three counties lost more than 400,000 people in 1961." In Fengyang's Qingang Village, "among the village's 34 households of 175 people, those who could flee did so, while others died, and only 10 households of 39 people were left."[18]

According to a report in February 1961, 60,245 Fengyang residents starved to death in 1959 and 1960.[19] This is consistent with the estimated population loss of 25 percent over the three years of 1958–61. More than

8,400 households were wiped out, and 27 villages became ghost towns. The principal of Fengyang County's experimental primary school, Wang Huanya, and his family of twelve all died of starvation. In the village of Zhaozhuangzi in Xiaoxihe Commune, the sister of Zhang Yupu was found alive in the arms of her father, who had died two days before.

A conference was called in January 1961 to rectify the Five Winds. At least 90 percent of the participants had lost at least one family member, and many wept as they spoke:

Wang Tinghua . . . called county deputy director Song Zhaoyin to account, saying, "In 1958 you led us to Guangou Reservoir to dig a canal but gave us nothing to eat, while making us work five days and nights without sleeping . . . Last year more than 100 people in our village starved to death, did you know that?"

A representative of Zongpu Commune's Guoguang production brigade said, "So many people died and you didn't dare to report it. In our village of just over 300 people, 87 died—it's too painful to talk about!"

Wu Shanlan, party branch secretary of the Zhanjia production team . . . said, "In the spring of 1960, the county party committee gave the masses dried sweet potatoes to eat, but they were already rotting, bitter, and reeking, and the masses said it was worse than drinking herbal medicine. The result was an increase in edema, and 27 people died within just ten days in April."

The party secretary of Wudian Commune, Wan Deyuan, said, "In 1959 Wudian held a tobacco-curing meeting, and the county party committee insisted that there were more tobacco leaves, even though they knew better. The secretary of the county party secretariat, Dong Anchun, loaded up one donkey-load of tobacco onto three donkeys to make it look like there was more. He also arranged for obviously starving commune members to be kept inside so outsiders couldn't see them. People who starved to death had to be buried a meter deep and had crops grown over them."

Li Jinming, a representative of Wudian Commune's Shanwang production brigade, said, "In 1958, we harvested 17,500 kilos of grain but called it 29,000 kilos for requisition purposes, so we had to hand over 16,500 kilos, leaving only 1,000 kilos for commune members to eat. There was really no grain to eat, and the masses ate hemp leaves or whatever else they could find. I reported to Dong Anchun: We have nothing to eat. He said I was raising a fuss and threatened to expel me from the party. As a result, of the 280 of us, only 170 were left. Of my family of five, four died and only I survived."

A representative of Wudian Commune's Quanxin production brigade said, ". . . Our brigade started out with more than 2,500 people, and now only around 1,300 are left. We reported this to Dong Anchun, and he said we were making things up. We took him to look at the dead and he said, 'If no one dies, there will be no room in the world for all the people.'"

[Commune member] Wang Xizhou said, "These two years there's been too much damn nonsense, all because of pressure from above . . . It was the devil's own wind that blew in, and it would kill us all in another year . . ." Party branch secretary Wang Huanya said, "In the spring of 1960, eleven members of work group head Qian Xuan's family died. When the deaths began, a letter came from his family, but he waved his hands and wouldn't allow anyone to speak of it, and he just sent some money back to deal with the situation. Finally only three people were left . . . so he asked that the three children, with their grain and oil rations, be transferred to his care. He made this request several times, but by the time permission was finally granted, the three children had all starved to death. He became mentally deranged."

. . . Zhang Yupu of the Banqiao work group said, ". . . People became so constipated from food substitutes that they couldn't defecate. There was blood in their stool, which they had to prod out with sticks. I reported this to the head of the inspectorate at my unit, but he accused me of opposing Chairman Mao and the party and of slandering the people's communes. I was struggled for three days and had to write six self-criticisms . . . In the spring of 1960, five members of my family died, and I saved only one child . . ."

Chen Xuemeng, whom Chairman Mao had praised for his leading role in the collectivization process, said at the meeting, ". . . Among thirty-seven households at Wangjiahu, almost all of the adults died, and all that's left are orphans with no one to care for them. When the children see me, they say, 'Sir, my parents can't see you, all that's left is me.' It's heartbreaking!"

. . . A representative of the Kaocheng production brigade said, "Our brigade started out with 5,000, and now we have only 3,200. Even the Jap invaders didn't kill so many people. When the Japs came, at least we could run away, but this year there was nowhere for us to go . . . All we could do was stay home and accept death. In my family of six, four died, and only two are left. I'm the last person left tending the buffalo . . . the other twelve buffalo herders all died."

. . . At the Zhengshan production team, commune member Chang Jiecui's mother was suffering from malnutrition, so Chang asked production team head Hua for a little flour to feed her. Hua said, "Why bother feeding her? She's about to die anyway. Why not just bury her and get it over with before the others come in from the fields for lunch?" When Chang disagreed, Hua said, "If you don't do what I say, she'll die in your home and be buried there." Chang then buried her mother alive.[20]

In some localities, there were "four no's" to be observed in relation to the dead: (1) no shallow graves; all corpses had to be buried one meter deep and have crops grown over them; (2) no crying; (3) no burials along the roadside; and (4) no mourning rites. At the Zhangwan production team, survivors were forbidden to wear white mourning garb, and were required to wear red clothes of celebration.[21]

From 1959 to 1960, sixty-three cases of cannibalism in Fengyang County were officially recorded. At Damiao Commune's Wuyi production brigade, Chen Zhangying and Zhao Xizhen strangled their eight-year-old son, Xiaoqing, then cooked and ate him. At the Banjing production brigade, Wang Lanying dug up a corpse, ate part of it, and sold a kilo as pork.[22]

Many cannibalism cases were reported at Wudian and Caodian communes. Tang Xiuqi said, "One evening I was returning home from a meeting when I saw someone at Tang Yongding's home chop up a human head, cook it in a wok, and eat it. Tang Yongding himself was in his doorway eating from a ladle. He said, 'I've already eaten several.' All the village children call Tang Yongding a hairy ape."[23]

At a meeting on August 9, 1961, a tractor station head surnamed Wang said, "In 1959 I was in charge of rectifying the Zhetang production brigade at Banqiao Commune. When reporting a death, we didn't dare attribute it to lack of food, but said it was because of inadequate sanitation efforts. A woman was found to have eaten a dead child, and after it was reported to Ji Wenxiang (the county's deputy party secretary), Ji sent a work group to bind up that woman and take her to the public security bureau, accusing her of sabotaging socialism."[24]

County party secretary Zhao Yushu took no effective measures to deal with cannibalism. Fearing the consequences of the truth being re-vealed, he classified these incidents as "political sabotage" and ordered the public security bureau to carry out secret arrests. If people died in custody, that would eliminate all trace of the crime. Sixty-three people were arrested, and thirty-three died in custody.[25] These cases occurred despite a strong taboo in Chinese tradition against eating human flesh; most people would rather die of starvation than resort to it.

County leaders such as Zhao Yushu and Dong Anchun absolutely refused to acknowledge that people were dying of hunger. When Zhao and Dong visited the Kaocheng production brigade, they asked physician Wang Shanliang, "Why can't you manage to cure edema? What medicine are you lacking?" Dr. Wang answered, "All we're lacking is food!" Zhao and Dong immediately had Wang subjected to mass criticism, after which he was arrested.[26]

Cadres at all levels carried out cover-ups. On July 2, 1960, the Bengbu prefectural party committee secretariat learned that a man named Zhang Shaobai (variously described as party secretary of Yinjian Commune or deputy director of the Fengyang County party committee secretariat) had written to Mao under the pseudonym Shi Qiuming. The letter said, "The number of deaths at the three communes and four villages I'm familiar with is extremely alarming. In one, the deaths have reached 5 percent, in another 15 percent, and in another more than 20 percent . . . Some villages are almost completely empty. I personally witnessed 300 or 400 parentless children rounded up, with around 100 deaths reported." It was subse-quently learned that the actual number of starvation deaths was much higher, but this letter was classified as "reactionary," and Zhang was vio-lently persecuted.

In the spring of 1960, Bengbu's deputy mayor, Ma Qian, heard that many people in his home village had died of starvation or fled the famine, so he arranged for 5,000 kilos of soy pulp (*okara*) to be sent to Linhuai, and notified villagers to come and fetch it. The emergency aid was re-fused by general branch deputy party secretary Yang Yunchun and deputy county head Miao Jian, who reported Ma Qian to the prefectural party committee for "right-deviating thinking."[27]

In 1961, Fengyang County party secretary Ma Weimin reported,

We all basically understood the situation with the deaths. At the outset we regarded individual deaths as exceptions and did not report them to the upper levels, deciding to deal with them ourselves. Subsequently, many more people died, and as the problem grew we panicked and were even less willing to report the deaths. It was clear that the dead had died of starvation, but we said it was from old age or illness, and we classified unnatural deaths as natural deaths. In some places, families were not allowed to mourn their dead or to bury them in proper graves, and letters mentioning deaths were confiscated and suppressed, with their writers sometimes attacked. Some cadres who truthfully reported the situation to the organization were subjected to struggle.

STARVING PEASANTS AND GORGING CADRES

Reports of deaths were accompanied by reports of cadre privilege. In the spring of 1960 many infants were abandoned, but county party secretary Zhao Yushu ordered that infants should not be taken in, and that anyone who rescued one would have to take responsibility for raising it. On the other hand, when a hen went missing from Zhao's household, he ordered an investigation by the local police and public security bureau, setting a three-day deadline for cracking the case. People commented that the Zhao family's old hen was valued more highly than an abandoned child. Zhao's household also enjoyed plenty of top-quality food all year round.[28]

In the spring of 1959 a county party secretary surnamed Yang brought a song-and-dance troupe to Zongpu Commune, filling stricken village streets with music and revelry, firing off pistols, and shooting photographs as if nothing were amiss.[29]

While peasants starved, cadres entertained at lavish feasts. Once, when the county party committee met, some committee members were so drunk that the meeting had to be adjourned. When the county's deputy head and party secretary of Xiaoxihe Commune, Miao Jian, went on inspection visits, he brought his own liquor, meat, and a chef. When the Zhetang production brigade leader was enjoying one of his lavish meals, a sick person asked for a swallow of fish broth, only to be slapped and sent off hungry. Lin Xingfu of the county party committee work group reported, "County party committee chairman Jiang Yizhou ate wheat flour and rice, with no limits on his consumption. He didn't eat at the communal kitchen, but had rice crusts fried in oil. [County party secretary] Zhou's family never ate coarse grain."

Yang Yiquan of the Wudian work group said, "County party committee members had special privileges. They ate everything, including wheat flour and rice . . . When the masses suffer from edema, they can't buy sugar, but the commerce department gives a packet to each member of the county party committee . . ." Qiang Hua said, "The Wudian on-the-spot meeting was very wasteful. There was no food at the communal kitchen, and thirteen people died at Zhoulou in two days, but at the meeting they still ate and drank—fried dough strips, fried glutinous rice cakes, boiled dumplings, steamed bread, twelve dishes in the morning and twenty-four at noon, and fancy liquor along with it. Edema patients at Shuangyingzi Village were locked in their homes to keep them out of sight." A member of the Zongpu work team said, "In the winter of 1959 and the spring of 1960, while the masses were dying of edema, the county party committee was inviting guests to feasts and convening commune party secretary meetings. The reservoir had to keep sending over fish, all for a few party secretaries and standing committee members, who didn't pay a penny for anything . . . The county party committee ate hundreds of kilos of grain every month. If this grain had been sent to the production teams, how many starving people could have been saved?"[30]

In Xiaoxihe Commune's Shanhe production brigade, every cadre, from production team secretary to work group cadre to kitchen staff, would eat a little more and a little better. Records indicate that these cadres consumed more than 900 kilos of beef. When deputy county head and commune party secretary Miao Jian inspected the brigade between harvests in May 1960, he spent the whole time feasting with local cadres. Deputy party secretary Shi Yuping ate in a private dining room, taking his meals at the communal kitchen only six times from July to November of 1960. He kept stores of salted fish and meat at home. Commune deputy party secretary Li had the local store supply all its eggs and sugar to him and continued to feast while on inspection visits. The party secretary and the accountant of the Qiaoshan production brigade operated an "International Women's Day" farm as a pretext for selecting women to rape or seduce.[31]

POLITICAL PRESSURE USED AGAINST THE ORDINARY PEOPLE

The Five Evil Winds had begun to impose tremendous political pressure on the province even before the Great Leap Forward. From October 1957 to June 13, 1958, rectifications and struggle campaigns had gathered data on "landlords, rich peasants, counterrevolutionaries, and bad elements." In Fengyang this resulted in the arrest of 1,327, with another 1,406 placed under surveillance, 1,025 subjected to struggle and supervision, and 127 otherwise disciplined, with 313 cases left unresolved. Other investigations of so-called counterrevolutionaries led to the arrest of 366 individuals, while another 45 were arrested in campaigns against infiltration by counterrevolutionaries and in the tracking down of fugitives. A purge of counterrevolutionaries and bad elements within state organs, enterprises, and schools resulted in 59 individuals being sent to reeducation through labor. About 1 percent of the county's population was affected by these campaigns.[32]

Those actions were aimed at "contradictions between the enemy and us," but the campaigns that began in 1958 focused on "internal dissent among the people." During the establishment of people's communes, 722 residents were subjected to struggle and mass debate.[33] The 1959 campaign against right deviation (called the Socialist Education Movement in the countryside) intensified the attack on dissenting views. Some who told the truth or pointed out the absurdity of chaotic directives were targeted and struggled as "anti-party," "right-deviating," "denier," "conservative," "negating achievement," or as "vilifying the Three Red Banners." County head Zhao Conghua was labeled a right opportunist for his views on the people's communes and communal kitchens.[34] Forty-one other party members and cadres were identified as problematic during the campaign against right deviation.[35] A model worker named Chen Xuemeng pointed out some problems and was labeled a "capitalist" with "right-deviating thinking." Dissent or theft of food brought brutal corporal punishment.

During the post-famine rectification in 1961, commune members exposed violations of law and discipline by more than one-third of all cadres at the level of production team leader or above, finding that one-eighth of the rural population had been subjected to corporal punishment, including 15,001 from whom food had been withheld. This abuse had resulted in 441 deaths and 383 cases of permanent disability. Of 2,078 people who were detained or arrested in 1960, only around 300 ever went through formal legal proceedings. Of the 2,078 detainees, 1,076 were starving people accused of stealing food. Overcrowding led to 382 deaths in custody.[36]

County party committee members appointed themselves police, judge, and jury, detaining people without authorization and setting up labor reform teams. In Wudian Commune, 1,285 people were subjected to corporal punishment in 1959 and 1960, with 95 executed. At Xiaoxihe Commune, nearly 40 percent of the cadres engaged in violations of law and discipline or wrongful coercion and commandism. Of the 3,175 people they subjected to corporal punishment, 96 died and 103 were crippled.

The party branch secretary of the Qiaoshan production brigade attempted to bury four children alive before others successfully appealed for the children to be spared. In May 1960 the head of the Daxihe production brigade discovered a small child plucking out corn stalks to eat and threw him into a field-side pit filled a meter deep with water. The child's mother arrived in time to save him. Yinchen production team member Guo Chuanliang was in charge of grazing the buffalo when they ate some crops, so the production team leader punished him by smashing his fingers with firewood.[37]

Leader Miao of the Shanxi production team beat 35 team members in March 1960. Insisting that a fifteen-year-old girl named Xiaomiao had eaten some sweet potato seeds, he beat her with a shovel and a bamboo pole, and when she fainted, he waited until she revived, then beat her again until she wet herself and her arm was broken. On March 24, Miao accused fifty-two-year-old Liu Jinyou of being late in grazing the cattle and withheld his meal ration. When Liu searched for wild herbs in the fields, Miao accused him of sabotaging production, then savagely beat him and exposed him to the cold. Too disabled to work, Liu was deprived of his meal rations. Five days later he died.

Of the Shanhe production brigade's 1,078 members, 36.3 percent were bound, beaten, strung up, deprived of meals, or paraded. Two were beaten to death and one was persecuted to death. Of the 240 members of the Beixia production team, 237 were beaten.

During the 1960 wheat harvest, party secretary Chen of the Shanhe production brigade forced commune members to work around the clock. When Lu Dianyou fell asleep in the field, Chen had him doused with boiling water. Production team leader Wang in the Fengxing production brigade caught a thief surnamed Li and had his lips branded with burning tongs. Leader Han of Yinjian Commune's Zhaoyao production team chopped four fingers off a child caught stealing unripened crops. Huaifeng production brigade leader Zhang found Wang Xiaojiao stealing unripened crops and had him suspended from a roof beam with wire strung from his ears and hands. Two children of Sanxiao production team member Wu Kaicong were driven by hunger to eat grain shoots. Team branch secretary Wang had his henchman string the children together with wire through their ears and told them, "Now you can telephone each other." Xinhuo production brigade branch secretary Zhong raped a woman after catching her stealing unripened grain. Another woman caught in the act at the Zhetang production brigade had a gun jammed into her vagina by the brigade leader.[38]

Liwu production brigade leader Su withheld medical treatment from Xu Kailan, an edema victim who had accused him of corruptly misappropriating oil. As Xu's condition deteriorated before a clinic examination, Su decided to have him buried alive. Xu's child was crying nearby at the time, so Su lured the child away with a cookie, then covered Xu with straw and had him carried out and buried.[39]

Wudian Commune's Zhaolou production team deputy leader Zhao was quoted as saying, "The masses are slaves, and they won't do anything unless beaten, berated, or deprived of food." He took part in the beating of more than thirty people in 1960, with some dying. Of the commune's 1,163 cadres at the production team level and above, 265 were found to have violated law and discipline.[40]

AT THE IRRIGATION WORKS

The Great Leap Forward launched many irrigation projects in Fengyang. Because they were undertaken with an unscientific approach, many were a waste of manpower and resources. Peasants working on irrigation projects were treated as slaves, and hunger exacerbated by arduous labor caused many to die.

One project was an electric pumping station, where workers were forced to take extra shifts and workloads while more than 60,000 kilos of their grain rations were embezzled. The secretary of the county party secretariat, Zhang Daohou, came up with the slogan of "Three days and nights without rice, work efficiency increases thrice; even when snowing, working shirtless is nice." County party committee member Du Sijian found some toiling with their shirts on and berated them for not working hard enough.

Work sites followed the rule of "More food for more labor, less food for less labor, no food for no labor." Workers requesting leave had to obtain permission in order to receive a meal ration. The sick were sent home, and because their meal rations were reduced or withheld, they sometimes died on the way. Available figures indicate that 2,474 peasants died working on the electric pumping station—17.3 percent of the county's public project labor force. This number does not include those who expired after dragging themselves home. Of the 500 members of Limin Commune who were sent to work on the electric pumping station, 307 died. Of 40 members of the Songji production brigade sent to the project, 29 died.[41]

County party committee member Li set up his own "court," "jail," and "labor reform squad" at Randeng Reservoir and had two dozen pairs of handcuffs made to deal with those who "acted up." He had more than seventy people locked up and fettered, of whom twenty-eight died.[42] Workers who failed to meet his quotas were sent to the Reform Through Labor team.

Workers were ordered to bury Daxihe Commune member Wang Zanman while he was still breathing, but they dragged him away instead. Wang revived and spent four days crawling home.[43] Ding Xueran was sent to the reservoir site after being caught butchering an old sow. He was forced to do heavy labor all day and at night he was shackled in a dark cell. After a month of this torment, he died. Song Weiqin, a member of the Nanliujia production team, attempted to run away from the reservoir site, but was captured and forced to work without food until he died. When workers died, no report was made, and families were not notified.[44]

In the spring of 1960, Shanhe production brigade deputy leader Miao brought workers to the reservoir and forced them to labor like slaves. He beat more than one hundred, of whom thirty-five died. Xinhua production brigade deputy head Zhang had Xu Shanyou bound and delivered to the reservoir site. When Xu refused to go, Zhang had his hands tied behind his back and then had him dragged by an ox. His skin scraped raw, Xu finally agreed to go, but died four days later.[45] Zhang retaliated against Shi Qianshan for criticizing him during the 1957 rectification campaign, deploying Shi and his wife separately to the reservoir and to the railway, respectively, and then persecuting Shi's elderly mother and two children at home. When the children fell ill under Zhang's abuse, their grandmother begged for them to be treated at the hospital. Zhang retorted, "Go to the hospital? I want to see your whole family extinguished!" Within a few days both children died, and their grandmother soon followed.[46]

ASSIGNING FIELDS TO HOUSEHOLDS TO SURVIVE THE FAMINE

Fengyang's situation grew desperate, with communal kitchens running out of food, corpses littering the ground, and no means of escape. Hovering on the brink of death, some production teams ignored communism and assigned plots of land to households, allowing peasants to raise their own food and survive. By 1961, Fucheng Commune's Sifeng production brigade had increased yields per *mu* beyond the 1957 levels. County officials promoted the brigade's experience countywide. As will be detailed later, the practice spread throughout the province. The fields were officially called "responsibility fields," but the peasants called them "salvation fields."[47] The CCP Central Committee called a halt to assigning fields to households in 1962. By then, less than 20 percent of Fengyang County's production teams were still under collective management. The peasants' desire for responsibility fields was never extinguished; years later, after the Cultural Revolution, household farming was revived in Fengyang's Xiaogang Village, helping to launch economic reform throughout China.

PART 2: THE WUWEI CRISIS[48]

In the spring of 1955, Wuwei County established 1,119 cooperatives. Soon after, Mao published "On the Question of Agricultural Cooperation," and the entire county achieved collectivization almost overnight. Many in Wuwei went hungry after the autumn harvest, and some demanded to withdraw from the collectives. Angry throngs raided the grain stores, and households divided up seed grain, denouncing the government and vilifying cadres. The higher levels responded by sending down groups to "carry out stringent criticism and education of the capitalist mentality of rich peasants and right-deviating conservatism, individualism, departmentalism, egalitarianism, and other erroneous thinking among cadres, party members, and Youth League members."[49]

A senior-grade propagandist told a mass gathering that whoever attempted to withdraw from the collective would have to first pay back the costs incurred when the army liberated the area, along with prior disaster relief. This dumbfounded the peasants, who muttered among themselves, "So that's how they renege on the so-called voluntary participation in cooperatives and freedom to withdraw." From then on, no one dared withdraw from the collectives.[50]

Wuwei County party committee first secretary Yao Kuijia heard that starving peasants had fled to Jiangxi Province. He reported it to the provincial party committee and sent agents to Jiangxi to return the refugees to their places of origin. He also required train stations and ferry ports to deny tickets to anyone lacking a permit. When the refugees returned, they were given no food and were left to await death by starvation.

In September 1958 the county's 435 collectives were amalgamated into 31 people's communes within just ten days.[51] Yanqiao district's Chen Guangfu had already implemented a Communist distribution system during the collectivization process in 1955, and while organizing the Xiangshan Agricultural Cooperative into a people's commune, he enthusiastically implemented a free-supply ration system. When Mao learned of it, he proclaimed, "Anhui's Wuwei County produced a Huang Wenbing[52] during the Three Kingdoms era, and now it has produced a Chen Guangfu." Only the poor transport links prevented Mao from visiting Xiangshan.

On October 9, 1958, *People's Daily* celebrated Chen Guangfu's efforts in an article, declaring, "This distribution system greatly promotes the maturation of commune members' Communist thinking, and accelerates the eradication of the last vestiges of private ownership of the means of production . . . It not only greatly helps accelerate the pace of successful socialist construction and accelerates increased production, but also creates an excellent foundation for the transition to a Communist distribution system. For that reason, it can be considered a ladder to communism, and the sprouting of communism."[53]

Wuwei's rationing system embodied the worst effects of the Communist Wind. Every asset was confiscated without compensating the owners. According to one source, 109 of the brigade's 471 living quarters were torn down.

In 1959, Dajiang Commune proposed realizing 10,000-head piggeries, 10,000-chicken hatcheries, 10,000-melon storehouses, 10,000-duck pens, 10,000-fish ponds, 10,000-goose embankments, and 10,000-kilo-per-*mu* fields. These assets had belonged to commune members. After the autumn of 1959 the county announced collectivization of poultry and livestock. This brought a wave of butchering, eating, and selling that wiped out almost all livestock and poultry. The villages were reduced to vast stretches of desolation and poverty.[54] The result was that starvation depleted the county's 1957 population of 982,979 to 662,557 by the end of 1960.[55]

OFFICIALS SNATCH GRAIN FROM THE MOUTHS OF PEASANTS

Wuwei County's 1958 grain yield of 310 million kilos was reported as 650 million kilos, and the 1959 yield of 220 million kilos was reported as 550 million. Xia Kewen, an official with the county grain bureau, recalls being ordered to inquire into actual crop yields in 1958. He found that the best fields produced an average of only 60 kilos per *mu*, and the poorest, 20 kilos. He reported these figures, but district-level cadres rejected them and made up statistics to report to the upper levels.[56]

At the end of 1958, with most peasants on the brink of starvation, first party secretary Yao Kuijia told the county party committee that food was plentiful. "The crux of the grain supply problem is the thinking and work style of the leaders and problems in operational methods."

At Hongmiao Commune, Yao used struggle sessions, hangings, beatings, stripping, and exposure to coerce the surrender of grain. More than 7,600 people starved to death, including 2,260 of the 4,944 members of the Zhabei production brigade.

Yao had "uncooperative" brigade and team leaders tortured, and ordered cadres to snatch every kernel of grain from the peasants during anti-hoarding campaigns. When the 1960 autumn harvest was brought to the storehouses, newspaper articles praised exaggerated reports. Kaicheng Commune sent 15,000 kilos of grain to the storehouse, and when the grain supply center head reported this truthfully, Yao said, "Tie up that son of a bitch and bring him in!" Yao telephoned Tuqiao Commune party secretary Ma Yugen and told him to keep sending grain. Ma said, "All we have left is 150,000 kilos of seed grain, and we can't send that in," but Yao retorted, "Send that and the grain rations as well!"

In October 1959, with many already dead at Shangli Commune, Yao told the commune's party secretary, Liu Yikuan, "You go back now, and if you haven't met your procurement quota of 120,000 kilos within three days, you can bring me your head on a platter at the next meeting." Liu eventually sent 150,000 kilos of seed grain to the state.

While Wuwei's peasants starved, the CCP Central Committee

honored the county in 1958 for surpassing agricultural program targets, and the prefectural party committee proclaimed it a "red flag" in 1959.

THE SUFFERING OF THE PEASANTS

Skeletal peasants tottered along village paths, even the young leaning on walking sticks. No one had the strength to work, yet cudgel-wielding cadres forced them to the fields. The peasants simply planted the edges of the paddies, while weeds took over the inner fields.[57]

Efforts to seize grain increased. A November 1960 investigative report found, "A minority of cadres arbitrarily imposed corporal punishment on the masses, such as binding, hanging, and beating, withholding of food, protracted kneeling, and exposure to cold or heat. Some set up unauthorized jails and labor reform teams. Others resorted to outrageous punishments such as smashing fingers with rocks, jabbing fingers with needles, cutting off ears, branding noses, sewing lips together, and so on."[58] Another investigative report found that at one commune, fourteen were severely injured, five died, and one was driven to suicide.[59]

Records show that weather conditions were normal in Wuwei from 1957 to 1961, yet three hundred thousand county residents starved to death.[60] Dead bodies were left covered in beds while family members fetched the deceased's portion of gruel or food substitute—until a suspicious cadre eventually barged in and discovered the truth. In some places, the desperate went from concealing the dead to eating them.[61]

In 2003, author Xie Guiping talked to a survivor named Su Xiufang, who during the famine had lived in Sulao Village, not quite two kilometers from Kunshan. Sulao Village originally had 570 inhabitants, but death and outward migration had reduced the population to just over 200, and some households had been completely extinguished. Su's family, all descendants of the same great-grandfather, had 72 members, but 53 of them had died of starvation or abuse. After her mother died, Su's two-year-old brother lay mewling pitifully at her side. In hopes of collecting one extra ration of congee, the family covered the corpse with a blanket and told no one of the mother's death. That extra gruel allowed Su and her little brother to cling to life. When Su's cousin starved to death, her uncle took the body into the hills behind the village and cut away the flesh to eat before burying the remains. Many villagers witnessed this incident.

Xia Kewen, an official with the county's grain bureau, told Xie Guiping that an itinerant peddler used his earnings to buy food but never shared it with his wife and son. When they begged for food, he beat them and threatened to kill them. The desperate wife and son finally strangled him while he slept, saving themselves with the food in his bundle.

Hu Dahai, who headed up Wuwei County's public security dispatch station, recalled, "At that time the criminals in our detention center might include a woman who'd killed her husband, a son who'd killed a parent, or a mother who'd killed her own child—all kinds of completely immoral crimes, and all of them arising from hunger."[62]

SUPPRESSING THE TRUTH TELLERS

The county party committee's "letters from the masses office" received 1,173 letters in 1959 and 1960, but the vast majority received no appropriate attention, and in some cases the writers were investigated as reactionaries.

After illness forced him to retire, Qian Hanxuan, former deputy director of the county party committee's organization department, wrote a pseudonymous letter to Mao describing the situation in Wuwei. Party first secretary Yao Kuijia intercepted the letter and had the public security police seek out the writer. Fearing an innocent person would be arrested, Qian admitted that he was the writer. Yao ordered him brought to the county headquarters and yelled, "You bastard, you're just the henchman and running dog of Zhang Kaifan.[63] You do nothing all day but eat, then go complaining to the Central Committee." He had Qian locked up and struggled.

Tianqiao Commune party secretary Ji Yongshan, Miaohou production brigade party secretary Yang Kecai, and Ganghe production brigade head Tang Shengchuan jointly wrote Mao a report on Yao Kuijia and Wuwei's hardships. When Yao found out, he had Ji and the others struggled, dismissed, or demoted, and sent to hard labor. When Yang Kecai took time off from hard labor to visit his wife and Ji Yongshan sought medical treatment, Yao had them arrested and jailed.

The vice-principal of Yanqiao's Nanyue Elementary School, Chen Ying, sent three letters to Yao Kuijia between July and October of 1959 to inform him of work style issues among Wuwei's grassroots cadres and problems with the people's livelihood. Yao passed the letters' contents to a committee in charge of rectifying incorrect work styles, then ordered Chen struggled and sent to hard labor.

Yao told the chairman of the county party committee secretariat to hold all letters to the Central Committee or State Council and inspect them. In Xiang'an Town, Yao saw a letter-writing stall[64] and took the attendant in for interrogation. He had the stall dismantled and threatened: "If you write any more letters, I'll have you arrested and brought to justice." The man fled, fearing for his life.

In early 1960, Premier Zhou Enlai received a letter describing starvation in Wuwei and elsewhere, and he wrote to Anhui's provincial party secretary, Zeng Xisheng, telling him to investigate:

> *Comrade Xisheng:*
> *I'm passing to you the enclosed letter. After reading it, please send someone to the two counties to investigate. This could be true, or it could be exaggerated, but every province has exceptional cases like this, especially the provinces that suffered the disaster last year, so it's worth taking notice. When the Chairman endorsed the document of Shandong's six-level cadre conference, he made a point of emphasizing this. After carrying out inquiries, please report back to me by letter.*
> *Respectfully yours,*
> *Zhou Enlai*
> *March 29, 1960*[65]

The situation Zhou described as "exaggerated" or an "exceptional case" was in fact even direr than the letter depicted.

ZHANG KAIFAN'S "BIG RUCKUS IN WUWEI"

At the Lushan Conference, Mao criticized Zhang Kaifan for "raising a ruckus in Wuwei" and designated him a right opportunist. The people of Wuwei, however, regarded Zhang as a hero.

Zhang joined the revolution in 1927, at one point being sent to Longhua Prison, where he wrote this poem:

Longhua has received many of noble character through the ages;
Countless warriors have met their ends here.

Blood stains within the walls, peach blossoms without;
Both are equally bright and red.

In spring 1959, while secretary-general of Anhui's provincial party committee and vice-governor, Zhang received reports of fallow fields, severe famine conditions, and people lacking means of subsistence. Uneasy, he went to Wuwei on July 4. His car was surrounded by peasants who kowtowed and begged him to solve the food shortage. Seeing with his own eyes the miserable conditions, he was deeply distressed. On July 7 he told the county party committee:

> During last year's Great Leap Forward, romanticism went too far; a girl who was pretty to begin with had too much powder applied to her face. For example, a yield that was clearly 200 kilos per *mu* was reported as 400 kilos or 500 kilos, and everyone tried to sound better than anyone else, with the more reported the better.
>
> Some of our comrades, for reasons of face, didn't relay the true situation to the upper levels. Let me ask you now: What matters more, your face or ensuring that the peasants get enough to eat!? This last time I came over from Shijian and saw many sick people. In particular I saw a great deal of edema, many people with grossly swollen legs, many women suffering from uterine prolapse and amenorrhea.
>
> If we take the road to impoverishing the peasants, who will take part in revolution? I, Zhang Kaifan, will have no part in it!
>
> What do the peasants get to eat? A family, young and old, gets an average of less than 50 grams per person. Some of our comrades are so foolhardy as to carelessly change the food ration standard without any thought of the survival of the masses. Don't they have any human decency?
>
> It's better not to bother with the communal kitchens—that doesn't affect the quality of the people's communes . . . In any case, the communal kitchens are poorly run. Many people are willing to go back to the old way—if they're given grain, firewood, farmland, and woks, they will gratefully receive them with both hands and happily attend to their own needs.[66]

Zhang recommended handing over millions of kilos of reserve grain to the sick and to the children, and he urged the provincial party committee to suspend operating the communal kitchens.

During his twenty days in Wuwei, Zhang observed relations between cadres and villagers, and local living standards and crop conditions. He saw waxen faces and emaciated bodies, people bedridden, walking with canes, or starving to death. Everywhere, he saw withered seedlings in desolate fields. Zhang urgently reported what he'd seen to the provincial and prefectural leaderships and requested emergency aid. He appealed to cadres and villagers to work together and urged peasants to plant more vegetables.

Zhang learned that the party secretary of the Wangfu production brigade, Zhang Dinggen, was tyrannizing villagers and had caused three deaths, but that he was protected by Yao Kuijia. Zhang Kaifan notified the politics and law department to have Zhang Dinggen arrested. He was likewise incensed to learn that a production team leader of the Xinhuan production brigade, Huang Daben, and a production team leader named Ni Jinzhang from Dougou's Ganghe production brigade had repeatedly beaten and abused commune members. He had their local party organizations immediately strip them of their positions.

Zhang Kaifan recommended returning commune-occupied residential quarters to their original owners, allowing people to prepare their own meals, returning plots of land for household use, and opening the market and fish ponds. On July 15 the county's 6,000-plus communal kitchens were closed, with only 120 refusing to disband.

On August 2 the Wuhu prefectural party committee complained to the provincial party committee: "Zhang Kaifan's proposed 'three returns,' especially the order to disband the communal kitchens, violates the Central Committee's and provincial party committee's guiding principles and policies on communal kitchens." They called attention to Zhang's concerns about "cadre work styles and various illnesses." The prefecture asked the provincial party committee to look into Zhang's behavior.

On August 4 the Anhui provincial party committee reported to the CCP Central Committee that Zhang "ordered that the communal kitchens be disbanded, and in a distrustful state of mind ordered the county party committee secretariat to investigate changes in various circumstances before and after communization, with the result that Wuwei County's work has been thrown into chaos. The Wuwei county party committee and the Wuhu prefectural party committee object very strongly to Zhang's methods and feel that they violate the Central Committee's general and specific policies."[67]

On August 10, Mao Zedong responded:

> Print off and distribute to all comrades. The Central Committee has its right opportunists, those comrades of the military club;[68] the provincial level also has them, one example being Anhui's provincial party secretary, Zhang Kaifan. I suspect that these people are opportunists who have infiltrated the party. During the transition period from capitalism to socialism, they maintain a capitalist standpoint and scheme to sabotage the dictatorship of the proletariat and split the party, organizing factions within the party and disseminating their influence, while causing a slackening of the proletarian vanguard as they establish their own opportunistic party. The essential components of this clique were originally the main members of the Gao Gang anti-party clique.[69] They were willing and revolutionary participants in the bourgeois democratic revolution. As to their revolutionary methods, they were usually wrong. They lacked the psychological preparation for socialist revolution, and upon reaching the stage of socialist revolution, they felt uncomfortable and early on began taking part in the Gao Gang anti-party clique, which used conspiratorial means to achieve its reactionary goals. The remnants of the Gao Gang clique who escaped capture are now stirring up trouble again, and are impatient and eager to launch their attack. Swift exposure is beneficial to the party and also to them. If they are willing to cleanse their brains, it may be possible to bring them back, because they possess both reactionary and revolutionary sides. Their current antisocialist agenda opposes the Great Leap Forward and the people's communes. Do not be deceived by their blandishments, for example when they say that the General Line is basically correct and it's only necessary to delay the people's communes a few years. In order to save them, we must expose them to all cadres so their market shrinks all the more.[70]

Zhang Kaifan was criticized from August 27 to September 21, 1959. The next target was the province's alternate party secretary and head of the provincial party committee's propaganda bureau, Lu Xuebin, who had agreed with Zhang Kaifan's methods in Wuwei.

Zhang and Lu were dubbed members of an "anti-party alliance," and a campaign was launched against any cadres and commune members who spoke the truth. Zhang was stripped of his party membership and official posts, struggled for fifty-one days, and jailed for more than two hundred days, then sent to labor in a mine. His family was expelled from the provincial government residential compound.

Zhang's brother Changxuan, cousins Shisan and Changshu, and a veteran democrat named Wang Shizhi were persecuted to death. Anyone connected with Zhang was subjected to ruthless struggle. Their homes were ransacked, and as "right opportunists" or "seriously right deviationists" they were sent to hard labor. At least 28,741 Wuwei cadres were implicated and subjected to struggle.[71] So many people were found guilty that Wuwei's prisons could not hold them all, and some prisoners were sent to labor camps. The marching prisoners were so numerous, observers said, that they resembled an army regiment.[72]

After the famine, Zhang Kaifan was rehabilitated, but he suffered devastating persecution once again during the Cultural Revolution. He was finally restored to office after Deng Xiaoping launched economic reform in December 1978.

PART 3: THE BO COUNTY TRAGEDY

In Bo County in Anhui's northwest, productivity plummeted for the same reasons as elsewhere, and much of the rural population was lost to unnatural death. During the famine years, Liang Zhiyuan was deputy secretary of the county party committee, while also serving as head of the party committee rural work department's productivity and welfare section, and as vice-director of the county party and government general office. As someone who personally experienced the famine years and regularly visited the countryside, he wrote up many valuable narratives relating to that time, and these serve as my primary sources on Bo County.[73]

In autumn 1958, Bo County joined the rest of the province in launching "satellites." Wuma Commune planned a rice paddy Sputnik of at least 5,000 kilos per *mu*, while the county aimed for average yields of 500 kilos per *mu* in 1958 and 5,000 kilos per *mu* in 1959. The county party secretary then took personal command of the campaign. A paddy in the Nidian production brigade was selected and fenced off, after which prime mature rice plants were selected from more than 100 *mu* of paddy fields and transplanted into the 1,389-*mu* satellite field. The ridges between the fields were planted with grass to make it look authentic. After days of hard, around-the-clock effort, the super-Sputnik was reported to the higher levels. All communal and production brigade cadres were summoned for group photos next to the miracle field, where a yield of 20,401.5 kilos was announced. The record-breaking harvest prompted ecstatic news reports followed by congratulatory telegrams from the upper levels.

Visiting cadres quickly caught on to the Nidian brigade's methods and copied them. In fields that did not allow for mass transplanting as rice paddies did, the crops from several fields were simply moved onto one field, with the combined harvest claimed for one small area. When sweet potatoes were harvested, the best were piled onto one field for inspection by higher-level cadres, who then confirmed the launching of the "satellite."

The exaggeration frenzy brought Bo County fame, and local cadres were invited to the 1959 assembly for national heroes, where they were presented with awards by the State Council.

The downside to this honor was procurement quotas based on the grossly exaggerated yields. In 1957 the actual procurement was 65 million kilos, but the quota rose to 150 million kilos for 1958. Failure to meet the quota resulted in grain-searching campaigns and criticism of right deviation. Grain handed in became the main standard for leftist, centrist, or rightist leanings. As communal kitchens shut down for lack of food, and peasants swelled with edema, the county party committee insisted that claims of food shortages were bogus. Every chest and cupboard of every home was overturned and emptied in search of hidden grain. Finally, a prefectural party committee work group inspection acknowledged the food crisis, and grain was sold back to the villages. The amount was inadequate, however, and ten days of rations were consumed in three.

Cadres who spoke the truth came under attack, and those who exaggerated most wildly basked in official praise. In 1958 the county party committee sent a newly promoted deputy secretary surnamed Song to Wuma Commune, where he joined the commune party committee's first secretary to launch the famous 20,000-kilo rice paddy Sputnik. On March 4, 1960, as the commune's peasants starved, the two cadres did not distribute the 125 grams of grain per day that the county had sold back to the commune as its February grain ration, but sent 2,250 kilos back to the county. The commune won extravagant praise at a county party committee meeting, but its peasants suffered one of the highest death rates.

Following the 1959 Lushan Conference, the county party committee on August 29 launched a campaign against right opportunism, mercilessly persecuting any party member or cadre who had spoken truthfully about the famine or who was seen as denying accomplishments. As a result, no one dared to speak the truth as starvation marched through Bo County's villages. The 1959 procurement rose to 39.5 percent of the actual yield, compared with 33.2 percent in 1958. In the spring of 1960, the amount of grain sold back for grain rations was only around 60 grams per person per day.

BO COUNTY'S COMMUNAL KITCHENS

From September 7 to 17, 1958, the county established more than 4,700 communal kitchens. Most were run by the production teams, with the accountants serving as mess officers. For the first month or so, the mess halls served three solid meals, and commune members thronged the red flag–emblazoned doorways as if attending a holiday feast. Guests were welcome, and payment in cash or ration coupons was seldom required. Officials and journalists watched as jubilant crowds shouted, "Long live the communal kitchens!"

Soon, however, most commune members found themselves waiting in long lines and squatting outside to eat. Those at the end of the line were often greeted with empty woks. Rainy days meant lining up in ankle-deep mud, and cold days meant gobbling down food that was cold by the time it was served. There was no way to accommodate the old and sick, and nothing to supplement the nutritional needs of weaning infants. Waste exhausted food supplies soon after the autumn harvest. Most communal kitchens were forced to close down, and failure to meet the 1958 procurement targets set off campaigns against hoarding. "Dissuasion stations" were set up along roads to block the escape of starving peasants. Edema was rampant by February and March of 1959, and many people fled to neighboring Henan Province. By early March only a few dozen communal kitchens were still operating, and spring plowing had ground to a halt. The winter wheat harvest allowed some communal kitchens to reopen, but famine followed in the summer, and few kitchens were able to continue operating.

Preservation of the communal kitchens became a top priority after the Lushan Conference led to a campaign against right deviation. There was no "voluntary participation and freedom to withdraw," and even with no food supplied, a glass of water or a bowl of soup could be obtained only at communal kitchens. Anyone who "slandered" or "attacked" the communal kitchens was subjected to harsh attack. The head of the Xiaochenzhuang production team, Cheng Zhongde, composed a jingle: "The communal kitchens / food have they none / and starving kids / cry for their moms." For this he was labeled a right deviationist, stripped of his position, and subjected to repeated struggle.

The county party committee forced every village to maintain a communal kitchen. Household grain and cooking implements were confiscated, and peasants were forced to trek in rain and snow for every meal. Large kitchens with limited equipment often imposed long waits for food, as captured in an anonymous doggerel: "Breakfast waits until the sun is due south / red sun lights the hills as lunch hits your mouth / dinner comes with the cock's dawn crow / wonder when we'll eat on the morrow." A full-scale investigation was launched to uncover the author of the ditty, but the "scoundrel" was never apprehended.

Villagers struggled for survival by eating weeds and tree bark. Some teams returned confiscated woks, but once harvest time arrived, all cooking pots were seized again to prevent commune members from consuming unharvested crops. Some peasants hid their woks in wood piles or rivers, furtively bringing them out under cover of darkness to cook up weeds and bark gathered during the day.

Communal kitchens that were reopened during the campaign against right deviation served only the poorest-quality food, with portions limited to around 100 grams per person per day. Most mess halls provided no oil in their meals for two years, much less a hint of meat. Some went months without even salt for flavoring. No hot or boiled water was provided during the winter, since most communal kitchens had no firewood. Rounding up firewood required cutting down trees or dismantling houses. More than 80 percent of the county's trees were cut, and more than one hundred thousand homes were stripped of their wood. In some localities, caskets were dug up, their scattered bones heightening the atmosphere of horror and desolation.

In the autumn of 1959, cadres at the rank of county party committee deputy director set up their own small canteens, where food was both plentiful and palatable. Visiting commune party secretaries also ate at these special canteens. Although the special canteens required ration tickets, they always exceeded their monthly ration of grain and oil. The deficit was made up by the county party committee's finance and trade department.

Communal kitchens had their public and hidden aspects. Some were able to supplement food needs from small farms, work units predominantly made up of militia (referred to as rocket camps), commune guesthouses, and communal vegetable gardens. These communes had more than enough to satisfy their members and visiting leaders, and even provided feasts.

Most cadres managed to eat their fill, even when canteen meals were inadequate. They picked and chose the better canteens, and some unlawfully seized foodstuffs to ensure the survival of their households. The worst paid no heed to the starving and grabbed whatever they could, even selling off what their families couldn't eat. At a time when the average commune member had to make due on a ration of 100 grams a day, cadres consumed about a third of the food.

A cadre from Gucheng Commune said, "Holding the communal kitchen's ladle and scale in my hand, I decide who lives and who dies." Cadres, their families and their relatives, kitchen staff, and upper-level inspectors all ate well, while meals were withheld from the ill and from those labeled malingerers, troublemakers, or thieves. The head of the Suzhuang production team stole food to procure sexual favors from ten female commune members while more than eighty members of his production team starved to death. The Qiaoyuan branch party secretary caused the death of eleven peasants from whom he withheld meals. A jingle went: "Big wind, big fog, everyone's starved but the cadres."

A few good cadres shared the fate of the peasants, and many who refused to take advantage of their power starved. Among those who died were Su Ruzhang and four other party members at the Chenlou production team.

On November 3, 1960, the CCP Central Committee at long last relaxed its demands on the communal kitchens. The county party committee then allowed households to prepare their own meals. The communal kitchens closed down in a flash; of the county's 4,438 collective canteens, only 287 did not disband, and those were all at small farms and old-people's homes, where disbanding would have proved disadvantageous. On April 26, 1961, the CCP Central Committee made communal kitchens voluntary, and they all closed down for good.

TWO HUNDRED THOUSAND STARVATION DEATHS
THROUGHOUT THE COUNTY

Peasants confronted starvation with gallows humor: "We don't fear the earth or skies, we only fear officials' lies," "Launching satellites in the air puts commune members in the ground," "Anti-rightist campaigns transform commune members into cannibals."

On March 17, 1961, a county party committee's investigation arrived at a total of 44,000 unnatural deaths for the county. In 1979 a Fuyang administrative office concluded that Bo County had lost 28,824 rural households in 1959 and 1960, a reduction of 150,503 people, or 21.1 percent of the population. The February 1996 *Bozhou Annals* states that the number of households in 1960 was 29,400 fewer than in 1958, a negative population growth of 96,000. As official figures, these can be considered gross understatements.

In May 1960 the county party committee had Liang Zhiyuan organize a survey of mortality rates, which was carried out by the head of the county party committee's livelihood inspection committee, Wang Xinzhai. The first brigade surveyed had lost 719 people from January 1 to May 8, 1960 (not counting those who died after fleeing elsewhere), comprising 25.3 percent of the population. Deaths continued after that.

The county party committee found these figures unacceptable and ordered another survey, at the Shihe production brigade. Liang Zhiyuan sent Li Yunceng to carry out the survey. The results showed that 909 people had died from January 1 to May 15, 1960, comprising 29.15 percent of the surveyed villagers. Including famine losses from 1959 and up until the end of 1960 would have resulted in mortality rates exceeding 30 percent for both brigades.

At the end of 1960, Liang led a survey of six villages in the Wangge production brigade. The original population of 575 people in 127 households had been reduced by 239 people, or 41.5 percent, in two years, and 18 households had been completely obliterated. Xiaolizhuang lost 48 percent of its people, and Xiaoxuzhuang, 49 percent. In a later survey of the Shihe production brigade, Liang found a village that had lost 70 percent of its population.

In mid-March 1960, during a recess at Gucheng Commune's Liyao Elementary School, two adolescent students died while sitting in the doorway of their classroom. Following a rainstorm around the same time, nineteen dead bodies lay exposed along the road.

Liang estimates that the county lost at least two hundred thousand people to unnatural death, with nearly thirty thousand households completely wiped out. Guantang Commune had more than four hundred orphans. The Yangmiao production brigade took in eleven orphans, but ten starved to death.

In a five-month period from January through May 1960, 28.25 percent of poor peasants, 12.5 percent of middle peasants, and 44 percent of landlords and rich peasants died of unnatural causes. The famine's victims included a number of local luminaries. The Housunwan production team lost the mother of a revolutionary martyr to starvation, and a well-known scholar from the late Qing era, Li Qindan, starved to death in the Mingwa production team. Su Ruzhang, a retired revolutionary, fed on his daughter's corpse but still failed to save his own life.

As elsewhere, deaths in Bo County were not always reported, so that surviving family members could continue to draw the deceased's food ration, and unburied corpses were a common sight, even in school classrooms. In spring 1960, carts dragged several bodies at a time to the burial ground, or corpses were thrown into dry wells. In October 1960, Liang Zhiyuan saw the skulls and feet of seven corpses protruding from shallow graves along a riverbank.

Thousands died after eating poisonous plants and mushrooms. At the Dengshuangmiao production team, the five-member family of Gao Sizeng died after eating rotten hemp seeds. Others died from overindulgence. In the Zaozhuang production team, ten people died after gorging themselves on unripened wheat in May 1960.

Party committees refused to acknowledge the starvation or to sell grain back to the villages. Only in spring 1960 was grain sent to the villages, but the supplement was only around 100 grams per person each day. Peasants appealed elsewhere for help, but their letters were labeled counterrevolutionary, and the writers were imprisoned.

Dissuasion stations along major roadways and at bus and train stations and ferry piers prevented the starving from fleeing. Intercepted persons were subjected to interrogation, body searches, detention, beating, trussing up, and jailing, and any food they carried was confiscated.

THE HORROR OF CANNIBALISM

Liang Zhiyuan recorded a large number of cases of cannibalism. He found,

> The extensiveness of the practice, the number of incidents, and the length of time that it continued is exceptional in human history. Based on the nearly one-million-word journal I kept of my work in the countryside over the course of three years, in which I checked and verified cases as well as recorded cases that I personally witnessed and heard, there was not a single commune where cannibalism was not discovered, and in some production brigades not a single village was untouched by the phenomenon.[74]

The county government initially imposed harsh penalties on cannibalism, but enforcement relaxed until these "special cases" were largely ignored. The cases were highly confidential, and disclosure could bring fierce attack even during the Cultural Revolution. For that reason, cases such as those described by Liang Zhiyuan remained all but unknown for decades.

The county party committee handled its first "desecration" case in spring 1959, when police at Wobei detained a vagrant cooking the flesh of a dead child. The county public security bureau had no idea how to handle the case, but finally designated it a "desecration of human remains" and formally arrested the perpetrator. The county party committee's secretary of politics and law decided that the "criminal" was in a state of emaciation and had no political objectives, whereupon he was given two steamed buns and a lecture and then released. The county party committee, however, had the criminal detained and jailed, only to release him again when further inquiries determined a lack of political objectives. Subsequently the head of the Wobei police station was heard repeating a line from a historical drama: "People eat people, dogs eat dogs, rats are so hungry they gnaw on bricks." During the 1959 campaign against right deviation, he and the secretary of politics and law were struggled, demoted, and transferred.

Cannibalism reached a peak in the spring of 1960. Human flesh was consumed cooked or raw; it was sliced from the bodies of the dead, or the living were killed to obtain it. Some people bought it at the market (already cooked), passed off as pork by vendors. About 40 percent of those who ate human flesh subsequently suffered attacks of diarrhea and died.

Others ate human flesh on a regular basis without ill effect, especially if they chose lean meat and mixed it with vegetables, ate smaller amounts spread over several meals, or ate more foods preserved through pickling and salting.

As elsewhere, cannibalism often involved family members. Zhu Li from Zhuzhai Village was the sole survivor of her four-member household. Desperate with hunger, she gnawed the flesh of her dead daughter, falling severely ill afterward. In Zhangzhuang Village, a survivor named Zhang Cuiliang recalled, "In the spring of 1960, a four-member family had been reduced to just the mother and her emaciated daughter. Driven to madness by starvation, the woman killed her daughter and cooked her flesh to eat, after which she became completely deranged and repeatedly cried out her daughter's name."

Cadre Yang Xinkuan recalled,

In the spring of 1960, I headed the organization department of Chengfu Commune. At Hanlaojia Village, a sixteen-year-old boy surnamed Han was left to care for his younger brother following the death of their parents. In March 1960, Han was driven by hunger to kill his brother. He discarded the head and spine in a mud pit and was cooking up the flesh to eat when he was discovered by a cadre. During interrogation he admitted to killing his brother and cooking and eating his flesh. Because the boy was not yet eighteen, the commune party committee decided, with my participation, to have him sent to the commune's "rocket camp" (set up for forced labor), and after several months in detention the boy was dead.

County party committee's livelihood inspection committee head Lu Mei reported on March 3, 1960, that twenty-five of the forty households in Haozhuang Village had engaged in cannibalism, and that bodies were being dug up and eaten nearly every night. Nothing could be done to stop it.

In Guantang Commune's Zhangzhuang Village, cannibalism was an open secret. One villager fed congee with human flesh in it to an orphan named Zhang Cuiliang and saved his life. At the age of fifty, Zhang Cuiliang still spoke of this matter.

In April 1960, Liang Zhiyuan inspected a county dissuasion station, where Dr. Yang Wende told him, "Vagrants who die at the dissuasion station are often dug up and eaten." Yang showed Liang a burial ground where vagrant graves had been dug up and the head of a middle-aged man lay half exposed. Yang said the public security bureau had done nothing.

A Lide education office accountant recalled that in Lizhai Village, cannibalism became so prevalent in the spring of 1960 that the authorities began making arrests and organizing struggle sessions. Anyone who refused to attend would have meals withheld. A woman who had eaten human flesh several times was censured for "unlawful" acts that "sullied the government's image," and villagers were warned that anyone engaging in this practice would be imprisoned. Cases of cannibalism decreased after that.

Banking cadre Wang Tizhong recalled that as starving residents of Wanglou Village were driven to cannibalism, the production brigade began arresting the most heinous offenders for public exposure. One woman was apprehended as she was ladling cooked meat into a big bowl, and she was immediately taken with her illicit meal to a mass criticism. Those attending were tantalized by the aroma of cooked flesh. Someone said, "I want to try some," and grabbed a piece of the meat and wolfed it down. Others immediately snatched pieces of the cooked meat, and the meeting devolved into chaos, with all the cooked human flesh disappearing in the blink of an eye. Wang Tizhong's own wife grabbed a piece and said it was delicious. There was nothing to do but adjourn the meeting.

Human flesh was bought and sold in urban outskirts, market towns, village street stalls, and among itinerant peddlers. In Guoqiao Village, a fifty-seven-year-old peasant killed a thirteen-year-old boy named Lianchen. After cooking and eating part of the boy's flesh, the man sold the remainder in the village as pork. Tian Chaozhen of the county public security bureau cracked the case, and the perpetrator was sentenced to death, but died in prison.

PART 4: THE OVERALL SITUATION IN ANHUI PROVINCE

Mao attached particular importance to Anhui. A *People's Daily* article approved by Mao and the Central Committee reported on his inspection tour of the province on September 16, 1958:

> Agriculture and tea leaf production at Shucha People's Commune have made great progress this year; this year's total grain output is estimated

at 36 million kilos, or an average of 800 kilos per *mu*, an increase of 138 percent over last year, and amounting to 950 kilos per capita, an increase of 136 percent over last year. Since communal kitchens began operating in this commune, they have reached the stage of serving meals free of charge. Chairman Mao says, "If one commune is able to serve free meals, other communes in similar circumstances should also be able to do so. And if meals can be provided free of charge, clothing should also be free sometime in the future." Comrade Zeng Xisheng told Chairman Mao that the 8,600 households of Shucha People's Commune are already raising 32,000 pigs, and the communal kitchen is able to serve 250 grams of meat to each commune member every week. It is estimated that the commune will eventually raise 60,000 pigs, at which time, if half are eaten and half are sold, each person will be able to eat an average of 200 grams of pork every day. Comrade Zeng Xisheng says, "At present the communal kitchen doesn't serve vegetables, and commune members bring their own vegetables to eat, but eventually vegetables will also be provided." Chairman Mao was very happy to hear this and pointed out, "The people's communes must collectively grow vegetables in the future, and vegetable farming must be professionalized."[75]

Local cadres took pride in constructing communism, while peasants long inured to hardship were inspired by guarantees of food and clothing.

With private ownership presented as the source of all evil, eliminating it was the ultimate righteous act, and cadres who opposed the Communist Wind were struck down as right opportunists. Provincial party secretariat secretaries Li Shinong and Zhang Kaifan and the deputy director of the Hui River regulatory committee's political department, Liu Xiushan, were targets of the campaign against right deviation, and their fall hastened the spread of the Five Winds.

THE EFFECT OF THE FIVE WINDS ON ANHUI'S PEASANTS

Anhui was a major contributor to the Communist Wind, Exaggeration Wind, Coercive Commandism Wind, Chaotic Directives Wind, and Cadre Privilege Wind that wreaked havoc throughout China. In 1958, parts of Anhui suffered drought, but *Anhui Daily* brushed aside the real situation in an article headlined "Turning Lake Chao into a Ladle, and Sending Water Wherever There's Drought." The Huaibei irrigation project, designed to relieve the drought situation in northern Anhui, had begun in the autumn of 1957, but the original plan to move 4 billion cubic meters of earth in ten years was whipped into exaggerated claims of 2.4 billion cubic meters moved in the first six months. As the article put it, "We can overturn heaven and earth and move mountains into the sea."

The main instigators of the Communist Wind in Anhui were rural cadres, who coerced the collectivization of all private and small-group assets without apology and even with a sense of pride. Mao's comments on free food and clothing during his visit to Anhui provided the wind with an added boost.

In 1959, Bengbu went all out for locally constructed machine tools. Lacking raw materials, commune members were told to dismantle the doors, door frames, and benches in their homes, and even coffins, to construct frames for the machinery. The machine tools produced were unusable. In the spring of 1960, Bengbu's municipal party committee proposed establishing fifteen collective piggeries, each with ten thousand pigs at five communes, and each production team was to run a 100-head piggery, along with several chicken and duck farms. Commune members were forced to surrender all of their pigs, goats, chickens, and ducks, and many had to move out of their homes to make way for the jumbo pigsties. The result was massive death among the collectivized livestock, while cadres made off with the survivors.[76]

The figures on grain yield and pig farming quoted in the *Anhui Daily* report on Mao's visit were preposterous, yet provincial leader Zeng Xisheng enjoyed Mao's endorsement. Once the lies were reproduced in *People's Daily*, cadres all over China felt compelled to spew out similar falsehoods.

In March 1961, Bengbu's party secretary, Cheng Guanghua, reflected on the Exaggeration Wind:

Our city's blind engagement in the trend was very serious, and we even engaged in fabrication. In 1958, seeing other localities launch their high-yield "Sputniks," in our suburbs we also fabricated a "satellite field," transplanting three and a half *mu* of rice plants into tiny plots of land and transforming a 100-kilo-per-*mu* yield into 5,500 kilos, then taking photographs, calling on-the-spot meetings, and having them published in the newspaper . . . We proposed that "whatever others have, we must have, and what others don't have, we also must have." Our cadres read through every newspaper in search of fresh items, and we sent cadres out all year picking up experiences from other places, emphasizing that "advanced experience expires overnight." Where there was smoke, we saw fire, and when we heard news about some other place, we didn't analyze it or consider whether it was necessary, but blindly did the same thing. The result was a severe Exaggeration Wind.[77]

High reported grain yields led to higher procurement targets, even as actual grain yields decreased from 1957 to 1961.

TABLE 8.1: GRAIN SUPPLIES IN ANHUI, 1957–61

Year	1957	1958	1959	1960	1961
GRAIN YIELD (BILLION KILOS):					
Unprocessed	10.2	9.2	7.35	7.524	6.875
Processed	8.8695	8.0	6.391	6.5425	5.2935
Procured	3.421	2.9235	2.8545	1.753	1.284
Sold	2.0475	2.955	2.5335	1.622	1.158
In hand	7.496	8.0315	6.07	6.4115	5.1675
Population (millions)	33.56	34.267	34.455	30.856	29.877
Per capita allotment (kilos)	223.36	234.38	176.17	207.785	172.96

Data source: Crop yield, procurement, and sales figures come from the August 25, 1962, issue of the Grain Bureau Project Command Grain Data Summary. Total population data come from China Population: Anhui.

Note: The yields in the table refer to the calendar year, while the procurement and sales figures refer to the "grain year."

The figures for grain "in hand" in Table 8.1 include grain rations, feed grain, seed grain, and grain for industrial use. Based on the figures for population and grain "in hand," the average per capita grain ration (trade grain) for these years was as follows: 1957–58: 156.35 kilos; 1958–59: 156.35 kilos; 1959–60: 123.32 kilos; 1960–61: 145.5 kilos; 1961–62: 121.05 kilos. These are average figures that do not take account of the greatly reduced amounts given to the rural population under the policy of squeezing the countryside to preserve the cities. The "deductions" at each level of the bureaucracy further reduced the grain that villagers actually received. The situation was, however, actually better in 1961–62 than the figures suggest, because by then Zeng Xisheng had begun allowing the assignment of output quotas to households and the cultivation of marginal land.

Anhui's famine began in the winter of 1958 and became severe by the spring of 1959. The blindness of the party bureaucracy to the predicament of the peasants is amply reflected in an article in *Economic News*, which started out:

> The Anhui provincial party committee work group recently conducted a survey of the grain supply situation in Tongcheng County. The survey data indicate that the present so-called grain supply problem in the countryside is not a matter of a grain shortage, or of excessively onerous state procurement targets, but rather an ideological problem. The Anhui provincial party committee believes that the Tongcheng County data are representative of the province as a whole, and calls on all localities to criticize those right-deviating conservatives and apply themselves wholeheartedly to current grain supply work.[78]

This article found "an ideological problem, especially among grassroots cadres. It turns out that false reporting of output and private withholding is widespread in all communes, and the underreported amounts are very large and take many forms. Some grain yields of 850 kilos per *mu* are reported as only 350 kilos, with the excess grain secretly taken to storehouses. One production team was found to have hidden 15,000 kilos in a gap between two walls, while another production team hid 20,000 to 25,000 kilos of grain in haystacks." The article continued, "As to reports of eating only chaff and vegetables and howling over lack of grain, these are preemptive attacks aimed at ensuring that procurement quotas are not raised further."

The solution was ideological education:

> Within one week, the situation underwent a fundamental change. Communal kitchens that had closed down resumed operation, and meals made up of only chaff and vegetables were transformed into two rices

and one congee. Hidden warehouses were brought into the open, and the outcry over grain from cadres and masses turned into discussions of a bumper harvest. Lack of strength to work in the fields became high-spirited effort, and the fields were transformed into scenes of fluttering red flags and bustling activity.

Mao nevertheless perceived hoarding as rooted in the system of ownership, and on February 28, 1959, he warned against proceeding too rapidly:

> The policy is correct, but its rationale has not been clearly explained. The system of ownership based on the production teams and partial ownership by the communes will predominate . . . for several years to come . . . ownership by the communes and partial ownership by the production teams . . . is a gradual process . . . Failure to acknowledge this objective truth will make it impossible to resolve the problem and persuade people to comply.[79]

This article and Mao's editorial comments reined in the Communist Wind of "big and collective," but the truth of grain shortages remained hidden, and continued campaigns against "false reporting" exacerbated starvation.

Meanwhile, cadres indulged themselves. Records preserved from that period report: "When Zeng Qingmei arrived in Bengbu for an inspection, the first thing he wanted to do was dance, and in his capacity as a standing committee member of the provincial party committee he had actresses brought in that same night to serve as his dance partners. At that time people were already starving to death in Bengbu, and this influence was very bad." Zeng was a provincial cadre in charge of party discipline.

"In 1960, the prefectural party committee rounded up a large number of people to build a new guesthouse. During the Mid-Autumn Festival, as starving people dropped dead in the streets, the prefectural and county party secretaries were holding extravagant banquets. Even during weekdays they brought women in for dancing and dinner parties."[80]

Less-educated grassroots cadres were easily carried away by a zeal for communism that made them capable of extreme acts, especially against those whose words or actions contradicted Communist ideals. On August 4, 1960, provincial control commission party secretary Zeng Qingmei reported that 40 percent of Xiao County's cadres had engaged in violations, including torture of commune members.[81] The situation was similar in virtually every county.

To preserve stability, Anhui deployed its public security resources, detaining more than eight thousand people in 1957. In 1958 the Central Committee handed down a detention quota of forty-thousand to fifty thousand people, and Anhui detained more than double that number. Most detainees were innocent working people who had expressed their dissatisfaction with the Great Leap Forward, the people's communes, the iron- and steel-forging campaign, the communal kitchens, or the Communist Wind, or who, in the throes of starvation, had stolen some unharvested grain or vegetables, concealed or stolen grain stores as a means of avoiding death, desperately joined in mob looting of grain stores, or attempted to flee the famine. Many died in custody. During the three years of the famine, more than fifty thousand people died at Anhui's labor reform farms or in detention centers, 31 percent of all detainees.[82]

In the spring of 1959 a denunciation was posted in the provincial capital: "Down with Fatty Zeng, Kill Slut Yu" (meaning Zeng Xisheng and his wife). Zeng Xisheng ordered the public security police to find the culprit, and party cadres were compelled to produce handwriting samples. Eighteen thousand people were inspected, and searches were carried out of four thousand homes. Some targets were put under surveillance, with their mail opened and listening devices installed in their homes. Three suspects were arrested or suspended. After half a year's effort and the suicides of two "suspects," the case remained unsolved. Zeng Xisheng continued to shout at the investigators, "My money would be better spent on a dog."

Anyone who aroused the wrath of a leader could be imprisoned. There were no formal procedures, and many were arrested and sentenced without evidence. A person could die in detention without his name even being recorded. Some people were simply shipped off to a labor reform farm and "disappeared" without a trace.[83]

COVERING AND UNCOVERING THE TRUTH

How many people starved to death in Anhui during the Great Famine? Statistics from *China Population: Anhui*[84] indicate 2,262,800 deaths, with an additional shortfall of 2,430,600 births. Given that the statistics are derived from official sources, it can be safely assumed that they understate the catastrophe.

The May 1961 report by Li Jian of the Central Committee investigation group found that 3 million had starved to death in Anhui. In the spring of 2001, Li Jian told me that the head of the Central Committee's Organization Department, An Ziwen, had carried out his own inquiries while sent down to Anhui for several years during the Cultural Revolution, and he calculated the number of unnatural deaths in Anhui as 5 million.[85] Cao Shuji concluded that unnatural deaths in Anhui totaled 6,306,000, or 18.3 percent of the pre-famine population.[86] Yin Shusheng, the former deputy bureau head in charge of day-to-day operations of Anhui's provincial public security bureau, found that the records backed a death toll of more than 4 million, and that this figure was not a matter of conjecture.[87]

After analyzing official Anhui reports, Wang Weizhi, a population expert working in the Public Security Ministry's Third Division (handling population statistics), reached conclusions that suggest a mortality rate exceeding 15 percent,[88] which is consistent with An Ziwen's figure of 5 million deaths.

Cannibalism cases numbered well over a thousand. An April 23, 1961, report by the provincial public security bureau identified nearly thirteen hundred such cases, the majority occurring in late 1959 and early 1960. A survey found that thirty-six cases involved selling human flesh for profit, while the rest were consumption for survival.[89]

Zeng's refusal to report the famine to the upper levels led Mao to have great faith in him, and he was appointed to a concurrent position as party secretary of Shandong Province, where he was entrusted with the task of "uncovering the truth." Soldiers, students, and cadres who returned home to find family members dead of starvation sent constant streams of letters to the Central Committee, for which they were invariably persecuted.

On March 13, 1960, the provincial party committee's finance and trade department, most directly responsible for grain supply, dismissively reported on the letters:

The number of letters received in January and February this year was more than during the same period last year. In January, 182 letters were received, and in February 283 were received, for a total of 476 [sic] compared with 187 letters received during January and February of last year . . . Eight letters, or 26 percent, were found to be partially factual, while 23 letters, or 74 percent, were completely false, and among thirteen anonymous letters, twelve were manufactured as vicious attacks. For example, a letter from He Chengcai (an Anhui native) of the Jiangxi Provincial Military Academy of Medical Sciences says, "The government has not given any grain to Jinzhai County's Guanmiao production team, and the life of the masses is very hard, with many people dying or flee-ing." An immediate investigation determined that in this locality the masses are able to eat 17.5–20 kilos of grain per month, in the form of one rice and two congees per day, with vegetables in addition to that, and no one has fled or died because of livelihood problems. This letter and the results of the investigation were forwarded to the academy . . .

People were persecuted for revealing what they learned while visiting their home villages. Around the time of the Spring Festival in 1960, Pan Kang, deputy director of the Fujian Air Force's logistics department, went home and witnessed the desperate circumstances in the Nanmao and Dahan work teams. Many of his own family members had starved to death, but commune cadres such as Miao Jian feasted. Pan argued with Miao, then used his own funds to buy seed grain for the work team. After Pan left, Miao had local cadres send letters to the Fujian Air Force, ac-cusing Pan of "right-deviating thinking" and of going home to "attack the people's communes and the Great Leap Forward." When the Fujian Air Force sent someone to Pan's home county to investigate, the county was able to deceive him, but a second investigation determined that sixty-six people had starved to death. Even so, Pan was disciplined.[90]

The authorities used various means to deceive visitors. Before vice president Dong Biwu arrived in Fuyang, provincial leaders removed all corpses from Dong's travel route and rounded up edema patients and placed them under watch.[91] When foreign employees of the Xinhua News Agency went on vacation in 1960, deputy minister of Internal Affairs Fang Shi accompanied them to Anhui. The Anhui provincial party com-mittee took them to scenic spots where beautifully dressed young women warbled in boats and street vendors offered a rich variety of tasty snacks. Ordinary people were barred from entering any of the venues the for-eigners visited.[92]

The cover-up resulted in delays in dealing with the mass starvation, and hunger remained a serious problem right through the autumn of 1961. A survey of Bengbu in September found children so debilitated by rickets that they could neither stand nor walk.[93] The cover-up became increasingly difficult as more died, however, and some letters reached the Central Committee. In April 1960 the Central Control Commission sent the head of its investigations division, Liu Lisheng, and the head of the letters and petitions section, Zhang Min, to Anhui's Qianshan County. In August, the commission sent Zhang Min and Cao Siheng to Anhui's Su, Xiao, and Quanjiao counties. In November the commission sent Li Hai to Fuyang Prefecture for an inquiry into outward migration. These investigations uncovered a portion of the truth, but lack of cooperation by cadres at all levels prevented a comprehensive understanding of Anhui's situation. The Central Committee in December sent a work group headed by Wang Weigang, a deputy chief justice of the Supreme People's Court, to learn more about edema and deaths in Anhui. Zeng Qingmei and Bengbu prefectural party secretary Shan Jingzhi soon complained to the Central Committee, saying that the work group took note only of what scoundrels were saying. The work group was then recalled.[94]

From December 28, 1960, to January 3, 1961, Wang Congwu convened a meeting of the Central Control Commission to hear from the work group, which reported on the suffering of the people and the official cover-up. Zeng Qingmei and Shan Jingzhi also attended, and insisted that the work group's findings were wrong.

Prior to this meeting, Wang Congwu had reported to the head of the Central Committee's Organization Department, An Ziwen, that the Anhui provincial party committee had prevented people from speaking the truth and had complained about the group to the Central Committee. As soon as the meeting was over, central leaders Tan Zhenlin and Ke Qingshi called in Zeng Qingmei and Shan Jingzhi and harshly criticized them, at which point Zeng and Shan finally acknowledged their wrongdoing.

In April and May 1961 the Central Control Commission sent the head of its rural work department, Li Jian, with others to Anhui. They went directly to the countryside and learned of massive starvation in Bengbu, Fuyang, and elsewhere. The party secretary of Bengbu's control commission, Deng Yancai, told them that one million people had starved to death in Bengbu Prefecture. Li Jian's team then went to the provincial capital and ordered the provincial control commission to reveal the true situation to the Central Committee. Upon reading the information Li Jian had collected, Zeng Xisheng slammed his fist on the table and yelled, "They're carrying out espionage in Anhui!"

Red Army veteran Weng Keye (deputy party secretary of the provincial control commission) had carried out inquiries in Bengbu and had reported his findings to the provincial party committee, only to be ignored. Now he provided his original draft to Li Jian. Li Jian wrote up a report to Wang Congwu stating that three million people had starved to death in Anhui Province.[95] Wang Congwu passed this report to the Central Committee secretariat. Confronted, Zeng Xisheng defended himself by saying those below had concealed the truth from him. Wang Congwu then produced the report that Weng Keye had given the provincial party committee and said, "Someone reported all this to you, so how can you say that those below didn't provide you with information?" Zeng Xisheng had nothing further to say.

At the time of the Seven Thousand Cadres Conference in January 1962, Anhui had still not been designated a disaster area, and as the conference drew to a close, Zeng Xisheng had still not revealed the true situation. A letter reached the Central Committee, however, so Mao decided to extend the conference. On January 30 and February 3, President Liu Shaoqi went to the Friendship Hotel, where the Anhui representatives were staying, to put an end to the cover-up. When the Seven Thousand Cadres Conference adjourned on February 7, the Anhui group stayed behind. On February 9, Liu went to talk with them a third time and announced that Zeng Xisheng was being transferred out of Anhui. Only then did the cover-up finally end.[96]

Ironically, Zeng Xisheng had to take responsibility for not only the massive starvation deaths, but also for the "responsibility fields" that curtailed the starvation. Although Mao had given a nod to the responsibility fields, they didn't contribute to the building of communism. The Central Committee declared that the responsibility fields had been implemented without going through a trial phase.

Zeng Xisheng remains a controversial figure. People loathed him because, under his leadership, millions starved to death in Anhui Province; yet they also cherish his memory because he allowed the responsibility fields that saved so many lives. Those within the party still committed to the commune movement gave him no quarter for the "salvation fields."

On a concurrent assignment as party chief of Shandong Province, Zeng opposed leftism and exposed the true situation there. In August 1965 the Central Committee transferred him to the Southwest bureau, but the Cultural Revolution was launched soon after that. Zeng was seized and struggled, and he died on July 15, 1968. He is now remembered above all for his role in the responsibility fields.

THE SALVATION FIELDS[97]

When the party modified Mao's disastrous "large and collective" communistic policies by permitting a three-level ownership system with production teams as the basic accounting unit, this served to contain the Five Winds, but brought no change to the system. Peasant wags depicted the crux of the problem in doggerel: "Down to the fields in a line / huffing and puffing in time / looking good and doing less / the iron rice bowl's still mine." With all rewarded regardless of their contribution, productivity could not improve.

The concept behind Anhui's responsibility fields began fermenting in the autumn of 1960, and it was tried out at the end of 1960. It took shape in the spring of 1961 and was brought to a close at the end of 1962. Mao's attitude toward the responsibility fields was ambivalent at best.

On August 28, 1960, Zeng Xisheng proposed creating three divisions under the production teams to handle production quotas: a food ration production group, a feed grain production group, and a commodity grain production group. In October he proposed that "production teams should set up production groups to avoid the problem of all talk and no action on production." In October, Zeng returned to Anhui from Shandong Province to defend the responsibility fields: "We have a three-and-a-half-level ownership system, with the production groups serving as half an ownership unit, as a means of strengthening the production responsibility system. The production contracts still implement a double contract system, with the production teams contracted to the production brigades, and the production groups contracted to the production teams." This system was extended throughout the province. Nevertheless, making the production groups the primary unit of production didn't change the overall problem of empty huffing and puffing to draw one's allotment—it just reduced the size of the iron rice bowl.

At the start of 1961 the Anhui provincial party committee sent leaders to Shandong to update Zeng. First, he advised that in order to revive the rural economy, it was acceptable to assign output quotas to households, and he had already initiated a trial household quota system. Second, Zeng had requested instructions from Mao on eliminating the communal kitchens and allowing commune members to prepare their own meals. Taking responsibility for the problems in Anhui, he had asked Mao for permission to no longer serve as Shandong's party secretary, and to return to Anhui to correct his errors and revive productivity. Apparently, Zeng Xisheng understood how serious Anhui's problems were, and hoped assigning output quotas to households would address the situation before the outside world became aware of it.

In February 1961, Zeng Xisheng was relieved of his position in Shandong and allowed to return to Anhui. While he was passing through Bengbu, Zhang Zuoyin, a provincial leader stationed there, told Zeng of a seventy-three-year-old peasant named Liu Qinglan who had taken his tubercular son up into the mountains and, without the aid of ox or plow, used a single shovel to cultivate a plot of virgin land, from which he harvested 1,650 kilos of grain. Apart from what he retained for food and seed, Liu sold 900 kilos of grain to the state and paid 60 yuan in cash to the commune. Household production seemed the way out of the crisis.[98]

On returning to the provincial capital, Hefei, Zeng proposed "assigning fields based on manpower, and assigning work points based on actual production." This meant first assessing a household's manpower based on a system of work points. Fields would be contracted out based on the household's labor capacity. The households were required to turn over grain to the state on the basis of their work points. The land and large farm machinery were still collectively owned, and the contracted grain would still be distributed by the state. Anything produced in excess of the contracted amount could be retained by the households. The system had "five centralizations": planning, distribution, farming technology, water resources, and action against natural disaster. Even so, cadres worried that they could be accused of dividing up land among households.

Zeng Xisheng reported this method to Mao at the CCP Central Committee's Guangzhou Conference on March 15 and 16, 1961. Mao replied, "Give it a try! If it doesn't work, carry out self-criticism. If it works well and can generate an additional 500 billion kilos of grain, that would be splendid!" Zeng telephoned the provincial party committee to report Mao's response and added, "It's clear sailing, we can launch." With that, the entire province adopted the responsibility field method.

Just as the practice was spreading, Mao sent a message to Zeng that the responsibility fields "could be tried out within a limited parameter." Noting Mao's change in attitude, Zeng sent a letter on March 20 to Mao and other leaders weighing the pros and cons. "We are undertaking this method not merely because of requests from a portion of the masses, nor without regard to its possible dangers, but because we want to gain its benefits, and with provisions made to guard against its disadvantages."[99] Mao made no comment on Zeng's letter.

On returning to Hefei on March 28, Zeng called a meeting to brief the provincial party committee's standing committee. He noted, "This method [the responsibility fields] could motivate the enthusiasm of the masses and increase production, so we're going to try it out for one year. If it proves effective, we'll continue it, and if it doesn't work, we'll discontinue it."

Mao was informed in a report on April 27, 1961, "Our province began a trial of the assignment of work and production quota responsibility on March 6, but suspended it immediately upon receiving a phone call from Comrade Xisheng on March 20. At that time, the production teams involved in the experiment constituted 39.2 percent of the province's production teams."[100] This implied responsiveness to Mao's reservations, even though Zeng did not actually discontinue the household responsibility system. The report went on to explain:

> During the trial period, the inadequate propaganda carried out in some localities led a minority of masses to misconstrue this method as an assignment of production quotas to households, or even as an allocation of fields, and some who hoped for access to more surplus grain intentionally described the method as assignment of production to households in letters to relatives working in factories and enlisted in the army, telling them to come home and work the fields. The fact is that this method is not an assignment of production to households or a division and allocation of fields. It is entirely consistent with the provision in the Central Committee's Sixty Agricultural Provisions that allows for the "implementation of a strict system of management and responsibility" entailing "assigning some responsibility to production teams and some responsibility to individuals."[101]

Zeng, again in Bengbu in July 1961, reported to Mao on the responsibility fields. Mao replied, "If you don't find any problems with it, you can apply the method universally." Zeng immediately notified Anhui's party apparatus of Mao's directive and ordered expansion of the responsibility fields. By mid-October, the practice was being applied to nearly 85 percent of the province's cultivated area.

The responsibility fields yielded excellent results. Most of the province eliminated fallow fields within one year, and livestock and farming tools rapidly increased. A survey found that in teams implementing responsibility fields, crop yields per *mu* increased 38.9 percent in one year. This meant that even after fulfilling procurement quotas, everyone's basic food needs could be met. Peasants began to refer to the responsibility fields as "salvation fields." To feed themselves, peasants mainly grew sweet potatoes the first year, and many hungry residents in neighboring Henan Province went to Anhui to gather sweet potatoes that had been left in the fields.

Then Mao's attitude changed yet again. In December 1961, he called Zeng to Wuxi and asked, "Now that production has revived, do you think we should change it [meaning the responsibility fields] back to the old method?" Zeng replied, "The masses are just beginning to enjoy the benefits of the system. Can we allow them to continue it a little longer?" Mao didn't say yes or no.

The responsibility field policy continued in 1962. In order to prevent others from claiming the method was capitalistic, an emphasis was placed on the "five centralizations." The Central Committee's attitude was nevertheless clear: the responsibility fields had to change. During a Central Committee work conference, Liu Shaoqi said, "The responsibility fields are a form of backtracking." The message passed back to Anhui was that responsibility fields led in the direction of individual production, and to the possibility of polarization and usury down the road. On March 20, 1962, the standing committee of the Anhui provincial party committee agreed that the responsibility fields ran counter to the Central Committee's Sixty Agricultural Provisions and would ultimately result in the disintegration of the collective economy and progression down the capitalist road. The orientation had to be corrected.

Some local cadres petitioned Mao and the provincial party committee, advocating continuation of the responsibility field method. Some in the central government agreed. In June 1962, State Council vice-premier Li Fuchun wrote a letter to Liu Shaoqi, Deng Xiaoping, and others in the secretariat expressing his support for the responsibility fields. In July the head of the Central Committee's Rural Work Department, Deng Zihui, sent people to Anhui. Their report endorsed the benefits of the responsibility fields and advised against "finishing them off with one blow and thoroughly repudiating them." When the Central Committee secretariat discussed this report, Deng Zihui said straight out that the production responsibility system was good and should be spread throughout the countryside. Not long afterward, at a Central Committee work conference, Deng Zihui incurred harsh criticism. He nevertheless reiterated, "I maintain my view of the responsibility fields." At the Tenth Plenum of the Eighth CCP Central Committee from September 24 to 27, 1962, Deng Zihui was dismissed, and the Central Committee's Rural Work Department was disbanded. The meeting appealed to the entire party to "never forget class struggle." Anhui Province's responsibility fields came under criticism as a "trend toward individual production" resulting in "a bourgeois restoration."

At the end of 1962, Anhui's provincial party committee required that "by spring 1963, some production teams should be corrected, with the remainder corrected by spring 1964." In many localities, however, a method of superficial but not substantive change was adopted, prolonging the practice of responsibility fields.

Mao's renewed emphasis on class struggle brought many cadres under criticism for the "trend toward individual production," and these attacks intensified with the Socialist Education Movement and the Cultural Revolution. Hundreds of thousands were subjected to struggle and criticism because of their involvement in the responsibility fields. Fifteen years later, in 1978, Anhui Province took the lead in reinstating the responsibility fields, after which the practice spread throughout China.

9 THE FOOD CRISIS

Severe food shortages became inevitable as industrialization increased the demand for food in the cities and collectivization dulled the productive zeal of the peasants. All resources were tightly controlled by the state, and the PRC regime had engaged in repeated "food wars" since coming to power. Starting in 1959 the battle intensified. It was a battle between the rulers and the peasants in which the peasants suffered the greatest number of casualties as the chief targets of relentless extractive pressure. The command that "procurement quotas must be met" rapidly set the formidable state machinery in motion, its weight increasing down the chain of command until it landed with crushing force on the shoulders of the peasants.

THE STATE MONOPOLY FOR PURCHASING
AND MARKETING AS A SOURCE OF PEASANT HUNGER

According to official statistics, in the five years from 1949 to 1954, the urban population increased 43 percent.[1] The Ministry of Food, calculating from the perspective of food supply, gave a 10 percent higher figure for the urban population in 1953. The state's grain tax and procurement more than doubled from 1950 to 1953 and still was unable to satisfy the urban demand. In the grain year from July 1, 1952, to June 30, 1953, the state recorded a grain deficit of 2 billion kilos. On June 30 the state grain reserves were reduced from 7.25 billion kilos to 5.25 billion kilos. The Food Committee of the National Conference on Financial and Economic Work in June 1953 concluded that the problem was great, the solutions limited, and the current situation unsustainable.[2]

Prior to the founding of the PRC, the wheat flour industries of China's coastal cities relied heavily on imported wheat. According to a survey by

Shanghai's Jiao Tong University, from 1922 to 1930 China imported an average of 125,847,800 kilos of wheat per year,[3] with reliance on imports much higher at certain places and times. By now the age of wheat imports had ended.

Faced with an acute food shortage, Mao tasked the Central Finance and Economic Commission with finding a solution. The commission settled on a state monopoly for purchasing and marketing, under which all foodstuffs would be controlled by the government. All food produced had to be sold to the state, and the amount of food left to the peasants for their own consumption was subject to state approval. Urban households were issued ration booklets for food. Without a ration ticket, not a mouthful of food could be had. The peasants were naturally extremely dissatisfied with this arrangement. At the National Food Conference on October 10, 1953, Chen Yun said, "If we don't manage the food issue, the market will become volatile; if we adopt a state monopoly for purchasing and marketing, the peasants are likely to oppose it. Whichever option we choose brings risk."[4]

Disregarding the views of the peasants, Mao and his Politburo forged ahead with the state monopoly, which came into effect in December 1953. In theory, surplus grain was to be sold to the state. In reality, careerist officials ensured that all requisition quotas were met or exceeded, even if this meant seizing the peasants' own grain rations, animal feed, and seed grain. Urban residents were allotted a set grain ration, but as each province deducted a percentage for itself, the actual grain ration was less than that set by the state.

In its February 2, 1955, "Report of the South China Sub-bureau Regarding Current Tensions in the Villages and Measures Taken," the CCP Central Committee's South China sub-bureau described the situation in the villages following implementation of the state food supply monopoly: (1) In the later stage of the food requisition drive (in the second half of 1954), all localities experienced a wide-scale slaughter of pigs and ducks. (2) In some areas of Zhongshan, Xinhui, and Nanhai, peasants withdrew from their land or even handed over their land certificates because they felt their fields were of insufficient quality to meet the requisition quota. (3) Peasants were not eating their fill and lacked enthusiasm in production, with a considerable drop in work attendance. (4) Peasants had grave misgivings over the food issue. Near Gangkou Town of Zhongshan County, villagers often crept off at night to see if grain had been transported from the granaries, and stood weeping on the riverbanks as ships left with foodstuffs for redistribution. Members of grain-deficient households who had not been issued grain ration cards went to the homes of cadres and wept. (5) Peasants frequently expressed dissatisfaction by saying things such as, "After working so hard all year, there's nothing to eat."[5]

A large number of revolts were met by harsh punishment. Hunan's Changde Prefecture resolved: "Those counterrevolutionary elements who sabotage the planned purchasing and planned supply will be punished under the 'Regulations of the PRC on Punishing Crimes of Counter-revolution.'"[6] In Yunnan Province during the early stages of the food monopoly, many died during criticism sessions, and there were instances of violent resistance.[7] Sichuan's Dechang County in 1954 convened twenty-five mass meetings at which judgments were delivered against twenty-nine individuals. One was sentenced to death, and twenty-three were given prison sentences.[8] In 1953, Sichuan's Shizhu County convened nine pub-lic judgment meetings at which two people were sentenced to death, five were sentenced to prison terms, and two were placed under surveillance and control.[9] Riots erupted in Fujian's Shaowu County in 1954, resulting in the arrest of 114 people for "counterrevolutionary incitement of the masses to sabotage the state monopoly for purchasing and marketing of grain." Sixteen were executed, fifty-six were given prison terms, and nine were placed under surveillance and control.[10]

Despite the revolts, the Food Ministry maintained that "the peasants' complaints about food shortages are false." This viewpoint dominated the thinking of the state leadership for a very long time. No matter how loud the peasants' laments of starvation, those in the top leadership re-garded them as the cries of opposition to socialism.

Guangxi early on exemplified the deadly dynamics. Because of its falsely reported crop yields, Guangxi's procurement quota was excessively high, and thousands died of hunger in 1955. Starvation deaths, edema, and other diseases of malnourishment were particularly rampant in Pingle, Lipu, and Heng counties in Pingle Prefecture. The Ministry of Supervi-sion investigated "Starvation Deaths from Famine in Guangxi Province in 1956," as the result of which the provincial first secretary and two pro-vincial party secretaries were stripped of their official positions and transferred out. A number of prefectural and county officials were also dismissed and put on probation within the party, had demerits recorded, or received severe warnings.[11] Cadres who refused to go along with this scapegoating and claimed that the starvation was caused by the state monopoly for purchasing and marketing were stripped of party membership.

The Great Famine occurred within a system that produced incentives for local officials to exaggerate production while the state monopoly stifled incentives for increasing production. The monopoly also deprived peasants of their right to obtain food and made them dependent on the government for every meal, while punishing them for applying individual effort in food production. The Great Famine was an inevitable consequence of intensifying the killer potential inherent in the system.

Entering 1958, the central government grew more apprehensive over food. On February 16 it pointed out that some places genuinely faced food shortages.[12] The Central Committee nevertheless demanded a strong effort to exceed the original targets in procuring grain, gaining control of even more of the food produced.

TABLE 9.1: GRAIN YIELD AND PROCUREMENT PRIOR TO THE GREAT LEAP FORWARD (IN BILLION KILOS)

Yield and procurement	1953–54	1954–55	1955–56	1956–57	1957–58
Yield	116.85	169.5	183.9	192.75	194.91
Procurement	50.15	53.9	52.05	49.7	51.915
(trade grain)	(41.4)	(45.15)	(43.0)	(41.924)	(42.737)
Percentage of yield	30.1	31.8	28.3	25.8	26.6

Source: The Food Ministry Statistical Department table for July 1957, and the Food Ministry's table for February 6, 1958, Central Archives: 1957–180-5-6; the figures for 1957 and 1958 are not the final figures, Central Archives: 1958-180-6-1.

Because too much grain was procured each year, part had to be sold back to the rural areas. In some years, more than 40 percent returned to the countryside, as shown in Table 9.2. The transportation back and forth brought enormous waste, but the state still wanted control over all foodstuffs.

TABLE 9.2: GRAIN SOLD BACK TO THE RURAL AREAS PRIOR TO THE GREAT LEAP FORWARD (IN BILLION KILOS)

	1954–55	1955–56	1956–57	1957–58
Grain sold to the countryside	24.7	20.25	24.5	21.45
(trade grain)	(20.05)	(16.7)	(20.1)	(17.5)
Percentage of procurement	45.8	38.9	49.3	41.3

Source: The Food Ministry Statistical Department table for July 1957, Central Archives: 1957-180-5-7; and the Food Ministry's table for February 6, 1958, Central Archives: 1957-180-5-12; the figures for 1957 and 1958 are not the final figures, Central Archives: 1958-180-6-1.

Prior to the Great Leap Forward, despite food shortages, China exported more than 2 billion kilos of grain per year to obtain foreign exchange and pay for imported equipment. This grain was snatched from the mouths of the peasants.

TABLE 9.3: GRAIN EXPORTS PRIOR TO THE GREAT LEAP FORWARD (IN BILLION KILOS)

Year	Grain exports	Unprocessed grain	Soybean content
1953–54	1.6	1.8	0.9
1954–55	2.05	2.3	1.15
1955–56	2.2	2.55	1.15
1956–57	2.2	2.55	1.2

Source: The Food Ministry Statistical Department table for July 1957, and the Food Ministry's table for February 6, 1958, Central Archives: 1957-180-5-6. Because the Food Ministry's figures are calculated on the basis of the grain year, and the China Economic Yearbook figures are based on the production year, there is some discrepancy between the grain export figures in this table and those presented for the years 1956–65 in chapter 12 on the official response to the crisis.

The conflict between the state and the peasants over food intensified in 1957. In some places, peasants organized to take grain by force, while others migrated out as emaciated plow oxen dropped dead in the fields.

Resistance to the state was strongest in Hebei, Shandong, Henan, Anhui, and northern Jiangsu provinces. In the atmosphere of the 1957 Anti-Rightist Campaign, "mass debates" were launched in the villages to "distinguish the cardinal questions of right and wrong on the food issue." In two prefectures of western Hunan, the "Main debate points on the state monopoly for purchasing and marketing grain" were: (1) Is the state monopoly for purchasing and marketing grain good or not? Do we want it or not? (2) Is the grain ration too low? Is the state cutting off the peasants? (3) Must we meet the grain monopoly's procurement quotas? If output is increased, should procurement also be increased? (4) Is it possible to plan grain consumption and to economize on grain consumption? Despite this effort, only one prefecture managed to exceed its procurement quotas.[13]

As the state applied political pressure for more grain procurement, anyone who dissented became a political target, and the media published articles with titles such as "The State Monopoly for Purchasing and Marketing Is Excellent—Rebutting the Rightist Elements," and "Those Who Oppose the State Monopoly for Purchasing and Marketing Are Opposing Socialism."[14]

By the spring of 1958 the food shortage was severe. From April 17 to 19 the Central Committee secretariat received telephone reports from Anhui, Fujian, Gansu, Guangdong, Guangxi, Hebei, Hunan, Inner Mongolia, Jiangsu, Jilin, Liaoning, Shandong, Shanxi, Sichuan, and Yunnan, during which it learned of food shortages and even the exhaustion of food supplies in some areas. In Anhui, 1.3 million people lacked food, and food supplies had been cut off to more than 670,000 rural inhabitants of Shandong Province and to 690,000 residents of 15 counties in Guangdong Province. Gansu had food shortages in 21 of its counties, and 735 famine deaths were recorded in the province's worst-hit county.[15]

Even before the Great Leap Forward, the party Center had become aware of food shortages. In his May 8, 1958, "Survey of the Food Situation over the Next Five Years," the Food Ministry's party group secretary wrote, "Food supply work has been tense over the past few years. We've had to push on procurements in winter, on supply in spring, and on both procurements and supply in summer. If we let up even a little, the food situation will experience problems . . . It would appear that food supplies will remain tight for at least ten more years." The Great Leap brought the crisis to a head.

MAO ZEDONG WORRIES ABOUT "TOO MUCH FOOD"

The Great Leap Forward devastated rural productivity. The total national grain output in 1956 was 192.75 billion kilos, and officials claimed a total of 200 billion kilos for 1958 (with the actual amount impossible to ascertain), but output remained below 170 billion kilos from 1959 to 1963. At its lowest point in 1960, output sank to 143.5 billion kilos, even lower than in 1951. It was not until 1965 that output returned to its 1956 level.

In the midst of this catastrophe, high-yield "satellites" were launched all over China in 1958, and grain output was projected at 425 billion kilos.

**TABLE 9.4: GRAIN OUTPUT RECORDED BEFORE,
DURING, AND AFTER THE GREAT FAMINE (IN BILLION KILOS)**

Year	Output
1956	192.75
1957	195.05
1958	200.0
1959	170.0
1960	143.5
1961	147.5
1962	160.0
1963	170.0
1964	187.5
1965	194.45

Source: China Statistical Yearbook (1984), *p. 141. These statistics are based on the production year (January 1 to December 31), while the Food Ministry's figures are based on the grain year (July 1 to June 30).*

The Sputnik-launching campaign is generally blamed on lower-level cadres, but it was Mao who first said at the Chengdu Conference, "We have to make an example of bumper harvests, dozens or hundreds of such examples."[16] After he uttered these words, party newspapers promoted "the example of bumper harvests" and "launching satellites." Those below scrambled to meet expectations. When Mao aspired to yields of 5,000 kilos per *mu*, his subordinates reported back with yields of 50,000. Exaggeration was pandering propelled by the state machine.

The Exaggeration Wind began with *People's Daily* reporting the launching of a "Sputnik" in Henan's Suiping County. Reports of miraculous wheat yields frequently occupied key spots on the newspaper's front page, often in special type or even highlighted in red, fueling fanaticism and fraud as each claimed greater "achievements" than the one preceding:

> June 8: Henan's Suiping Sputnik Commune reports an average wheat yield of 1007.5 kilos per *mu*;
>
> June 9: wheat yields of 1178.5 kilos per *mu* are reported at Lemin People's Commune in Hubei's Gucheng County, and yields of 750 to 1,000 kilos per *mu* on 7 million *mu* of farmland in Xiangyang, Hubei Province;
>
> June 11: 1,197 kilos at Liuzuolou Commune in Hubei's Wei County;
>
> June 12: 1,765 kilos at Henan's Suiping Sputnik Commune;
>
> June 15: a front-page banner headline reads "Paeans to Bumper Harvests Fill the Air: Beaming Smiles on Millions of Faces," followed by an article entitled "Henan's Wheat Yields More Than Double," with the subtitle "Fence Sitters and Bean Counters Need to Wake Up";
>
> June 16: 2,176.5 kilos in Gucheng, Hubei Province;
>
> June 18: 2,206 kilos at Shuanglou Commune in Henan's Shangqiu County;
>
> June 21: 2,267.5 kilos at Tianzhuang Commune in Henan's Hui County;
>
> June 23: 2,344.5 kilos at Xianfeng Commune in Gucheng, Hubei Province;
>
> June 30: 2,551.5 kilos at Anguo, Hubei Province;
>
> July 12: 3,660 kilos at Xiping, Henan Province; and
>
> September 22: a yield of 4,292.8 kilos per *mu* on a farm 2,797 meters above sea level in Qaidam Basin, Qinghai Province.

At the beginning of July, *People's Daily* began reporting the launch of high-yield satellites in the early rice harvests:

July 12: 1,637.5 kilos per *mu* at Chengmenxiang Commune in Minhou, Fujian Province;

July 18: 2,903 kilos at Lianban Commune in Minhou, Fujian Province;

July 26: 4,597.5 kilos at Boyang, Jiangxi Province;

July 31: 5,298.5 kilos at Chunguang Commune in Yingcheng, Hubei Province;

August 1: 7,680.5 kilos at Changfeng Commune in Xiaogan, Hubei Province;

August 10: 8,113.5 kilos at Gaofeng Commune in Congyang, Anhui Province;

August 13: 18,478 kilos at Jianguo Commune in Macheng, Hubei Province;

August 22: nearly 21,538 kilos at Fanchang, Anhui Province; and

September 5: 30,263.5 kilos in Lian County in the northern hill country of Guangdong Province.

The fabrications disseminated by the propaganda organs put political pressure on those who were skeptical of the fantastical claims. Doubters became political targets. In an atmosphere in which lies were encouraged and truth was attacked, exaggeration became the order of the day. Once the Exaggeration Wind gained strength, its interactive force stoked it into a devastating gale.

Qian Xuesen, a renowned rocket scientist and idol of the nation's youth, wrote:

Is there an upper limit to the amount of food the earth can produce for humanity? Scientific calculations say this upper limit is not even close to being reached! In the years to come, the efforts of the peasants and agricultural scientists will bring about bumper crops that far exceed present levels. This is because the maximum agricultural output is predicated on the amount of solar power over a given surface area in a given year. If this solar power can be converted into agricultural products, the yield will be much higher than it is now.

Let's make a calculation: if 30 percent of the solar power that shines on one *mu* of cropland can be put to use by plants, and the plants can use this portion of solar power to convert the moisture and carbon dioxide in the air into nutrients to feed themselves and develop and grow strong, and if only one-fifth of this becomes edible crops, then the grain yield of one *mu* of rice paddy would not be the mere 1,000 kilos or 1,500 kilos we see at present, but rather twenty times that amount!

. . . What today's conditions do not allow, we will create the conditions to produce tomorrow; what we don't yet have today, we will surely have tomorrow![17]

In March 1959, veteran revolutionary Li Rui asked Mao why he had been so credulous about high-yield satellites, and Mao said it was because of Qian's essay.[18]

On August 15, 1958, the first party secretary of the CCP Central Committee's South Central bureau, Tao Zhu, published an essay in *Red Flag* entitled "Refuting the Argument That There Are Limits to Crop Yield Increases," in which he averred that Guangdong's rice paddies could achieve an output of 5,000 kilos per *mu*. On August 11, 1958, Tan Zhenlin, China's vice-premier in charge of agriculture, published a long essay in *People's Daily* endorsing the great political significance of the exaggerated figures. On September 26 the famously straight-talking vice-premier Chen Yi published an article in *People's Daily* offering personal testimony of fields that produced 500,000 kilos of sweet potatoes, 300,000 kilos of sugarcane, and 25,000 kilos of rice per *mu*.

On August 22, Anhui Province announced that it had achieved an average early rice yield of 500 kilos per *mu*. On September 13, Henan proclaimed itself the second province to reach that goal. On October 20, Sichuan joined the club. On September 29, *People's Daily* reported, "Gansu's crop yields have more than doubled . . . So we see prosperity coming to Gansu Province, which has always suffered food shortages." *People's Daily* went on to report the national summer harvest as 69 percent higher than the year before.

A summary report to the Central Committee by the Food Ministry's leading party group on August 15 concluded: "Based on information reported from all localities, the national grain yield this year is estimated at 314.15 billion kilos, an increase of 119.2 billion kilos, or 61.44 percent, over last year's yield of 194.95 billion kilos."[19]

To express doubts about the phony numbers was to "cast aspersions on the excellent situation," and no one wanted to be labeled a "denier." In Xinyang, anyone claiming that the high-yield model farms were fake was subjected to struggle. According to the memoirs of Xinyang's prefectural commissioner, Zhang Shufan, some twelve thousand struggle sessions were mounted in the prefecture.[20] The result was even sharper blasts of the Exaggeration Wind.

During Central Committee work conferences, Mao sometimes expressed skepticism regarding the high-yield satellites, but at other times, he proclaimed his belief in them. He expressed unreserved belief in the doubling and redoubling of crop yields in 1958. When in Wuhan one day in mid-September, he said, "Over the past nine years, the food supply has increased very slowly, and we've always had to worry about there not being enough. Now we've seen the supply increase by hundreds of billions of kilos in just one year. This year it's doubled, maybe next year it will double again, and then we'll find ourselves with more food than we know what to do with. It's the same with steel. In the past nine years we've produced a few million tons, but in just a few months this year we've increased production by millions of tons . . . It's odd, isn't it?"[21]

On November 16, 1958, the vice-premier in charge of agriculture and the agriculture minister jointly submitted to the CCP Central Committee and Chairman Mao a document claiming, "The total crop yield for 1958 will reach 425 billion kilos. This is after the provinces, cities, and autonomous regions reduced the figures provided by the counties by 10 to 30 percent . . . The figure of 425 billion kilos is relatively reliable . . . the total will not be lower than 375 billion kilos, and can be published as such. This is . . . a very great leap forward. This point must be affirmed; this overall total cannot be cast into doubt by a small minority of false or exaggerated reports."[22]

The report reflected a massive fraud. Based on these figures, "In 1959 the amount of land set aside for cash crops will be increased, and that set aside for food crops will be reduced by about 400 million *mu*, or 20 percent less than in 1958. But the food grain output will be set at 525 billion kilos."

The high-yield myth fed Mao's optimism. When he went on an inspection visit to Hebei's Xushui County on August 4, he believed the lies told to him by the county party secretary and joyfully said, "How can this county of just over 310,000 people eat so much grain? What will you do with the extra food? From now on, people will eat mostly wheat, with corn and yams used to feed animals, especially pigs. With more pigs being raised, people will be able to eat more meat." He also said, "With more food available, we can plant less in the future, and people will only have to put in half a day's labor."[23]

During an inspection tour of Jiangsu at the end of September, Liu Shaoqi advocated "planting one-third of the land with grain and one-third with trees, and leaving one-third fallow," as well as "planting less and harvesting more."[24] The Eighth CCP Central Committee in December stipulated:

> In the past there were always worries over our large population and small amount of cultivated land. But the fact of the bumper harvest in 1958 has overturned this . . . The amount of cultivated land is not inadequate, but excessive . . . Within a few years . . . land used for crops can be reduced to about one-third. Some of the excess land can be left fallow part of the time, in rotation with use as pastureland or for growing herbal fertilizer, while another part can be applied to afforestation or to digging ponds so that the earth will become a garden with a dazzling array of flowering plants on flatlands and hillsides and in the ponds.[25]

In the spirit of "less planting, higher yields, bigger harvest," the Huzhuang production brigade in Jiangsu carried out an autumn planting covering only 54.5 percent of the arable land. Commune members were distressed by so much fallow land, and secretly planted another 200 *mu*.[26] The vice-premier in charge of agriculture, Tan Zhenlin, subsequently acknowledged, "The amount of land area cultivated in 1959 was 177 million *mu* less than in 1958, a decrease of nearly 10 percent. That was probably one of the reasons for reduced output in 1959."[27]

The Chinese Academy of Sciences (CAS) convened an enlarged meeting on August 6, 1959, to discuss Mao's question of "what to do with the extra food." After strenuous debate, the academy's leading party group assigned research into the utilization of excess grain to six research institutes, placing many important research projects on hold and redeploying a large number of researchers to the question. A year later, the scientists carrying out research into the use of excess food were themselves suffering extreme food deprivation. They were then mobilized to develop food substitutes.[28] On November 9, 1960, the CAS leading party group submitted its "Recommendations Regarding a Food Substitute Campaign" to the CCP Central Committee and Chairman Mao.

THE RUTHLESS GRAIN PROCUREMENT CAMPAIGN

The myth of high grain yields led to excessive consumption and elevated state procurement. The wasteful consumption occurred only in the autumn of 1958, but still contributed to the Great Famine in 1959. Some localities launched "feasting Sputniks." Others served food at staggered intervals to the convenience of anyone passing by. At that time I was a senior high school student, and during the school holidays I was engaged in a work-study program in which I helped deliver mail. On one delivery trip from the county seat in Xishui to Xianma Town, I encountered a communal kitchen serving lunch, and decided to test the claim of "Free Meals" proclaimed on the red banners that decorated its walls. Without a second glance, the dining hall staff gave me a big bowl of food, and I relished the joy of a "Communist" white rice feast. The communal kitchen in my home village served luxuries peasants never enjoyed even on major holidays.

Because many workers had been deployed to steel and irrigation projects, in many villages only the elderly, women, and children were left to tend the crops, and much grain rotted unharvested in the fields. In some localities rice was harvested late, and wasteful harvesting caused losses of around 10 percent of the crop yield. In some localities, production of cotton, peanuts, and sweet potatoes dropped 20 to 30 percent.[29]

The mortal blow to peasants, however, was the state's high procurement quotas. Because the total output for 1958 was projected at 425 billion kilos,[30] procurement targets were raised accordingly. For the 1958/59 grain year (July 1, 1958, to June 30, 1959), procurement was 55,667,500,000 kilos, 9,757,000,000 kilos more than the previous year, an increase of 21.25 percent. The output was calculated as 200 billion kilos, an increase of only 0.26 percent over the previous year.[31]

Not enough grain was left to feed farm households. Total grain output for Fujian Province in 1959 was 12.2 percent less than in 1957, but the gross procurement (subtracting the amount sold back to the villages) increased by 40.9 percent. The total grain output for 1960 was 1.145 billion kilos less than that for 1957, but the gross procurement was still 140 million kilos greater. The percentage of total output procured was 16.8 percent in 1957, but rose to 31.9 percent and 27.2 percent in 1959 and 1960. The province's per capita grain ration fell from 294 kilos in 1957 to 240 kilos in 1959 and 215 kilos in 1960, and commune members were barred from making up the difference by growing sideline crops for their own consumption. According to provincial statistics, unnatural deaths and reductions in births totaled 870,000 from 1959 to 1961.[32] Fujian was far from the worst hit of China's provinces.

In one classic fraud in August 1958, Macheng County's Jianguo Commune claimed a rice yield of more than 18,450 kilos per *mu* by transplanting mature rice plants from other fields into the 1.016-*mu* paddy field of the No. 2 production team. This deception brought disaster. From the second half of 1959 through 1960, more than seventy of the four hundred residents of the production team's village starved to death. Neighbors were pitiless, saying, "In your thirst for glory, you forced the rest of us to sell off too much grain."[33]

Despite the claims of gargantuan harvests, the Food Ministry reported on October 4 that total procurement was down 2.45 billion kilos. "Grain reserves in the nation's storehouses decreased 3.4 billion kilos from the same time last year. Grain reserves decreased in seventeen provinces and cities, with supplies weakest in Tianjin, Beijing, Liaoning, and Jilin."[34]

According to data compiled by departments of the CCP Central Committee, as of early April 1959, as many as 25.17 million people were going without food.[35] In the spring of 1959 people began dying in droves. Because local officials covered up or underreported the deaths, the central government regarded starvation as an anomaly and continued its food requisition drive. On February 21, 1959, Tan Zhenlin, the top party official for agriculture, declared, "The current food supply problem is largely a matter of attitude . . . Why are people hiding away grain during a bumper harvest? It's all a matter of attitude."[36] His remarks reflected an ongoing debate among senior officials.

On January 27, 1959, the secretary of the Guangdong provincial party secretariat, Zhao Ziyang, offered information supporting the myth of ample food: "Leinan County took a great leap forward in production, but at the end of last year an abnormal food shortage emerged. The county launched a series of cadre conferences, as the result of which 35 million kilos of secretly withheld grain was discovered. The experience of Leinan County bears out that there is plenty of food in the countryside and that the food shortage is bogus and the result of private withholding."

The Guangdong provincial party committee then agreed to "conduct a struggle against false reporting of output and selfish departmentalism in order to guarantee that the transfer of foodstuffs is accomplished." On February 22, 1959, Mao wrote a long memo on Zhao Ziyang's report, expressing the view that "the matter of false reporting of output and private withholding . . . is very serious . . . It is a widespread problem throughout the country and must be immediately solved."[37]

Mao on February 28 wrote a long memo asserting that the hoarding problem could be solved only by implementing "asset ownership based on production teams with partial ownership by communes."

Du Daozheng, who was then head of the Guangdong branch of the Xinhua News Agency, attended provincial party committee meetings as a nonvoting delegate. He later told me that the anti-hoarding campaign was Tao Zhu's idea and that only Madame Chen Yu expressed a different view. Tao carried out the campaign in Dongwan, and Zhao Ziyang in Zhanjiang. Zhao was much milder; Tao persecuted people, while Zhao did not. In April, however, Tao Zhu saw that there really was no grain, and he took the initiative to end the campaign.

During the Zhengzhou Conference from February 27 to March 5, 1959, even with constant reports of food shortages, the CCP Central Committee refused to acknowledge a problem. In a speech, Mao said:

> Everyone can see that there is a certain amount of strain in our relations with the peasants at this time over some matters. An obvious phenomenon is that following the bumper harvest in 1958, part of the procurement of grain, cotton, oil crops, and other agricultural products has still not been met. Moreover (apart from a minority of disaster areas), there has been widespread incidence of false reporting of output and private withholding throughout the country, with unrest over claimed shortages of grain, oil, pork, and vegetables. The scale is by no means inferior to the food-related unrest in 1953 and 1955. Comrades, I ask all of you to consider, what is this actually all about? . . . I believe we should search for the answers in our knowledge of the system of ownership under the rural people's communes and the policies we've adopted.[38]

While Mao acknowledged problems with communal ownership, he still did not believe there was a food shortage, or that villagers were starving. Rather, he believed that adjustments to the system of ownership would allow the state to collect more grain.

TABLE 9.5: A GENERAL SURVEY OF STATE GRAIN MANAGEMENT DURING THE GREAT FAMINE
(TRADE GRAIN, IN BILLION KILOS)

Input and outflow		1957/58	1958/59	1959/60	1960/61	1961/62
Input	Total	46.0055	56.272	60.7145	41.187	39.7335
	Procurement	46.0055	56.272	60.7145	39.042	33.957
	Grain year	(43.790)	(54.601)	(59.76)	(42.6335)	(34.124)
	Imports	–	–	–	2.145	5.7765
Outflow	Total	44.9825	58.3285	63.0255	47.4545	38.855
	Sales	42.1045	52.6005	55.9565	44.3485	36.816
	Urban sales	21.1215	27.316	29.6325	26.2445	23.3935
	Rural sales	20.983	25.2595	26.324	18.104	13.4225
	Gov't supply	6.215	6.16	6.56	6.09	6.225
	Exports	2.084	3.628	4.3255	11.96	8.775
	Wastage	0.1725	1.484	2.0875	1.301	0.539
Reserves		19.2205	17.164	14.853	8.5855	9.464
(Stale reserves)		(14.584)	(10.857)	(7.5915)	(5.4695)	(6.515)

Source: "Food Ministry Planning Division Grain Data Summary," August 25, 1962, Central Archives: 1962-180-10-109.

Note: In the three grain years of 1957/58, 1958/59, and 1959/60, the purchase and sale figures include turnover grain and variety conversion, but the grain year 1960/61 does not. Government supply refers to army provisions.

When peasants saw that high procurement targets would deprive them of their grain rations, animal feed, and seed grain, some did hide grain, but the government greatly overestimated the amount. Even as peasants died, officials would not believe there was a food shortage, and bore down even harder on grain procurement. Under heavy pressure, grassroots cadres pillaged homes with a violence and degradation that exacerbated the misery of the starving.

On December 9, 1959, Sichuan's Fengdu County party committee met to "oppose false reporting of output" in one commune. The party committee head suggested that they "first attack the front line (district branch secretaries, production brigade leaders, accountants, and supervisors), then the rear line (production team leaders), and finally the well-to-do middle peasants." Seven people were strung up and beaten at the meeting, among whom one died at the scene. In subsequent meetings elsewhere, 173 people were beaten to death, and 1,179 cadres were dismissed.[39]

During a grain-search campaign at Fanhe Commune in Tieling, Liaoning Province, it was announced that "concealing one kernel of grain was the same as concealing a bullet," and that "anyone hiding one kernel of grain was a counterrevolutionary." Cadres were told that "only those with the heart of a killer can get the grain." Commune party secretary Xu swung a rope over the table and said, "Do you all know what this is? Size up whether there's grain and act accordingly!" At the meeting, the branch party secretary of the Yaowangmiao production team, Cui Fengwu, was struggled to the point that he wet himself.

When a production team cadre meeting was held at Yaowangmiao, a cadre in charge of grain purchasing surnamed Wei (section chief of the county agricultural commission) demanded that a production team member named Liu Yuqing hand over some grain. When Liu said he had none, Wei had him bound and forced to kneel, then kicked him and had him paraded for a day. Liu committed suicide, and his wife went mad.

When section chief Wei held a mass meeting at the Laohe production team to call on villagers to hand over their grain, he had them march double-time while he stood on a platform and used the caricatured speech and mannerisms of their earlier Japanese oppressors to order them: "You must hand over all grain, many many, chop chop!" After the meeting he led more than thirty people on a house-to-house search for grain.

Commune secretary Li Xingmin set up a tribunal at the Chengnan-bao production team, where he conducted a kangaroo court to force the surrender of grain. Sixty-seven commune cadres took part in physical assaults on 88 individuals and the "debating" of 112.[40]

The anti-hoarding campaigns produced little grain. Finally, in early summer 1959, the CCP Central Committee conceded that there actually was a food shortage, yet it refused to acknowledge that there had been no increase in output. During a Central Committee telephone conference on April 19, Li Xiannian said, "The peculiar feature of this year is the big increase in output combined with a big food shortage." He held that the grain yield for the 1958/59 grain year was 35 percent higher than that for the year before, while noting that state grain reserves were down: "By June of this year, we won't even be able to maintain the minimum reserve of 18 billion kilos; it's the lowest reserve level since implementation of the state monopoly for purchasing and marketing of grain."[41]

Scientist Qian Xuesen "proved" that the peasants were still hoarding grain in an article in September 1959 that claimed yields should have been 18,000 kilos per *mu*.[42] Given such attitudes at the Center, the elevated procurement targets continued in 1959 and 1960.

THE FOOD MINISTRY CELEBRATES AS THE PEASANTS WEEP

The grain yield for 1959 was down 15 percent, but on November 2, 1959, the Food Ministry reported that the food supply situation was "superb."[43] Earlier, during the Lushan Conference, the Food Ministry party group secretary had suggested high state procurement premised on a bountiful harvest. At 6:00 a.m. on July 5, Mao wrote, "I agree overall with the views in this report. Have it printed and distributed to all conference participants." His memo stated:

(1) If it is found that this year's harvest actually was better than last year's, we can strive for a procurement of 55 billion kilos in the first step from passivity to taking the initiative. (2) . . . Tell the peasants to resume eating chaff and herbs for half the year, and after some hardship for one or two or three years things will turn around. We should build up our reserves and consume less, fix the ration on a per capita basis, and distribute food rations to households, with meals taken in the communal kitchens and any savings passed back to the peasants. People should eat more when busy and less when work is slow, eat congee as well as cooked rice, and mix grain with vegetables, and they'll still have plenty to eat. (3) . . . Those who plant can harvest the proceeds without being taxed or requisitioned. The main thing is to provide enough for animal feed and partially for human consumption. Resume private garden plots and by all means reassign plots of land for private use. (4) . . . Is it possible to arrange for the people's livelihoods on the basis of the actual grain yield for 1957? Life was pretty good in 1957, wasn't it? By doing this, the peasants' grain reserves can be increased more. With grain in hand, they won't be so anxious, and . . . they can have a cheerful outlook.[44]

Given that the estimated yield was far above the actual yield, meeting the procurement quota for 1959/60 required a new anti-hoarding campaign in concert with the campaign against right deviation. The oppressive tactics were a success. During a national telephone conference on October 15, Li Xiannian said, "From July 1 to October 10, we took in . . . 7.84 billion kilos more than this time last year." He emphasized that obtaining grain required "a struggle between the two roads of socialism and capitalism, and a struggle of political warfare . . . We need to . . . carry out criticism of right-deviationist thinking."[45]

This brutal political struggle that snatched grain from hungry peasants resulted in glowing reports at the highest levels. The Food Ministry reported on November 27: "The grain procurement drive . . . has been a brilliant success."[46] The report went on to promise that the 1959/60 procurement target set by the CCP Central Committee would be exceeded.

Statistics indicate the cost of this success. Out of all the deaths resulting from China's Great Famine, 60 percent occurred from the winter of 1959 to the winter of 1960.

TABLE 9.6: STATE GRAIN SALES TO THE COUNTRYSIDE DURING THE GREAT FAMINE PERIOD (TRADE GRAIN, IN BILLION KILOS)

	1957/58	1958/59	1959/60	1960/61	1961/62
Full year	20.983	25.2595	26.324	18.1045	13.4225
2nd half year	6.7015	10.0505	8.3465	6.6335	2.858
3rd quarter	4.203	5.11	5.057	4.2235	2.662
July	1.9365	2.109	1.8775	1.757	1.2985
August	1.151	1.578	1.4685	1.3565	0.9865
September	0.9655	1.423	1.211	1.11	0.677
4th quarter	2.4985	4.9405	3.7925	2.41	1.896
October	0.8375	1.803	1.4295	0.898	0.593
November	0.774	1.551	1.105	0.677	0.588
December	0.884	1.5865	1.258	0.835	0.715

(Continued)

TABLE 9.6 (*Continued*)

	1957/58	1958/59	1959/60	1960/61	1961/62
1st half year	14.2815	15.209	17.9745	11.4705	8.5645
1st quarter	4.723	5.513	7.1355	4.473	8.5645
January	1.1095	1.509	1.6815	1.0815	0.8305
February	1.148	1.494	2.0455	1.3065	0.7965
March	2.2065	2.51	3.4085	2.085	1.552
2nd quarter	9.5585	9.691	10.839	6.9975	5.3855
April	2.9545	3.4835	3.401	2.4745	1.909
May	3.6355	3.6435	3.896	2.4715	1.873
June	2.9685	2.569	3.042	2.0515	1.6035

Source: "Food Ministry Planning Bureau Grain Data Summary," August 25, 1962, Central Archives: 1962-180-10-109.

PRESSURING THE VILLAGES TO PRESERVE THE CITIES

The glow of illusory success was short-lived, as a Food Ministry report on July 12, 1960, described a state of emergency in Beijing, Shanghai, and Tianjin, and in ten cities in Liaoning Province and portions of Jilin Province. Grain reserves in Beijing and Tianjin would last only four more days; those in Shanghai, two; and in Liaoning, six.[47]

Most localities no longer dared overreport their grain yields in the summer of 1960. At the National Finance and Trade Secretaries Conference in October, the grain yields reported by each province were even less than the 1957 total output of 180 billion kilos. Procurement proceeded at a glacial pace, and reserves were steadily being depleted. By the end of September, China's eighty-two large and medium-size cities, with a total population of sixty-one million people, held grain reserves at half the level of the year before. Grain was being sold off as fast as it came in. In a report at the National Finance and Trade Secretaries Conference on October 16, Li Xiannian said the sales target for the next nine months (from October through June) had been set about 25 percent lower than that in the previous year. The food ration for the countryside was set even lower. Li said that if the average monthly sales volume were not reduced by 1.3 billion kilos from the year before, the current year's target of increasing the grain reserves by 1.65 billion kilos could not be met. Li insisted that the urban reserves took precedence over the stomachs of the peasants. Without plentiful reserves, he had no way of guaranteeing food provisions for the urban areas.

While the urban food ration fell, rural dwellers were in a much worse position. According to Tan Zhenlin, from October 1960 to June 1961, the monthly per capita food ration was: Shandong, 5.565 kilos; Henan, 8.5 kilos; Hebei, 8.5 kilos; Shanxi, 10 kilos; Liaoning, 10 kilos. These rations were composed primarily of yams. In Henan only 2.5 kilos of the 8.5-kilo food ration was grain, and in Shandong the food ration included no grain at all.[48] This was the amount set by the Center, but as each step of the bureaucracy deducted a portion, the actual amount of food that reached rural households was considerably less.

Throughout the Great Famine, villagers starved so that urban dwellers could live. Wang Minsan, then head of Guizhou's provincial food bureau, recalls a Central Committee disaster-relief telephone conference in late 1959 during which Peng Zhen, the secretary of the Central Committee secretariat, enjoined all provinces to send food aid to Beijing as soon as possible. Peng Zhen said, "The dead in each province are the problem of that province, but deaths in Beijing are a problem for the People's Republic of China." Guizhou was assigned to allocate 50 million kilos of food. Provincial party secretary Zhou Lin displayed great determination, immediately promising that the provincial food bureau would put the shipment together that very night.[49] When Deng Xiaoping went to Sichuan, his comments to Li Jingquan echoed Peng Zhen's: a food shortage in Sichuan had less serious political ramifications than food shortages in the big cities, and Li Jingquan should consider the political situation and send more food to save the cities.[50]

"Saving the cities at the expense of the villages" became explicit policy during the Central Committee work meeting at Lushan in August 1961. In a speech on August 2, Zhou Enlai said,

> As of June of last year, the reserves stood at 15 billion kilos. This year they're down to only 7.35 billion kilos, of which 2.75 billion kilos is new grain. We can't dig further into the reserves. We're preparing to import

5 million tons of food, but foreign exchange is tight. Since adjustments are implemented first in the villages, the situation must also turn for the better there before it can happen in the cities. The problem in the cities is harder to solve. We need to retrench in the villages to preserve the large and medium-sized cities.

From June 1960 to September 1962, Zhou spoke of the food crisis 115 times, and 994 notations in his handwriting can be found in 32 statistical reports that have been preserved by the Food Ministry. His main concern was food supply to the cities.

The Food Ministry's calculations showed that the central reserves would end up with a deficit of 6 billion kilos of trade grain for the year 1961 to 1962. The state planned to import 5 billion kilos to fill that gap, but the Ministry of Foreign Trade believed this would be difficult due to droughts in Canada and Australia and a shortage of foreign exchange. The only solution was to squeeze the peasants. The grain yield for 1961 was only 142.5 billion kilos, and even if this were all retained in the countryside, it would be less than the total rural food ration for 1957 (156.5 billion kilos). In fact, the amount of grain shifted from the villages that year stood at 19.15 billion kilos (derived from 23 billion kilos of unprocessed grain), so the per capita rural grain food ration was 61.5 kilos less than that in 1957.[51] Fortunately, many localities had by then relaxed their collectivization policies. Grain was being produced in private garden plots and on marginal land, and areas that assigned output to households experienced a turnaround; otherwise the death toll in 1961 would have been much higher.

From 1961 to 1962, there were 120 million people on urban food rations. Grain rations totaled 20 billion kilos, not including an additional 5 billion kilos of grain needed for the food industry, nonstaple and condiment production, and industrial use. Even extracting an extra 19.15 billion kilos of grain from the villages would not meet the needs of China's urban areas. For that reason, there was no choice but to reduce the volume of grain sold to the urban areas. The urban grain sales volume in 1961–62 was 6.1 billion kilos lower than that in 1959–60, but was still 2.4 billion kilos greater than that in 1957–58. Imported grain was the only means of making up the deficit. In 1961–62, China imported 5.775 billion kilos of grain. (The imports began in the first half of 1961, and a total of 2.145 billion kilos was imported in 1960–61.)

Beginning in 1961, Tianjin, Beijing, and Shanghai survived on imported grain. During a speech at a conference on August 26, 1961, Li Xiannian said, "We now have more money than commodities. Purchasing power in 1961 stands at 67.5 billion yuan, but we can supply only 65.5 billion yuan in commodities . . . In order to import grain, we must squeeze out each and every exportable item."[52] Export commodities such as pork, eggs, and oil had to be snatched from the peasants, but the imported grain that these exports purchased was supplied to the cities. Again, the cities were preserved at the expense of people in the countryside.

The emergency implementation of household-based output quotas had resulted in more food being produced than in the previous two years, and procurement levels had decreased dramatically, to only 33.95 billion kilos. This concession was forced on the government by the tens of millions dying in the villages. With reserves depleted, however, the government's provision of grain to the countryside also decreased, by 7.5 billion kilos, and peasants were still fighting starvation. According to Food Ministry statistics, in 1960 the per capita rural food supply had decreased by more than 95 kilos from the average in 1955 to 1957. From 1961 to 1962, some 100 million rural residents had access to a maximum of only 250 grams of food per day.

Edible oil exemplified the pressure put on the villages. In the spring of 1959, oil supplies were short, and neither export quotas nor the demand for industrial oil could be met. The CCP Central Committee decided to keep edible oil supplies from the villages. Apart from the rapeseed-growing regions, China's rural areas were not supplied with any edible oil from June to September.[53]

Calorie-deprived peasants were stripped of their one source of fat, in part for the sake of export. From 1958 to 1959, 219 million kilos of edible oil was exported, leaving less than 950 million kilos for domestic consumption. Villagers were also deprived of meat and eggs, which were requisitioned by force for supply to the cities and for export.

THE GREAT FAMINE'S FOOD SUBSTITUTE CAMPAIGN

Faced with food shortages, the entire country sought to develop food substitutes. The Central Committee in November 1960 circulated "Recommendations on the Food Substitute Campaign" by the Chinese Academy of Sciences, which suggested a number of pseudo-foods:

1. *Acorn flour.* Acorns were shelled and crushed, then soaked in a so-
dium carbonate solution for one or two days to remove inedible
tannins and produce an edible starch. The annual production of
acorns was estimated at 4 billion kilos or more. If 20 percent of this
quantity were used to make starch, it would produce 300 million to
350 million kilos.

2. *Powdered roots of corn and wheat.* Roots were ground and crushed
into a powder, with a color and flavor resembling parched flour.
Flour made from corn root and wheat root could produce billions
of kilos of food substitute.

3. *Leaf protein.* Fresh grass, crop leaves, and tree leaves selected for
edibility could produce 1 to 5 kilos of leaf protein powder per 50
kilos of leaves. Obtaining leaf protein from leaves resembled the
process of making bean curd. The gathered leaves (which had to be
processed on the day of collection) were minced, then mixed with
water and ground into syrup. The leaf juice was extracted and then
heated to 70–80 degrees Celsius, a process which formed a protein
sediment. This sediment was then filtered and dried, resulting in the
leaf protein powder.

4. *Man-made meat essence.* This was a food made from enzymes, with
a nutritional content similar to that of meat. An enzyme called "white
mold" (*Geotrichum candidum*) was selected for this purpose from
more than four hundred types of bacteria. The white mold was
placed in a culture solution—this culture could be created by boiling
water left over from washing rice or scouring pots, and from the
outer leaves of vegetables, spoiled fruit, nontoxic tree leaves, weeds,
and the leaves, roots, and runners of crop plants—and maintained
at a temperature of 20–30 degrees Celsius. In two or three days a
white membrane would begin growing on the surface of the solution. This membrane was then dissolved through heating at 50 to 60
degrees Celsius, forming a paste that was the meat substitute essence.

5. *Chlorella*, *Scenedesmus algae*, and *Tetraselmis algae*. Dried algae
powder had a protein content of 20–40 percent and a fat content of
4–6 percent. *Chlorella* and *Scenedesmus* grew in freshwater, and
Tetraselmis in saltwater.

The Central Committee forwarded recommendations from the Chinese Academy of Sciences' Entomology Research Institute on November

14, 1960, on eating insects: "In the space of two weeks we collected more than 600 kilos of edible insects. The bodies of insects are rich in protein and fat. Insects can therefore be used to make soy sauce, *fuyong* (salty fermented bean) sauce, dried meat floss, and edible oils, and with further processing can be made into various kinds of pastries and biscuits." The Entomology Institute suggested toasting, deep-frying, drying, and grinding into powder; oil extraction; and making insects into soy sauce, pastries, and biscuits, particularly recommending thirteen types of insects.

TABLE 9.7: ANALYSIS OF THE NUTRITIONAL CONTENT OF THIRTEEN TYPES OF INSECTS (EXPRESSED AS PERCENTAGE OF THE INSECT'S BODY WEIGHT)

Insect type	Gross protein	Gross fat
Larva of bean hawk moth (dried)	50.8	23.3
Larva of scarab beetle (dung beetle) (dried)	48.1	21.0
Fly maggot (dried)	63.1	25.9
Fly pupa (dried)	41.7	25.1
Larva of corn borer (dried)	41.2	44.8
Larva of tussock moth (dried)	50.6	37.7
Mature larva of cabbage butterfly (dried)	60.6	21.4
Cabbage butterfly pupa (dried)	53.9	24.4
Army worm pupa (fresh)	13.8	6.2
Cotton locust (fresh)	21.3	2.8
Locust (fresh)	18.7	4.1
Termite (fresh)	23.2	28.3
Silkworm pupa (fresh)	23.1	14.2

Source: Chinese Academy of Sciences, Entomology Research Institute, November 1960.

Every locality sent people up to the mountains and into the waters to seek these food substitutes. Food alternatives did help mitigate starvation, but they also caused food poisoning, often with fatal results. In any case, the fundamental source of the famine was not addressed.

THE CALORIC INTAKE LEVEL OF THE PEASANTS

A man from my native village, Wang Meisong, gained expertise in the physiological mechanism of death by starvation. Wang graduated from the Hunan Medical University and worked at the Environmental Medicine Research Institute of the Academy of Military Medical Sciences, researching the physiological changes that occur under special circumstances. He then taught at Tianjin University of Medical Sciences. Back in 1960–61, he led a medical team that treated starvation victims in Hunan Province. His father and uncle both starved to death during the Great Famine. The following comes from Wang's written records and from published materials he provided.

The energy required by the human body for movement

The human body has different energy requirements under different conditions. Even at rest, a human consumes a certain amount of energy to maintain the appropriate body temperature, heart rate, respiration, and muscular tension. This basal metabolic rate is a function of body size, sex, age, and climate. Generally, an adult male weighing 65 kilograms has a basal metabolic rate of 1,560 kilocalories for a 24-hour period.

Labor requires further energy. Light work done while seated, such as office work or watch repair, consumes 2,400 kilocalories per day. Light work conducted in a standing position by, for example, a shop clerk or a teacher, requires 2,600 kilocalories. Moderate labor involving the operation of heavy machinery or driving a tractor or motor vehicle consumes 3,000 kilocalories. Heavy, nonmechanized agricultural labor or semimechanized transport work requires 3,400 kilocalories. Extremely heavy nonmechanized labor such as loading work, mining, tree cutting, or wasteland reclamation consumes 4,000 kilocalories per day.[54] In addition, working outdoors in winter requires more calories.

Most farm work in China was heavy or extremely heavy labor undertaken out of doors, requiring a daily intake of 3,400–4,000 kilocalories.

The caloric intake of Chinese peasants during the Great Famine

During the three years of the Great Famine, the average unprocessed grain ration for a Chinese peasant did not exceed 250 grams per day, equivalent to about 175 grams of processed grain. This ration was largely substituted with sweet potatoes, melons, and vegetables. There was no oil or meat, so the grain ration was the basic source of sustenance.

The average grain ration of 175 grams of rice amounted to 618 calories. Rice was seldom available, however, and eating even sweet potatoes was a stroke of luck. A typical sweet potato ration of 1.25 kilos provided 1,313 calories, which is 337 calories lower than the basal metabolic requirement for an adult male. In some localities vegetables were substituted for grain, and a kilo of cabbage provided only about 160 calories. In some places where the famine hit hardest, even 1.25 kilos of sweet potato or 2.5 kilos of cabbage were beyond reach, and when communal kitchens closed down for lack of food, villagers foraged for grass and tree bark, which provided virtually no calories or nourishment.

When food is inadequate, the lack of protein, hydrocarbons, fat, vitamins, salt, and trace elements results in a variety of illnesses. In the statistical records of that time, deaths from these illnesses were recorded as natural deaths rather than as deaths from starvation.

According to Professor Wang Meisong, the government promoted unscientific hunger alleviation methods that actually exacerbated the suffering of the peasants:

Double-cooked rice: Cooking rice with water in a clay basin, then adding water and cooking again, was said to increase the size of the rice grains and make the rice more filling. In fact, this rice was no different from congee, and hunger returned even faster after the rice was eaten. The government also disseminated the factoid that double-cooking rice increased its nutritional content. In fact, the additional cooking destroyed vitamins, making this rice less nutritious.

Vegetable supplements: Newspapers suggested that replacing grain with vegetables and melons was beneficial to health. In fact, vegetables cannot take the place of grains with regard to either caloric or nutritional value. In addition, vegetables contain relatively large amounts of nitrite, which oxidizes iron in the hemoglobin of the red blood cells and reduces their ability to transport oxygen, resulting in cyanosis of the lips, fingernails, and skin and causing breathing irregularities and death in severe cases, especially in young children. This brought a high incidence of death from what was called Blue Baby Syndrome [*qingzi bing*].

Chaff in steamed buns: Rice straw was soaked in limewater, then minced and added to flour to make steamed buns. The main constituents of rice straw are cellulose and xylem, which have a much more complex carbohydrate structure than sugar. The digestive tracts of grazing animals allow them to put on flesh by eating this material, but the human digestive tract lacks this capacity. Limewater is alkaline and also cannot break down cellulose, so when rice straw is soaked in limewater, humans gain no nourishment from it.

Aged bones: In some localities, the bones of animals that had died years ago were gathered up, smashed into fragments, and boiled into soup. After years of environmental and bacterial decomposition, the bones had no nutritional value apart from some calcium and phosphorus.

THE FATAL PATHOLOGIES OF STARVATION

Medical practitioners divide starvation into three categories: complete starvation (the organism cannot take in any food), incomplete starvation (inadequate caloric intake and inadequate food intake), and partial (qualitative) starvation (adequate caloric intake, but lack of one or more nutritional components essential to the organism).[55] During the Great Famine, peasants in some regions experienced episodic complete starvation conditions, while the country as a whole, including the urban and rural areas, experienced incomplete starvation.

When the body expends more energy than it takes in, it draws on its own glycogen reserves for energy, but these reserves are not enough to sustain the body's basal metabolism for one day. Once the body's glycogen is consumed, the next stage is the depletion of the body's fat content. Complete dependence on the body's fat reserves produces side effects such as the production of large amounts of ketones, which can result in metabolic acidic toxicosis.

Once fat reserves have been depleted, the protein in the internal organs and muscles begins to dissolve. The muscles then become emaciated and the visceral organs begin to atrophy.

When the cardiac muscles begin to atrophy, blood circulation is reduced, and blood pressure drops until heart failure occurs. Professor Wang Meisong's medical team treated edema victims in a commune school, typically two hundred at a time. He observed that most edema patients ultimately died of heart failure.

The next stage in starvation is atrophy of the kidneys, pituitary gland, thyroid gland, sex glands, and other endocrine glands. The gastrointestinal tract's mucous membrane shrinks, reducing its ability to digest and absorb nutrients.

Atrophy of the reproductive organs caused by lack of protein leads to improper development of the uterus in young females, known as uterine hypoplasia. Amenorrhea is even more common. Atrophy of the supporting structure of the uterus may also cause the uterus to drop into the vaginal canal, a condition known as uterine prolapse.

Reports to the central government attested to the pervasiveness of amenorrhea and uterine prolapse in the countryside.[56] They were consistent with the surveys carried out by Professor Wang Meisong's medical team, which found entire counties where only a tiny minority of premenopausal women menstruated. This minority belonged to cadre families who took more than their fair share of food and other resources. Among men in the prime of life, it was common to find atrophy of the testicles and inability to produce semen. Starvation was therefore accompanied by a severe drop in the birth rate.

During a food shortage, the first symptom that becomes apparent is protein-energy malnutrition. An individual cannot perform various physical movements, the body loses strength, and all functions decline. Reduced protein content in the blood plasma brings a drop in the osmotic pressure of the plasma colloids, accompanied by an increase in the permeability of the blood vessels. This allows fluids to seep through the blood vessel walls into the surrounding subcutaneous tissue, causing edema throughout the body.

The body's various enzymes and hormones are made up primarily of protein, and the inability to synthesize enzymes and hormones, such as insulin and anterior pituitary hormones, results in symptoms such as an inability to digest and absorb protein and fats. Without sufficient protein, the body cannot generate antibodies and loses its resistance to disease. Inadequate intake of protein and carbohydrates over the long term depletes the body's internal fats and exhausts muscle proteins, causing the sufferer to appear emaciated and skeletal, a condition known as marasmus.

The length of time that life can be sustained in starvation conditions depends on the degree of energy and protein deprivation and the body's original nutritional level. Life may continue for as long as several years, or as short as a few months. Once body weight drops below 70 percent of its normal level, the victim can seldom be saved.

These descriptions apply to conditions of "incomplete starvation." During the Great Famine, peasants in some parts of China experienced "complete starvation" with access to water. This process can be divided into three stages: (1) the euphoric stage, lasting three to four days; (2) the inhibition stage, lasting thirty-five to forty days; and (3) the paralysis stage, lasting two to three days.

The euphoric stage occurs primarily during the depletion of the body's glycogen. When the glycogen is almost completely used up, the process switches over to breaking down the body's fat content. When the fats are almost entirely depleted, the metabolic regulating function is severely obstructed, and protein formation experiences a sharp breakdown.

Edema is less common in complete starvation. It is most likely to emerge in the last stage, when blood plasma protein is reduced and there is a drop in the blood colloid osmotic pressure.

Changes in the visceral organs are not as apparent in complete starvation as they are in incomplete starvation. In particular, the heart usually shrinks more slowly. However, heart failure progresses much more quickly, because the heart's strength is related to the supply of sugar. The other internal organs are consumed at a rate inverse to their importance to survival.[57] In comparison with incomplete starvation, complete starvation may involve the loss of 40 percent or even more than half of body weight before death occurs.

In conditions of extreme hunger, all of the human body's functions, movements, and capacities decline, and at a certain stage, an instinctual and extremely intense hunger reflex kicks in. The instinct for survival drives a starvation victim to seek out anything that can be eaten. Survival takes precedence over all else, and animal nature overtakes human nature. Human beings at the extreme of hunger pay no regard to affection, morality, or dignity; hence the incomplete statistics showing thousands of instances of cannibalism during the Great Famine.

10 TURNAROUND IN LUSHAN

Following the Beidaihe Conference in August 1958, the Great Leap Forward created general chaos. To control the situation, Mao and the Central Committee adopted rectification measures from November 1958 to June 1959. By June and July of 1959, the worst fanaticism had subsided, and many attending the Lushan Conference believed its purpose was to rectify leftist errors.

The Lushan Conference was held for forty-six days, from July 2 through August 16, 1959. An enlarged meeting of the CCP Central Committee Politburo went until August 2. The Eighth Plenum of the Eighth CCP Central Committee was held from August 2 to 16. Had it not been for the Lushan Conference, the momentum of the rectification efforts in the first half of 1959 might have soon ended the food crisis, reducing the death toll by more than two-thirds. Instead, the Lushan Conference intensified the policies of 1958, thereby extending the devastating effect of the Great Famine by an additional three to four years.

Mao's feelings were complicated. What he feared most was being accused of line errors. In CCP history, line errors led to reshuffles in the central leadership. The leader could only step down, and a leader obliged to step down over a line error would come to no good end. If the situation reached such a turn, Mao might follow in the footsteps of Chen Duxiu, Zhang Guotao, Wang Ming, Bo Gu, and Li Lisan.[1] Mao's supporters therefore spared no effort in protecting him and attacking his detractors.

Chen Yun had been in charge of economic work until 1958, when Mao demanded, "Is it only Chen Yun who can manage the economy? Can't I do it?" In 1959, Mao acknowledged his error, telling Wu Lengxi, "I'm afraid people like us aren't suited to economic affairs," and "Last year I fought a losing battle."[2]

Already in the summer of 1959, when the Central Committee leaders in frontline operations issued rectification policies, Mao considered the policies right deviating.[3] Prior to the Lushan Conference, he was depressed, aggrieved, apprehensive, and resentful.

Mao carried out self-criticism of his 1958 errors during the expanded Politburo meeting held on June 12–13. He said, "This was the first time I took charge of industry, and like the Autumn Harvest Uprising I led in 1927, I lost this first battle. But it wasn't only my mistake—the rest of you here were also involved." He described how back in 1927 he had hidden in the fields all night and hadn't dared move even the next day, only rejoining his troops on the third day. "I was completely disoriented at the time because I had never before led troops in battle; I had no experience. I also had no experience handling the economy, and my first battle in this area was also a failure."

He said,

Last year [1958] we committed at least three major errors: First, the plan was too ambitious and the targets too high; it had to be forced through, which inevitably upset the equilibrium and dislocated the economy. Second, too much power was delegated to the lower levels, and everyone went in their own direction. Policy descended into chaos, and too much money was spent. Third, the commune system was developed too quickly and didn't go through experimentation and testing; it was just pushed out in one fell swoop and stirred up the Communist Wind, and the cadres couldn't manage it. Now food supplies are tight, mostly because of falsely reporting output as well as providing free meals and letting everyone eat to their hearts' content.[4]

Mao also said, "A man has to be better than a pig; when you hit a wall, you need to change directions." Such words led some leaders to believe Mao was prepared to "change direction."

On June 29, while taking the boat from Wuchang to attend the Lushan Conference, Mao convened a meeting of the heads of the region. On the key issue of assessing the current situation and evaluating 1958, he set the tone: "The achievements have been great, the problems many, and the future is bright."[5]

Many other top leaders and senior provincial officials resolutely defended the Three Red Banners. Ke Qingshi in Shanghai and Li Jingquan in Sichuan were two of Mao's mainstays. Among the senior Beijing officials, Lin Biao and Kang Sheng were also staunch supporters. Zhou Enlai, who had recently been criticized for opposing rash advance, now stood firmly behind Mao. Most officials adopted an attitude of self-preservation and bent with the wind, while some hoped a new round of political infighting might give them an advantage over political rivals.

Mao had formulated his verdict that "the achievements have been great, the problems many, and the future is bright" while on an inspection visit of Hunan in the company of Zhou Xiaozhou on June 23. During this trip he also returned to his native village for the first time in thirty-two years before proceeding to Wuhan and arriving at Lushan by boat on June 29.

Discontent was seething. Even in a system in which subordinates tended to report only what the leader wanted to hear, Mao had received documents criticizing the Three Red Banners prepared for the Lushan Conference: In May 1959, more than eighty county party committee cadres at the Jiangxi Provincial Party School blasted the Three Red Banners as devoid of merit, and a report by the political department of the Guangzhou Military Region's Forty-second Group Army called for the Central Committee to take responsibility for "line errors." Cadres of the State Council secretariat criticized the communes and the steel-forging campaign; party cadres throughout Tianjin were "virtually unanimous in negating the Great Leap Forward"; and the leaders of the democratic parties were even more scathing in their criticism of the Three Red Banners. The outcry among lower-level cadres was actually much more vociferous than these carefully selected reports conveyed.

Even a substantial number of officials within Mao's inner circle considered the problems of 1958 very grave. From June 27 to July 1, members of the central leadership traveling to the Lushan Conference took a reserved train from Beijing to Wuhan, then a boat to Jiujiang, during which there was unfettered discussion of the many problems that had arisen during the Great Leap Forward. CCP Central Committee Propaganda Department chief and State Council vice-premier Lu Dingyi accompanied defense minister Peng Dehuai throughout the journey. Shortly before setting off for Lushan, Lu had been ordered by Zhou Enlai to conduct inquiries regarding the great steel-forging campaign. Lu had found much that troubled him, in particular widespread fraud and deception, enormous waste, and the deployment of the strongest laborers to the steel

foundries, leaving grain unharvested in the fields. He shared these observations with Peng Dehuai, who was extremely concerned.[6]

Like other officials attending the Lushan Conference, Li Rui believed
its purpose was to counter leftism. He later told me, "Even the materials
Ke Qingshi brought up the hill were for opposing leftism, and when the
conference changed directions, he was obliged to have anti-rightist materials sent up from Shanghai."

In hindsight, it seems Mao's actual intention was never that simple.
Having already perceived the precariousness of his position and that
people were challenging the Three Red Banners, he opened the conference on the afternoon of July 10 with an emphasis on evaluating the situation according to one's views on the Three Red Banners. He warned,
"If we don't share common ground on this question, the party cannot
achieve unity; this is a major issue that affects the entire party and all the
people."[7] It appears that he wished to correct some specific errors, but he
would not allow criticism of the Three Red Banners.

During the first few days, attendees freely aired their views on problems brought on by the Great Leap Forward. Mao, however, resisted such
criticism in a speech on July 23:

> So an advanced cooperative (now called a production brigade) commits
> one error. For 700,000-odd production brigades, that's hundreds of thou-
> sands of errors. Even in a year's time, you couldn't report on all of them,
> and what would we get for it? The country would collapse. Even without
> an invasion by the imperialists, the peasants would rise up in revolt and
> overthrow the lot of us . . . If nine out of ten matters are bad and all of
> them are reported, everything will be wiped out—and should be. I'll just
> leave, go back to the countryside, and lead the peasants to overthrow the
> government. If the People's Liberation Army [PLA] isn't willing to go
> with me, I'll get the Red Army—I'll organize a new liberation army. But I
> think the PLA would go with me.[8]

Since Mao was fundamentally opposed to any criticism of 1958, why
arrange for a conference of unfettered discussion? It was simply to lure
the snakes from their dens, a method he had used with spectacular success in the run-up to the 1957 Anti-Rightist Campaign. During the Shanghai Conference in March and April 1959, he had talked up Hai Rui[9] and

advocated the "Hai Rui spirit," while giving a copy of *The Biography of Hai Rui* to Peng Dehuai. At that same conference, Mao spoke of Peng Dehuai, saying, "Many people hate me, especially Comrade Peng Dehuai—he absolutely loathes me, or at least certainly hates me to a substantial degree. My policy toward Comrade Peng Dehuai is this: 'If you don't mess with me, I won't mess with you; if you mess with me, I'll certainly mess with you.' This isn't my approach toward Comrade Peng Dehuai alone, but toward all other comrades as well."[10] According to one insider, "At one point the Chairman said jokingly to Peng, 'Marshal, let's reach an agreement: after I die, don't stage a revolt. Can you manage that?'"[11] During the Lushan Conference, Mao drew Peng out to "mess with him," then leveled his heavy artillery to "mess with" Peng.

During the first days of the conference, Henan's provincial first secretary, Wu Zhipu, acknowledged that the Communist Wind and Exaggeration Wind had been virulent in Henan and had affected the whole country, for which he apologized to all the other provinces. Hubei's provincial first secretary spoke with a heavy heart of the situation in Hubei. Hunan's provincial first secretary said the overall situation gave little ground for optimism. Yet others constantly interrupted to defend the Great Leap Forward, making some critics reluctant to speak frankly. The defenders included top officials such as senior general Luo Ruiqing and vice-premier Tan Zhenlin.

Among the reference materials for the conference were several documents negating the Three Red Banners, which Mao distributed without comment.[12] While suggesting an "anti-leftist" agenda, they served as bait for Mao's trap. On two occasions between July 10 and 16, Mao made a point of calling in his "rightist friends" Zhou Xiaozhou, Zhou Hui, and Li Rui for a chat, and the tone of the conversation was light and friendly. The bookish Li Rui naïvely felt that "the midsummer hillside was bathed with a spring breeze that facilitated heartfelt expression," and that "going further upstairs to the hall of sundry voices," "from everyone's heart flowed the ultimate words of truth." In fact, these two meetings turned out to be "reconnaissance missions" for Mao.

Scheduled to last half a month, the conference continued with no sign of adjournment. Mao delivered all his speeches off the cuff and steered the direction of the conference, giving him the advantage of surprise in his attacks.

PENG DEHUAI PLEADS ON BEHALF OF THE PEOPLE

Peng Dehuai had been Mao's comrade-in-arms at Jinggang Mountain from 1927 to 1934, when Mao developed his strategy of guerrilla warfare. Relations between the two had been very close; Peng would come in and chat with Mao without ceremony, and if Mao was in bed, Peng would push aside his quilt to sit down and chat. Even after Mao "ascended the throne," Peng had no patience for yelling out "Long live!" to Mao or singing "The East Is Red," and rather than addressing Mao as "Chairman," he continued to refer to him as "Old Mao." This breached the imperial tone of the new regime.

During the Great Leap Forward, Peng served as a member of the CCP Central Committee Politburo and the Central Military Commission, as vice-premier of the State Council, and as defense minister. At the outset he joined in the enthusiasm, but when he became aware of the actual situation, his views changed.[13]

At the Wuchang Conference in November 1958, Peng objected to announcing a grain yield of 500 billion kilos for 1958. Eventually Mao proposed announcing a yield of 375 billion kilos, and Peng went along, although he harbored doubts.[14] After the Wuchang Conference, Peng accompanied Hunan's provincial first secretary, Zhou Xiaozhou, on an inspection tour of Hunan and concluded that the grain yield could not be as high as the figure announced. After learning of falsified figures, he felt that the procurement quota based on the announced total grain yield would prove excessive, and he sent a telegram to the Central Committee saying that the procurement target should be lowered by 25 percent. During his Hunan inspection tour, Peng found peasants suffering from hunger, with residents of one senior center fed only 100 to 150 grams of rice per day. A crippled veteran slipped Peng a note: "The grain is scattered, the potato leaves withered, and the young and strong are sent to the steel mills, leaving children and women to bring in the harvest; how are we to survive the coming year? Please get word back on behalf of the people!" The misery of the peasants and the criminal folly of the cadres struck Peng with full force in his own native place. How could he fail to "get word back" to Lushan on behalf of the people?

In May 1959, Peng visited several countries in Eastern Europe, returning to Beijing in mid-June. While in Hungary, Peng had learned that the main cause of the 1956 Hungarian uprising had been an expansion of purges and leftist errors in economic work. He told Hungarian leader János Kádár, "It's not our enemies who are the greatest threat—worst of all is when the party's line is incorrect and the party's work becomes disconnected from the masses. This is the most important lesson we've gained from experience."

When Peng returned to Beijing, he carefully read internal reference documents and sent the Chairman items showing that the situation was serious. There were many such documents. At the end of June, Peng was sent a notice requiring his attendance at the Lushan Conference. He went with great reluctance.[15]

On the train from Beijing to Wuhan, he shared a compartment with Zhang Wentian, He Long, Kang Sheng, and others, and there was much casual conversation. Peng mentioned that in Hungary people ate 20 kilos of meat per year and still revolted, and said it was only the decency of China's workers and peasants that prevented the Red Army from having to be called in.[16] These remarks of his were later deemed a serious political error.

During the open discussion at the outset of the conference, Peng frankly expressed his views, with some of his comments touching upon Mao Zedong:

> July 3—"The grain yield figures provided by the commune in the Chairman's home village were higher than the reality. From what I've learned, the yield increased by just 16 percent. I asked Comrade Zhou Xiaozhou, and he said that the commune's yield increased by only 14 percent, and that was with a great deal of help and financial loans from the state. The Chairman has also visited that commune, and I asked him, 'What do you think of it?' He said he didn't discuss this matter, but I believe he did."

> July 4—"We have to learn from experience without grumbling or calling to account. Everyone shares the blame, including Comrade Mao Zedong. The figure of 10.7 [million tons of steel in a year] was Chairman Mao's idea, so why should he not share responsibility? At the Shanghai Conference he performed a self-criticism and admitted he'd gotten a little hotheaded."

> July 6—"In our party it's usually hard to correct 'leftism,' while 'rightism' is relatively easy to correct. Once 'leftism' starts, it takes over everything else, and no one dares to speak out."

July 7—"I think we started on the people's communes a bit too early. The advantages of the collectives were just beginning to show themselves, and they hadn't reached their full potential when we started on the communization movement. In addition, we didn't carry out trial runs. If we'd tested the method for a year before launching it, that would have been better."

July 8—"There are different rules for politics and economics, and that's why ideological education cannot replace economic work. Chairman Mao and the party have a popular credibility unequaled anywhere else in the world, but it's wrong to abuse this public trust. The chaotic transmission of the Chairman's ideas last year caused a lot of problems."

"No one pays any attention these days to collective decisions by the party committees—instead, one man makes the decisions. The first secretary's decision counts, but not the second secretary's. There's been no building up of collective credibility, only individual credibility. This is irregular and dangerous."

Ke Qingshi passed along these sharp comments to Mao, and they later became ammunition against Peng.[17]

According to Peng, Hunan's first party secretary, Zhou Xiaozhou, came to talk with him twice during the opening stage of the conference.[18] During their initial chat on July 5, Peng told Zhou that in January, Mao had called in several people to discuss the iron and steel targets, and that Chen Yun had considered the target of 20 million tons impossible to achieve. Peng said that upon his return from Europe, he reported to Mao, and that when he talked of dozens of people around Yugoslavia's Tito fleeing to Albania, Mao's face suddenly flushed red. Peng also told Zhou that it was difficult to launch discussions on some issues within the Central Committee's standing committee; some members found it inconvenient to speak, some were incapable of speaking, and some said very little. Peng told Zhou that he had some views he wanted to discuss with Mao, but he was afraid of misspeaking and causing Mao's displeasure. On the other hand, the worst he would suffer for his offense would be dismissal, and that was of no consequence.

During their second conversation, on July 12, Zhou said the grain figures for the previous year were bogus, and he mentioned the problems of the communal kitchens. Peng suggested that these problems be truthfully relayed to the Chairman. Zhou said that he and others had recently been called in for a chat with Mao, observing, "We spoke very freely, and the Chairman was able to accept it." He hoped Peng would seek out the Chairman for a talk. Peng said he was afraid he'd express himself poorly; some of his ideas weren't yet completely thought out, and he hadn't yet brought them up. For that reason he was considering writing a letter, and Zhou Xiaozhou agreed with this idea.[19]

By that afternoon, however, Peng decided it would be better to talk with Mao. He went to Mao's quarters, but found him asleep. Mindful that the conference would end in a few days' time, Peng resolved to write a letter.[20]

On the morning of July 13, an outline in hand, Peng dictated the detailed contents to his aide-de-camp. After rearranging and editing the record, he made two copies and had one delivered to Mao on the afternoon of July 14. Peng may never have anticipated that this letter would have such an explosive impact, or that it would leave such a deep imprint on Chinese history.

Peng started his letter affirming that "the accomplishments of the 1958 Great Leap Forward are absolutely undeniable." He found that

the capital construction projects of 1958 now look to have been a bit too numerous and carried out a bit too hastily; funding had been diverted from some necessary projects, which had been postponed, and that was a shortcoming . . . For that reason, the plans for next year (1960) should be drawn up on a practical, realistic, safe, and reliable basis and be handled with careful consideration. Regarding some capital construction projects that could not in fact be completed in 1958 and the first half of 1959, we must employ the utmost resolution to suspend them. We'll have to cut our losses to make the best of the situation; otherwise the serious imbalance will be prolonged, and it will be difficult to shake off our disadvantaged situation in some areas.

Peng also affirmed, "The 1958 rural communization movement was of enormous significance; it will not only allow China's peasants to thoroughly shake off poverty but will expedite . . . China's transition from socialism to communism. There was a period of confusion related to the ownership question, and some shortcomings and errors emerged in the course of concrete operations, which of course must be taken seriously.

However, these problems have been largely resolved through a series of conferences."

Peng found much to praise: "During the 1958 Great Leap Forward, we solved the problem of unemployment. In a populous, economically backward country such as ours, such a rapid resolution is no small matter but a very great one."

On the steel-forging campaign, Peng said, "Setting up too many backyard blast furnaces and wasting some resources (material and financial) and manpower inevitably incurred substantial losses. But what we gained from it was a preliminary nationwide geological survey on an enormous scale and the training of a substantial number of technical personnel. A large number of cadres were also trained and improved through this campaign. Although we had to 'pay some tuition' (in the order of 2 billion yuan in subsidies), even in this respect there were both losses and gains." (Mao noted that Peng placed "losses" before "gains.")

In summation:

Some of the shortcomings and errors that emerged during the 1958 Great Leap Forward were largely unavoidable. Just as in the repeated revolutions of our party over more than thirty years, the great accomplishments have been accompanied by some shortcomings; they're two sides of the same coin. The obvious contradictions we're now facing . . . arise from an imbalance that has caused strains . . . They have affected relations between workers and peasants, and between the different social classes in the urban areas and among the peasants. In this respect they are political in nature and are critical to our continued ability to mobilize the masses and further implement the leap forward.

The shortcomings . . . had various causes. The objective factor was our inadequate familiarity with the process of building socialism and our relative lack of experience. Our understanding of the laws of socialism's planned proportional development was not deep enough, and the guiding principle of the two-pronged approach was not implemented on the ground in all cases. In handling the problems of building the economy, we've proved less proficient than in our handling of political problems such as the shelling of Jinmen and suppressing the uprising in Tibet.[21]

Peng took note of "the burgeoning climate of exaggeration" and "petty bourgeois fanaticism, which easily leads to leftist error." He held that "political commandism cannot replace the laws of economics, and even less can it replace concrete measures in economic work." He concluded, "Correcting these leftist phenomena will generally be more difficult than countering right-deviating conservatism; this has been borne out by the historical experience of our party."[22]

Peng's measured and moderate letter was intolerable to Mao. After receiving the letter, Mao on July 16 had it printed and distributed "to all comrades as reference" under the heading "Comrade Peng Dehuai's Written Opinions."

Peng hadn't expected his letter to be distributed as a "written opinion." On July 18 he requested that the letter be withdrawn, declaring that it had been written on the spur of the moment and that it did not express his views with sufficient clarity.[23] Kang Sheng, an expert in political persecution, wrote a note to Mao on the same day that Peng's letter was distributed, saying, "I boldly suggest that this cannot be handled with lenience."[24]

Most attendees agreed with Peng's letter, but quite a few felt that some phrases could be reconsidered. The second part of the letter was considered too critical. Hu Qiaomu, Zhou Xiaozhou, and Li Rui strongly supported the letter. A Shanxi official said, "We need Marshal Peng's spirit at this time." A military cadre also fully endorsed Peng's letter.[25] All those who supported Peng were subsequently criticized and punished.

Huang Kecheng, the People's Liberation Army general chief of staff, was summoned to Lushan on July 17 as Mao's first move in his attack on Peng Dehuai. Having Huang retain command of the military in Beijing while Peng was being criticized in Lushan left Mao feeling vulnerable. Now Mao could have the whole "gang" rounded up. On the evening that Huang arrived, Peng told him that he'd written a letter to Mao and he gave Huang a copy. Huang responded, "I agree with the views in this letter, but it's poorly phrased; some of the wording is too harsh. What were you thinking?" Peng said, "The situation is so serious, but no one has been willing to speak out at the conference, so I hoped to write something that would be taken seriously."[26]

On July 18, Zhou Xiaozhou, Zhou Hui, and Li Rui called on Huang and told him of the pressure preventing people from talking of shortcomings. Huang said that at this point speaking out "didn't seem advisable." Around this time, Huang had a tiff with a radical promoter of the Great Leap Forward, Tan Zhenlin, who angrily said, "We brought you up the mountain as a means of calling in reinforcements; we expect you to support us." Huang replied, "Then you made a mistake; I'm not your reinforcement, I'm your opponent."[27] Huang was subsequently criticized for "plotting rebellion."

Before Mao launched his counterattack, few at the conference criticized Peng. Critics included Chen Zhengren, who was involved in the Communist experiment in Xushui and was influenced by Ke Qingshi, with whom he shared quarters during the conference. Another critic was He Long, who on July 21 said, "The main problem at present is a lack of drive, not an overheated mentality or false reporting." He criticized Peng's letter, saying,

> Our shortcomings don't even constitute one finger. In such a huge country with such an enormous population, how can we not expect shortcomings and errors? In any case, these were very quickly addressed due to the brilliant leadership of the Central Committee and Chairman Mao . . . For this reason, my view of Marshal Peng's letter to the Chairman is that its overall assessment is inappropriate and that it places too much emphasis on problems . . . I remember Marshal Peng once said on the train, "If it weren't for the decency of China's workers and peasants, the Red Army would have been called in by now." This is obviously a great overstatement of the case.[28]

He Long's harsh attack on Peng can probably be attributed in large part to their different power bases in the military. Both Peng and Mao referred to the Red Army in terms of a new revolution. Deng Liqun, however, in a conversation about the Lushan Conference on April 16, 1998,[29] added the term *Soviet* before *Red Army*, stubbornly maintaining his allegation of Peng having "illicit relations with a foreign country."

On July 17, two days after Peng submitted his letter, Mao called in Zhou Xiaozhou, Zhou Hui, Li Rui, Hu Qiaomu, and Tian Jiaying for a chat that lasted from 5:00 to 10:00 p.m. as they ate, drank Maotai, and bantered. Li Rui felt that "Mao Zedong had not yet made a full turn to the left and did not yet intend to launch a counterattack."[30]

As it happened, not long after Peng returned to China, on July 18, Soviet leader Nikita Khrushchev addressed a mass rally in Poland, stating that the communes organized shortly after the Russian Civil War had achieved little due to the economic and political conditions at the time.

They had then been abandoned, and the peasants organized into coopera-tives. Deng Liqun subsequently blamed Khrushchev's remarks for the victimization of Peng,[31] observing, "The Soviet Union's newspaper and its leader's remarks criticized our errors, and these remarks were very similar to Peng Dehuai's. For that reason, the suspicion arose of col-laboration inside and outside of China."[32] It is clear, however, that Mao had turned against Peng before learning of Khrushchev's criticism of the communes, so Deng Liqun's words do not reflect the truth of the matter.

MAO ZEDONG'S AGGRESSION OVERTURNS
HEAVEN AND EARTH

By July 21 the leftists had denounced Peng's letter as "targeting Chairman Mao." It is uncertain how much they influenced Mao. Many sensed which way Mao was going. Zhang Wentian had prepared a speech, but Hu Qiaomu, who had already gotten wind of what was coming, telephoned Zhang and advised him to make little mention of shortcomings.[33] Zhang Wentian ignored the advice, and his three-hour-long speech was repeat-edly interrupted by group head Ke Qingshi and several others expressing dissenting views.

Zhang Wentian, also known as Luo Fu, had joined the party in 1925 and was appointed head of the Central Committee's Propaganda De-partment in 1931. During the Yan'an period, Zhang was one of the CCP's top leaders, along with Mao Zedong, Zhou Enlai, Liu Shaoqi, and Zhu De, and he had served as ambassador to the Soviet Union and first vice-foreign minister, and as an alternate member of the Politburo.[34] Zhang's views were straightforward, incisive, and highly focused. Regarding the causes of the problems, he said, "It is not enough to attribute them to lack of experience; they should be explored in terms of ideological and work methods." Leading the economy "purely through political command was untenable." He believed that the crux of the problems lay in strengthen-ing democracy within the party.

> The Chairman always says we must dare to express differing views, even if it means death from a thousand cuts or beheading, and so on. This is right. But it's not enough to simply tell people not to fear death; people will always fear death. It doesn't matter so much to die at the hands of

the Kuomintang, but dying at the hands of the Communist Party would bring eternal disgrace. So the other side of the coin is that the leadership must create an environment that encourages those below to dare to express their opinions and create a situation that is lively, vital, and free.

Zhang's speech mentioned Peng's letter at the end. He noted that the part of Peng's letter that had drawn the most criticism was his comment about "petty bourgeois fanaticism," and even people who supported Peng had found that objectionable. In Zhang Wentian's view, "It may have been better not to mention this problem, but bringing it up caused no harm—it can be considered either way. But I'm afraid that the 'Communist Wind' was also petty bourgeois fanaticism."[35]

That evening, Zhang encountered Peng and said, "I spoke for three hours today defending you." Peng took a copy of Zhang Wentian's outline and read it. Afterward he told Zhang, "You were very comprehensive."

Some said that Zhang's speech "comprehensively and systematically elaborated" on Peng's letter, and that it was "an attack on the General Line, the Great Leap Forward, and the people's communes, and opposed the party's guiding principles." A textual analysis of the speech's 9,000 words showed only 270 words devoted to accomplishments. The word *but* was used thirty-nine times, and in all but one instance was followed by something negative.[36]

At that time, Zhang was vice-foreign minister. On the train to the Lushan Conference, he had shared a compartment with Peng Dehuai, He Long, and Kang Sheng. Upon arrival at Lushan, he stayed next door to Peng's quarters. From July 2 to 16, Zhang was in the North China group. He told the group that the Great Leap Forward had put the Foreign Ministry's work in a disadvantaged position. Early on during the conference, while reading the Soviet Union's *Textbook on Political Economy* (third edition), he told his secretary that the backyard steel-smelting furnaces were useless, that the economy had gone out of balance, and that distribution according to work done should not be violated. He found it was all a result of hubris.

During a conversation with Peng on July 12, Zhang complained, "We're only allowed to talk about the good things, not about the bad things. There's pressure." Peng said, "It's the same in our group." Zhang said, "Comrade Mao Zedong is very sharp and ruthless in persecuting others, just like Stalin in his last years. Comrade Mao Zedong has learned many good things from Chinese history, but he's also learned some of the political tricks of Old China's ruling class. We have to prevent the errors of Stalin's last years."[37] In early and mid-July, Peng and Zhang had a number of conversations about the long, meaningless speeches in Politburo meetings.[38] On July 14, Zhang walked over to Peng's quarters and learned that Peng was planning to write a letter to Mao. He expressed agreement with Peng's intention of laying out the problems in a way that was both wide-ranging and in-depth. Peng wanted Zhang to look at the letter, but Zhang declined. Peng began reading it to him, but before he finished, Zhang walked away.[39]

From July 17 to August 1, Zhang Wentian was assigned to the second group (East China group), and on July 18 he began preparing the outline for his speech to the group. The next day, after the group meeting, Tian Jiaying invited Zhang to his quarters for a talk. On the way there, they came upon Zhou Xiaozhou, Chen Boda, Hu Qiaomu, Wu Lengxi, and Li Rui and invited them along. All acknowledged feeling under pressure and thought that after affirming accomplishments, they should be allowed to bring up shortcomings. Zhang also had subsequent one-on-one conversations with critics. Then, around July 20, Tian Jiaying telephoned Zhang and advised him to avoid certain topics, because "those above" had different opinions. This was followed by a phone call from Hu Qiaomu, who said that Mao was preparing to attack Peng. He advised Zhang to keep his thoughts to himself. Zhang's secretary likewise felt that Zhang's speech was not consistent with the tone the conference had adopted toward Peng, and worried that Zhang would also come under criticism. Zhang ignored all this advice.[40]

In Li Rui's view, "There were many reasons leading to Mao Zedong's speech on July 23. Zhang Wentian's long and pointed speech may have been the last straw."[41]

On July 22, Mao called in several people. Ke Qingshi and Li Jingquan criticized attempts to correct leftism. Ke said, "We really need Chairman Mao to speak out and block further development of this trend; otherwise the ranks will disperse." In his view, Peng's speech targeted the General Line and Chairman Mao. That evening, Mao met with Liu Shaoqi and Zhou Enlai to prepare for a plenary session the following day.[42]

On the morning of July 23 everyone was called to a meeting at which the Chairman would speak. The contents of Mao's speech had not been discussed in advance with members of the standing committee, who like all the other conference attendees had not been notified of Mao's intention to speak until that morning.

Mao began by saying he'd taken three sleeping pills without being able to fall asleep. He described "two trends" at the conference: "One is not to touch on certain matters and to jump if they are touched upon . . . I've advised these comrades that we have to listen to the negative comments." The other trend was "being attacked from both inside and outside the party . . . There is a group of people who regard the present situation as a complete mess." "The more we're told that things are a mess, the more we must listen. 'We must brace ourselves to bear up under it' . . . The Celestial Kingdom will not sink into the ground, the sky will not fall. And why not? Because we've done some good things, and we have strong support." "Why aren't we being tough? It's just a matter of having a little less pork for a time, or fewer hairpins, or a shortage of soap. It's called a proportional imbalance—industrial, agricultural, commercial, and communications supplies are all strained, and that makes people tense. But I don't see any reason to be nervous."

Mao then targeted Peng for "saying we've disconnected ourselves from the masses. I think this was temporary, a matter of two or three months . . . There has been a little bit of petty bourgeois fanaticism, but not so much . . . Because we're so poor, we want to introduce communism sooner. Now we hear of these places actually implementing communism, so why not go for a look? What view should we take of this enthusiasm?" "These cadres are leading hundreds of millions of people . . . They want communes, communal kitchens, large-scale cooperatives, large-scale farming—they're very enthusiastic. If they want to do these things, does it have to be called petty bourgeois fanaticism?"

Of the Communist Wind and reallocation without compensation, Mao said, "We spent more than a month suppressing the wind in March and April this year, and where retreat was called for, it was carried out. The accounting between the communes and production teams was clarified, and the accounting between the production teams and the masses in some places was also clarified, and where it's not yet clear, the process is ongoing."

Overenthusiastic cadres had "carried out who knows how many self-criticisms. Since . . . last November there have been . . . conferences where all had to criticize themselves . . . We've criticized ourselves so many times; wasn't anybody paying attention?" "[Criticism of the Great Leap Forward] has been nothing more than blather; they cursed three generations of ancestors . . . When I was a young fellow, hearing this kind of slander made me boil with anger. I'm the kind of person who doesn't mess with others if they don't mess with me, but if someone messes with me, I'll definitely mess with them; someone has to mess with me before I'll mess with them. I've never abandoned this principle to this day."

Next Mao pointed out, "I advise another group of comrades, at this crucial juncture, don't vacillate . . . If now we're supposed to talk about petty bourgeois fanaticism, then let's turn it around—that campaign against rash development, it was a kind of petty bourgeois what? Fanaticism? The bourgeois mentality is not fanatical; it's cold, cheerless, heart-breaking despair, and pessimism."

To Mao, those who criticized the Great Leap Forward were "going down the same path as those comrades who erred in the last half of 1956 and the first half of 1957" by criticizing rash advance.

Mao conceded he had committed "two offenses":

First, the 10.7 million tons of steel was my decision and my suggestion. As a result, 90 million people went to the steel mills along with 4 billion yuan in subsidies, and the results didn't match the expenditure. Second, I didn't invent the people's communes, but I promoted them . . . When I discovered the model commune of Chayashan . . . I felt I had gained possession of a great treasure. If that's what you call petty bourgeois fanaticism, so be it . . . You see, "The creator of bad precedent will be cursed with a lack of progeny." Am I without heirs? In Chinese custom, only male offspring count. My one son was killed, and another son is mad, so I regard this as having no offspring. One big steel-forging campaign, one people's commune . . . The creator of bad precedent is me, and my line should be extinguished.

After the meeting, Peng stood outside the door, and when Mao emerged, he hurried over and said, "Chairman, I'm your student; if I've said something wrong, you can criticize and instruct me to my face. Why do you have to do it this way?" Mao waved Peng off and strode away.[43]

Returning to their quarters, Peng and Huang Kecheng had no appetite and were silent.[44] After that, Peng Dehuai didn't join the others in the dining hall. On July 24 or 25, Zhang Wentian ran into Peng and said,

"We can't talk about shortcomings anymore, we can't criticize; criticism is dangerous. We did nothing wrong. Mao Zedong's speech was meant to suppress and stigmatize us."[45]

On the night of July 23, Peng Dehuai could not sleep. He kept asking himself, "How did my letter for the Chairman's reference become a Written Opinion? How can it have become an agenda of right opportunism? Why does he say it was organized, planned, and purposeful?"[46]

POSITIONS SHIFT FOR SELF-PRESERVATION

Under China's system at the time, once Mao took an idea in hand, the vast majority of the leadership would rapidly join in an overwhelming mainstream consensus, and anyone with alternative views would be isolated and put under group attack. There was virtually no chance of anyone rising to the defense of the unjustly persecuted; only years later, after the political climate and mainstream view had changed, might one hope for some redress of injustice.

As opposed to parliamentary politics, China at that time had "conference politics." The Chinese language artfully reverses the characters for *parliament* (*yihui*) to make the phrase for *conference* (*huiyi*)—in the process, transforming a democratic institution into an autocratic tool for implementing the intentions of the supreme leader and besieging those with dissenting views. In imperial politics, the ruler states his views, but if he attempts to wrongfully punish someone, another can speak in that person's defense. "Conference politics" imposes a more devastating "dictatorship of the majority" in which all chime in to support the supreme leader, and it is impossible for an individual to intercede on behalf of the oppressed.

After Mao's speech, no one spoke against the Left. The rest of the conference focused on criticizing Peng Dehuai, Huang Kecheng, Zhang Wentian, Zhou Xiaozhou, and others, and forcing them to endure self-criticism. The senior officials joined in lockstep. Men who had fearlessly faced hails of bullets on the battlefield and had refused to surrender under the torture of the enemy became as submissive as lambs, while others willingly served as the falcons and hounds of evil. Many more trimmed their sails to the wind and toadied to whatever side gained the upper hand. Their rationalizations included preserving the overall situation for the sake of party unity. During the revolution, most had been single and lacking possessions. They had believed their opponents were evil, and that the sacrifice of their lives would be honorable. In their rise through the ranks, they had acquired wives and children, honor and wealth. The higher authority positioned to punish them was cloaked in idealism; punishment would be accompanied by a disgrace shared by their loved ones. So it was that totalitarianism turned yesterday's heroes into today's slaves.[47]

LIU SHAOQI

In April 1959, Liu Shaoqi became president of the People's Republic, formalizing Mao's decision. Unwilling to serve as president, Mao remained chairman of the CCP Central Committee and chairman of the Central Military Commission, which held the greatest actual power. If Liu had genuinely been second in command, Mao could not have done as he pleased at the Lushan Conference. Liu was no more than Mao's submissive minister, and his fate was entirely in Mao's hands.

On July 4, Liu stated that the Great Leap Forward in 1958 had consumed the grain reserves of 1957 as well as drawing on the reserves for 1959. The errors of the previous year had greatly affected the economy and the people's livelihood. Nevertheless, Liu defended the errors in the name of revolution.[48]

Liu's speech on July 16 opened the conference by putting forward the slogan "Saying enough about accomplishments, thoroughly exploring shortcomings, going all out."[49] In Li Rui's view, Liu implicitly advocated opposing leftism. According to Li Rui, Liu Shaoqi had sought out Mao's confidant, Hu Qiaomu, to discuss opposing leftism, but Hu Qiaomu had not dared to pass this along to Mao.[50] Although nominally second-in-command, Liu could not even express his views directly to Mao.

Liu's wife, Wang Guangmei, and son, Liu Yuan, likewise say that "before and after the Lushan Conference, Liu Shaoqi opposed the leftists."[51] They recall that when Mao gave his sudden notice on the morning of July 23 of a plenary meeting at which he would give a speech, Liu Shaoqi was deep in sleep after taking a sleeping pill late the previous night, and his bodyguards half-carried him to the assembly in a semiconscious state. After hearing Mao's criticism of Peng, Liu had Hu Qiaomu come to his quarters and recommended that criticism of Peng be kept on a small scale. Liu wanted Hu Qiaomu to draft a document opposing leftism. Hu suggested Liu discuss this with Mao first, to which Liu retorted, "Once you've drafted it, of course I'll discuss it with him." Subsequently Hu had Peng Zhen talk with Liu, and the idea of drafting a document was abandoned.[52]

On July 31 and August 1, while Peng came under attack, Liu, who had largely shared Peng's views, spoke not a single word in his defense, and even interjected his own remarks supporting Mao's criticism. When others tried to extort a confession from Peng, Liu enthusiastically joined in. On August 1, Liu declared, "It's worth considering whether Peng Dehuai's concept of socialism is entirely the same as the party's . . . Peng has his own way of thinking. I agree with the Chairman that he is ambitious and wants to reshape the party and the world in his own image. That's where the problem lies." Liu revealed that Peng objected to singing "The East Is Red" and that Peng thought China was under a personality cult that should be opposed. Liu suggested that Peng was responsible for dropping a provision on Mao Zedong Thought from the party constitution of the Eighth National Party Congress.[53] Liu's revelations were meant to attack Peng and curry favor with Mao.

Huang Kecheng recalled, "A comrade from the Central Committee came and talked to me twice, advising me to get out of my fix by 'turning against Peng once and for all.' I said, '. . . I absolutely refuse to frame someone in order to save myself.'"[54] Li Rui's book reveals that the Central Committee comrade who visited Huang Kecheng these two times was Liu Shaoqi.[55]

On August 17, the day after the Lushan Conference was adjourned, a work meeting of the Central Committee was held under Mao's direction, with Liu Shaoqi as the main speaker. He began: "The fact that we can hold this meeting represents a great victory for our party." He defended the errors of the Great Leap Forward, saying that while "some people see this as disorder . . . it is the normal manifestation and order of revolution." Liu went on: "I consider myself an enthusiastic proponent of the 'cult of personality' and of raising the personal prestige of some people . . . Some oppose the 'cult of personality' for Comrade Mao Zedong, but I think this is completely wrong and is in fact a form of sabotage against the party, the proletarian cause, and the people's cause."[56] At the Lushan Conference, Liu Shaoqi and Lin Biao engaged in competition over who could offer Mao the most extravagant flattery. Lin's shameless fawning during the standing committee meeting on August 1 was exceeded only by Liu's on August 17.

Liu Shaoqi was by no means ignorant of the dangers of the Three Red Banners. Less than a month after the Lushan Conference, during the National Day celebration at Tiananmen on October 1, 1959, Liu remarked to Deng Zihui, "Who could have guessed that the people's communes would have such a devastating effect on productivity!"[57] From this it can be seen that Liu took part in the group attack on Peng in spite of sharing Peng's deep-seated convictions.

In their book *The Unknown Liu Shaoqi*, Liu's son and wife say that Liu committed two errors in his life: one was failing to prevent the Great Leap Forward, and the other was failing to prevent the Cultural Revolution.[58] In fact, Liu had no power to stop Mao. They are more justified in another pronouncement they make: "Mao Zedong ultimately placed himself above the party and the people, and people will inevitably trace the blame back to him . . . [Mao] was ultimately destroyed by his self-created mythos."[59]

ZHOU ENLAI

Zhou Enlai's status within the party was once higher than Mao's. At the Zunyi Conference, during the Long March, Zhou was "entrusted by the party with taking the final decision on military matters," and Mao was "Comrade Enlai's assistant in military command,"[60] though Zhou transferred the actual power of military command to Mao. After the founding of the PRC, Zhou was premier of the State Council, but he put himself in a submissive relationship to Mao. Following their opposition to rash advance in 1956, Zhou and Chen Yun lost their say in economic work, and as the Great Leap Forward rose in response to the campaign against rash advance, Zhou "sincerely mended his ways" and closely collaborated with Mao.

Zhou arrived at Lushan on July 1, and he met with Mao on July 2. At various meetings, he pointed out a series of shortcomings and errors. Production targets were too high, and capital construction projects were on too large a scale. Zhou knew he could criticize leftist errors to a certain extent, but it was out of the question to undermine the Three Red Banners. The author of a biography of Zhou believes, "During the Lushan Conference, Zhou Enlai's view of the situation was similar to Peng Dehuai's, but he didn't adopt the same methods."[61]

Obliged to defend the Three Red Banners and their consequences,

Zhou felt deeply conflicted. This was manifested in his schizophrenic performance at the Lushan Conference as he exerted great effort to resolve practical issues while pandering to Mao at every opportunity.

On July 10, Mao defended the shortcomings and errors of the Great Leap Forward. Zhou interjected to relate how a vice-chairman of the Soviet Union's Council of Ministers who had visited in 1958 had praised the Great Leap Forward. In fact, that Soviet official had expressed critical views, but Zhou only passed on his praise.[62]

In a lengthy speech on July 12, Zhou held that the previous year had represented a new revolution. Problems had arisen, and the old equilibrium was shattered; what was needed was a new equilibrium.[63] Zhou devoted considerable time to professional work, in part to prevent political infighting.

In a speech on July 16, Zhou assessed the steelmaking campaign positively.

During Mao's July 23 speech criticizing Peng Dehuai, Zhou sat by Mao's side. Mao said, "Premier, you opposed rash advance, but now you're standing firm." Conversely, Peng and his supporters "repeated the erroneous path of the comrades in the second half of 1956 and first half of 1957." After Mao's speech, Zhou called in the vice-premiers for a talk, during which he had an exchange with Peng Dehuai:

ZHOU: Placing losses in front of gains was intentional; you should have separated the practical from the discouraging.

PENG: . . . Why did I want to write this letter for the Chairman's reference during this conference? I had a feeling that there was a lack of willingness to criticize within the Communist Party . . . Not being able to voice criticisms within the Communist Party violates the party's basic principles.

Zhou then mentioned a number of problems that had arisen.

PENG: Why not mention this during the conference plenum?

ZHOU: If I start out talking about these difficulties, it would sound like a meeting for airing grievances, and misunderstandings would dampen the atmosphere.

PENG: You people are really too wise to the ways of the world. Very cunning.

ZHOU: This is a tactic. The opposition to rash advance in 1956 was a
mistake, wasn't it? At that time I just blurted something out . . . I
should have been more cautious; that's the lesson to be drawn. This
year you took my place. In fact, having seen what happened to me,
you even wrote that the General Line was basically correct; you didn't
use the term "rash advance."[64]

On July 26, after Mao recommended "dealing with incidents and also
with individuals," the denunciations escalated. Peng's writing of the letter was labeled as a "right-deviating movement" and a "vicious attack."
On that afternoon, Zhou delivered a lengthy speech in which he defended
the General Line and called for a practical and realistic approach to work.
He considered Peng Dehuai's letter to be a matter of political direction. He
warned his subordinates not to take the wrong side in this political
struggle and to focus on economic work to get past the current crisis.[65]

At the standing committee meeting on August 1, it was mainly Mao
who talked. When Peng spoke of some historical situations, Zhou asked
about their trip to the Soviet Union: After they talked with Stalin, what
did Stalin say to Peng as he escorted him to the door?[66] This was an inquiry into Peng's supposed "illicit relations with a foreign country." Zhou
also commented that Peng's letter was an "attack on the General Line,
taking a right-deviating position." "When the Chairman spoke, what he
said wasn't taken in." When Lin Biao told Peng that "many people say
you're a liar and have ambitions" and accused him of "failing to accept the
Marxist-Leninist worldview," Zhou cut in, describing Peng as "very arrogant and insubordinate."

When Liu Shaoqi exposed Peng Dehuai's opposition to singing "The
East Is Red," Zhou interposed, "This is a matter of sentiment." When
Mao said that in the past Peng had cooperated with him 70 percent of the
time, Zhou hastily interposed, "When we were in the North he was always taking an independent stand, and during the three years in Yan'an
he was always incompatible with others. There was cooperation in the
War of Liberation and in the War to Resist America and Support Korea,
but once he returned to the Central Military Commission, he made little
effort to fall in line."

On August 1, Central Committee members and alternate members
arrived to attend the Eighth Plenum of the Eighth CCP Central Committee. Briefing them, Zhou said,

There are symptoms of a trend in the conference of talking a great deal about shortcomings and exaggerating them, as exemplified by Comrade Peng Dehuai. On the train he said that if it weren't for the decency of China's workers and peasants, we'd have had our own Hungarian Incident, and during the report to the Chairman on July 7, he also expressed this view. When we heard it, we considered it unacceptable . . . The standing committee called Peng in to talk, feeling that there was a plan, preparation, organization, and purpose behind his letter and that it constituted an agenda to oppose the party Central Committee, oppose the General Line, and oppose Chairman Mao . . . Zhang Wentian spoke for three hours, promoting himself and Peng as a civilian-military team heading up Foreign Affairs [Zhang] and Defense [Peng]. Zhou Xiaozhou from the provinces also raised the proletarian banner in an attack against "petty bourgeois fanaticism" . . . Once Peng's letter came out, the nature of the problem changed . . . After leftist errors were corrected, right opportunism reared its head—on and off the mountain, within and outside the party, in China and outside, everywhere. Comrade Peng Dehuai is a prime example of this dangerous right opportunism. For that reason, Chairman Mao has proposed that the mission of this conference is to defend the General Line, oppose right opportunism, and oppose power struggles that cause divisions in the party. That is the essence of the problem.[67]

On August 24, at an enlarged meeting of the Central Military Commission in Beijing, Zhou communicated Peng's crimes and exposed his historical errors.[68] Throughout the Lushan Conference, Zhou never said a word in Peng's defense. During the Cultural Revolution, seven years later, he also joined with Mao to "overthrow" Liu Shaoqi and led the special investigation team that pronounced Liu a "traitor, inside agent, and scab." This verdict was signed by Zhou Enlai and transmitted to every party branch in China.

ZHU DE

During the revolution, Zhu De joined forces with Mao Zedong to establish a revolutionary base at Jinggang Mountain, and for a long time many referred to the CCP leadership as "Zhu-Mao," with Zhu's name coming before Mao's. After the founding of the PRC, however, Zhu had little power. He resigned himself to a leisurely existence and took no part in power struggles, modeling his submissive and courtly attitude toward Mao on General Xu Da's relationship with the first Ming emperor, Zhu Yuanzhang. Zhu De had a strong foundation in ancient Chinese culture, and knew what happened when a new empire was founded: "When the cunning hare dies, the running dog is cooked; when the flying birds are killed off, the fine bow is put into storage."[69] In his awareness that he couldn't hope to retain the status he'd enjoyed during wartime, Zhu De was much more "literate" than Peng Dehuai.

Inspection visits in 1958 and 1959 enlightened Zhu on China's situation. At Lushan on July 6, he said, "We have to attach more importance to private ownership among the peasants. If workers are still given wages, why should the peasants be willing to accept communism? . . . If we can't manage communal kitchens properly, we shouldn't stick with them, and it's no disaster if they all close down. We should allow peasants to prosper rather than allowing them to fall into poverty. The family system should be strengthened. Provinces needn't operate their own industrial systems."[70]

On July 23, Zhu De supported the spirit of the Great Leap Forward but criticized its particulars: "The Great Leap Forward arose from heat, and heat is the source of revolution . . . We had a good harvest last year, so why are food supplies still tight? The main reason is that everything was consumed in the communal kitchens. All the good food was eaten and the bad food was left to rot. The peasants are used to private ownership, and decentralizing consumption might result in savings."[71]

By July 25, Zhu had joined the criticism of Peng's letter, which he said "put undue emphasis on shortcomings and errors. This does not conform to reality. One of Marshal Peng's characteristics is his tendency to stubbornly maintain his opinions. If the opinions are correct, of course they should be maintained, but if they're wrong, it's necessary to accept criticism and correct errors. Peng Dehuai's letter served a useful purpose, but his views are incorrect, and he should take the opportunity to carry out a thorough self-criticism regarding his over-emphasis on shortcomings."

Commenting on this quote, Li Rui says, "Zhu De and Peng Dehuai had been comrades-in-arms for thirty years, and they knew each other well. It would appear that [Zhu] had no choice at the time but to say what he did."[72] On July 26, after Peng carried out self-criticism, Zhu was conciliatory:

> Marshal Peng has expressed himself with a good attitude; I believe he has held nothing back. Marshal Peng's speech contained one sentence: It is easier to move a river or a mountain than to change one's character. This is peasant wisdom. All of us here move forward daily, so how can we not change? That's where his subjectivity and one-sidedness come from. Everyone is right to criticize Marshal Peng, and Peng accepted our criticisms. In the past they weren't accepted and caused disagreement. I believe that after this meeting, with our thinking and understanding united, we won't need to continue carrying this baggage around.[73]

Zhu De was the first person to speak at the standing committee meeting on August 1, and his criticism of Peng's letter was tempered. Mao interrupted by lifting up his leg and scratching at his shoe, saying, "It's like scratching your foot through a boot." Zhu flushed red and stopped speaking, offering only a few more comments at the end of the meeting.[74]

On August 4, after a long speech by Lin Biao, Zhu said, "My original assessment was incorrect; I thought Comrade Peng Dehuai's letter was written on the spur of the moment, but now it seems this was not the case . . . Now Chairman Mao is still here, and I don't believe anyone wants to see Chairman Mao opposed or for Chairman Mao to give up his position. The basic problem behind Comrade Dehuai's vacillation on the General Line is a lack of understanding of the masses and of the party. This is where his greatest error lies."[75] If even Zhu De was forced to join the chorus, others could hardly do otherwise.

LIN BIAO

In the People's Liberation Army, no one could match the outstanding military service of Lin Biao. In May 1958, at Mao's suggestion, Lin was promoted to vice-chairman of the Central Committee and appointed a member of the Politburo standing committee.

Lin Biao was not originally in attendance at the Lushan Conference, but Mao called him in after receiving Peng Dehuai's letter. Immediately after his arrival on July 17, Lin took a resolute anti-rightist stand. His criticism of Peng Dehuai was raised to the highest plane of principle, and his attack was the fiercest.

At a standing committee meeting on July 31, Mao emphasized the importance of keeping up the mood of mass movements. When Peng expressed doubt, Lin Biao quickly sided with Mao: "It's hard to keep up the mood and easy for it to dissipate, and once it has dissipated it's even harder to pump it up."[76] Dismissing Peng's objections to having his letter to Mao distributed as a "written opinion," Mao said, "It's not necessarily true that you're unhappy that your letter was made public. The purpose of this letter was to rally public opinion and organize the ranks." Lin Biao immediately put in, "I completely agree with this view."[77]

On August 1, Lin berated Peng as a careerist, hypocrite, and warlord in the mold of Feng Yuxiang. Given that China had a great hero such as Mao Zedong, he said, no one else could aspire to be a hero.[78] Later Lin denigrated Peng's character:

> You said you weren't prepared for your letter to be published, but in fact that was your intention . . . The wind has been stirred up inside and outside of China, and it seemed an opportune moment . . . On the surface your intentions look good, but in fact it's an attempt to seize on shortcomings . . . The facts bear out that it's right-deviating, and the motivation proceeds from personal ambition. Only Chairman Mao can be considered a great hero; you and I can't even come close, so don't even make such a suggestion . . . [79]

On August 4, during a briefing for new arrivals at Lushan, Lin Biao was the first to speak. He said, "I was the first of the reinforcements to arrive, you're the last-stage reinforcements." He said that Peng's letter

> is generally right-deviating, opposes the General Line, opposes the Great Leap Forward, opposes the people's communes . . . He didn't mention Chairman Mao by name, but before and after, inside and outside the conference, and between the lines, the target of his attack has been extremely apparent, and that is his opposition to Chairman Mao . . . He raised the banner of opposing "petty bourgeois fanaticism" to carry out an assault on the party and against Chairman Mao . . . My direct impression is that this person is obsessed with making himself into a hero; he's

extremely arrogant and conceited and looks down on others . . . He's extremely ambitious; he'll go all out to make his name, seize power, establish his position, and gain illustrious fame that will last through one hundred generations. He's extremely aggressive, his head held high, wanting to be a hero, a very great hero . . . Chairman Mao is the only real hero.[80]

On August 17, the day after the Lushan Conference ended, Peng Dehuai was removed from office. In accordance with Mao's suggestion, Lin Biao took over Peng Dehuai's work. During an enlarged meeting of the Central Military Commission after the Lushan Conference, Lin Biao personally took charge of a struggle session against Peng Dehuai, Huang Kecheng, and others.

TAN ZHENLIN

Tan Zhenlin was the State Council's vice-premier in charge of agriculture. He was an enthusiastic proponent of the Great Leap Forward, and during the Lushan Conference he staunchly defended the Three Red Banners. Even so, he showed reluctance to vilify Peng. On July 26, following Huang Kecheng's self-criticism, Tan spoke at the fifth group meeting, saying,

> This letter is poisonous gas added to a smokescreen. Peng Dehuai is a loyal and devoted comrade who always acts for the party and the country. He made an immortal contribution to the revolutionary cause, and this is something that no one can in any way deny. There is no way that this letter can make me deny his past. He's an honest and selfless man. For him to have the courage to write this letter and raise this controversy is a very good thing . . . This fight does not prevent my respecting his past or the contributions he will continue to make in the future.[81]

Two days later, however, someone criticized Tan for affirming Peng's character and historical contribution. Tan then changed his tone, saying, "I say he is no Zhang Fei, but rather more like Wei Yan."[82] In the classic *Romance of the Three Kingdoms*, Zhang Fei was loyal and devoted, frank and outspoken, while Wei Yan was a traitor.

CHEN BODA

Chen Boda was director of the Central Committee's political research office and secretary to Mao. Soon after arriving at Lushan, he and several other of Mao's secretaries (referred to as *xiucai*)[83] launched a debate criticizing the errors of 1958. On July 18 and 19, Chen argued that the side effects of the Great Leap Forward should not be ignored, but that the focus should be on issues and not individuals. He said, "I fired a barrage at Comrade Chen Zhengren," saying the Central Committee Rural Work Department should carry out self-criticism, because Chen Zhengren felt there were no great problems in agriculture, and there were merely some strains on food supplies in a minority of areas. Chen Boda described how he'd been deceived: "Some of the things I saw and heard last year during my trip to Suiping, Henan Province, and Fan County, Shandong Province, were not true. They were arranged in advance by lower-level cadres. Recently a comrade from *Red Flag* magazine went to these two counties and found out the true situation. I sent a letter with these views to comrades Shu Tong and Wu Zhipu, and both of them were very upset." Prior to Lushan, Chen had gone home to Fujian and learned about conditions there, which he described.[84]

Prior to Mao's attack on July 23, Chen shared the views of Tian Jiaying, Wu Lengxi, Li Rui, and others, making himself a target of criticism following Mao's speech.[85] To extricate himself, Chen Boda edited the text of his speech and delivered a lengthy tirade against Peng Dehuai's letter. Writing as a theorist, he quoted authoritative works to support Mao's July 23 speech and equated the Great Leap Forward with the Paris Commune. "I'm in total agreement with the views the Chairman expressed in his speech. Last year I visited Suiping, Fan County, Guangdong, and Fujian and was deeply moved by the soaring heroic spirit of the masses. I never doubted the boundless enthusiasm of the masses, even though I mentioned some operational shortcomings." Peng's appraisals, he said, "were wrong."[86]

On October 9, Chen delivered to Mao an essay entitled "Please Examine Comrade Peng Dehuai's Political Outlook." On October 11, Mao sent it back with a note: "I've read this, it's very good. I've made a few edits. Discussion with comrades Kang Sheng and Qiaomu should make it even better." Chen followed Mao's advice, and the revised article, retitled "The Battle Between the Proletarian Worldview and the Capitalist Worldview," was sent to Mao for approval. After Mao's further revisions, it was published in *Red Flag* magazine. On December 13 the CCP Central Committee distributed the article to cadres at all levels.[87]

Having scored political points through his criticism of Peng, Chen Boda emerged from the shadow of criticism at the Zhengzhou Conference and regained Mao's confidence. During the Cultural Revolution, he was appointed head of the Central Cultural Revolution Group and eventually became the fourth-highest-ranking official in the CCP.

HU QIAOMU

Hu Qiaomu was Mao's secretary and favored courtier. On the train to Lushan, Hu called the policy of "making steel the key link" (*yigang weigang*) nothing but clever wordplay.[88] On July 3 he remarked to others that Mao seemed to have forgotten his own dictum to observe first of all the rules of warfare, then the rules of revolutionary warfare, then the rules of Chinese revolutionary warfare.[89]

On the evening of July 6, Li Rui, Hu Qiaomu, and Chen Boda met for a chat in the quarters shared by Tian Jiaying and Wu Lengxi. Among other things, Hu recalled that during the Wuchang Conference, Wang Jiaxiang had told Liu Shaoqi that the decision regarding the people's communes should not be announced. Liu told Mao, and Mao became very angry, but Hu felt that Wang should have been commended. They went on to talk about how Ke Qingshi and others had been praised and promoted, resulting in an even more sycophantic atmosphere; after the Anti-Rightist Movement, no one dared to speak the truth.[90]

Chatting in Tian Jiaying's quarters around July 18, Tian, Hu Qiaomu, Wu Lengxi, Chen Boda, and Li Rui all felt the substance of Peng's letter in line with their own thinking. Hu Qiaomu said, "This letter may cause trouble."[91] During a speech on July 18, however, Hu voiced support for the content of Peng's letter without specifically mentioning it.

Following Mao's July 23 speech, Hu held his peace, and a few days later he fell in line. On August 10, Hu delivered a lengthy speech attacking Peng for "the slander of 'Stalin's last years.'"[92] He said that this comparison of Mao with Stalin's errors was a serious matter of principle and a "very great insult and vicious slander" against Chairman Mao and the CCP Central Committee. He then went on to flatter Mao with a six-point comparison of his leadership with that of Stalin's last years.

Hu Qiaomu and the other *xiucai* who abandoned Peng were warmly embraced by Mao. Li Rui, however, was excluded as a member of Peng's "club."

After leaving Lushan, Hu Qiaomu sent Mao a long essay that criticized Peng's letter from the standpoint of a two-line struggle. Mao wrote a memo on the document, which was then printed and distributed throughout the country.

It is worth mentioning here the last of the *xiucai*, Wu Lengxi, who was director of both the Xinhua News Agency and *People's Daily*. Prior to Lushan, Wu directed the Xinhua branch offices to collect data related to the Great Leap Forward. The fact-filled reports published by the Xinhua branches often contained a measure of truth, and impressed Peng Dehuai when he read them after his return from Eastern Europe. After the wind shifted at Lushan, however, Wu Lengxi made a radical turnaround and had the Xinhua materials sent to Lushan as evidence of crimes of "right opportunism," and seven Xinhua branch directors suffered persecution as a result.

HE LONG AND OTHER SENIOR MILITARY OFFICERS

Marshal He Long was a man of courage. After raiding a salt tax office with two meat choppers in 1916, he helped lead the Communist forces in the 1927 Nanchang Uprising that led to the founding of the PLA. Moving through the CCP ranks, he became vice-chairman of the Central Military Commission, vice-premier of the State Council, and chairman of the State Sports Commission. No longer fired with the spirit of his "meat chopper revolutionary" days, he served as one of Mao's most effective henchmen at Lushan.

It was He Long who exposed Peng Dehuai's comments on "calling in the Red Army," and on July 24 he voiced Mao's long-standing grievance over Peng's refusal to follow his guerrilla strategy in 1937 during the War of Resistance.[93] Mao had brought up this old matter during his extended chat with Zhou Xiaozhou, Zhou Hui, Hu Qiaomu, Tian Jiaying, and Li Rui on July 17, claiming that a pamphlet distributed by the North China Military Commission under Peng's leadership had served the interests of Mao's opponent at the time, Wang Ming. Mao cited this as an example of Peng's record of disunity with him.[94] Although none of the five people at that meeting disclosed Mao's comments to anyone else, He Long expressed views identical to Mao's in his speech.

Following Mao's July 23 speech, He Long said on August 3, "I believe that Comrade Dehuai's letter has an anti-party agenda. He has vacillated at several crucial junctures in the past and has demonstrated considerable insubordination to Comrade Mao Zedong, serving as an accomplice to line error. His impetuous production of this anti-party agenda this time is also directed entirely at the party Central Committee and Chairman Mao."[95]

Military cadres Luo Ruiqing, Su Zhenhua, Huang Yongsheng, and Xiao Hua also directed virulent criticism at Peng Dehuai. Luo had supported the Great Leap Forward even before Mao's Lushan speech.

Following Mao's attack on Peng on July 23, Li Rui, Zhou Xiaozhou, and Zhou Hui worried that the speech would cause a situation to develop like that in the last years of Stalin's reign, with no real collective leadership and all left to the arbitrary actions of a single individual. The three then sought out Huang Kecheng, after which Peng Dehuai joined them. Emerging from Zhou Hui's quarters, they encountered Luo Ruiqing.[96] Luo of course had no way of knowing what they had been discussing, but he reported seeing these people together. This "July 23 incident" became a target of investigation and group attack during the conference.

On August 3, Luo Ruiqing said that Peng's lifestyle resembled Feng Yuxiang's (referring to his appearance of hard work and plain living) but that it was pure hypocrisy. "This façade of hard work and plain living is largely bogus. His political ambitions are enormous . . . He has lost some of his party spirit and has become self-interested rather than upright and selfless; he is seriously individualistic. Quite apart from his lifestyle, much of his conduct is pretense, and the part of it that is genuine is opposed to the party, opposed to the party's correct leadership, and opposed to the General Line. So what use is this so-called hard work and plain living?" Luo repeated this to Peng's face afterward.[97]

On August 10, Luo frog-marched Li Rui to a meeting to confront Huang Kecheng over the "July 23 incident" and the discussion of "Stalin's last years." The session exploded into an uproar. Luo averred that Peng's and Huang's quarters had become a base of conspiracy for the anti-party opposition. "When you heard someone comparing Comrade Mao Zedong with 'Stalin's last years,' why weren't you enraged? Why didn't you roundly curse those members of the 'military club'? Why didn't you expose them?"[98]

After the Lushan Conference, Luo Ruiqing was promoted to chief of general staff, joining Lin Biao in managing the work of the Central Military Commission, reportedly at Lin's suggestion. His glowing prospects were short-lived, however. Luo came under attack during the Cultural Revolution and he attempted suicide by leaping from a building, succeeding only in breaking his legs.

Xiao Hua also kicked Peng while he was down. He had accompanied Peng on the trip to Eastern Europe, and on August 9 he said, "Comrade Peng Dehuai said something in Albania; he said the greatest danger to our party during the revolution was right deviation but that after taking political power, the greatest danger was bureaucratism and 'left' deviation." He added, "I'm suspicious about the second conversation he had with Khrushchev. They were sitting together at one table, and the rest of us were at another table, and there was no embassy interpreter present."[99]

While Peng Dehuai was suffering under these unjust accusations, none of his fellow military commanders said a word in his defense; those who didn't chime in on the criticism spoke for Mao by urging Peng to surrender and admit his guilt. Marshals Nie Rongzhen and Ye Jianying went to Peng's quarters and advised him to undergo self-criticism. Peng later wrote:

> They asked me if I had thought it through. I said the letter I wrote to the Chairman was based on specific domestic circumstances and the conditions at the Lushan Conference, and I had no preparation and harbored no ulterior motives. They also asked me if I had exchanged views with other comrades before writing the letter. I said, "Apart from Comrade Zhou Xiaozhou coming twice to my quarters to talk about concrete work conditions in Hunan Province, at which time I told him I was preparing to write a letter to the Chairman (but didn't mention the contents), I did not discuss it with other comrades. Comrade Zhang Wentian came to my quarters several times to discuss some national-level economic construction work, but I didn't discuss the letter with him." They also said, "You can't look at the letter alone; you have to consider how to best serve the interests of the overall situation." "You have to set aside the letter itself and carry out self-criticism from the standpoint of the overall interest."[100]

On August 24, marshal and foreign minister Chen Yi convened a mass denunciation meeting against Zhang Wentian. The chief criticism was of "illicit relations with a foreign country." Buckets of sewage water were dumped on Zhang's head as he was ordered to thoroughly confess his wrongdoing.[101]

The two Zhous from Hunan (Zhou Xiaozhou and Zhou Hui) had originally supported Peng Dehuai, and Zhou Hui came under considerable criticism. Taking a "divide and conquer" position, Mao decided to "undermine Peng Dehuai's foundation" by having Zhou Hui come in for a private conversation. Zhou admitted his error and wasn't named as part of the anti-party clique.

Mao wanted to bring Zhou Xiaozhou over as well. He told Zhou that if he wrote a self-criticism and exposed Peng Dehuai, he would be allowed to return to his work in Hunan. Zhou Xiaozhou tearfully told Mao, "Chairman, I can't do this. A lot of the information in Marshal Peng's letter originally came from me, and it was I who advised him to speak with you. I felt it would serve a good purpose for someone in his position to speak with the Chairman, and that's why he wrote the letter, so how can I criticize him?" With a wave of his hand, Mao said, "Get out." Zhou Xiaozhou stood up and said sincerely, "I can't return to Hunan, and the new secretary may not be familiar with the situation when he arrives. I request the Chairman to consider letting Zhou Hui go back to act as an assistant to the new secretary."

So it was that Zhou Xiaozhou took all the responsibility upon himself. As they prepared to leave Lushan, Zhou Xiaozhou tearfully embraced Zhou Hui, enjoining him to work well for Hunan and asking him to look after his wife and children.[102] Zhou Xiaozhou came under fierce group attack, but stood firm throughout. When the cases of right deviationists were reassessed for possible rehabilitation in 1962, the Central Committee stipulated that Zhou Xiaozhou should not be included.

After the Lushan Conference, Zhou Hui descended the mountain like a tiger. Upon returning to Hunan he joined in the attacks against Zhou Xiaozhou and other "right opportunists," implicating more than twenty thousand cadres. Years later, some journalists whom Zhou victimized wrote, "History will ultimately arrive at a just conclusion as to who was true gold and who was dung and dirt, including one individual who has persisted in his shamelessness to this very day."[103]

THE STANDING COMMITTEE TURNS AGAINST
CONSCIENCE AND VIRTUE

On July 31 and August 1, Mao convened a meeting of the CCP Central Committee Politburo standing committee on the upper floor of his living quarters and led a criticism of Peng Dehuai that continued through lunch. The attendees included Liu Shaoqi, Zhou Enlai, Zhu De, Lin Biao, Peng Zhen, and He Long, while Huang Kecheng, Zhou Xiaozhou, Zhou Hui, and Li Rui attended without voting rights.[104] This two-day meeting established the nature of Peng Dehuai's "errors," and put his entire career under scrutiny and evaluation. The remarks made at Politburo standing committee meetings cannot be published, but fortunately Li Rui was there and he made a detailed record of the proceedings that serves as the main source of what follows.[105]

On July 31, Mao did almost all of the talking and set the tone while others interposed remarks supporting his views. On August 1, Mao again dominated the conversation while the others carried out interrogations and group attacks. Among them, Lin Biao raised the accusations to the highest level and employed the most strident tone. No one expressed a dissenting view, and the discussion was completely one-sided.

Since 1949, the CCP had established the premise that Mao was invariably correct. Anyone whose views differed from his in the course of the revolution had historical problems and blemishes on their political records. Anyone who subsequently disagreed with Mao had to have these past errors scrutinized and evaluated.

During the two-day standing committee meeting, Mao carried out his own evaluation of Peng Dehuai's past actions, saying that in the thirty-one years they had worked together, Peng had cooperated with him only 30 percent of the time and had been uncooperative 70 percent of the time.[106] He brought up all of their past differences for criticism on the basis of principle and the two roads, and carried out a new evaluation of which side Peng had stood on throughout past line struggles.

After rehashing these old historical accounts, Mao said, "While the two of us have been in Beijing, there have been only nine telephone calls between us in ten years—that's less than one phone call per year." He said Peng had become alienated from him and too seldom reported back to him or asked him for instructions.[107] Regarding the July 14 letter, Mao said, "At other important junctures, you didn't take the trouble to write to me, so why did you choose to write this long memorial at just this time?"[108] "In speaking of 'petty bourgeois fanaticism,' you're primarily referring to the central leadership organs, not to the provinces and even less to the masses. This is how I see it. In speaking of being 'facile,' you're referring to the leading organs, but in fact your real target is the Central Committee."[109] "You were preparing to publish it to win over the masses, rally the troops, and remold the face of the party and the world in your own image." "You want to amend the General Line, you want to make a new one . . . You're ambitious, you always have been." "All along you've wanted to remold the party and the world to suit you, but for various reasons you've never gotten the opportunity. This time you went abroad and brought back the sutras (or so it seems)."[110] "You're a right opportunist; according to the latter part of the letter, the leadership and the party are equally useless."

The others attending the meeting, apart from pursuing Peng Dehuai's political transgressions, also denigrated his personal integrity while seizing the opportunity to flatter Mao. While exposing and criticizing Peng Dehuai's comments opposing the cult of personality, Lin Biao, Liu Shaoqi, Peng Zhen, and others affirmed the cult of personality for Mao. The Politburo standing committee was originally meant to serve as a form of group leadership, and Mao should have been no more than a convener. In actuality, however, he set himself above the committee, and collective leadership became a dictatorship. While Mao himself undeniably bore the primary responsibility for this development, how could his "sedan bearers" and worshippers of his personal cult escape blame?

This two-day meeting set the tone for Peng Dehuai and the others, and wrapped up the unjust case against them. The "Peng, Huang, Zhang, Zhou" anti-party clique and "military club" were manufactured out of thin air for labeling the scapegoats. The day after the meeting, on the afternoon of August 2, the Eighth Plenum of the Eighth CCP Central Committee was convened to rubber-stamp this injustice and to mobilize the entire party in a campaign against right deviation.

Mao's speech opening the plenary session was not long, but it explicitly and resolutely mobilized the party to counter the "savage assault of right opportunism." Mao said,

Is our line actually correct or not? Some of our comrades are expressing doubts . . . Soon after arriving at Lushan, some comrades called for

democracy, saying we're not democratic now, we can't speak freely, there's a kind of pressure that prevents us from daring to speak... Only later did it become clear that they wanted to attack this General Line, that they wanted to sabotage this General Line. When they say they want freedom of expression, what they want is freedom to destroy the General Line with their speech, and freedom to criticize the General Line... We've spent nine months opposing left deviation, and that's not the problem now. The Lushan Conference is not a matter of opposing the Left, but of opposing the Right, because [right] opportunism is a vicious attack on the party and the party's leading organs, and an attack against the people's undertakings—against the dynamic socialist undertaking in which six hundred million people have been engaged.[111]

It was also on the opening day of the plenum that Mao wrote his "Letter to Zhang Wentian" and had it immediately printed and distributed. Although only five hundred words long, the letter contained a number of classical allusions and employed a stridently cynical and sarcastic tone. It framed the scapegoated officials as members of a "military club," and added that the members of this club "combined literary and military skill to mutual advantage."[112]

After the opening of the Eighth Plenum, the struggle against Peng Dehuai reached an intense phase, and evening parties were suspended. Small groups were merged into three large groups; the one headed by Li Jingquan dealt with Peng Dehuai, that headed by Zhang Desheng dealt with Huang Kecheng, and Ke Qingshi's group dealt with Zhang Wentian and Zhou Xiaozhou—all employing biting criticism and interrogation.[113] These criticism meetings went on to encircle and suppress the "military club" and to pursue Zhou Xiaozhou's comments on "Stalin's last years." The intensity and ferocity of the criticism and the oppressiveness of the atmosphere are comparable to struggle sessions during the Cultural Revolution that was to follow. Under a barrage of interrogation, Peng Dehuai said, "You want to hear that I had ambition and that I wanted to unseat Mao, but there's no way I can say that." When someone blamed him for a bad attitude, Peng Dehuai said, "I have no defense counsel, but you're acting like judge and jury."[114]

On August 10, Mao wrote a memo on the "Report on the Order by Anhui Provincial Party Secretariat Secretary Zhang Kaifan to Close the Communal Kitchens in Wuwei County," and had it printed and distributed to the entire assembly. Speaking of Peng Dehuai and others, Mao wrote, "In the transition period from capitalism to socialism, [they] took the side of the bourgeoisie and deliberately sabotaged the dictatorship of the proletariat, caused division within the Communist Party, organized factions within the party to spread their influence and cause a slackening of the proletarian vanguard, and established their opportunistic party." "The remnants of the Gao Gang clique who evaded punishment are now stirring up trouble again, impatient and eager to launch their attack."[115]

In order to provide theoretical ammunition to those criticizing Peng Dehuai and the others, Liu Lantao, who was neither a theoretician nor someone engaged in theoretical work (at that time he was serving as an alternate secretary of the CCP Central Committee secretariat), took the initiative to organize the compiling of "How Marxists Should Deal with Revolutionary Mass Movements," comprised of quotes by Marx, Engels, Lenin, Stalin, and Mao. Upon receiving it, Mao embraced it like a rare treasure and wrote two lengthy memos on August 15 and 16. The August 15 memo stated,

> To those splittists within the Communist Party, those friends at the most extreme right . . . You're unwilling to listen to me; I'm already in "Stalin's last years," and have become "arbitrary and rampaging," not giving you "freedom" or "democracy," while "subordinates magnify the actions of their superiors." It's all about "erring to the utmost and then making a 180 degree turnaround," and "deceiving" you and treating you like "big fish pulled up on the line," while also "somewhat resembling Tito." No one is able to speak frankly to my face, only your leader is qualified to do so. It's just too deplorable, and apparently only your emergence can save the day, etc., etc. Your barrage of bombs nearly blew away half of Mount Lushan.

The August 16 memo stated, "The struggle that emerged at Lushan was a class struggle, and a continuation of the life-and-death struggle that has been going on between the bourgeois class and the proletarian class in the course of the socialist revolution for more than ten years now. In China, in our party, it would appear that this struggle will have to continue for at least another twenty years or half a century—in any case, until classes are completely eliminated; only then will the struggle end."[116]

On August 16, the full party plenum adopted a resolution.

The resolution regarding Peng Dehuai started off by defining the clique: "A right-deviating opportunist anti-party clique led by Comrade Peng Dehuai and including comrades Huang Kecheng, Zhang Wentian, Zhou Xiaozhou, and others," which at Lushan launched a "savage attack against the party's General Line, against the Great Leap Forward, and against the people's communes." The resolution observed that "an attack from within the party, especially from within the party's Central Committee, is clearly more dangerous than an attack from outside the party"; therefore, "insistently crushing the activities of the right-deviating opportunistic anti-party clique led by Comrade Peng Dehuai is absolutely essential, not only for defending the party's General Line, but also for defending the central leadership of the party headed by Comrade Mao Zedong, defending the unity of the party, and defending the socialist undertaking of the party and the people."

It was claimed that Peng "carried out a savage attack on the leadership of the CCP Central Committee and Comrade Mao Zedong," causing "the leadership of Comrade Mao Zedong" to come under threat. The resolution found that Peng Dehuai, Huang Kecheng, Zhang Wentian, Zhou Xiaozhou, and other comrades formed an anti-party clique, led by Comrade Peng Dehuai, during and prior to the Lushan Conference. The resolution tasked the entire party with "exposing the true face of this hypocrite, careerist, and conspirator." Looking back at supposed errors in party history, the first Wang Ming line, the second Wang Ming line, and the Gao-Rao anti-party alliance incident, Peng supposedly stood on the side of the "erring lines in opposition to the correct line represented by Comrade Mao Zedong." These disagreements with Mao supposedly "represented the interests of bourgeois revolutionaries who participated in our party during the democratic revolution."

In short, it was not the serious consequences of Mao's badly misguided policies that aroused the criticism of Peng and the others, but rather the success of the General Line that spurred disruption by exploiters facing the threat of imminent demise:

> The success of the party's General Line, the Great Leap Forward, and the People's Commune Movement clearly dealt a fatal blow to the capitalist and individual economy. Under these conditions, the remnants of the Gao Gang clique, led by Peng Dehuai, along with various and sundry other right-deviating opportunists, were pressed to take what

they considered an "advantageous" opportunity to stir up trouble, and came out in opposition to the party's General Line, the Great Leap Forward, and the people's communes, and to the leadership of the party Central Committee and Comrade Mao Zedong.

The members of this so-called anti-party clique included Li Rui. Although his lower rank made him unworthy of mention, Li was stripped of all his official positions, expelled from the party, and sent to a labor camp.

After the Lushan Conference, the erroneous policies of 1958 were intensified, causing an already profoundly troubled country to sink into an even deeper calamity. Mao's cult of personality and personal dictatorship, on the other hand, were strengthened, foreshadowing the Cultural Revolution that was to follow only a few years later.

ENGULFED IN THE CAMPAIGN AGAINST
RIGHT DEVIATION

Mao's overwhelming victory at the Lushan Conference raised his fanaticism to an even more extreme level, as reflected in a letter he wrote to the editors of the poetry journal *Shi kan* when he submitted his poems "Arriving at Shaoshan" and "Ascending Lushan" on September 1, 1959:

> A vicious right-deviating opportunistic attack in recent days has stated that the people's undertaking is flawed in this or that respect. Anti-China and anti-Communist elements from all over the world, as well as bourgeois and petty bourgeois opportunists who previously managed to infiltrate the ranks of the proletariat and the party, have joined forces for a vicious joint attack. Good heavens! They want to bring down the entire Kunlun Mountain range! But hold on there, Comrade! A smattering of opportunists within China who hang the "Communist" shingle have seized on a few trifles to raise their banner vilifying the party's General Line, the Great Leap Forward, and the people's communes. They have ludicrously overrated their influence, like a swarm of ants attempting to shake a mighty tree. Reactionaries across the world have been hurling their verbal voodoo at us since last year. I say, bring it on! The only surprise would be if the mighty undertaking of the 650 million great Chinese people were not cursed and vilified by imperialism and its

running dogs throughout the world. The more virulent their curses, the happier I am. Let them berate us for half a century, and then we'll see who has come out ahead. These two poems are a response to those sons of bitches.[117]

Mao's reduction of the starvation of multitudes of peasants to a "trifle" and his vilification of their defenders as "sons of bitches" was replicated in the party organization at every level. In a twinkling, every publication and every meeting of every party committee and government body focused on criticizing right-deviating thought. Defense of the Three Red Banners rose to fever pitch. Vast numbers of people were attacked as "right-deviating opportunists" or "seriously right-deviating" for trying to stop the deadly policies. Anyone who found shortcomings in the Great Leap Forward or tried to tame its excesses was denounced as a right-deviating opportunist. Those who refused to publicly acknowledge their errors were persecuted even more harshly.[118]

A total of 1,900 individuals within the party committees of state organs and party organs directly subordinate to the Central Committee were classified as key targets for criticism from August 1959 to January 1960, comprising 3 percent of the party members in these organs. (This included 287 individuals, or 9.3 percent of the total, at the departmental rank or above.) Another 2,714 people were classified as key targets "requiring help," making up another 4.4 percent of all party members. The number of party members singled out to be criticized, and therefore helped, made up 7.5 percent of the overall total. Following exposure and criticism, 224 of those party members were designated right-deviating opportunists, including 61 at the departmental level or above. This campaign also labeled more than 90 individuals as alien-class elements, degenerate elements, or other bad elements.[119]

At the beginning of September, local authorities had to report back to the CCP Central Committee on their progress in the battle against right deviation. As of early September, reports had come in from Gansu, Qinghai, Xinjiang, Guizhou, Hunan, Anhui, Heilongjiang, Henan, Shaanxi, Jilin, Guangdong, and Jiangxi, detailing the right-deviating errors of cadres as high in rank as provincial party secretary. Their errors included criticizing the Great Leap Forward and undemocratic cadre work styles, disbanding communal kitchens, and "dashing cold water on the great iron and steel campaign."

The CCP Central Committee commented:

> Although the number of right-deviating elements is not great and comprises a very small percentage of high-level cadres, in a climate favorable to them they could still stir up trouble and whip up a countercurrent, and if not exposed and criticized in a timely manner they could obstruct the leap forward in the cause of socialist construction and cause very great damage to our work. Your due notice is requested.[120]

Provinces identified whipping boys as members of "anti-party cliques."[121] In factory and mining enterprises, workers and staff were evaluated on the basis of their attitudes toward the Three Red Banners, and those with serious problems were subjected to criticism. The Central Committee demanded thorough eradication of these "human contaminants."[122]

On October 15, 1959, the Central Committee commented on a report of the Agricultural Ministry:

> In May, June, and July of this year, an evil and unhealthy trend of right deviation emerged in the countryside in the form of "basic ownership in production teams," "freedom in minor affairs," an upsurge in private sideline occupations, and sabotage of the collective economy, as well as disbanding a portion of the rationing system and the communal kitchens, etc. This is in fact a fierce countercurrent against the socialist road. Following the Lushan Conference, all localities have begun to expose large quantities of these reactionary, repulsive things through the struggle to counter right deviation, while drumming up enthusiasm and defending the party's General Line. Please take serious note and thoroughly carry out criticism.[123]

This document not only completely negated rectification measures undertaken in the spring and summer of 1959, but actually designated them as "fierce countercurrents against the socialist road."

While the campaign against right deviation was being undertaken in the cities, a Socialist Education Movement was launched in the villages as "a very intense, very profound class struggle." "In the countryside, a portion of well-to-do middle peasants, along with a minority of right-deviating opportunists among cadres who represent the interests of well-to-do middle peasants, have fiercely opposed the people's communes, the rationing system, and communal kitchens, the Great Leap Forward, the General Line, and the leadership of the party; essentially, they opposed socialism." "If the fierce attack by a portion of well-to-do middle peasants against the party and socialism in the countryside is not thoroughly crushed, it will be impossible to further consolidate the people's communes, or to continue the Great Leap Forward in agriculture and the implementation and execution of the party's General Line."[124]

The Socialist Education Movement attributed all the serious problems of 1958 to "right deviation." In places where, for example, the grain yield had unexpectedly dropped by 30.8 percent, the number of live pigs was reduced by 51 percent, the death rate among plow oxen was 12 percent, and only 50 percent of commune members turned out to work the fields; or where "serious capitalist inclinations resulted in fields lying fallow, with production dropping year after year and disease spreading," the solution was to intensify Great Leap policies. This use of the Left to counter the Right had increasingly serious consequences.[125]

According to statistics from the 1962 reexamination and rehabilitation, between 3 and 4 million cadres and party members were targeted for criticism and designated as right-deviating opportunists.[126] In a speech on May 11, 1962, Deng Xiaoping said in reference to the reexamination and rehabilitation exercise, "We now have figures from the regions that have carried out reexamination and rehabilitation. For example, 400,000 in Henan—the actual number is certainly greater. The estimate for the entire country is 10 million. The total number of people affected is in the tens of millions."[127]

The 1957 Anti-Rightist Movement silenced intellectuals, the Lushan Conference silenced high-level cadres, and the 1959 campaign against right deviation took the process right down to the grass roots. China became a country with only one voice. Whatever Mao said was the "directive from the highest level." Regarding his directives, the rule was, "When you understand them, carry them out; when you don't understand them, carry them out anyway, and while carrying them out gain a better understanding of them."

The campaign against right deviation revived the Communist Wind, Exaggeration Wind, Coercive Commandism Wind, and Chaotic Directives Wind that had been restrained during the first half of 1959. The Socialist Education Movement in the countryside was integrated with the campaign against private withholding and with the fulfilling of the grain procurement targets. This exacerbated the food shortage and greatly intensified the famine.

It is because of this that starvation surged in 1959, with deaths reaching a peak in 1960 and continuing into 1961. It was only then that Mao remarked:

> What was the nature of our error after the Lushan Conference? The mistake was that we should not have transmitted the resolution against Peng, Huang, Zhang, and Zhou below the county level. The transmission should have ended at the county level, and below that level only the summary of the Zhengzhou Conference, the spirit of the eighteen items of the Shanghai Conference, and the measures against "leftism" should have been disseminated. Once the measures against rightism commenced, they created a false impression that all was well and that there was great progress in production, when that was not actually the case. The problems of Peng, Huang, Zhang, and Zhou should have been restricted to only 100,000-odd people; it was not necessary for the military to carry the issue to the company level, and the localities didn't need to carry it to the level of the communes and below. Carrying it further resulted in a large number of people being accused as right-deviating opportunists. Now we can see that this was a mistake, and that good people who spoke the truth were labeled as right-deviating opportunists or even as counterrevolutionaries.[128]

By the time Mao expressed this superficial repentance, tens of millions of people were dead.

11 CHINA'S POPULATION LOSS IN THE GREAT LEAP FORWARD

During the Great Leap Forward, China was highly centralized politically, and the state held a monopoly over economic resources. Any systemic disaster therefore affected the entire country, leaving victims nowhere to turn. All provinces had edema, exaggerated reports of crop yields, and correspondingly high requisition targets, failure to meet procurement targets followed by anti-hoarding campaigns, the launching and disbanding of communal kitchens, and starvation and death. The Five Winds blew throughout the country, Sputniks were launched everywhere, and every locality had ludicrous iron- and steel-forging campaigns.

Even so, the famine hit some places harder than others. The rate of death by unnatural causes was highest in Sichuan, Anhui, Gansu, Henan, Shandong, Qinghai, and Hunan, and lowest in Shanxi, Zhejiang, Jiangxi, and Jilin. According to official statistics, the mortality rates for 1960 were: Anhui 6.858 percent, Sichuan 5.397 percent, Guizhou 5.233 percent, Gansu 4.3 percent, Qinghai 4.073 percent, Henan 3.96 percent, Hunan 2.942 percent, Shandong 2.36 percent, and so on. In some provinces the famine waned by 1961, as in Shandong and Henan. In others, covering up the disaster prolonged the starvation.

In Sichuan, starvation deaths persisted to 1962. The mortality rate in Sichuan from 1958 to 1962 was 1.517 percent, 4.69 percent, 5.39 percent, 2.942 percent, and 1.482 percent. Twelve of China's twenty-nine provinces experienced negative population growth in 1960, but Sichuan was the only province that experienced negative population growth during all four years. Four other provinces experienced negative population growth in both 1960 and 1961: Guizhou, Guangxi, Qinghai, and Hunan.

Wang Weizhi, who worked in the Public Security Ministry's Third Division in the 1960s, provided me with the mortality figures in all localities for the year 1960. In 675 counties and cities the death rate exceeded 2 percent. These counties were in 12 provinces and autonomous regions: 75 in Sichuan, 72 in Guangxi, 68 in Anhui, 68 in Shandong, 64 in Hunan, 63 in Henan, 60 in Yunnan, 53 in Gansu, 48 in Jiangsu, 43 in Guizhou, 38 in Hubei, and 23 in Qinghai. In 40 counties, the death rate exceeded 10 percent: 11 were in Anhui, 11 in Sichuan, 10 in Henan, 4 in Guizhou, 3 in Qinghai, and 1 in Guangxi.

Wang Weizhi's figures are incomplete, however. At least five other localities in Sichuan Province had mortality rates exceeding 10 percent in 1960, and Henan's Huaibin County suffered a mortality rate of 38.32 percent. Counties with death rates exceeding 2 percent were also far more than the 675 listed by Wang Weizhi.

A succinct summary of the famine casualties with provincial differentiation, as shown in Table 11.1, has been provided by Cao Shuji, the chairman of the history department of Shanghai's Jiao Tong University, who calculated unnatural deaths by means that will be explained in greater detail later in this chapter.

TABLE 11.1: CAO SHUJI'S CALCULATIONS FOR UNNATURAL DEATHS IN EACH PROVINCE

Province	Unnatural deaths (millions)	Unnatural death rate (%)
Anhui	6.33	18.37
Sichuan	9.402	13.07
Guizhou	1.746	10.23
Hunan	2.486	6.81
Gansu	1.023	6.45
Henan	2.939	6.12
Guangxi	0.931	4.63
Yunnan	0.804	4.19
Shandong	1.806	3.38
Jiangsu	1.527	2.88

(Continued)

TABLE 11.1 (*Continued*)

Province	Unnatural deaths (millions)	Unnatural death rate (%)
Hubei	0.675	2.20
Fujian	0.313	2.02
Liaoning	0.33	1.71
Guangdong	0.657	1.71
Heilongjiang	0.19	1.21
Hebei	0.61	1.10
Jiangxi	0.181	1.06
Shaanxi	0.187	1.02
Jilin	0.12	0.94
Zhejiang	0.141	0.55
Shanxi	0.06	0.37
Total	32.458	5.11

Sources: Cao Shuji, The Great Famine: China's Population 1959–1961, *Hong Kong: Xianggang shidai guoji youxian gongsi, 2005, p. 282; Li Chengrui,* China Population Censuses and Analysis of Results, *Beijing: Zhongguo caizheng jingji chubanshe, 1983, p. 58.*

REASONS FOR DISPARITY IN THE EFFECTS OF THE GREAT FAMINE

Given China's highly centralized system, why did the Great Famine hit some regions harder? To sociologist Li Ruojian, location and natural resources were key factors. The inland provinces suffered more than the coast, and mountain regions more than the plains.[1]

Cao Shuji believes that places where popular memory of past famine was strong built up resistance to renewed famine. During the Taiping era, Jiangxi suffered many deaths, and Shanxi and Shaanxi also experienced famines over the preceding century. Local people therefore attached much greater importance to food supply, and during the Great Leap Forward they resisted pressure from the upper levels to hand over their grain. Their mortality rates during the famine were lower as a result.

I believe that two additional factors contributed to the severity of the famine:

Factor No. 1: The consequences of the Great Famine were harshest where officials fell under Mao Zedong's influence most strongly.

Different provinces fell under Beijing's centrifugal force to varying degrees. Where the central influence was strongest, the effects of the famine were harshest, and where that influence exerted less pull, the effects of the famine were somewhat ameliorated. Plainly put, provincial party secretaries who kept in step with Mao during the Great Leap Forward, and who displayed the greatest "creativity" in promoting the government's policies, brought the greatest disaster upon their people. In the spring of 1959 the CCP Central Committee granted some concessions to the peasants, but some provincial party secretaries implemented them only partially or not at all, anticipating (as it turned out, correctly) that Mao did not genuinely endorse these reforms.

In localities where the leading cadre's political attitude most closely matched Mao's, the effect of the famine was felt most harshly. Even if the cadre was located far from Beijing and had reached only the county level of the bureaucracy, he could still read the party newspapers, access Central Committee documents, and hear leaders' broadcasted speeches. Consequently, a province where the provincial party secretary evaded irrational directives might have a relatively low death rate, but certain localities within it might still suffer disaster.

Most provinces were lackluster in their implementation of central policies, and as a result, the mortality rate in many provinces did not exceed 2 percent, even in 1960. The famine was generally less devastating among the remote minorities of Tibet, Xinjiang, and Inner Mongolia. However, the Guangxi Zhuang Minority Autonomous Region had a mortality rate of 2.946 percent, and Yunnan, with its many autonomous minority counties, recorded a death rate of 2.62 percent. Here the leading cadres were mostly Han Chinese with stronger ties to the Center.

Cadres who heeded Mao were swiftly promoted, whereas those who lagged risked political peril. Some policies demanded strict compliance.

Procurement quotas had to be met, people's communes had to be established, and iron- and steel-forging and irrigation campaigns had to be launched. It was possible to haggle with the Center over procurement quotas, or to take local circumstances into account in steelmaking and irrigation projects, but typically at the expense of individual careers.

Even where political pressure was a greater factor than central stipulations, most officials still went along with the flow. Lagging brought the risk of being labeled right-deviating, so most officials preferred to aim for rapid development, as in the case of the communal kitchens. It might be possible to ignore a social trend and to pay no attention to media reports about high-yield "Sputnik" fields, for example, but this risked an impression of backwardness.

Revealing the effects of the famine was also perilous. When food supplies were inadequate, a local leader had to decide whether to fulfill the procurement quota at the expense of lives or request a reduction in the quota. The leader had to decide whether to cover up the famine in reports. When communal kitchens increased suffering, should they be maintained in name only while allowing households to prepare their own meals? When peasants reached the brink of death, did one dare open the grain stores and distribute emergency provisions? When peasants tried to save themselves through household production, should a local leader oppose it, turn a blind eye, or support their efforts? These decisions tested the humanity of local officials, and it was those most in thrall to Mao who tended to ignore the call of conscience.

Changle County party secretary Wang Yongcheng was a positive example. When he learned that the communal kitchens had virtually nothing edible to serve, and that homes had no food, he made it his priority to solve the food problem and save the peasants from starvation. Wang informed the prefectural party committee and suspended the campaign against right deviation. He requested grain from the upper levels and led peasants in "self-help production projects." Sweet potatoes, a high-yield crop that grew quickly, were planted, producing an excellent crop that prevented the worst of the famine. Since pumpkins ripened early, Wang ordered the planting of pumpkins, which produced a bumper harvest of what villagers referred to as "life-saver melons." The county leadership allotted land for household cultivation at the upper limit of the 7 percent stipulated by the central government, while ensuring that this included the best land. Peasants were allowed to grow crops around their homes, in gullies, along roadsides and slopes, and on all marginal land.[2] The result was that while Shandong suffered one of the highest percentages of starvation deaths, no one starved to death in Changle County.

Factor No. 2: The famine hit hardest where procurement quotas were highest and sales of grain to the countryside were lowest.

The statistical table compiled by the Food Ministry's planning department in August 1962 recorded grain yields for each province during the years of the Great Famine, along with the procurement figures and grain sales figures, which allow for calculation of the per capita consumption of grain for each province.

TABLE 11.2: GRAIN PRODUCTION DURING THE GREAT FAMINE (IN BILLION KILOS)

Region	1957	1958	1959	1960	1961
National total	181.95	199.0	170.0	144.05	133.85
Northern Region	1.33	1.02	0.90	0.67	0.71
Beijing	0.79	0.89	0.58	0.55	0.61
Hebei	9.1	10.05	9.05	7.33	131.97
Tianjin	0.21	0.16	0.18	0.10	0.12
Shanxi	3.56	4.63	4.07	3.37	3.49
Inner Mongolia	2.96	4.75	4.25	3.5	3.4
Northeast Region	16.92	21.05	19.7	12.99	14.47
Liaoning	5.87	7.0	6.3	3.49	4.07
Jilin	4.3	5.25	5.4	4.0	4.4
Heilongjiang	6.65	8.8	8.0	5.5	5.0
Eastern Region	52.61	55.57	48.69	43.4	40.34

(Continued)

TABLE 11.2 (*Continued*)

Region	1957	1958	1959	1960	1961
Shanghai	1.02	1.16	1.1	1.16	1.1
Jiangsu	11.0	11.5	10.09	9.75	9.0
Zhejiang	7.25	7.85	7.75	6.45	6.25
Anhui	10.2	9.2	7.35	7.52	6.09
Jiangxi	6.2	6.75	6.25	6.10	5.91
Fujian	4.44	4.76	4.0	3.29	3.0
Shandong	12.11	14.35	12.15	9.12	9.0
South Central Region	50.12	53.41	44.39	39.3	36.06
Guangdong	11.45	11.75	9.65	9.5	9.75
Guangxi	5.25	5.3	5.05	4.6	4.4
Hubei	9.8	10.0	7.7	7.9	6.7
Hunan	11.3	12.25	11.09	8.0	8.0
Henan	12.3	14.05	10.88	9.3	7.21
Southwest Region	34.69	36.02	27.78	24.45	21.1915
Sichuan	23.26	24.75	18.42	16.2	13.0
Yunnan	6.08	5.54	5.12	4.86	5.02
Guizhou	5.36	5.73	4.24	3.39	3.18
Northwest Region	11.12	12.5	11.34	9.11	8.6
Shaanxi	4.44	5.38	4.89	4.16	3.73
Gansu	3.73	3.83	3.25	2.07	2.25
Qinghai	0.59	0.57	0.5	0.41	0.37
Xinjiang	1.82	2.03	2.07	2.017	1.8
Ningxia	0.55	0.7	0.64	0.46	0.46

Source: "Food Ministry Planning Department Grain Data Summary," August 25, 1962.

TABLE 11.3: GRAIN PROCUREMENT DURING THE GREAT FAMINE
(TRADE GRAIN IN BILLION KILOS)

Region	1957–58	1958–59	1959–60	1960–61	1961–62
National total	46.01	56.27	60.71	39.04	33.96
Northern Region	4.02	6.22	6.89	3.64	3.77
Beijing	0.22	0.21	0.15	0.06	0.10
Hebei	2.16	3.22	3.58	1.58	1.63
Tianjin	0.12	0.088	0.10	0.059	0.07
Shanxi	0.72	1.32	1.47	0.77	0.9
Inner Mongolia	0.81	1.38	1.6	1.17	1.07
Northeast Region	5.81	8.78	9.67	6.58	5.49
Liaoning	1.31	1.99	2.22	1.25	1.29
Jilin	1.48	2.48	2.59	2.23	1.93
Heilongjiang	3.02	4.26	4.86	3.10	2.27
Eastern Region	14.32	15.24	16.84	10.8	9.94
Shanghai	0.41	0.44	0.50	0.35	0.38
Jiangsu	3.28	3.73	3.71	2.94	2.20
Zhejiang	2.12	2.38	2.66	1.65	1.65
Anhui	3.42	2.92	2.85	1.75	1.28
Jiangxi	1.54	1.66	2.06	1.76	1.55
Fujian	1.0	1.01	1.3	0.87	0.73
Shandong	2.55	3.09	3.73	1.48	2.15
South Central Region	11.46	14.07	13.69	8.83	7.37
Guangdong	2.54	2.45	3.05	2.34	2.10
Guangxi	0.94	1.14	1.49	1.08	0.89
Hubei	2.5	2.83	2.77	2.29	1.69

(Continued)

TABLE 11.3 (*Continued*)

Region	1957–58	1958–59	1959–60	1960–61	1961–62
Hunan	2.29	2.66	2.99	1.75	1.55
Henan	3.19	4.99	3.38	1.33	1.13
Southwest Region	7.66	8.58	9.48	6.92	5.07
Sichuan	5.54	6.08	6.46	4.77	3.28
Yunnan	1.01	1.11	1.34	0.98	1.00
Guizhou	1.10	1.39	1.68	1.18	0.79
Northwest Region	2.74	3.44	4.15	2.28	2.32
Shaanxi	1.1	1.21	1.54	0.69	1.12
Gansu	0.85	1.11	1.25	0.62	0.48
Qinghai	0.16	0.22	0.26	0.18	0.08
Xinjiang	0.46	0.67	0.83	0.66	0.51
Ningxia	0.18	0.23	0.27	0.14	0.13

Source: "Food Ministry Planning Department Grain Data Summary," August 25, 1962.

TABLE 11.4: GRAIN SALES DURING THE GREAT FAMINE (TRADE GRAIN IN BILLION KILOS)

Region	1957–58	1958–59	1959–60	1960–61	1961–62
National total	42.10	52.60	55.96	41.85	36.82
Northern Region	6.16	7.53	8.30	6.44	5.49
Beijing	1.0	1.25	1.48	1.2	1.14
Hebei	2.64	3.20	3.30	2.18	1.85
Tianjin	0.77	0.97	0.99	0.86	0.82
Shanxi	1.01	1.18	1.39	1.07	0.87
Inner Mongolia	0.75	0.94	1.14	1.13	0.82
Northeast Region	6.02	6.81	7.83	7.66	6.45
Liaoning	2.77	2.91	3.39	3.12	2.71

(*Continued*)

TABLE 11.4 (*Continued*)

Region	1957–58	1958–59	1959–60	1960–61	1961–62
Jilin	1.31	1.62	1.67	1.77	1.53
Heilongjiang	1.94	2.29	2.77	2.77	2.21
Eastern Region	13.38	16.34	16.33	11.86	10.19
Shanghai	1.63	1.83	2.01	1.73	1.70
Jiangsu	3.19	3.53	3.66	2.47	2.04
Zhejiang	1.72	2.11	2.19	1.58	1.35
Anhui	2.05	2.96	2.53	1.62	1.16
Jiangxi	1.13	1.29	1.42	1.32	1.085
Fujian	0.87	1.06	1.18	0.87	0.81
Shandong	2.78	3.57	3.34	2.27	2.05
South Central Region	9.67	11.73	12.47	8.77	7.25
Guangdong	2.37	2.46	2.71	2.25	1.88
Guangxi	1.04	1.12	1.19	0.90	0.8
Hubei	2.25	2.58	2.66	1.99	1.63
Hunan	1.70	1.89	2.25	1.61	1.38
Henan	2.31	3.67	3.66	2.01	1.56
Southwest Region	4.60	7.15	7.64	6.68	5.01
Sichuan	2.95	4.64	5.07	4.37	3.48
Yunnan	0.89	1.24	1.21	0.99	0.81
Guizhou	0.76	1.28	1.35	1.32	0.71
Northwest Region	2.27	3.032	3.39	2.94	2.20
Shaanxi	0.90	1.027	1.14	0.99	0.89
Gansu	0.65	1.019	0.96	0.9	0.54
Qinghai	0.17	0.25	0.2	0.25	0.16
Xinjiang	0.44	0.56	0.80	0.68	0.49
Ningxia	0.11	0.17	0.19	0.13	0.12

Source: "Food Ministry Planning Department Grain Data Summary," August 25, 1962.

The grain requisitioned was the amount each province was required to provide to the state. Grain needed in the countryside for food rations, seed, and livestock feed had to be sold back to the localities. The state gathered grain into state warehouses and then sold the grain from those warehouses. From the point of view of the Food Ministry, the procurement was income and what was sold was disbursement, and income minus disbursement equaled reserves. For a province, procurement was a disbursement and the sale of grain to the localities was income, and production minus procurement plus sales equaled the province's grain budget.

The grain "in hand" included meal rations, animal feed, seed grain, and grain for industrial use. Following deduction of the last three items, only 30 percent of the grain in hand was left for meal rations. The policy of squeezing the villages to save the cities made the per capita consumption of peasants much lower than official figures indicate. Deductions were made at each level of the bureaucracy, so the amount that each peasant received was lower yet. Although the per capita consumption for 1961 and 1962 was the lowest, by that time many localities had assigned output quotas to households and encouraged the cultivation of marginal land, so the amount of grain to which peasants had access was greater than in the prior three years.

TABLE 11.5: PER CAPITA GRAIN BUDGET FOR EACH PROVINCE DURING THE GREAT FAMINE (TRADE GRAIN IN KILOS)

Location	1957	1958	1959	1960	1961
Hebei	228.8	233.7	200.3	184.6	213.3
Shanxi	213.0	239.4	207.7	190.0	175.6
Inner Mongolia	267.7	373.6	304.8	251.8	232.6
Liaoning	273.9	286.6	265.7	191.4	197.0
Jilin	286.3	289.0	287.5	215.9	242.2
Heilongjiang	317.8	363.0	289.6	246.4	236.6
Jiangsu	226.4	230.2	203.2	188.7	180.5
Zhejiang	236.0	255.6	241.2	211.8	192.7

(*Continued*)

TABLE 11.5 (Continued)

Location	1957	1958	1959	1960	1961
Anhui	223.4	234.4	176.2	207.1	173.0
Jiangxi	288.0	287.4	242.7	243.1	233.4
Fujian	256.8	280.1	217.6	181.8	168.6
Shandong	200.2	239.0	189.2	183.1	146.7
Guangdong	272.3	278.7	215.1	214.6	216.1
Guangxi	217.3	209.8	185.4	176.3	172.8
Hubei	269.9	268.5	216.9	208.5	181.3
Hunan	256.6	269.6	241.1	190.0	193.5
Henan	202.8	220.6	195.6	181.8	138.8
Sichuan	253.9	283.5	206.5	198.4	178.0
Yunnan	276.6	258.4	226.0	223.7	220.6
Guizhou	256.4	284.6	193.0	187.9	165.1
Shaanxi	203.2	244.6	204.8	201.4	153.1
Gansu	242.8	252.8	195.7	167.2	166.1
Qinghai	257.8	232	180.2	171.1	188.7

Source: Calculated from the figures in Tables 11.2, 11.3, and 11.4, and the population figures for each province recorded in the China Population *series.*

The areas hardest hit by the famine tended to be those with a per capita grain allocation of 210 kilos or less. In 1959 and 1960, these included Hebei (200.3, 184.6), Shanxi (207.7, 190.0), Jiangsu (203.3, 188.7), Anhui (176.2, 207.1), Shandong (189.2, 183.1), Henan (195.6, 181.8), Sichuan (206.5, 198.4), Guizhou (193.0, 187.9), Gansu (195.7, 167.2), and Qinghai (180.2, 171.1). The 1960 per capita grain allocation was also lower than 210 kilos in Hubei, Hunan, and Fujian, but they were hit less hard by the famine. In a small number of provinces, including Jiangsu, Hebei, and Shanxi, the per capita grain allocation was low, but the famine's effects were less severe.

Clearly per capita grain allocation wasn't the only cause of severe famine. Other factors included: whether policies allowed peasants to seek their own food supplies by cultivating small plots and marginal land; whether irrigation and other big projects exhausted labor resources; and the duration of mandatory participation in the communal kitchens. Decisions on all these matters hinged greatly on the local leadership's allegiance to Mao and his policies.

TOTAL POPULATION LOSS DURING THE GREAT FAMINE

The number of starvation deaths during the Great Famine remains a sensitive issue. Given that the government did its utmost to cover up or shrink the death figures, the records on starvation deaths are incomplete and unreliable, and extensive research in China and overseas has been able to produce only rough estimates.

Population figures from the State Statistical Bureau were reported by the Ministry of Public Security based on household registration (*hukou*) records. These are the official figures acknowledged by the central government, and although deaths were underreported, the trends in population change reflected by the data are reliable. The data indicate that the "three-year famine" (1959, 1960, and 1961) actually began in the winter of 1958, reflected in a higher-than-normal mortality rate and a lower-than-normal birth rate. By 1962 the death rate throughout the country, except for Sichuan and a few other provinces, had returned to a normal level, and the post-famine recovery led to above-normal birth rates.

Wang Weizhi, an official in the Public Security Ministry responsible for population statistics, said that data on deaths at that time were top secret. Data on Shandong Province could be accessed by only five people: the party secretary and deputy party secretary of the provincial party committee, the provincial governor and vice-governor, and the public security head. Food minister Chen Guodong, Vice-Minister Zhou Boping, and the director of the State Bureau of Statistics, Jia Qiyun, were charged in 1961 with directing each province to compile data on food supply and demographics. The data indicated a population loss of tens of millions. This information was reported to only two people: Premier Zhou Enlai and Mao Zedong. After reading the report, the premier contacted Zhou Boping and told him to destroy it immediately and make sure that no one else saw it. Zhou Boping, Chen Guoding, and Jia Qiyun supervised the destruction of the original data and copies of the report. Premier Zhou relaxed only once Zhou Boping had assured him that all copies had been destroyed.[3] From then on, no population figures were published, and every level of government did its best to cover up or minimize the number of starvation deaths recorded. By reporting fewer deaths, local officials were less vulnerable and could also claim grain rations for the unreported dead.

China staged its third national census in 1982, and published the results along with the census results from 1953 and 1964. The figures indicate a 1960 population decrease of 10 million, from 672 million in 1959 to 662 million in 1960.[4]

Professor Zhang Qingwu of Chinese People's Public Security University carried out population statistical work within the Public Security Ministry from 1955 to 1986. He told me the ministry's figures were all provided by the provincial public security bureaus, which obtained their figures from the county public security bureaus, and the county bureaus obtained their figures from lower-level units. The figures were taken as reported, except in cases of obvious error, and the Public Security Ministry's Third Division almost never modified the data it received.

Since grassroots cadres feared bearing political responsibility for excessive deaths, they would never overreport deaths. In addition, local officials could claim a food ration for each living person, whereas deaths decreased rations. The reported number of deaths could therefore be assumed to be less than reality.

The population figures published in 1984, including total population and mortality and birth rates, are laid out in Table 11.6.

TABLE 11.6: OFFICIALLY PUBLISHED POPULATION FIGURES BY YEAR (IN MILLIONS), BIRTH RATES, AND MORTALITY RATES (%)

Year	Year-end population	Birth rate	Mortality rate	Natural population growth
1953	587.96	3.7	1.4	2.3
1954	602.66	3.78	1.32	2.48
1955	616.45	3.26	1.23	2.032

(*Continued*)

TABLE 11.6 (*Continued*)

Year	Year-end population	Birth rate	Mortality rate	Natural population growth
1956	628.28	3.19	1.14	2.05
1957	646.53	3.40	1.01	2.32
1958	659.94	2.92	1.2	1.72
1959	672.07	2.48	1.46	1.02
1960	662.07	2.07	2.5	−0.46
1961	658.59	1.80	1.42	0.38
1962	672.95	3.70	1.00	2.7
1963	691.72	4.34	1.00	3.33
1964	704.99	3.91	1.15	2.76
1965	725.38	3.79	0.95	2.84
1966	745.42	3.51	0.88	2.62

Source: China Population Yearbook (1984), *Beijing: Zhongguo tongji chubanshe, 1984, p. 83.*

Using this data, it is possible to calculate how many people were born or died in a given year. Once the number of deaths during the famine years is calculated, the number of deaths by unnatural causes can be calculated by subtracting the number of deaths by natural causes; i.e.:

Unnatural deaths = (year n death rate − normal death rate) × year n total population

In order to calculate how many people starved to death in a given year, it is important to know the normal mortality rate for that year and the total population (given as the average of the population at the beginning and the end of that year). The higher the rate of normal deaths, the lower the rate of unnatural deaths, and vice versa. In calculating the number of unnatural deaths for the years 1958 to 1962, some scholars use the 1957 mortality rate as the normal death rate.

When I made my own calculations, I took into account that in the peacetime years following 1949, the birth rate gradually increased, and the mortality rate decreased. This trend continued right up until the government began implementing its population-control policy in 1972. Under normal circumstances, these population trends should have continued in the years 1957 through 1964.

I used the average figures for the three years prior to 1958 (1955–57) as the starting point, and the average figures for the three years after 1962 (1964–66) as the end point. I calculated the end point figures starting in 1964 to avoid the immediate aftereffects of the famine, such as compensatory increases. However, the 1964 census made a one-time elimination of 8.2 million in overreported population over the previous two years,[*] resulting in an unusually high "mortality rate" for 1964. For this reason, in calculating the normal mortality rate, I used the mortality rate figures from 1963, 1965, and 1966.

On the basis of these figures, I made the following calculations:

Normal mortality rate $= \{(1.228 + 1.14 + 1.08)\%/3 + (1.004 + 0.95 + 0.883)\%/3\}/2 = 1.047\%$

Normal birth rate $= \{(3.260 + 3.190 + 3.403)\%/3 + (3.914 + 3.788 + 3.505)\%/3\}/2 = 3.51\%$

By this method, I calculated unnatural deaths as 1958 = .986 million, 1959 = 2.744 million, 1960 = 9.979 million, 1961 = 2.489 million. The total number of unnatural deaths in the three years of the Great Famine then comes to 16.198 million.

During the famine, birth rates dropped due to malnutrition, gynecological disorders, and reduced sperm count, and the disruption of normal marital relations. The birth rate often decreased even faster than the mortality rate increased. Shanghai experienced few starvation deaths during the famine, but it had a shortfall of about 140,000 births.

The shortfall in the number of births during the famine years can be calculated from the normal birth rates and the actual number of births in a given year following a similar process to that used for unnatural deaths. Based on the official figures, I arrived at the following birth shortfalls: 1958 = 3.854 million, 1959 = 6.873 million, 1960 = 9.499 million, 1961 = 11.278 million. The total shortfall in births during the three famine years is thus 31.5 million.

[*]As reported to me by Wang Weizhi, who was involved in the process.

By this calculation method, the Great Famine caused a total population loss of more than 47.7 million.

The total population loss can be calculated from a different angle. We can combine the natural population growth with the normal mortality rate and normal birth rate to arrive at the normal population growth rate. By this method, the population under normal circumstances at the end of 1961 should have been 711.92 million. That means that the total population loss for the famine years was 53.33 million. This includes the number of unnatural deaths as well as the shortfall in births.

The total population reduction figures arrived at by the two methods differ because figures for each year compound inaccuracies from the year before.

FIGURE 11.1: THE POPULATION PYRAMID

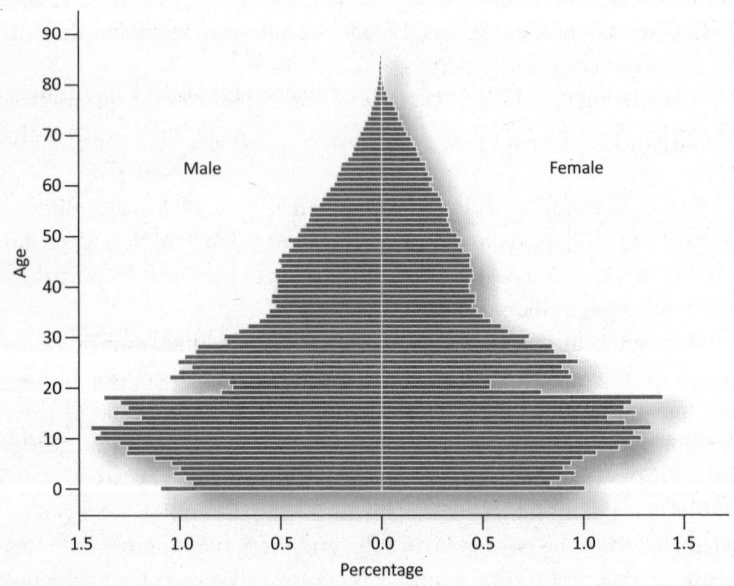

The population pyramid uses a linear format to incorporate the age and sex distribution of the population for each year. The ordinal axis represents age, and the transverse axis represents the proportion of the population. The left side of the transverse axis represents the male population, and the right side of the transverse axis represents the female population. Age advances upward on the ordinal axis.

China's three sets of census data each produced a population pyramid. From Figure 11.1 it can be seen that the Great Famine produced horrific gaps in the age structure.

CALCULATIONS DERIVED FROM THE FIGURES
PROVIDED BY EACH PROVINCE

China's national borders cover a vast territory with large disparities in local conditions that were reflected in the statistics relating to the famine. The population figures for each province presented in the *China Population* series since 1986 are compiled by an editorial committee under the leadership of the Education Ministry, the National Population and Family Planning Commission, and the State Council's Population Census Office. The figures on unnatural deaths have been reduced, but they can be considered closer to the truth.

Calculating the normal mortality rate based on average figures from the three years preceding and three years following the Great Famine (1955, 1956, 1957, 1963, 1965, 1966), the results are as follows:

TABLE 11.7: EFFECT OF THE GREAT FAMINE ON EACH PROVINCE (IN MILLIONS)

Location	1958	1959	1960	1961	1962	Total
SICHUAN						
Unnatural deaths	0.9853	2.5337	2.9942	1.2304	0.2265	7.9701
Shortfall in births	0.8696	1.3961	1.7259	1.6553	0.545	6.1919
ANHUI						
Unnatural deaths	0.0946	0.2412	1.927			2.2628
Shortfall in births	0.3974	0.5381	0.7903	0.7048		2.4306

(*Continued*)

TABLE 11.7 (*Continued*)

Location	1958	1959	1960	1961	1962	Total
HENAN						
Unnatural deaths	0.0989	0.1718	1.3938			1.6645
Shortfall in births	0.0744	0.3279	1.0125	0.9352		2.35
SHANDONG						
Unnatural deaths	0.143	0.435	0.7118	0.4375	0.1171	1.8443
Shortfall in births	0.0535	0.7849	0.8417	0.5765		2.2566
HUNAN						
Unnatural deaths		0.0493	0.6467	0.2072		0.9032
Shortfall in births	0.2186	0.4404	0.5997	0.8318		2.0905
GUIZHOU						
Unnatural deaths	0.0119	0.1005	0.6396	0.1434		0.8959
Shortfall in births	0.1388	0.247	0.3709	0.413		1.1697
GUANGXI						
Unnatural deaths	0.0143	0.1407	0.4023	0.1823		0.7396
Shortfall in births	0.0741	0.2584	0.3687	0.402		1.1032
GANSU						
Unnatural deaths	0.1445	0.0991	0.401	0.0221		0.6667
Shortfall in births	0.059	0.2169	0.262	0.2621		0.8
JIANGSU						
Unnatural deaths		0.1752	0.3397	0.123		0.6379
Shortfall in births	0.4343	0.6069	0.7078	0.0923	0.0793	1.9206
LIAONING						
Unnatural deaths	0.0242	0.0989	0.0936	0.2463	0.0177	0.4807
Shortfall in births		0.2164	0.1253	0.4965	0.0672	0.9054
GUANGDONG						
Unnatural deaths	0.018	0.1149	0.2438	0.0772	0.0263	0.4802
Shortfall in births	0.1551	0.3594	0.5798	0.48		1.57

(*Continued*)

TABLE 11.7 (*Continued*)

Location	1958	1959	1960	1961	1962	Total
YUNNAN						
Unnatural deaths	0.1512	0.0828	0.2404			0.4744
Shortfall in births	0.2853	0.3396	0.276	0.365		1.2659
HUBEI						
Unnatural deaths		0.1311	0.3428			0.4739
Shortfall in births	0.063	0.1928	0.5092	0.1641		0.9291
HEBEI						
Unnatural deaths	0.0178	0.0696	0.2044	0.1208		0.4126
Shortfall in births	0.2487	0.304	0.4039	0.6075	0.0975	1.6616
FUJIAN						
Unnatural deaths			0.1156	0.0626	0.0058	0.184
Shortfall in births	0.0884	0.1148	0.1559	0.2806		0.6397
JIANGXI						
Unnatural deaths		0.0332	0.0949	0.0048		0.1329
Shortfall in births	0.1037	0.139	0.1796	0.2967		0.719
JILIN						
Unnatural deaths	0.0009	0.0567	0.0145	0.0417	0.014	0.1278
Shortfall in births	0.0612	0.1311	0.0764	0.1645		0.4332
ZHEJIANG						
Unnatural deaths		0.0261	0.0673	0.0143		0.1077
Shortfall in births	0.0337	0.2362	0.3106	0.4712		1.0517
QINGHAI						
Unnatural deaths	0.0061	0.0156	0.0777	0.0035		0.1029
Shortfall in births	0.0218	0.0365	0.0636	0.0613	0.0049	0.1881
HEILONGJIANG						
Unnatural deaths		0.0571	0.0213	0.0329		0.1113
Shortfall in births	0.0746	0.1217	0.0942	0.1916	0.0444	0.5265

(*Continued*)

TABLE 11.7 (*Continued*)

Location	1958	1959	1960	1961	1962	Total
SHANDONG						
Unnatural deaths	0.0024	0.0206	0.0446	0.0111		0.0787
Shortfall in births	0.0685	0.0899	0.0955	0.2367		0.4906
SHAANXI						
Unnatural deaths		0.0278	0.021			0.0488
Shortfall in births	0.1185	0.1229	0.1058	0.2395		0.5867
NINGXIA						
Unnatural deaths	0.0091	0.0115	0.0079	0.0012		0.0298
Shortfall in births	0.0047	0.0363	0.0533	0.0599		0.1542
XINJIANG						
Unnatural deaths		0.0345	0.0162			0.0507
Shortfall in births		0.0367	0.0517	0.0748		0.1632
INNER MONGOLIA						
Unnatural deaths		0.012				0.012
Shortfall in births		0.0638	0.086	0.1757		0.3255
BEIJING						
Unnatural deaths			0.0098	0.0155		0.0253
Shortfall in births				0.0539		0.0539
TIANJIN						
Unnatural deaths		0.0097	0.0127	0.0102		0.0326
Shortfall in births		0.0111	0.0178	0.0587		0.0876
SHANGHAI						
Unnatural deaths			0.0049	0.0144	0.0102	0.0295
Shortfall in births			0.025	0.0801	0.0391	0.1442
NATIONAL TOTAL						
Unnatural deaths	1.72	4.75	11.09	3.0	0.42	20.98
Shortfall in births	3.65	7.35	9.89	10.44	0.87	32.2
TOTAL POPULATION LOSS	5.37	12.1	20.98	13.44	1.29	53.18

These figures indicate a total population loss of 53.18 million, including 20.98 million unnatural deaths. After Mao's death, provinces revised their previously reported figures, bringing them somewhat closer to reality. But even in the 1980s, starvation deaths remained a highly sensitive political issue, and unnatural deaths based on figures provided by some provinces are smaller than those reported by investigators. For example, the investigation carried out in Anhui by Li Jian of the Central Control Commission estimated 3 million unnatural deaths. During the Cultural Revolution, the former head of the Central Committee's Organization Department, An Ziwen, found that 5 million people starved to death in Anhui. My calculation based on provincial data arrives at a figure of only 2.26 million. Bo Yibo reported that 3 million people starved to death in Shandong, but my calculation produces a figure of only 1.8443 million. The president of Sichuan's provincial people's consultative conference, Liao Bokang, wrote that 12 million people starved to death in Sichuan, but my calculation produces a figure of 7.87 million. A 2001 article in *Fujian Party History Monthly*[5] puts the total number of unnatural deaths in Fujian Province for those three years at 220,000, based on figures from the provincial public security bureau. But my method gives a total of only 180,000 unnatural deaths.

My inquiries uncovered cases of provincial leaders from the famine years continuing to interfere with mortality figures in the 1980s. In any case, as with all official figures, the figures on unnatural deaths drawn

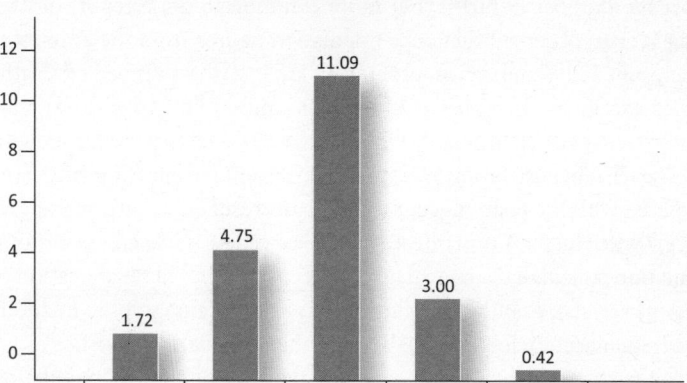

FIGURE 11.2: UNNATURAL DEATHS BASED ON OFFICIAL FIGURES
FROM THE PROVINCES (IN MILLIONS)

from provincial statistics must be considered an underestimate, although somewhat closer to reality than those based on State Statistical Bureau data.

The official provincial data show 1.72 million unnatural deaths in 1958 and 4.75 million in 1959, reaching a peak of 11.09 million in 1960. Following the implementation of famine-relief measures, unnatural deaths rapidly decreased to 3 million in 1961. By 1962 the vast majority of provinces no longer suffered from famine, but a few provinces such as Sichuan contributed to a nationwide total of 420,000 unnatural deaths. While lower than reality, the figures for unnatural deaths still provide a reliable indication of the yearly trends.

RESEARCH BY POPULATION EXPERTS OVERSEAS

Considerable research has been carried out by foreign scholars into the population loss brought about by China's Great Famine. Some of them start out by applying demographic methods to revise the unreliable population figures reported in the *China Statistical Yearbook*.

As noted earlier, the figures in the *China Statistical Yearbook* depended on the recollections of local officials, and as a result there were often discrepancies in these figures as reported by the provinces. The largest discrepancies occur in the birth rates and death rates, mainly due to misreporting. Once population-control policies were strictly enforced, misreporting of births increased. During the era when material goods were allocated according to head count, it was less common to misreport the number of births, but more common to underreport deaths. Wang Weizhi observed that once population figures from the grassroots level reached the county or provincial level, if the number of deaths seemed excessive, the upper-level officials would ask, "Are these figures accurate? Go over them again!" Figures were changed to pass muster with upper-level officials. From 1958 to 1962, the underreporting of deaths compared with the relative accuracy of births resulted in natural population growth (births minus deaths) that exceeded the increase in total population (calculated somewhat more accurately based on allocation of living materials). Population scholars have used demographic methods to address inaccuracies in officially published population statistics.

Compared with the yearly household registration figures, population census figures are more accurate. The censuses conducted in 1953 and

1964 surveyed a limited number of items, such as age, sex, and ethnicity. The third census, in 1982, included a survey of births and deaths for the preceding year, among other additional items. The National Population and Family Planning Commission in 1983 carried out a random birth rate survey, in a population of around one million people, of some three hundred thousand women ages fifteen to sixty-seven to provide a retrospective survey of marriage and birth in the years since 1940. The survey was conducted door-to-door, so it is relatively reliable. Using these different sets of data, demographers applied statistical methods to revise birth rates and death rates.

The head of the China branch of the Center for International Research in the U.S. Census Bureau, Judith Banister, used the Family Planning Commission's survey to recalculate the birth rate and then used the population census data to recalculate the mortality rate. Her main focus was on general trends in China's birth rate and mortality rate. The birth and mortality rates she calculated provide basic data for estimating the changes in China's population during the three years of the Great Famine.

Ansley J. Coale served as president of the Population Association of America and of the International Union for the Scientific Study of Population, and was for many years director of the Office of Population Research at Princeton. He based his research on the Family Planning Commission and census data.

Gérard Calot, director for twenty years of the French National Institute for Demographic Studies, used his own methods to revise the birth rates and death rates for China.

Using the revised birth and mortality rates calculated by these demographers, along with the average total population for each year, it is possible to calculate the number of unnatural deaths and shortfall of births during the three years of the Great Famine. The calculation method uses the three-year average for 1955 to 1957 as a starting point, and the three-year average for 1964 to 1966 as the end point. If there had been no Great Famine, the birth rates and mortality rates should each have formed a continuum, and the mortality rates and birth rates for the years from 1959 to 1961 would have appeared on the line drawn between these two points. An even simpler method is to use the averages of the two points as the normal mortality and birth rates.

Using Banister's data, unnatural deaths come to 3.001 million for 1958, 3.868 million for 1959, 18.335 million for 1960, and 4.567 million for 1961.

TABLE 11.8: REVISED DEATH RATES AND BIRTH RATES CALCULATED BY SEVERAL DEMOGRAPHIC EXPERTS

Year	Birth rate (%)			Mortality rate (%)		
	BANISTER	COALE	CALOT	BANISTER	COALE	CALOT
1954	4.344	4.44	4.191	2.42	2.91	1.996
1955	4.304	4.13	4.137	2.233	2.24	2.231
1956	3.989	4.002	3.828	2.011	2.08	1.685
1957	4.325	4.11	4.145	1.812	1.9	1.324
1958	3.776	3.77	3.622	2.065	2.04	1.598
1959	2.853	2.83	2.724	2.206	2.33	1.92
1960	2.676	2.52	2.565	4.46	3.88	4.076
1961	2.243	2.23	2.17	2.301	2.05	2.703
1962	4.102	4.09	3.979	1.402	1.37	1.828
1963	4.979	4.73	4.869	1.381	1.3	2.122
1964	4.029	4.07	3.982	1.245	1.35	2.082
1965	3.898	3.97	3.877	1.161	1.11	1.026
1966	3.983	3.83	3.952	1.112	1.04	1.227

Sources: Li Chengrui, "Demographic Fluctuation Caused by the 'Great Leap Forward,'" Chinese Communist Party History Research, no. 2 (1997): 1–14; Ansley J. Coale, Rapid Population Change in China, 1952–1982, Washington, D.C.: National Academy Press, 1984.

The total number of unnatural deaths for 1958–61 is 28.871 million. The shortfall in births is 1.997 million for 1958, 8.034 for 1959, 9.2133 for 1960, and 11.951 for 1961, for a four-year total of 31.195 million. Using Banister's data, China's total population loss was 61.066 million.

Using Coale's revised data produces 2.71 million unnatural deaths in 1958, 4.63 million in 1959, 14.68 million in 1960, and 2.78 million in 1961, for a four-year total of 24.80 million. His data produce a four-year total shortfall in births of 30.683 million. China's total population loss is then 55.483 million.

Calculations using the birth and death rates resulting from Calot's revised data produce a five-year total of unnatural deaths of 28.509 million (1.303 million for 1958, 2.14 million for 1959, 16.328 million for 1960, 7.214 million for 1961, and 1.524 million for 1962), and a total shortfall in births of 31.9785 million (2.378 million for 1958, 8.345 million for 1959, 9.362 million for 1960, 11.841 for 1961, and 52,500 for 1962). The total population loss is then 60.488 million.

TABLE 11.9: DEMOGRAPHIC CHANGE BASED ON THE REVISED DATA OF THREE FOREIGN EXPERTS (IN MILLIONS)

	Year	Banister	Coale	Calot
Number of unnatural deaths	1958	3.001	2.71	1.303
	1959	3.968	4.632	2.140
	1960	18.335	14.689	16.328
	1961	4.567	2.7769	7.214
	1962			1.524
	Total	29.871	24.81	28.509
Shortfall in births	1958	1.997	1.613	2.378
	1959	8.034	7.763	8.345
	1960	9.213	9.749	9.362
	1961	11.951	11.558	11.841
	1962			0.0525
	Total	31.195	30.683	31.979
Total population loss		61.066	55.493	60.488

RESEARCH BY CHINESE SCHOLARS

JIANG ZHENGHUA'S RESEARCH

The conclusion reached by Jiang Zhenghua's research is that the total number of unnatural deaths during the Great Famine was 17 million. His conclusion is the mainstream viewpoint in China.

Jiang's research was carried out under impetus from Li Chengrui, a senior revolutionary cadre at the rank of deputy minister with a steadfast faith in communism. Li served for many years as secretary to finance minister Li Xiannian, and was then appointed director of the State Statistical Bureau. At the bureau, Li took charge of the census in 1982, and as a result acquired a fairly deep knowledge of population issues. In June 1985 he attended the Twentieth Conference of the International Union for the Scientific Study of Population and became acquainted with international experts such as Coale, Banister, and Calot. He then decided to study the death and birth rates during the Great Famine, and suggested to the head of the National Population and Family Planning Commission that this question be included on the national research agenda. Jiang Zhenghua, the head of Xi'an Jiaotong University's Population Research Institute, accepted the assignment.

Born in October 1937, Jiang studied at the International Institute for Population Sciences in Bombay (now Mumbai), India, from 1980 to 1982. He established Xi'an Jiaotong University's Population Research Institute in 1984. About a year after the institute was founded, Jiang accepted the assignment from Li Chengrui. The total of 17 million deaths arrived at by Jiang and his assistant Li Nan was endorsed by the relevant state organs.

TABLE 11.10: THREE DIFFERENT SETS OF FIGURES PRESENTED BY JIANG ZHENGHUA (%)

YEAR	*China Population: General Introduction*		*China Population Yearbook 1987*		Xi'an Jiaotong University Journal	
	BIRTH RATE	MORTALITY RATE	BIRTH RATE	MORTALITY RATE	BIRTH RATE	MORTALITY RATE
1955	3.654	1.723	3.732	2.254	3.798	1.268
1956	3.52	1.677	3.592	2.152	3.639	1.28
1957	3.645	1.655	3.684	2.053	3.719	1.301
1958	3.162	1.725	3.177	2.006	3.229	1.336

(Continued)

TABLE 11.10 (*Continued*)

	China Population: General Introduction		*China Population Yearbook 1987*		Xi'an Jiaotong University Journal	
YEAR	BIRTH RATE	MORTALITY RATE	BIRTH RATE	MORTALITY RATE	BIRTH RATE	MORTALITY RATE
1959	2.846	1.896	2.786	2.691	2.777	1.729
1960	2.384	3.125	2.424	3.158	2.467	3.24
1961	2.078	2.457	2.503	2.438	2.45	1.652
1962	4.473	1.808	3.965	1.784	3.837	1.36
1963	4.557	1.672	4.623	1.635	4.537	1.327
1964	4.048	1.303	4.363	1.493	4.123	1.264
1965	3.846	1.128	3.951	1.304	3.943	1.086
1966	3.576	0.964	3.654	1.162	3.666	0.96

TABLE 11.11: JIANG ZHENGHUA'S REVISED TOTAL POPULATION FIGURES (IN MILLIONS)

Year	Estimated year-end population	Estimated mid-year population
1954	603.1	594.68
1955	614.84	607.85
1956	626.36	618.73
1957	638.93	630.57
1958	648.29	643.54
1959	654.76	649.99
1960	652.39	655.04
1961	649.26	649.32

(*Continued*)

TABLE 11.11 (*Continued*)

Year	Estimated year-end population	Estimated mid-year population
1962	667.6	654.89
1963	687.49	676.03
1964	704	694.61
1965	723.58	712.63
1966	743.25	733.56

Source: Yuan Yongxi, ed., China Population: General Introduction, *Beijing: Zhongguo caizheng jingji chubanshe, 1991, p. 618.*

Li Chengrui maintains that Jiang's research was "more scientific" than that of the international scholars. However, I found that Jiang produced three completely different sets of birth and mortality rates.[6]

Jiang reached his total of 17 million unnatural deaths by subtracting natural deaths from total deaths. He arrived at his lower number of unnatural deaths by attributing a larger proportion of deaths to natural causes. The total number of deaths he calculated was only 3.0 million lower than that calculated by Ansley Coale, but the number he attributed to natural causes was 6.62 million higher.

Using Jiang Zhenghua's calculated total deaths of 82.99 million, along with the natural death rate resulting from his revised figures, the result is actually 39.41 million unnatural deaths.

Using the figures presented in *China Population: General Introduction* produces a natural mortality rate of 1.41 percent, which is then used to calculate a total of 55.383 million natural deaths for the years 1958 to 1963, and 27.6 million unnatural deaths.

Using the natural mortality rate of 1.736 percent derived from the data presented in *China Population Yearbook (1987)*, the total number of natural deaths for those six years is 68.188 million, and the total of unnatural deaths is 14.78 million.

The total number of unnatural deaths during the Great Famine that Jiang Zhenghua announced in his 1987 article resulted from his stating death rates prior to the Great Famine that were much higher. The higher non-famine death rates resulted in lower figures for unnatural deaths.

These calculations used Jiang Zhenghua's estimated total deaths and Jiang's revised mortality rates to arrive at the number of natural deaths, and after that the number of unnatural deaths.

It is possible to check Jiang's calculations using his revised birth and mortality rates and the revised average total populations for each year. Because Jiang provided three different sets of figures, we'll carry out these calculations three times:

Calculations using the data published by Xi'an Jiaotong University produce unnatural deaths of 0.9203 million in 1958, 3.4839 million in 1959, 13.4086 million in 1960, 2.9803 million in 1961, and 1.0936 million in 1962, for a five-year total of 21.8867 million. The shortfall in births totals 28.21 million. The total loss to China's population thus comes to 50.097 million lives.

Calculations based on the data Jiang Zhenghua presents in *China Population: General Introduction* produce a total of 23.37 million unnatural deaths and a shortfall of 28.685 million births, for a total population loss of 52.055 million lives.

Calculations based on the data presented in "Methods and Results of Estimating China's Population Trends" produce 22.099 million unnatural deaths and a shortfall of 27.489 million births, for a total population loss of 49.588 million lives.

Calculations attempting to verify Jiang's results produce large discrepancies, and none produce the figure of 17 million unnatural deaths he reported and the government endorsed. In an attempt to get to the bottom of these discrepancies, I wrote to Jiang in 2002, but he did not reply. I surmised that the number of unnatural deaths Jiang initially calculated too greatly exceeded the State Statistical Bureau figures, so he subsequently put forward other figures that employed a higher natural mortality to reduce the number of unnatural deaths and thereby reduce the political risk. Of the figures Jiang published, those in the most "official" format, *China Population Yearbook (1987)*, give the highest natural death rate, possibly with this consideration in mind.

In June 2005, I wrote to Jiang again, and this time received a reply on October 19, written by hand on the stationery of the National People's Congress standing committee secretariat, but with the letterhead in black, indicating that what I had received was a photocopy:

Comrade Jisheng:

My apologies for my delayed response to your letter.

The change in China's population during its time of economic hardship is a matter of concern both inside and outside of China, and is a past event that we should clarify for history. The calculations by foreign scholars of unnatural deaths during those years use the mortality rate for 1957 or earlier, or the mortality rate for 1964 or adjoining years, as the standard for estimating the natural mortality rate in the intervening years, and consider its difference from the actual mortality rate during those years as the number of unnatural deaths. This kind of estimate has two major flaws: first, mortality rates differ among different age groups, and using a general mortality rate cannot take into account the influence of the different patterns among age groups from 1957 to 1964. Under the mortality rate levels of that time, the mortality rate of infants and children dropped relatively fast, while the change in the mortality rate among other age brackets was relatively less, or none at all. Second, among the deaths from unnatural causes, elderly people made up a relatively larger proportion because that group is more seriously affected by unfavorable living conditions and has less ability to escape a detrimental environment. For that reason, some scholars have arrived at excessively high calculation results. The 1982 population census provided us with very good data, and following the fourth and fifth censuses, we carried out analysis of the data and discovered that the quality of the data in these two censuses was inferior to that of the third census. We therefore felt that using the detailed data for mortality rate divisions by age group in that census was most reliable. We used the 1982 data to compile a life expectancy table based on age, then used optimization technology to reconstruct life expectancy tables for previous years. The differentials between the mortality rates and unnatural mortality rates for 1957 to 1965 that we calculated from these are, from a methodological standpoint, more rigorous than those of the foreign scholars. Our advantage was having the full support of Comrade Chengrui, who provided us with micro data collected firsthand for the third (1982) census.

The reason for the differences between the three sets of figures is that during the optimization it was necessary to adopt a historical point for the standard criteria; the optimization technology can also *have different criteria for general optimization and age group optimization. The historical starting point can use the mortality rate from one year, or the average of the years before and after, as the standard. It can also adapt the mortality rate of each year. The first results published in the* Xi'an Jiaotong University Journal *used general optimization and timepoint standard criteria for the calculation. When the results were published in the* Yearbook, *we had already used general optimization to adapt the historical mortality rate for each year, and this caused changes to the life expectancy tables. While calculating the figures for* China Population: General Introduction, *we made another improvement to the optimization technology, adopting an age bracket optimization method, which methodologically speaking is the most rigorous. In my personal opinion, these particular results are the ones I would recommend as the standard for you to consult. I don't have the detailed data in hand, and many of the calculation results are buried in piles of manuscripts and data; I wish I had an opportunity to sort through them. I remember that the results of the three calculations differed by only around 2 million, and 17 million was the round number. If I find the original materials, I will provide you with the exact figures.*

I offer you the above circumstances for your reference. It is sincerely worthy of respect that you maintain your interest in state affairs after your retirement.

In haste and with best wishes for the autumn months,
Jiang Zhenghua
October 17, 2005

Jiang said there was a discrepancy of only around 2 million between his three figures, but the discrepancy is much larger according to my computation. He says the three sets of figures are different because of different "optimization" methods carried out on the data. On the issue of Jiang Zhenghua's "optimization" techniques, demographers can pass their own scientific judgments.

DING SHU'S RESEARCH

Another person who has carried out research into population loss during the Great Famine is the overseas Chinese scholar Ding Shu. He holds:

1. If there is a reliable mortality rate, then:

the number of unnatural deaths in year n = (year n mortality rate – the natural mortality rate) × the population at the end of the previous year (n–1)

2. If there is a reliable birth rate, then:

the number of unnatural deaths in year n = the population at the end of year n – {1 + (birth rate – natural mortality rate)} × population at the end of the previous year (n–1)

Lacking either a reliable birth rate or a reliable mortality rate, Ding treated the 1957 mortality rate as the natural mortality rate (1.080 percent). If not for the Great Famine, the mortality rate should have decreased, so using the 1957 mortality rate as the natural mortality rate for the famine would not underestimate the natural mortality rate. Based on the 1964 census data, he did his own calculation for the birth rates for the years 1958–62 and used the second of these formulas to make his computations. His conclusion is a total of 35 million unnatural deaths from 1958 through 1962.[7]

JIN HUI'S RESEARCH

Jin Hui in Shanghai has also put forward a number. In 1993, Jin Hui used the population figures the Chinese government published for 1953–66 to point out that China's population was reduced by 13.48 million in 1960 and 1961. Based on the birth rates published by the government, he also calculated a total of 25.68 million births for 1960 and 1961. Finally, he calculated a natural mortality rate for 1959–61 based on the average mortality rate for the years 1956, 1957, 1962, and 1963, from which he estimated a total of 13.95 million natural deaths for 1960 and 1961.

Births – natural deaths + population decrease = unnatural deaths

According to this method, the number of unnatural deaths in 1960 and 1961 totaled 25.21 million. Applying the same calculation method to the year 1959 arrives at a total of 27.91 million unnatural deaths for the three years.

Jin Hui feels that the value for the population decrease is also unreliable because the urban population was still growing. Deducting the figure for urban population growth, the absolute figure for unnatural deaths in China's countryside would require increasing the nationwide figure for unnatural deaths by another 6.8 million. The total number of unnatural deaths in China's countryside during the three years of the famine then comes to 34.71 million.[8]

CHEN YIZI'S DATA

In *Hungry Ghosts: Mao's Secret Famine*, Jasper Becker reports that Chen Yizi, former head of China's Economic System Reform Institute, told him that the institute possessed a research report showing that around 43 million people starved to death during the Great Famine, and that another reference document supplied to the central leadership gave a figure of 50 to 60 million.[9] There is no way to verify this, however.

CAO SHUJI'S RESEARCH

Historical geographer Cao Shuji used demographic and historical geography methods to re-create figures for unnatural deaths in 1959–61 based on administrative districts such as those used in the Qing era.

His method was to start out with the 1953, 1964, and 1982 census data for each county as the foundation for his analysis. He then used information recorded in local annals to calculate the population growth rate for each locality before and after the famine, and to determine the population of each locality before and after the famine, and in that way he arrived at the number of unnatural deaths in each locality. By subtracting the 1961 population from the 1958 population, he obtained the net reduction in population. He then added in the portion of natural population growth that exceeded the natural mortality rate during the Great Famine. To this total population loss he added the net migration, which gave him the number of unnatural deaths in a given locality.

The information in annals is incomplete but is adequate as a sampling. Coordinating the two types of information can greatly reduce discrepancies. The results of Cao's research were that unnatural deaths during the three-year Great Famine totaled 32.458 million.[10]

THE PERSUASIVENESS OF WANG WEIZHI'S CONCLUSIONS

Wang Weizhi majored in population statistics at Moscow's Institute of Economic Analysis from 1955 to 1959. After returning to China, he spent more than twenty years carrying out population statistical work in the Public Security Ministry's Third Division for administration of household registration. In the early 1960s he went to several provinces to verify population data and became aware of actual circumstances. During and after the 1980s he carried out research at the Population Institute of the Chinese Academy of Social Sciences. In Wang's opinion, Jiang Zheng-hua's calculation of 17 million unnatural deaths is much lower than the reality. Wang concluded that unnatural deaths from the three-year Great Famine totaled 33 to 35 million.

Wang Weizhi revised the published population figures for the years 1959–61 based on his own practical experience and theoretical research.

TABLE 11.12: TOTAL POPULATION AND NATURAL POPULATION GROWTH 1959–61 (IN MILLIONS)

Year	Total population	Total population growth	Natural population growth
1958	659.94	–	–
1959	672.07	12.13	+6.77
1960	662.07	−10.00	− 3.04
1961	658.59	−3.48	+2.49

Source: China Statistical Yearbook (1984), p. 83.

The figures the Chinese government published for these years are contradictory. The three-year cumulative figure based on total population growth shows a reduction of 1.35 million, while the figure based on natural population change comes out to an increase of 6.22 million. Wang Weizhi felt that both figures were problematic. Assuming 1959 as the first year of the famine, there would have been a reduction in births that year, and mortality figures would have begun to increase. The officially reported total population increase of 12.13 million, a scant 1.28

million decrease from the previous year's increase, is not consistent with actual circumstances. For the year 1960, both the 10 million decrease in total population and the 3.04 million natural population decrease are too low. The inaccuracy results from a desire to report a larger population and fewer deaths. For the year 1961 the total population continued to decrease, while the natural population showed an increase of 2.49 million, a contradiction demonstrating that these figures are also inaccurate.

A re-creation of the data based on the 1964 population census shows that the 1961 population should have been 645.08 million, a decrease of 14.86 million from the original statistical tally. Wang calculated that in 1960 and 1961 the population decreased by 21.63 million. That represented an additional decrease of 8.15 million above the original statistical data.

The birth statistics that the Public Security Ministry published for those three years are as follows: 16.474 million for 1959, 13.893 million for 1960, and 11.886 million for 1961.[11] Population control was not yet being implemented, and reporting births meant obtaining state allocation quotas, so it would have been exceptional for births to be underreported. These figures therefore can be assumed to be accurate. The number of births for a given year minus the natural population increase produces the number of deaths: 9.804 million in 1959, 28.893 million in 1960, and 18.516 million in 1961, for a total of 57.213 million deaths. Subtracting the number of natural deaths produces unnatural (i.e., starvation) deaths. Based on the official population data for 1958, Wang calculated 23.43 million natural deaths from 1959 to 1961, which he subtracted from the total of 57.213 million deaths to arrive at 33.783 million unnatural deaths.

In fact, during the fourth quarter of 1958, some localities were already experiencing the famine, so the actual number of deaths for that year would actually be higher than the number of natural deaths. If the average number of deaths for the years 1956–58 is treated as natural deaths, then the total number of natural deaths for 1959–61 comes out to 21.747 million. Subtracting this number from the 57.213 million total deaths for that period produces 35.466 starvation deaths during those three years.

According to Wang's revised figures, the mortality rate for 1960 was 4.433 percent, not the 2.543 percent reported in the *Statistical Yearbook*. His mortality rate is close to the rates of 4.46 percent and 4.067 percent calculated by Banister and Calot, and is much higher than Jiang Zheng-hua's 3.125 percent (in *China Population: General Introduction*), 3.158 percent (in Li Chengrui's book), and 3.24 percent (in *Xi'an Jiaotong University Journal*).

Wang Weizhi's calculations carried out adjustments on the statistical data based on his many years of practical firsthand experience. He knew how inaccurate the figures were that each locality reported, and that using precise mathematical tools to handle such data was simply absurd.

Unnatural death totals calculated by the three Chinese scholars Jin Hui, Cao Shuji, and Wang Weizhi range from 32.5 million to 35 million. Each used a different method, but their results are close. However, Jin Hui and Wang Weizhi didn't add in unnatural deaths from 1958 and 1962, even though there were starvation deaths in the winter of 1958 and the spring of 1962. Cao Shuji's calculations include only a portion of the deaths in 1958 and 1962. If the starvation deaths from 1958 and 1962 are added in (based on official figures reported by the provinces, these total 1.81 million for 1958 and 420,000 for 1962, for an overall total of 2.23 million), the total number of starvation deaths during the Great Famine reaches 35 million to 37 million.

My research in more than a dozen provinces leads me to conclude that the figure of 36 million approaches the reality but is still too low. Figures provided by those who experienced the Great Famine far exceed the figures used by the statisticians.

If outward migration for each province is taken into account, unnatural deaths might come out somewhat lower, but the floating population was very limited. Based on figures provided by the Public Security Ministry, intraprovincial migration in 1960, when population movement was greatest, did not exceed 6 million people, and interprovincial movement was very much lower.[12] Only interprovincial migration would have had any effect on the unnatural deaths calculated for each province. The testimony of on-the-spot witnesses such as Liao Bokang, An Ziwen, and Liang Zhiyuan suggests that the number of unnatural deaths was not lower than 36 million, even taking migration into account.

Based on this analysis and on opinions from various quarters, I estimate that the Great Famine brought about 36 million unnatural deaths, and a shortfall of 40 million births. China's total population loss during the Great Famine then comes to 76 million.

12 THE OFFICIAL RESPONSE TO THE CRISIS

In the face of a nationwide famine and unprecedented chaos arising from the Great Leap Forward, Mao's thinking underwent a transformation, and his passion for a Communist transition waned. The CCP government embarked on a series of policy adjustments and attempted to rectify errors, mainly from November 1958 until the Lushan Conference in August 1959. These rectification measures were limited, however, by Mao's insistence that they should cause no harm to the Three Red Banners—even though it was these very policies that were the direct cause of the Great Famine. Mao's secretary Ye Zilong said, "Mao Zedong's approach to rectifying errors was only partial and carried the prerequisite that no vacillation over the Three Red Banners could result."[1]

After the Lushan Conference, even this limited rectification fell by the wayside. A new Great Leap Forward was launched in 1960, accompanied by a new Communist Wind. Another rectification followed in 1961, but it was too late; too much damage had already been done, and the insular and fossilized nature of the system and the abuses of its leadership precluded an effective corrective mechanism.

The eight months prior to the Lushan Conference saw a series of conferences that attempted to unite the thinking of the leadership around rectification. Starting in November 1958 these meetings[2] affirmed that China was currently in the socialist rather than Communist stage, and emphasized realistic targets and the use of "bourgeois prerogatives" such as commodities, currency, and distribution according to work done in the service of socialism. Recent trends toward equal distribution and excessive centralization were reversed, and production teams became the basic accounting unit. The last of these conferences, the enlarged Politburo meeting and Seventh Plenum of the Eighth CCP Central Committee in Shanghai, passed the "Draft 1959 National Economic Plan" and adjusted economic targets for iron and steel and other commodities.

Mao nevertheless continued to push for achieving communism as soon as possible. While conceding that the transition from collective ownership to full public ownership could not be done in three or four years, he advocated "struggling hard" so communism could be achieved in fifteen years. He spoke out against indiscriminate and uncompensated transfer of assets, but described uncompensated transfer of resources within the communes as a sort of "mini–public ownership system."[3] He insisted that "the system of commodity production is not for profit, but for developing production in the interests of the peasants and the worker-peasant alliance."[4] Through it all, Mao required the Propaganda Department to continue praising the Three Red Banners, and endorsed media emphasis on the accomplishments of the people's communes: "Due to the excessive publicity given to operational shortcomings during the 1956 campaign against rash advance, the enthusiasm of the masses suffered an attack that resulted in a saddle shape. Yet subsequent examination found that these so-called shortcomings amounted to only one finger out of ten, or not even one finger. At that time, however, some people were excessively skittish and lapsed into a panic. It was a manifestation of right-deviating sentiment. This is a lesson that we should by no means forget."[5]

The peasants were granted some concrete concessions during the rectification: in May and June 1959 the CCP Central Committee issued directives that relaxed restrictions on households raising poultry and livestock and cultivating household garden plots.[6]

These reforms were blown into oblivion by the Lushan Conference and the campaign against right deviation that followed. A report by the leading party group of the Agriculture Ministry on September 29, 1959, found that an undesirable right-deviating trend in the countryside in May, June, and July had made work teams the basic accounting unit; had begun assigning work quotas to households in what was essentially a reversion to individual farming; had encouraged private sideline occupations; and had obliterated the partial rationing system and the communal kitchens.[7]

In fact, these "problems" all resulted from implementing the Central Committee's policy concessions to the peasants in May and June. The Central Committee nonetheless described the problems revealed by the leading party group as "a savage countercurrent opposing the socialist road," and called for "thorough exposure and criticism."[8] The truth was that Mao had never approved of the Central Committee's May and June concessions; his confidant, Sichuan party secretary Li Jingquan, divulged as much in February 1960, saying, "The Chairman says that some of the things issued by the Central Committee in May and June last year were negative things . . . But we should understand these things from a positive angle. For instance, on the communal kitchens, we should take a positive approach to running them, and voluntary participation is aimed at this."[9]

Following the campaign against right deviation, the Great Leap Forward was revived in 1960, and that was the year in which the most people starved to death. In January 1961 the Ninth Plenum of the Eighth CCP Central Committee once again decided on a direction of "adjustment, consolidation, replenishment, and enhancement" for the national economy, and a retreat from the Great Leap Forward. China's political system made it difficult for the policy makers in the Central Committee to understand what was actually going on at ground level, however. They learned of problems only several months after the fact, and what they were told was inevitably a pale shadow of the actual situation. The hindrance that the campaign against right deviation posed to rectification resulted in the Great Famine persisting for an extra three or four years.

MAO LETS OTHERS TAKE THE STAGE

Mao was no fool, as demonstrated during the First Zhengzhou Conference in November 1958. On the second day of the conference, while listening to reports on the problems of the communization movement from Wu Zhipu, Wang Renzhong, Zhou Xiaozhou, and other provincial party secretaries, Mao took the wind out of their sails by observing, "The price we're paying right now is too high, I'm afraid it's not good."[10] While listening to Wu Zhipu and other others discuss the Ten-Year Plan on November 4, he said, "It all comes back to the topic of socialism. We shouldn't always veer off into communism right away . . . If you say we can manage the transition in ten years, I don't necessarily believe it."[11] On November 5, Zhou Xiaozhou, Shu Tong, and Zeng Xisheng reported public concern that paper currency would be abolished and that all assets would be handed over to state ownership, resulting in bank runs and panic purchasing. Mao said, "As to the scrapping of currency, Chen Boda has that inclination. Beijing is in a state of chaos right now; there are no regulations, and everything's in disorder. I'm afraid we won't be able to implement the people's communes in the cities." Mao also said that in iron and steel production, it was enough to catch up with Britain without trying to catch up with the United States. "I now have misgivings over our mentioning at Beidaihe that in a minimum of three or four years or a maximum of five or six years we could move from collective ownership to full public ownership . . . that was speaking too soon."[12] On November 9, responding to some who were inclined to avoid a commodity economy, Mao said, "We have to continue developing socialist commodity production and commodity exchange . . . At present there's a certain tendency toward engaging in communism as quickly as possible, and preferably within two years. In Shandong's Fan County they talk in the most fabulous terms about embarking on communism in two years, but I'm doubtful."

At this First Zhengzhou Conference, Mao repeatedly affirmed the General Line, Great Leap Forward, and people's communes, but emphasized that the establishment of the people's communes had given rise to an excessively rash push toward communism. He pointed out that the people's communes remained under a system of collective ownership, and that even the implementation of full public ownership might not be tantamount to communism. He called on leaders to distinguish between collective and public ownership, and between socialism and communism. He then expounded on the need to develop a commodity economy, and criticized scrapping commodity production and stripping peasants of their assets. Regarding the mass around-the-clock mobilizations for the iron- and steel-forging campaign, he called on all localities to "strike a balance between work and rest" and to "take both production and livelihood in hand."[13]

Only Mao could have gotten away with saying such things, however; anyone else would have been accused of right deviation. Mao's relatively realistic utterances earned him praise from his subordinates, but the ruthless campaigns against critics of rash advance and against right deviation had left a deep impression on cadres at all levels, who felt compelled to continue their high-flown rhetoric. At the Wuchang Conference, for example, Liu Shaoqi suggested that some communes start making the transition to full public ownership upon reaching a consumption level of

150 to 200 yuan. Peng Zhen likewise voiced the opinion that waiting for everyone to reach a set consumption would cause too much delay to the transition; it was better to strike while the iron was hot, and to make the transition sooner rather than later, say within three or four years.[14] As officials at the top talked up communism, their imitators in the lower echelons proliferated.

It was well known that Mao was deeply committed to the Three Red Banners, and that he was particularly enamored of mass movements; these were the central themes behind everything he did. Everyone saw Mao's shift into a lower gear as temporary and not fundamental. In any case, Mao's low-key pronouncements were accompanied by newspaper articles extolling the glories of the Great Leap Forward and the people's communes, and Mao's subordinates dared not act on his more realistic directives. Shandong provincial party secretary Shu Tong, for example, never made a sincere effort to transmit Mao's more measured pronouncements following the Zhengzhou Conference. He said that he was afraid of dashing cold water on the mass movement, and he believed the campaign against the Three Winds (Communist Wind, Exaggeration Wind, and Chaotic Directives Wind) was only a short-term matter, while the campaign against right deviation was long term.[15] Shanxi's provincial first secretary, Tao Lujia, said, "In the process of rectifying the error of elevated production targets, it was necessary to show one's colors and demonstrate a firm resolve . . . At the same time, I felt that Chairman Mao sometimes revealed an admiration for high targets, and seemed to demonstrate a conflicted mentality."[16]

Sensing the difficulty of putting his views into practice, Mao wrote an "internal party communiqué" on April 29, 1959, to cadres from the provincial level downward expressing his thoughts on rectification. In order to counter high production targets, Mao declared that production team cadres "are simply not required to pay any attention to the targets set by the upper levels . . . Only act according to what is genuinely practicable." On close-planting: "It can't be too far apart or too close . . . The inflexible directives from above on close-planting are useless and cause considerable harm to the people. For that reason, you don't need to follow those inflexible directives." On food supplies: "Rations are to be set on a per capita basis, with more food allocated during the busy season and less during lax periods. People should be provided with cooked rice during busy times, and half-rice half-congee during lax times, mixed with other foods such as sweet potatoes, green vegetables, turnips, melons, beans, and taro." "After ten or eight years of struggle, we'll be able to resolve the food supply issue. Within these ten years, boasting and high-sounding words are forbidden, as this is very dangerous."

Mao also negated the policy of cultivating less land in anticipation of bigger harvests, and said that all available land must continue to be cultivated. While seeing mechanization as "the way forward in agriculture," he said, "this will require ten years' time." The final issue was speaking truthfully: "State exactly how much you've actually harvested, and don't say what doesn't conform to fact." "Honest people who speak the truth are, in the final analysis, beneficial to the people's undertaking, and should not suffer for it. Those who are untruthful hurt the people and themselves, and ultimately they will come to grief. It should be said that much of the falsehood has resulted from pressure from above. The policy above has been 'boasting, pressuring, and rewarding,' and this has given little choice to those below."[17]

Mao concluded, "If the actual situation is not as bad as I have said, and higher goals can be achieved, I can be considered a conservative, and thank heaven for that great honor." This indicated that he still hoped to achieve the higher targets, and his more perceptive subordinates, such as Wu Zhipu and Li Jingquan, acted accordingly. This bypassing of the upper-level cadres and direct communication with the lower levels was, in fact, a typical tactic of Mao's, and one that he employed again in the Cultural Revolution. It created the impression that Chairman Mao was wise and sagacious, and that any existing problems were created by others.

When mass starvation developed, Mao felt he had been duped by lower-level cadres, and in early 1961 he called for a thorough investigation. He sent teams headed by Tian Jiaying, Hu Qiaomu, and Chen Boda to carry out investigations in Zhejiang, Hunan, and Sichuan. Liu Shaoqi, Zhou Enlai, Zhu De, and Deng Xiaoping went to Hunan, Sichuan, Beijing, and other places. Liu Shaoqi spent more than forty days investigating the situation in his home village in Hunan Province. These officials learned a great deal about the actual situation in the countryside, but the damage had already been done.

In November 1960, the CCP Central Committee made a decisive effort toward a nationwide rectification of the Five Winds through an "urgent memorandum" drafted by Zhou Enlai, which became known as the "Twelve Agricultural Provisions":

1. Three-level ownership, with the production team as the basic accounting unit, is the basic system for the current stage of the people's communes.
2. Resolutely oppose and thoroughly rectify indiscriminate and uncompensated transfer of resources.
3. Strengthen ownership by the production teams.
4. Uphold partial ownership by the work teams.
5. Allow commune members to manage small amounts of land for private cultivation and small-scale household sideline production.
6. Minimize deductions and maximize work points to increase income for 90 percent of commune members.
7. Insist on the principles of "from each according to his ability" and distribution according to work done, and remunerate labor in a ratio of 30 percent through rations and 70 percent through wages.
8. Save labor in all areas and strengthen the frontline agricultural labor force.
9. Make adequate arrangements in food supply and operate the communal kitchens effectively.
10. Guide the resumption of rural markets to stimulate the rural economy.
11. Strike a genuine balance between work and rest.
12. Let up on mass mobilization, and rectify work styles and the communes.[18]

About twenty days later, Mao said, "I have also committed errors and definitely need to correct them." His self-criticism took the form of a memo on a provincial party committee report:

Comrade Mao Zedong . . . said that he shares the same fate and breathes in concert with all those comrades who are willing to correct their errors. He said that he had committed errors, and that he definitely needed to correct them. The first error was in the Beidaihe Resolution, which envisaged an excessively rapid transition to communal ownership . . . This viewpoint was impractical. It has now been corrected, and starting from now, the current system of ownership by the communes will not be changed for at least (comrades, please note, this is "at least") seven years. If there is a change in the future, it will be the production teams taking over commune assets, and not communes taking over production team assets. It is also stipulated that starting from now, the socialist system (from each according to his ability, and remuneration based on work done) will absolutely not be changed for at least twenty years . . . In summation, regardless of the time frame, the production team's property will be owned and used by the team in perpetuity, and no indiscriminate and uncompensated transfer of resources will ever be allowed. The accumulation of public assets cannot be excessive, and public projects must also by no means be excessive. There will be no inflexible stipulations on changing the character of the countryside in a few years; rather, these changes will take place step-by-step in accordance with the situation.[19]

Despite Mao's self-criticism, the Communist Wind continued blustering right through 1961. The ideals of communism had made too deep an impression on cadres, not only as a result of China's effective mass media apparatus, but also because implementation of communism had been written into the party constitution, and a key criterion for assessing a cadre was the steadfastness of his faith in communism. Even while rectifying hasty implementation of full public ownership, the advantages of "big and collective" could not be negated, nor could the achievements of the Great Leap Forward. In a speech on February 27, 1959, Mao said:

The relationship between our achievements and our shortcomings is, as we usually say, the relationship between nine fingers and one finger out of ten fingers. Some people suspect or deny the 1958 Great Leap Forward, and suspect or deny the advantages of the people's communes, and this viewpoint is obviously completely wrong.

. . . the advantages of the "big and collective" extra-large communes are the best means for us to achieve the transition from the rural socialist collective system to the socialist system of full public ownership, and are also the best means of accomplishing the transition from socialism to communism. If suspicions develop regarding this basic issue, this is completely wrong, and it is right deviation.

It is necessary to anticipate, on the one hand, that those members of the "wave gazing" and "autumn reckoning" factions will come out jeering at us, and on the other hand, that those landlords, rich peasants, counterrevolutionaries, and bad elements will carry out acts of sabotage. However, we must tell the cadres and the masses that when they come up against these circumstances, there is absolutely no need to fear. We should maintain our equanimity and hold our peace for a time, bracing ourselves and allowing these people to expose themselves. When the time comes, the masses as a group will very quickly distinguish right from wrong and make a distinction between the enemy and us, and they will rise up and crush the ridicule of those backward elements and the assaults by those hostile elements.[20]

Cadres carried out rectification with a Sword of Damocles hanging over their heads, a sword on which were written the phrases "right opportunism," "wave-gazing faction," "autumn-reckoning faction," "landlord," "rich peasant," "counterrevolutionary," and "bad element." The threat of this dangling sword caused cadres to err on the side of the Left rather than the Right. Assessing error as more than one finger out of ten might bring the sword plummeting down on one's head.

Rectification required full restitution of all assets confiscated from households and production teams; but where homes had been destroyed, it was difficult to build new ones, and where seized assets had already been squandered, it was difficult to compensate the original owners. Localities reported compensation paid out to production teams and households, but most of these figures were bogus. The restitution process began in the spring of 1959 but made very slow progress.

IDEOLOGICAL IMPEDIMENTS TO THE EXPANSION OF PEASANTS' FREEDOM

If the collective was unable to guarantee peasants' livelihood, the least it could do was to allow commune members to eke out their own survival. As spring transitioned to summer in 1959, the Central Committee instructed regions to address the massive decrease in pig stock by allowing some household-reared pigs, chickens, and ducks. This necessitated providing commune members with plots of land, but not to exceed 5 percent of the landholding of the commune. The allocation could also be made on the basis of head of livestock, with 0.1 or 0.2 *mu* of land allocated for each pig a household reared.[21]

The Central Committee on June 11, 1959, directed:

1. The proceeds from the sale of any home-raised pigs, sheep, chicken, ducks, or rabbits are to be remitted to individual commune members, and every commune member is to be granted several days each month for tending household garden plots and livestock.
2. Allocating plots for household cultivation is to be resumed, regardless of whether or not a household raises pigs. The crops raised on these plots are not subject to grain tax or requisition quotas, but commune members are not allowed to sell, rent, or transfer the plots.
3. Commune members are encouraged to use all land around their homes, on the outskirts of the villages, and along rivers and roadways. Crops harvested from this land are not subject to agricultural tax or requisition quotas.
4. Scattered trees and shrubs around homes are to be returned to the use of commune members.[22]

These reforms revived rural markets (referred to in some localities as "free markets"), and by 1962 it was possible once again to buy fresh gingerroot, lily buds, lotus root, water chestnuts, and arrowheads not seen for years. When the village markets started operating, their prices were at least double state prices. High prices stimulated production, which in turn brought prices down, and by June of 1962, privately raised produce cost only a fraction more than state produce.[23] These free markets were still considered capitalistic, and party members were not allowed to buy produce from them.

The increasing self-sufficiency of the peasants invited an official backlash, however. Mao said that the flourishing trade in rural by-products was "a great problem, and measures must be taken across the board to change the status quo." The Central Committee on August 19 demanded "appropriate restrictions on self-sufficiency, as far as possible increasing the commodity portion in accordance with urban and rural needs."[24] This was in effect neglecting the peasants' needs in order to provide for the cities and to ensure exports.

The fact is that some localities did not allocate the stipulated amount of land for household cultivation. Some cadres considered private gardens and free markets to be "capitalism," and worried that they would affect collective production, so their compliance with the Central Committee directive was superficial at best.[25] Sichuan Province didn't bother executing the directive at all.

RESPONSIBILITY FIELDS AS A TEMPORARY MEASURE

After collectivization, work points were allocated for labor, with remuneration based on work points. Allocation was initially set at twelve points for one day of hard labor, ten points for ordinary labor, and five or six points or less a day for women and children. This type of allocation tended to result in people putting in a minimum of effort, so meetings were held every evening to evaluate each person's actual effort that day. Since this involved issues of face, honest evaluations were difficult. The system was further amended to assign work quotas, the satisfactory completion of which brought a certain number of work points. The allocation of work quotas turned into production quotas for work teams, and finally into allocation of production to households. Now land was contracted to a family, with a certain amount of produce handed over to the collective and any surplus retained by the household. The clearer the responsibility, and the closer the relationship between labor and allocation, the greater the initiative applied to the labor in this system, which became known as "responsibility fields."

However, putting production under the management of individual households shattered the principle of a collective economy with centralized management, collective labor, and centralized allocation, and brought accusations of embarking on the capitalist road. To solve the food supply crisis, some localities managed to disguise the responsibility system, with participation reaching 70 percent in some areas. By May 1962, Liu Shaoqi and Deng Xiaoping believed that production had been individually contracted to at least 20 percent of all peasant households.[26]

The fact remained that allocation of production to households contradicted Communist ideals. A similar system implemented in Zhejiang Province in 1956, three years before the famine, had been declared a "directional error" by Mao, and the cadres in charge had been punished as rightists.[27] Although this measure saved countless lives during the famine, it was the people themselves who spontaneously took this initiative to save themselves while sympathetic local officials turned a blind eye. Not yet fully aware of the actual famine situation, Mao and the Central

Committee cracked down harshly. On November 2, 1959, *People's Daily* declared that "the poisonous weed of allocation of production to households must be torn up by the roots!" On December 4, *Guangming Daily* published an article entitled "Allocation of Production to Households Is the Guiding Principle of Right Opportunists in the Countryside for the Restoration of Capitalism."

On October 13, 1959, the Central Committee stated, "Allocating all or a portion of agricultural labor or production to households is in fact a means of opposing the socialist road in the countryside and following the capitalist road. All localities taking this view and undertaking such activities must be thoroughly exposed and criticized."[28]

On October 12, 1959, the Central Committee criticized Geng Qichang and Wang Huizhi, both prefectural-level party secretaries in Henan Province, saying that they

> . . . took advantage of the rectification of the communes and allocation of work and production to practice a so-called "sectional responsibility system," under which they remeasured land plots, set boundary markers, and advocated the allocation of land, livestock, farming implements, and labor to heads of households, then carried out labor under the direction of household heads and commended the individualistic vision of so-called "fields full of people, but not in groups." They wished to revert the "big and collective" people's communes to a "small and private" system of mutual-aid groups or individual households. This clearly reveals that the true intention and essence of right opportunists toward the people's communes is one of fundamentally opposing agricultural collectivization, and opposing the socialist road. This thinking directly reflects the demands of a portion of well-to-do middle peasants. But in the final analysis, it ultimately follows the capitalist road, aims for the restoration of capitalism in the countryside, and essentially reflects an anti-party, anti-people capitalist mentality within the party . . . The party committees of all localities should search out a set of typical materials and mobilize party cadres in a campaign to expose and criticize the threatening visage of the right opportunists . . . so as to ensure that the party's General Line for socialist construction can be effectively implemented.[29]

On October 15, 1959, the Central Committee endorsed a report criticizing "the evil and unhealthy right-deviating trend that arose in May,

June, and July this year and produced 'basic ownership by production teams' and 'allocation of production to households,' and used small-scale private ownership and small freedom to launch private sideline occupations and sabotage the collective economy."[30]

The Central Committee elsewhere declared, "A struggle between the two roads is currently ongoing in the countryside. This struggle is a continuation of the struggle between the two roads of capitalism and socialism that has been carried out in the countryside over the past ten years, and it is an intense and profound class struggle."[31] In general, opposition to the "salvation fields" within the government structure was formidable, and some leaders were more opposed to right deviation than Mao himself.

Only at the end of 1960 did Mao and the other central government leaders acknowledge how serious the famine was. Scrambling for a solution, they gave their tacit consent to allocation of production to households. Mao remained ambivalent, however. Once the worst of the famine had passed in the autumn of 1962, the Central Committee condemned the allocation of production to households as following the capitalist road, and ordered all localities to "correct" this trend. Grassroots cadres who had used the method to rescue peasants from the brink of death came under harsh attack and persecution. During the Socialist Education Movement and the Cultural Revolution, this political demerit was called to even more serious account.

RELEASE OF URBAN LABOR RELIEVES STRAIN ON FOOD SUPPLIES

Grain procurement was a means of feeding the urban populace. With the rapid development of industry, the urban population soon grew beyond what agricultural resources could sustain. Chen Yun said, "In the last three years we've recruited more than 25 million workers, causing the urban population to reach 130 million, and it now looks as if this is inappropriate."[32] Irrational industrial projects were to be abandoned, and Chen Yun ordered that all workers called up from the countryside over the past three years should be sent back, noting, "Sending 10 million people back to the countryside will reduce the food provision by 2.25 billion kilos, and sending 20 million back will reduce it by 4.5 billion kilos."[33] Some capital construction projects were also halted, and tens of thousands of workers suddenly found themselves out of work. A large-scale reduction in the workforce was finally implemented in 1961.

On May 31, 1961, Chen Yun gave the CCP Central Committee four proposals for resolving the food shortage: (1) continue to adjust the party's rural policies; (2) have industry strongly assist agriculture; (3) import food—although foreign exchange and transport capacity were inadequate; and (4) deploy urban residents to the countryside. He considered the first of these to be fundamental, and the fourth to be absolutely essential.[34] The Central Committee accepted Chen Yun's recommendations and began taking measures to reduce the urban population by at least 20 million within the next three years. By July 31, 1963, the Central Committee concluded that the number of people consuming government grain rations had been reduced by 28 million.

In the usual fashion, localities exceeded the Central Committee quotas for sending people back to the countryside. Jilin Province had a target of 812,000, but actually sent back 980,000.[35] Henan's target was 1.099 million, but 1.206 million were sent back.[36] Apart from rural residents who had been recruited to urban factories over the past three years, members of the urban population's disadvantaged groups were also forced out. From 1961 to 1963, Shanghai rounded up 6,000 under- or unemployed households and sent 26,000 people to rural Anhui Province.[37] In Qiqihar, Heilongjiang Province, 114,000 people were sent to the countryside in 1960, among them 35,000 roving migrants and 56,000 others who lacked fixed employment.[38] In some localities, family members of persons undergoing labor reform or reeducation were sent to the countryside if they had family there.

The process of downsizing the workforce and reducing the urban population met with resistance. Some retrenched workers were registered as permanent urban residents and had no means of livelihood in the countryside. Others had left their home villages long ago. Such people were ill prepared to support themselves through agricultural labor, and village residents did not welcome their arrival. In Bengbu, Anhui Province, the plan was to reduce the urban population by 35,600 in 1961, but the reduction had reached only 28,390 by the end of October. In November the municipal party committee required every enterprise and work unit to suspend operations and merge, reducing the workforce so that all cullable workers could be sent back to the countryside as soon as possible. The city finally met its 1961 target, only to have a new reduction of 25,000 people ordered for 1962.[39]

Changzhou, Jiangsu Province, experienced a mass uprising from May 20 to 23, 1960, by seventy veteran employees of the Daming Textile Mill who were to be sent to the countryside. It took several days of negotiation to keep the situation from escalating and to persuade the workers to go peacefully to the villages.[40] In other cities, some urban residents set for rustification found various illegal means to linger. Generally speaking, however, the relocation of more than 20 million people from the cities to the countryside without any significant turmoil could only have occurred under China's system at that time. Mao once said, "Our people are really good! Tens of millions can be called up at a moment's notice and be sent off with a wave of the hand."[41] The truth was, however, that many whose interests were violated in the process continued to petition the government for decades afterward. Only a small minority ever saw their grievances redressed.

RECTIFICATION OF WORK STYLES AND COMMUNES SHIFTS THE BLAME TO GRASSROOTS CADRES

The rectification measures targeted the excesses of the Three Red Banners, but this touched a raw nerve with Mao and other leaders, who pronounced such moves part of a "fierce countercurrent in opposition to the socialist road." They blamed the starvation deaths on this countercurrent rather than on the Three Red Banners.

Mao held that at the upper levels this countercurrent originated among right opportunists, while at the lower levels it arose from landlords, rich peasants, counterrevolutionaries, bad elements, and rightists, whose opposition to the Three Red Banners had created the serious problems in the countryside. Once the party's top leaders acknowledged the Xinyang Incident at the end of 1960, Mao changed his nine-to-one achievement-to-shortcoming formulation to three-to-one at the local level. The problems that constituted the one out of three were attributed to scoundrels who had seized power at the grass roots.

On November 15, 1960, Mao wrote: "The situation is very good in two-thirds of the country, while the situation is very bad in one-third. Within five months all of these situations must be turned around . . . All evildoers and wrongdoings must be put to right; evil influences must be stamped out and a healthy atmosphere must prevail." On this same report, Mao sent the following message to Zhou Enlai: "A certain amount of time must be spent talking about the bad situation in one out of three localities, where scoundrels have taken power, people have been beaten to death, food production has dropped, people are going hungry, the democratic revolution has been incomplete, and feudalist powers are making major mischief, increasing hostility to socialism and sabotaging socialism's production relations and productive forces . . ."[42]

A Central Committee directive on December 8, 1960, stated:

You are all aware of the serious problems that have arisen in some parts of Shandong, Henan, and Gansu provinces. This Work Situation Report No. 215 . . . describes the serious situation . . . in particular the extremely serious problems among cadres of extravagance and waste, corruption and degeneration, violation of the party constitution, violation of law and discipline, and paying no heed to the life and death of the people. Some of these wrongdoings are simply inconceivable, among them acts of counterrevolutionary sabotage that are clearly the despair-inducing destructive retaliation of feudalistic forces that have usurped leadership in some localities. It is the most intense manifestation of class struggle in the countryside. It must be borne in mind that China's rural population still includes 8 percent comprised of landlords and rich peasants and their family members, which when combined with urban capitalists, bourgeois intellectuals, and upper-level petty bourgeoisie and their family members, amounts to around 10 percent of the country's population. The vast majority of these people have undergone socialist transformation in varying degrees . . . For that reason, it is essential that we reform them. However, among them exist greater or lesser degrees of feudalistic and bourgeois spontaneous power, which influence and corrupt us on a daily basis. Among them are the most resolute and most covert counterrevolutionaries who have not been reformed and who have not accepted reform. They feel an extreme hatred for socialism, and are consciously prepared at any moment to "reincarnate" themselves by usurping leadership as a means of carrying out retaliation and unbridled struggle. Comrade Mao Zedong says, "We must not only continue to carry out the socialist revolution, but must also thoroughly complete the unfinished tasks of the democratic revolution."

. . . If we leaders are negligent or lacking in vigilance, or if deviations arise in policy, the counterrevolutionaries will take the opportunity to drag away those among us who are weak or vacillating in revolutionary resolve, and bring about the corruption of the party leadership in some places and in some work units . . . it can be seen that the transformation of the entire society is a long-term and arduous task of class struggle . . . Sun Yatsen said, "Until the revolution has succeeded, comrades must continue to exert great effort." We can borrow this slogan . . . [43]

Rather than look to the system, policies, and guiding ideology, Mao and the Central Committee blamed the massive death toll on political and class enemies who had usurped leadership at the grassroots level as a result of "insufficient thoroughness of the democratic revolution." Wherever starvation deaths had been particularly numerous, supplemental training in democratic revolution was carried out by means similar to those employed during Land Reform, with grassroots cadres replacing landlords and local despots as the targets of struggle and brutal persecution.

Some grassroots cadres had indeed abused their authority, but the greatest injury had resulted from faithful execution of the Central Committee's policies. The poor quality of some cadres exacerbated the situation, but the Central Committee was ultimately responsible.

SEVERAL MAJOR ERRORS MAINTAINED TO THE END

Although the Central Committee under Mao's leadership made various adjustments to extreme leftist polices, it failed to adopt practical measures on major issues. It ignored the obvious distress of starving peasants while maintaining elevated procurement targets and food exports, and it persisted with the Great Leap Forward and delayed adjustment of economic targets.

The State Council secretariat on April 6, 1959, reported on food shortages in Shandong, Jiangsu, Henan, Hebei, and Anhui, and on April 9 sent up a statistical table showing that 25.17 million people were going without food in fifteen provinces. Mao wrote a memo requesting that the first secretaries of each of the fifteen provinces promptly address the issue. Mao believed this was a "temporary (two-month) urgent crisis,"[44] and he made no effort to relax food supply policies.

Lower-level officials continued to send up reports meant to deceive Mao. In April 1959, as the famine deepened, a report claimed that Henan and Hebei had arrested the spread of the spring famine, that the outward migration of Shandong peasants had been largely brought to a halt, and that the overall incidence of edema had begun to decline.[45] On April 26, Mao wrote in a memo, "Plant more melons and vegetables and pay attention to both eating and economizing on food, eating less during quiet times and more during busy times."[46]

On October 26, 1960, Mao read a report stating that hundreds of thousands of people had starved to death in Xinyang Prefecture. He responded with a blasé memo of a dozen words: "Liu [Shaoqi] and Zhou [Enlai], please read today and this afternoon discuss ways to deal with this."[47] He treated the Xinyang Incident as an isolated incident to be handled as routine work, and made no move to relax policies on supplying or procuring grain.

In respect to grain procurement and the sale of grain back to rural households, procurement for the 1958/59 grain year increased by 22.32 percent. In 1959, when the Great Famine had become pervasive, procurement levels continued to rise, while sale of grain back to the countryside increased only marginally. That is to say, during the height of the Great Famine in 1959–60, the state provided no relief aid to the countryside, but rather extracted an additional 3.378 billion kilos of grain. Snatching grain from the mouths of starving peasants was no easy matter, and resulted in the horrendous violence and tragedy described elsewhere in this book. Only in autumn 1960 did the government cut back on grain procurement. For 1960–61, it was reduced to 39.042 billion kilos, which was 21.68 billion kilos less than the previous year. At the same time, however, the sale of grain back to the countryside was also reduced by 8.22 billion kilos, so the peasants' burden was actually reduced by only 13.46 billion kilos.

TABLE 12.1: STATE GRAIN PROCUREMENT AND SUPPLY TO THE COUNTRYSIDE DURING THE GREAT FAMINE (IN BILLION KILOS)

Procurement and sale	1957–58	1958–59	1959–60	1960–61	1961–62
Procured from the countryside	46.0055	56.272	60.7145	39.042	33.957
Sold to the countryside	20.983	25.2595	26.324	18.104	13.4225

Source: "Food Ministry Project Command Grain Data Summary," August 25, 1962.

In January 1960 the Central Committee not only refused to relax procurement quotas and release grain reserves to save peasant lives, but actually increased the grain in state storehouses. In its endorsement of a Food Ministry report, the Central Committee noted, "It is not only necessary but also possible to gradually increase the state grain reserves on the basis of the continuing leap forward in grain production."[48] In 1960, when the number of starvation deaths reached its peak, the state still possessed tens of billions of kilos in grain reserves, but made no large-scale release of grain for emergency relief.

The figures for grain reserves in Table 12.2 clearly show that as tens of millions of people starved to death, tens of billions of kilos of grain were being held in the government storehouses. The period from April 1959 to April 1960 represented the largest number of starvation deaths, but during this year, grain reserves reached 44.3515 billion kilos (as of early November 1959), and never dipped below 14.311 billion kilos (in May 1960). In April 1960, when the famine was most severe, the grain reserves

TABLE 12.2: GRAIN RESERVES DURING THE GREAT FAMINE (TRADE GRAIN, IN BILLION KILOS)

	1957–58	1958–59	1959–60	1960–61	1961–62
July	17.7425	19.447	16.9395	13.294	7.873
August	20.095	19.9355	19.792	14.4555	9.565
September	24.3155	20.8615	25.1575	17.051	11.7405
October	28.0105	20.906	32.7605	19.3465	15.2475
November	34.533	32.901	44.3515	27.004	23.0285
December	37.8455	37.4215	42.449	28.6055	24.501
January	36.254	35.721	38.2075	25.5175	21.9395
February	33.8375	32.728	33.6595	22.225	19.744
March	30.083	27.8005	27.227	17.9915	16.443
April	25.381	21.675	20.1755	13.3945	12.899
May	20.2265	15.95	14.311	9.543	10.046
June	19.2205	17.164	14.853	8.5855	9.464

Source: "Food Ministry Project Command Grain Data Summary," August 25, 1962.

stood at 20.1755 billion kilos. That would have been enough to feed 140 million people for an entire year. If just half of these grain reserves had been released, no one needed to have starved.

Reserve figures show that while more than a million people starved to death in Xinyang, Henan Province held at least 1.25 billion kilos of grain reserves in its storehouses at the end of June 1960, and nearby Hubei Province held 661 million kilos of grain. If the grain stores of these two provinces had been released to the 8 million residents of Xinyang, each would have received more than 25 kilos of grain, and no one would have starved. What was the purpose of the state's obsession with increasing grain reserves? What were these reserves meant for, if not to save the lives of starving people? The situation is simply incomprehensible.

Even more intolerable is the fact that while China's people starved, the government continued to export large quantities of grain. While grain output in 1959 was 25 million tons less than in 1957,[49] grain exports reached a historic high, doubling to 4,157,500 tons. The exported trade grain was equivalent to 5 million tons of unprocessed grain, which could have fed 24.5 million people for one year. In 1960, at the height of the famine, China continued to export 2,720,400 tons of grain. There were virtually no grain imports in 1959, and very few in 1960. It was only two years after the famine began that some grain and small amounts of sugar began to be imported. Imported foodstuffs were all supplied to the cities.

Exports also included large quantities of oil, fresh eggs, meat, and fruit. During a nationwide telephone conference convened by the Central Committee on April 19, 1959, Li Xiannian brought up "the issue of pork and egg exports." At that time, the countryside was littered with the corpses of the starved, and the pigs that survived were thin and stunted. Once pigs weighed a few dozen kilos, they were taken off for state procurement. Li said, "We've only met a little more than 10,000 tons of our export target of 26,000 tons of pork for the first quarter of this year. This is unacceptable. All provincial party committees should consider the necessity of command as well as persuasion." He went on to grumble, "The pigs we're producing are of very poor quality—they look more like dogs. In Hong Kong they ridicule us and incinerate our exported pigs, saying they're diseased and that a pig weighing less than twenty kilos isn't worth bringing to market. The Czech prime minister, Široký, sent our premier a letter of protest saying, 'First you don't send us the amount you promised, then what you send us can't be sold in the market because of its inferior quality.'" Speaking of eggs, Li likewise complained of the failure to meet export quotas. He demanded that the commerce system "launch a crash acquisition drive" and "adopt drastic measures to resolve the export issue."[50]

Snatching food for export from the lips of starving people necessitated atrocities on a vast scale. One example was a chicken-and-egg-procurement drive held in April 1960 in Sichuan's Shizi Commune. The appropriation was based on head count, regardless of whether a household owned chickens or whether those chickens had actually laid eggs. Those who failed to meet their quota were penalized by the withholding of food rations. Production team member Ke Zhengguo could provide no eggs, so his entire seven-member family was deprived of food. Ke's mother had to borrow six eggs from relatives to hand over to cadres before the family's food rations were restored. Apart from being turned away from the communal kitchens, commune members who failed to provide eggs were not allowed to purchase salt, kerosene, cigarettes, or other daily necessities. Some supply and marketing cadres and production team cadres met their egg-procurement quotas by barging into homes in the depths of night and snatching chickens in an atmosphere of clamor and terror.[51]

The apparatus under the Ministry of Commerce supplied 3.03 billion yuan worth of exported foodstuffs, exceeding its export quota by 10.8 percent. This represented an increase of 28.9 percent over 1958. These exported goods included 233,000 tons of pork, the largest amount exported since the founding of the People's Republic; 20,000 tons of frozen beef and mutton, exceeding the export projection by 25 percent; more than 26 million kilos of fresh eggs and 6,208 tons of frozen eggs; and 9.54 million live fowl and 7,022 tons of frozen poultry. In addition, 102,000 tons of apples and 91,000 tons of citrus fruits were also exported.[52]

From January 7 to 17, 1960, Mao convened an enlarged Politburo meeting during which he continued to trumpet the Great Leap Forward: "Things have gone well since the Lushan Conference; production has increased every month, and it appears that this year will not be inferior to last year, and may even be a bit better."[53] This meeting took the view that 1960 would mark another Great Leap Forward. Steel output was set at 18.4 million tons and grain output at 300 billion kilos. Modernization would be basically accomplished within eight years, accompanied by completion of the transition to full public ownership. The meeting called for wide-scale implementation of communal kitchens and pilot programs extending the people's communes throughout the urban areas. The meeting was followed by nationwide mass campaigns for industrialization, irrigation works, communal kitchens, and communal livestock rearing. Some sidelined capital construction projects were revived, and the Five Winds began blasting their way across the country once again.[54]

In July, the Soviet Union withdrew its specialists, and in a counterattack against "Soviet revisionism," the Chinese people were exhorted to grit their teeth and "battle for steel," not just 18 million tons, but over 20 million tons. Apart from steel, the campaign against right deviation ensured that production targets in all other areas also rose rather than dropped in 1960. China became a massive construction site, only to leave the landscape cluttered with half-completed projects when the construction campaign had to be abandoned in 1961.

BLAMING NATURAL DISASTER AND THE SOVIET UNION

How could the government account to history for the deaths of tens of millions of people? The leadership blamed it all on Mother Nature. On October 1, 1960, *People's Daily* stated, "Over the past two years, regions throughout China have suffered the serious effects of a natural calamity."

In January 1961 the Central Committee made the same point more emphatically: "Following the serious natural calamity in 1959, another exceptional natural calamity was encountered in 1960." From then on, official documents, speeches by top leaders, and media reports all publicized the "natural calamity." In an exception, Liu Shaoqi bluntly told a Central Committee work conference on May 31, 1961, "In most localities, natural disaster was not the chief cause; rather, deficiencies and errors in our operations were the chief cause."[55]

During the Seven Thousand Cadres Conference in January 1962, Liu went further with his pronouncement of "three parts natural disaster and seven parts man-made disaster."[56] Mao was highly displeased with this formulation, and during the Tenth Plenum of the Eighth CCP Central Committee in September 1962, he criticized this bleak assessment of the situation and attributed the hardship entirely to "natural calamity." The expression "three-year natural calamity" continued to be used right through to the early 1980s. A Central Committee resolution on "Certain

Questions in the History of Our Party Since the Founding of the PRC," which was passed on June 27, 1981, claimed: "Mainly due to the errors of the 'Great Leap Forward' and the 'Campaign Against Right Deviation,' coupled with a concurrent natural calamity and the Soviet Union's perfidious breach of contract, our national economy suffered serious hardship from 1959 to 1961, causing heavy losses to the country and the people."[57] This followed the formulation of "three parts natural disaster and seven parts man-made disaster" with an emphasis on the "errors of the 'Great Leap Forward' and the 'Campaign Against Right Deviation,'" with the additional factor of the Soviet Union's breach of contract. But what were the actual historical facts?

Was the Great Famine brought about by a natural calamity? In order to answer this question, I consulted meteorologists and referred to historical data. The conclusion I reached was that natural calamities have occurred regularly, including during the three years of the famine, but that those three years were in no way exceptional.

The *China Atlas of Agriculture, Climate, and Natural Resources and Major Changes in Crop Yield*[58] analyzes climate data collected at 350 meteorological stations from 1951 to 1990. Let's view the circumstances of the natural calamity during 1959–61 according to several indicators in this book and then interpret the data in combination with other information.

1. Precipitation anomaly percentage

In order to evaluate natural calamity, meteorologists typically use "precipitation anomaly percentage" to classify various levels of drought. If the precipitation in a given year is close to the average precipitation over the course of several years, no drought is regarded as having occurred.

The precipitation anomaly percentage for 1960 was -30 percent, which is a moderate drought much less serious than in 1955, 1963, 1966, 1971, 1978, 1986, and 1988. The drought conditions in 1978 were far more severe than in 1960, and occurred during the "near economic collapse" following the Cultural Revolution, yet no starvation deaths resulted.

The precipitation anomaly percentages for 1959 and 1961 were around 80 percent, which qualified them as flood years, but the degree of flooding was far less than in 1954, 1973, and many other years. Meteorologists divide floods into flooding and severe flooding, with severe flooding classified as conditions in which the precipitation anomaly percentage exceeds 200 percent in the course of one month, 100 percent over two months, or 50 percent over three months.[59] The conditions for the years of 1959 and 1961 qualify as moderate flooding. Flooding was most severe in 1954, with some people drowning in flood torrents, yet there was no large-scale starvation that year.

FIGURE 12.1: GRAPH OF CHINA'S PRECIPITATION ANOMALY PERCENTAGES FOR THE YEARS 1951–90

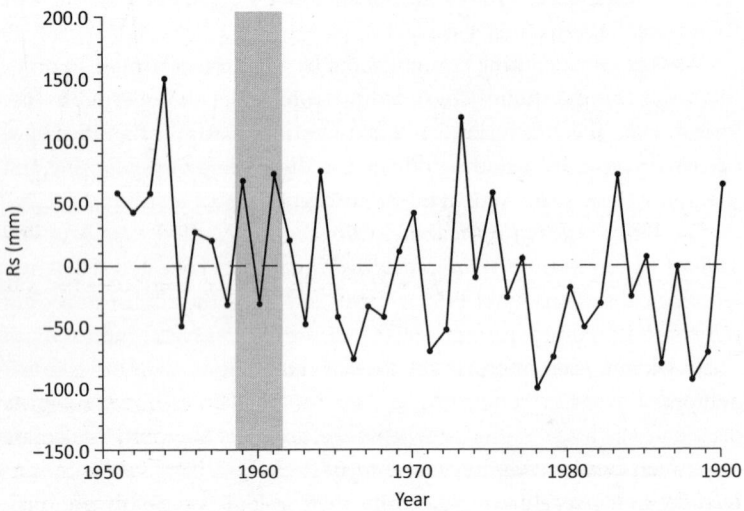

Source: China Atlas of Agriculture, Climate, and Natural Resources and Major Changes in Crop Yield, *p. 50.*

2. Precipitation anomaly percentage during the growing season

The growing season runs from April to October, and precipitation levels during this period affect crop yields. The graph of growing season precipitation anomaly percentages is basically the same as the graph for the annual precipitation anomaly percentages. Because different regions have different seasonal precipitation patterns, their growing season precipitation anomaly percentages also differ. Generally speaking, however, the range of the growing season precipitation anomaly for 1959 to 1961 was actually the smallest for the forty-year period, and far lower than in 1954, 1965, 1972, 1973, 1978, and 1989. The years from 1959 to 1961, therefore, qualify as normal years and cannot be considered years of natural calamity.

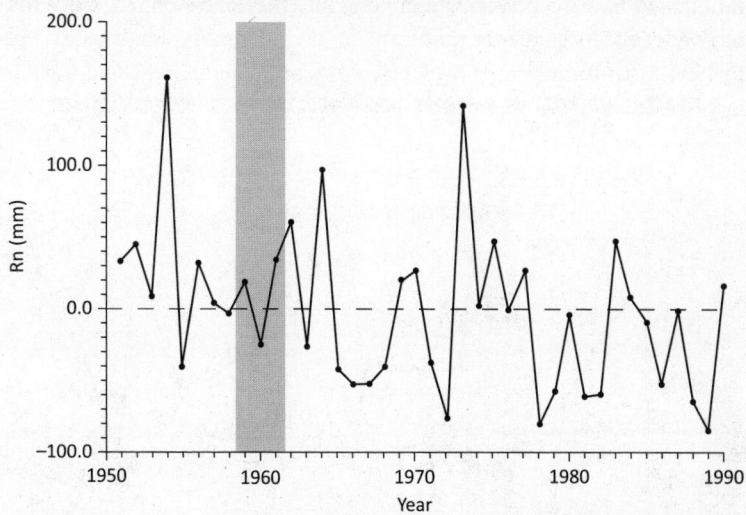

FIGURE 12.2: GRAPH OF GROWING SEASON PRECIPITATION ANOMALY PERCENTAGES FOR THE YEARS 1951–90

Source: China Atlas of Agriculture, Climate, and Natural Resources and Major Changes in Crop Yield, *p. 53.*

3. Annual mean temperature anomaly curve

Temperature has a strong effect on crop growth. Chinese meteorologists used data from the 350 nationwide meteorological stations to calculate the annual mean temperature for 1951 to 1990. The divergence in the annual mean temperature for the years 1958 to 1961 was not exceptional, and the conditions in these years were close to normal.

4. Temperature productivity time curve (TSPt)

Precipitation productivity (TSPn) and temperature productivity (TSPt) are both constituents of "climate productivity." Climate productivity is a means of using climate conditions to estimate agricultural production potential. In other words, a locality's sunlight, temperature, precipitation, and other climatic factors are used to estimate the maximum crop yield that can be expected with the optimal use of crop selection, soil fertility, and farming techniques. This is the most direct scientific formulation of how natural conditions can influence crop yield.

The natural development of crops is related to climate, and in particular to temperature and precipitation. The TSPt (temperature productivity) curve shows a given year's degree of divergence from the historical mean. Years where the divergence is small are considered normal years. Figure 12.3 shows that the divergence in TSPt for the years 1958–61 is not the largest for the forty-year period.

FIGURE 12.3: DIVERGENCE IN TEMPERATURE PRODUCTIVITY, FOR THE YEARS 1951–90

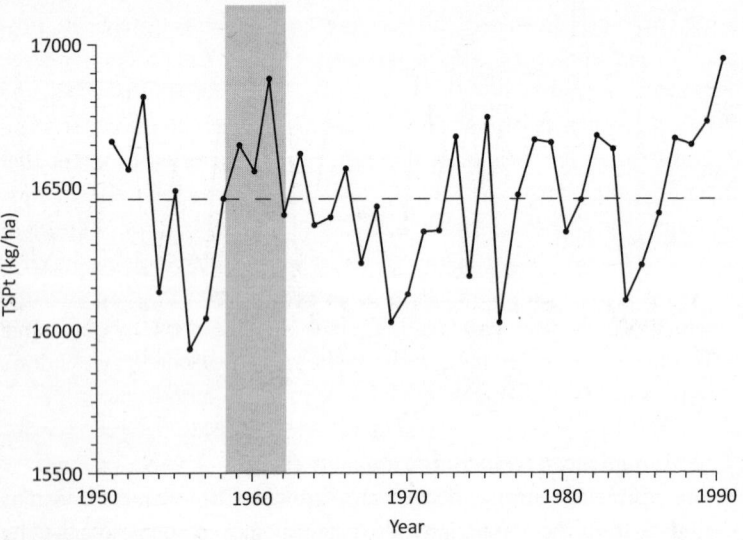

After writing this section, I was still not entirely certain about my findings, so I decided to seek a face-to-face interview with the chief compiler of this data, meteorological expert Gao Suhua, who before her retirement was a researcher with the Chinese Academy of Meteorological Sciences for more than thirty years. She concurred with my findings and said, "From 1958 to 1961, there were no large-scale droughts or floods within China, nor was there any large-scale occurrence of damagingly low temperatures. Conditions in those three years were normal."

And what of the Soviet Union's reneging on its contracts with China? China's August 23, 1958, military assault on Jinmen (then known in the West as Kinmen or Quemoy) enraged Soviet leader Nikita Khrushchev, who feared that once Mao obtained nuclear weapons, he would drag the Soviet Union into a war with the United States over the Taiwan Strait. China's aggressive development targets in the Great Leap Forward also weighed on his mind. In June 1959 the USSR tore up the agreement it had signed with China for new defense technology and refused to supply China with atomic bomb samples and the technology and materials to manufacture nuclear bombs.[60] By that time, China's Great Famine had already been ongoing for more than half a year, and, in any case, the agreement from which the Soviet Union withdrew had no effect on agriculture or industry. The agriculture-related assistance project in which the Soviet Union was involved, the Luoyang Tractor Factory, went into production on November 1, 1959, and achieved its planned production level.

Relations continued to deteriorate. On July 16, 1960, the USSR tore up 600 agreements it had signed with China (343 relating to experts and 257 relating to technology) and notified the Chinese government that from July 28 to September 1, 1960, it would withdraw all of its 1,390 experts currently in China while terminating the dispatch of more than 900 additional experts.[61] However, the expert and technological agreements that the Soviet Union scuppered were unrelated to agriculture, and, in any case, were abandoned in the second half of 1960, more than a year into the Great Famine. To blame the famine on the Soviet Union's abrogation of its agreements is in clear contradiction to the facts.

Another claim is that China's starvation deaths resulted from the Soviet Union's pressure on China to repay its debts. Again, this has no basis in fact. By agreement, China was to repay its debts to the Soviet Union by 1965. In 1964, China made an advance repayment of all the remaining principal and interest owed to the Soviet Union, and before October 1965 also fully repaid all cane sugar loans and trade debt. China's early repayment arose from Mao's wish to show that China could hold its own. After the Soviet Union announced the recall of its experts, Mao began talking up the virtues of reconstruction through one's own efforts, and instructed Zhou Enlai to calculate how long it would take to repay the remaining debt. Zhou said, "Based on 8 billion rubles, in the past we repaid 500 million per year, and at that level of repayment we'll need sixteen years to clear the debt. If we make payments of 800 million, it will take ten years to repay." Mao then told the Politburo, "The Yan'an period was so difficult, but we managed to survive on nothing but chili peppers. Things are much better now than they were then. We just need to tighten our belts and struggle to repay the debt within five years." After discussion, the Politburo agreed, and every province established a foreign trade committee to squeeze out any products that could be used to repay the debt.[62]

In December 1964, Zhou Enlai proudly stated that in a time of economic hardship, "Not only did we not borrow one yuan in foreign debt, but we also repaid nearly all of our past foreign debt . . . The remaining sum of 17 million rubles we propose to repay early through a portion of this year's trade surplus. In addition, we've produced capital and goods of much greater value than the amount of debt repaid during this period for use as aid to socialist countries and nationalist countries."[63] The full version of the work report states, "Estimated to the end of 1964, our country's foreign aid totals 6.67 billion yuan, of which 3.55 billion yuan, or 53 percent, was disbursed from 1961 to 1964." China's substantial foreign aid indicates that repayment of its foreign debt did not in fact constitute an enormous burden and was not a factor in the Great Famine.

ABSOLUTE POWER CORRUPTS ABSOLUTELY

While famine paralyzed the countryside, the cities also suffered extreme shortages. The commerce departments controlled the distribution of goods, and as commodities grew scarce, these departments used their privileged access for their own enrichment.

An investigation by provincial cadres in Suzhou revealed rampant backdoor distribution, extravagance, and waste:

All cadres in the vegetable, aquatic products, and foodstuffs companies under the Suzhou municipal commerce department engage in backdoor methods to consume large quantities of nonstaple foods. The vegetable company sold off a total of more than 169,500 kilos of potatoes, cowpeas, water chestnuts, cabbage, and carrots through the back door from January to August of this year. The company's fruit wholesale department purchased more than 1,000 kilos of apples from January to August, of which more than 750 kilos were eaten by the company's own staff. The 114 cadres in the aquatic products company privately purchased 2,346.5 kilos of fish from January to September, an average of more than 20 kilos per person, and twelve people bought more than 50 kilos each. From January to September of this year, the market owed the masses 580,000 meat ration tickets, equivalent to 85,000 kilos of pork and poultry meat, while the foodstuffs company staff purchased and sold through the back door more than 14,000 kilos of meat products, equivalent to 400,000 meat ration tickets. That company's fresh meat wholesale director, surnamed Xia, in April of this year purchased 48 kilos of pork and pig tripe. Of the 494 staff of the Jinchang District Food Market, 432 staff, or 87.5 percent, took part in private distribution of foodstuffs among themselves. Prior to this year's Spring Festival, the former head of the Nanhao Street distribution division, surnamed Jin, and another surnamed Li, secretly took a cart of cabbages from the storehouse, and they also made off with the fried bean curd provided to residents for the May Day celebration. Staff of the Zhujiazhuang Food Market each took 5 kilos of lotus root, 2.5 kilos of water chestnuts, and 1.5 kilos of bean sprouts at the time of the National Day celebrations. It is estimated that market staff in this district made off with around 1,000 kilos of fresh vegetables every day.[64]

This report further revealed that in the first half of 1960, Suzhou's municipal finance and trade departments took away extremely scarce nonstaple foods for meaningless coordination work in Wuxi, Inner Mongolia, the Northeast, and other places. The food included more than 25,000 kilos of meat and more than 19,000 kilos of fish. During their so-called coordination work, officials invited guests and gave gifts in an orgy of feasting. The commerce bureau had in the previous year invited guests seventy-six times, totaling seventy-five tables, and so far in 1960 had invited guests thirty-six times, with fifty-nine tables. Even more distressing was that during severe famine conditions, large quantities of food had simply rotted in the departmental storehouses over the past half year, including 75,000 kilos of pears, 10,000 kilos of peaches, 10,000 kilos of tangerines, more than 15,000 kilos of turnips, 13,000 kilos of pork and pig tripe, 25,000 kilos of fish and prawns, 3,000 kilos of shrimp paste, and 100,000 preserved eggs.

Similar incidents are recorded in every provincial archive.

Corruption among grassroots cadres centered on eating more and better, while for higher-level cadres it was in the pursuit of pleasure. Sichuan's provincial first secretary, Li Jingquan, ate and drank his fill every day, then went to parties with hired performers. When Gansu's provincial first secretary went to the countryside for inspection tours, the province's famous Lanzhou Restaurant sent meals to him by special car. Shandong's provincial first secretary, Shu Tong, caused a major disruption through a sexual dalliance. Shu called a conference in early August 1960 to pass along instructions from a conference at Beidaihe. The conference lasted for more than forty days, and a subsequent investigation revealed that Shu spent most of this time in his room playing poker with a female nurse, or taking her out dancing or on scenic tours. Meanwhile, no move was made to implement relief measures, and Shandong's famine conditions continued to deteriorate.

Many local archives contain records of cadres engaging in large-scale construction projects for entertainment purposes during the famine. As ordinary people exhausted their food supplies, edema became epidemic, and people began succumbing en masse to starvation, Guizhou's famine-stricken Zunyi Prefecture indulged in nonessential construction projects that included four large theaters, three guesthouses, and a multistory service center of over 8,000 square meters housing a dance hall, photography studio, and elevators. The doors, windows, and floors of the guesthouses were constructed of camphor and sandalwood, and their rooms were furnished with antique calligraphy scrolls, ivory carvings, leather sofas, and brocaded cushions. A neighborhood beautification project entailed dismantling all the houses along the river. Some displaced residents were forced to seek refuge in remote mountain areas, while others were never provided with any resettlement at all.[65]

This kind of recreational construction originated with the Central Committee. In 1959 many provinces and cities built special villas for the use of Mao and Politburo standing committee members. Apart from provincial capitals, some medium-size cities vied to follow this negative example. Famous establishments such as Hunan's "Lotus Garden," Sichuan's Jinniuba Guesthouse, Hubei's East Lake Guesthouse, Jiangsu's Purple Mountain Guesthouse, Shandong's Nanjiao Guesthouse, Hangzhou's Liuzhuang Guesthouse and Wangzhuang Guesthouse, and Shanghai's Xijiao Guesthouse were all built around 1960. These "abodes for the touring emperor" were lavishly appointed, their quality sometimes exceeding Beijing's Diaoyutai Guesthouse. They consumed enormous financial resources when the country was in the throes of crisis.

The main courtyard of the Tianjin Guesthouse consisted of four villas that were reportedly reserved for Mao Zedong, Liu Shaoqi, Zhou Enlai, and Zhu De. Their size, luxuriousness, furnishings, and landscaping, graded scrupulously in accordance with the ranks of their tenants, inspired gasps of admiration and awe. The enormous facilities constructed at Dishuidong, Hunan's "Dripping Cave" scenic area, were located near Mao's ancestral home. Mao's paternal great-grandparents, grandparents, and other forebears were buried here. Mao said, "This is a good place.

When I was young I used to graze buffalo here, collect firewood, cut grass, and wrestle with my playmates." In June 1959, when Mao went back for a visit, he said to Hunan's provincial first secretary, Zhou Xiaozhou, "Xiaozhou, this place is so peaceful; after I retire, can you build me a thatched hut to live in? Other leaders can also come here for a rest!"[66] Several months later, Zhou Xiaozhou was attacked as part of Peng De-huai's anti-party clique and had no opportunity to act on Mao's request. In May 1960, Mao brought up the matter again with Hunan's new first secretary, Zhang Pinghua. Zhang quickly arranged for the code-named Project 203, relocating local villagers and closing off the entire area for construction of three multistory buildings. The building occupied by Mao included a master bedroom, guest bedroom, conference room, dining room, recreation room, and other facilities. At the same time, a highway was built to Dishuidong. The two-year construction period coincided with peak starvation deaths. From October 1958 to March 1961, three pro-duction brigades in nearby Dongjiao Commune (subsequently renamed Longdong Commune) lost 707 members, or 13.5 percent of their total population. The mortality rate in Chengeng Commune's Nanxiang and Shijiang production brigades reached around 20 percent. A total of thirty thousand people died throughout Shaoshan County.[67]

Publications in the 1980s continued to spread the propaganda that Mao gave up meat during the years of hardship. I was deeply moved by the thought of Mao sharing in the suffering of his people. More recent information from Mao's personal chef presents a less deprived picture, however:

I remember in October 1960, Beijing was already frigid with the onset of winter. This was during the Three Years of Hardship, and Premier Zhou suggested that the Central Committee set an example by "eating vegetarian" . . .

Chairman Mao likewise substituted vegetables for meat and fish. At that time, there were no fresh vegetables in Beijing except for cabbage. One day, the head of the service department asked me, "Does Shanghai have any vegetables that we can't get in Beijing? In particular, vegetable dishes that can be made under Beijing's conditions?" I said, "Yes, things like stir-fried gluten, steamed gluten, and vegetarian chicken, these are things Beijing doesn't have." He asked, "Do you know how to make them?" I said, "I can give it a try." The next day, Wang Dongxing [at that time the Central Committee's head of security] and the head of the service department came to me and had me go to Division No. 1 to cook some dishes. At that time, Division No. 1 was Chairman Mao, Division No. 2 was Liu Shaoqi, Division No. 3 was Zhou Enlai, Division No. 4 was Zhu De, Division No. 5 was Peng Zhen, Division No. 6 was Deng Xiaoping, and Division No. 7 was Lin Biao. In this way I began cooking at Chairman Mao's residence, making Shanghai vegetarian dishes such as stir-fried gluten, steamed gluten, vegetarian ham, vegetarian duck, and so on. Then the previous chef was transferred elsewhere, and I became Chairman Mao's personal chef, continuing there for five years, right up until the beginning of the Cultural Revolution . . . Chairman Mao "ate vegetables in place of meat and fish" right up until the end of 1961.[68]

The vegetarian Shanghai specialties that Mao's personal chef prepared were basically soybean products that required a great deal of vegetable oil to prepare. Both in terms of fat content and protein, these dishes were highly nutritious and in no way inferior to meat. A menu that Mao's chef drew up for him in April 1961 included seventeen types of special fish and prawn dishes:

Steamed fish with turnip cubes, braised mandarin fish, fried mandarin fish, soft-fried mandarin fish, Moscow-style baked fish, cheese-baked fish, fish roasted with vegetables, Poland-style poached fish, braised jumbo prawns, roasted prawn filets, prawn toast, deep-fried jumbo prawns, curried prawns, slow-cooked prawns, soft-fried prawns, prawns with lettuce.[69]

According to an account by He Fang, a party insider and history expert:

Mao Zedong's going several months without meat during the Three Years of Hardship was publicized to a fantastic degree. The truth was that his doctor had advised him to switch to beef and mutton because of the elevated cholesterol content of pork. Also, during the early 1960s, Mao developed a preference for Western food. As a result, on April 26, 1961, Mao's staff and chef drew up a Western-style menu for him made up of a dozen or so beef, mutton, and vegetable dishes and sixteen or seventeen kinds of Western-style soup.[70]

The claim that Mao went without meat was therefore largely myth. On a postprandial stroll one evening during the Chengdu Conference in March 1958, Mao told Guizhou provincial party secretary Zhou Lin to dramatically increase production of the province's famous Maotai liquor while maintaining the quality. Zhou Lin followed orders, and production of the liquor, used almost exclusively for export, gift presentation, and consumption by senior officials, achieved a Great Leap Forward to 912 tons in 1960, a production level that was not surpassed until 1978.[71] Producing 1 kilo of the liquor required 5 kilos of grain, and total production of 2,079 tons of liquor from 1959 to 1961 consumed 10,040 tons of unprocessed grain.

The Maotai production center, Guizhou's Renhuai County, was home to some 200,000 peasants, many of whom died of starvation or suffered the effects of edema. If the grain used to produce Maotai had been distributed to the county's residents, all would have survived the worst of the famine. Instead, when the Maotai distillery encountered a shortage of raw material in 1960, the entire province was required to contribute grain. This upsurge in production contrasted sharply with the prerevolutionary practice of banning production of grain alcohol during famine years.[72]

Regarding the CCP's ineffectual relief efforts, Luo Longji observed:

> They know there's a problem, but even now they don't know the source of the problem; their examinations and corrections don't touch on the fundamental issue, and the measures they've decided on have failed to tackle the main points, only managing to make matters even worse and increasing the number of problems . . . The Communist Party speaks of materialism, but in fact they are the most idealistic; they speak of objective law, but it is they who show the least respect for objective law. Now they grasp a copy of *Das Kapital*, published in 1848,[73] to solve the problems of 1958. What kind of system is this? In all justice, I must fulfill my responsibility to humanity and cannot approve of such a system.

Luo said, "The extreme shortage of material goods, not just temporary but permanent, has been created by the social system." He expressed this opinion in private, but subsequently someone informed Mao, who condemned his views as reactionary.

Luo Longji also said,

The great shortage of material goods at present is a chaotic situation that has never before existed in China or elsewhere. In my view, everything was ruined in 1956. There were problems with the reform of privately owned industry and commerce; large factories can only solve big problems, but the problems of daily life must depend on small factories. Now we only see large factories and no small ones. After the reform of private industry and commerce came the Anti-Rightist Campaign, and that was followed by politics in command, the Great Leap Forward, and the people's communes.[74]

Half a century later, the sagacity of Luo Longji's "reactionary speech" is recognized and appreciated.

13 SOCIAL STABILITY DURING THE GREAT FAMINE

Throughout Chinese history, major famines have typically given rise to peasant revolts. In some cases, mass peasant uprisings brought dynastic change. The Great Famine of the 1960s was unprecedented in scale. Why did it not give rise to major social turmoil?

PART 1: PUBLIC ORDER BEFORE AND DURING THE GREAT FAMINE

From 1958 to 1962, China's oppressive tyranny and starvation led to intense dissatisfaction with the government. According to statistics from the area around Shaanxi's Baoji City, at least 116 "reactionary posters" and letters were issued in 1960, with half targeting food supply.[1] Public order did deteriorate during the Great Famine, with small-scale disturbances and rioting, outward migration, and an increase in crime. Yet there was no large-scale unrest.

Disturbances and riots were more likely in the ethnic minority regions, with fewer occurring in the Han-dominated Central Plains. In Han regions, few possessed weapons, and there were no autonomous social organizations. Conversely, some ethnic minorities were more bellicose in temperament and owned weapons, and some local headmen exercised a greater leadership and organizational role. Ethnic discontent and rioting occurred regularly from the 1950s onward, but the causes were complex and could not be attributed purely to the Great Leap Forward. Even so, the hardships imposed on peasants by the state purchasing monopoly and radical collectivization policies, and the devastation wreaked by the Great Leap Forward, were undoubtedly contributing factors. The government kept such incidents a closely guarded secret, and newspapers did not report them, but local annals and official archives record many such incidents.

Summary of Major Events in Modern Yunnan records that on June 5, 1957, the Diqing CCP work group reported to the provincial party committee on its suppression of an armed rebellion. Three counties inhabited by Tibetans had experienced armed rebellions of varying scales over the past year. A rebellion in Deqin in June 1956 had been reduced to a few stragglers, while a rebellion in Zhongdian in March still had some "stubborn pockets of resistance." The sixth district of Weixi Lisu Autonomous County also experienced some localized rioting.[2]

The Lijiang Xiaoliangshan Riot was reported by the Kunming Military Region on April 12, 1956:

> The armed rebellion situation in Lijiang Prefecture: Yongsheng, Ninglang, and Huaping had armed rebellions involving a total of more than 3,500 people . . .
>
> (1) More than 200 bandit rebels in Yangping, Shaoping, and other areas began rioting on April 6, stealing 1,500 kilos of rice, more than 100 kilos of beans, and 450 kilos of vegetables. We provided more than twenty armed escorts (seven people's police, four public security officers) and caravans with more than fifty horses, and except for four caravans that escaped, the others disappeared without a trace. At the same time, our work teams were surrounded at Shaoping and Mo'erping, and ten of our people were killed or wounded, with four rifles and handguns stolen along with all of the goods. That same night, more than 200 people surrounded our Yangchang office and killed two of our messengers. (2) The Shuiping and Maoniuping areas in western Huaping have more than 300 bandits with more than 200 firearms. On April 8, they surrounded our Tongda district government office, and at dawn on the 9th, our Huaping people's police officers and militia engaged in armed combat with the enemy, killing or wounding more than 50 of them. (3) Xinying Village (southern Ninglang) has more than 600 bandits who on April 8 began rioting and carried off 1,500 kilos of grain and all of the trade group's goods. On April 7, more than 1,000 of the enemy surrounded us at Paomaping. We immediately dispatched four platoons to Ninglang for attack, and as of April 8 reinforcements had arrived at the scene to lend their assistance.[3]

The Kunming Military Region reported armed rebellions involving more than 4,000 people during three weeks in April 1956. Troops were deployed in 36 armed combats with "enemies," with 363 killed, 397 wounded, and 470 taken prisoner.[4]

During the same period, the Yunnan Province public security bureau reported unrest involving around 2,500 people in portions of Huaping County, and a riot by 3,000 at the Ninglang County border.[5]

Disturbances among the Yao minority of Yunnan's Funing County were reported on September 25, 1956. The report observed "The question is why after several years of effort on our part, the counterrevolutionary elements are still able to carry out such substantial acts of sabotage, and why the masses continue to give credence to counterrevolutionary incitement . . . This requires an examination of our subjective operations."[6]

A report by the Wenshan Prefecture party committee elaborated further on the unrest[7]:

The problem of members of the Yao minority in Landian, Funing County, insisting on withdrawing from the collective has been mitigated after a period of effort. However, there have been new developments in the disturbances among the Shanyao and Heiyao groups, ranging from withdrawals from the collective to fighting with village cadres, seizing firearms, and organizing armed riots. Landlord Zhang Shangjie (Heiyao, warrant issued for arrest, fugitive) led an armed band of landlords and rich peasants and ordinary members of the collective totaling more than forty people to attack our Jinglong town government. They seized five firearms, the official party branch seal, a bundle of documents, 40 yuan in cash, and clothing, and chased down and pursued our town secretary with intent to kill. When the town secretary opened fire and injured one of them, they withdrew. Subsequently eighty-six men from eight stockaded villages of Jinglong Township all ran off. In addition, members of the Shanyao minority in Longshao and Longwan also forcibly withdrew from the collective and fought with the head of the collective, a member of the Tu minority, seizing five firearms. Most of the men of the Shanyao minority go to the mountains night and day to hold meetings and repair firearms and prepare sand gunpowder. There are differences between rioting by ethnic minorities to withdraw from the collectives and armed insurrections by bandits. There is still plotting and incitement by the enemy, but it takes an ethnic form, and most of the participants in the disturbances are ordinary masses who have been deceived. After these incidents, we reinforced the cadre strength and stationed troops at the garrison to maintain control, and maintaining a peaceful ethnic resolution resulted in pacification of most of the masses.

Weixi County reported an ambush in December 1956 in which eighty people snatched six packloads of foodstuffs, killing five police escorts and wounding two others in the process.[8]

The Guihua Temple Incident occurred around the same time.

In the fighting at Sicun Ruoyimu in December 1956, we shot dead seven bandit rebels and displayed their corpses on a side street (near the Lama Temple), inciting family members to claim the bodies. More than 200 rebel family members arrived, and an armed conflict took place. One staff member was lost at the scene, and we also shot dead one lama. At the sound of gunfire, troops immediately rushed to the scene, and they were fired on. The Guihua Temple is the largest monastery in Diqing Autonomous Prefecture.[9]

Violence also erupted in Zhaotong Prefecture in November 1958, with forty-six "bandits" killing a dozen cadres and township office staff in Zhaolu Integrated Area, while raising slogans against communal kitchens and nurseries and around-the-clock labor. Local officials subsequently rounded up 180 miscreants, killing 12. Another riot raising similar anticommunal slogans rose up at the border between Dali and Yongsheng around the time of the National Day celebrations.[10]

A counterrevolutionary rebellion by the "Chinese People's Insurrectionary Army" under Li Guangrong occurred at Dasongshu New Village coal mine in Yunnan's Luquan County on October 26, 1958. The ringleader and mainstays of the rebellion were captured the next day. On October 28 a rebellion-suppression task force arrived and arrested 117 people, from whom confessions were extorted. Twenty-four people were executed, with crippling injuries inflicted on thirty-six (of whom seven eventually died), and fifty were sentenced to imprisonment.[11]

At Chonggang Commune on December 27, 1958, rioters in Jinping County's Chonggang Commune seized fabric, clothing, rubber-soled shoes, and piecemeal goods and more than 1,300 yuan in cash, killing a grain bureau cadre and a salesclerk. "After leaving the scene, the rioters cooked food, and after five or six hours of commotion, the forty-three ringleaders retreated to the mountains."[12]

Another report analyzed a rebellion in the communes of Xuanwei County in December 1960[13]:

On the night of December 24, 1960, a counterrevolutionary rebellion occurred at Adu Commune in Yunnan's Xuanwei County, and also affected Zengping and Cuihua communes. This is the border region between Yunnan and Guizhou provinces, and two regiments of railway corps troops and 30,000 peasant workers were in the vicinity . . . The rebellion involved . . . 417 commune members. They included 138 cadres of the rank of production team leader or above, finance and trade officials, and primary school teachers, comprising 9 percent of all cadres in the affected region. They included two members of the commune party committee, seven party branch secretaries, forty-seven party members, and forty-five Youth League members. During the rebellion, thirteen cadres were killed, along with one ordinary commune member, and eleven firearms were seized. After our troops arrived on December 25, the bandits scattered in all directions, and by the 26th the rebellion was effectively quelled.

This counterrevolutionary rebellion began fermenting on July 28 of this year. The bandit rebel unit was known as the "Yunnan Branch of the Central Command of the China Construction," boasting four regiments. The rebellion arose in only one of these "regiments." The others were in six Xuanwei communes, including Baoshan and Shuanghe, as well as the three civilian public works "regiments" set up under the twenty-four railway corps regiments, making a total of more than two thousand bandits, and they were rounded up on the eve of the riots. By November 25, the main bandit ringleader, Xu Rujun, was executed, and the rest were all captured. Following investigation, 54 percent of the thirty-nine hard-core bandits of "battalion" rank or higher were found to be landlords, rich peasants, counterrevolutionaries, or bad elements.

In this rebellion, counterrevolutionary elements targeted the Three Red Banners and shortcomings in our work, and raised political slogans to dupe the masses, such as "implement the second land reform, distribute land equally to households, no grain tax, no selling of surplus grain," "disband the communal kitchens, distribute food rations to households, take meals at will," "resume free markets, no grain coupons, cloth coupons, or meal coupons," and "return the land to the old families, land returned to individual ownership."

Yunnan's provincial first secretary, Xie Fuzhi, reported to Premier Zhou Enlai that in 1960 "at least twelve large and small rebellions have occurred in the three southwestern provinces, including at least five in Sichuan, five in Guizhou, and two in Yunnan."[14]

Annals[15] record many riots and rebellions during this period:

Yunnan Province: Bandits rioted in the Sijiao Mountains in July 1958.[16] In the same year, discontent over the Great Leap Forward in Mouding County resulted in the killing of public security officers and an attack on the district office.[17] A rebellion occurred on April 16 in Jianshui County. Production team leader Li Wancheng was killed, and fourteen firearms were snatched from the people's militia. The rebellion was quelled on April 26.[18] A military revolt occurred in Nanhua County on November 10, 1962, but was quelled on November 22.[19] Zhenyuan County experienced a riot involving more than thirty people in 1962.[20]

Qinghai Province: On April 18, 1958, Han Yinu, commander of the 200-strong "Anti-Communist National Salvation Army," coerced more than 4,000 others to join an insurrection in Xunhua County,[21] which continued for five years. "From April 1958 to March 1962, there were 3,639 battles of varying sizes (including 2,811 in which army troops took part and 828 in which local cadres and the people's militia took part), in which 16,000 of the enemy were killed and 4,876 wounded, and entailing 46,800 captures and 58,800 surrenders. Four recoilless rifles were seized, along with four machine guns and large quantities of other firearms."[22] In 1959 a tribal rebellion occurred in Haixi Prefecture.[23]

Gansu Province: On the night of March 18, 1958, an armed rebellion in the Luzhu district of Zhuoni County spread to the Shangdie, Zhagana, and Beishan districts.[24] On August 15, 1958, large-scale riots broke out in Guanghe and Dongxiang: "They cried out counterrevolutionary slogans, sabotaged the government, killed and injured cadres, plundered banks, destroyed highways and communications routes, and so forth. In the second half of August, Lanzhou army troops assisted by militia suppressed the rebellion."[25] On December 20, 1960, Zhenyuan County's Tunzi Commune experienced a rebellion by the "Five-Point Army of the National Salvation Revolt on Behalf of the People."[26] A military rebellion occurred in 1963 in Jiayuguan Commune in Jiayuguan City.[27]

Sichuan Province: In 1958, Rongchang County uncovered restorationist activities by secret societies.[28] On May 28, 1960, Liu Zhishan led more than 300 temple adherents in Kai County in seizing 18 firearms and more than 1,200 rounds of ammunition from the Manyue Commune militia, then looted the commune's dry goods store and supply and marketing cooperative and took over the state-owned tree farm, killing or wounding four party cadres and abducting sixteen others. In July 1961 the "Workers and Peasants Democratic Party," led by Xu Shiqing, stole five handguns and fifty rounds of ammunition, then robbed grain depots and food transports in Meishan, Qionglai, and Xinjin.[29] In April 1961 the public security bureau of Jianhe County arrested leaders of the "Chinese Heroes Party" in Taiyong Commune. In August 1962 public security police captured members of the "Chinese People's Anti-Communist National Salvation Military and Government Command" active in Jianhe and Sansui counties.[30] In the same year, a plot by the "Chinese National Revolutionary Army" was uncovered in Dianjiang County, and five ringleaders were captured.[31] Aba Prefecture experienced intermittent military rebellions by ethnic minority leaders from 1956 until the beginning of 1961.[32]

Guizhou Province: At least twenty-four counterrevolutionary incidents were reported in Qiandongnan Prefecture in 1958. The more influential included the counterrevolutionary rebellion in Tianzhu County by the "Free China Democratic League Southwest Allied Anti-Communist Combat Force," the counterrevolutionary plot among inmates of Laiping County's Zhonghuang Labor Reform Farm, a planned rebellion in Guiyang, and revived plans for rebellion by the Cendong "4-1" counterrevolutionary clique. Thirty-five key instigators were arrested in these four cases alone. At least nineteen more counterrevolutionary plots were uncovered in this prefecture in 1959, and Zhenyuan County uncovered plans for a rebellion by the "China Free Democracy Party" in October 1960. Plans for a counterrevolutionary rebellion by the "China Border Region Guerrilla Warfare Headquarters" were uncovered in January 1961 in the Qingshan (Green Mountain) area.[33]

As of June 1960, Guizhou's Jiangkou County had lost forty thousand of its original population of less than one hundred thousand to starvation. Those who survived rose up, led by commune party secretaries who had watched their own children starve to death. The unarmed peasants were quickly suppressed by troops with modern weapons. The county head, who had at one point opened storehouses to feed the starving, killed himself with a bullet to the head, and a county party secretary whose exaggerated output reports had contributed to the disaster drowned himself.[34]

Guangxi Zhuang Autonomous Region: This region reported a riot in Baise County in 1958.[35]

Anhui Province: Yuexi County experienced a riot in 1959.[36]

Hubei Province: Someone proclaimed himself emperor in Baokang County in 1959 and assembled more than two hundred peasants in an attempted insurrection.[37]

Hebei Province: A woman named Yan Puzhen established an armed organization called the "Army of Benevolence and Righteousness," which attempted to take over the old county town of Yongnian on December 13, 1960. All ninety-five members were captured.[38]

Hunan Province: On October 28, 1960, security forces in La'ershan and Tuojiang townships arrested more than forty people planning a revolt by the "Chinese Democratic Liberation Party."[39]

Jilin Province: In July 1961, the provincial public security bureau uncovered a "Chinese Democratic Party," led by the former propaganda chief of the Huaide County party committee, Zhao Gedong.[40]

Guangdong Province: This province experienced a riot in Yangshan County, as well as in the Yao minority areas of Liannan and Lianshan counties in 1958.[41] Riots also occurred in 1958 and 1959 in two locations in Guangdong's Wengyuan County.[42]

This is but a sampling of the many incidents reported in local annals. The vast majority of the riots and revolts were small-scale and aimed purely at filling hungry bellies. Some local officials tended to label as "counterrevolutionary rebellion" even routine expressions of opinion. For example, in December 1957 a party member in Tonghai, Yunnan Province, wrote a letter to the upper levels describing the locality's food shortage and collected more than eight hundred signatures. Officials labeled the action a "counterrevolutionary disturbance" and imprisoned fourteen people, who were not rehabilitated until 1979.[43]

Tyranny, starvation, and abusive cadres compelled many residents of border areas to flee. According to the information I was able to gather, mass migration occurred in three main regions: Along the southwestern border, 80,000 people were reported to have fled Yunnan counties and prefectures, but the actual number was greater. Nearly 60,000 people fled Dehong Prefecture alone.[44] Near Shenzhen in the southeast, large numbers fled to Hong Kong starting in 1958. However, the real upsurge in refugees occurred in 1961 and 1962, due to the forced return of urban residents to the countryside. More than 110,000 people joined this illegal migration, with some 60,000 arriving safely in Hong Kong. The Hong Kong British government repatriated 40,000. The third site of mass migration was in Xinjiang's Ili Kazakh Autonomous Prefecture. During the spring and summer of 1962, more than 60,000 people fled to the Soviet Union with livestock, farming implements, and vehicles.

Archives contain numerous records of looting of food supplies. Most occurred along railway lines, where bands of peasants attacked grain transports. Grain depots were also looted.

In January 1961, starving hoards thronged food transports arriving at Gansu's Wuwei train station. Some five hundred to six hundred people took part in the looting in broad daylight on January 5, and more than two hundred young people arrived that night, stealing coal and more than ninety sacks of barley weighing over 9,000 kilos. The train station's artillery regiment and armed guards were unable to stop the looting and withdrew when some in the mob began throwing stones. Some looters shouted, "You don't dare open fire on us!" Others engaged in hand-to-hand fighting with soldiers while their companions raided the cargo. By afternoon the throng had grown to around one thousand. The armed police set up a machine gun. County party committee standing committee member Huang Jinzhong deployed two more platoons from an artillery regiment, while instructing department and bureau heads to learn more about the situation in nearby production teams and make arrangements to improve the people's livelihood. After being apprised of the situation, the Zhangye prefectural party committee withdrew its soldiers and ordered that no members of the public should be beaten, berated, detained, or fired upon. Those who had traveled long distances were to be fed and persuaded to return home.[45]

Elsewhere in Gansu around the same time, mobs four hundred strong besieged the flour mill in Jiuquan with ladders, sacks, cudgels, knives, and iron bars. Some took advantage of nightfall to intercept and rob wagon-borne grain supplies, cutting open grain sacks with knives and filling the sacks they were carrying. Guns were fired to ward off the looters, but thefts continued over the next two days.[46]

The Gansu provincial party committee was informed in January 1961 that social order had broken down along the railway lines, with constant train robberies of increasing scope and seriousness. An investigation found that 142 of the 338 trains arriving at the northern train station had been robbed. Other figures showed that 420 train robberies had occurred from October 1960 to January 22, 1961, including 184 in the first twenty days of January. The locations of the robberies had progressed from small locales to larger towns, and from train stations to railway lines, with a progression from robberies by individuals to robberies by bands, from petty pilfering to mass looting, and from stealthy nighttime thefts to attacks in broad daylight.[47]

Gansu Province recorded five hundred to six hundred incidents of food looting in January 1961, with losses of at least 500,000 kilos of food and nearly 10,000 head of livestock, and the pillaging of large amounts of dry goods and the paralysis of transport routes.[48] Later in 1961, mass lootings were reported at granaries in Zhangye City and Anxi County.[49]

In December 1960, Anhui's Wuhu Prefecture experienced at least 180 food thefts. In ninety-six cases, a total of 18,000 kilos of grain were stolen. Another 65 food thefts occurred throughout the province in early 1961, with more than 5,000 kilos of food stolen, and robberies continued into the spring of 1962. Most food thefts occurred where people were suffering great hardship. Nearly 5,500 people were reported to have taken part in 22 food robberies in thirteen counties.[50]

Guizhou's Leishan County reported numerous lootings of state grain depots in 1960.[51] From December 1960 to January 1961, Liping County experienced more than 4,000 lootings of storehouses by starving people.[52] Guangdong's Chaozhou City also reported robberies at collective storehouses.[53]

Published crime data show a marked increase in crimes during the height of the famine in 1960 and 1961.

Sichuan's Lu County experienced such a serious breakdown in law and order that some production teams and administrative districts were

TABLE 13.1 CRIMINAL CASES IN JILIN PROVINCE, 1957–63

Year	Murder	Rape	Theft	Maiming or killing of livestock	Fraud	Arson	Total
1957	140	603	4,537	79	366	74	10,753
1958	165	671	7,867	73	203	64	6,148
1959	107	493	4,395	24	125	26	5,278
1960	106	542	4,295	60	163	32	6,557
1961	114	263	5,478	397	297	38	12,945
1962	146	388	11,284	159	260	28	10,593
1963	136	967	9,443	27	366	48	9,540

Source: Jilin Provincial Annals, vol. 12, Public Security and Judicial Annals: Public Security, Changchun: Jilin renmin chubanshe, 1998, p. 172.

unable to hold meetings. Yangjiu Commune experienced at least seventeen lootings and thefts from January 6 to 10, 1961. Commune member Yang Yunzhang was robbed by a cudgel-bearing mob that burst into his home and took away six geese, twelve chicken eggs, and three sheep. Caoshi Commune experienced at least 104 cases of plundering and theft from the end of December 1960. Internal statistics show that thirty-six of Lu County's sixty-nine communes reported thefts during one week in the spring of 1961.[54]

Courts tended to treat such cases on an ideological basis. Gansu Province's *Minqin County Annals* records: "During the Three Years of Hardship from 1959 to 1961, the people's livelihood was in a precarious state, with many people fleeing elsewhere or dying. In order to survive, some commune members slaughtered livestock and stole grain. During this time, the court trial work came under leftist influence, and these activities came under attack as acts of sabotage. Of all the cases heard in 1959, 492 cases, or 55.8 percent of the total, were classified as criminal cases."[55] The observations are echoed in other localities.

Professor Zhang Qingwu of Chinese People's Public Security University, who researches public order, worked in the Ministry of Public Security at that time. He told me that the majority of criminal cases involved starving people stealing food to survive. There were very few murders. A statistical report from Jilin Province similarly found that during the time of greatest hardship, the number of cases of murder, arson, and fraud remained about the same, while there was a substantial decrease in cases of rape and a large increase in cases of theft and of maiming or killing of livestock (for food).

PART 2: REASONS FOR THE LACK OF LARGE-SCALE SOCIAL TURMOIL

The reason for the lack of large-scale social conflict and turmoil during the three-year Great Famine was the CCP's totalitarian social controls.

MAINTAINING LARGE-SCALE SUPPRESSION OF COUNTERREVOLUTIONARY ACTIVITY

In 1950 and 1951, the state issued a directive and then a law against "counterrevolutionary" activities. This was followed by the arrest of 2.62 million people (of whom 380,000 were released after reeducation due to the insignificance of their "crimes"), with 712,000 executed, 1.29 million imprisoned, and 1.2 million placed under surveillance and control.[56]

Further decrees on counterrevolutionary crime continued to be issued into the mid-1950s, each followed by a new upsurge in campaigns against the so-called counterrevolutionaries.

These unending campaigns sapped the forces of social resistance, and no one dared step forward as an opposition leader. According to the leading party group of the Jilin provincial people's procuratorate: "The enormous achievements of the struggle to suppress counterrevolutionaries in recent years, coupled with the work by political organs at all levels under the leadership of the party committees . . . have dealt a succession of heavy blows to the enemy . . . Although some counterrevolutionaries remain, they are fewer, weaker, and more isolated."[57]

THE "GREAT LEAP FORWARD" IN PUBLIC SECURITY WORK

With the launch of the Great Leap Forward, the organs of dictatorship carried out their own Great Leap by identifying and attacking with utmost severity any word or action opposed to the government. Every level of the bureaucracy formulated an arrest plan and assigned arrest quotas that increased as they passed down each rung of government. Arrests from 1958 to 1960 exceeded the total number for the nine years from 1949 through 1957. Anhui Province arrested more than 8,000 criminal suspects in 1957. When the central government assigned the province an arrest quota of 45,000 for 1958, it surpassed that quota with 101,000 arrests. From 1958 to 1960, 173,000 people were arrested in the province; at least a third died in custody.[58]

During that same period, Qinghai Province's labor reform and labor reeducation system recorded 49,304 deaths—30 percent of those in custody or newly released. Qinghai arrested 63,064 people in those three years, 2.58 percent of the population and more than triple the arrests made from 1949 to 1957. The arrests included 40,602 for opposing the launch of the Great Leap Forward in 1958.[59]

When Mao took the initiative to correct leftist tendencies in late 1958 and early 1959, the number of arrests and detentions decreased. But the drive in 1960 to implement the spirit of the Lushan Conference and beat back right deviation led to a new upsurge in arrests and detentions—18,177 arrests in Qinghai, for instance, and more than 50,000 in Anhui.[60]

A National Public Security Conference in mid-1958 resolved to reinforce efforts against counterrevolutionaries, which led to an upsurge in crackdowns.[61] According to incomplete statistics, from winter 1958 until June 1959, Jilin Province unearthed 9,058 counterrevolutionary remnants and 943 mainstays of reactionary secret societies, and exposed 4,959 landlords and rich peasants. The campaign collected 26,839 reports from informers, of which 16,538 were found to be substantiated. Pressure impelled the surrender of 2,232 counterrevolutionaries and criminal fugitives. In July 1960, Jilin authorized more arrests in areas where "the democratic revolution had been inadequately thorough."[62] Available information indicates that Jilin's experience was representative.

In 1958–60, Anhui's Tianchang County Court prepared blank judgments affixed with official seals and supplied them to the countryside so that anyone whose conduct was found wanting could be immediately convicted and placed under control and surveillance. Public security and procuratorial organs and communal cadres could also fill in these blank judgments on the spot, and in some cases oral judgments sufficed.[63]

The Chuxiong Yizu Autonomous Prefecture of Yunnan Province

cracked down on 5,813 active counterrevolutionaries from 1958 to 1961, and on 10,549 individuals in other undesirable categories in the year 1958 alone. Thirty-seven were sentenced to death, 3,238 were arrested, and 702 were sent to reeducation through labor.[64] A large number of the accusations were baseless.

Localities also organized targeted attacks. In mid-December 1961, Jilin Province assembled a large-scale joint task force along railway lines to attack theft and profiteering. The operation enlisted more than 20,000 cadres in investigations at 12,487 target locations. More than 9,900 suspects were uncovered at 12,487 locations, among whom 8,733 were subjected to group investigation and 1,172 detained. Ultimately 39 were arrested, 79 sent to reeducation through labor, 143 sentenced to forced labor, and 315 put into administrative detention. The others were released after criticism and reeducation. More than 10,000 leads resulted in 52 criminals arrested. The momentum of the campaign led to the additional surrender of more than 2,000 thieves, profiteers, and smugglers and 21 criminal cliques in just seven days.[65]

In 1961, Sichuan's Chongqing County launched a seven-day "public order movement," during which 909 petty thieves were subjected to struggle, resulting in twelve deaths from beatings or suicide.[66]

Once the Great Leap Forward was launched, the grass roots tightened control over "hostile influences." Sichuan's *Dianjiang County Annals* record: "Starting in 1959, 'wrapping committees' made up of party members, Youth League members, militia, and public security officers began monitoring landlords, rich peasants, counterrevolutionaries, and bad elements, implementing a system of one admonishment per month, one evaluation per quarter, and one overall appraisal per year. Depending on performance, each person had a label applied or removed, and the results were published."[67] These measures were typical.

A CLOSELY MAINTAINED SYSTEM OF SOCIAL CONTROL

Once in power, the Chinese Communist Party established an ironclad system of social control that included an impermeable organizational structure, a household registration system, food rationing, and controls on population movement.

Political and economic powers were concentrated in the party, which by the time of the Great Leap Forward had fifteen million members.

Under the disciplinary restraint of "each person submitting to the organization, lower levels submitting to the higher levels, and the entire party submitting to the Central Committee," every party member was obliged to comply with the party's will and also drive and supervise the execution of this will among the people. The party's control penetrated every village, every workshop, every school, every shop, and every military unit. The party also led the Communist Youth League, labor unions, Women's Federation, Young Pioneers, and other "mass organizations." In China, virtually every individual worked, studied, and learned within an organization controlled by the CCP. Each relied on the party for all means of livelihood and information. Every individual's behavior and thinking was under organizational control. Only a tiny minority ever expressed views at variance with those of the government, and opposition was considered exceptional and extreme behavior.

Loss of control over a floating population easily led to social turmoil. For that reason, once the PRC was established, the government focused on minimizing and controlling the floating population. Once the state monopoly for purchasing and marketing grain, cotton, and oil was put into effect in 1953, urban residents received all means of livelihood through state-issued ration coupons, which could be redeemed only in one's residential district. In January 1958 the State Council assigned household registration work to the public security bureaus. This gave the public security apparatus an intimate familiarity with the situation of every resident. Anyone who left his residential district for even a short length of time required a written permit from the local government and had to carry his ration tickets with him. Upon arrival at his destination, the traveler was required to present his permit to the local public security substation, and he had to use his ration tickets to obtain daily necessities. Peasants were tightly bound to the land. They were not allowed to leave their villages for nonagricultural work, and leaving the village for any other reason required permission from the production team head. The result was that China had virtually no floating population.

The Great Famine brought an increase in refugees, but all levels of government continued to control population movement. Local officials were required to prevent peasants from leaving their home villages, while peasants who fled to other parts were detained, beaten, paraded as "criminal fugitives," and repatriated to their points of origin. The minister of public security, Xie Fuzhi, told a National Politics and Law Conference in October 1962 that the floating population reached 6 million in 1960. The government had taken 2.07 million people into custody from January to August 1961, and another 1.4 million from January to August 1962, with the total for that year expected to reach nearly 2 million.

Following a meeting of the ministries of Public Security and Internal Affairs in 1961, cities in Jilin Province introduced specific measures to improve public order and control the floating population:[68]

1. Stem the flow of refugees. The first step was to block exit routes and educate peasants not to leave their homes. The second was to man checkpoints at train stations, with strict inspection of train tickets and food coupons on the trains. All refugees discovered in the cities or on the railways were to be taken into custody and either repatriated or resettled elsewhere in the countryside. Those who resisted repatriation or produced falsified household registrations were to be sent to labor camps.

2. Eliminate the idle urban population. Household registration work should be strengthened with increased manpower. Household registration police were to be remunerated as cadres and could not be transferred at will. Tight control was ordered at hostels, restaurants, and bathhouses. Dance halls should be forbidden from selling tickets to outsiders.

3. Strengthen security work on major highways. Additionally, each factory, party organ, and school should carry out rectification and reinforce discipline so as to plug existing loopholes.

The Ministry of Public Security instructed each major city to select representative cases and carry out executions, with a smaller number of executions in midsize cities and villages. Executions should be carried out at mass rallies at which the top official would make a speech and the judgment would be passed and carried out forthwith. Notices would be put up to inform all households of the event, so that the death of one would serve to warn multitudes.

TIGHT IDEOLOGICAL CONTROL

At that time, the Communist Party held the banner of truth firmly in its grip. After half a century of chaos and warfare and the corruption of the

Kuomintang regime, the Communists had won the public's trust. People believed the CCP would lead them to a glorious future under communism, and many were willing to sacrifice their own lives to this cause.

Every newspaper, conference, classroom, and public forum disseminated the unified voice of the government and released information advantageous to the government. Party branches, the Communist Youth League, the people's militia, the Women's Federation, labor unions, and schools all instilled the will of the Central Committee, and eliminated all "static" interfering with transmission of the central government's voice. China's propaganda machinery and all of its cultural and educational activities oriented every individual's thoughts and actions in the same direction.

This massive ideological effort made people docile, and the closing off of information sources kept them in ignorance. The Xinyang Incident, in which more than a million people starved to death, and the Tongwei Incident, in which a third of the population died, were unknown to neighboring regions at that time, and remained closely guarded secrets for decades. Major incidents were handled as isolated rather than systemic problems, and starvation deaths were reckoned as merely "one finger" in the context of "nine fingers" of achievement. Anyone who cast doubts on the "nine fingers" was considered a negator of the Three Red Banners.

Official propaganda depicted life overseas as an abyss of suffering, and the lack of positive comparison ameliorated the dissatisfaction that China's peasants felt toward their lot.

NIPPING REBELLION IN THE BUD

In earlier times, China's oppressed retreated to the hills and forests and rose up in rebellion. Mao himself in his youth had established such a "revolutionary base" against the government of that time. With the establishment of the People's Republic, however, such tactics had become irretrievable relics of history. It was now all but impossible for the populace to draw on military force to overturn the regime, for a number of reasons:

1. Lack of leadership. Past peasant uprisings had relied on local strongmen and landlords as their mainstays, but repeated political campaigns since 1949 had resulted in the killing, imprisonment, or surveillance of everyone who had previously held a position of influence.

2. Lack of financial resources. Before the CCP came to power, it was possible to expropriate monies from the rich and powerful to fund rebellions. In the New China, however, all financial resources were controlled by the state, and there were no wealthy citizens from whom funds could be extracted.

3. Lack of weapons to use against the government. Any band of rebels fell within the range of the government's weapons, and the state military could penetrate even the most remote "base area" through modern transport routes.

4. Lack of organization. Without the right to free assembly, any political organization could be stamped out as soon as it emerged. Modern totalitarian systems allow very little possibility for successful popular revolts on the order of Song Jiang's bandit mob at Mount Liang (in the novel *Water Margin*) or Mao Zedong's Red Army at Jinggang Mountain.

From 1958 to 1962, the government maintained a military strength of more than four million. These armed forces were well equipped and prepared to deal with both foreign aggression and domestic strife. It was impossible for citizens to contend with the might of the government armed forces.

GRASSROOTS CADRES SCAPEGOATED TO ALLEVIATE DISSATISFACTION

The places suffering the heaviest toll from starvation were typically those most oppressed by abusive cadres, and where the Five Winds blasted most severely. The Central Committee's campaign to rectify the Five Winds disciplined many errant grassroots cadres. In Sichuan's Hechuan County, for example, 5,184 of the county's 25,283 cadres were disciplined from 1959 to 1961. The pretext was the "inadequate thoroughness of the democratic revolution," with the disciplined cadres described as "the dregs of the Kuomintang." This appeased many victimized peasants and led them to feel that "the central government is wise and good, and it is only the local cadres who are bad." Thus the Communist Party was able to shift the blame for its own shortcomings onto the long-vanquished Guomindang (or Kuomindang) regime.

14 THE SYSTEMIC CAUSES OF THE GREAT FAMINE

Why did no one expose the blatant lies of the "high-yield satellite" fields?

Why did tens of millions of people arrive at death's door without being saved?

Why did the policies that caused starvation continue for three years?

Why were cadres able to inflict such cruel abuse on peasants?

Why were most of those who starved the very peasants who produced China's food?

Why was it possible to keep the catastrophic death of tens of millions secret for half a century?

The answers to these questions lie in the system.

China's totalitarianism combined features of Stalinist autocracy with those of China's traditional monarchy; that is, it drew on the political framework of the first Qin emperor to implement a comprehensive dictatorship of the proletariat. In Mao's own words, it was a system that "combined Marx with Qin Shihuang."

MAO ZEDONG, CHINA'S LAST EMPEROR

On August 5, 1973, Mao summoned his wife, Jiang Qing, and had her transcribe a poem that criticized Guo Moruo's *Ten Critiques*.[1]

The gentleman is advised not to berate Qin Shihuang,
The business of burning and burying requires discussion;
Although the ancient dragon is dead, his empire lives on,
While the lofty fame of Confucianism is but chaff.
The Qin political system has continued for 100 generations,
The *Ten Critiques* is not a good essay;

Familiarize yourself with the Tang *Discourse on Feudalism*,
And don't retreat from Zihou back to Wen Wang.[2]

China's history had been one of despotism, and Mao embraced autocratic thinking. The Tang *Discourse on Feudalism* discussed fiefdoms prior to the Qin dynasty, when the feudal lord enjoyed a great measure of independence, and the central government could not exercise complete control. Emperor Qin Shihuang abolished fiefdoms and established an administrative system of prefectures and counties. The Tang scholar Liu Zongyuan, in his *Discourse on Feudalism*, found the new system to be superior in terms of its centralization of power. The emperor appointed all local officials, and those who met with disfavor found themselves unseated. This administrative system carried on for more than two thousand years. The Old China is commonly referred to as feudalistic, but historian Liu Zehua holds that under Qin Shihuang, China became monarchic.[3]

Although CCP rule served as a mere coda of the Chinese imperial despotism it inherited, its access to modern weaponry, transportation, communication, and methods of organization gave it an even tighter and more detailed, extensive, and penetrating control over society, officialdom, and the people than the former imperial autocracy had ever accomplished. This stranglehold encompassed all of society's political, economic, cultural, and ideological workings and all aspects of daily life. The dictatorship's coercive power penetrated every corner of even the most remote village, to every member of every family, into the minds and entrails of every individual. Thus Mao's rule was not just monarchy but totalitarianism, which denotes the expansion of executive power to its ultimate extreme. Totalitarianism is characterized by powerful central rule that uses coercion and repression to control all aspects of an individual's life, thereby imprisoning an entire society within the state machinery. Totalitarianism will pay any cost and expend all necessary effort to achieve national objectives decided by state rulers, who declare themselves the sole representatives of the majority whose interests the objectives purport to serve. Large-scale, organized violence is rationalized by unlimited loyalty to the state.

The national objective the leaders of Mao's generation pursued was communism, presented as a system in which there would be no exploitation or oppression, and under which all contributed according to their ability and took according to their need under conditions of complete equality. Why did the system they actually established fall so short of these ideals? Friedrich Hayek provides a profound answer to this question in his book *The Road to Serfdom*. I don't doubt the sincerity of the creators of this system, many of whom hoped to rescue the people from misery. When they began applying their ideals to actual life, they could not anticipate the results.

The construction of a system involves too many factors to predict or control the outcome. Once the system is in place, it imposes restraints on the people it intends to serve, and forces its executors to act in accordance with the system's logic and inertia, even if these acts run contrary to the aspirations of its creators. Hayek remarks on the tragedy that "the pursuit of some of our most cherished ideals has apparently produced results utterly different from those which we expected."[4] This is the experience of the Chinese people.

In power, Mao became immersed in China's traditional monarchal culture and Lenin and Stalin's "dictatorship of the proletariat." Disregarding the democracy he had promoted in his early years, he positioned himself as China's last and most powerful emperor. During the Yan'an period,[5] Mao once asked his Russian interpreter Shi Zhe the difference between a president and an emperor. Shi Zhe provided a systematic answer based on his political knowledge, but Mao just laughed and said, "In fact, they're the same!"[6] In 1950, on the first International Labor Day (May 1) celebration under the New China, when Mao was provided with a list of slogans for his approval, he personally added one: "Long live Chairman Mao!" Clearly Mao regarded himself as an emperor.[7]

Mao grew up in China's agrarian society and had had no experience with Western democracy and rule of law; rather, his aspiration was for regime change of the kind brought about by peasant revolts. In his eyes, both presidents and emperors reigned over the multitudes, and mass kowtowing and cries of "Long live the emperor!" were a matter of course. André Malraux recalled in 1972, "I once asked Mao if he considered himself a successor to China's last great emperors, and he replied, 'Of course I'm their successor.'"[8]

Seeking to unite divisions and govern chaos, Mao's generation constructed a pyramidal power structure on the soil of China's imperial culture. The party, the army, the highly concentrated economic and political systems, strong ideological control, and integrated social structure complemented one another to form an extremely stable, highly centralized pyramid. Mao was positioned at the pinnacle, where his iron grip on the party and the military made him China's ultimate political and ideological authority. In this structure, ordinary individuals could serve only one purpose: to give their all for communism.

China's earlier emperors had been able to say, like France's Louis XIV, "L'état, c'est moi"—"I am the state." But Mao could go further and say, "I am society." The leading organs at every level were subject to Mao, but within their own jurisdictions, their power was as all-encompassing as Mao's, so that each was a local despot. Each official wore two faces: before his superiors he was a slave, and before his subordinates, a tyrant.

THE STATE'S MONOPOLY OVER ECONOMIC RESOURCES AND CONTROL OF THE ECONOMY

Hayek says, "The various kinds of collectivism, communism, fascism, etc., differ among themselves in the nature of the goal toward which they want to direct the efforts of society. But they all differ from liberalism and individualism in wanting to organize the whole of society and all its resources for this unitary end and in refusing to recognize autonomous spheres in which the ends of the individuals are supreme."[9]

"Organizing the whole of society and all its resources" to achieve communism's "unitary end" required the party's highly centralized planned economy, which completely expropriated the autonomous sphere of the individual. In the countryside, collectivization involved seizing all means of production for the collective, and placing all foodstuffs, cotton, oil, and other agricultural products under the state monopoly for purchasing and marketing. The peasants and production team cadres had no say in terms of which crops to plant or how to cultivate them.

The urban population likewise received all means of livelihood through the state rationing system, and urban industry was directly operated and managed by the state. What China's factories produced, and how much and by what means, were all determined by the state. When socialist transformation was completed in 1957, the three major categories of enterprises—state-owned industry, collectively owned enterprises, and businesses under joint state-private ownership—were all effectively controlled by the state and accounted for 99.1 percent of the gross industrial output value and 94.5 percent of the total value of retail sales.

Major policy decisions for economic construction were concentrated in the Central Committee, and within that context, Mao's views carried the greatest weight. Many economic targets were proposed by him.[10] The state economic apparatus was like a huge machine in which hundreds of millions worked according to directives from the highest levels. Ensuring that these directives were implemented without interference required a highly centralized political system that eliminated all "noise" and "static" through the construction of uniform public opinion.

TOTALITARIAN PARTY LEADERSHIP

China's political and economic power was concentrated in the CCP, whose members had to share the same faith in Marxism-Leninism and Mao Zedong Thought, and had to venerate the same leader: Mao Zedong. Under the one-party dictatorship, whatever party members were required to do was also expected of the general populace.

The CCP had been established with the same iron discipline as the Soviet Communist Party, and alternative views were difficult to express. This tightly integrated party easily became a tool of the supreme leader's arbitrary rule. The party dominated society through a structure that operated in tandem with government departments and work units at every level. The party's supreme leading body was supposedly the National Party Congress and the Central Committee that arose from it, but in actuality, the chairman of the party reigned supreme. On the appointment of cadres and all other important questions, the party's first in command held absolute power, while local party committees established standing committees to handle daily practical authority. The party's full-time cadres were state cadres, and their salaries and the party's operating expenses were drawn from the state coffers.

The founding principle of the CCP was "democratic centralism," but the reality was centralism without democracy, or democracy as merely a means toward centralism. Following the 1957 Anti-Rightist Movement, no one outside the party dared criticize the party, and following the 1959 campaign against right deviation, no one within the party dared criticize the leadership or its policies. All levels of the party were subject to a single command; party secretaries at each level were like patriarchs, with

Mao himself serving as the supreme patriarch. With the party leadership at all levels lacking both external and internal monitoring, special privileges began to develop rapidly after 1957.

Opinions within the CCP were resolved through discussion in which the minority ultimately submitted to the majority. Under normal circumstances, Mao had the final say. Disputes over major issues were resolved through "line struggle," in which the proponents of different viewpoints battled it out until one emerged victorious. Those who executed the "erroneous line" then stepped down, while those who had persisted in the "correct line" consolidated power. Considered a "manifestation of class struggle within the party," line struggle tended toward a fight to the death. Once Mao achieved absolute power, line struggle became his tool for striking down dissenters.

Although China had other parties, none existed to acquire governing power, and all submitted to the CCP. The leaders of these "democratic parties" were CCP members whom the party had deployed, and the parties' funds were allocated by the CCP. In any meaningful sense, therefore, China's democratic parties were merely social organizations under the leadership of, and in service to, the Communist Party.

As a revolutionary in the 1930s, Mao had proposed "abolishing the Kuomintang's one-party dictatorship and establishing a democratic coalition government." The actual result, however, was just another "one-party dictatorship," with the Communist Party simply replacing its predecessor, just as peasant revolts had overthrown and replaced dynasties over the past two thousand years.

PRESERVING POWER THROUGH THE BARREL OF A GUN

The army—in this case the People's Liberation Army—was the backbone and guardian of state power. From June 1946 to June 1950, the PLA annihilated 8.07 million troops from Chiang Kai-shek's Nationalist forces and brought about "rule from the barrel of a gun."

This was an army incomparably immense by world standards, reaching 6.11 million by 1951.[11] It was—and still is—an army backed by an enormous technology contingent. China has hundreds of national defense institutes and more than one hundred military academies and national defense research organs absorbing the best talent from the country's technical and engineering institutions, and backed by the country's heavy industry.

Mao held this huge military force firmly in his grip. The party's command of the gun was not merely dependent on military officers' loyalty to the party; it was ensured through a series of institutions.

The Central Committee's Central Military Commission (CMC) commands the military. The post of chairman of the CMC is held simultaneously by the chairman of the Central Committee, who has the final decision-making power on major issues. The top leaders of the Central Committee are also members of the CMC, and the principal military cadres are appointed by the CMC. As in the government structure, every level of the military has a corresponding party organization, and military cadres are all members of the party committee at their level, through which the army's major issues are discussed and approved. The party's leadership safeguards the party's command of the gun, while the additional reinforcement of ideological and political work ensures that each soldier is familiar with this principle. In addition, Mao absorbed the experience of the military inspection system from Chinese history to form comprehensive and watertight military discipline inspection methods:

1. Officers were transferred frequently, preventing personal bonds that could engender conspiracies against the Center or transform a military unit into a commander's personal army.
2. Separation of the power to deploy and to lead troops ensured that all military actions were decided by the Center. The CMC chairman had the ultimate decision-making power.
3. Military payroll and equipment were issued through the Center's General Logistics Department, preventing the creation of warlords through local support.
4. Military and administrative leadership were separated at the local level, putting them in a state of mutual supervision and control and making it impossible for a separatist military regime to be established at the local level. Mutual supervision likewise existed between the commanding officer and the political commissar of any army unit.
5. Military, executive, and logistical operations were separate hierarchies, each subordinate to a party committee at its level.
6. The Center was strong and the branches weak. If problems arose in a local unit, the Center could use its superior military in the capital to quash a revolt. Military units (and their commanders) stationed

outside the capital were required to obtain permission to carry weapons when entering Beijing. Military aircraft were not allowed to enter the airspace of the capital.

Since ultimate decision-making power rested with the chairman of the Central Military Commission, Mao commanded the gun that controlled the party, and used the party to control the people.

A POLITICAL SYSTEM DEMOCRATIC IN NAME ONLY

At three o'clock in the afternoon on October 1, 1949, three hundred thousand people gathered in Tiananmen Square for a grand ceremony during which Mao declared the establishment of the People's Republic of China.

In his battles with Chiang Kai-shek, Mao had repeatedly raised democratic political slogans,[12] but during a Politburo meeting in August 1949, he said, "We'll adopt a system of democratic centralism rather than one of bourgeois parliamentarianism . . . It's unnecessary to have a bourgeois parliament and tripartite separation of powers."[13] Thus he fundamentally negated a modern political system.

Mao divided the formation of the country into separate issues of state and government. He said that the state is the country's class character. Problems of state are problems of the status of social classes within the country.[14] In June 1949 he proposed a "people's democratic dictatorship"—that is, "democratic toward the people and dictatorial toward the enemy." The scope of "the people" gradually narrowed to exclude landlords, rich peasants, counterrevolutionaries, bad elements, and rightists, and urban intellectuals were labeled as bourgeoisie and brought under attack along with well-to-do middle peasants. The "people" and the "enemy" never had clear-cut legal definitions. Every cadre could define as an "enemy" anyone who opposed him, and thereby designate that person a target of dictatorship.

The National People's Congress (NPC) was central to the PRC's system of government. The nation's president and vice president were elected by the NPC. The premier of the State Council, after being nominated by the country's president, was confirmed by the NPC. The NPC also elected the heads of the Supreme People's Court and the Supreme People's Procuratorate. The Constitution stipulated that the NPC was also empowered to make decisions on all major national issues, such as examining and approving the National Economic Plan and state budget, approving the division of the country into provinces, cities, and autonomous regions, and declaring war or peace.

The 1954 Constitution stipulated that the president was the PRC's representative to the outside world. At the same time, the president could exercise only certain powers as head of state in coordination with the standing committee of the NPC. Under these circumstances, the head of state was a collective made up of the national president and the NPC standing committee. After the term of the First National People's Congress expired, Mao was no longer willing to serve as president and was replaced by Liu Shaoqi. After Liu was "overthrown" during the Cultural Revolution, China no longer had a president, as Mao was willing neither to serve as president nor to allow anyone else to serve.

Montesquieu defined republics as governmental systems in which the populace or a portion of the populace holds the ultimate political power; monarchies as governments in which a single person governs in compliance with law; and dictatorships as governments with no law or regulations and in which an individual governs according to his own will. Based on the provisions of its Constitution, the PRC was a republic, not a dictatorship. But during the Mao era, China had only two legal statutes: the Constitution and the Marriage Law. During his later years, Mao was able to ignore the Constitution and act in accordance with his own wishes. At the Beidaihe Conference on the afternoon of August 21, 1958, he said:

> We can't rely on law to govern the majority of people; the majority needs to cultivate habits. The armed forces rely on military law to rule and can't manage it; in fact the 1,400-man plenum [referring to the enlarged 1958 CMC meeting] governed people. Who can remember so many civil and criminal laws? I took part in formulating the Constitution, and even I can't remember it. Han Fei[15] talked about rule of law, but then the Confucians came along and talked of rule by man. Each of our resolutions is a law, and holding meetings is law. The provisions on public order have to become a matter of habit before they will be observed, and by the time they become part of the social consensus and awareness we will have achieved communism. Each of our regulations, the majority, 90 percent, are created at the departmental level. We don't rely on these, but mainly

on resolutions and conferences, four times a year; we don't rely on the civil law or the criminal law to maintain public order. The National People's Congress and State Council meetings also have their own way, and what we rely on is our own way.[16]

In short, modern Western countries were ruled by democratic parliamentary politics, but China was ruled by dictatorial "conference politics," in which all major issues were decided at meetings controlled by the supreme leader. The conference was a tool for carrying out the will of the supreme leader, and its "resolutions" were a written expression of that will. This will penetrated every corner and household of China through tens of thousands of CCP branches. There was no division between party and government, and the party's top leaders enjoyed absolute power. While the Constitution stipulated that the National People's Congress was the organ of highest authority, the ultimate authority was actually held by the standing committee of the CCP Central Committee Politburo. The National People's Congress was nothing more than a rubber stamp.

To the political system of Qin Shihuang was grafted a Leninist-Stalinist system referred to as the "revolutionary regime." Opposing this regime was an act of "counterrevolution" to be handled with the utmost severity.

TOTALITARIAN IDEOLOGICAL CONTROL

Matching the highly centralized system was a unified propaganda mechanism through which "all people were brought into line" so that "all laughed, cried, and cursed in unison."[17] The importance the party placed on ideological control was reflected in its emphasis on firmly grasping "two barrels": the gun barrel and the pen barrel; seizing and ruling its domain relied on both.

The propaganda machine aimed at making all of China's people submit themselves to the ultimate goal of communism. The message was that it was necessary, glorious, and sublime to sacrifice the individual self for the sake of the "greater self," and that unwillingness to make this sacrifice was shameful. The general public, especially ignorant youths, heard only one voice and learned only one theory, in order to ensure that their thinking was completely "pure" and that their "love and hate" were intense and clearly demarcated. These "pure" youths were in fact the "fundamentalists" of communism, sincere and formidable in rejecting and attacking non-Communist thinking. The Communist Wind's ability to blast repeatedly throughout the Great Famine was a result of these years of Communist indoctrination.

There were only two major national newspapers, the party-run *People's Daily*, and *Guangming Daily*, which targeted an intellectual readership. Their leading ideology was identical. Each province had its own newspaper, which had the same content as *People's Daily* except for local news authorized by the provincial party committee. On a given day, it was far from unusual for the articles, titles, and layouts of the first page of every newspaper in the country to be virtually identical. The Central People's Broadcasting Station and the Xinhua News Agency were also the mouthpieces of the Central Committee, their articles submitted to censors who approved or rejected them on the basis of whether they strengthened or weakened belief in communism and loyalty to the party and its leaders. Ordinary people were not informed of actual conditions overseas, or of negative domestic events. The state jammed "enemy broadcasts," and listening to Voice of America was considered a tremendous crime. Few people possessed radios, and few radios were able to receive shortwave signals.

Social science research topics, ideology, and the reporting of research were all decided by party officials. The sole objective of social science research was to explain and expound on official viewpoints and defend official error. Academic publications such as *Philosophical Research* (*Zhexue yanjiu*) and *Economic Research* (*Jingji yanjiu*) were propaganda tools for the CCP.

Books and publications with views diverging from those of the CCP were removed from library shelves, while others were locked away and still others were destroyed. Culture and art were considered the "cogs and screws" of the great revolutionary apparatus. The great majority of literary and artistic works were dedicated to praising the CCP and Mao and creating a simulacrum of peace and prosperity. While the media used propaganda to mobilize loyalty to the party and the social sciences used theory, literature and art used pure emotion to even more effectively deify the leadership.

In his last years, Mao repeatedly expressed his approval of Qin Shihuang's "burning of books and burial of scholars," observing that the

Qin emperor had only "buried" a few hundred scholars, while "we" had "buried" many multiples of that number. The truth of this statement led almost all of China's great scholars and experts to relinquish their freedom of thought and independent characters and thoroughly reform themselves. Those who refused while preserving their lives were a tiny minority, such as Liang Shuming and Chen Yinque.[18] Repeated political struggles, such as the 1956–57 Anti-Rightist Movement that purged nearly six hundred thousand intellectuals, reinforced unanimity of thought.

This imposed consensus centered on Mao Zedong Thought made Mao the ultimate wielder of both political and military power and ideological "enlightenment" in a secular theocracy that united the center of power with the center of truth. Countless cadres took upon themselves the heavy responsibility of "fighting for humanity's most beautiful ideal" and righting wrongs according to heaven's decree. With no time to waste on persuading the reluctant, violence was inevitable. These cadres then became the scapegoats for all that went wrong during the Great Famine, while the victims of the disaster continued to venerate Chairman Mao as a brilliant sage, and the central government as unerring.

A FULLY INTEGRATED SOCIAL STRUCTURE

Modernized transportation and communication facilitated achievement of the imperial ideal of complete subjugation. Every locality shared the same institutional structure and executed the same policies. Every individual lived within an organization led by the CCP, cried out the same slogans, and used the same political jargon. Officials in every locality convened meetings on the same subjects at the same time. With all of society operating under similar conditions, policy disasters were all-encompassing, and there was no place of refuge to which victims could flee.

Chinese society was fully integrated into a pyramidal structure. In the urban areas, this pyramid took the form of city, district, subdistrict office, neighborhood committee, residents' group, resident. In the countryside, the pyramid took the form of province, prefecture, county, commune, production brigade, production team, commune member. A production team in Guangdong Province was basically identical to one in far-off Heilongjiang, and the living conditions of a Guangdong commune member differed in no substantial degree from those of his Heilongjiang counterpart. This structure produced a stable system in which members behaved uniformly. The government, urban, and rural pyramids combined into a pyramidal network that confined every member of society to one cell on a particular level of that network. This social structure facilitated highly centralized control and extinguished individual freedom. Policies spread unobstructed through this network; if erroneous, they were impossible to resist or correct, and their repercussions were magnified by zealous implementation at each level.

In this fully uniform and integrated social structure, no one was "beyond the pale." When the renowned writer Zhang Yihe was struck down as a counterrevolutionary in Sichuan Province, her father, Zhang Bojun, told her, "You must survive—even if you have to flee to the marshes as an outlaw, you must survive!" Zhang Yihe sorrowfully replied, "Where are those marshes?" In this social structure, refugees from famine likewise had nowhere to flee.

THE INVISIBLE SYSTEM OF BEHAVIORAL RESTRAINT

The visible system just described was reinforced by an invisible system that was often even more effective at standardizing individual behavior. This invisible system comprised two aspects: the value system formed through ideological instruction, and China's cultural traditions.

The value system that Mao promoted included Communist ideals, a theory of class struggle, a philosophy of unceasing and irreconcilable conflict and confrontation, and moral concepts that subordinated the individual to collective interests. This value system was etched into every soul and became the standard for discerning right from wrong, good from evil, and beauty from ugliness.

Thousands of years of imperial thinking led to an even more deepseated acknowledgment of the supremacy of the monarch as the patriarchal head of all society, the embodiment of law and order, the deciding factor in the rise and fall of the nation, the supreme source of enlightenment, and the supreme adjudicator. The ruler/father was owed respect, and his subjects/children were obligated to submit themselves in an integrated relationship of loyalty and filial devotion. Antithetical to the concepts of equality, personal dignity, and independent character, monarchism produced dependence, blind loyalty, and servility.

Aspects of this culture of monarchism were integrated with the Communist value system to form the ideological foundation for collectivism. The traditional concept of "dying for a just cause" became "sacrificing the small self for the greater self," with the "just cause" understood as communism. People worshipped their leaders, venerated authority, and resigned themselves to adversity. In the face of persecution, people saved themselves through deception and by selling out their friends. With every level of the bureaucracy presenting the dual face of slave and master, the voice of the lower levels was suppressed by the levels above in a system that acknowledged only positive feedback. The whip of authority and the lure of paradise deprived cadres of rationality and turned them into fanatics, swindlers, and slave drivers.

The invisible value system not only restrained individual behavior but also formed a social psychology and ethical environment that made every individual both victim and oppressor. In this way, everyone bore responsibility for this system to varying degrees, and every person was complicit in the operation of this machine.

THE LACK OF A CORRECTIVE MECHANISM

Under a totalitarian system, even a ruler of the highest integrity would have difficulty avoiding error, not to mention one of flawed character. Lacking access to alternative viewpoints, he cannot draw on collective wisdom. Once he falls into error, he hears no criticism, but only fawning and flattery; a small error then becomes greater, and a localized problem quickly develops into a general problem. In trying to control the ears and eyes of the ordinary people, the supreme ruler inevitably ends up blocking his own ears and eyes. As a result, the formulation of erroneous policies is exacerbated by false information passed to the upper levels by lower-level officials for the purposes of pleasing their superiors and advancing themselves. Thus the bogus reports in 1958 of "high-yield satellite launches" led Mao to ponder the problem of what to do with excess food and to propose allowing enormous swaths of land to lie fallow. A lack of accurate information led him to believe that the mass starvation from late 1958 to early 1960 was isolated and temporary and should pose no impediment to the onward leap of the national economy, with the result that the 1959 Lushan Conference pushed policies even farther left. In the spring of 1960, Mao continued to promote communal kitchens on the basis of false reports of successful communal kitchens in Guizhou, Hunan, Shandong, and other provinces where residents were actually starving.[19]

Former Propaganda Department chief Zhu Houze once told me, "When you stand in the middle of the Circular Mound Altar in the Temple of Heaven and call out, echoes come back at you from every direction. But what you hear is still just your own voice." In a monarchal political system, the supreme ruler hears only voices that conform to his own will.

Mao believed some lies, and even when he was skeptical of others, it was to no avail. According to the memoirs of his personal secretary, Ye Zilong, at the outset, Mao believed the reports of "satellite launches," and read the reports of exaggerated crop yields with genuine thoroughness, circling and underlining portions with a red pencil.[20] Later on, he took note of many problems that emerged with the Great Leap Forward. He inspected many localities, and saw through some of the satellite launches and lies. On August 13, 1958, when Mao toured Tianjin's Xinli Village, commune leaders claimed that a paddy field had yielded 50,000 kilos per *mu*. Mao said, "You're exaggerating. That's not possible, and you're just shooting off your mouth. I've worked in the fields and you haven't. That's unreliable—50,000 kilos, I don't believe it. You can't even pile up that much grain!" The commune leaders told a child to go stand on top of the rice plants, but Mao said, "Child, don't do it. The higher you stand, the harder you fall!"[21]

Mao was vexed at his lack of access to facts. One time, in Ye Zilong's presence, he muttered, "Why won't they tell me the truth? Why?"[22] Ye Zilong recalls, "As early as the Nanning Conference in January 1958, Mao Zedong called for everyone to be honest, to speak the truth, and to act honestly. But in the course of actual work, what Mao heard was not always the truth." He would call people in to gain an understanding of the situation, but all he heard was how good things were, and no one spoke of the problems.[23] In order to shake off the vexation of falsehood, in 1961 Mao and other leaders carried out their own investigations, and Mao sent subordinates to carry out surveys in Sichuan, Hunan, and Zhejiang. Without these investigations by the top leaders themselves, no decision would have been taken to disband the communal kitchens.

A system without a corrective mechanism is the most dangerous of all systems, and democracy is the best of all corrective mechanisms. In the emergence and correction of error, the system is a far more critical factor than an individual leader. Good leaders in a bad system can mitigate losses, but only up to a point. During the Great Famine, the quality of leadership varied, so the severity of the famine likewise varied in different provinces, yet the entire country still suffered tens of millions of starvation deaths. Conversely, bad leaders in a good system can also cause damage, but it's easier to discover and correct, and the bad leaders will be ousted from power.

15 THE GREAT FAMINE'S IMPACT ON CHINESE POLITICS

Events in China in the second half of the twentieth century appear to have proceeded along this chain of logic: without the Anti-Rightist Campaign, there would have been no Three Red Banners; without the Three Red Banners, there would have been no Great Famine; without the Great Famine, there would have been no campaign against right deviation, no Socialist Education Movement, and no Cultural Revolution; if the Cultural Revolution had not carried matters to an extreme, there would have been no economic reform.

At the beginning of 1962, as the government faced tens of millions of starvation deaths and an overwhelming crisis in the national economy, diverging opinions once again surfaced among the top leaders. Liu Shaoqi replaced Peng Dehuai as Mao's chief opponent, and the struggle between them lasted from the Seven Thousand Cadres Conference in 1962 until the launch of the Cultural Revolution in 1966.

DIVISIONS EMERGE DURING THE SEVEN THOUSAND CADRES CONFERENCE

Liu Shaoqi kept in close step with Mao in 1958. His personal secretary, Yao Liwen, believes Liu's thinking began to change during his visit to his home village in 1961, or perhaps even earlier, when he observed the disastrous 1959 autumn harvest. In any case, by the time of the Seven Thousand Cadres Conference, he was no longer singing Mao's tune.

The Ninth Plenum of the Eighth CCP Central Committee in January 1961 formally approved a policy of "adjustment, consolidation, replenishment, and enhancement" to the national economy. A lack of ideological unity limited the effectiveness of reform, however, and the economic situation remained dire. The Central Committee decided on November 12 to convene a five-level cadre conference for the purpose of unifying thinking and surmounting the current difficulties, and Liu and Deng Xiaoping were put in charge of drafting a report for the conference, scheduled for January 10, 1962. With a total of 7,118 participants, this twenty-eight-day meeting became known as the Seven Thousand Cadres Conference.

Mao declined to comment on the drafts Liu sent him shortly before the conference, and directed that the existing version of the report be immediately printed and distributed. Everyone would be allowed to comment on the report during three days of group discussion, and it would be amended in accordance with everyone's views before being submitted to the Politburo for discussion and formal approval.[1]

The conference formally opened on January 11, with small-group discussions initially focusing on the draft of Liu's report and the issue of "opposing decentralism and bolstering centralization." Liu Shaoqi, Zhou Enlai, Chen Yun, and other central leaders treated any economic activity outside the National Economic Plan as "decentralism," and opposed it as such.[2] Local representatives presented an alternative view: "There is decentralism in industry, but in the countryside there has been excessive centralism, not decentralism."[3] As the discussion progressed to shortcomings and errors arising from the Great Leap Forward, disputes intensified. The majority of delegates continued to endorse the correctness of the Three Red Banners, but some dared to ask why food shortages and market tensions had arisen during the leap, while others challenged various specifics of the banners.[4]

Given the unanticipated range of opinions on Liu's draft report, Mao proposed setting up a new drafting committee, headed by Liu, which could amend or completely redraft the report as necessary. Disputes arose among the committee's twenty-one members, however, when discussing responsibility for the shortcomings and errors of the last few years. Peng Zhen said, "Our errors are first and foremost the responsibility of the Central Committee secretariat. Does that include the Chairman, Shaoqi, and the comrades on the Central Committee standing committee? They should be included as appropriate for however many errors were committed. Chairman Mao has not been without error. The three-to-five-year transition and the organization of the communal kitchens were approved by Chairman Mao."

At this point, Deng Xiaoping interposed, "Chairman Mao said, 'Your report paints me as a sage, and there's no such thing. Everyone has shortcomings and errors, it's just a matter of how many. Don't be afraid to mention my shortcomings.'"

Peng Zhen said, "Chairman Mao's prestige ranks with Mount Everest or Mount Tai—even if you cart off several tons of soil, it remains as formidable. It's like the East China Sea—even if you carry off cartloads of water, it remains as vast. There's currently a trend within the party of fearing to express views and fearing to discuss errors. Any criticism leads to ruin. If Chairman Mao's 1 percent or one-tenth of 1 percent of error cannot be criticized, it will leave behind a bad influence on our party . . . From Chairman Mao to every branch secretary, each bears a share of responsibility."[5]

Zhou Enlai defended Mao, saying, "We need to look for the causes among ourselves; during the present difficulties we need to stand firm and bear the responsibility, as the whole world is watching us . . . If not for violations of the Three Red Banners and Mao Zedong Thought, the achievements really would have been greater . . . The Chairman discovered problems early on and was prepared for them, and the errors were ours. He couldn't fight against the tide all on his own. Now our entire party must be of one heart and mind to strengthen unity, obey our 'helmsman,' and obey the Central Committee, with the Central Committee listening to Chairman Mao. That is the main issue in our present work."[6]

Chen Boda then said, "Peng Zhen's remarks regarding Chairman Mao are worth further study. Is Chairman Mao responsible for the many messes we stirred up? Do we need to inspect Chairman Mao's work? The basic problem now is that the Central Committee is unable to exercise power collectively. The peasants believe in the Central Committee and in Chairman Mao. It's not the Chairman's policies that made such a mess of things."

Mao endorsed the "direction" of the new draft of the report produced on January 22, and after the report was adopted by an enlarged Politburo meeting on January 25, Liu delivered it orally to the full conference on January 27. This three-hour presentation was sometimes deeply unpleasant for Mao.

Liu noted in the report, "On the economic front we face rather significant difficulties; the people have inadequate food, clothing, and other necessities. Why are these inadequate? Because during the three years of 1959, 1960, and 1961, our agricultural production drastically decreased. Industrial output also decreased, by at least 40 percent . . . We originally believed that in these few years we would have a Great Leap Forward in agriculture and industry. We didn't leap forward, however, but actually fell significantly backward, resulting in a big saddle shape."

The report pointed out that the straitened circumstances arose from work errors. Liu observed, "When I went to Hunan, the peasants said it was three parts natural disaster and seven parts man-made disaster. If you don't acknowledge this, people won't accept it." He also proposed a "seven-three ratio" of accomplishments to errors to replace Mao Zedong's "nine fingers and one finger." He observed, "In some places the shortcomings and errors comprise more than three fingers. In a portion of places all over the country, it could be said that shortcomings and errors outnumber accomplishments. If we fundamentally refuse to acknowledge that there have been shortcomings and errors, or claim they're just on minor issues and try to beat around the bush or cover things up, and don't practically, realistically, and thoroughly acknowledge our past and existing failings, then no summing up of the experience can be carried out, and bad cannot be turned to good."

The report assigned the Central Committee chief responsibility for the errors of the last few years and called for the Three Red Banners to undergo further testing. "The 'Three Red Banners' are an experiment, and whether they're correct requires testing them in practice. We're not abolishing the 'Three Red Banners' now, and will continue to maintain them and struggle for them. Some problems cannot be seen so clearly at present, but after five or ten years, we can summarize the experience, and at that time go a step further in reaching a conclusion."[7]

Mao was clearly dissatisfied with Liu's oral presentation. Years later, Mao told a foreign delegation head, "For many years, the fighting within our party was not publicized. During the Seven Thousand Cadres Conference in 1962, I made a statement that revisionism would topple us, and that in as little as a few years, or after as many as a dozen years or several decades, it was possible that China would change colors. That statement wasn't published at the time, but I could already see some problems back then."[8]

The conference had been scheduled to end on January 30 or 31. On the afternoon of January 29, however, the delegates said they hadn't finished expressing their views and still had things to get off their chests. Mao said, "We'll let off steam during the day, watch shows at night, have a good meal, and everyone will be satisfied,"[9] and the conference continued.

Lin Biao addressed the conference on January 29 with a resolute and high-toned affirmation of the Three Red Banners. He attributed the Great Famine to "an exceptionally serious and long-running natural calamity that was devastating to some localities," and said, "We also committed some errors in our work, but these were just operational errors and not line errors." He also completely absolved Mao of blame. Like Zhou Enlai, he contended that "these difficulties were in certain respects and to a certain extent because we didn't act in accordance with Chairman Mao's directives, Chairman Mao's warnings, and Chairman Mao's thinking. If we had listened to Chairman Mao and learned from him, we would have made fewer wrong turns, and would be facing fewer difficulties today . . . If Chairman Mao's views are not respected or encounter major interference, that's when problems arise. The history of our party over several decades bears this out."[10]

Presiding over the conference, Mao expressed delight with Lin's spirited defense: "Comrade Lin Biao spoke very well regarding the party's line and the party's military policies. I hope his speech can be put in order [for publication]. I'll give you a week or half a month to do it."[11] Mao later had the edited speech sent to Tian Jiaying and Luo Ruiqing with the memo, "Read this all the way through. It's a very good and meaty essay that's a joy to read."[12]

When Mao addressed the conference on January 30, he did not refer to the Great Famine, but expounded on democratic centralism:

> Without a high degree of centralism, it will not be possible to establish a socialist economy. If our country does not establish a socialist economy . . . we'll become a country like Yugoslavia, a country that is effectively capitalist. Our proletarian dictatorship will be transformed into a bourgeois dictatorship, and what is more, into a reactionary, fascist style of dictatorship. We need to be highly alert to this issue, and I hope comrades will give a great deal of thought to it.[13]

Mao also elaborated on the Three Red Banners, indicating his opposition to Liu's call for the policies to be tested in practice.

The Seven Thousand Cadres Conference ended up promoting the policy of "adjustment, consolidation, replenishment, and enhancement," and while raising a number of criticisms against the Central Committee's work, it thoroughly affirmed the Three Red Banners and declined to overrule the Lushan Conference.

After the conference resolutions were transmitted to the provinces, many grassroots cadres were dissatisfied. A discussion in Gansu Province raised many criticisms. A cadre from the provincial party school said, "Five hundred million of our country's six hundred million people produce our food but don't have enough to eat; how can we say it's the achievements that matter?" A cadre in the provincial health bureau said, "In the last few years there have been no achievements; rather, the situation has actually deteriorated, and this damage has been felt not only materially, but also in political ethics." A cadre in the provincial finance and trade office said, "The problems of these few years have been both widespread and protracted, so it can't be said that there are no problems with the Central Committee's leading ideology." A comrade from *Gansu Daily*'s printing factory said, "Listening to this report, it's like the Central Committee did no wrong, and the main errors were all in the execution at the lower level. I feel the Central Committee hasn't examined the shortcomings and errors thoroughly enough, and they've looked too little at fundamental problems."

Some directly targeted Mao and other central leaders: "The Central Committee had several conferences and [issued] some documents that were inappropriate and had a great influence on the lower levels." "The big iron and steel campaign targets kept being revised, and the autumn harvest rotted in the fields—it was that way in Gansu and in Hebei, so it wasn't just a local problem." Xie Xianqing of the provincial grain bureau said, "Chairman Mao said there would be so much food that we wouldn't be able to eat it all. There was no survey or research on this. The Chairman may have done as Stalin did, making subjectivist errors in his later years." The head of the light industry office, Du Xilin, said, "I've heard the ordinary people berating Chairman Mao, saying the Chairman listened to treacherous courtiers rather than to loyal officials, and that Chairman Mao had dug himself into a cave somewhere. They wondered if he knew what was happening down here." A cadre from the party's mass apparatus said, "Chairman Mao must have known that people were starving to death in Gansu. I wonder how many people have died throughout the whole country!"[14] Similar briefing papers came in from every province.

The Seven Thousand Cadres Conference revealed serious divisions within the party's senior leadership based on attitudes toward the Three Red Banners: either a complete affirmation or a skeptical attitude. The main divisions centered on whether the Great Famine was natural or man-made, on the seriousness of the famine and assessments of the situation over the course of several years, and on assigning responsibility for the Great Famine. Mao retained deep in his heart the memory of who supported and opposed him in his moment of crisis. This "most important question of revolution"—"who is our enemy, and who is our friend"—laid the groundwork for "whom to rely on and whom to strike down" in the Cultural Revolution four years later.

THE XILOU CONFERENCE AND MAY CONFERENCE FURTHER INFURIATE MAO

Once the Seven Thousand Cadres Conference ended, Mao went to Wuhan, while Liu Shaoqi convened an enlarged Politburo standing committee meeting at Zhongnanhai's Xilou (Western Pavilion) conference room on February 21, 1962.

The Xilou Conference's assessment of the situation was even grimmer than that of the Seven Thousand Cadres Conference. Chen Yun pointed to reduced agricultural productivity, overly ambitious capital construction projects, inflation, currency speculation, profiteering, and lower living standards among urban residents.[15] Liu Shaoqi said that the Seven Thousand Cadres Conference "didn't disclose the difficulties thoroughly enough and was unwilling to uncover problems for fear of accusations of painting a bleak picture. What's to fear about revealing the situation's true colors? Painting it black can make people pessimistic, but it can also arouse people to courageously struggle against adversity!" "It's an abnormal time with the characteristics of a time of emergency; we don't need routine measures but rather emergency measures to readjust the economy."[16]

The Xilou Conference, followed by an enlarged State Council meeting on February 26 and an enlarged Politburo standing committee meeting on March 13, recommended measures to readjust the economy and surmount the crisis. On March 14, Liu Shaoqi, Zhou Enlai, and Deng Xiaoping flew to Wuhan to report to Mao, who agreed with the views of the majority of the standing committee and accepted Liu's suggestion that Chen Yun take over the leadership of the Central Committee Finance Committee. He still felt it was wrong to paint a uniformly bleak picture of the situation, however, and said the deficit was not genuine and required further discussion.

From May 7 to 11, 1962, Liu presided over a working conference of the Central Committee, which became known as the "May Conference." The focus was a plan for restructuring the economy. Although Mao had requested that participants not paint a uniformly bleak picture, Liu called again for a thorough estimation of the difficulties, and observed, "From the economic standpoint, generally speaking, the situation is not very good; rather, we're in straitened circumstances." "The foundation is unstable, and under difficult conditions it's possible that the political situation will take a turn for the worse."[17]

Since finances were handled through a centralized bursary system that both received and allocated key goods, leaders in charge of practical operations were receiving appeals for reduced requisition quotas from the same provincial officials who were telling Mao of their excellent situation. It was therefore officials such as Liu Shaoqi and Zhou Enlai who perceived the extent of the crisis.[18]

Acting on Liu Shaoqi's guiding principle of "adequate retrenchment" and Chen Yun's views, the Xilou Conference and the May Conference adopted measures to put the national economy on a more balanced, sustainable, and stable footing within the next three to five years. The urban population was to be further reduced by 10 million by the year's end, capital works projects would be cut back and agricultural output revived, while inflation was to be brought under control. Even more important was that all party members who had come under criticism and discipline for right deviation were to have their cases reexamined. The question was whether Mao would tolerate these adjustments, and Liu requested his instructions.

When Mao returned to Beijing in July 1962, Chen Yun reported the viewpoints upon which the standing committee members had reached agreement. He gained the impression that Mao did not oppose the ideas, but was merely considering them. Soon after that, Mao called Liu Shaoqi in for a meeting while he swam. Liu rushed to the pool and warmly greeted him, only to have Mao start firing questions at him: "What's your hurry? Can't you hold the line? Why can't you keep things under control?"

Caught by surprise, Liu went into the changing room and waited for Mao to come out of the pool before replying, "The views Chen Yun and Tian Jiaying expressed within the party didn't violate organizational principles. There's nothing wrong with them having ideas to discuss with you."

Mao said, "It's not a matter of organizational principle but of content! They came to you, Deng Zihui spouted off for so long, the picture painted at the Xilou meeting was so bleak, what's the rush?"

Mao was releasing resentment that had been building up for a long time, and Liu, just as eager to get the issue off his chest, responded, "History will record the role you and I played in the starvation of so many people, and the cannibalism will also be memorialized!"

Mao said, "The Three Red Banners have been refuted, the land has been divided up, and you did nothing? What will happen after I die?"

Liu calmly stated his views: the Three Red Banners would not be overturned, the people's communes would not be disbanded, there would be no more elevated targets, the communal kitchens would no longer be operated. Mao also calmed down and agreed to continue with the economic restructuring. Liu returned feeling under great pressure, but believing that the worst was over.[19]

A former vice-minister of the Food Ministry, Zhou Boping, later told me that soon after the Xilou Conference, Chen Yun went to Shanghai and sent aides to the countryside to observe the situation. In the major food-producing regions of Hubei Province they saw vast collective fields lying fallow, while crops on household plots of land flourished. When the group reported back, Chen Yun said, "It appears that agricultural collectivization has done a lot of harm. But now is not the time to talk about it—the political risk is too great. Chairman Mao sets too great a store by agricultural collectivization." Chen Yun warned the aides to say nothing of what they had seen once they returned to Beijing. He personally discussed these matters with Mao for an hour when he reported to him in July.[20]

Mao eventually retaliated against Liu in his "Bombarding the Headquarters—My First Big-character Poster," in which he squared the accounts of the "1962 right deviation." But the hard line Mao was prepared to take first emerged in September 1962, during the Tenth Plenum of the Eighth CCP Central Committee.

THE TENTH PLENUM AS THE SILVER BULLET OF CLASS STRUGGLE

Chen Yun, carrying out the frontline work to resolve China's economic crisis, was profoundly affected by the differing assessments of the problem among the top leadership. At a meeting of the leading party groups of State Council ministries and commissions, he said, "The views of senior cadres are not completely unanimous regarding the extent of the difficulties and how quickly they can be surmounted." "Will agricultural recovery proceed quickly or slowly? Assessments on this also differ." "We can't cover up this lack of agreement."[21]

As household responsibility was increasingly implemented in 1961 and 1962 after earlier false starts, Deng Zihui repeatedly voiced his support of the system. In April 1962 he said, "There's no need for misgivings or fearing accusations of individual farming or right deviation—we need to be practical and realistic."[22] At a meeting of the Central Committee secretariat in June 1962, response to a report on Anhui's "responsibility fields" was divided. Deng Zihui felt Anhui's responsibility fields did not constitute a directional error, and Deng Xiaoping shared this view, observing, "In regions where the peasants are suffering hardship, all kinds of measures are being taken. Anhui comrades have good reason for saying, 'It doesn't matter whether a cat is black or yellow; as long as it catches mice, it's a good cat.' The responsibility fields are a novelty, so let's give them a try."[23] When Chen Yun reported to Mao in July, he also spoke of reviving the practice of dividing the fields among the peasants.

Mao, however, declined to embrace a "retreat" from the Three Red Banners, because it was contrary to Communist ideals. Also causing great anxiety to Mao at that time was a trend toward reversing verdicts, in particular a reexamination of the case against Peng Dehuai. The Seven Thousand Cadres Conference had decided to reexamine the cases of all party cadres who had been criticized in the last few years, but drew the line at cases of those labeled members of an anti-party clique during the Lushan Conference. Liu Shaoqi said the struggle to oppose Peng's right-opportunistic anti-party clique was absolutely essential; Peng had not been criticized because of his letter, a great deal of which was consistent with fact, but because he had continued subversive anti-party activities as an evil remnant of the Gao-Rao clique.[24]

When Peng subsequently learned of this frame-up, he defended himself in an eighty-thousand-word appeal to the Central Committee and Mao on June 16, 1962 (subsequently referred to as the "Eighty-Thousand-Word Memorial"). The reexamination of Peng Dehuai's case thus became a matter of great vexation to Mao.

Economic readjustments were accompanied by reexamination of cases of injustice, concessions to intellectuals, and greater respect paid to the democratic parties. At the Guangzhou Conference in March 1962, Zhou Enlai, Chen Yi, and others made remarks that were respectful of intellectuals, and Chen Yi proposed "removing the label of bourgeois intellectual, and adding the accolade of working-class intellectual."[25] These initiatives irritated Mao.

In February 1962, Wang Jiaxiang, who was then head of the Central Committee's International Liaison Department, felt that with so many domestic worries, it was inadvisable to invite foreign aggression. He wrote a letter to the officials in charge of foreign affairs, Zhou Enlai, Deng Xiaoping, and Chen Yi, that included five points: (1) Conciliation was desirable, and it was unnecessary to overthrow imperialism in order to have worldwide peaceful coexistence; (2) China should avoid an open rupture in Sino-Soviet relations and should consolidate the Sino-Soviet alliance; (3) China should adopt a relatively appeasing attitude toward the American imperialists and should no longer send troops abroad at another country's request; (4) In Sino-Indian relations, China should raise the banner of the Five Principles of Peaceful Coexistence[26] while resolving existing Sino-Indian disputes through negotiations; (5) Assisting the people's revolution in other countries required "being practical and realistic and acting according to capabilities." Armed conflict was not the only means of achieving national independence; China should not encourage the people of other countries to rise up in revolution and should not interfere in the internal affairs of other countries.[27]

When China sent a delegation to a disarmament conference of the World Peace Council in Moscow in July 1962, Wang Jiaxiang took charge of setting the delegation's guiding principles and drafting the speech the delegation head would give. Delegations from several African nations subsequently expressed dissatisfaction with the Chinese delegation's approach and speech. When Mao learned of it, he criticized the delegation's actions as "alienating the leftists, reinforcing the rightists, and increasing vacillation among the centrists." He also criticized Wang for "an attempt to appease U.S.-led imperialism, Soviet-led revisionism, and reactionaries in all countries, especially India, which is called the 'three appeasements,' along with minimizing support to national liberation struggles and revolutionary movements."[28]

Around the same time, some people summed up certain domestic restructuring measures as the "three freedoms and one contract," namely, more freedom to peasants to plant their own crops, further opening of free markets, more responsibility of enterprises for their own profits and losses, and assignment of output to households. The "three freedoms and one contract" and "three appeasements and one reduction" were then attacked as part of a "program for capitalist restoration."

All of these events following the Seven Thousand Cadres Conference were very displeasing to Mao, who perceived the Central Committee under Liu's leadership to be departing ever further from his line in economics, politics, and domestic and foreign policy. Most alarming to Mao was his perception that Liu's remarks betrayed overtones of an "autumn reckoning." In March 1962, Liu called in Public Security head Xie Fuzhi and others and asked the Public Security Ministry to summarize the lessons of beating deaths and abuse of the innocent over the past few years. Liu said, "If we don't uncover it while living, it will be uncovered by the next generation after we're dead." Liu's words made Mao think of Khrushchev's exposure and criticism of Stalin.

Popular resistance to collectivization policies had been reduced to an undercurrent by the powerful state machinery, but Mao still felt the pressure of this undercurrent. In addition, the starvation deaths of tens of millions had engendered skepticism or outright opposition to the Three Red Banners within the party. As his increasing isolation converged with the social undercurrent following the Seven Thousand Cadres Conference, Mao sensed the gathering of a powerful force hostile to him. He chose the opportunity of the Tenth Plenum of the Eighth CCP Central Committee to fight back.

The plenum lasted only from September 24 to 27, 1962, but the preparatory meetings ran from August 26 to September 23, and were preceded by a Central Committee working conference from July 25 to August 24 that set the tone of the Tenth Plenum.

Departing from the original agricultural focus of this working conference at Beidaihe, Mao on August 6 gave a speech on class without having discussed his intentions with anyone in advance.[29] He continued to express his views during committee meetings, and ultimately changed the theme of the conference to a criticism of the "Wind of Gloom" (hei'an feng), the "Go-alone" or "Individual Farming Wind" (dan'gan feng), and the "Verdict-reversing Wind" (fan'an feng).

Mao repeatedly objected to the "Wind of Gloom," saying, "A portion of our comrades . . . encourage gloom, encourage talking about shortcomings and errors. But when it comes to talking about the bright spots, or about achievements, or about the collective economy, they have no enthusiasm. What should we do?"[30] Remarks like these showed that Mao had rejected the lessons of the Great Leap Forward and had never wholeheartedly embraced the "regressionist" measures of the last few years. Liu Shaoqi felt obliged to offer some explanations and self-criticism.

Criticism of the "Individual Farming Wind" was particularly virulent. Alleging increasing class polarization, Mao asked, "Have we arrived at socialism or at capitalism? Do we still want agricultural collectivization? Are we going to divide up the fields and assign production quotas to households or have collectivization?" He blamed the trend on a "certain petty bourgeois component" within the party. "Some comrades have become Marxist, but to varying degrees; in some cases the transformation has been inadequate. There are quite a few comrades within our party who lack adequate psychological preparation for socialist revolution." Deng Zihui suffered Mao's harshest criticism: "He's vacillating, his view of the situation is almost uniformly gloomy, and he vigorously encourages assignment of production quotas to households. This is all associated with his persistent unwillingness to carry out collectivization before the 1955 Summer Conference, and his subsequent hacking away at collectivization, which he never valued."[31] Deng was removed as head of the Central Committee's Rural Work Department and was relegated to a nominal position as deputy director of the State Planning Commission.

Criticism of the "Verdict-reversing Wind" mainly targeted Peng Dehuai, who had continued to deny the existence of an anti-party clique attempting to usurp leadership or of any conspiracy with foreigners to subvert the government. Mao said, "The campaign against right deviation in 1959 for the most part targeted the wrong people, but I think Peng Dehuai's demand for a reexamination of his case and rehabilitation means that we can't cancel the whole movement." Right up until the plenum concluded, every conference and subcommittee session included criticism of Peng Dehuai. Huang Kecheng, Zhang Wentian, Zhou Xiaozhou, Tan Zheng, Deng Hua, Gan Siqi, and Hong Xuezhi were also forced to undergo self-criticism,[32] and the Central Committee organized a team to investigate Peng, Huang, and Zhang.[33]

After resurrecting class struggle at the Beidaihe Conference, Mao summarized his thoughts in the bulletin of the Tenth Plenum of the Eighth CCP Central Committee:

Throughout the entire history of the proletarian revolution and proletarian dictatorship, and in the entire historical period of the transition from capitalism to communism (this period requires several decades or even more), there exists a class struggle between the proletarian and bourgeois classes and a struggle between the two roads of socialism and capitalism. The overthrown reactionary ruling class has not resigned itself to its demise; they're still scheming for a restoration to power. At the same time, society retains some bourgeois influence and the force of custom from the old society, as well as a tendency toward spontaneous capitalism among a portion of small producers. For that reason, among the people there are still some who have not undergone socialist transformation; their numbers are not many, only a few percentage points, but once they have the opportunity, they intend to depart from the socialist road and go along the capitalist road. Under these circumstances, class struggle cannot be avoided. This is a historical pattern upon which Marxism-Leninism expounded early on, and we must absolutely not forget it. This class struggle is complex, tortuous, varying in intensity, and sometimes fierce. It's unavoidable that this class struggle should be reflected within the party. The influence of foreign imperialism and domestic bourgeoisie are the social roots of revisionist thinking within the party. While carrying out struggle against class enemies at home and abroad, we must be at all times on guard and resolute in our opposition to all types of opportunistic ideological tendencies within the party.[34]

Liu Shaoqi immediately fell in line with Mao's formulations on class struggle, and some of his pronouncements were even more radical than Mao's. Little did Liu know that these words would become the guiding ideology for the Cultural Revolution and the embryo of the theory of continuous revolution under the proletarian dictatorship; even less did he know that they would ultimately spell his own doom.

After October 1962 all the provinces responded with reports describing intense class struggle and attempted capitalist restoration. This upsurge in class struggle was followed by a Socialist Education Movement.

FROM "SUPPLEMENTARY TRAINING IN DEMOCRATIC REVOLUTION" TO THE "FOUR CLEAN-UPS"

Following the Tenth Plenum of the Eighth CCP Central Committee, Mao launched a nationwide Socialist Education Movement and large-scale class struggle in the urban and rural areas as a means of "combating revisionism" and preventing "peaceful evolution." The movement in the countryside was devoted to inventory, financial affairs, work points, and cleaning up accounts, and was therefore referred to as the "Four Clean-Ups" (*siqing*) movement.

The Central Committee issued a series of documents providing increasingly dire assessments of class struggle. One in early 1965, "Some Current Questions Raised in the Rural Socialist Education Movement" (known as the "Twenty-three Provisions"), redefined the "Four Clean-Ups" as political, economic, organizational, and ideological cleansing, thereby broadening and elevating the scope of the campaign. Increasing emphasis was placed on the leadership of work groups dispatched from above, who were to push aside and "clean up" grassroots cadres. University students and military cadres were recruited into an immense "clean-up" workforce. I myself served as a member of a Beijing municipal party committee work group that carried out an eight-month "clean-up" of a production brigade at Dabailao Commune. Before being sent to the countryside, we had to be educated so that "the strings of class struggle" were "stretched very tight" in every one of us. We intended to ferret out a "counterrevolutionary clique," and assumed that the village's branch party secretary was a "capitalist roader."

The Four Clean-Ups campaign in the countryside was originally carried out on the premise that the "democratic revolution had not being thorough enough." This observation is typically traced back to Mao's memo on the Xinyang Incident in December 1960, but it had already appeared half a year earlier in a report on Hebei's Handan County.[35] At that time, Liu Shaoqi was very concerned about problems in Hebei's villages, and the need for class struggle in the countryside to reclaim "power that is not in our hands" was a notion shared by Mao and Liu. However, a disagreement developed between Mao and Liu on the Four Clean-Ups, resulting in a personal rupture.

This rupture came to a head through the participation of Liu's wife, Wang Guangmei, in a "clean-up" of the Taoyuan production brigade of

Hebei's Luwangzhuang Commune. Rather than following Mao's preference for "holding a fact-finding meeting," Wang's team infiltrated the village covertly, establishing contacts and visiting the poor. Wang's five months of "work experience" convinced her that Taoyuan's leading party branch was "a counterrevolutionary double-faced regime" and that the branch party secretary, Wu Chen, was a "Kuomintang element" who had "infiltrated the party."[36] Wang described her Taoyuan experience at a meeting of the Hebei provincial party committee and heard some encouraging comments.[37] While Mao Zedong suffered a setback in the Great Leap Forward, Liu Shaoqi found himself on the ascendance, and from June until August 1964, he took Wang on a tour of a dozen or so provinces and cities to present the "Taoyuan experience." On August 1, Liu himself gave a major report to the heads of the central party, political, and military organs in Beijing's Great Hall of the People. This report was to sow the seeds of endless trouble for him.

A participant at the meeting, Li Xin, recalls:

> Liu Shaoqi began to talk, and although there was a microphone on the table, he didn't sit down, but strode back and forth across the stage with his hands clasped behind his back . . . Liu spoke of the necessity for all cadres to be seconded to units for work experience, and called on everyone to emulate Wang Guangmei. He said, "Wang Guangmei went down to the countryside, and isn't that how she discovered so many new problems? And she wrote up everything and summarized many new experiences very meaningfully. I suggest you all go to the countryside—hurry and go!" At this point, Liu looked at Premier Zhou for a moment, and then addressed the group again: Anyone who didn't want to go should be made to go! Having spoken to this point, he stopped abruptly.[38]

Li Xin writes that upon walking out of the meeting, he heard others discussing what had transpired. " 'What was that all about? Were we being lectured?' . . . Walking down the steps from the Great Hall of the People, up ahead of me two or three military cadres were cursing up a storm, in particular berating Liu Shaoqi for stepping forward personally to flatter his 'old bag.' As I drew closer, they turned around and looked at me, and it turned out that we knew one another, so we shared a laugh."[39]

During his speech, Liu not only pumped up Wang Guangmei but also criticized Mao, although without naming names: "He said that we should not be dogmatic regarding Chairman Mao's works and that the method of fact-finding meetings was outdated. People who didn't go through secondment for work experience could not become members of the Central Committee or join the secretariat or Politburo."[40]

Mao vacillated on whether to distribute Wang Guangmei's report, especially after the teary comments of his wife Jiang Qing on Liu's speech: "After Stalin died, Khrushchev made a secret report, and now you aren't even dead and someone is making an open report."[41] Pushed by Liu, however, the Central Committee disseminated "The Taoyuan Experience" throughout the country on September 1, along with an editorial comment emphasizing the report's "universal significance."[42]

Sharing Mao's grave assessment of the class struggle situation in the countryside, Liu followed "The Taoyuan Experience" with several documents that pushed the Four Clean-Ups further into left-deviating error and led to even more cases of injustice throughout the country. Although the methods and terminology employed in the Four Clean-Ups were largely identical to those of Mao's 1961 "rectification in work styles and communes" and were clearly a Maoist legacy of the Great Famine years, Mao nevertheless denounced Liu at the outset of the Cultural Revolution, and referred to his massive purge as "left in form but right in essence."[43]

The split between Mao and Liu came to the surface during a month-long Central Committee work conference starting on December 15, 1964, to discuss the Four Clean-Ups and formulate the "Twenty-three Provisions." Wang Guangmei and Liu Yuan describe the previously docile Liu engaging in an open wrangle with Mao:

> Liu Shaoqi proposed that the main contradiction was between the "four cleans" and the "four not-cleans," and that its nature was the "interweaving of the contradiction among the people with the contradiction between the enemy and us."
>
> Mao Zedong said that the landlords and rich peasants were the back-stage operators and the "unclean" cadres their frontmen. The unclean cadres were the persons holding authority, and merely attacking the landlords and rich peasants would not allow the poor and lower-middle

peasants to rise. It was essential to target the cadres, and to mobilize the masses to rectify the party.

Liu Shaoqi said that all kinds of contradictions had come together during the "Four Clean-Ups" campaign, and the situation was complicated. It was better to use facts as a starting point and to resolve contradictions as they were discovered rather than to elevate all of them to contradictions between the enemy and us.

Mao became agitated and said, "This movement of ours is called the Socialist Education Movement, not some kind of 'four cleans' or 'four not-cleans' or some kind of interweaving of multiple contradictions— who says there's all this interweaving? . . . That doesn't serve to define the nature of the contradiction! This is no other kind of ideological education movement than a Socialist Education Movement, and its main focus is to attack the faction of capitalist roaders who have gained power within the party!".

Liu Shaoqi stood his ground and asked, as if seeking advice, "I still don't understand much about this 'faction.' Individual capitalist roaders exist, but the capitalist class is about to die out, so how can there be a faction? Referring to a faction implies numerous people, and contradictions between the enemy and us are not all that prevalent. Where do we find capitalist roaders in the Coal Ministry or Metallurgy Ministry?"

Without thinking, Mao blurted out, "Zhang Linzhi is one!"[44]

Liu Shaoqi did not pursue the matter further, because under those circumstances, once Mao Zedong mentioned a name, that person would be struck down.[45]

December 26, 1964, just a few days after this confrontation, was Mao's seventy-first birthday, and he hosted a dinner at the Great Hall of the People. He shared a table with several model workers and scientists, with the other central government leaders at another table. Mao was normally ebullient at such events, but this time his demeanor was solemn. He started off by saying he had not invited his own children to the dinner because they had contributed nothing to the revolution. He went on to criticize some phrases used in the Socialist Education Movement, such as the "four cleans" or the "overlap of contradictions inside and outside the party," saying they were not Marxist. He also censured some central organs as "independent kingdoms," and spoke of the danger of revisionism within the party. No one else dared utter a word.[46]

The Four Clean-Ups campaign was still under discussion on January 28, 1965, when Deng Xiaoping was to preside over a meeting of the Central Committee secretariat. Thinking it was a routine briefing, Deng told Mao, "Chairman, you're not feeling well. You don't have to attend the meeting." Mao marched into the meeting with a copy of the PRC Constitution and the party constitution in each hand. He said, "One person told me not to come to the meeting (alluding to Deng Xiaoping), and one didn't want me to speak (alluding to Liu Shaoqi). Why am I being stripped of the rights to which I'm entitled under the party constitution and the Constitution?" What was Mao insinuating when he said someone didn't let him speak? In his later years, Chen Boda recounted:

> At a Central Committee meeting discussing the "Twenty-three Provisions," Chairman Mao spoke first, but he had spoken only a few sentences when Liu Shaoqi interrupted him. It's fine to interpose a few comments, as long as you then let the other person finish. But Liu Shaoqi just kept going on and on, and Chairman Mao had no opportunity to pick up where he'd left off. During the next day's meeting, Chairman Mao picked up a copy of the party constitution and said it stipulated that party members had the right to speak at party meetings. Everyone present immediately understood that he was saying Liu Shaoqi didn't allow him to speak.[47]

This showed how deep the rift had grown between Mao and Liu. As Wang Guangmei and Liu Yuan put it, "Mao Zedong could not tolerate even the slightest challenge to his authority. A discussion between equals implied a scorning of his authority, and even the smallest contradiction could send him into a rage. He told Liu Shaoqi, 'Who do you think you are? All I have to do is lift a finger and you're finished!'"[48]

In a conversation with the American journalist Edgar Snow in 1970, Mao confirmed that he had decided to strike down Liu Shaoqi during the discussions on the Twenty-three Provisions in January 1965.

Mao did strike down Liu Shaoqi during the Cultural Revolution. Of course, this involved not just lifting a finger but launching a large-scale political movement. It would be overly simplistic to attribute the Cultural Revolution to nothing more than the power struggle between Mao and Liu or to Mao's idiosyncrasies; all the same, Mao's suspicion and dissatisfaction toward Liu were factors. Democratic systems provide a normal mechanism for changing leaders, but in an autocratic system, the supreme leader is surrounded by toadies and conspirators, and any change in leadership is accompanied by brutality and violence. The person occupying the position of supreme power finds himself in the hot seat (the Three Kingdoms warlord Cao Cao said crowning him emperor would be like putting him on the stove). Mao's deep familiarity with Chinese history made him naturally suspicious and wary of all those around him.

CRITICIZING "REVISIONISM" PROGRESSES TO "FUNDAMENTALISM"

The ultimate program of the CCP was to build a Communist society in China. The party not only required its members to steadfastly uphold Communist ideals but also used that ideology to educate all Chinese. In the actual practice of constructing communism, however, these ideals suffered the repeated assaults of reality. In the mid-1950s a divergence of opinion began to emerge among the CCP's top leaders: should they adhere to communism in its purest form, or make revisions based on actual conditions? Should socialism be constructed rapidly, or more progressively in line with practical circumstances? The resolution of the 1956 Eighth National Congress of the CCP was in fact a concession of ideals to reality, but Mao overturned that resolution during the Third Plenum of the Eighth National Congress without consulting the Central Committee, and then forcibly put forward the Three Red Banners of the General Line, the Great Leap Forward, and people's communes to accelerate China's progress toward communism. By using the totalitarian system and class struggle to force an overly hasty application of Communist ideals, Mao and his followers brought about the Great Famine.

Following the Great Famine, the CCP could be viewed as consisting of roughly two factions: One faction had retreated from Communist ideals to doing what reality required. They could be referred to as the "pragmatists." The other faction persisted with political struggle to push forward the realization of Communist ideals. They could be referred to as the "idealists." This is, of course, a simplistic demarcation, and the line could not always be drawn so clearly. The pragmatists sometimes felt conflicted when dealing practically with concrete matters required them to go against their ideals; likewise, the idealists often ran up against a cold reality, and in defending their ideals were prone to assume a crisis of class struggle and attack from hostile forces. China's political environment at the time was disadvantageous to the pragmatists, but when the idealists brought about economic chaos, it was left to the pragmatists to salvage the situation. In the process, the pragmatists departed even further from their ideals, causing the idealists to regard them as even more of a threat.

The most powerful weapon Mao could wield against the pragmatists was criticizing revisionism, as he did when class struggle was resurrected during the Tenth Plenum of the Eighth National Party Congress. "Revisionism" was first used in a pejorative sense by Lenin, when the Second International criticized Russia's October Revolution and the system that had arisen from it. Criticizing revisionism served Mao as a weapon in domestic political infighting, but was also related to his ambitions to assume leadership of the International Communist Movement. Success in the Korean War, the establishment of an industrial foundation through the First Five-Year Plan, and China's contribution to the "satisfactory resolution" of the uprisings in Poland and Hungary had all raised the status of the CCP and Mao personally in the socialist camp, and it was in the frame of mind of an international leader that Mao made his second trip to Moscow in November 1957.

At a ceremony marking the fortieth anniversary of the October Revolution, Mao's speech aroused a standing ovation from the audience. During the summit, each speaker stood at the lectern and read a speech approved by the Central Committee of his or her party; only Mao delivered an unscripted address from where he was seated. After the conference, he acted like a cohost, lobbying the leaders of the Eastern European parties and busily reconciling conflicts between them and the Soviet Communist Party. If the Soviet Union had been the undisputed leader of the socialist camp in the past, Mao now appeared to have risen to an equal footing with Khrushchev.[49]

Khrushchev's wholesale criticism of Stalin in 1956 both gladdened and worried Mao. Toppling Stalin from his pedestal raised Mao's own status within the International Communist Movement, but the challenge to Stalin's prestige also threatened Mao, who was the Stalin of China. Mao therefore maintained that Stalin's "merits outweighed his demerits," and castigated Khrushchev for tossing away the "daggers of Leninism and Stalinism." The truth was that tossing away these "daggers" would undermine Chinese socialism.

Just as Mao began dreaming of attaining the leadership of the International Communist Movement, Khrushchev proposed a peaceful competition with the capitalist world and suggested that the Soviet Union would outstrip the United States in fifteen years. This was when Mao jumped in with China's new goal: "In fifteen years, we can catch up with or surpass the United Kingdom." He went further in August 1958, saying, "In only ten to twenty years, the Soviet Union can become two United States, and we can become four United States." Some scholars therefore believe that both international and domestic factors caused Mao to embark on the Great Leap Forward, as he strove for leadership of the International Communist Movement.[50]

In addition, the Soviet leadership maintained a critical stance toward China's Great Leap Forward and people's communes, and it was Soviet skepticism, ridicule, and criticism that spurred Mao's propaganda campaign against Moscow, in particular against the concepts of "peaceful coexistence" and "peaceful transition." In April 1960, the Central Committee published its article "Long Live Leninism" as a direct attack on the Central Committee of the Soviet Communist Party.

These strident criticisms of the Soviet government and Khrushchev did not pass unnoticed; in June 1960, Khrushchev responded by openly criticizing CCP policies. From this point forward, the Central Committee became even firmer in its opposition to revisionism, and *Soviet revisionism* became part of everyday language in China, equated with *right opportunism*. Mao labeled Peng Dehuai a revisionist, and later placed that cap on Liu Shaoqi as well. In the early 1960s, Mao made "countering and preventing revisionism" one of the party's chief political tasks.

This campaign against revisionism reached its height in 1963. The Central Committee organized a "Central Committee Leading Group to Counter Revisionism," headed by Deng Xiaoping, which spent the months from September 1963 to March 1964 hunkered down at the Diaoyutai Guesthouse, writing nine essays criticizing "Khrushchev's revisionism." These essays, which became known as the "Nine Critiques," were published in *People's Daily* and *Red Flag*, and were read out in a strident and bellicose tone over the Central People's Broadcasting Station to impress them on every Chinese mind.

The "Nine Critiques" pushed the CCP's line even further left. From the present perspective, we can describe the guiding ideology behind the antirevisionist rhetoric as Marxist fundamentalism. Marxist fundamentalism began to be practiced in China in 1958, and after the failure of the

Great Leap Forward, the Cultural Revolution practiced this fundamentalism even more fanatically.

At the same time, Marxist fundamentalism was being widely adopted in Pol Pot's Cambodia, one of the "great achievements" of Mao's exported revolution. Mao once expressed his complete satisfaction with his star pupil, telling Pol Pot, "You've done well. You've managed to do things that we wanted but were unable to do."[51] Mao did not know at this time that Cambodia was to lose a quarter of its population under the rule of the Communist Party of Kampuchea (known to the outside world as the Khmer Rouge).

Following the Great Leap Forward, the struggle between China's "idealists" and "pragmatists" was repeated again and again, leaving behind ever deeper scars. As the struggle intensified, it ultimately led to the Cultural Revolution. The Cultural Revolution took the stand of the idealists to an extreme—and toward destruction. By the end of the twentieth century the banner of communism had lost all the glory of its former days, both in China and across the world. The pragmatists salvaged the situation after Mao's death by pushing China onto the road of "reform and opening."

Reform brought unprecedented development of China's economy, but at the same time intensified the crisis of faith: the majority of Chinese people, and even many within the CCP, no longer believed in communism. Even so, the rulers dared not call Communist ideals into question, because abandoning the flag of communism meant losing their own legitimacy. The only way out was to relegate communism to the far-distant future.

By abandoning attempts to mold the country's future and individual behavior through the forcible imposition of ideals, leaders could focus on facing reality as effective managers of society. This could be considered progress, but a ruling clique serving as society's managers should have its powers conferred, and limited, by the people, and the assessment of its managerial effectiveness should be based on practical experience, not on a priori criteria. This conferment and assessment of managerial authority can be expressed only through the people's ballots in a democratic system. The other alternative is to replace Communist ideals with preservation of the CCP's leadership status as the highest goal. This is extremely dangerous, because a regime that takes as its highest priority the preservation of the interests of the ruling clique will never gain popular respect and can have no long-term future. Judging from the political practice and developmental direction after Deng Xiaoping, China should be moving toward a democratic system and not toward one of this latter type.

We cannot be too optimistic, however. The French sociologist Gustave Le Bon once said:

> A long time is necessary for ideas to establish themselves in the minds of crowds, but just as long a time is needed for them to be eradicated. For this reason crowds, as far as ideas are concerned, are always several generations behind learned men and philosophers. All statesmen are well aware to-day of the admixture of error contained in the fundamental ideas I referred to a short while back, but as the influence of these ideas is still very powerful they are obliged to govern in accordance with principles in the truth of which they have ceased to believe.[52]

That is why it will take a very long time for a modern democratic system to be established in China.

We must not wait passively for that eventuality, however; each and every one of us should use all available resources to push for democracy. At the same time, it should be borne in mind that the transformation of a political system cannot be too radical or hasty. Over the past one hundred years, the Chinese have suffered too much from radicalism, and they have learned a profound lesson. Radical methods can cause society to spin out of control. An overnight imposition of democracy combined with the radical actions of anarchists could cause a weak regime to lose its ability to control society and allow the emergence of a new dictator— because autocracy is the most effective means of restoring order out of chaos. Those members of the public who find anarchy intolerable will welcome a dictator as a savior. In that way, the very people who are most radical and hasty in their opposition to autocracy may be the very ones who facilitate the rise of a new autocratic power.

NOTES

AN EVERLASTING TOMBSTONE

1. Translator's note (TN): A common practice in China of posting information, opinions, and propaganda on community walls.
2. TN: Zaociling and Wanli were villages under the township of Mayuanxiang.
3. TN: The tax was paid in the form of a share of a farmer's crop rather than in cash.
4. TN: The Communist Party launched its Land Reform movement in 1946, three years before the founding of the People's Republic. All rural land held privately or by the rival Kuomintang was seized and reallocated to rural peasants.
5. TN: A *mu* is a Chinese unit of land measurement equivalent to approximately 0.066 hectare or 0.165 acre.
6. Literally, 12 *dan*, equivalent to about 600 kilos.
7. TN: Literally, 20 *li*, a traditional Chinese unit of distance now calculated at half a kilometer (1,640 feet).
8. TN: (1906–67) China's last emperor, the Manchu Aisin-Gioro Puyi, also known as Henry P'u Yi, ruled China as the Xuantong emperor from 1908 to 1912, and then as a puppet emperor from 1917 to 1924. The Japanese then made him the Kangde emperor of Manchukuo from 1934 to 1945. He finally abdicated the throne and, after serving time in prison, was appointed a member of the Chinese People's Political Consultative Conference from 1964 until his death.
9. TN: Once a city in its own right, Hankou is now a district of the city of Wuhan, capital of Hubei Province. It remains a key port on the Yangtze River, and serves as Wuhan's business center.
10. TN: Josip Broz Tito (b. 1892) was leader of Yugoslavia from 1945 until his death in 1980. Although a Communist, he resisted Soviet influence and promoted the Non-Aligned Movement.
11. TN: Generally regarded as one of China's top universities, established in Beijing in 1911.
12. TN: Wen Yiduo (1899–1946), a critic of the Nationalist government, died at the hands of the Kuomintang. Zhu Ziqing (1898–1948), an anti-imperialist, died of starvation after refusing American food aid. Both Chen Yinque (1890–1969, sometimes also spelled Chen Yinke) and Wu Mi (1894–1978), on the other hand, were foreign-educated intellectuals who maintained a distance from the Communist Party. Wu Mi was tortured during the Cultural Revolution.

13. TN: Yang and Li (also known as Tsung-Dao Lee) were scholars in the United States when they became the first Chinese Nobel Prize winners.

14. TN: Launched by Mao Zedong in 1966 and continuing until the arrest of the Gang of Four and the death of Mao in 1976.

15. TN: Written in black ink with pen brushes on large sheets of paper and pasted on walls for a standing crowd to read, the big-character poster was a major vehicle of public expression and mass communication during political campaigns, especially during the Cultural Revolution.

16. TN: From Mao's poem "Song wenshen" ("Sending Off the God of the Plague"). Mao wrote the poem on July 1, 1958, upon learning of parasitic disease control efforts in Yujiang, Jiangxi Province.

17. On August 6, 1945, U.S. military jets dropped an atomic bomb on the Japanese city of Hiroshima, killing seventy-one thousand people. On August 9, the United States dropped another bomb on Nagasaki, killing eighty thousand people.

18. An estimated 240,000 people died in the Tangshan earthquake.

19. Henri Michel, *The Second World War* (Chinese edition), vol. 2, Beijing: Commercial Press, 1981, p. 427. (TN: English edition published by Praeger in 1974.)

20. Deng Yunte, *History of Famine Relief in China*, Beijing: Commercial Press, 1993, pp. 142–43.

21. TN: Full citations for these works by Li Wenhai, a professor at Renmin University, and others, can be found at qss.ruc.edu.cn/en/100964/101137/20249.html.

22. TN: Kaolin clay, also known as "Guanyin clay" because it is a key ingredient in the porcelain used in producing Guanyin figurines, was eaten by peasants during the famine to stave off hunger. As it was indigestible, it tended to block the intestines, often resulting in death.

23. In the first seven printings of the Chinese edition of this book, I used Li Rui's estimate, which put the number of cannibalism cases throughout China in excess of 1,000. In July 2009 the former deputy commissioner of the Anhui provincial public security bureau, Yin Shusheng, provided me with the following information: In 1961 the Anhui provincial public security bureau reported to the provincial party committee that there had been 1,289 cases of cannibalism in the province. There were more than 300 cases of cannibalism reported in Xining City and Huangzhong County in Qinghai Province. Added to the figures reported for Sichuan, Shandong, Henan, and other places in China, an estimated total of several thousand is no exaggeration.

24. TN: Greene (1909–85) was a British American journalist who visited and wrote about a number of Communist countries during the 1960s and '70s. His works on China include *A Curtain of Ignorance: How the American Public Has Been Misinformed About China*, New York: Doubleday, 1964.

25. TN: Snow (1905–72) is believed to be the first Western journalist to have interviewed Mao Zedong. His *Red Star Over China* (1937) was for some time the seminal account in the West of the early years of the Chinese Communist Party.

26. Wang Guangmei, Liu Yuan et al., *The Unknown Liu Shaoqi*, Zhengzhou: Henan renmin chubanshe, 2000, p. 90.

27. Deng Liqun, *My Words on Behalf of Comrade Shaoqi*, Beijing: Dangdai Zhongguo chubanshe, 1998, pp. 107–108.

28. Amartya Sen, "Democracy as a Universal Value," *Journal of Democracy* 10, no. 3 (1999): 3–17. Translated into Chinese by Cheng Xiaonong in *Modern China Studies* 69, no. 2 (2000).

29. Liu Shaoqi, "Speech at an Enlarged Working Conference of the Central Committee," January 27, 1962, in Central Committee Documents Editorial Committee, ed., *Selected Works of Liu Shaoqi*, vol. 2, Beijing: Renmin chubanshe, 1985, pp. 441–42.

1. THE EPICENTER OF THE DISASTER

1. Zhang Linnan, "Regarding the Pan, Yang, Wang Incident," February 1993, in Henan Party History Working Committee, ed., *Fengyu chunqiu*, Zhengzhou: Henan renmin chubanshe, 1993.

2. Ibid. Zhang's article states that the large number of "rightists" in Henan arose from the "supplemental" Anti-Rightist Movement following the Pan, Yang, Wang incident.

3. Conversation with Li Jian at Li's home on Wanshou Road, Beijing, on March 9, 2001.

4. Xinyang Incident Special Investigation Group, "Regarding the Problem of Ma Longshan," November 20, 1960. Henan provincial archives, 1960, permanent collection, vol. 2403.

5. TN: The CCP's Lushan Conference was held from July 2 to August 16, 1959, in the form of an enlarged meeting of the CCP Central Committee Politburo, followed by the Eighth Plenum of the Eighth CCP Central Committee. During this meeting, Mao gained the upper hand against his critics and reversed corrective measures taken against "rash advance" earlier in the year. Full details are provided in chapter 10 of this book on the Lushan Conference.

6. Zhang Shufan, "The Xinyang Incident: A Bitter Lesson," *Bainian chao*, no. 6 (1998): 39–44.

7. Ibid.

8. Ibid.

9. General Office of the Central Committee of the Chinese Communist Party, and Yu Sang and Wu Renwen of the Henan Provincial Party Committee Work Group, "Investigation Report Regarding the Problem of Deaths and Food Supply in Henan Province's Xinyang Prefecture," June 18, 1960 (hereafter "Yu Sang and Wu Renwen").

10. "Self-examination by the Communist Party Committee of Henan Province Regarding the Xinyang Incident," November 1, 1960, Henan provincial archives.

11. Lu Xianwen's report to Mao Zedong, in "Chairman Mao's Remarks at Xinyang," November 13, 1958.

12. Yu Dehong (secretary to Zhang Shufan), "Recollections of the Xinyang Incident," September 17, 2001, typescript mailed to the author on November 9, 2001, p. 11.

13. Conversation with Li Ruiying in her home on Qianmen West Ave., Beijing, in March 2001.

14. Qiao Peihua, "The Xinyang Incident," unpublished typescript, July 19, 2000, pp. 70–72. The author gratefully acknowledges Qiao Peihua's permission to quote from his account. TN: Qiao Peihua's book was published by Open Books (Hong Kong) in 2009.

15. TN: "Lighting the celestial lantern" is an ancient torture in which a person is stripped bare, wrapped in cloth, doused in oil, and then suspended and lit on fire.

16. Li Li, report to Wu Zhipu, November 28, 1960. "Desecration" in this context refers to flesh being cut from corpses to be eaten.

17. Conversation with Yu Dehong, September 1999.

18. Conversation with Yu Wenhai (of Fanghuxiang, Huaibin County), September 1999.

19. Chinese Communist Party Committee of Huangchuan County, "Report on the Problem of Grain Procurement," October 30, 1959.

20. Taolin Subgroup of the Provincial Party Committee Investigation Group, "Investigation Report on Deaths Due to the Inadequate Living Arrangements by Huangchuan County's Taolin Commune," June 3, 1960 (hereafter "Taolin Subgroup").

21. "Second Self-examination by the Chinese Communist Party Committee of Huangchuan County Regarding the Problem of Deaths," June 3, 1960.

22. Henan Investigation Group of the Organization Department of the Central Committee of the Chinese Communist Party, "Regarding Xi County and Fanghu's Campaign Against False Reporting of Output and Private Withholding," October 9, 1960.

23. Li Zhenhai, Tao Mosheng, and He Dizhong, "Investigation Regarding the Situation in Xi County," October 9, 1960.

24. Kang Jian, Vanished Glory: The Lessons and Warnings of the People's Communes, Beijing: Zhongguo shehui chubanshe, 1998, pp. 418–24.

25. "Comrade Song Zhihe's Report Regarding Several Current Major Items in the Work Situation in Several Counties of Xinyang Prefecture," December 4, 1959.

26. Qiao Peihua, "The Xinyang Incident," pp. 69–70.

27. "Instructions Requested by the Chinese Communist Party Committee of Henan Province Regarding the Stripping of Xinyang Prefectural Party Secretary Lu Xianwen's Party Membership, the Death Sentence Imposed on Guangshan County Party Committee First Secretary Ma Longshan, and Several Policy Questions Regarding the Handling of the Incidents of Death in the Xinyang Prefectural Party Committee," November 1, 1960.

28. Taolin Subgroup.

29. Kang Jian, Vanished Glory, pp. 463–65.

30. The Xinyang Annals record 483,000 deaths.

31. Yu Dehong, "Recollections of the Xinyang Incident."

32. Report by Wei Zhen of the Central Committee Work Team, "Regarding Several Exceptional Problems Brought to Light in Tangyi County," December 21, 1960 (hereafter "Report by Wei Zhen").

33. Yu Sang and Wu Renwen.

34. Sanpisi Commune Subgroup of the Provincial Party Committee Joint Investigation

Group, "Investigation Report Regarding Deaths at Huangchuan County's Sanpisi Commune," June 3, 1960 (hereafter "Sanpisi Subgroup").

35. Zhang Shufan, "The Xinyang Incident." This paragraph from the original manuscript was edited out when *Bainian chao* published Zhang's memoir.

36. Yang Weiping, "Investigation Report Regarding the Xinyang Incident," October 15, 1960.

37. Li Zhenhai, Tao Mosheng, and He Dizhong, "Investigation."

38. Chinese Communist Party Committee of Huaibin County, "Second Investigation into Deaths from Edema and Other Epidemic Diseases," June 7, 1960 (hereafter "Huaibin Party Committee").

39. Chinese Communist Party Committee of Henan Province, "Self-criticism Regarding the Xinyang Incident," November 1, 1960.

40. From Comrade Xu Zirong's speech to the standing committee of the provincial party committee, December 6, 1960.

41. Yang Weiping, "Investigation."

42. Huaibin Party Committee.

43. Kang Jian, *Vanished Glory*, pp. 454–55.

44. Ibid.

45. Ibid.

46. Qiao Peihua, "The Xinyang Incident."

47. Ibid., p. 70.

48. Chinese Communist Party Changge County Control Commission, "Investigation Report on Serious Coercion and Commandism and Violations of Law and Discipline by Party Cadres of the No. 1 Administrative District of Pohu Commune," included in Yu Xiguang, *The Great Leap Forward: Memorial of a Time of Hardship*, Hong Kong: Shidai chaoliu chuban youxian gongsi, 2005, pp. 66–67.

49. CCP Central Committee Party Literature Research Center, ed., *Manuscripts by Mao Zedong Since the Founding of the State*, vol. 7, Beijing: Zhongyang wenxian chubanshe, 1992, p. 594.

50. Zhang Shufan, "The Xinyang Incident."

51. Qiao Peihua, "The Xinyang Incident," p. 86.

52. Li Zhenhai, Tao Mosheng, and He Dizhong, "Investigation."

53. Conversation with Li Ruiying.

54. Interview in 1999 with Lu Baoguo, a Xinhua News Agency journalist stationed in Xinyang during the Great Famine.

55. "Account of the Suppression of Comrade Zhang Fu Following His Reporting of the Situation to the Party Central Committee."

56. Sanpisi Subgroup.

57. Report by Wei Zhen.

58. Chinese Communist Party Committee of Xinyang Prefecture, "Report on the Rectification Campaign and Production Disaster Relief Efforts," December 22, 1960 (hereafter "Xinyang Prefectural Party Committee").

59. "Wang Binglin's Materials Exposing Yang Weiping," December 1960.

60. Ibid.

61. Yu Dehong, "Recollections of the Xinyang Incident."
62. Ibid.
63. Zhang Shufan, "The Xinyang Incident."
64. Ibid.
65. *Manuscripts by Mao Zedong Since the Founding of the State*, vol. 9, 1996, p. 326.
66. Qiao Peihua, "The Xinyang Incident."
67. Quoted in "Report by the Xinyang Prefectural Party Committee on the Rectification Movement and Production Disaster Relief Work," CCP Central Committee Document [61], no. 4, December 22, 1960.
68. Wang Congwu and Xu Zirong, "Report on the Large-scale Class Retaliation Carried out in the Feudalistic Restoration in Xinyang Prefecture," December 1, 1960.
69. According to materials in the Gansu provincial archives transmitted by Zhang Desheng, an official of the Northwest bureau and first secretary of the Shaanxi provincial party committee, quoting statements by Mao on October 27 and 28, 1960.
70. Qiao Peihua, "The Xinyang Incident," p. 97.
71. Xinyang Prefectural Party Committee.
72. Central Committee Special Investigation Group, "Situation Report of the Special Investigation into the Xinyang Incident," November 20, 1960.
73. From Comrade Wang Renzhong's remarks at the meeting of the standing committee of the provincial party committee, December 6, 1960.
74. Comrade Xu Zirong's speech to the standing committee of the provincial party committee, December 6, 1960.
75. From Comrade Wang Congwu's speech to the meeting of the standing committee of the provincial party committee, December 6, 1960.
76. "Ma Longshan's Report on Xinyang, October 21, 1960, Respectfully Transmitted by Section Chief Liu to the Province's Two Directors."
77. TN: *Mu Guiying Takes Command* is a famous Peking opera about the eponymous woman warrior.
78. The content of this section, unless otherwise noted, is drawn from the author's three conversations with Yang Jue and Ji Yu from March to May 2001, and from written materials mailed to the author by Wang Tingdong from Shanxi later in 2001. This section was submitted to Yang Jue, Ji Yu, and Wang Tingdong for their examination and approval prior to publication.
79. TN: The Guangzhou Peasant Movement Training Institute was founded in 1924, and Mao Zedong and Zhou Enlai were among the notables who lectured there until the institute was closed in 1926 due to deteriorating relations between the Chinese Communist Party and the Kuomintang. It was reopened as a commemorative site in the 1950s. Peng Pai was one of the institute's directors, and also the founder of the short-lived Hailufeng Soviet in Guangdong in 1927.
80. See chapter 9 in this book, on the food crisis.
81. See chapter 4 in this book, on the people's communes.
82. The content of this section on Henan's irrigation projects, unless otherwise noted, is drawn from Henan Province Water Resources Department, ed., "Henan's Water

Resources During the Great Leap Forward," 1998; Henan Province Water Resources Department, *Brief Overview of Henan's Water Resources Over the Last Forty Years*; and Xu Ming, "Wu Zhipu and Henan's Great Leap Forward Movement," *Twenty-first Century*, no. 48 (August 1998): 37–47.

83. TN: According to a directive of the CCP Central Committee and the State Council, the "pests" to be wiped out in a nationwide campaign were rats, sparrows, flies, and mosquitoes.

84. From Comrade Wang Congwu's speech to the meeting of the standing committee of the provincial party committee, December 6, 1960.

85. TN: These numbers refer to the following: grain yields of 400 *jin* (200 kilos) per *mu* in fields north of the Yellow River, 500 *jin* (250 kilos) per *mu* south of the Yellow River, and 800 *jin* (400 kilos) per *mu* south of the Huai and Yangtze rivers. These were some of the long-term goals in Mao's National Program for Agricultural Development, which Henan nevertheless claimed it could achieve within one year.

86. Mao Zedong's remarks at the Chengdu Conference (3), March 20, 1958, in *Long Live Mao Zedong Thought, 1958–1960*, p. 35.

87. Kang Jian, *Vanished Glory*, pp. 110–17.

88. Editorial, "Congratulating Our Peasant Brothers on Creating a Miracle," *People's Daily*, June 12, 1958.

89. Wang Binglin referred to "Xiping's Heping Agricultural Commune Launches Bumper Crop Satellite of 3,660 Kilos per Mu," *Henan Daily*, July 11, 1958, p. 1 headline.

90. Qiao Peihua, "The Xinyang Incident," pp. 70–72.

91. TN: American scholar Edward Friedman found "cartification" and "bearingification" ongoing when he visited rural China in 1978.

92. Xu Ming, "Wu Zhipu and Henan's Great Leap Forward."

93. TN: This short-lived movement began and ended in early 1871 as the world's first workers' government. For a full history, see www.marxists.org/history/france /paris-commune/index.htm.

94. Conversation with Yang Jue and Ji Yu on March 19, 2001. TN: *Baidu Encyclopedia* describes the incident in detail and reports that Zou (born Su Han in 1910) drowned himself in 1959: baike.baidu.com/view/221978.html. Zou was posthumously rehabilitated, following Peng Dehuai's rehabilitation in 1978.

95. Xu Ming, "Wu Zhipu and Henan's Great Leap Forward."

96. Conversation with Yang Jue and Ji Yu.

97. Ibid.

98. Xu Ming, "Wu Zhipu and Henan's Great Leap Forward."

99. Yu Xiguang, *The Great Leap Forward*, pp. 85, 91.

100. He Libo, "Wu Zhipu, Criminal Instigator of the 'Communist Wind' in Henan During the Great Leap Forward," *Dangshi zonglan*, no. 2 (2006): 36–41.

101. Zhao Zongli, "The Tanghe Incident Brought About by 'Leftists' Opposing 'Rightists,'" *Yanhuang chunqiu*, no. 10 (2010): 62–66.

102. See chapter 11 in this book, on population loss, and Cao Shuji, *The Great Famine: China's Population 1959–1961*, Hong Kong: Shidai guoji youxian gongsi, 2005, p. 263.

103. Conversation with Yang Jue and Ji Yu.

104. From Comrade Wang Renzhong's remarks at the meeting of the standing committee of the provincial party committee, February 10, 1961. See also Qiao Peihua, "The Xinyang Incident," pp. 130–32.

105. He Libo, "Wu Zhipu, Criminal Instigator."

106. Conversation with Yang Jue and Ji Yu.

2. THE THREE RED BANNERS: SOURCE OF THE FAMINE

1. TN: In Mao's words at the Second Plenum of the Eighth National Congress of the CCP in May 1958. Cf. *People's Daily*, "Historical Slogans of the Chinese Communist Party," June 8, 2001.

2. Vladimir Lenin, "The Tasks of the Youth Leagues," 1920, published in China as "Qingniantuan de renwu," in *Selected Works of Lenin*, vol. 2, Beijing: Renmin chubanshe, 1954, pp. 807–11. TN: This English translation of Lenin's speech is provided by the Marxists Internet Archive, at www.search.marxists.org/archive /lenin/works/1920/oct/02.htm.

3. The CCP's "mass movements" used executive power and the propaganda machinery to mobilize the masses in an all-out effort to achieve a particular objective designated by the Communist Party.

4. The transition period referred to here denotes that from new democracy to socialism. The main task of the transition period proposed in 1953 was "accomplishing socialist industrialization, and implementing socialist transformation in agriculture, handicrafts, and industry and commerce," abbreviated by the Chinese phrase *yihua sangai*. At that time, the plan anticipated that completion of this task would require ten to fifteen years. Later the deadline was brought forward to achieve implementation in two to three years.

5. Bo Yibo, *Looking Back on a Number of Significant Policy Decisions and Events*, vol. 1, Beijing: Zhonggong zhongyang dangxiao chubanshe, 1991, p. 522.

6. *Selected Works of Mao Zedong*, vol. 5, Beijing: Renmin chubanshe, 1977, pp. 223, 224.

7. Bo Yibo, *Looking Back*, vol. 1, p. 527.

8. TN: The Chinese characters for *empty* and *poor* not only look similar in their written form, but also have a pronunciation close enough to cause confusion, given Mao's heavy Hunan accent.

9. Bo Yibo, *Looking Back*, vol. 1, p. 528.

10. Ibid., p. 532.

11. Ibid., pp. 532–33.

12. *Selected Writings of Zhou Enlai*, vol. 2, Beijing: Renmin chubanshe, 1984, pp. 190–91.

13. Jin Chongji, ed., *The Biography of Zhou Enlai*, vol. 3, Beijing: Zhongyang wenxian chubanshe, 1991, pp. 1126–27.

14. Bo Yibo, *Looking Back*, vol. 1, p. 534.

15. Wu Lengxi, *Remembering Chairman Mao: Fragments of My Personal Experience in Several Significant Historical Events*, Beijing: Xinhua chubanshe, 1995, p. 49.

16. Bo Yibo, *Looking Back*, vol. 1, pp. 545–46.

17. "On Being Promoters of Revolution," October 9, 1957, in *Selected Works of Mao Zedong*, vol. 5, pp. 474–75. TN: The "rightist Zhang-Luo Alliance" refers to "right-

ist" intellectuals epitomized by Zhang Bojun and Luo Longji, who promoted an increased role for the democratic parties.

18. "On Being Promoters," p. 475.
19. TN: Harry Pollitt and John Gollan were leaders of the Communist Party of Great Britain.
20. "Speech at the Congress of Communist and Workers' Parties in Moscow," November 18, 1957, in CCP Central Committee Party Literature Research Center, ed., *Collected Works of Mao Zedong*, vol. 7, Beijing: Renmin chubanshe, 1999, pp. 325–26.
21. Bo Yibo, *Looking Back on a Number of Significant Policy Decisions and Events*, vol. 2, Beijing: Zhonggong zhongyang wenxian chubanshe, 1993, pp. 635–57; Zhang Zhanbin, Liu Jiehui, Zhang Guohua, eds., *The Great Leap Forward and the Three Years of Hardship in China*, Beijing: China Commercial Press, 2001, pp. 1–4.
22. Mao Zedong, "Annotations on an Extract of a Document Apparently Opposing Rash Advance," January 1958, *Manuscripts by Mao Zedong Since the Founding of the State*, vol. 7, pp. 32–36.
23. Mao Zedong's speech at the Nanning Conference, in Li Rui, *A Personal Record of the Great Leap Forward: The Notes of Mao Zedong's Secretary*, Haikou: Nanfang chubanshe, vol. 1, p. 71.
24. Bo Yibo, *Looking Back*, vol. 2, p. 673.
25. TN: Chen Mingshu served on the standing committees of the Chinese People's Political Consultative Conference and the National People's Congress before being forced out of politics during the 1957 Anti-Rightist Movement. Zhang Xiruo, minister of education from 1952 to 1958, bitterly opposed the dismantling of Beijing's archways and city walls.
26. Mao Zedong's speech at the Nanning Conference, in Li Rui, *A Personal Record*, vol. 1: 36–82.
27. Jin Chongji, ed., *The Biography of Zhou Enlai*, vol. 3, p. 1367.
28. Li Rui, *A Personal Record*, vol. 1, p. 80; Bo Yibo, *Looking Back*, vol. 2, p. 639.
29. Jin Chongji, ed., *The Biography of Zhou Enlai*, vol. 3, p. 1396.
30. Yang Mingwei, "The 'Great Leap Forward' Sweeps Through China, Zhou Enlai Comes Close to Resigning," *Yanhuang chunqiu*, no. 2 (2000): 6–11.
31. Wu Lengxi, *Remembering Chairman Mao*, p. 60.
32. Li Rui, *A Personal Record*, vol. 1, p. 170.
33. Mao Zedong's speech at the Chengdu Conference, March 22, 1958, in *Long Live Mao Zedong Thought, 1958–1960*, p. 40.
34. Ibid., pp. 35–36.
35. Li Rui, *A Personal Record*, vol. 1, p. 252.
36. Yang Mingwei, "Zhou Enlai's Request to Resign as Premier," in Zhang Zhanbin et al., eds., *The Great Leap Forward*, p. 10.
37. Li Rui, *A Personal Record*, vol. 1, pp. 223–35.
38. Bo Yibo, *Looking Back*, vol. 2, p. 663.
39. "Speech at the Chengdu Conference," March 1958, in CCP Central Committee Party Literature Research Center, ed., *Collected Works of Mao Zedong*, vol. 7, p. 369.

40. Li Rui, *A Personal Record*, vol. 1, pp. 212–13, 215.

41. Ibid., pp. 215, 244, 288.

42. CCP Central Committee Party Literature Research Center, ed., *The Life of Mao Zedong, 1949–1976*, vol. 1, Beijing: Zhongyang wenxian chubanshe, 2003, pp. 798–99.

43. TN: Mao was here slightly misquoting a poem by Tang dynasty poet Song Zhiwen.

44. Li Rui, *A Personal Record*, vol. 1, p. 293.

45. TN: *"Shang you hao zhe, xia bi shen yan,"* Mencius (372–289 B.C.E.), Teng Wen Gong, part 1; translated by James Legge as "What the superior loves, his inferiors will be found to love exceedingly." Mencius follows by writing, "The relation between superior and inferior is like that between the wind and grass. The grass must bend when the wind blows upon it."

46. Li Rui, *A Personal Record*, vol. 1, p. 319.

47. Mao Zedong, "The Lowly Are the Cleverest, the Noble Are the Stupidest," in *Manuscripts by Mao Zedong Since the Founding of the State*, vol. 7, p. 236.

48. "Mao Zedong's Speech at the Second Plenum of the Eighth Party Congress," May 8, 1958, 4:50 p.m., in *Long Live Mao Zedong Thought, 1958–1960*, p. 72.

49. As quoted ibid.; and in Li Rui, *A Personal Record*, vol. 1, pp. 332, 380, 390.

50. Chen Yun, in "Speeches at the Second Plenum of the Eighth National Congress of the CCP," May 16, 1958.

51. Li Rui, *A Personal Record*, vol. 1, p. 369.

52. Ibid., p. 370.

53. Ibid., p. 359.

54. TN: Mao referred to setting up good "revolutionary" models and denouncing bad "bourgeois" ones, as elaborated on in his speech to the Second Session of the Eighth Party Congress on May 8.

55. TN: Li Bai, or Li Po (701–762), is one of the greatest poets of the Tang dynasty. Lu Xun (1881–1936) is a major modern Chinese writer. Nie Er (1912–1935) is a composer whose *March of the Volunteers* was named the national anthem of the People's Republic of China.

56. TN: Although other Chinese measurements such as *jin* are converted to the metric system throughout this book, *mu* will be retained as a land measure in order to preserve the "round" targets set on cultivation and crop yields.

57. Li Rui, *A Personal Record*, vol. 1, pp. 340–46.

58. TN: Yu the Great, or Da Yu, was the legendary founder of the Xia dynasty, venerated for teaching the people flood-control techniques. Mao here quotes the Tang philosopher Han Yu, who described the triumph of Mencius over Yang Zhu and Mozi in establishing the status of the Confucian school as an "achievement by no means less than that of Yu."

59. "Letter Written After Rereading the *People's Daily* Editorial 'Mobilize the Populace, Discuss the Program for Agricultural Development, Lift Agricultural Productivity to a New Climax,'" May 26, 1958, in *Manuscripts by Mao Zedong Since the Founding of the State*, vol. 7, p. 254.

60. Li Danhui, "Further Discussion of the Substitution of 'Rash Advance' with 'Leap Forward,'" *Modern China Historical Research*, no. 2 (1999): 89–92; Comrade

Zhou Enlai's letter: source of the phrase 'leap forward,'" Jilin provincial archives, Category 1, Catalogue 1–14, vol. 75, p. 9.

3. HARD TIMES IN GANSU

1. Zhang Zhongliang, "Go All Out, Battle Hard for Three Years, Aim High for a Leap Forward in Agriculture, and Leap Forward Once Again!," February 9, 1958.

2. "Report to the Provincial Party Committee by Li Busheng, Li Shenghua, and Tian Yuan of the Dingxi Work Group," in *Bulletin No. 3 of the Enlarged Meeting of the Dingxi Prefectural Party Committee*, January 12, 1961, Gansu (received) [61], no. 2164.

3. *Gansu Provincial Annals: Major Events.*

4. "Inspection Report by the Gansu Provincial Party Committee on Several Issues Relating to the Implementation and Execution of the Spirit of the Northwest Bureau's Lanzhou Conference over the Last Two Years," adopted by the Fourth Plenum of the Third Provincial Party Congress on December 3, 1962, archives of the Gansu provincial party committee, Gansu (issued) [63], no. 6 (hereafter "Gansu provincial party committee").

5. "Remarks on the Gansu Provincial Party Committee Report on Food Supply Work," in *Manuscripts by Mao Zedong Since the Founding of the State*, vol. 8, p. 529.

6. "Opinions Put Forward to the Central Committee and Its Leaders and Related Departments During a Meeting in Gansu Province of Party Cadres of Provincial Units of Grade 19 or Above to Study and Discuss Documents from the Meeting of the Enlarged Central Committee Work Conference," February 28, 1962, compiled by the provincial party office. TN: The "Enlarged Central Committee Work Conference" refers to the Seven Thousand Cadres Conference.

7. Zhenyuan County Party Committee History Group, "Cases of Injustice in Zhenyuan County During the Great Leap Forward," *Bainian chao*, no. 4 (1999): 48–53.

8. TN: The region comprising the provinces of Shaanxi, Gansu, and Ningxia was a key power base in the early development of the Chinese Communist Party.

9. CCP Gansu Provincial Committee Office, ed., *Bulletin of the CCP Gansu Provincial Committee Three-level Cadre Conference*, no. 4, November 9, 1960.

10. CCP Gansu Provincial Committee Office, ed., *Bulletin of the CCP Gansu Provincial Committee Three-level Cadre Conference*, no. 13, November 11, 1960.

11. Ibid.

12. TN: Commonly romanized as General Tso Tsung-t'ang.

13. TN: It is worth noting that another "Yintao Project" was started in 2006, with the aim of bringing more drinking water to Gansu Province. See, for example, "Gansu to Start Eight Large Projects," AsiaInfo Services, January 11, 2005.

14. The figures in Table 3.1 must be accompanied by two clarifications: (1) The yields in the "Food Ministry Planning Department Grain Data Summary" are for unprocessed food grain, while the procurement and sales figures are for trade (i.e., processed) grain. In order to facilitate the calculations, processed grain yields have

been calculated by dividing the unprocessed yield by a factor of 1.15. (2) Gansu's grain "in hand" in the table is calculated by subtracting the procurement amount from the processed yield and then adding the amount sold back to the province. However, in the "Food Ministry Planning Department Grain Data Summary" the figures provided for yield apply to the calendar year from January to December, while the procurement and sales figures apply to the "grain year," July 1 of the stated year to June 30 of the following year. For example, the processed grain yield of 12.217 billion kilos for 1958 refers to the summer and autumn harvests of that year, but the actual 1958/1959 grain yield would include the 1958 autumn harvest and the 1959 summer harvest. For that reason, the calculation of grain in hand in Gansu Province in any particular year can be considered only an approximation. The divergence comes in replacing the given year's summer harvest with that of the following year. Because the summer harvest makes up a relatively smaller share of the total annual harvest, the divergence is not great. The grain "in hand" in the province includes grain for industrial use, animal feed, seed, and urban consumption. In subsequent chapters of this book, the calculations are made on the same basis without further annotation.

15. "Gansu provincial party committee."

16. "Telephone Report by the Qingshui County Party Committee Regarding Livelihood Arrangements and the Situation of Outward Migration," February 17, 1960. The Gansu provincial party committee on February 19 printed copies of the report and distributed it to members of the standing committee, secretariat, rectification office, and other bodies, a total of twenty-eight copies.

17. "Gansu provincial party committee."

18. Ibid.

19. Ibid.

20. Su Runyu, ed., *China Population: Gansu*, Beijing: Zhongguo caizheng jingji chubanshe, 1988, p. 83.

21. Li Lei, *Long Years*, self-published, October 1999, p. 149.

22. Yun Xiaosu, "Accurately Acknowledging the Food Supply Problem in Gansu," *Gansu Economic Daily*, January 7, 1998, p. 1.

23. Fu Shanglun, Hu Guohua, Feng Dongshu, and Dai Guoqiang, *Farewell Hunger*, Beijing: Renmin chubanshe, 1999, p. 21.

24. Cao Shuji, *The Great Famine*, p. 277.

25. CCP Tianshui Prefectural Party Committee, "Request for Funding for Free Medical Treatment," December 24, 1960; dispatch to the Gansu provincial party committee, receipt no. [60]1725. The report was copied and distributed to all party secretaries, the secretary-general, the secretariat, leading cadres of the livelihood arrangements committee, and the health and medical treatment office, a total of twenty-six copies.

26. Provincial Party Committee Rural Work Department, "Report on the Problems in Min County," August 19, 1960. The report was copied and distributed to the standing committee, secretariat, water conservancy bureau, weather bureau, farming machinery bureau, and wasteland reclamation bureau, a total of twenty-five copies.

27. "Telephone Report by the Wuwei Prefectural Party Committee Regarding the Incidence of Sickness, Food and Fuel Shortages, and Outward Migration in Yongchang County," January 15, 1962, Gansu, receipt no. [62]20049.

28. CCP Gannan Prefectural Party Committee, "Report on Livelihood Arrangements and Increasing the Rural Grain Rations," April 8, 1962; dispatch to the Gansu provincial party committee, receipt no. [62]20638, forty-four copies printed.

29. Linxia Prefectural Party Committee, "Briefing on the Living Conditions at Linxia County's Dahejia Bonan Minority Commune," May 11, 1962, Gansu provincial party committee receipt no. [62]20864, twenty-three copies printed.

30. Li Lei, *Long Years*, pp. 122–50.

31. Provincial Industry and Communications Departments, "The Incidence of Edema in the Industry and Communications System," printed on December 9, 1960, by the CCP Gansu provincial party committee office and issued to members of the provincial party standing committee and others, a total of thirty-six copies.

32. CCP Baiyin Municipal Party Committee, "Report Regarding Vigorously Preventing and Curing the Spread of Edema, and Suggestions Going Forward," December 18, 1960.

33. CCP Yumen Municipal Party Committee, "Report Regarding the Situation of Edema in Factories and Mines, Enterprises, Organizations, and Party Schools," December 11, 1960.

34. CCP Lanzhou Municipal Party Committee, "Situational Report Regarding the Incidence of Edema Among Cadres and Staff," December 3, 1960, Lanzhou municipal party committee document [60]846.

35. He Fengming, *Experience: My 1957*, Lanzhou: Dunhuang wenyi chubanshe, 2001, p. 420.

36. Ibid., pp. 394–97.

37. TN: The relevance of the various locales in this poem is helpfully decoded at wapedia.mobi/en/Poetry_of_Mao_Zedong.

38. *Tongwei County Annals*, Lanzhou: Lanzhou daxue chubanshe, 1990, pp. 146–47.

39. "Report by the Provincial Party Committee Health Department Inspection Group to the Health Department's Leading Party Group and the Dingxi Prefectural Party Committee," January 8, 1961.

40. Zhang Dafa, *On the Golden Bridge*, Dingxi Writers Association, 2005, pp. 35, 37.

41. CCP Tongwei County Committee, "Regarding the Historical Experience and Lessons of Tongwei," July 5, 1965, CCP Gansu provincial committee document, issued [65]347.

42. Fu Shanglun et al., *Farewell Hunger*, p. 26.

43. Zhang Dafa, *On the Golden Bridge*, pp. 33–38.

44. CCP Dingxi Prefectural Committee Organization Department, "Situational Report Regarding the Examination of the 1958 'Pulling Down of White Flags' and 'Planting of Red Flags,'" October 19, 1959.

45. CCP Tongwei County Committee, "Regarding the Historical Experience."

46. Ibid.

47. Ibid.

48. Ibid.

49. Ibid.

50. "Report to the Provincial Party Committee on January 12, 1961, by the Dingxi Work Group's Li Busheng, Li Shenghua, and Tian Yuan," *Bulletin of the Enlarged Dingxi Prefectural Party Committee*, no. 3 (telephoned by Comrade He Yayi on January 12 at 11:00 p.m.), Gansu receipt no. [61]2164.

51. CCP Tongwei County Committee, "Regarding the Historical Experience."

52. TN: Xi is here quoting Mao Zedong: "A revolution is not a dinner party, or writing an essay, or painting a picture, or doing embroidery; it cannot be so refined, so leisurely and gentle, so temperate, kind, courteous, restrained, and magnanimous. A revolution is an insurrection, an act of violence by which one class overthrows another." From "Report on an Investigation of the Peasant Movement in Hunan," March 1927.

53. This incident of the countywide telephone conference was related during a seminar of veteran Tongwei cadres that I arranged on August 10, 2000.

54. TN: Huang Shiren is the evil landlord character in the revolutionary opera *The White-haired Girl*.

55. This information was related during a seminar of veteran Tongwei cadres that I arranged on August 10, 2000.

56. Gansu Provincial People's Procuratorate, Dingxi Branch, "Investigation Report Regarding Tongwei's Handling of Reeducation Through Labor," March 30, 1960.

57. "Central Committee Transmission with Instructions: Gansu Provincial Party Committee's Situational Report Regarding the Complete Deterioration of the Tongwei County Party Committee," April 21, 1960, CCP Central Committee document issued [60]364.4.

58. "Gansu Provincial Party Committee's Situational Report Regarding the Complete Deterioration of the Tongwei County Party Committee," April 6, 1960.

59. CCP Tongwei Party Committee, "Regarding the Historical Experience."

60. "CCP Gansu Provincial Committee Report on 'The Historical Experience and Lessons of Tongwei,'" July 5, 1965, dispatches from the CCP Gansu provincial committee, receipt no. [65]347.

61. "Inspection Report by the Gansu Provincial Party Committee on Several Issues Relating to the Implementation and Execution of the Spirit of the Northwest Bureau's Lanzhou Conference Over the Last Two Years," approved by the Fourth Session of the Third Plenum of the Gansu provincial party committee on December 3, 1962.

62. TN: The development of "rope-drawn plowing" is described in greater detail in chapter 4, on Sichuan Province.

63. "Transmission by the Dingxi Prefectural Party Committee of Some Opinions Expressed at an Enlarged Meeting of All County Party Committees to Leading Comrades of the Central Committee and the Provincial Party Committee," November 28, 1961.

64. "Inspection Report by the Gansu Provincial Party Committee on Several Issues Relating to the Implementation."

65. Ibid.

4. THE PEOPLE'S COMMUNE: FOUNDATION OF THE TOTALITARIAN SYSTEM

1. Bo Yibo, *Looking Back*, vol. 1, pp. 194–202.
2. Mo Rida, ed., *The Development of Agricultural Cooperatives in Our Country*, Beijing: Tongji chubanshe, 1957, p. 31, as quoted in Gao Huamin, "Research on Well-to-do Middle Peasants in the 1950s," *Party History Research Materials*, no. 4 (1996): 1.
3. "North China Bureau's Directives on Rectifying Rash Advance in the Development of Agricultural Cooperatives," March 1953, in Huang Daoxia et al., eds., *Compilation of Historical Documents on the Agricultural Cooperative Movement Since the Founding of the PRC*, Beijing: Zhonggong dangshi chubanshe, 1992, p. 128.
4. "Speech by Wu Zhichuan, head of Zhejiang Rural Work Department at the Third National Rural Work Conference," April 1955, in Huang Daoxia et al., eds., *Compilation*, p. 243.
5. Bo Yibo, *Looking Back*, vol. 1, p. 337.
6. *Selected Works of Mao Zedong*, vol. 5, pp. 257–58.
7. Yang Xinpei, "Report on the Mass Disturbance in Xianju County," June 1957, in Huang Daoxia et al., eds., *Compilation*, p. 432.
8. TN: One online source describes the Daqihui as a huge organization made up of peasants and fishermen existing for some three hundred to four hundred years along Zhejiang's coast. See "Shehui xisu: Shangyu Daqihui" (Social Customs: Shangyu's Daqihui), daoxuol.cn/wap.aspx?nid=42218&cid=15&sp=10, accessed October 1, 2009.
9. He Zuming and Xu Jingrao, "The Daqihui Disturbance in Shangyu County," *Historical Materials on China's Agricultural Cooperatives*, no. 1 (1989).
10. "Newsletter of the Henan Provincial Party Committee Rural Work Department," March 28, 1957, in Huang Daoxia et al., eds., *Compilation*, p. 424.
11. "Guangdong Provincial Party Committee Report on Withdrawal from the Cooperatives," December 24, 1956, in Huang Daoxia et al., eds., *Compilation*, p. 405.
12. "Briefing Paper of the Liaoning Provincial Party Committee on a Minority of Co-operative Members Withdrawing and Stealing Horses," April 4, 1957, in Huang Daoxia et al., eds., *Compilation*, p. 405.
13. "Directives of the Jiangsu Provincial Party Committee on the Proper Handling of Rural Mass Disturbances," June 2, 1957, in Huang Daoxia et al., eds., *Compilation*, p. 430.
14. "Report of the CCP Central Committee Rural Work Department on Withdrawal from the Cooperatives and Problems with Large Cooperatives," December 6, 1956, in Huang Daoxia et al., eds., *Compilation*, p. 408.
15. "Directives from the CCP Central Committee Regarding Conducting Large-scale Socialist Education Among the Rural Population," August 8, 1957, in Huang Daoxia et al., eds., *Compilation*, p. 435.
16. CCP Central Committee Secretariat, comp., "The Status of Rectification in the Rural Areas of Thirteen Provinces," in Huang Daoxia et al., eds., *Compilation*, p. 443.

17. Liu Jiemei's oral testimony, transcribed by Jie Min and Nie Bin, published as "Uprooting Capitalist Thinking," *People's Daily*, September 30, 1957.

18. Kang Jian, *Vanished Glory*, pp. 55–85.

19. Zhou Cheng'en, "People's Communes and Utopian Theory in Socialist Construction," *Chinese Communist Party History Research*, no. 5 (1988): 44–50.

20. Chen Qingquan and Song Guangwei, *The Biography of Lu Dingyi*, Beijing: Zhonggong dangshi chubanshe, 1999.

21. Bo Yibo, *Looking Back*, vol. 2, pp. 732–33.

22. Chen Qingquan and Song Guangwei, *The Biography of Lu Dingyi*, pp. 447–48.

23. "Henan Provincial Party Committee Report Concerning the Establishment of People's Communes," August 22, 1958, in Huang Daoxia et al., eds., *Compilation*, p. 480.

24. Bo Yibo, *Looking Back*, vol. 2, p. 740.

25. CCP Central Committee Rural Work Department, *Renmin gongshehua yundong jianbao* (People's Commune Movement Bulletin), no. 4: "China Has Basically Achieved Complete Organization Under the People's Communes," September 30, 1958, in Huang Daoxia et al., eds., *Compilation*, p. 503.

26. Bo Yibo, *Looking Back*, vol. 2, p. 749.

27. "Comrade Yan Hongyan's Letter to the Chairman," May 9, 1961, sent from Midu County, no. [61]380, to the provincial party office; Sichuan provincial office [61], receipt no. 2564.

28. Ling Zhijun, *History No Longer Wavers: The Rise and Fall of the People's Communes in China*, Beijing: Renmin chubanshe, 1996, p. 330.

29. Kang Jian, *Vanished Glory*, pp. 95–98.

30. Mao Zedong, "The Student's Work," *Hunan Education Monthly*, 1, no. 2 (December 1919).

31. Japan's New Village Movement envisaged communes based on mutual aid and shared resources, with the ultimate goal of creating a peaceful, classless, and anarchist society.

32. Mao Zedong, "On the People's Democratic Dictatorship," June 30, 1949, *Selected Works of Mao Zedong*, vol. 4, Beijing: Renmin chubanshe, 1960, p. 1408.

33. Mao Zedong's speech at the enlarged meeting of the CCP Politburo at Beidaihe on the morning of August 21, 1958, in Li Rui, *A Personal Record*, vol. 2, pp. 105, 107.

34. "Record of the Zhengzhou Meeting," enlarged Central Committee Politburo meeting, February 27–March 5, 1959, in Huang Daoxia et al., eds., *Compilation*, p. 528.

35. Further details are provided in chapter 12 of this book, on the official response to the famine.

5. THE COMMUNAL KITCHENS

1. Mao Zedong, "Speeches at the Chengdu Conference," no. 4, March 22, 1958, in *Long Live Mao Zedong Thought, 1958–1960*, p. 39.

2. TN: Also known as the Way of the Celestial Master, a Daoist movement founded by Zhang Lu's grandfather, Zhang Daoling, in 142 C.E. At its height, the movement controlled a theocratic state in the Hanzhong Valley, north of Sichuan, which was

incorporated into Cao Cao's Kingdom of Wei in 215 C.E. See en.wikipedia.org /wiki/Five_Pecks_of_Rice_Rebellion.

3. Mao Zedong, "Comments on Printing and Distributing the *Biography of Zhang Lu*," December 7, 1958, in *Manuscripts by Mao Zedong Since the Founding of the State*, vol. 7, p. 627.

4. Kang Jian, *Vanished Glory*, pp. 153–60.

5. Liu Shaoqi, "Talk to the All-China Women's Federation," in *Materials for Criticism: Collected Counterrevolutionary Revisionist Discourse of the Chinese Khrushchev, Liu Shaoqi, June 1958 to July 1967*, Beijing: Renmin chubanshe ziliaoshi, September 10, 1967.

6. Yuzhong County party secretary Lie Bingrang, "Report on the Communal Kitchens," May 1961, dispatches to the Gansu provincial party committee, receipt no. [61]21697.

7. Luo Pinghan, *The Big Iron Rice Bowl: The Beginning and End of the Communal Kitchens*, Nanning: Guangxi renmin chubanshe, 2001, p. 31.

8. "Survey of Canteens in the People's Communes of Xinfan County," July 3, 1959.

9. Hu Qiaomu et al., "Report on Resolving the Communal Kitchen Problems at Shaoshan Commune," April 10, 1961, in *Several Important Documents Transmitted by the Central Committee to the Chairman for Instructions*.

10. Zhang Buzhen, *A Thirst for Truth: Liu Shaoqi in 1961*, Zhuhai: Zhuhai chubanshe, 1998, p. 140.

11. Hui Wen, "A Record of the Rectification of the Rural Cooperatives During the Time of Hardship," at www.yhcw.net/famine.

12. Huang Daoxia et al., eds., *Compilation*, p. 326.

13. Ibid., p. 495.

14. "Summary of the Symposium Convened by Comrade [Li] Jingquan of the Party Secretaries of Fuling, Neijiang, Luzhou, Wenjiang, Mianyang, and Nanchong Prefectures," February 14, 1960.

15. "Urgent Directive from the CCP Central Committee Regarding Current Policy Problems of the Rural People's Communes," also known as the "Twelve Provisions on Agriculture," November 3, 1960, in Huang Daoxia et al., eds., *Compilation*, pp. 614–15.

16. Yuzhong County party secretary Lie Bingrang, "Report on the Communal Kitchens."

17. Mao Zedong's speech at the Sixth Plenum of the Eighth CCP Central Committee.

18. Shaanxi Provincial Party Committee Propaganda Bureau, "Ideological Trends: Some Grassroots Cadres and Commune Members Suggest Disbanding the Communal Kitchens," in CCP Central Committee Propaganda Department, *Propaganda and Education Trends*, May 23, 1959.

19. Huang Daoxia et al., eds., *Compilation*, p. 567.

20. "Closure of Communal Kitchens in Some Localities," in Zhejiang Provincial Party Committee Rural Work Department, ed., *Qingkuang ziliao*, no. 3 (January 13, 1961).

21. An Faxiao, member of the Luzhou Subgroup of the Sichuan Provincial Party Committee Production Inspection Group for Rectifying the Communes, "Investigation

Report on Several Problems Arising in the Course of Rectifying and Consolidating the People's Communes in Luzhou Prefecture," September 1, 1959, printed on September 9, 1959, by the Sichuan provincial party committee office.

22. See chapter 8, for further details on the situation in Anhui Province.

23. Luo Pinghan, *The Big Iron Rice Bowl*, p. 153.

24. Ibid., p. 134.

25. Ibid., p. 136.

26. Peng Dehuai, *The Autobiography of Peng Dehuai*, Beijing: Renmin chubanshe, 1981, p. 286.

27. Li Rui, "Seeking Truth from Facts at the Expense of Official Position: In Cherished Memory of Comrade Zhou Xiaozhou," in *Ten Essays in Memoriam*, Beijing: Renmin chubanshe, 1983, p. 64.

28. *Selected Works of Zhang Wentian*, Beijing: Renmin chubanshe, 1985, p. 497.

29. Mao Zedong's speech at the Lushan Conference, July 23, 1959, in *Long Live Mao Zedong Thought, 1958–1960*, p. 239.

30. TN: Sun Yatsen, *Plans for National Reconstruction, 1919*.

31. Mao Zedong, "Remarks on Data Relating to the Closure and Reopening of Dozens of Communal Kitchens in the Daozhu Production Brigade of Hunan's Pingjiang County," August 5, 1959, in *Manuscripts by Mao Zedong Since the Founding of the State*, vol. 8, p. 410.

32. An Faxiao, "Investigation Report."

33. "Directives of the Sichuan Provincial Party Committee Regarding Resolutely Opposing Right-deviationist Thinking and Successfully Tiding Over the Famine by Increasing Production and Economizing on Grain," September 2, 1959.

34. "Development of the Rural Communal Kitchens Throughout China as of the End of 1959," in Huang Daoxia et al., eds., *Compilation*, p. 602.

35. General Office of the CCP Central Committee, comp., "The Situation of the Rural Communal Kitchens in Eight Provinces," in "Memo from the CCP Central Committee Regarding Strengthening the Leadership of the Communal Kitchens," March 18, 1960.

36. "CCP Central Committee's Comments on the Report of the Guizhou Provincial Party Committee Regarding the Current Situation of the Rural Communal Kitchens," March 4, 1960, in *Manuscripts by Mao Zedong Since the Founding of the State*, vol. 9, pp. 44–45.

37. "CCP Central Committee's Endorsement of the Guizhou Provincial Party Committee's 'Report on the Current Situation of the Rural Communal Kitchens,'" March 6, 1960.

38. "Central Committee's Transmission of the Hebei Provincial Party Committee's Provisions on the Participation of Cadres in the Communal Kitchens," March 7, 1960.

39. "The Situation of Rural Communal Kitchens in Eight Provinces," issued by the CCP Central Committee on March 18, 1960.

40. Office of the PRC Agricultural Commission, *Compilation of Important Documents Regarding Agricultural Collectivization*, Beijing: Zhonggong zhongyang dangxiao chubanshe, 1981, vol. 2, p. 293.

41. *People's Daily*, "Taking Charge of Daily Life as Well as Production," June 21, 1960.
42. Long Yuwen, "The Communal Kitchens' Long Abuse and Instant Closure: A Contemporary Record of the Communal Kitchens in Fengcheng County's Xiaogang Commune," in *Historical Materials on China's Agricultural Cooperatives*, no. 4 (1988).
43. Kang Jian, *Vanished Glory*, p. 93.
44. Wei Junyi, "Burning Era, Burning Hearts," quoted in Zhang Zhanbin et al., eds., *The Great Leap Forward*, p. 144.
45. Zhou Demin, "Fragmentary Recollections of the 'Five Winds' in Ningxiang," in *Literary and Historical Materials on Changsha*, vol. 7, December 1988.
46. Document of the General Office of the CCP Central Committee, September 1959. Filed in the Shandong provincial archives.
47. Zhang Buzhen, *A Thirst for Truth*, p. 112.
48. "Comrade Wang Feng's Report to the Chairman Regarding the Rural Communal Kitchens and Other Problems," May 9, 1961, in Linxia, documents of the Gansu provincial party committee, no. [61]0296.
49. Hu Qiaomu et al., "Report on Resolving the Communal Kitchen Problems."
50. Ibid.
51. Liu Bingxun, "Mao Zedong's Reasons for Closing the Rural Communal Kitchens," *Bainian chao*, no. 6 (1997): 48–52.
52. Jiang Weiqing, *A Seventy-Year Journey: The Memoirs of Jiang Weiqing*, Nanjing: Jiangsu renmin chubanshe, 1996, pp. 454–56.
53. Liu Bingxun, "Mao Zedong's Reasons."
54. "Central Committee Dispatch of Several Important Documents on Instructions from the Chairman," CCP Central Committee document, no. [61]323.
55. "Comrade Wang Feng's Report to the Chairman Regarding the Rural Communal Kitchens and Other Problems," May 9, 1961.
56. Office of the PRC Agricultural Commission, Compilation of Important Documents Regarding Agricultural Collectivization, vol. 2, Zhonggong Zhongyang dangxiao chubanshe, 1982, p. 484.

6. HUNGRY GHOSTS IN HEAVEN'S PANTRY

1. I made many work trips to Sichuan, also collecting information on the famine. Veteran Xinhua reporters who had spent the famine years in Sichuan were most helpful. Later I came across a book on the Internet by Dong Fu, *Green Wheat Seedlings and Yellow Rape Flowers: A Record of the Great Leap Forward in Western Sichuan*. This excellent book is the basis for the following material on Wenjiang Prefecture, unless otherwise noted.
2. CCP Pi County Committee, "Summary of Chairman Mao's Remarks at Hongguang Collective in Hexing Town, Pi County," March 20, 1958.
3. Dong Fu, *Green Wheat Seedlings*.
4. Gao Yilu (Pi County first party secretary), "Preliminary Examination of the Losses Brought About by the Communist Wind," December 1, 1960.
5. Ibid.

6. Zhang Shouyu and Liu Jingzhou, "Report to the Provincial Party Committee on the Problems in Rong County," November 30, 1960.

7. Gao Yilu, "Preliminary Examination."

8. Sichuan Province Rural Work Department Investigation Group, "The Serious Loss of Farming Implements Caused by Indiscriminate Transfer of Resources in Baiyang Administrative District of Leshan County's Tongjiang Commune," January 5, 1961. The office of the rural work department printed forty-five copies, sending the master copy to the provincial party committee.

9. Leshan County Mianzhu Commune Working Group of the Provincial Party Committee Work Team, "Severe Loss in Productivity Brought About by the Chaotic Orders Issued by Cadres of the No. 2 Administrative District of Leshan's Mianzhu Commune," January 16, 1961.

10. Li Lin, "Situational Report of Chunhua Administrative District of Dianjiang County's Chengxi Commune," submitted to the provincial party committee and party secretary Liao, January 31, 1961.

11. Li Huaipei (first secretary of Chengdu's Jinniu Commune), "Regarding the Problem of Egalitarianism and Indiscriminate Transfer of Resources," speech given during the second stage of the second-term working conference of the Sichuan provincial party committee, December 1, 1960. Sichuan Provincial Party Committee Inspection Group, Yibin Subgroup, Jiang'an Work Team, "Situational Report on the Backwardness of Changning County's Taoping Commune (summary)," July 9, 1959.

12. "Comrade Li Jingquan's Remarks at the Provincial Party Committee Six-level Cadre Conference (notes)," March 11, 1959.

13. "Comrade [Li] Jingquan's Remarks at the Meeting of Municipal and Prefectural Party Secretaries on the Morning of November 7, 1959, at Panjiaping, Chongqing."

14. Dangdai Zhongguo Editorial Committee, *Modern China's Sichuan*, vol. 1, Beijing: Dangdai Zhongguo chubanshe, 1990, p. 94.

15. *Manuscripts by Mao Zedong Since the Founding of the State*, vol. 8, pp. 235–38.

16. TN: Tailism (*weibazhuyi*) is the term applied to abdicating the party's leadership of the masses and blindly following uninformed popular demand.

17. Li Rui, *A True Record of the Lushan Conference*, revised and expanded 3rd ed., Zhengzhou: Henan renmin chubanshe, 1999, p. 71.

18. CCP Central Committee Party Literature Research Center, ed., *A Selection of Important Historical Documents Since the Founding of the State*, vol. 12, Beijing: Zhongyang wenxian chubanshe, 1996, pp. 293, 294, 382–84.

19. Li Rui, *A True Record*, p. 72.

20. Ibid., p. 137.

21. "Minutes of the Meeting Called by Comrade [Li] Jingquan of the Party Secretaries of Fuling, Neijiang, Luzhou, Wenjiang, Mianyang, and Nanchong Prefectures," evening of February 14, 1960 (hereafter "Minutes of the Meeting Called by Comrade [Li] Jingquan").

22. Mianzhu Working Group of the Provincial Party Committee Inspection Group, "Report Regarding the Problem and Resolution of the Grain Shortage at Mianzhu's Hongqi Commune," March 9, 1959.

23. "Comrade Li Jingquan's Remarks at the Provincial Party Committee Six-level Cadre Conference (notes)."

24. Sichuan Provincial Party Committee Inspection Group, Yibin Subgroup, Jiang'an Work Team.

25. Yan Hongyan, "Report to the Provincial Party Committee and Comrade Dazhang Regarding Several Problems with Rural Work Learned of at Renshou," dispatches to the provincial party committee, receipt no. 4873. The office copied and sent the report on July 23, 1959, to "Comrades Mengxia, Cangbi, and Zhou Yi" and the committee office (three copies).

26. Mianyang Working Group of the Provincial Party Committee Rectification of Work Styles and Communes Work Team, "Materials Relating to the Transformation of the Backward Aspects of Mianyang's Shima Commune," January 12, 1961 (hereafter "Mianyang Working Group").

27. Li Lin, "Situational Report."

28. "Minutes of the Meeting Called by Comrade [Li] Jingquan."

29. Li Jingquan, "Remarks at the Second Conference of Prefectural Party Secretaries at Nanchong (notes)," March 26, 1960.

30. "Bulletin of the National Conference of Food Bureau Heads," February 9, 1960, Nanchong, Sichuan Province.

31. Fan Sui, "Reporting from Heaven's Pantry," in Xinhua News Agency Retired Cadres Department, ed., *Laonian shenghuo*, no. 4 (2006): 24. Fan Sui's figure for the grain shipped out is larger than the "requisition amount" provided by the Food Ministry in the official files. Perhaps the central government required Sichuan to provide additional quantities of grain after procurement quotas were met. It is also possible that Fan Sui's figures are for unprocessed food grain, as opposed to the figures for trade grain provided by the Food Ministry. One kilo of trade grain is equivalent to roughly 1.15–1.2 kilos of unprocessed grain.

32. *True Record of Important Events in Modern Sichuan*, 1st ed., Chengdu: Sichuan renmin chubanshe, November 2005, pp. 66–67.

33. Liang Qishan's letter to the provincial party committee and Wanxian prefectural party committee, September 26, 1960. The Sichuan provincial party committee office copied and distributed the letter on September 26, 1960, to all party secretaries, Comrade Shaofang, the rural work department, the secretary-general, and the secretariat (seventeen copies total).

34. Bishan County Party Committee, "Twelve Emergency Measures for Rapid Treatment of Edema," October 22, 1960, copied and distributed by the Bishan County party committee office on October 24, 1960.

35. Bishan County Party Committee, "Report on 1961 Prevention and Cure of Diseases and Views on Operations Hereafter," January 2, 1960, dispatches to the Sichuan provincial party committee, receipt no. [62]208, printed and distributed

by the Sichuan provincial party committee to secretaries Liao and Du and Secretary-general Zhou and the secretariat on January 11, 1962.

36. Mianyang Working Group.

37. Wenjiang Prefectural Party Committee Office, record of a telephone call from the Dayi County party committee office, April 25, 1960.

38. Guan County Party Committee Office, "Report to the Wenjiang Prefectural Party Committee Regarding Two Incidents of Unnatural Death," March 26, 1960.

39. Da County Work Team of the Provincial Party Committee Rectification of Work Styles and Communes Inspection Group, "Investigative Report Regarding the Eating of Guanyin Clay by the Masses in Parts of Qu County Due to Inadequate Living Arrangements," August 31, 1961. The Sichuan provincial party committee office on August 6, 1961, copied and distributed the report to party secretaries Liao, Xu, and Zhao, deputy secretary-general Zhou, the secretariat, the finance and trade department, and the organization department (a total of twelve copies).

40. Jiangjin Prefectural Party Committee, "Report on the Edema Situation," dispatches to the Sichuan provincial party committee, receipt no. [62]4171.

41. Ma Jiliang (Changshou County party committee work group), "Telephone Report Regarding Some Circumstances and Problems in Changshou County," January 25, 1962, dispatches to the Sichuan provincial party committee, receipt no. [62]519, printed by the committee office on January 25.

42. "Report by the Wanxian Prefectural Party Committee Office on Edema in the Countryside," January 15, 1962, dispatches to the Sichuan provincial party committee, receipt no. [62]295.

43. "Comrade Chen Guodong's Report to Vice-premier Li Xiannian," March 17, 1962.

44. Zhou Yi, "Situational Report on Xichang Prefecture," May 27, 1962.

45. Li Dingbang (Provincial Party Committee Office), "The Production and Livelihood Situation in the Ya'an Region," September 4, 1962, printed by the Sichuan provincial party office on September 5, 1962, to all party secretaries, the finance and trade department, and the committee office.

46. CCP Central Committee Propaganda Department, *Propaganda and Education Trends*, May 23, 1959.

47. *Manuscripts by Mao Zedong Since the Founding of the State*, vol. 9, p. 8.

48. Health Ministry Leading Communist Party Group, "Report on the Prevention and Treatment of Current Major Diseases," February 1, 1961.

49. Yang Wanxuan, "Report on the Situation of Drought and Edema in Changning County," August 9, 1959, in Nanxi, dispatches to the provincial party committee, receipt no. 5268.

50. Luzhou Prefectural Party Committee Office, "Report on the Disease Situation in Gulin County," December 7, 1959.

51. "Comrade [Li] Jingquan's Memo on the 'Luzhou Prefectural Party Committee Office Report on the Disease Situation in Gulin County,'" December 8, 1959.

52. "Luzhou Prefectural Party Committee's Written Comments and Transmission of the Situational Report by the Gulin Epidemic Investigation Working Group on the

Recent Situation of Disease and Death in Gulin," Sichuan provincial party committee 1960 first meeting of prefectural party secretaries, document no. 6.

53. Provincial Party Committee Office for the Eradication of Diseases and Pests, "The Working Group's Report on the Present Situation of Preventing and Curing Edema," January 18, 1961, Sichuan provincial party committee office, receipt no. 343.

54. Qiao Zhongling and Zhai Rong to the Provincial Party Committee and Neijiang Prefectural Party Committee, April 16, 1960.

55. Provincial Party Committee Office for the Eradication of Diseases and Pests, "Situation on the Prevention and Cure of Edema," March 7, 1961.

56. Ibid.

57. Wei Ping and Tan Wancai (Provincial Party Committee Office for the Eradication of Diseases and Pests), "Investigation Report on the Current Situation of Preventing and Treating Edema at Fuling County's Mingjia Commune," August 26, 1961.

58. Prefectural Party Committee Office for the Eradication of Diseases and Pests, "Briefing on the Investigation of Disease in Some Communes in Fuling and Wulong," August 12, 1961.

59. Li Dingbang, "The Production and Livelihood Situation in the Ya'an Region."

60. "Report by Comrade Zhou Yi on Scattered Circumstances in Xichang Prefecture," May 27, 1962, dispatches to the provincial party committee office, receipt no. [62]2290.

61. Dong Fu, *Green Wheat Seedlings*.

62. Wang Shuben's report to the Wenjiang prefectural party committee, December 13, 1960, as reported in Dong Fu, *Green Wheat Seedlings*.

63. Dong Fu, *Green Wheat Seedlings*.

64. Ibid.

65. Yibin Prefectural Party Committee Leading Committee for the Eradication of Diseases and Pests, "Report on the Development of Edema Throughout the Prefecture," July 5, 1961, dispatches to the Sichuan prefectural party committee office, receipt no. [61]4302.

66. Li Yin (Yibin Production Inspection Committee), "Empty Fields in Yibin's Anbian Commune," July 26, 1961, dispatches to the provincial party committee office, receipt no. [61]3597.

67. "Telephone Report of the Yibin Prefectural Party Committee Regarding the Current Treatment Situation," February 2, 1962.

68. Sichuan Provincial Party Committee Inspection Group, Yibin Subgroup, Jiang'an Work Team.

69. United Front Department of the Central Committee Work Group, "Survey of the Problem of Production Brigade and Production Team Cadres Taking More Than Their Share at Tuqiao Commune in Dazu County, Sichuan Province," August 24, 1962.

70. Li Lin, "To the Provincial Party Committee and Party Secretary Liao," January 31, 1961.

71. Dianjiang Working Group of the Provincial Party Committee Inspection Group, "Report on the Situation at Jiefeng Commune for Third-stage Rectification of Work

Styles and Communes Relating to the Recovery of Stolen and Embezzled Funds," April 8, 1961.

72. Dong Fu, *Green Wheat Seedlings*.

73. Liao Bokang, "An Eddy in the Long River of History: Recalling the 'Xiao, Li, Liao Incident,'" typescript no. 2, p. 27. Liao was a deputy director of Chongqing's municipal party office.

74. Provincial Party Committee Inspection Group, "Report on Several Serious Problems in Rong County," January 16, 1961, dispatches to the Sichuan provincial party committee office, receipt no. [62]313.

75. Gan Tang, Wang Shanqing, and Li Maoyun (Provincial Party Committee Inspection Group's Luzhou Investigation Subgroup), "Combined Report Regarding the Inspection of Production and Livelihood in Luzhou Prefecture"; "Report on Some Violations of Law and Discipline in Luzhou Prefecture," June 3, 1960.

76. Prefectural Party Committee Rectification of Work Styles and Communes, Wenjiang Work Team, "Report on Serious Violations of Law and Discipline by Cadres Uncovered During the Five-level Cadre Meeting in Jintang County," January 16, 1961, dispatches to the Sichuan provincial party office, receipt no. [61]447 (hereafter "Wenjiang Work Team").

77. Sichuan Provincial Party Committee Inspection Group, Yibin Subgroup, Jiang'an Work Team.

78. Qiao Zhimin, "Comrade Qiao Zhimin's Report Regarding the Rectification of Hechuan's Nanping Commune," November 29, 1960, the Sichuan provincial party committee office copied and distributed the report on December 2, 1960, to the members of the provincial party committee standing committee, secretary-general, and committee office.

79. "Comrade Fan Zhizhong's Report on Cadres Violating Law and Discipline at Hechuan County's Nanping Commune," November 13, 1960, dispatches to the provincial party committee office, receipt no. 7266; the Sichuan provincial party committee office copied and distributed the report on November 14, 1960, to all party secretaries, secretary-generals, and the leading party groups of the control commission and branch public security office.

80. Ibid.

81. Wenjiang Work Team.

82. "Comrade Wang Ziqing's October 3, 1960, Report to the Rural Work Department Regarding Some Problems in Rong County"; Zhang Shouyu and Liu Jingzhou, "Report to the Provincial Party Committee."

83. Liu Wenzhen, "Report on the Guiding Ideology for Rectification of Work Styles at the County-, District-, and Commune-level Party Committees of Jiangjin, Hechuan, Jiangbei, Yongchuan, and Rongchang," January 22, 1961.

84. Prefectural Party Committee Inspection Group, Fuling Subgroup, "Investigation Report Regarding Integrated Work at Ma'an Commune for Self-help Production and Economizing to Get Through the Famine and for the Launch of Disease Prevention and Cure," September 20, 1961.

85. Provincial Party Committee Agricultural Inspection Group, Jiangjin Subgroup, "Report to the Sichuan Provincial Party Committee," May 2, 1960.

86. "Comrade Liu Wenzhen's Telephone Report Regarding Serious Problems Discovered During an Inspection of Rural Communal Kitchens in Bishan County," January 6, 1961, dispatches to the Sichuan provincial party committee office, receipt no. [61]126; the office sent this report to all party secretaries, Comrade Jiangzhen, the secretary-general, the finance and trade department, Comrade Shaofang, the committee office, and the food bureau leading party group.

87. Prefectural Party Committee Inspection Group, Luzhou Subgroup, Xuyong Inspection Committee, "Report Regarding 'Output Quotas Assigned to Households and Work Points Based on Production' in Some Production Teams of Xuyong County's Tiantang Commune," August 4, 1959, Sichuan provincial archives office, file no. 1485.

88. An Faxiao (Provincial Party Committee Rectification and Production Inspection Group, Luzhou Subgroup), "Investigation Report Regarding Several Problems in Rectification and Consolidation Work at the People's Communes in Luzhou Prefecture," September 1, 1959.

89. Sichuan Provincial Party Committee, "Report on Circumstances Following the Jiangbei County Party Committee's Rectification of the Right-deviating Regressionist Error of Assigning Output Quotas to Households," September 19, 1961, [61.9], prefectural party committee party secretary conference document no. 000002.

90. CCP Central Committee Work Group, United Front Department Small Group, "The Situation of Output Quotas Assigned to Households in Xinglong District of Jiangbei County, Sichuan Province," in United Front Department, ed., *Situation Briefing*, no. 12 (August 28, 1962).

91. Pingshan County Party Committee Working Group, "The Experience of the Wuyi Production Brigade of Pingshan County's Qingliang Commune in Rectifying the Assignment of Output Quotas to Households," August 25, 1961; Mou Haixiu recommended this experience in a letter to Liao Zhigao on September 19. See [61.9], prefectural party committee party secretary conference document no. 000002.

92. "Comrade [Li] Jingquan's Transmission of the Resolution of the Eighth Plenum of the Eighth CCP Central Committee Regarding the Peng Dehuai Anti-Party Clique (notes)," morning of August 30, 1959.

93. Li Dazhang, "Speech at the Meeting of the Prefectural Party Committee Secretaries," Jinniuba, September 7, 1959.

94. Liao Bokang, "An Eddy in the Long River," p. 19.

95. Dispatches from the CCP Central Committee, receipt no. [59]807.

96. "Directives of the Sichuan Provincial Party Committee Regarding Resolutely Opposing Right-deviationist Thinking and Successfully Tiding Over the Famine by Increasing Production and Economizing on Grain," September 2, 1959, Sichuan party committee directive, no. [59]418. Printed and issued by the Sichuan provincial party committee office on September 3, 1959.

97. Ibid.

98. These figures do not include non-party cadres from Chengdu or figures from the counties in Luzhou and Liangshan prefectures.

99. "Sichuan Provincial Party Committee Office Telephone Report to the Central Committee Secretariat Regarding the Campaign Against Right Deviation at the Provincial, Prefectural, and County Levels," November 21, 1959. "Statistical Table of Key Individuals Targeted in the Campaign Against Right Deviation Among Party Cadres in District-level Government Agencies and Party Secretaries of People's Communes," Sichuan provincial party office, December 25, 1959. "Statistical Table of Key Individuals Targeted in the Campaign Against Right Deviation Among Party Cadres of Manufacturing and Mining Enterprises," Sichuan provincial party office, December 25, 1959. "Statistical Table of Key Party Cadres Targeted in the Campaign Against Right Deviation in Universities, Colleges, and Secondary Schools," Sichuan provincial party office, December 25, 1959. "Statistical Table of Key Non-Party Cadres Targeted in the Campaign Against Right Deviation in Manufacturing and Mining Enterprises," and "Statistical Table of Key Non-Party Cadres Targeted in the Campaign Against Right Deviation in Universities, Colleges, and Secondary Schools," Sichuan provincial party office, December 25, 1959.

100. CCP Central Committee Work Group, United Front Department Small Group, ed., *Situation Briefing*, no. 24 (October 13, 1962).

101. Ibid., no. 12 (August 28, 1962).

102. "Suggestions for Resolving Several Concrete Problems in the Reexamination of Cases (draft)," September 19, 1961. On September 21, Xu Mengxia submitted this draft to the prefectural party committee party secretary conference to solicit feedback [61.9], prefectural party committee party secretary conference document no. 16.

103. Liao Bokang, "An Eddy in the Long River."

104. Sichuan Provincial Planning Committee, "Analysis of Historical Grain Yields in Our Province (data)," July 25, 1962, printed by the Sichuan provincial party committee office, July 26, 1962.

105. "Situation in the Reduction in the Number of Pigs in Neijiang," *Rural Work Bulletin*, no. 83 (November 3, 1960).

106. Provincial Party Committee Work Group, "Problems at Xinfan County's Hetun Commune and Suggestions on How to Solve Them," March 1962.

107. Sichuan Provincial Public Security Bureau, CCP Qionglai County Committee Joint Task Force, "Initial Report on the Verified Facts Regarding the Serious Violations of Law and Discipline, Corruption, and Degeneration of the Accused Individual, Daozuo Commune Second Party Secretary Yang Shulou," December 6, 1960.

108. Wenjiang Prefectural Party Committee Work Group, "The Case of Pan Tingguang's Violation of Law and Discipline," December 1, 1960. Quoted in Dong Fu, *Green Wheat Seedlings*.

109. *True Record of Important Events in Modern Sichuan*, p. 156.

110. Dong Fu, *Green Wheat Seedlings*.

111. Liao Bokang, "An Eddy in the Long River."

112. "Comrade Wang Ziqing's October 3, 1960 Report."

113. CCP Pi County Committee, "Pi County Five-level Cadre Meeting to Discuss the Labor Force Problem."

114. CCP Chengdu Municipal Party Committee Party History Research Room, *CCP Wenjiang Prefecture Chronicle of Major Events*, Chengdu: Chengdu chubanshe, 1995.

115. Liu Hongkang, ed., *China Population: Sichuan*, Beijing: Zhongguo caizheng jingji chubanshe, 1988.

116. Dong Fu, *Green Wheat Seedlings*.

117. Liao Bokang, "An Eddy in the Long River," p. 35.

118. Ming Lang's January 1962 letter to the CCP Central Committee, in *Dangdai shi ziliao*, no. 2 (2006): 8.

119. Xiao Feng, "Sichuan's Situation," 1962. Quoted in Liao Bokang, "An Eddy in the Long River."

120. Cao Shuji, *The Great Famine*, p. 214.

121. Dong Fu, *Green Wheat Seedlings*.

7. THE RAVAGES OF THE FIVE WINDS

1. Li Rui, *A Personal Record*, vol. 2, p. 123.

2. TN: A Shanghai journalist and party propaganda chief who later became a member of the Gang of Four.

3. TN: Guan Feng, head of the philosophy group at the newly formed party journal *Red Flag*, would soon become the journal's deputy editor-in-chief, and later a member of the Central Cultural Revolution Small Group.

4. TN: Hu Sheng was a political theorist, party historian, and propagandist who went on to serve as president of the Chinese Academy of Social Sciences from 1985 to 1998.

5. Xushui County Party Committee, "Plan for Accelerating the Construction of Socialism to Forge Ahead to Communism (draft)," August 22, 1958.

6. Li Rui, *A Personal Record*, vol. 2, p. 34.

7. Mao Zedong, "Remarks on 'Shandong's Fan County Proposes Achieving the Transition to Communism in 1960,'" November 6, 1958, in *Manuscripts by Mao Zedong Since the Founding of the State*, vol. 7, p. 494.

8. Feng Youlin and Wei Huli, "The Communist Test of Paoma Commune in Dangyang, Hubei," *Chinese Communist Party History Research*, no. 4 (1998): 92–94.

9. CCP Liaoning Provincial Committee Work Group, "Summary of the Experimental Rectification of Tieling County's Fanhe Commune," December 15, 1960.

10. Mao Zedong, "Comments Written on the Final Draft of the Central Committee Resolution Regarding Problems in Establishing People's Communes in the Countryside," August 1958, in *Manuscripts by Mao Zedong Since the Founding of the State*, vol. 7, p. 360.

11. Mao Zedong's Speech to the First Zhengzhou Conference, November 6, 1958, in *Long Live Mao Zedong Thought (1958–1960)*, p. 143.

12. Mao Zedong's Speech to the Wuchang Conference, November 21, 1958, ibid.

13. Mao Zedong, "Annotations Regarding Problems in the Transition from Socialism to Full Collective Ownership," in *Manuscripts by Mao Zedong Since the Founding of the State,* vol. 8, p. 148.

14. CCP Central Committee Rural Work Department, *National Rural Work Department Heads Conference Bulletin,* no. 10 (January 22, 1959).

15. Ibid.

16. Modern China Series, *Modern China's Yunnan,* vol. 1, Beijing: Dangdai Zhongguo chubanshe, 1991, p. 142.

17. *China Situation Series: Jingning,* Beijing: Zhongguo dabaike quanshu chubanshe, 1992, p. 16.

18. *China Situation Series: Zhenning,* Beijing: Zhongguo dabaike quanshu chubanshe, 1993, pp. 397, 537.

19. Li Zhenzhen, "The Propaganda Department's Science Division During the Great Leap Forward: An Interview with Yu Guangyuan and Li Peishan," *Bainian chao,* no. 6 (1999): 23-30. TN: Yu Guangyuan was a genuine scientist, having obtained a degree in physics from Tsinghua University.

20. Ibid.

21. *Guangming ribao,* August 7, 1958.

22. *Guangming ribao,* September 11, 1958.

23. *Guangming ribao,* August 12, 1958.

24. Kang Jian, *Vanished Glory,* p. 275.

25. Lu Xun (1881-1936) and Guo Moruo (1892-1978) are leading lights in modern Chinese literature.

26. Xie Chuntao, *The Raging Waves of the Great Leap Forward,* Zhengzhou: Henan renmin chubanshe, 1990, p. 69.

27. Wei Junyi, "Burning Era, Burning Hearts," quoted in Zhang Zhanbin et al., eds., *The Great Leap Forward,* p. 143.

28. Quoted in Kang Jian, *Vanished Glory,* p. 189. TN: The translators regretfully affirm that the original Chinese is actually as bad as this.

29. Zhao Shengzhong, "The Formation and Consequences of a 'Leaping' Statistical System," *Twenty-first Century,* no. 60 (August 2000): 47-55.

30. Xue Muqiao, "Fight Hard for Three Months to Change the Face of China's Statistical Work and Implement a Great Leap Forward in National Statistical Work!," *Statistical Work,* no. 14 (1958): 3.

31. "Summary of Remarks by Director Jia Qiyun at the Conference of All Provincial and Municipal Statistical Bureau Heads," Jiangsu provincial archives, series no. 3133, vol. 2125.

32. "Record of Remarks by State Bureau of Statistics Director Xue Muqiao at the Henan Province Statistical Work Symposium," *Statistical Work,* no. 12 (1958).

33. Xue Muqiao, "How Statistical Work Can Leap Forward," *Statistical Work,* no. 5 (1958).

34. Xue Muqiao, *The Memoirs of Xue Muqiao,* Tianjin: Tianjin renmin chubanshe, 1996, p. 256.

35. "Counter Right Deviation, Encourage Enthusiasm, Work Hard to Strengthen the Party Spirit of Statistical Work!," summary of remarks by Director Jia Qiyun at the conference of all provincial and municipal statistical bureau heads, Jiangsu provincial archives, series no. 3133, vol. 2125.

36. Record of remarks by Mao Zedong at the enlarged Politburo meeting, in CCP Central Committee Party Literature Research Center, ed., *The Life of Mao Zedong, 1949–1976*, vol. 1, p. 1130.

37. Wang Jinglin, "Experiencing Hardship on the Road to Prosperity: The Development of the Paoziyan Agricultural Collective," *Historical Materials on China's Agriculture Cooperatives*, no. 2 (1998).

38. CCP Liaoning Provincial Committee Work Group, "Summary of the Experimental Rectification of Tieling County's Fanhe Commune," December 15, 1960.

39. "Investigation Report on the Situation of the 'Fourth Wind' in the No. 8 Production Brigade of Huaiyang City's Wuli Commune," November 16, 1960.

40. *Materials for Criticism*, p. 2.

41. Ibid., pp. 17, 18.

42. Huang Zheng, ed., *PRC President Liu Shaoqi*, vol. 2, Beijing: Zhonggong dangshi chubanshe, 1998, p. 1124.

43. Lu Tong and Feng Laigang, *Liu Shaoqi in the Twenty Years After the Founding of the PRC*, Shenyang: Liaoning renmin chubanshe, 2001, p. 221.

44. *Materials for Criticism*, pp. 33, 34, 37.

45. Kang Zhuo, "Comrade Liu Shaoqi at Xushui," *People's Daily*, September 8, 1958.

46. Xinhua News Agency, "Comrade Shaoqi Visits Jiangsu's Cities and Villages," *People's Daily*, September 30, 1958.

47. Ibid.

48. Ibid.

49. *Selected Writings of Deng Xiaoping*, vol. 2, Beijing: Renmin chubanshe, 1983, p. 260.

50. CCP Mianyang County Committee, "Summary of Mianyang County's First-stage Implementation of Policy," November 3, 1960, in Huang Daoxia et al., eds., *Compilation*, p. 620.

51. "Central Committee Directive on Correcting the 'Five Winds' Problem," November 15, 1960, in *Manuscripts by Mao Zedong Since the Founding of the State*, vol. 9, p. 352.

52. Mao Zedong, "Remarks Interposed While Being Debriefed at the CCP Central Committee Work Conference," December 30, 1960. This meeting was held in Beijing from December 24, 1960, to January 13, 1961.

53. Bo Yibo, *Looking Back*, vol. 2, p. 758.

8. ANXIOUS IN ANHUI

1. TN: *Lespedeza striata*, a bitter-tasting medicinal herb from the pea family known in English as Japan clover herb. In the United States, it is grown to feed livestock.

2. Zhao Yushu's self-criticism as a representative of the county party committee at the enlarged five-level cadre conference, January 7, 1960.

3. Comrade Ma Weiman's speech at the three-level cadre conference, "The Experience and Lessons of Fengyang County Over the Last Two Years," August 24, 1961.

4. Zhao Yushu's self-criticism.

5. CCP Fengyang County Committee, "Pilot Project Survey on Implementing the 'CCP Central Committee's Urgent Directives Regarding Current Policy Problems in the Rural People's Communes,'" November 24, 1960.

6. Zhao Yushu's self-criticism.

7. CCP Fengyang County Committee, "Pilot Project Survey."

8. Ibid.

9. Chen Zhenya (deputy director of Anhui's rural work department), "Report on the Fengyang Problem," February 1, 1961.

10. Zhao Yushu's self-criticism.

11. CCP Fengyang County Committee, "Pilot Project Survey."

12. Fengyang County Party Committee, "Brief Report on the Rectification of Work Styles and Communes," no. 16, March 14, 1961.

13. Ibid.

14. CCP Fengyang County Committee, "Pilot Project Survey."

15. *Bulletin of the Fengyang County Party Committee's Enlarged Five-level Cadre Conference*, no. 6, January 10, 1961.

16. Zhao Yushu's self-criticism; Ma Weimin's speech.

17. Guo Shutian et al., *China Out of Balance: Part 1: The Past, Present, and Future of Urbanization*, Shijiazhuang: Hebei renmin chubanshe, 1990, p. 19.

18. Zhang Wanshu, *The Laughter of My Hometown People*, Beijing: Xinhua chubanshe, 1986, pp. 29, 57.

19. Chen Zhenya, "Report on the Fengyang Problem."

20. *Bulletin of the Fengyang County Party Committee Enlarged Five-level Cadre Conference*, no. 4, January 8, 1961; no. 5, January 9, 1961; and no. 6, January 10, 1961.

21. Chen Zhenya, "Report on the Fengyang Problem."

22. Ibid.

23. *Bulletin of the Fengyang County Party Committee Enlarged Five-level Cadre Conference*, no. 6, January 10, 1961.

24. "Record of the Department Head Rectification Meeting," August 9, 1961.

25. Chen Zhenya, "Report on the Fengyang Problem."

26. Ibid.

27. Ibid.

28. Ibid.

29. Ibid.

30. *Bulletin of the Fengyang County Party Committee Enlarged Five-level Cadre Conference*, no. 5, January 9, 1961.

31. Ibid.

32. Wang Gengjin et al., eds., *Thirty Years in the Countryside: A True Record of Social*

and Economic Development in the Villages of Fengyang County (1949–1983), vol. 2, Beijing: Nongcun duwu chubanshe, 1989, pp. 162–64.

33. Ibid., p. 169.

34. CCP Fengyang County Committee, "Material Regarding the Anti-Party Crimes of Zhao Conghua," October 30, 1959.

35. CCP Fengyang County Committee, "The Launch of the Rectification of Work Styles in Fengyang County," December 8, 1959.

36. Chen Zhenya, "Report on the Fengyang Problem."

37. CCP Fengyang County Committee, "Pilot Project Survey."

38. Chen Zhenya, "Report on the Fengyang Problem."

39. CCP Fengyang County Committee, "Investigation Report Regarding Evildoers Holding Sway in Xiaoxihe Commune," February 10, 1961.

40. "Report of the Wudian Commune Party Committee Regarding Rectification of Work Styles and Communes," April 18, 1961.

41. Chen Zhenya, "Report on the Fengyang Problem."

42. "Supplementary Self-criticism by Comrade Zhao Yushu of the Fengyang County Party Committee at the Enlarged Five-level Cadre Conference," January 15, 1961.

43. Ibid.

44. CCP Fengyang County Committee, "Regarding the Situation of the Five Winds," November 7, 1961.

45. CCP Fengyang County Committee, "Investigation Report Regarding Evildoers."

46. Ibid.

47. Fengyang County Committee Investigation and Research Group, "Briefing Report on Work on the Three Includes and Four Fixes at Zhengfucheng Commune's Sifeng Production Brigade," nos. 1 and 2.

48. Information in this section is drawn from Ding Renbu, "Wuwei's Calamitous 'Communist' Dream," in Qiu Shi, ed., *Episodes of the Republic*, vol. 2, Beijing: Jingji ribao chubanshe, 1998; Xie Guiping, "The Great Leap Forward and Its Consequences in Wuwei County, Anhui Province," *Dangdai Zhongguo yanjiu*, no. 2 (2006): 118–27; Yang Jinsheng, "My Time of Melons and Vegetables," *Yanhuang chunqiu*, no. 7 (2002): 40–41; and Yu Naiyun, "Zhang Kaifan's Iron Soul and Poetic Spirit," *Yanhuang chunqiu*, no. 4 (1997): 50–53.

49. Ding Renbu, "Wuwei's Calamitous 'Communist' Dream."

50. Ibid.

51. Ibid.

52. TN: Ironically, Mao is referring here to a somewhat disreputable character in the classic *Water Margin*.

53. "Pulling Out the Roots of Capitalism's Spontaneous Power, Building a Ladder to Communism: Anhui's Xiangshan Commune Becomes the First to Implement a Rationing System," *People's Daily*, October 9, 1958, p. 3.

54. Ding Renbu, "Wuwei's Calamitous 'Communist' Dream."

55. Yang Jinsheng, "My Time of Melons and Vegetables."

56. Xie Guiping, "The Great Leap Forward and Its Consequences."

57. Ibid.

58. CCP Wuwei County Committee, "On the Implementation of the Central Committee's Twelve-point Urgent Directive," November 27, 1960.

59. "Dougou Commune's Summary Report Regarding the Launch of a Campaign Against Corruption, Waste, and Bureaucracy and a Rectification of Work Styles," July 18, 1960, transmitted by the Wuwei County party committee.

60. Yang Jinsheng, "My Time of Melons and Vegetables."

61. Ibid.

62. Ibid.

63. TN: Zhang Kaifan was secretary-general of Anhui's provincial party committee and the province's vice-governor. His heroic attempts to address the famine realistically will be detailed in the next section, "Zhang Kaifan's 'Big Ruckus in Wuwei.'"

64. TN: A common service provided to those who lacked the ability to write their own letters.

65. CCP Central Committee Party Literature Editorial Committee, ed., *Selected Letters of Zhou Enlai*, Beijing: Zhongyang wenxian chubanshe, 1998, p. 556.

66. Yu Naiyun, "Zhang Kaifan's Iron Backbone and Poetic Spirit," *Yanhuang chunqiu*, no. 4 (1997): 50–53.

67. Qiu Shi, ed., *Episodes of the Republic*, vol. 2, pp. 462–76.

68. TN: The allegations against the "military club" will be detailed in chapter 10.

69. The incident of the Gao Gang anti-party clique was explained to me by Gao Gang's private secretary, Zhao Jialiang. Gao Gang was a founder of the northern Shaanxi revolutionary base that had provided the Red Army with a crucial foothold during the Long March. After the PRC was established, Gao sided with Mao against Liu Shaoqi in promoting agricultural collectivization at the expense of consolidating the new democratic order. Mao began grooming Gao as a replacement for Liu, but when Gao came out openly against Liu and claimed Mao's backing, Mao found himself at a disadvantage. In 1954, Mao accused Gao Gang of forming an anti-party clique with Rao Shushi, who was head of the Central Committee's Organization Department. During the political infighting of what came to be known as the "Gao Rao Incident," Gao Gang killed himself.

70. *Manuscripts by Mao Zedong Since the Founding of the State*, vol. 8, pp. 431–32.

71. Wuwei County Annals Office, ed., *Wuwei County Annals*, Beijing: Shehui kexue wenxian chubanshe, 1993, pp. 342–43.

72. Xie Guiping, "The Great Leap Forward and Its Consequences."

73. Liang Zhiyuan, "The Revised Records of an Official of the Bo County Agricultural Satellite Experience," *Yanhuang chunqiu*, no. 1 (2003): 22–25; "The Serious Consequences of Bo County's State Monopoly for Purchasing and Marketing Grain," *Yanhuang chunqiu*, no. 7 (2003): 25–27; "Bo County's People's Congress, People's Committee, and People's Political Consultative Conference During the Great Leap Forward," *Yanhuang chunqiu*, no. 3 (2006): 18–21. In addition, Liang wrote "A Painful Historical Lesson: The True Record of Unnatural Deaths Among Bo

County's Rural Population," "Report on 'Special Cases': Cannibalism Heard of and Seen in Anhui's Bo County," and "The Campaign for Communist Kitchens in Anhui's Bo County." Edited versions of the last two were published in a highly restricted internal publication, *Chunqiu wencun*, but "A Painful Historical Lesson" has never been published in any form.

74. The content of this section is drawn from Liang Zhiyuan's "Report on 'Special Cases': Cannibalism Heard of and Seen in Anhui's Bo County," which was published in *Yanhuang chunqiu*'s internal circulation edition, *Chunqiu wencun*, in an edition of several dozen copies. Later an unknown person submitted the article to Hong Kong's *Open Magazine* (*Kaifang*), where it was published under the pseudonym "Beijing scholar Lu Ping" in October 2003.

75. "Chairman Mao in Anhui," *People's Daily*, October 4, 1958.

76. "Self-criticism by Comrade Cheng Guanghua Representing the Bengbu Municipal Party Committee (notes)," March 18, 1961.

77. Ibid.

78. "Is It a Grain Shortage Problem or an Ideological Problem?," *Economic News*, no. 9 (1959). *Economic News* is an internal publication of the State Planning Commission that provides mainly policy-related materials to the central leadership. This publication revealed a portion of the truth, but this particular article had an extremely deleterious effect.

79. Mao Zedong, "Remarks on the Current Problems Arising from Collective Ownership in the Countryside," in *Manuscripts of Mao Zedong Since the Founding of the State*, vol. 8, p. 80.

80. "Opinions and Requests to the Provincial Party Committee," *Bulletin of the Bengbu City 1961 Three-level Cadre Conference*.

81. Zeng Qingmei, "Situational Report Regarding a Portion of Cadres Violating Law and Discipline at Xiao County's Majing Commune," August 4, 1960.

82. Yin Shusheng, "How Public Security Work Was Carried Out During the Great Leap Forward," *Yanhuang chunqiu*, no. 1 (2010): 17–23. Before retiring, Yin Shusheng was the deputy bureau head in charge of everyday operations for the Anhui provincial public security bureau. He had previously worked in Qinghai Province, and provided information for this book regarding the situation in Qinghai during the Great Famine.

83. Ibid.

84. Zheng Yulin and Gao Benhua, eds., *China Population: Anhui*, Beijing: Zhongguo caizheng jingji chubanshe, 1987.

85. Li Jian's conversation with the author, April 2001.

86. Cao Shuji, *The Great Famine*, p. 66.

87. Yin Shusheng, "Original Records of Anhui's Special Cases," *Yanhuang chunqiu*, no. 10 (2009): 62–63.

88. From Wang Weizhi's contemporary notebooks, which Wang allowed the author to copy.

89. Yin Shusheng, "Original Records of Anhui's Special Cases," *Yanhuang chunqiu*, no. 10 (2009): 62–63. Provincial party secretary Zeng Xisheng circulated the report to

only a few party secretaries while ordering the public security bureau to destroy the original records. Yin Shusheng came across the report while editing the Anhui provincial public security annals.

90. Chen Zhenya, "Report on the Fengyang Problem."

91. Li Jian's conversation with the author in his home on the afternoon of April 9, 2001.

92. Fang Shi is an old leader and colleague of the author's, and he disclosed this incident in a conversation with him, May 1961.

93. Bengbu City Leading Group on Eradicating Disease, "Opinions Regarding Efforts to Eradicate Disease and Going Forward," November 17, 1961, document no. 20 for the enlarged meeting of the municipal party committee.

94. Li Jian's conversation with the author in his home on the afternoon of April 9, 2001. The following information regarding the Central Control Commission is drawn from this conversation.

95. Li Jian, "Situation Report on Edema, Blocking of Information, and Large-scale Disciplinary Actions Against Cadres in Anhui Province."

96. Zhang Suhua, *Crisis Point: The Beginning and End of the Seven Thousand Cadres Conference*, Beijing: Zhongguo qingnian chubanshe, 2006, pp. 235–37.

97. Unless otherwise noted, the information in this section is drawn from the following sources: Deng Liqun, ed., *Modern China Anhui*, Beijing: Dangdai Zhongguo chubanshe, 1992, in particular the section entitled "Systemic Reform of the Rural Economy"; CCP Anhui Provincial Party Committee Rural Policy Research Office, "The Whole Story of Anhui's Practice of Responsibility Fields," in *Historical Materials on China's Agricultural Collectivization*, no. 1 (1986): 7.

98. Portions of the section entitled "Systemic Reform of the Rural Economy" in Deng Liqun, ed., *Modern China Anhui* are quoted in *Historical Materials on China's Agricultural Collectivization*, no. 1 (1994): 36.

99. "A Letter from Comrade Zeng Xisheng to Mao Zedong and Other Comrades," in Huang Daoxia et al., eds., *Compilation*, p. 649.

100. CCP Anhui Provincial Committee, "Report on Anhui Province's Experiment with Assigning Work and Production Quota Responsibility," April 27, 1961.

101. "Central Committee Secretariat's Transmission of the Anhui Provincial Party Committee's Report Regarding Trial Implementation of Assigning Work and Production Responsibility," May 3, 1961, CCP Central Committee secretariat document [61]30.

9. THE FOOD CRISIS

1. *China Statistical Yearbook (1984)*, Beijing: Zhongguo tongji chubanshe, 1984, p. 81.

2. Bo Yibo, *Looking Back*, vol. 1, pp. 255–56.

3. Jiao Tong University Research Institute Investigation Report, "Grain Imports from Foreign Countries Prior to Liberation," 1954, Central Archives: 1954-180-2-54.

4. CCP Central Committee Documents Editorial Committee, ed., *Selected Writings of Chen Yun, 1949–1956*, Beijing: Renmin chubanshe, 1995, p. 208.

5. Huang Daoxia et al., eds., *Compilation*, pp. 231–32.

6. *Changde Prefecture Annals—Grain and Oil Trade*, Beijing: Zhongguo kexue jishu chubanshe, 1992, p. 32.

7. *Yunnan Province Annals—Grain and Oil*, Kunming: Yunnan renmin chubanshe, 1993, pp. 41–51.

8. *Dechang County Annals—Grain and Oil*, Chengdu: Sichuan renmin chubanshe, 1998, p. 615.

9. *Shizhu County Annals*, Chengdu: Sichuan cishu chubanshe, 1994, p. 449.

10. *Shaowu City Annals*, Beijing: Qunzhong chubanshe, 1993, pp. 1297–99.

11. *People's Daily* editorial, "Resolutely Wage Struggle Against Bureaucratism That Ignores Human Life," June 18, 1956.

12. "CCP Central Committee Directive on Going a Step Further in the Buying and Selling of Foodstuffs," CCP Central Committee document [58]104.

13. "Main Debate Points on the State Monopoly for Purchasing and Marketing Grain in Xiangxi Autonomous Prefecture," "Yiyang County Through Mass Debate Exceeds Procurement Quota for Early Rice," December 1957, Central Archives: 1957-180-5-72.

14. Shandong *Dazhong ribao*, October 20, 1957.

15. Central Committee's Transmission of General Office of the Central Committee, comp., "Brief Report on Food Shortages and Food Emergencies in Sixteen Provinces and Regions and the Solutions Proposed by the Local Party Committees," April 25, 1958, CCP Central Committee document, Zhongfa [58]333.

16. Mao Zedong, "Speech at the Chengdu Conference (3), March 20, 1958," in *Long Live Mao Zedong Thought, 1958–1960*, p. 36. TN: Mao elaborates on the unity of opposites and the law of contradiction in his essay "On Contradiction," an English translation of which can be found online at www.lastsuperpower.net/docs/mao-contradiction.

17. Qian Xuesen, "How High Will Grain Yields Be?," *China Youth News*, June 16, 1958, p. 4.

18. It is possible, of course, that Mao was trying to shrug off personal responsibility with a less-than-truthful reply, as Li Rui suggested to me in 2004.

19. Food Ministry leading Communist Party group report to the Central Committee, August 15, 1958, Central Archives: 1958-180-6-7.

20. Zhang Shufan, "The Xinyang Incident."

21. Wang Renzhong, "Chairman Mao in Hubei," *Qi-Yi zazhi*, no. 5 (1958).

22. "Central Committee's Approval of 'The Overall Situation, Problems, and Views Regarding Agricultural Production and the Rural People's Communes,' by Comrades Tan Zhenlin and Liao Luyan," in Huang Daoxia et al., eds., *Compilation*, p. 513.

23. Kang Zhuo, "Chairman Mao Arrives at Xushui," *People's Daily*, August 11, 1958.

24. "Comrade Liu Shaoqi Inspects the Cities and Villages of Jiangsu," *People's Daily*, September 30, 1958.

25. "Resolution on Several Issues Related to the People's Communes," in Huang Daoxia et al., eds., *Compilation*, p. 519.

26. Provincial and County Work Group Stationed in Qutang, "Situation Report on the Redress of Indiscriminate Transfer of Resources at the Huzhuang Production

Brigade of Qutang Commune," January 23, 1960, Jiangsu provincial archives: 3011-891.

27. "Tan Zhenlin's Speech to the Conference," February 12, 1960, "Reference Document 17 on the February 1960 National Conference of Finance and Trade Secretaries," Central Archives: 1960-180-3-3.

28. Xue Pangao, "The Lesson of Natural Science Research Blindly Following Political Orders—The Absurd Scientific Research Assignment on 'What to Do with Excess Food,'" *Yanhuang chunqiu*, no. 8 (1997): 24–26.

29. "Situational Report of the Hubei Provincial Party Committee Regarding the Enlarged Meeting of the Provincial Party Committee," in Huang Daoxia et al., eds., *Compilation*, p. 563.

30. It was eventually reported as 375 billion kilos, but two or three years later, the Food Ministry's figure was 199 billion kilos, and the figure provided by the State Statistical Bureau in the 1980s was 200 billion kilos. Only heaven knows what the actual amount was.

31. Materials for the 1959 National Conference of Food Bureau Heads, Central Archives: 1959-180-7-82.

32. Lin Qiang, "Natural Disaster or Man-made Disaster? Fujian's Great Leap Forward Campaign Revisited," *Fujian Party History Monthly*, no. 1 (2001): 25–28.

33. Zhang Yuebing, "Empty Fame Brings Genuine Disaster Through the 'First Among All Fields Under Heaven,'" *Yanhuang chunqiu*, no. 3 (1995): 31–33.

34. Food Ministry Leading Party Group, "Situation Report on the Current Purchase, Sale, and Allocation of Grain," Central Archives: 1958-180-6-3.

35. Bo Yibo, *Looking Back*, vol. 2, p. 714.

36. "Comrade Tan Zhenlin's Summing Up at the Wheat Symposium for Ten Provinces and Cities," minutes of February 21, 1959, printed and distributed by the CCP Shandong provincial party committee rural work department on February 26, 1959.

37. *Manuscripts by Mao Zedong Since the Founding of the State*, vol. 8, p. 53; Zhang Yubin et al., eds., *China in the Great Leap Forward and the Three Years of Hardship*, Beijing: China Commercial Press, 2001, p. 170.

38. Mao Zedong, "Speech at the Chengdu Conference, February 2, 1959," in *Long Live Mao Zedong Thought, 1958–1960*, p. 200.

39. *Fengdu County Annals*, Chengdu: Sichuan keji chubanshe, 1991, p. 31.

40. CCP Liaoning Provincial Committee Work Group, "Summary of the Experimental Rectification of Tieling County's Fanhe Commune," December 15, 1960, Jilin provincial archives: 1-212.

41. "Comrade Li Xiannian's Remarks During a Central Committee Telephone Conference," April 19, 1959. This document is available in the archives of Jilin, Jiangsu, Shandong, and Sichuan provinces.

42. Qian Xuesen, "Mechanics Issues in Agriculture," *Zhishi yu liliang*, nos. 8 and 9 (September 25, 1959).

43. Sha Qianli, "Fight Right Deviation, Go All Out, and Set Off a New Surge in the Red Flag Movement," November 2, 1959, Central Archives: 1959-180-7-20.

44. Mao Zedong, "The Grain Problem," in *Manuscripts by Mao Zedong Since the Founding of the State*, vol. 8, p. 336.

45. "Summary of Remarks by Comrade Li Xiannian During Two Central Committee Secretariat Telephone Conferences on October 15, 1959," Shandong provincial archives: AB1-02-510.

46. Food Ministry Leading Party Group, "Views Regarding the Current Food Supply Problem and Future Food Supply Work," November 27, 1959, Central Archives: 1959-180-7-20.

47. Niu Peicong and Chen Guodong, "Urgent Report on Food Supplies," July 12, 1960, Central Archives: 1960-180-8-1.

48. "Tan Zhenlin's Remarks During the National Telephone Conference," November 2, 1960, Central Archives: 1960-180-8-4.

49. Wang Minsan, "Tightrope-walking Days," *China Grain Economy*, no. 7 (2001): 10–12.

50. Conversation with veteran Xinhua Sichuan branch journalist Liu Zongtang in Chengdu on December 13, 2000.

51. PRC Food Ministry, "Outline of a Report on the Food Supply Problem," May 7, 1961.

52. Li Xiannian, "Speech to the Conference of Food and Commerce Bureau Heads," August 26, 1961, Central Archives: 1961-180-9-79.

53. National Finance and Trade Conference Office, "Talking Point Memo Prepared for Li Xiannian's Speech to the National Conference of Finance and Trade Secretaries," September 10, 1959, *Bulletin No. 1 of the National Finance and Trade Conference*, p. 7, Shandong provincial archives: AB1-02-511.

54. Wuhan University School of Medicine, ed., *Nutrition and Food Hygiene Studies*, Beijing: Renmin weisheng chubanshe, 1981, pp. 20–21.

55. Dalian Medical University Pathophysiology Teaching and Research Section, ed., *Pathophysiology*, Beijing: Renmin weisheng chubanshe, 1962, p. 154.

56. All-China Women's Federation, "Report on the First-stage Experience of Uterine Prolapse and Amenorrhea," February 2, 1961; Gansu Provincial Party Committee, "Gansu Provincial Party Committee's Transmission of Comrade Wang Feng's Report to the Chairman Regarding Problems in the Rural Communal Kitchens," May 9, 1961.

57. Dalian Medical University Pathophysiology Teaching and Research Section, ed., *Pathophysiology*, p. 159.

10. TURNAROUND IN LUSHAN

1. TN: Chen Duxiu, a leader of the May Fourth Movement and cofounder of the Chinese Communist Party, was forced out of the party in 1929 when he took the side of the Trotskyists in opposition to the Comintern. Zhang Guotao, another CCP founder, disagreed with Mao over strategy during the Long March, and his failure in a key battle led the Comintern to favor Mao. He was purged in 1937. Wang Ming, the leader of a Bolshevik faction within the CCP, was sidelined after leaving Yan'an to take charge of the Yangtze division, which was abolished in 1938. Mao targeted

Wang as a dogmatist during the party's 1942–45 "rectification." Bo Gu was another member of the Bolsheviks, and although he subsequently criticized Wang Ming, he never regained favor with Mao. Li Lisan, who led the CCP from 1928 to 1930, turned toward extremist calls for the revolution to be extended throughout the country, which became known as the "Li Lisan line" and led to his being marginalized and eventually purged.

2. Li Rui, *A True Record*, pp. 12–13.

3. This view was expressed by Mao's trusted lieutenant, Li Jingquan. For further details, see chapter 6, on Sichuan.

4. Wu Lengxi, *Remembering Chairman Mao*, pp. 134–36.

5. *Manuscripts by Mao Zedong Since the Founding of the State*, vol. 8, pp. 331–32.

6. Chen Qingquan and Song Guangwei, *The Biography of Lu Dingyi*, pp. 451–52.

7. CCP Central Committee Party Literature Research Center, ed., *The Life of Mao Zedong, 1949–1976*, vol. 2, p. 970.

8. Mao Zedong, "Speeches at the Lushan Conference," *Long Live Mao Zedong Thought, 1958–1960*, p. 239.

9. TN: Hai Rui was a Ming dynasty official who served as a model of integrity and honesty. His example was also cited prominently in the early 1960s, which inspired Wu Han to write the play *Hai Rui Dismissed from Office*. Yao Wenyuan's critique of this piece, published toward the end of 1965, is known as the blasting fuse of the Cultural Revolution.

10. Li Rui, *A Personal Record*, vol. 2, pp. 467–68.

11. Huang Kecheng, *The Autobiography of Huang Kecheng*, Beijing: Renmin chubanshe, 1994, p. 262.

12. *Manuscripts by Mao Zedong Since the Founding of the State*, vol. 8, pp. 342, 343, 346.

13. Huang Kecheng, *Autobiography*, p. 248.

14. Peng Dehuai, *Autobiography*, p. 265.

15. Huang Kecheng, *Autobiography*, p. 248.

16. Cheng Zhongyuan, "Zhang Wentian's Speeches," in Zhang Zhanbin et al., eds., *The Great Leap Forward*, pp. 247–48.

17. Cong Jin, *An Era of Twists and Turns*, Zhengzhou: Henan renmin chubanshe, 1989, pp. 198–200.

18. Li Rui's journal also recorded the time and content of these conversations. Li Rui, *A True Record*, p. 99.

19. Peng Dehuai, *Autobiography*, pp. 267–68.

20. Cong Jin, *An Era of Twists and Turns*, p. 203.

21. TN: Also known as Quemoy, the island of Jinmen, situated between mainland China and Taiwan, has, along with the island of Matsu, provoked a number of cross-Strait crises. The most recent instance occurred in August 1958, when Mao shelled the island to arouse a reaction from the United States that might persuade the Soviet Union to provide China with more weapons—an exercise from which Peng was excluded and which he apparently opposed. See Jung Chang and Jon Halliday, *Mao: The Unknown Story*, New York: Alfred A. Knopf, 2005, pp. 441–42. The Beijing gov-

ernment also put down a major uprising in Tibet in March 1959, following which the Dalai Lama sought political refuge in India.

22. Peng Dehuai, *Autobiography*, pp. 281–87.

23. Ibid., p. 276.

24. Wang Guangmei, Liu Yuan et al., *The Unknown Liu Shaoqi*, p. 135.

25. Li Weimin, "General Wan Yi at the Lushan Conference," *Yanhuang chunqiu*, no. 3 (1995): 17–20.

26. Huang Kecheng, *Autobiography*, p. 249.

27. Ibid., p. 250.

28. Li Rui, *A True Record*, pp. 110–12.

29. CCP Central Committee Party Literature Research Center, ed., *The Biography of Chen Yun*, vol. 2, Beijing: Zhongyang wenxian chubanshe, 2005, p. 1190.

30. Li Rui, *A True Record*, p. 73.

31. Roderick MacFarquhar has also suggested that Khrushchev's July 18 remarks provided Mao Zedong with a pretext to criticize Peng Dehuai (Roderick MacFarquhar, *The Origins of the Cultural Revolution* [Chinese edition], vol. 2, Beijing: Zhongguo shehui kexue chubanshe, 1990, pp. 204–206). The full text of Khrushchev's speech was not published in *Pravda* until July 21, however, and only that text contains criticism of the communes. China's *Internal Reference* (*Neibu cankao*) on July 27 contained an article on Khrushchev's comment, and Hu Qiaomu passed it to Mao on July 28. Mao then distributed it to the conference attendees on July 29. This means that Mao did not learn about Khrushchev's July 18 speech until after his own July 23 speech. Mao had Peng Dehuai's "Written Opinions" distributed on July 16, and began positioning himself for retaliation by reorganizing the conference and sending for reinforcements even before Khrushchev had made his speech.

32. CCP Central Committee Party Literature Research Center, ed., *The Biography of Chen Yun*, vol. 2, p. 1190.

33. Zhang Peisen, ed., *The Life and Times of Zhang Wentian*, vol. 2, Beijing: Zhonggong dangshi chubanshe, 2000, p. 1149. Here it is said that Hu Qiaomu's telephone call came "around this time," while Li Rui's *A True Record* clearly states that it occurred on the morning of July 21.

34. Roderick MacFarquhar has suggested Zhang Wentian was the chief strategist behind the criticism of the Three Red Banners at the Lushan Conference, with Peng Dehuai playing only a supporting role (MacFarquhar, *Origins of the Cultural Revolution*, vol. 2, p. 332). However, neither Li Rui nor Yao Liwen (Liu Shaoqi's secretary) concur with this assessment.

35. Zhang Peisen, ed., *The Life and Times of Zhang Wentian*, vol. 2, pp. 1149–50.

36. Bo Yibo, *Looking Back*, vol. 2, pp. 862–63.

37. Zhang Peisen, ed., *The Life and Times of Zhang Wentian*, vol. 2, p. 1148.

38. Ibid.

39. Ibid.

40. Ibid., pp. 1148–49.

41. Li Rui, *A True Record*, p. 129.

42. Wu Lengxi's recollections of the Lushan Conference, in CCP Central Committee Party Literature Research Center, ed., *The Life of Mao Zedong, 1949–1976*, vol. 2, p. 978.

43. Li Weimin, "General Wan Yi at the Lushan Conference."

44. Huang Kecheng, *Autobiography*, pp. 252–53.

45. Zhang Peisen, ed., *The Life and Times of Zhang Wentian*, vol. 2, p. 1151.

46. Peng Dehuai, *Autobiography*, p. 277.

47. The only currently available reliable account of the shift in attitude among senior officials before and after Mao spoke on July 23 is in Li Rui's *A True Record*, which is based on Li's conference notes. What follows relies heavily on this book, supplemented by other sources.

48. Li Rui, *A True Record*, p. 32.

49. Ibid., p. 67.

50. Ibid., p. 68.

51. Wang Guangmei, Liu Yuan et al., *The Unknown Liu Shaoqi*, p. 82.

52. Ibid., pp. 137–38.

53. Li Rui, *A True Record*, p. 207.

54. Huang Kecheng, *Autobiography*, p. 258.

55. Li Rui, *A True Record*, p. 253.

56. Ibid., pp. 351–52.

57. Deng Zihui's secretary was there at the time and related this matter to Liu Shaoqi's secretary, Yao Liwen. Forty years later, Yao Liwen told me.

58. Wang Guangmei, Liu Yuan et al., *The Unknown Liu Shaoqi*, p. 83.

59. Ibid., p. 85.

60. He Fang, *Notes on Party History: From the Zunyi Conference to the Yan'an Rectification*, vol. 1, Hong Kong: Liwen chubanshe, 2005, pp. 4–5.

61. Jin Chongji, ed., *The Biography of Zhou Enlai*, vol. 3, p. 1477.

62. Li Rui, *A True Record*, p. 58.

63. Ibid., p. 66.

64. Jin Chongji, ed., *The Biography of Zhou Enlai*, vol. 3, p. 1478.

65. Li Rui, *A True Record*, pp. 164–65.

66. TN: This interrogation by Zhou Enlai related by Li Rui clearly did not refer to Peng Dehuai's most recent visit to the Soviet Union, which was after Stalin's death, but to an earlier visit in which Zhou and Peng both took part.

67. Li Rui, *A True Record*, pp. 218–21.

68. Jin Chongji, ed., *The Biography of Zhou Enlai*, vol. 3, p. 1485.

69. TN: The quote comes from Sima Qian's *Historical Records*, "The Biography of Han Xin": "When the enemy kingdom has been broadened, the emperor's counselors die."

70. Li Rui, *A True Record*, pp. 32–33.

71. CCP Central Committee Party Literature Editorial Committee, ed., *Selected Works of Zhu De*, Beijing: Renmin chubanshe, 1983, p. 373.

72. Li Rui, *A True Record*, pp. 147–48.

73. Ibid., p. 160.
74. Ibid., p. 189.
75. Ibid., p. 218.
76. Ibid., p. 183.
77. Ibid., p. 187.
78. Ibid., p. 189.
79. Ibid., pp. 204–206.
80. Ibid., pp. 214–18.
81. Ibid., pp. 148–49.
82. Ibid., p. 149.
83. TN: *Xiucai*, a term for a "district-level entry scholar" under the imperial exam system, refers to someone beginning to make his way up the ranks of the bureaucracy through intellectual rather than military acumen. Mao's personal secretaries, such as Chen Boda, Hu Qiaomu, and Li Rui, enjoyed considerable influence with Mao in spite of their lack of party rank. However, their lack of revolutionary credentials and their dependence on Mao's capricious favor made them vulnerable to attack from other senior cadres. See Frederick C. Teiwes and Warren Sun, *China's Road to Disaster: Mao, Central Politicians, and Provincial Leaders*, Armonk, NY: M.E. Sharpe, 1999, p. 167.
84. Li Rui, *A True Record*, p. 153.
85. Ibid., p. 142.
86. Ibid., p. 154.
87. *Manuscripts by Mao Zedong Since the Founding of the State*, vol. 8, pp. 546–47.
88. Li Rui, *A True Record*, p. 30.
89. Ibid., p. 36.
90. Ibid., pp. 37–38.
91. Ibid., pp. 74–75.
92. Ibid., pp. 287–88.
93. Ibid., p. 153.
94. Ibid., p. 73.
95. Ibid., p. 239.
96. Huang Kecheng, *Autobiography*, p. 253; Li Rui, *A True Record*, p. 144.
97. Li Rui, *A True Record*, p. 239.
98. Huang Kecheng, *Autobiography*, p. 259; Li Rui, *A True Record*, p. 280.
99. Li Rui, *A True Record*, p. 251.
100. Peng Dehuai, *Autobiography*, p. 278; Li Rui, *A True Record*, pp. 171–72.
101. Cheng Zhongyuan, "Zhang Wentian's Speeches," p. 275.
102. Yang Difu, "Zhou Xiaozhou's Refusal to Criticize Peng Dehuai During the Lushan Conference," *Yanhuang chunqiu*, no. 1 (2001): 28–29.
103. Zhu Zheng, ed., *1957 New Hunan Journalists*, Changsha: Jinggang yinshuachang, 2002.
104. Huang Kecheng, *Autobiography*, p. 255.
105. Li Rui, *A True Record*.

106. Ibid., p. 185.

107. Ibid., p. 194.

108. TN: Literally a *wanyanshu*, or ten-thousand-word memorial, of the type previously written to the emperor.

109. Li Rui, *A True Record*, p. 196.

110. Ibid., pp. 196–97. TN: Mao's last remark compares Peng's trip to Eastern Europe to the pilgrims going to India to bring back the Buddhist sutras in *The Journey to the West*.

111. Record of Mao Zedong's Speech to the Eighth Plenary Session of the Eighth Central Committee of the CCP, August 2, 1959, in CCP Central Committee Party Literature Research Center, *The Life of Mao Zedong, 1949–1976*, vol. 2, pp. 991–93.

112. *Manuscripts by Mao Zedong Since the Founding of the State*, vol. 8, p. 399.

113. "Wang Renzhong's Journal," in CCP Central Committee Party Literature Research Center, ed., *The Life of Mao Zedong, 1949–1976*, vol. 2, p. 999.

114. Bo Yibo, *Looking Back*, vol. 2, p. 865.

115. *Manuscripts by Mao Zedong Since the Founding of the State*, vol. 8, pp. 431–32.

116. Ibid., pp. 447–48, 451–52.

117. Ibid., p. 488.

118. "Standards and Principles Approved by the Central Committee for Party Committees of Organs Directly Subordinate to the Central Committee and Party Committees of Central State Organs for Submitting Reports on the Rectification of Erring Comrades in the Course of the Campaign Against Right Deviation and for Identifying Right-deviating Opportunists," January 15, 1960.

119. Ibid.

120. "Materials Transmitted by the Central Committee Relating to the Right-deviationist Thinking and Activities of a Portion of High-level Cadres Exposed in the Provinces, Cities, and Districts," September 8, 1959.

121. "Central Committee Approves the Resolution of the Qinghai Provincial Party Committee Regarding the Errors of the Anti-Party Clique Led by Zhang Guosheng," October 14, 1959.

122. CCP Central Committee Memo on the "Report on the Situation of the Eleventh Session (enlarged) of the First Sichuan Provincial Party Committee," October 3, 1959.

123. Huang Daoxia et al., eds., *Compilation*, p. 573.

124. Ibid., pp. 573–74.

125. "Report by the Mianyang Prefectural Party Committee Regarding the Reform of Backward Societies and Teams in the Socialist Education Movement," January 8, 1960.

126. Hu Sheng, ed., *Seventy Years of the Chinese Communist Party*, Beijing: Zhonggong dangshi chubanshe, 1991, p. 367.

127. Deng Xiaoping, "Remarks at the Central Committee Working Conference." The figures were edited out of the version of this speech included in the *Selected Writings of Deng Xiaoping*.

128. Mao Zedong, "Mao Zedong's Remarks at the Central Committee Working Conference in Beijing," June 12, 1961.

11. CHINA'S POPULATION LOSS IN THE GREAT LEAP FORWARD

1. Li Ruojian, "Several Questions Regarding Population Loss After the Great Leap Forward," *Chinese Journal of Population Science*, no. 4 (1998): 41–45.

2. Ma Zhongyue, "County Party Secretary Wang Yongcheng During the Great Famine," *Yanhuang chunqiu*, no. 3 (2007): 43–45.

3. Zhou Boping's conversation with the author on September 25, 2003.

4. *China Statistical Yearbook (1984)*, Beijing: Zhongguo tongji chubanshe, 1984, p. 81.

5. Lin Qiang, "Natural Disaster or Man-made disaster?"

6. These different results were published in: Jiang Zhenghua and Li Nan, "A Correction of China's Population Trend Parameters," *Xi'an Jiaotong University Journal*, no. 3 (1986); "Methods and Results of Estimating China's Population Trends," *China Population Yearbook (1987)*, Beijing: Zhongguo tongji chubanshe, 1987; Yuan Yongxi, ed., *China Population: General Introduction*, Beijing: Zhongguo caizheng jingji chubanshe, 1991, p. 617.

7. Ding Shu, *Man-made Disaster*, Hong Kong: Nineties Monthly Press, 1996, Appendix: "How Many People Starved to Death During the Great Leap Forward?"

8. Jin Hui, "Memorandum on the 'Three-year Natural Disaster,'" *Society*, nos. 4–5 (1993): 13–22.

9. Jasper Becker, *Hungry Ghosts: Mao's Secret Famine*, New York: The Free Press, 1966, pp. 271–72. Published in a Chinese translation by Jiang Heping by Mirror Books (New York), 2005.

10. Cao Shuji, "Deaths in the Chinese Population 1959–1961 and Contributing Factors," *Chinese Journal Population Science*, no. 1 (2005): 16–30, 97.

11. *Compilation of PRC Population Statistical Data*, Beijing: Zhongguo caizheng jingji chubanshe, 1988, p. 268.

12. Xie Fuzhi, "Speech at the State Politics and Law Working Conference," October 19, 1962, Jilin provincial archives: 1:126.

12. THE OFFICIAL RESPONSE TO THE CRISIS

1. Ye Zilong, *The Memoirs of Ye Zilong*, Beijing: Zhongyang wenxian chubanshe, 2000, pp. 222–23.

2. These conferences included the First Zhengzhou Conference (November 2–10, 1958), the Wuchang Conference (November 21–27, 1958), the Sixth Plenum of the Eighth CCP Central Committee (November 28–December 10, 1958), the Second Zhengzhou Conference (February 27–March 5, 1959), and the enlarged Politburo meeting and Seventh Plenum of the Eighth CCP Central Committee (March 25–April 5, 1959).

3. Mao Zedong's second speech at the First Zhengzhou Conference, November 6, 1958, in *Long Live Mao Zedong Thought, 1958–1960*, p. 143.

4. Ibid., p. 152.

5. *Manuscripts by Mao Zedong Since the Founding of the State*, vol. 8, p. 8.

6. CCP Central Committee Party Literature Research Center, ed., *A Selection of Important Historical Documents Since the Founding of the State*, vol. 12, pp. 293, 294, 382–84.

7. Huang Daoxia et al., eds., *Compilation*, p. 573.

8. Ibid., p. 572.

9. "Minutes of the Symposium of the Party Secretaries of the Fuling, Neijiang, Luzhou, Wenjiang, Mianyang, and Nanchong Prefectural Party Committees Convened by Comrade Jingquan," February 14, 1960, evening.

10. Bo Yibo, *Looking Back*, vol. 2, p. 808.

11. Li Rui, *A Personal Record*, vol. 2, p. 346.

12. Bo Yibo, *Looking Back*, vol. 2, pp. 808–10.

13. Mao Zedong's speeches at the Zhengzhou Conference, November 2, 6, 7, 9, 1958, in *Long Live Mao Zedong Thought, 1958–1960*, pp. 141–46.

14. Li Rui, *A Personal Record*, vol. 2, p. 358.

15. Shu Tong, "My Self-examination," December 13, 1960, document for the enlarged meeting of the Shandong provincial party committee.

16. Tao Lujia, *Chairman Mao Taught Us to Be Provincial Party Secretaries*, Beijing: Zhongyang wenxian chubanshe, 1996, p. 76.

17. Internal party communiqué, April 29, 1959, in *Manuscripts by Mao Zedong Since the Founding of the State*, vol. 8, p. 235.

18. "CCP Central Committee's Urgent Memorandum Regarding the Current Policy Problems in the Rural People's Communes," November 3, 1960, in Huang Daoxia et al., eds., *Compilation*, pp. 613–17.

19. "CCP Central Committee's Remarks on Transmitting the Fourth Report of the Gansu Provincial Party Committee Regarding Implementation of the Central Committee's Urgent Directives," November 25, 1960, in *Manuscripts by Mao Zedong Since the Founding of the State*, vol. 9, pp. 364–65.

20. Mao Zedong's Speech to the Second Zhengzhou Conference, February 27, 1959, in *Long Live Mao Zedong Thought, 1958–1960*, pp. 200–201.

21. "Central Committee Directive Regarding Allocating Plots of Land for Private Cultivation to Facilitate Developing Pigs, Chickens, Geese, and Ducks," May 7, 1959, in Huang Daoxia et al., eds., *Compilation*, p. 568.

22. "Central Committee Directive Regarding Four Problems, Including Commune Members Privately Rearing Poultry and Livestock and Plots of Land Allocated for Private Cultivation," June 11, 1959, in Huang Daoxia et al., eds., *Compilation*, p. 568.

23. Office of the Jiangsu Provincial People's Committee, "A Survey of the Situation at Jinsha and Five Other Open Town Markets," July 15, 1962.

24. "Remarks on the Printing and Distribution of the Guangdong Provincial Party Committee's Materials on Correcting the Occurrence of Excessive Self-sufficiency in Agricultural By-products," August 1, 1959, *Manuscripts by Mao Zedong Since the Founding of the State*, vol. 8, pp. 395–96.

25. CCP Central Committee Rural Work Department, "The Situation and Problems with Implementing and Carrying Out the Sixty Provisions in All Localities," August 24, 1961.

26. Ling Zhijun, *History No Longer Wavers*, p. 84.

27. Ibid., p. 55.

28. "Central Committee's Transmission of the Jiangsu Provincial Party Committee's Notice Regarding Immediately Correcting the Assignment of Agricultural Work and Production to Households," October 13, 1959.

29. CCP Central Committee Transmission of the September 29, 1959, "Henan Provincial Party Committee Report Regarding Several Typical Materials," October 12, 1959.

30. Leading Party Group of the Ministry of Agriculture, "Report on Agricultural Trends Since the Lushan Conference," transmitted by the CCP Central Committee on October 15, 1959.

31. *Manuscripts by Mao Zedong Since the Founding of the State*, vol. 8, p. 555.

32. CCP Central Committee Documents Editorial Committee, ed., *Selected Writings of Chen Yun, 1956–1985*, p. 159.

33. Ibid., p. 160.

34. Ibid., p. 151.

35. Jilin Province Annals Compilation Committee, *Jilin Annals*, Changchun: Jilin renmin chubanshe, 1998, p. 206.

36. Henan Province Annals Compilation Committee, *Henan Annals*, Zhengzhou: Henan renmin chubanshe, 1991, p. 57.

37. Hu Huanyong, ed., *China Population: Shanghai*, Beijing: Zhongguo caizheng jingji chubanshe, 1987, p. 143.

38. Qiqihar Annals Compilation Committee, *Qiqihar Annals* (draft), internally printed and distributed, 1994, p. 124.

39. (Bengbu) Municipal Party Committee Leading Group for Reducing the Urban Population, "Suggestions Regarding Efforts to Further Reduce the Urban Population and Cut Down Staffing," November 17, 1961.

40. "Briefing Paper by the Changzhou Municipal Party Committee Regarding Mass Disturbances Occurring During Retrenchment at the Daming Textile Factory," June 10, 1962.

41. Feng Tongqing, "Genuinely Surprised, But Hoping for No Danger," *Human Resource Development of China*, no. 1 (1995): 10–14.

42. "Remarks on the Situation Report on Central Organs Transferring 10,000 Cadres to Grassroots Units," November 15, 1960, in *Manuscripts by Mao Zedong Since the Founding of the State*, vol. 9, pp. 349–50.

43. "Central Committee's Directive Regarding the Serious Situation Occurring in Some Prefectures of Shandong, Henan, Gansu, and Guizhou," December 8, 1960.

44. "Remarks Regarding Solving the Spring Famine Food Shortage Problem," April 17, 1959, in *Manuscripts by Mao Zedong Since the Founding of the State*, vol. 8, p. 209.

45. "Report by the Ministry of Internal Affairs Regarding Improvements in the Spring Famine Following Reinforced Effort in All Localities," April 23, 1959.

46. CCP Central Committee Party Literature Research Center, ed., *The Life of Mao Zedong, 1949–1976*, vol. 2, p. 939.

47. "Remarks on the Investigation Materials of the Central Committee Organization Department and the Central Control Commission Regarding the Xinyang Problem," October 26, 1960, in *Manuscripts by Mao Zedong Since the Founding of the State*, vol. 9, p. 326.

48. "Central Committee's Transmission of the Food Ministry's Report on Increasing the State Grain Reserves to Fifty Billion Kilos Within Three Years," January 26, 1969.

49. *China Statistical Yearbook (1984)*, p. 141.

50. Comrade Li Xiannian's remarks during the Central Committee telephone conference on April 19, 1959.

51. "Material Relating to Several Problems in Finance and Trade Work," Appendix 3 of "Report of the Jiangjin Group of the Provincial Party Committee's Agricultural Inspection Party," May 3, 1960, pp. 56–59.

52. Leading Party Group of the Commerce Department, "Report on the Situation in Fulfilling the 1959 Export Plan," January 8, 1960 (60), *Documents of the Shanghai Conference*, no. 97.

53. CCP Central Committee Party Literature Research Center, ed., *The Life of Mao Zedong 1949–1976*, vol. 2, p. 1044.

54. Ibid., p. 1045.

55. Liu Shaoqi, "The Causes and Ways of Surmounting the Present Economic Difficulties," May 31, 1961, in Central Committee Documents Editorial Committee, ed., *Selected Works of Liu Shaoqi*, vol. 2, p. 337.

56. See chapter 15 in this book.

57. *Anthology of Important Documents since the Third Plenary Session of the Central Committee*, vol. 2, Beijing: Renmin chubanshe, 1982, pp. 754–55.

58. Gao Suhua, ed., *China Atlas of Agriculture, Climate, and Natural Resources and Major Changes in Crop Yield*, Beijing: Qixiang chubanshe, 1993.

59. State Science and Technology Commission, State Planning Commission, and State Commission for Economics and Trade Joint Research Group on Natural Calamity, eds., *Progress Report on the Regional Study of China's Natural Disasters*, Beijing: Haiyang chubanshe, 1998, p. 44.

60. *PLA Daily*, August 13, 1981.

61. Ibid.

62. Wu Lengxi, *The Ten-year Debate: A Memoir of Sino-Soviet Relations*, vol. 1, Beijing: Zhongyang wenxian chubanshe, 1999, pp. 336–37.

63. Zhou Enlai, "Government Work Report," *People's Daily*, December 31, 1964.

64. Sun Haiguang and Qiu Lu, "Investigation Report Regarding the Supply Situation in the Suzhou Municipal Nonstaple Food Market," November 4, 1960.

65. CCP Central Commission for Discipline Inspection, ed., "Chronicle of the Central Commission for Discipline Inspection," CCP Central Committee documents, issued [60] no. 1036.

66. When I visited Dishuidong in 1995 to copy down the materials set down here, my guide also mentioned this.

67. Hu Qiaomu's Letter to Mao Zedong dated April 14, 1961, "Central Committee Transmission of Several Important Documents with Memos from the Chairman," April 26, 1961, dispatches from the CCP Central Committee documents, receipt no. [61]323 *mao*.

68. "I was Chairman Mao's Chef," recounted orally by Su Linda, transcribed by Zhao Guang; circumstances of the original publication unclear, circulated on the Internet.

69. Gu Jun, "Chinese People First Taste Western Food," *China Reading Weekly*, May 24, 2000.

70. He Fang, *Notes on Party History*, vol. 1, p. 101. He Fang's text notes that he drew this information from *The Archive of Mao Zedong's Life*, vol. 2, Beijing: Zhonggong dangshi chubanshe, 1999, p. 701.

71. Shuai Hao, *Wine as God: A Chronicle of Maotai During China's Great Famine*, published online.

72. Zhou Mengsheng, "The Maotai Distillery, Yesterday and Today," in Renhuai Political Consulative Conference and Municipal Party Committee, ed., *Renhuai Historical Materials*, vol. 6, pp. 75, 76.

73. TN: Luo Longji provides the incorrect year of publication for *Das Kapital*, the first volume of which was not published until 1867.

74. "Recent Reactionary Remarks by Luo Longji Regarding Problems in the Supply of Goods," "Luo Longji Improperly Claims That the Present Shortage in the Supply of Goods Was Created by the Socialist System." Mao had these reports distributed at the Lushan Conference on July 19, 1959.

13. SOCIAL STABILITY DURING THE GREAT FAMINE

1. "Central Committee Northwest Bureau Transmission with Instructions: Severe Handling of Behavior in Violation of Food Policies in Shaanxi, Gansu, Xinjiang, and Other Provinces and Regions," December 19, 1960, Central Committee Northwest bureau document, issued [60]16.12.

2. Modern Yunnan Editorial Committee, *Summary of Major Events in Modern Yunnan*, Beijing: Dangdai Zhongguo chubanshe, 1996, p. 168.

3. This document is held in the Yunnan provincial archives, category 2, catalogue 1, file no. 2401.

4. Ibid., file no. 2402.

5. Ibid.

6. "Report Regarding Disturbances Among Funing's Yao Minority." This document is held in the Yunnan provincial archives, category 2, catalogue 1, file no. 2296.

7. Wenshan CCP Prefectural Committee, "Report Regarding Ethnic Disturbances in Funing County," October 7, 1956, held in the Yunnan provincial archives, category 2, catalogue 1, file no. 2296.

8. The record of this telephone call by the Lijiang public security bureau is held in the Yunnan provincial archives, category 2, catalogue 1, file no. 2402.

9. This document is held in the Yunnan provincial archives, category 2, catalogue 1, file no. 3331.

10. "Situational Report of the Zhaotong Prefectural Party Committee Regarding the Riot in the Zhaolu Integrated Area." This document is held in the Yunnan provincial archives, category 2, catalogue 1, file no. 3348.

11. Luquan Yizu, *Annals of Luquan Yi and Miao Autonomous County*, Kunming: Yunnan renmin chubanshe, 1995, p. 26.

12. This document is held in the Yunnan provincial archives, category 2, catalogue 1, file no. 3946.

13. "Investigation Report on the Xuanwei Counterrevolutionary Rebellion," November 30, 1960. This document is held in the Yunnan provincial archives, category 2, catalogue 1, file no. 4108.

14. "Comrade Xie Fuzhi's Report to the Premier and [Li] Fuchun Regarding the Counterrevolutionary Rebellion and Food Supply Situation in Xuanwei, Yunnan," December 2, 1960, Yunnan provincial archives, category 2, catalogue 1, file no. 4105.

15. Comprehensive collections of these annals are held in China's National Library and in the Chinese University of Hong Kong's Universities Service Centre for China Studies.

16. *Heqing County Annals*, Kunming: Yunnan renmin chubanshe, 1991, p. 23.

17. *Mouding County Annals*, Kunming: Yunnan renmin chubanshe, 1993, p. 23.

18. *Jianshui County Annals*, Beijing: Zhonghua shuju chubanshe, 1994, p. 27.

19. *Nanhua County Annals*, Kunming: Yunnan renmin chubanshe, 1995, pp. 483–84.

20. *Simao Prefecture Annals*, Kunming: Yunnan minzu chubanshe, 1996, pp. 34–38.

21. *Qinghai Provincial Annals: Public Security*, Hefei: Huangshan shushe, 1994, p. 10.

22. *Qinghai Provincial Annals: Military*, Xining: Qinghai renmin chubanshe, 2001, p. 524.

23. *Haixi Prefecture Annals*, Xi'an: Shaanxi renmin chubanshe, 1995, pp. 41, 45.

24. *Gannan Prefecture Annals*, vol. 1, Beijing: Minzu chubanshe, 1999, p. 100.

25. *Linxia Hui Autonomous Prefecture Annals*, vol. 1, Lanzhou: Gansu renmin chubanshe, 1993, p. 52.

26. *Jingchuan County Annals*, Lanzhou: Gansu renmin chubanshe, 1996, p. 40.

27. *Jiayuguan City Annals*, Lanzhou: Gansu renmin chubanshe, 1990, p. 5.

28. *Rongchang County Annals*, Chengdu: Sichuan renmin chubanshe, 2000, p. 245.

29. Sichuan Provincial Public Security Bureau, ed., *Sichuan Province Public Security Annals*, Chengdu: Sichuan renmin chubanshe, July 1995, p. 54.

30. *Jianhe County Annals*, Guiyang: Guizhou renmin chubanshe, 1994, p. 245.

31. *Dianjiang County Annals*, Chengdu: Sichuan renmin chubanshe, 1993, p. 31.

32. *Aba Prefecture Annals*, Beijing: Minzu chubanshe, 1994, p. 771.

33. *Annals of Qiandongnan Miao and Dong Autonomous Prefecture: Public Security*, Guiyang: Guizhou renmin chubanshe, 1992, pp. 91–92.

34. Zheng Yi, "The Tragedy of the Countryside During the Great Leap Forward—An Outline of the Jiangkou Incident," *Zheng Ming* (Hong Kong), January 1993.

35. *Baise County Annals*, Nanning: Guangxi renmin chubanshe, 1993, p. 16.

36. *Yuexi County Annals*, Hefei: Huangshan shushe, 1996, p. 37.

37. *Baokang County Annals*, Beijing: Zhongguo shijieyu chubanshe, 1991, p. 684.

38. *Hebei Provincial Annals*, vol. 71, *Public Security*, Beijing: Zhonghua shuju chubanshe, 1993, pp. 34–35.

39. *Hunan Provincial Annals*, vol. 6, *Politics and Law Annals: Public Security*, Changsha: Hunan chubanshe, 1997, pp. 139–40.

40. *Jilin Provincial Annals*, vol. 12, *Public Security and Judicial Annals: Public Security*, Changchun: Jilin renmin chubanshe, 1998, p. 170.

41. *Lian County Annals*, Guangzhou: Guangdong renmin chubanshe, 1985, p. 452; *Liannan Yao Minority Autonomous County Annals*, Guangzhou: Guangdong renmin chubanshe, 1996, pp. 33, 34, 530.

42. *Wengyuan County Annals*, Guangzhou: Guangdong renmin chubanshe, 1997, pp. 39–42.

43. *Tonghai County Annals*, Kunming: Yunnan renmin chubanshe, 1992, p. 19.

44. *Yunnan Provincial Annals*, vol. 8, Kunming: Yunnan renmin chubanshe, 1995, p. 330. Further details are provided in the chapter on Yunnan in the Chinese edition of this book.

45. Telegram from the Zhangye prefectural party committee to the Gansu provincial party committee, January 7, 1961, dispatch to the Gansu provincial party committee office, receipt no. [61]2060.

46. CCP Jiuquan Municipal Party Committee, "Investigation Report Regarding the Flour Mill Wrongfully Firing Shots at Masses Stealing Grain," January 11 and 14, 1961, dispatch to the Gansu provincial party committee office, receipt no. [61]2060, [61]2189.

47. Provincial Party Committee Tianshui Work Group, Tianshui Prefectural Party Committee, "Report by the Provincial Party Committee Tianshui Work Group and the Tianshui Prefectural Party Committee Regarding Efforts to Protect the Safety of Railway Transport," January 23, 1961, dispatch to the Gansu provincial party committee office, receipt no. [61]2381.

48. *Gansu Provincial Annals*, vol. 2, Lanzhou: Gansu renmin chubanshe, 1989, p. 403.

49. *Zhangye City Annals*, Lanzhou: Gansu renmin chubanshe, 1995, p. 29; *Anxi County Annals*, Beijing: Zhishi chubanshe, 1992, p. 27.

50. *Anhui Provincial Annals: Public Security*, Hefei: Anhui renmin chubanshe, 1993, p. 238.

51. *Leishan County Annals*, Guiyang: Guizhou renmin chubanshe, 1992, p. 26.

52. *Liping County Annals*, Chengdu: Bashu shushe, 1989, p. 35.

53. *Chaozhou City Annals*, Guangzhou: Guangdong renmin chubanshe, 1995, p. 115.

54. Zhang Guangqin, "Report Regarding the Public Security Situation and Disorder in the Countryside," January 12, 1961, dispatch to the Sichuan provincial party committee office, receipt no. (61)214.

55. *Minqin County Annals*, Lanzhou: Lanzhou daxue chubanshe, 1994, p. 544.

56. Xu Zirong, "Statistical Report on Key Figures Since the Campaign to Suppress Counterrevolutionaries," January 14, 1954.

57. "CCP Jilin Provincial Committee Transmission with Instructions: Situational Report by the Leading Party Group of the Provincial People's Procuratorate Regarding Arrests of Criminals Throughout the Province in 1959," April 4, 1960.

58. Yin Shusheng, "How the Great Leap Forward in Public Security Work Was Launched," *Yanhuang chunqiu*, no. 1 (2010): 17–23.

59. Ibid.

60. Yin Shusheng, "Original Records of Anhui's Special Cases," *Yanhuang chunqiu*, no. 10 (2009): 62–63.

61. Jilin Province Politics and Law Coordination Office, "Opinions Regarding the Basic Situation in the Battle and Future Work (draft)," August 10, 1959.

62. CCP Jilin provincial committee's reply to the report by the leading party group of the Jilin provincial politics and law committee, July 19, 1960.

63. *Tianchang County Annals*, Beijing: Shehui kexue chubanshe, 1992, p. 149.

64. *Chuxiong Yizu Autonomous Prefecture Annals*, vol. 2, Kunming: Yunnan renmin chubanshe, 1993, pp. 204–32.

65. "Summary Remarks by Comrade Cui Cifeng at the Seminar for the Provincewide Unified Action to Attack Theft and Profiteering Activities," January 10, 1962.

66. *Chongqing County Annals*, Chengdu: Sichuan renmin chubanshe, 1991, p. 362.

67. *Dianjiang County Annals*, Chengdu: Sichuan renmin chubanshe, 1993, p. 216.

68. "Comrade Xu Shoushen's Remarks During the Telephone Conference Convened by the Provincial Party Committee Regarding Rectifying Public Security and Order in the Cities," November 2, 1961, printed and distributed by the CCP Jilin provincial committee office on November 6, 1961.

14. THE SYSTEMIC CAUSES OF THE GREAT FAMINE

1. Guo Moruo, *Ten Critiques*, Dongbei: Qunyi chubanshe, 1947. Subsequently included in *The Collected Works of Guo Moruo, Historical Works*, vol. 2, Beijing: Dongfang chubanshe, March 1996; also reissued as an independent volume.

2. This poem was circulated verbally. In 1974, during the campaign to "Criticize Lin Biao and Confucius," I heard a formal transmission of this poem at the Tianjin branch of the Xinhua News Agency. I have not seen it openly published to date.

TN: This poem includes a number of historical allusions. In particular, the "business of burning and burying" refers to China's first emperor Qin Shihuang's burning of books and burying of scholars alive; the "ancient dragon" refers to Qin Shihuang; the *Discourse on Feudalism* was written by Liu Zongyuan (773–819, courtesy name Zihou, of the Tang dynasty), who debunked the sacred character of feudalism and endorsed a system of prefectures and counties adopted by Qin Shihuang; Wen Wang (1152–1056 B.C.E.), the father of Zhou dynasty founder Wu Wang, implemented a relatively comprehensive feudalistic system in China.

3. Liu Zehua, *Chinese Monarchism*, Shanghai: Shanghai renmin chubanshe, October 2000, Introduction, p. 3.

4. F. A. Hayek, *The Road to Serfdom*, vol. 2, in *The Collected Works of F. A. Hayek*, Chi-

cago: University of Chicago Press, 2007, p. 60; published in a Chinese translation, by Wang Mingyi and Feng Xingyuan, by Beijing's Zhongguo shehui kexue chubanshe, 1997, pp. 13–14.

5. TN: 1935–47, the period following the end of the Long March, when the remnants of the Communist Party and the Red Army stopped in Yan'an, Shaanxi Province, for a time, then consolidated Mao's personal rule and refined their policies and party mythos.

6. Li Rui, who had once served as Mao Zedong's personal secretary, recounted this incident in my presence during an informal conversation in 2000.

7. "Comrade Chen Youqun's November 14 speech," *Bulletin of Discussions by Organs and the Central Jurisdiction on the Historical Resolutions (draft)*, vol. 5, no. 32 [215], November 17, 1980. I read an original copy of this briefing paper in the home of Li Rui, who was deputy director of the Central Committee Organization Department at that time.

8. Richard M. Nixon, *RN: The Memoirs of Richard Nixon*, New York: Grosset & Dunlap, 1978. TN: This quote is translated from the Chinese edition, published by Commercial Press, 1979, vol. 2, p. 246.

9. Hayek, *The Road to Serfdom*, p. 59. TN: English edition, p. 100.

10. A typical example was the iron- and steel-forging campaign, which Mao launched after leading a delegation to the Soviet Union in November 1957 and hearing that Khrushchev planned for the Soviet Union to overtake the United States in fifteen years.

11. Social Survey Institute of China, *Report on National Conditions in China*, Shenyang: Liaoning renmin chubanshe, 1990, p. 1084.

12. Xiao Shu, ed., *The Harbinger of History: The Solemn Promise Half a Century Ago*, Shantou: Shantou daxue chubanshe, 1988.

13. Website of the standing committee of the Beijing Municipal People's Congress, www.bjrd.gov.cn/, February 27, 2007. Originally published on the website of the National People's Congress, www.npc.gov.cn/.

14. *Selected Works of Mao Zedong*, vol. 2, Beijing: Renmin chubanshe, 1967, p. 637.

15. TN: A legalist philosopher of the third century B.C.E.

16. Mao Zedong, "Speech at the Enlarged Politburo Meeting at Beidaihe," in *Long Live Mao Zedong Thought, 1958–1960*, p. 109; *Study Materials (1)*, Beijing: Tsinghua University, 1967, p. 140.

17. TN: Plato, *The Laws*, quoted in Karl R. Popper, *The Open Society and Its Enemies*, vol. 1, *Plato*, 1945. The author quotes the Chinese translation by Zheng Yiming, published by Beijing's Zhongguo shehui kexue chubanshe, August 1999, p. 203. In English, Popper's exact quote from Plato runs as follows: "All men are moulded to be unanimous in the utmost degree in bestowing praise and blame, and they even rejoice and grieve about the same things, and at the same time," Princeton University Press, paperback printing, 1971, pp. 101–102.

18. TN: Liang Shuming (1893–1988) drew fame and repeated persecution for disagreeing with Mao's agricultural policies and protesting the suffering of peasants under

PRC rule. Chen Yinque (1890–1969, sometimes also spelled Chen Yinke) was a foreign-educated historian who maintained a distance from the Communist Party at the expense of his academic career.

19. *Manuscripts by Mao Zedong Since the Founding of the State*, vol. 9, pp. 44–46, 62–63, 64–65, 68, 73–75.

20. Ye Zilong, *The Memoirs of Ye Zilong*, p. 219.

21. Ibid., p. 220.

22. Ibid., p. 258.

23. Ibid., p. 221.

15. THE GREAT FAMINE'S IMPACT ON CHINESE POLITICS

1. Zhang Suhua, *Crisis Point*, pp. 46–47.

2. Ibid., p. 99.

3. *The Journal of Yang Shangkun*, vol. 2, Beijing: Zhongyang wenxian chubanshe, September 2001, p. 110.

4. Zhang Suhua, *Crisis Point*, p. 75.

5. Bo Yibo, *Looking Back,* vol. 2, pp. 1026–27.

6. Zhang Suhua, *Crisis Point*, pp. 110–11.

7. CCP Central Committee Documents Editorial Committee, ed., *Selected Works of Liu Shaoqi*, vol. 2, pp. 418–43.

8. Mao Zedong, "My Conversation with Comrades Kapo and Balluku, February 3, 1967," in *Long Live Mao Zedong Thought, 1961–1968*, p. 88.

9. Bo Yibo, *Looking Back,* vol. 2, p. 1019.

10. Zhang Suhua, *Crisis Point*, pp. 143–45.

11. CCP Central Committee Party Literature Research Center, ed., *The Life of Mao Zedong, 1949–1976*, vol. 2, p. 1190.

12. Bo Yibo, *Looking Back*, vol. 2, p. 1046.

13. Mao Zedong, "Speech at the Enlarged Central Committee Working Conference, January 30, 1962," in *Long Live Mao Zedong Thought, 1961–1968*, p. 17.

14. "Opinions Put Forward to the Central Committee and Its Leaders and Related Departments During a Meeting in Gansu Province of Party Cadres of Provincial Units of Grade Nineteen or Above to Study and Discuss the Documents from the Enlarged Central Committee Work Conference," February 28, 1962, compiled by the provincial party office.

15. Chen Yun, "The Current Financial and Political Difficulties and Several Ways to Surmount the Difficulties," February 26, 1962, in CCP Central Committee Documents Editorial Committee, ed., *Selected Writings of Chen Yun, 1956–1985*, pp. 183–98.

16. Bo Yibo, *Looking Back*, vol. 2, pp. 1051–52.

17. Liu Shaoqi, "What Is the Actual Economic Situation?," May 11, 1962, in CCP Central Committee Documents Editorial Committee, ed., *Selected Works of Liu Shaoqi*, vol. 2, pp. 444–49.

18. Bo Yibo, *Looking Back*, vol. 2, p. 1073.

19. Wang Guangmei, Liu Yuan et al., *The Unknown Liu Shaoqi*, p. 90.

20. Author's conversation with former vice-minister of the Food Ministry, Zhou Bo-ping, on September 25, 2003.

21. Chen Yun, "The Current Financial and Political Difficulties."

22. Deng Zihui, "Regarding Longsheng County's Problem of Assigning Output to Households," April 11, 1962, in Deng Zihui Collected Works Editorial Committee, ed., *The Collected Works of Deng Zihui*, Beijing: Renmin chubanshe, 1996, p. 544.

23. Bo Yibo, *Looking Back*, vol. 2, pp. 1084–85.

24. *Materials for Criticism*, pp. 206–208. This content was edited out of the *Selected Works of Liu Shaoqi*.

25. Bo Yibo, *Looking Back*, vol. 2, p. 998.

26. TN: A series of agreements between India and the People's Republic of China drafted in 1954 within the context of decolonization. The principles included mutual respect for each other's territorial integrity and sovereignty, mutual nonaggression, mutual noninterference in each other's internal affairs, equality and mutual benefit, and peaceful coexistence.

27. Zhu Liang, "Wang Jiaxiang in Selfless and Fearless Pursuit of Truth—The Truth Behind the Accusations of 'Three Appeasements and One Reduction' Revisionism," *Yanhuang chunqiu*, no. 8 (2006): 1–7.

28. Yan Mingfu, "Looking at Kang Sheng from My Personal Experience," *Yanhuang chunqiu*, no. 5 (2005): 40–45.

29. *Long Live Mao Zedong Thought, 1961–1968*, pp. 29–30.

30. Bo Yibo, *Looking Back*, vol. 2, pp. 1074–88.

31. Ibid., pp. 1092–93.

32. Ibid., p. 1093.

33. Huang Kecheng, *Autobiography*, p. 270.

34. Central Party School Party History Research Room, ed., *Collected Documents from Several Important CCP Meetings*, vol. 2, Shanghai: Shanghai renmin chubanshe, 1983, pp. 196–97.

35. CCP Handan Municipal Party Committee, "Report to the Provincial Party Committee Regarding the Basic Summing Up of the Three Oppositions Pilot Project in Thirty-two Villages and Suggestions for the Next-stage Arrangements," June 2, 1960, CCP Handan municipal party committee document, no. [60]141.

36. Wang Guangmei, "Summary of One Production Brigade's Experience with the Socialist Education Movement" (also known as "The Taoyuan Experience"), July 5, 1964. See *Materials for Criticism*, pp. 471–570.

37. Ibid.

38. Li Xin, "Record of the 'Socialist Education Movement,'" in Li Xin, *Looking Back at Fleeting Time: Sequel to Li Xin's Memoirs*, Beijing: Beijing tushuguan chubanshe, 1998, pp. 120–21.

39. Ibid.

40. Wang Li, *Wang Li's Posthumous Manuscript: A Record of Wang Li's Rethinking*, vol. 2, Hong Kong: Baixing chubanshe, 2001, p. 573.

41. Ibid., vol. 2, p. 573.

42. "Central Committee's Memo on the Transmission of 'Summary of One Production Brigade's Experience with the Socialist Education Movement,'" September 1, 1964, dispatches from the CCP Central Committee document, receipt no. [64]527.

43. Mao Zedong, "Bombarding the Headquarters—My First Big-character Poster," August 5, 1966.

44. TN: Zhang Linzhi, minister of coal and mining, died in early 1967 after being virulently denounced. His death was attributed to suicide, but he was found to have been brutally beaten.

45. Wang Guangmei, Liu Yuan et al., *The Unknown Liu Shaoqi*, pp. 115–18.

46. Bo Yibo, *Looking Back*, vol. 2, p. 1131.

47. Chen Xiaonong, *Chen Boda's Final Oral Recollections*, unpublished manuscript, 2004, p. 251. TN: The book was subsequently published in Hong Kong in 2005 by Yangguang huanqiu chubanshe.

48. Wang Guangmei, Liu Yuan et al., *The Unknown Liu Shaoqi*, p. 118.

49. Shen Zhihua, "The 'Great Leap Forward,' the People's Communes, and the Rupturing of the Sino-Soviet Alliance," personal website of Shen Zhihua and Li Danhui. The article can be accessed at Fenghuang gang (Phoenix online), at news.ifeng.com /history/zl/zj/shenzhihua/200906/0608_6016_1193227.shtml, posted June 8, 2009.

50. Ibid.

51. Conversation between the author and Yang Mu, the top Xinhua journalist stationed in Cambodia.

52. Gustave Le Bon, *The Crowd: A Study of the Popular Mind*, 1896, published in Chinese as *Wuhezhizhong*, Feng Keli trans., Beijing: Zhongyang bianyi chubanshe, 2004, p. 46. TN: An English translation by Batoche Books, 2001, is accessible online at socserv.mcmaster.ca/econ/ugcm/3ll3/lebon/Crowds.pdf. This quote is found on pp. 38–39.

BIBLIOGRAPHY

The following is a selective bibliography comprised of the first four of the ten sections in the original Chinese edition. It includes works referenced in chapters of the full Chinese version of *Tombstone* (*Mubei*) that were not translated for this English edition.

The last six sections of the original Chinese bibliography are omitted in this English version, but most of the works are referenced in the footnotes. They include book-length studies of the Great Famine and relevant book-length publications; scholarly articles published in journals and newspapers; memoirs; collections of statistical data, historical documents, and other relevant historical materials; provincial, municipal, and county annals; and standard works by Marx, Engels, Lenin, Stalin, and Mao, and by other ranking Chinese leaders.

1. PRIMARY SOURCES

ANHUI PROVINCE

Anhui Provincial Public Security Bureau. "Report on the Occurrence of Special Cases," April 23, 1961.

Bengbu City Leading Group on Eradicating Disease and Pests. "Opinions Regarding Efforts to Eradicate Disease and Going Forward," November 17, 1961.

(Bengbu) Municipal Party Committee Leading Group for Reducing the Urban Population. "Suggestions Regarding Efforts to Further Reduce the Urban Population and Cut Down on Staffing," November 17, 1961.

Bulletin of the Bengbu City 1961 Three-level Cadre Conference. "Opinions and Requests to the Provincial Party Committee."

"Bulletin of the Fengyang County Party Committee's Enlarged Five-level Cadre Meeting," no. 4, January 8, 1961; no. 5, January 9, 1961; no. 6, January 10, 1961.

CCP Bengbu Municipal Committee. "Directives for Further Mobilizing and Organizing the Masses to Collect Wild Herbs," March 26, 1961.

CCP Fengyang County Committee. "Brief Report on the Rectification of Work Styles and Communes," no. 16, March 14, 1961.

———. "Investigation Report Regarding Evildoers Holding Sway in Xiaoxihe Commune," February 10, 1961.

———. "Material Regarding the Anti-Party Crimes of Zhao Conghua," October 30, 1959.

———. "The Launch of Rectification of Work Styles in Fengyang County," December 8, 1959.

———. "Pilot Project Survey on Implementing the 'CCP Central Committee's Urgent Directives Regarding Current Policy Problems in the Rural People's Communes,'" November 24, 1960.

———. "Regarding the Situation of the Five Winds," November 7, 1961.

———. "Situational Report on Efforts to Correct the 'Responsibility Fields' and to Correct Assignments of Production Quotas to Production Teams," March 10, 1963.

CCP Fengyang County Party Committee Industry and Communications Department. "Summary Report of the Industry and Communications Department for 1958," December 1958.

CCP Fengyang County Party Committee Investigation and Research Group. "Brief Report on Work on the 'Three Includes' and 'Four Fixes' at Zhengfucheng Commune's Sifeng Production Brigade," nos. 1 and 2.

CCP Wuwei County Committee. "On Implementation of the Central Committee's Twelve-point Urgent Directive," November 27, 1960.

Chen Zhenya. "Report on the Fengyang Problem," February 1, 1961.

Cheng Guanghua. "All People Should Join in Producing Food Substitutes," November 29, 1960.

Comrade Ma Weiman's Speech at the Three-level Cadre Conference. "The Experience and Lessons of Fengyang County Over the Last Two Years," August 24, 1961.

"Dougou Commune's Summary Report Regarding the Launch of a Campaign Against Corruption, Waste, and Bureaucracy and a Rectification of Work Styles," July 18, 1960.

Fengyang County. "Record of the Department Head Rectification Meeting," August 9, 1961.

Office of the CCP Bengbu Municipal Committee Leading Group on Saving Grain. "Report Regarding Promoting Advanced Food Preparation Methods Throughout the City," January 26, 1960.

"Report of the Wudian Commune Party Committee Regarding Rectification of Work Styles and Communes," April 18, 1961.

"Self-examination by Comrade Cheng Guanghua Representing the Bengbu Municipal Party Committee (notes)," March 18, 1961.

"Supplementary Self-criticism by Comrade Zhao Yushu of the Fengyang County Party Committee at the Enlarged Five-level Cadre Conference," January 15, 1961.

Zeng Qingmei. "Situational Report Regarding a Portion of Cadres Violating Law and Discipline at Xiao County's Majing Commune," August 4, 1960.

Zhao Yushu's "Self-criticism as a Representative of the County Party Committee at the Enlarged Five-level Cadre Conference (the first self-criticism)," January 7, 1960.

GANSU PROVINCE

CCP Baiyin Municipal Party Committee. "Report Regarding Vigorously Preventing and Curing the Spread of Edema, and Suggestions Going Forward," December 18, 1960.

CCP Dingxi Prefectural Party Committee Organization Department. "Situational Report Regarding Reexamination of the 1958 'Pulling Down of White Flags' and 'Planting of Red Flags,'" October 19, 1959.

CCP Gannan Prefectural Party Committee. "Report on Livelihood Arrangements and Increasing Rural Grain Rations," April 8, 1962.

CCP Gansu Provincial Party Committee. "Regulations on Conducting Group Training and Special Training," February 27, 1961.

CCP Gansu Provincial Party Committee Secretariat, ed. "Bulletin of the CCP Gansu Provincial Party Committee Three-level Cadre Conference," nos. 4, 6, and 13, November 9, 1960.

CCP Jiuquan Municipal Party Committee. "Investigation Report Regarding the Flour Mill Wrongfully Firing Shots at Masses Stealing Grain," January 11 and 14, 1961, dispatch to the Gansu Provincial Party Committee Office, receipt no. [61]2060, [61]2189.

CCP Lanzhou Municipal Party Committee. "Situational Report Regarding the Incidence of Edema Among Cadres and Staff," December 3, 1960.

CCP Tianshui Prefectural Party Committee. "Request for Funding for Free Medical Treatment," December 24, 1960.

CCP Yumen Municipal Party Committee. "Report Regarding the Situation of Edema in Factories and Mines, Enterprises, Organizations, and Party Schools," December 11, 1960.

Central Committee Work Group Led by Central Supervisory Committee Deputy Secretary Qian Ying. "Regarding a Large Number of Cadres Suffering Serious Persecution During the Campaign Against Right Deviation in Tianshui Prefecture, Gansu Province," January 5, 1961.

Gansu Provincial People's Procuratorate Dingxi Branch. "Investigation Report Regarding Tongwei's Handling of Reeducation Through Labor," March 30, 1960.

Jiuquan Iron and Steel Company Party Committee. "Situational Report on Edema Among Workers and Staff," December 30, 1960.

Linxia Prefectural Party Committee. "Briefing on the Living Conditions at Lingxia County's Dahejia Bonan Minority Commune," May 11, 1962.

———. "Bulletin on the Living Conditions at Linxia County's Dahejia Bonan Minority Commune," May 11, 1962.

"Opinions Put Forward to the Central Committee and Its Leaders and Related Departments During a Meeting in Gansu Province of Party Cadres of Provincial Units of Grade 19 or Above to Study and Discuss Documents from the Enlarged Central Committee Work Conference," February 28, 1962.

Provincial Industry and Communications Department. "The Incidence of Edema in the Industry and Communications System," December 9, 1960.

Provincial Party Committee Rural Work Department. "Report on the Problems in Min County," August 19, 1960.

"Report by the Provincial Party Committee Health Department Inspection Group to the Health Department's Leading Party Group and the Dingxi Prefectural Party Committee," January 8, 1961.

"Report by the Provincial Party Committee Tianshui Work Group and the Tianshui Prefectural Party Committee Regarding Efforts to Protect the Safety of Railway Transport," January 23, 1961.

"Report to the Provincial Party Committee by Li Busheng, Li Shenghua, and Tian Yuan of the Dingxi Work Group." Bulletin no. 3 of the Enlarged Meeting of the Dingxi Prefectural Party Committee, January 12, 1961.

Telephone Report by the Qingshui County Party Committee Regarding Livelihood Arrangements and the Situation of Outward Migration, February 17, 1960.

"Telephone Report by the Wuwei Prefectural Party Committee Regarding the Incidence of Sickness, Food, and Fuel Shortages and Outward Migration in Yongchang County," January 15, 1961.

Yuzhong County Party Secretary Lie Bingrang. "Report on the Communal Kitchens," May 1961.

Zhang Zhongliang. "Go All Out, Fight Hard for Three Years, Strive for a Leap Forward in Agriculture, Then Leap Forward Again!," February 9, 1958.

Zhangye Prefectural Party Committee's Report to the Provincial Party Committee on the Evening of January 7, 1961.

GUANGDONG PROVINCE

CCP Wenchang County Committee. "Summary Report Regarding the Enlarged Four-level Cadre Conference," January 11, 1961.

Guangdong Provincial People's Government Public Security Bureau. "Summation Report on the Campaign to Eliminate Counterrevolutionaries in Guangdong," April 11, 1951.

Prefectural Party Committee Investigation Group. "Investigation Report Regarding the Situation of Organizational Impurity and Domination by Scoundrels at Gaoyao County's Sijia Production Brigade," March 12, 1961.

"Report of the Zengcheng County Four-level Cadre Conference," January 4, 1961.

"Report of the Zhongshan County Four-level Cadre Conference," January 5, 1961.

"Situational Report of the Jiangmen City Outskirts Four-level Cadre Conference," January 21, 1961.

"Summary Report of the Bao'an County Four-level Cadre Conference," January 3, 1961.

"Summary Report of the CCP Shende County Committee Four-level Cadre Conference," January 3, 1961.

Wu Nansheng. "Report Regarding the Situation of Large Numbers of Deaths from Edema in Hepu County," May 5, 1960.

Zhang Jinqi. "Report to the Provincial Party Committee Regarding the Emergence of Edema and Deaths in Luoding County," September 20, 1960.

Zheng Qun, Cheng Jiaying, and Zhang Lemin. "Investigation Report Regarding Serious Violations of Law and Discipline and Widespread Incidence of Death at Nanxiong County's Shixing Commune," July 31, 1960.

HEBEI PROVINCE

CCP Central Committee General Office Anguo Work Group. "Investigation Report Regarding the Problem of Restricting the Masses from Withdrawing from Communal Kitchens by the Party Committee of Anguo County's Wuren Commune and the Wuren Village Party Branch," July 18, 1960.

CCP Central Committee Work Conference Documents. Letters from Central Committee Leaders, 1961.

Feng Yunting to Secretary Pei, January 7, 1961.

Handan Municipal Party Committee. "Report to the Provincial Party Committee Regarding the Basic Summing Up of the 'Three Antis' Pilot Project in Thirty-two Villages and Suggestions for the Next-stage Arrangements," June 2, 1960.

Hebei Daily Zhangjiakou Reporting Team. "The Situation in Wei County," January 1961.

Hebei Provincial Party Committee. Encoded Telegram to the Prefectural and Municipal Party Committees: "Urgent Notice Regarding the Need to Promptly Discover and Prevent Deaths," December 28, 1960.

———. "Report on the Prevention of Edema," February 18, 1960.

———. "Report Regarding the Food Situation," April 16, 1959.

Hebei Provincial Party Committee Office. "Fourth Briefing on Food Supply Work in All Localities," October 14, 1961.

Hebei Provincial Party Committee Office for Rectification of Work Styles and Communes, and Provincial Supervision Commission. "Summary of the Organization and Handling of the Rural Campaign to Rectify Work Styles and Communes from the Winter of 1960 to the Spring of 1961," April 28, 1962.

Hebei Provincial Party Committee Supervision Commission. "Report on the Continued Incidence of Edema in Some Rural Areas," October 13, 1960.

"Hebei Provincial Party Committee's Urgent Notice on Making Practical Arrangements for the Livelihood of the Masses," November 8, 1960.

Hu Kaiming's Letter to Liu Zihou, January 21, 1961.

Leading Party Group of the Hebei Provincial Agriculture Bureau. "Preliminary Examination of the Chaotic Directives Wind (discussion draft)," January 17, 1961.

Leading Party Group of the Hebei Provincial Health Bureau. "Report on the Immediate Launch of a Disease Treatment and Prevention Campaign," August 12, 1961.

Letter of the Provincial Supervision Commission to the Provincial Party Committee, January 26, 1960.

Letters from CCP Central Committee Leaders and Important Memos from Chairman Mao, 1961.

Liu Zihou. "Urgent Telephone Call Regarding the Need to Get a Grip on Procurement Work," October 6, 1961.

Materials for the 301st Meeting of the Provincial Party Committee Secretariat, 1961.

Municipal Party Committees on the Situation of Railway Grain Robberies and Cadre Violations of Law and Discipline, 1961.

Provincial Agricultural Bureau Party Committee Work Group. "Compilation of Surveys of Present Agricultural Conditions in Ten Production Brigades in Cangzhou Area," July 1, 1962.

Provincial Inspection Group for Efforts Against Food Poisoning. "Report on the Investigation of the Food Poisoning Incidents in Zhuo, Ningjin, and Tang Counties," May 15, 1960.

Provincial Party Committee Office. "Viewpoints of the Prefectural Party Committees Expressed in Their Studies of the Spirit of the Provincial Party Committee Telephone Conference," September 17, 1961.

Provincial Party Committee on the Current Struggle Against the Enemy, at the Provincial Politics and Law Work Conference, 1961.

Report of the Hebei Provincial Party Committee and the Provincial People's Committee to the CCP Central Committee and the State Council: "Report on Convening the 1959 Agricultural Products Purchase and Sales Agreement Conference," March 14, 1959.

Survey Data on Rural Food Supplies, the People's Livelihood, Deaths, and the Rectification of Work Styles and Communes, reprinted by the Office of the Hebei Provincial Party Committee in 1960.

Tangshan Municipal Party Committee. "Report to the Provincial Party Committee on the Previous Phase of the Rural Rectification Campaign for Work Styles and Communes and Suggestions Going Forward," January 21, 1960.

The 132rd Session of the First Provincial Party Committee Standing Committee Regarding Problems in Food Supply Arrangements, 1961.

Transmitted by the Hebei Provincial Party Committee: Leading Party Group of the Hebei Provincial Public Security Bureau. "Report on Current Food Poisoning Mishaps and Suggestions Going Forward," August 1960.

Transmitted with Comments by the Hebei Provincial Party Committee: Xie Xuegong. "Survey Report on Edema," January 22, 1959.

Zhangjiakou Municipal Party Committee. "Comprehensive Report on the Rectification Campaign to Counter Right Deviation and the Rural Rectification Movement," January 16, 1960.

HENAN PROVINCE

CCP Henan Provincial Party Committee. "Self-criticism Regarding the Xinyang Incident," November 1, 1960.

CCP Huaibin County Party Committee. "Second Investigation into Deaths from Edema and Other Epidemic Diseases," June 7, 1960.

CCP Huangchuan County Party Committee. "Report on the Grain Procurement Issue," October 30, 1959.

Central Committee Special Investigation Group. "Situation Report on the Special Investigation into the Xinyang Incident," November 20, 1960.

"Comrade Song Zhihe's Report Regarding Several Current Major Items in the Work Situation in Several Counties of Xinyang Prefecture," December 4, 1959.

Comrade Wang Renzhong's Remarks at the Meeting of the Standing Committee of the Provincial Party Committee, December 6, 1960.

Henan Investigation Group of the Organization Department of the CCP Central Committee. "Regarding Xi County and Fanghu's Campaign Against False Reporting of Output and Private Withholding," October 9, 1960.

"How Comrade Zhang Futong Was Suppressed for Reporting on the Situation to the Central Committee," December 1960.

"Instructions Requested by the Henan Provincial Party Committee Regarding the Stripping of Xinyang Prefectural Party Secretary Lu Xianwen's Party Membership, the Death Sentence Imposed on Guangshan County First Secretary Ma Longshan, and Several Policy Questions Regarding the Handling of the Incidents of Death by the Xinyang Prefectural Party Committee," November 1, 1960.

Li Li. Report to Wu Zhipu, November 28, 1960.

Li Zhenhai, Tao Mosheng, and He Dizhong. "Investigation Regarding the Situation in Xi County," October 9, 1960.

"Lu Xianwen's Examination of His Own Errors (draft)," October 1960.

Lu Xianwen's Report to Mao Zedong. "Chairman Mao's Remarks at Xinyang," evening of November 13, 1958.

Ma Longshan. Report on Xinyang. "Respectfully Transmitted to Section Chief Liu and the Province's Two Directors," October 21, 1960.

Sanpisi Commune Subgroup of the Provincial Party Committee Joint Investigation Group. "Investigation Report Regarding Deaths at Huangchuan County's Sanpisi Commune," June 3, 1960.

"Second Investigation by the Chinese Communist Party Committee of Huangchuan County Regarding the Problem of Deaths," June 3, 1960.

Taolin Subgroup of the Provincial Party Committee Investigation Group. "Investigation Report Regarding Deaths Resulting from Inadequate Living Arrangements at Taolin Commune of Huangchuan County," June 3, 1960.

"Wang Binglin's Materials Exposing Yang Weiping," November 1960.

Wang Congwu and Xu Zirong. "Report on the Large-scale Class Retaliation Carried Out During the Feudalistic Restoration in Xinyang Prefecture," December 1, 1960.

Wei Zhen of the Central Committee Work Group. "Regarding Several Outstanding Problems Uncovered in Luyi County," December 21, 1960.

Xinyang Incident Special Investigation Group. "Regarding the Problem of Ma Longshan," November 20, 1960.

Yang Weiping. "Investigation Report Regarding the Xinyang Incident," October 15, 1960.

Yu Sang and Wu Renwen of the Secretariat of the CCP Central Committee and the Henan Provincial Party Committee Work Group. "Investigation Report Regarding the Problems of Deaths and Food Supply in Henan Province's Xinyang Prefecture," June 18, 1960.

JIANGSU PROVINCE

Baoying County Party Committee Work Group. "Situation Report on Baoying County's Tianping Commune," June 10, 1961.

CCP Jiangsu Provincial Committee. "Notice Regarding the Study and Dissemination of the Conference Report and Resolution of the Second Session of the Eighth CCP National Congress," May 8, 1958.

CCP Jiangsu Provincial Committee Work Group at the Zhengnan Production Brigade of Jianhu County's Tianmei Commune. "Investigation Materials Regarding the

Indiscriminate Transfer of Resources, the 'Communist Wind,' and the 'Exaggeration Wind,'" November 15, 1960.

CCP Suzhou Prefectural Committee. "Preliminary Situational Bulletin on Implementation of the 'Twelve Provisions' at Mocheng Commune," November 1960.

"Eight Suggestions to Cadres," Rectification of Work Styles and Communes Bulletin, no. 2, July 28, 1960.

Feng Guangcai. "Deduction of Commune Members' Grain Rations at Huaiyang City's Wangxing Commune," December 28, 1960.

Finance Office Secretariat of the Jiangsu Provincial People's Committee. "A Survey of the Situation at Jinsha and Five Other Open Town Markets," July 15, 1962.

"First Report by the Provincial Party Committee Work Group Stationed at the Haolun Production Brigade of Jianhu County's Tianmei Commune," September 18, 1960.

Food Ministry Work Group. "Investigation Report Regarding the Food Problem in Baoying and Yixing Counties," June 25, 1960.

Investigation and Research Team on Rectification at Guabu Commune. "Preliminary Investigation into the Problem of Cadre Work Styles at Liuhe County's Guabu Commune," April 1961.

Jiang Weiqing's Speech to the Second Session of the Eighth CCP National Congress. "With Politics in Command and Production Centrally Focused, All Work Items Shall Advance," May 1958.

Jiangsu Provincial Party Committee. "Report on the Current Situation in the Lixiahe Region of Northern Jiangsu," May 30, 1962.

Jiangsu Provincial Party Committee and County Party Committee Work Group at Qutang Commune. "Situational Report Regarding Rectification of Indiscriminate Transfer of Resources in Qutang Commune's Huzhuang Production Brigade," November 23, 1960.

Letter by Song Chao, Guo Tiesong, and Li Zhen to the Provincial Party Committee, Yangzhou Prefectural Party Committee, and Jiangdu County Party Committee, September 25, 1960.

Lishui Work Group of the Jiangsu Provincial Party Committee and Zhenjiang Prefectural Party Committee. "Situational Report Regarding Rectification of the Standing Committee of the Lishui County Party Committee," October 19, 1960.

Liu Zijian of the Jiangsu Provincial Party Committee Work Group at Dongtai County. "Work Report Regarding Rectification of the 'Communist Wind' at the Lu'nan Production Brigade," November 19, 1960.

Lu Jing's Letter to the Provincial Party Committee: "Why Coercive Commandism and Violations of Law and Discipline Are So Serious in Wu County's Dongqiao Commune," September 5, 1960.

Nantong County Investigation Report Regarding the Food Problem at Shigang People's Commune, March 24, 1959.

"Notice by the Changzhou Municipal Party Committee Regarding Mass Disturbances Occurring During Retrenchment at the Daming Textile Factory," June 10, 1962.

Provincial Party Committee Work Group. "Investigation Report on the Situation of the

'Four Winds' in the No. 8 Production Brigade of Huaiyang City's Wuli Commune," November 16, 1960.

———. "Investigation Report Regarding Exaggerated Output Claims at Changshu County's Baimao Commune," October 18, 1960.

"Remarks by Comrade Yin Bingshan at the Meeting of County and Municipal First Secretaries," July 22, 1960.

"Report to the Prefectural Party Committee by Director Yang of the Shanghai Bureau Regarding the Situation at Feng, Pei, and Donghai Counties," October 20, 1960.

Report to the Provincial Party Committee by the Provincial Party Committee Work Group Sent to Danyang County, September 20, 1960.

Shanghai Bureau Office. "Letter from the Jiangsu Provincial Work Group," August 24, 1960.

Sun Haiguang. "To Department Heads Xin and Sun and the Provincial Party Committee," December 27, 1960.

Sun Haiguang's Letter to the Provincial Party Committee and Committee Member Han's Comments, July 25, 1960.

"Why There Has Been No Great Leap Forward in the Xiping Production Brigade in Recent Years," August 4, 1960.

Xu Shenxing of the Jiangsu Provincial Party Committee Rural Work Department. "Report Regarding the Food Problem in Siyang County," December 2, 1960.

Yan Jingzhan's Telephone Report on the Morning of April 15, 1959: "Regarding Problems with the People's Livelihood."

Yangzhou Branch of the Jiangsu Provincial Party Committee Commune Rectification Investigation Group. "Report to the Provincial Party Committee Regarding Several Problems Sensed During Work," February 12, 1959.

JILIN PROVINCE

CCP Central Committee Northeast China Bureau. "Report Regarding the Production of Food Substitutes in the Northeastern Region," January 18, 1961.

CCP Changchun Municipal Committee Office. "Report Regarding Stopping Some of the Masses from Stripping Tree Bark and Damaging Public Facilities," May 11, 1961.

CCP Jilin Provincial Committee. "Authorizing Issuance of the Summary Statement Regarding Grain Work by Comrade Li Youwen at the Provincial Three-level Cadre Conference," October 31, 1960.

———. "Investigation Report Regarding the Participation of Family Members of Employees in Self-supporting Agricultural and Sideline Production," November 9, 1962.

———. "Notice Regarding the Need in Rural Work to Resolutely Implement Policy and Thoroughly Put an End to Suicides," February 20, 1960.

———. "Report Regarding Factory and Mining Enterprises Setting Up Agricultural and Sideline Production Bases," January 20, 1961.

———. "Report Regarding Grain Work," November 14, 1960.

———. "Report Regarding Preventing Unnatural Deaths Among Travelers," February 10, 1961.

———. "Report Regarding the Current Grain Situation," June 9, 1959.

———. "Report Regarding the Grain Situation and Livelihood Arrangement Problems," February 11, 1961.

———. "Urgent Notice: Rigorously Prevent All State-owned Facilities, Enterprises, and Work Units from Taking Over Communes and Cultivated Land Without Permission," April 17, 1961.

CCP Jilin Provincial Committee Finance and Trade Department. "Report on the Convening of a Meeting on Livelihood Arrangements in the Countryside," March 5, 1962.

CCP Jilin Provincial Committee Office. "Bulletin of the Jilin Province Six-level Cadre Conference," vol. 1, March 11, 1959.

CCP Liaoning Provincial-Municipal-County Committee Work Group. "Summary of the Experimental Rectification of Tieling County's Fanhe Commune," December 15, 1960.

CCP Siping Prefectural Committee. "Report Regarding Heedless Outward Migration Among Village Residents in Shuangliao County," June 15, 1960.

"Comrade Xu Shoushen's Remarks During the Telephone Conference Convened by the Provincial Party Committee to Rectify Public Security and Order in the Cities," November 2, 1961.

Documents of the Enlarged Provincial Party Committee Meeting for Transmitting and Implementing the Resolution of the Lushan Conference, August 26 to September 10, 1959.

"First Letter from Comrade Wu De to the Chairman," May 9, 1961.

Issued with Comments by the CCP Jilin Provincial Party Committee: "Situational Report by the Leading Party Group of the Provincial People's Procuratorate Regarding Arrests of Criminals Throughout the Province in 1959," April 4, 1960.

Jilin Province Politics and Law Coordination Office. "Opinions Regarding the Basic Situation in the Battle and Future Work (draft)," August 10, 1959.

Jilin Provincial Party Committee Office. "Jilin's Campaign to Produce Food Substitutes," January 7, 1961.

Jilin Provincial Procuratorate, Jilin Province Higher People's Court, Jilin Provincial Supervision Department. "Preliminary Suggestions Regarding Promptly Punishing Criminal Elements Who Violate and Sabotage Grain Policies, and Ensuring That Grain Procurement Work Is Carried Out Smoothly," January 9, 1959.

Leading Party Group of the CCP Jilin Provincial Politics and Law Commission. "Report on Adjusting the Limit to the Number of Arrests and Executions for the Year 1960," July 18, 1960.

Leading Party Group of the Jilin Provincial Health Department. "Investigation Report Regarding the Edema Situation in Two Administrative Districts of Tao'an County," March 11, 1961.

———. "Report Regarding Treating and Preventing Several of the Current Main Illnesses," June 2, 1961.

Leading Party Group of the Jilin Provincial Procuratorate. "Report Regarding the Current Grain Shortage in Some Localities," April 30, 1958.

——. "Report Regarding Violations of Law and Discipline Among a Minority of Grass-roots Cadres," August 5, 1959.

——. "Situational Report Regarding Action Against the Crimes of Violating Grain Policy and Sabotaging Grain Procurement," February 13, 1958.

Leading Party Group of the Jilin Provincial Public Security and Civil Affairs Departments. "Suggestions Regarding Resolutely Halting the Free Movement of the Population," October 20, 1961.

Northeast Bureau Agricultural Commission Work Group, Heilongjiang Provincial Party Committee Work Group. "Report on Experimental Rectification Work at Xiangyangchuan People's Commune," February 15, 1961.

Northeast Bureau Finance Commission. "Report on Views at the Symposium of Finance and Trade Department Heads of Three Provinces on Dealing Well with Food Substitutes and the People's Livelihood Arrangements," January 25, 1961.

"Outline Report Regarding the Grain Situation (draft)," November 29, 1961.

Record of a Telephone Call from Yanbian Prefectural Party Committee Cadre He Jianzhong Reporting on the Local Starvation Situation, evening of March 4, 1961.

Ruan Bosheng. "Report on the Current Situation of Production and Livelihood Arrangements in Huaide County," July 27, 1961.

"Second Letter from Comrade Wu De to the Chairman," May 10, 1961.

Song Zhenting. "Report Regarding the Main Operational Problems in Huaide County and Further Rectification of the Party and Communes," May 10, 1961.

Speech by Second Party Secretary Yue Lin of the CCP Jilin Provincial Committee Supervisory Committee at the First Session of the Second Jilin Provincial Party Congress, March 1960.

Speech by Vice-Governor Wang Huanru at the First Session of the Jilin Provincial Party Congress. "Regarding Arrangements for the People's Livelihood," March 21, 1960.

"Summary Remarks by Comrade Cui Cifeng at the Seminar on the Provincewide Unified Action to Attack Theft and Profiteering Activities," January 10, 1962.

Wu De. "Summing Up of the Jilin Province Six-level Cadre Conference," March 21, 1959.

Wu De's Remarks During the Provincial Party Committee Telephone Conference. "Regarding Grain Procurement and Problems with Arranging Livelihood," December 17, 1960.

Wu De's Summary Report at the Jilin Provincial Three-Level Cadre Conference, November 10, 1960.

Zhang Shiying. "Report on the Question of Developing Ginseng Production in Fusong County," December 7, 1961.

LIAONING PROVINCE

CCP Anshan Municipal Committee. "Situational Report Regarding Carrying Out an Education Campaign Centered on Foodstuffs Among the Family Members of Employees, and Successfully Arranging the Livelihood of the Masses," January 19, 1961.

CCP Liaoning Provincial Committee Work Group. "Summary of Experimental Work in the Rectification of Work Styles and Communes at Tieling County's Fanhe Commune," December 15, 1960.

SHANDONG PROVINCE

Bulletin of the Enlarged Meeting of the Shandong Provincial Party Committee, December 13–15, 1960.

CCP Shandong Provincial Committee. "Main Facts Regarding Comrade Zhao Jianmin's Localism, Decentralism, and Right-opportunistic Errors," October 21, 1958.

———. "Report to the CCP Central Committee Regarding Transmission and Implementation of the Report of the Beidaihe Conference," September 20, 1960.

———. Work Conference Documents. Bulletin dated August 14, 1960.

"Changwei Prefectural Grain Bureau Report to the Provincial Grain Bureau Requesting Instructions on the Purchase of Mildewed Dried Melon," October 29, 1961.

Comrade Mu Lin's Speech at the Enlarged Provincial Party Committee Meeting, December 13, 1960.

"Investigation Report by the Shandong Provincial Party Committee and the Provincial People's Committee Regarding the Closure of Communal Kitchens and Fleeing from the Famine," January 16, 1959.

"Notice of the Shandong Provincial Grain Bureau Regarding the Printing and Distribution of the Summary of Remarks by Comrade Fan Peihua During the Provincial Grain Telephone Conference," January 14, 1961.

"Report of the Leading Party Group of the Shandong Grain Bureau Regarding Adjustments to the State Grain Monopoly Annual Quota," February 25, 1960.

Shandong Provincial Grain Bureau. "Regarding the Rough Calculations for 1960–1961 by the City and Prefectural Party Committees of the Grain Requirements of the Villages and the State."

———. "Shandong's Grain Problem (report data)," May 12, 1961.

Shandong Provincial "Party Committee Office." *News and Materials*, no. 31, July 1960.

Shu Tong. "My Self-criticism," December 13, 1960.

Tan Qilong's Letter to Shu Tong, January 18, 1958.

Tan Qilong's Letter to Shu Tong, March 23, 1959

Tan Qilong's Letter to Shu Tong, April 11, 1959.

Transmitted via the Central Supervisory Committee: Report by the Shandong Provincial Supervision Commission Regarding Errors Occurring During the Launch of the Competition to "Pluck out White Flags and Plant Red Flags" in Jining Prefecture, April 30, 1959.

Wang Ying. "Brief Report Regarding Inspection of Edema Prevention in Jinxiang County," April 29, 1959.

Xia Zhengnong. "Comrade Xia Zhengnong's Report to the Provincial Party Committee Regarding Inspection of the Work Situation in Shouzhang," June 18, 1959.

Zeng Xisheng's Speech at the Enlarged Meeting of the Shandong Provincial Party Committee: "Urgent Mobilization of the Party and Government, Military, and

Civilians in the Battle to Vanquish Famine and Surmount Difficulties," October 29, 1960.

Zhao Jianmin's Speech at the Enlarged Provincial Party Committee Meeting, December 15, 1960.

SICHUAN PROVINCE

An Faxiao (Provincial Party Committee Rectification and Production Inspection Group, Luzhou Subgroup). "Investigation Report Regarding Several Problems in Rectification and Consolidation Work in the People's Communes in Luzhou Prefecture," September 1, 1959.

Bishan County Party Committee. "Report on 1961 Prevention and Cure of Diseases and Views on Operations Hereafter," January 2, 1960.

———. "Twelve Emergency Measures for the Rapid Treatment of Edema," October 22, 1960.

"Bulletin of the National Conference of Food Bureau Heads," February 9, 1960.

CCP Pi County Committee. "Pi County Five-level Cadre Meeting to Discuss the Labor Force Problem."

"Comrade Chen Guodong's Report to Vice-Premier Li Xiannian," March 17, 1962.

"Comrade Fan Zhizhong's Report on Cadres Violating Law and Discipline at Hechuan County's Nanping Commune," November 13, 1960.

"Comrade Li Dazhang's Report on the Lushan Central Committee Work Conference at the Meeting of Provincial and Prefectural Party Secretaries (edited notes)," September 20, 1961.

"Comrade [Li] Jingquan's Memo on the 'Luzhou Prefectural Party Committee Secretariat Report on the Disease Situation in Gulin County,'" December 8, 1959.

"Comrade [Li] Jingquan's Remarks at the Meeting of Municipal and Prefectural Party Secretaries on the Morning of November 7, 1959, at Panjiaping, Chongqing."

"Comrade Li Jingquan's Remarks at the Provincial Party Committee Six-level Cadre Conference (notes)," March 11, 1959.

"Comrade [Li] Jingquan's Transmission of the Resolution of the Eighth Plenum of the Eighth CCP Central Committee Regarding the Peng Dehuai Anti-Party Clique (notes)," August 30, 1959.

"Comrade Liu Wenzhen's Telephone Report Regarding Serious Problems Discovered During an Inspection of Rural Communal Kitchens in Bishan County," January 6, 1961.

"Comrade Wang Ziqing's Report to the Rural Work Department Regarding Some Problems in Rong County," October 3, 1960.

Da County Work Group of the Provincial Party Committee Rectification of Work Styles and Communes Inspection Team. "Investigation Report Regarding the Eating of Guanyin Clay by the Masses in Parts of Qu County Due to Inadequate Living Arrangements," August 31, 1961.

Dianjiang Work Group of the Provincial Party Committee Inspection Team. "Report on the Situation at Jiefang Commune for Third-stage Rectification of Work Styles and Communes Relating to the Recovery of Stolen and Embezzled Funds," April 8, 1961.

"Directives of the Sichuan Provincial Party Committee Regarding Resolutely Opposing Right-deviationist Thinking and Successfully Tiding Over the Famine by Increasing Production and Economizing on Grain," September 2, 1959.

Gan Tang, Wang Shanqing, and Li Maoyun. "Combined Report Regarding the Inspection of Production and Livelihood in Luzhou Prefecture"; "Report on Some Violations of Law and Discipline in Luzhou Prefecture," June 3, 1960.

Gao Yilu (Pi County First Party Secretary). "Preliminary Examination of the Losses Brought About by the Communist Wind," December 1, 1960.

Guan County Party Committee Office. "Report to the Wenjiang Prefectural Party Committee Regarding Two Incidents of Unnatural Death," March 26, 1960.

Guo Binglin's Letter to Section Head Xia, July 29, 1959.

Jiangjin Prefectural Party Committee. "Report on the Edema Situation," January 21, 1962.

Joint Task Force of the Sichuan Provincial Public Security Bureau and the CCP Qionglai County Party Committee. "Initial Report on the Verified Facts Regarding the Serious Violations of Law and Discipline, Corruption, and Degeneration of the Accused Individual, Yuandaozuo Commune Second Party Secretary Yang Shulou," December 6, 1960.

Leshan County Mianzhu Commune Work Group of the Provincial Party Committee Work Team. "Severe Loss in Productivity Brought About by the Chaotic Orders Issued by Cadres of the No. 2 Administrative District of Leshan's Mianzhu Commune," January 16, 1961.

Li Dazhang. "Speech at the Meeting of Prefectural Party Committee Secretaries," September 7, 1959.

Li Dingbang. "The Production and Livelihood Situation in the Ya'an Region," September 4, 1962.

Li Huaipei. "Regarding the Problem of Egalitarianism and Indiscriminate Transfer of Resources," December 1, 1960.

Li Jingquan. "Letter to the Chairman Regarding the Situation of the Rural Communal Kitchen Experiment," May 5, 1961.

———. "Remarks at the Second Conference of Prefectural Party Secretaries at Nanchong (notes)," March 26, 1960.

Li Jingquan's Letter to Vice-Premier Li Xiannian, August 5, 1960.

Li Lin. "Situational Report of the Chunhua Administrative District of Dianjiang County's Chengxi Commune." Submitted to the Provincial Party Committee and party secretary Liao, January 31, 1961.

Li Yin. "Empty Fields in Yibin's Anbian Commune," July 26, 1961.

Liang Qishan's Letter to the Provincial Party Committee and Wanxian Prefectural Party Committee, September 26, 1960.

Lin Piantian and Wu Guoxian. "Report Regarding the Situation in Sichuan," March 2, 1962.

Liu Wenzhen. "Report on the Guiding Ideology for Rectification of Work Styles at the County-, District-, and Commune-level Party Committees of Jiangjin, Hechuan, Jiangbei, Yongchuan, and Rongchang," January 22, 1961.

Liu Zhongwu, Wang Zheng, and Xiao Lin. "Report on the Situation of the Communal Kitchens in the Wu'ai Administrative District of Jintang County's Sanxing Commune," April 4, 1960.

Luzhou Prefectural Party Committee Secretariat. "Report on the Disease Situation in Gulin County," December 7, 1959.

Ma Jiliang. "Telephone Report Regarding Some Circumstances and Problems in Changshou County," January 25, 1962.

"Material Relating to Several Problems in Finance and Trade Work." Appendix 3 of the "Report of the Jiangjin Group of the Provincial Party Committee's Agricultural Inspection Group," May 3, 1960, pp. 56–59.

Mianyang Work Group of the Provincial Party Committee Commune Rectification Work Team. "Investigation Materials Regarding the Backward Conditions at Mianyang County's Songya Commune," January 17, 1961.

Mianyang Work Group of the Provincial Party Committee Rectification of Work Styles and Communes Work Team. "Materials Relating to the Transformation of the Backward Aspects of Mianyang's Shima Commune," January 12, 1961.

Mianzhu Work Group of the Provincial Party Committee Inspection Group. "Report Regarding the Problem and Resolution of the Grain Shortage at Mianzhu's Hongqi [Red Flag] Commune," March 9, 1959.

"Minutes of the Meeting Called by Comrade [Li] Jingquan of the Party Secretaries of Fuling, Neijiang, Luzhou, Wenjiang, Mianyang, and Nanchong Prefectures," February 14, 1960.

"Overall Situation of Restitution in Meishan County," June 2, 1961, sent to Comrade Li Dazhang and copied to Comrades Liao Qigao and Xu Mengxia.

Pingshan County Party Committee Work Group. "The Experience of the Wuyi Production Brigade of Pingshan County's Qingliang Commune in Rectifying the Assignment of Output Quotas to Households," August 25, 1961.

Prefectural Party Committee Inspection Group, Fuling Subgroup. "Investigation Report Regarding Integrated Work at Ma'an Commune for Self-help Production and Economizing to Get Through the Famine and the Launch of Disease Prevention and Cure," September 20, 1961.

Prefectural Party Committee Inspection Group, Luzhou Subgroup, Xuyong Inspection Committee. "Report Regarding the 'Output Quotas of Sweet Potatoes Assigned to Households and Work Points Based on Production' in Some Production Teams of Xuyong County's Tiantang Commune," August 4, 1959.

Prefectural Party Committee Office for Eradication of Diseases and Pests. "Briefing on the Investigation of Disease in Some Communes of Fuling and Wulong," August 12, 1961.

Prefectural Party Committee Rectification of Work Styles and Communes Wenjiang Work Team. "Report on Serious Violations of Law and Discipline by Cadres Uncovered During the Five-level Cadre Meeting in Jintang County," January 16, 1961.

Provincial Party Committee Agricultural Inspection Group, Jiangjin Subgroup. "Report to the Sichuan Provincial Party Committee," May 2, 1960.

Provincial Party Committee Inspection Group. "Report on Several Serious Problems in Rong County," January 16, 1961.

Provincial Party Committee Jianyang Work Group. "Brief Report to Section Head Yang and Party Secretary Liao Regarding Several Current Production Issues at Jiefang [Liberation] Commune," April 8, 1959.

Provincial Party Committee Office for Eradication of Disease and Pests. "Situation on the Prevention and Cure of Edema," March 7, 1961.

———. "The Disease Situation," July 24, 1962.

———. "The Work Group's Report on the Present Situation of Preventing and Curing Edema," January 18, 1961.

Provincial Party Committee Work Group. "Problems at Xinfan County's Hetun Commune and Suggestions on How to Solve Them," March 1962.

Qiao Zhimin. "Comrade Qiao Zhimin's Report Regarding the Rectification of Hechuan's Nanping Commune," November 29, 1961.

Qiao Zhongling and Zhai Rong to the Provincial Party Committee and Neijiang Prefectural Party Committee, April 16, 1960.

"Report by Comrade Zhou Yi on Scattered Circumstances in Xichang Prefecture," May 27, 1962.

"Report by the Mianyang Prefectural Party Committee Regarding the Reform of Backward Societies and Teams in the Socialist Education Movement," January 8, 1960.

"Report by the Wanxian Prefectural Party Committee Office on Edema in the Countryside," January 15, 1962.

Sichuan Province Rural Work Department Investigation Group. "The Serious Loss of Farming Implements Caused by Indiscriminate Transfer of Resources in the Baiyang Administrative District of Leshan County's Tongjiang Commune," January 5, 1961.

Sichuan Provincial Economic Planning Committee. "Analysis of Historical Grain Yields in Our Province (data)", July 25, 1962.

Sichuan Provincial Party Committee Inspection Group, Yibin Subgroup, Jiang'an Work Team. "Situational Report on the Backwardness of Changning County's Taoping Commune (summary)", July 9, 1959.

Sichuan Provincial Party Committee Restitution Committee Office. "Suggestions Regarding Several Problems in Current Restitution Work," September 19, 1961.

"Sichuan Provincial Party Committee Secretariat Telephone Report to the Central Committee Secretariat Regarding the Campaign Against Right Deviation at the Provincial, Prefectural, and County Levels," November 21, 1959.

State Council Finance Office Task Force. "Rough Calculations from the Investigation of the Settling and Restituting of Accounts in the Rectification of Sichuan Province's Indiscriminately Egalitarian Transfer of Resources (draft)", December 1960.

"Statistical Table of Key Individuals Targeted in the Campaign Against Right Deviation Among Party Cadres in District-level Government Agencies and Party Secretaries of People's Communes," December 25, 1959.

"Statistical Table of Key Non-Party Cadres Targeted in the Campaign Against Right Deviation in Manufacturing and Mining Enterprises," December 25, 1959.

"Statistical Table of Key Non-Party Cadres Targeted in the Campaign Against Right Deviation in Universities, Colleges, and Secondary Schools," December 25, 1959.

"Statistical Table of Key Party Cadres Targeted in the Campaign Against Right Deviation in Manufacturing and Mining Enterprises," December 25, 1959.

"Statistical Table of Key Party Cadres Targeted in the Campaign Against Right Deviation in Universities, Colleges, and Secondary Schools," December 25, 1959.

"Suggestions for Resolving Several Concrete Problems in the Reexamination of Cases (draft)," September 19, 1961.

Sun Chuanxue of the Xichang Branch of the Sichuan Provincial Party Committee Production and Commune Rectification Inspection Team. "To the Prefectural and Provincial Party Committees," June 29, 1959.

"Survey of Canteens in the People's Communes of Xinfan County," July 3, 1959.

United Front Department Subgroup of the CCP Central Committee Work Group. "Criticism and Discipline Rate Reaches 60 Percent Among Commune Party Secretaries in Hechuan County, Sichuan Province, During the Three Years," October 13, 1962.

———. "Investigation of Violations of Law and Discipline by Cadres in the Xingfu Production Brigade of Changtian Commune," September 3, 1961.

———. "The Situation of Output Quotas Assigned to Households in Xinglong District of Jiangbei County, Sichuan Province," August 28, 1962.

Wang Daoyi. "Report on Emergency Medical Treatment at Liuying District's Shiba Commune," January 28, 1962.

Wei Ping and Tan Wancai. "Investigation Report on the Current Situation of Preventing and Treating Edema at Fuling County's Mingjia Commune," August 26, 1961.

Wenjiang Prefectural Party Committee Office. Record of a Telephone Call from the Dayi County Party Committee Office, April 25, 1960.

Wenjiang Prefectural Party Committee Work Group. "The Case of Pan Tingguang's Violation of Law and Discipline," December 1, 1960.

Work Group of the Central Committee United Front Department. "Survey of the Problem of Production Brigade and Production Team Cadres Taking More Than Their Share at Tuqiao Commune in Dazu County, Sichuan Province," August 24, 1962.

Xue Zhiqiang of the Provincial Party Committee Wanxian Prefecture Grain Work Inspection Group to the Provincial and Prefectural Party Committees, October 28, 1960.

Yan Hongyan. "To the Provincial Party Committee and Comrade [Li] Dazhang Regarding Several Problems with Rural Work in Renshou," July 23, 1959.

Yang Wanxuan. "Report on the Situation of Drought and Edema in Changning County," August 9, 1959.

Yibin Prefectural Party Committee Leading Group for the Eradication of Disease and Pests. "Report on the Development of Edema Throughout the Prefecture," July 5, 1961.

Zhang Guangqin. "Report Regarding the Public Security Situation and Disorder in the Countryside," January 12, 1961.

Zhang Shouyu and Liu Jingzhou. "Report to the Provincial Party Committee on the Problems in Rong County," November 30, 1960.

YUNNAN PROVINCE

CCP Dehong Prefectural Party Committee. "Investigation Report Regarding Ethnic Minorities Fleeing," December 6, 1958.

CCP Wenshan Prefectural Committee. "Report Regarding Ethnic Disturbances in Funing County," October 7, 1956.

CCP Yunnan Provincial Committee. "Report Regarding Disturbances Among Funing's Yao Minority," September 25, 1956.

Chuxiong Prefectural Party Committee. "Report to the Provincial Party Committee Regarding Problems in Taoyuan Administrative District of Chuxiong County's Cangling Commune," December 9, 1960.

———. "Report to the Provincial Party Committee Regarding the Edema Situation," July 29, 1960.

"Comrade Xie Fuzhi's Report to the Premier and [Li] Fuchun Regarding the Counterrevolutionary Rebellion and Food Supply Situation in Xuanwei, Yunnan," December 2, 1960.

"Comrade Yu Yichuan's Summary Remarks at the Enlarged Provincial Party Committee Meeting on April 20 (minutes)," April 22, 1958.

Dali Prefectural Party Committee. "Situational Report Regarding Current Tool Reforms," October 3, 1958.

"Directives from the Simao Prefectural Party Committee and the Simao Military Subdistrict Regarding the Problem of Outward Migration Since This Spring," April 14, 1954.

"Edema and Death in Luliang County: A Summary of a Report by the Luliang County Party Secretary, Comrade Kong Xiangzhu," November 14, 1958.

"Investigation Report by the CCP Yunnan Provincial Committee Regarding the Incidence of Edema and Death," November 18, 1958.

"Investigation Report on the Xuanwei Counterrevolutionary Rebellion," November 30, 1960.

Letter by Ma Li and Jia Xingfu to the Provincial Supervision Commission, September 16, 1958.

Lijiang Prefectural Party Committee. "Report on Launching Local Manufacturing of Ball Bearings with Indigenous Methods," October 1958.

"Lijiang Prefectural Party Committee and the Military Subdistrict's Directives Regarding the Bijiang Military Department's Telephone Request for Troops to Be Deployed to Assist in Dissuading Residents from Fleeing," April 16, 1958.

Lincang Prefectural Party Committee. "Report on Deaths in Lincang County in 1956," July 22, 1957.

Liu Zhuofu. "Situational Report Regarding Edema in Qijing Prefecture," September 3, 1958.

Luxi Inspection Group. "Summary Report on Violations of Law and Discipline in Luxi Prior to the Inspection," February 28, 1959.

Provincial Party Committee Inspection Group. "Investigation Report Regarding the Incidence of Edema in Luoping County," September 2, 1958.

Provincial Party Committee Office. "Compilation of the Incidence of Edema Through-out the Province," July 30, 1959.

Provincial Party Committee Rural Work Department. "Situational Report on Edema and Deaths in Luliang County's Chahua Township," August 22, 1958.

Provincial Party Committee Work Group. "Report Regarding the Practice of Chaotic Struggle to the Detriment of the Livelihood of the Masses in Yanshan County," June 8, 1960.

"Record of Comrade Shi Huaibi's Telephone Report on the Grain Situation and People Fleeing the Country in Lancang and Other Localities," April 26, 1960.

"Report by the CCP Yunnan Provincial Committee on the Incidence of Edema in Qu-jing and Some Other Localities," July 27, 1958.

Report of the Qujing Group of the Provincial Party Committee Inspection Group's Kunming Division. "Situational Report Regarding the Launching of Iron and Steel Satellites in Fuyuan, Shizong, and Other Counties of Qujing Prefecture," December 14, 1958.

"Report on Discussions at the Prefectural Party Secretaries' Meeting," November 17 and November 21, 1958.

"Report on the Guihua Temple Problem," December 1956.

"Report on the Tiejiangzhai Incident in Laojie Administrative District of Jinping County's Chonggang Commune," December 29, 1958.

Resolution of the Eighth Plenum of the First Yunnan Provincial Party Committee. "Resolution Regarding Resolutely Implementing the Resolution of the Eighth Ple-num of the Eighth CCP Central Committee, Defending the Party's General Line Through Concrete Action, and Striving to Achieve in Advance and Exceed the 1959 Production Quotas," September 24, 1959.

"Second Batch of Materials for the Conference of Prefectural Party Secretaries (Starva-tion in Fuyuan County, Qujing County, and Malong County)," September 1958.

Simao Prefectural Party Committee. "Self-criticism Report Regarding Edema and Deaths in Lancang County," September 3, 1960.

"Simao Prefectural Party Committee's Second Set of Urgent Directives Regarding Re-solving the Present Grain Shortage in the Border Areas," August 20, 1956.

"Simao Prefectural Party Committee's Urgent Directives Regarding Leading the Masses to Surmount the Grain Shortage," August 4, 1956.

"Situational Report of the Zhaotong Prefectural Party Committee Regarding the Riot on the Border of Zhaoyang and Ludian," December 2, 1958.

Speech by Secretary Ma Jikong of the Provincial Party Committee Secretariat, Decem-ber 2, 1958.

Sun Yuting. "Drawing Lessons from the Struggle Against the Zheng Dun, Wang Jingru Anti-Party Clique to Strengthen the Party's Combat Effectiveness: Report to the Third Session of the First Yunnan Provincial Party Congress," September 25, 1958.

"Transmitted with Comments by the Provincial Party Committee: Report by the Rural Work Department Regarding Jinning County's Earnest Handling of the Resettle-ment of Commune Members Following Demolitions," March 27, 1958.

"Two Reports Regarding Claims of Grain Shortages in Maguan and Xichou of Wenshan Prefecture," June 26, 1961.

Yunnan Province Commission for Discipline Inspection. "Report on Widespread Death and Serious Violations of Law and Discipline During the 1952 Spring Famine in Mojiang County's Baliu and Longtan Districts, and Suggestions on How to Handle the Cadres Involved," May 3, 1955.

Yunnan Provincial Party Committee Inspection Group. "Situational Briefing on the Inspection of Luliang's Chahua Township," November 20, 1958.

"Yunnan Provincial Party Committee's Report Regarding Several Key Experiences in the Struggle Against Landlords, Rich Peasants, and Counterrevolutionaries," September 12, 1957.

ZHEJIANG PROVINCE

CCP Zhejiang Provincial Committee Office. "A Survey of the Basic Situation in Zhejiang's Rural Markets," March 18, 1954.

———. "Viewing the Basic Situation and Peculiarities in Zhejiang's Rural Markets Through a Representative Survey," March 15, 1954.

CCP Zhejiang Provincial Committee Rural Work Department Office. "Materials Regarding the Current Situation of Rectifying the Communal Kitchens and Arranging the People's Livelihood," May 9, 1960.

CCP Zhejiang Provincial Committee Work Group. "Some Circumstances and Problems in the Rural Work in Huangyan County's Luqiao Town (draft)," May 28, 1961.

CCP Zhejiang Provincial Committee's Investigation Group for Huangyan County's Luqiao Commune. "A Comparison of Two Production Brigades," May 18, 1961.

"Central Committee Rural Work Department's Self-criticism Regarding Zhejiang Province's Collectivization Problems," September 13, 1955.

"Closure of Communal Kitchens in Some Localities." In Zhejiang Provincial Party Committee Rural Work Department Office, ed., Situation Brief, no. 3 (January 13, 1961).

"Comrade Jiang Hua's Speech to a Meeting of First Secretaries of the County Party Committee," March 21, 1960.

"Dali Production Team's Food Substitute Campaign." In Zhejiang Provincial Party Committee Rural Work Department Office, ed., Situation Brief, no. 3 (January 13, 1961).

Documents printed by the Secretariat for the [Zhejiang] Provincial Grain Conference, May 14, 1962.

"Extra-urgent Telegram (On Taking the Initiative to Increase the Transfer of Grain from Zhejiang): 'From Jiang Hua to Comrade [Li] Xiannian and Reported to the Chairman, the Central Committee, and the Shanghai Bureau,'" April 21, 1959, 8:00 p.m.

Health Branch of the Wuxing County People's Committee. "Notice Regarding Edema," May 20, 1960.

Issued with Comments by the Provincial Party Committee: Report by the Leading Party Group of the Provincial Grain Bureau on the First Provincial Grain Meeting of 1959, July 1, 1959.

Jiang Hua. "High Speed Is the Spirit of Constructing Socialism: A Report to the Party Secretaries of All Communes in the Province," March 3, 1960.

———. "Work Report at the Second Session of the Second Zhejiang Provincial Party Congress," December 9, 1957.

Jiaxing County Sanitation Bureau. "Summary of Efforts to Prevent and Treat Edema," June 4, 1960.

Lin Hujia. "Speech at a Provincial On-the-Spot Meeting to Transform Backward Production Teams," May 10, 1960.

Provincial Party Committee Office. "The Situation Throughout the Province of Making Good on the Indiscriminate Transfer of Resources," March 1961.

Provincial Party Committee Rural Work Department Distribution Office. "The Current Situation of Rural Livelihood Arrangements," December 15, 1961. In CCP Zhejiang Provincial Committee Rural Work Department Office, ed., *Situation Brief*, no. 35 (December 18, 1961).

Provincial Party Committee's Investigation Group for Huangyan County's Luqiao Commune. "Survey Data on the Living Conditions of the Masses in the Lifeng Production Brigade (draft)," April 23, 1961.

Qu County Work Group. "Data on the Basic Conditions at the Lutou Production Brigade," May 4, 1961.

Report by Director Zeng Shaowen at the National Conference of Grain Bureau Heads. "Regarding Problems in Grain Work," July 16, 1961.

"Reports from All Localities to the Provincial Party Committee Requesting Aid," May 8, 1959.

"Strive to Continue the Great Leap Forward in the Province's Grain and Oil Efforts in 1960," February 12, 1960.

"The Situation of the Rectification of the Grassroots Organization of the Liming Production Team." In Zhejiang Provincial Party Committee Rural Work Department Office, ed., *Situation Brief*, no. 10 (February 9, 1961).

Transmitted via the Provincial Party Committee: Two Sets of Material by the Provincial Party Committee Office Regarding the Food Shortage in Some Areas, May 25, 1959.

Wenzhou Prefecture. "Sanitation Work Bulletin," August 18, 1959.

Zhejiang Provincial Health Department. "Investigation Report Regarding Cyanotic Illness," April 6, 1960.

Zhejiang Provincial Party Committee Office. "A Survey of the Grain Situation in Key Grain-producing Counties" (parts 1–17), 1961.

2. CENTRAL GOVERNMENT MINISTRIES

CCP CENTRAL COMMITTEE RURAL WORK DEPARTMENT

CCP Central Committee Rural Work Department. "National Rural Work Department Heads Conference Bulletin," no. 10, January 22, 1959.

———. "The Situation and Problems with Implementing and Carrying Out the Sixty Provisions in All Localities," August 24, 1961.

CCP CENTRAL COMMITTEE UNITED FRONT DEPARTMENT

CCP Central Committee Work Group, United Front Department Subgroup, ed. "Situational Bulletin," no. 12, August 28, 1962.

———. "Situational Bulletin," no. 24, October 13, 1962.

FOOD MINISTRY

"Comrade Chen Guodong's Report to Vice-premier Li Xiannian," March 17, 1962.

"Documents for the Second National Food Conference, 1957," August 1957.

Food Ministry. "Central People's Government State Planning Commission Program Targets Handed Down to the Food Ministry," June 15, 1954.

———. "Outline of the Report on the Food Supply Problem," May 7, 1961.

———. "Provisions on Reporting the Provision of Feed Grain," May 17, 1957.

———. "Report Regarding Problems in the Buying and Selling of Grain," August 1957.

———. "Urban Supply Bulletin," November 1957.

Food Ministry and the Central Finance and Economic Commission. "The Situation on the Month-by-Month Depletion of the Nation's Grain Reserves," July 1954.

Food Ministry Leading Party Group. Report to the CCP Central Committee: "Report on Arrangements for Tuber Production and Sale," March 7, 1958.

———. "Report to the Central Committee," May 20, 1958.

———. "Report to the Central Committee," August 15, 1958.

———. "Report on the Current Grain Procurement, Sale, and Allocation Situation," October 4, 1958.

———. "Views Regarding the Current Food Supply Problem and Future Food Supply Work," November 27, 1959.

Food Ministry Office, ed. "Grain Work Bulletin," no. 28, August 20, 1962.

Food Ministry Planning Department. "Grain Data Summary," August 25, 1962.

———. Statistical Data: "A Comparison of Nationwide Grain Requisition and Output, 1950–1953," 1954.

———. Statistical Data: "1953 Urban and Rural Demand for a Grain Ration Supply in Terms of Population and Quantity (Trade Grain)," 1954.

———. Statistical Data, 1956.

———. Statistics Calculated on July 5, 1960.

Food Ministry Statistics Department. Tables, July 1957, and Food Ministry Tables, February 6, 1958.

"Issued with Comments by the Central Committee: Report by the Food Ministry on Increasing the State Grain Reserves to 50 Billion Kilos Within Three Years," January 26, 1969.

Li Jingquan's Letter to Vice-premier Li Xiannian Regarding Sichuan Province's Grain Procurement Figures, August 5, 1960.

"Main Debate Points on the State Monopoly for Purchasing and Marketing Grain in Xiangxi Autonomous Prefecture," "Through Mass Debate Yiyang County Exceeds Procurement Quota for Early Rice," December 1957.

"Material Provided by the Food Ministry to Vice-premier Li Xiannian for His Speech to the National People's Congress," 1955.

Materials for the 1959 National Conference of Food Bureau Heads.

"National Food Conference Documents," July 1957.

Niu Peicong and Chen Guodong. "Urgent Report on Food Supplies," July 12, 1960.

Sha Qianli. "Fight Right Deviation, Go All Out, and Set Off a New Surge in the Red Flag Movement," November 2, 1959.

State Council Office No. 1. "Survey of the Rural Grain Shortage," April 22, 1955.

Zhang Naiqi. "The Situation of Food Supply Work Over the Last Five Years—Speech to the National People's Congress," September 25, 1954.

MINISTRY OF COMMERCE

Leading Party Group of the Ministry of Commerce. "Report on the Situation in Fulfilling the 1959 Export Plan," January 8, 1960.

MINISTRY OF HEALTH

Leading Party Group of the Ministry of Health. "Report on the Prevention and Treatment of Current Major Diseases," February 1, 1961.

MINISTRY OF PUBLIC SECURITY

"Guangxi Province's Suppression of Counterrevolutionaries and the Current Problem of Ideological Paralysis," May 15, 1951. In Guangxi Public Security Bureau, ed., "Situation and Material," no. 6, 1950–1951.

Ninth National Public Security Conference. "Resolution Regarding Thoroughly Eliminating the Counterrevolutionaries and Criminals At Large Who Have Slipped Through the Net in the Mountain Regions, Transitional Areas, Maritime Regions, and Backward Regions," August 16, 1958.

Xu Zirong. "Statistical Report on Key Figures Since the Campaign to Suppress Counter-revolutionaries," January 14, 1954.

3. OFFICIAL DOCUMENTS: CENTRAL GOVERNMENT

All-China Federation of Trade Unions Leading Party Group. "Report on the Development of Urban People's Communes and Several Problems," June 8, 1960.

"Bulletin of the Eighth Plenum of the Eighth CCP Central Committee," August 26, 1959.

"Bulletin of the Enlarged Meeting of the CCP Central Committee Politburo at Beidaihe," August 31, 1958.

"Bulletin of the Ninth Plenum of the Eighth CCP Central Committee," January 20, 1961.

"Bulletin of the Sixth Plenum of the Eighth CCP Central Committee," December 17, 1958.

"Bulletin of the Tenth Plenum of the Eighth CCP Central Committee," September 27, 1962.

"CCP Central Committee Directive Regarding Lowering Rural and Urban Grain Ration Levels," September 7, 1960.

"CCP Central Committee Directive Regarding the Dissemination of Speeches by Chen Yun and Other Comrades," March 18, 1962.

"CCP Central Committee Directive Regarding Urban People's Communes," March 9, 1960.

"CCP Central Committee Directives on the Launch of the 'Three Antis' Movement in the Countryside," May 15, 1960.

"CCP Central Committee Directives Regarding Grain Work," July 31, 1959.

CCP Central Committee Northeast Bureau. "Northeast Bureau Circular on Stabilizing the Ranks of the Labor Force," May 16, 1961.

"CCP Central Committee Resolution Regarding the Establishment of People's Communes in the Countryside," August 29, 1958.

"CCP Central Committee Transmission of Hebei Provincial Party Committee Transmission with Instructions: 'Baoding Municipal Party Committe Report on Mobilizing the Masses to Hold Eat-well Meetings,'" November 26, 1960.

"CCP Central Committee Transmission: Brief Report Compiled by the General Office of the Central Committee Regarding Food Shortages and Food Emergencies in Sixteen Provinces and Regions, and the Solutions Proposed by Local Party Committees," April 25, 1958.

"CCP Central Committee Transmission with Instructions: Guizhou Provincial Party Committee's 'Report on the Current Situation of the Rural Communal Kitchens,'" March 6, 1960.

"CCP Central Committee Transmission: 'Report by the CCP Xinyang Prefectural Committee on the Rectification Campaign and Production Disaster Relief Efforts,'" December 22, 1960.

"CCP Central Committee Transmission: 'Report by the Five-member Group on Adjusting the Rural Labor Force and Problems in Reducing and Demoting Workers and Staff,'" April 9, 1961.

"CCP Central Committee Transmission: Yunnan Provincial Party Committee's Preliminary Summary of the First Use of Peaceful Consultations to Carry Out Land Reform in Six Border Counties and Districts," December 10, 1955.

"CCP Central Committee Transmission with Instructions: Investigation Report by the Shandong Provincial Party Committee and Provincial People's Committee Regarding the Closure of Communal Kitchens and Fleeing from the Famine," January 22, 1959.

"CCP Central Committee Transmission with Instructions: Li Xiannian's Report on Immediate Allocation and Transfer of Grain, Oil, and Cotton and the Establishment of an Allocation and Transportation Department," February 21, 1960.

"CCP Central Committee Transmission with Instructions: Report on the Eleventh Meeting of the First Sichuan Provincial Party Committee," October 13, 1959.

"CCP Central Committee's Urgent Directives Regarding the All-Party Campaign for Foreign Trade Purchases and Exports," August 10, 1960.

"CCP Central Committee's Urgent Directives Regarding Verifying the Urban Population and Staple Food Supplies," June 16, 1961.

"Central Committee Directive on Countering Right-deviating Thought," August 7, 1959.

"Central Committee Directives Regarding the Serious Problems Arising in Some Areas of Shandong, Henan, Gansu, and Guizhou," December 8, 1960.

"Central Committee Memo on Transmission of Three Documents by the Henan Provincial Party Committee and the Luoyang Prefectural Party Committee Regarding Problems in Adhering to Policy," February 4, 1961.

"Central Committee Memo Regarding Strengthening the Leadership of the Communal Kitchens," March 18, 1960.

"[Central Committee] Northeast Bureau Directives Regarding Further Suppressing Counterrevolutionary Activities," February 28, 1951.

"Central Committee Northwest Bureau Transmission with Instructions: [Report] on the Severe Handling of Behavior in Violation of Food Policies in Shaanxi, Gansu, Xinjiang, and Other Provinces and Regions," December 19, 1960.

"Central Committee Resolution Regarding Continuing to Reduce the Urban Population by Seven Million in the First Half of 1962," February 14, 1962.

"Central Committee Secretariat Transmission: Report by the Anhui Provincial Party Committee Regarding Trial Implementation of Assigning Work and Production Responsibility," May 3, 1961.

"Central Committee Transmission: Comrade Gu Mu's 'Opinions Regarding Rapidly Overcoming the Phenomenon of Workers Secretly Leaving Their Factories and Consolidating the Worker Ranks,' and Comrade Jia Bubin's Letter," April 30, 1961.

"Central Committee Transmission: Hebei Provincial Party Committee's Provisions on the Participation of Cadres in the Communal Kitchens," March 7, 1960.

"Central Committee Transmission: Materials from Some Provinces, Cities, and Prefectures Uncovering Right-deviating Thought and Activity Among Some High-level Cadres," September 8, 1959.

"Central Committee Transmission with Approval: Military Commission General Political Department's 'Classification Criteria and Handling Methods for Right-deviating Elements,'" November 27, 1959.

"Central Committee Transmission with Approval: Report by Party Committees of Organs Directly Subordinate to the Central Committee and Party Committees of Central State Organs on Handling the Cases of Comrades Erring During the Rectification Movement in the Course of the Campaign Against Right Deviation, and on Standards and Principles for Identifying Right-deviating Opportunists," January 15, 1960.

"Central Committee Transmission with Approval: Resolution of the Qinghai Provincial Party Committee Regarding the Errors of the Anti-Party Clique led by Zhang Guosheng," October 14, 1959.

Central Committee Transmission with Instructions: All-China Federation of Trade Unions, "Report on the Present Development of Urban People's Communes and Several Problems," June 8, 1960.

"Central Committee Transmission with Instructions: Circular by the Jiangsu Provincial Party Committee Regarding Immediately Correcting the Assignment of Agricultural Work and Production to Households," October 13, 1959.

"Central Committee Transmission with Instructions: Comrade Qi Yanming's Report on Special-need Supplies for Ranking Cadres and High-level Intellectuals in Beijing," November 9, 1960.

"Central Committee Transmission with Instructions: Gansu Provincial Party Committee's Situational Report on the Complete Deterioration of the Tongwei County Party Committee," April 21, 1960.

"[Central Committee] Transmission with Instructions: Investigative Report by the Construction and Engineering Ministry Leading Party Group on Problems in Suspending or Delaying Construction Projects," January 6, 1962.

"Central Committee Transmission with Instructions: Materials Compiled by the Central State Organs Party Committees on Why Veteran Cadres Can't Meet the Test of Socialism."

"Central Committee Transmission with Instructions: Report by the Finance and Trade Office and the United Front Department on the Campaign Against the 'Backdoor' Sale of Commodities," May 9, 1962.

"Central Committee Transmission with Instructions: Report by the Zhejiang Provincial Party Committee on Violations of Policy in a Minority of Localities in Wenzhou and Jinhua Prefectures During the Socialist Education Movement," December 21, 1959.

"Central Committee Transmission with Instructions: Shanghai Municipal Party Committee's Report on Neighborhood Work and Plans to Establish Urban People's Communes," April 18, 1960.

"Central Committee Transmission with Instructions: State Council Finance and Trade Office and Beijing Municipal Party Committee, 'Request for Instructions on the Question of Supplying Nonstaple Foods to High-level Intellectuals and a Portion of Leading Cadres in Beijing,'" December 17, 1961.

"Central Committee Transmission with Instructions: The Hubei Provincial Party Committee's Summary Report on the Second Stage of Rectification of Work Styles and Communes at Mianyang's Tonghaikou Commune," January 31, 1961.

Central Committee Transmission with Instructions: "The Situation of Anhui Province's Correction of the 'Responsibility Fields,'" December 11, 1962.

"Central Committee Work Conference: Nine Ways to Reduce the Urban Population and Reduce Urban Grain Sales" (approved by the Central Committee on June 16, 1961).

"Central Committee's Memo on the Transmission of the 'Summary of One Production Brigade's Experience with the Socialist Education Movement,'" September 1, 1964.

"Chairman Mao's Transmission with Instructions: Comrade Hu Qiaomu's May 8 Letter to the Chairman," May 9, 1961.

"Chairman Mao's Transmission with Instructions: Comrades Deng Xiaoping and Peng Zhen's May 10 Letter to the Chairman," May 13, 1961.

"Comrade Mao Zedong's Directives Regarding Printing and Distributing Records of the Symposium on Consolidating the Collective Economy in the Production Teams," July 22, 1962.

"Comrade Yan Hongyan's Letter to the Chairman from Midu County," May 9, 1961.

General Office of the CCP Central Committee, comp. "The Situation of the Rural Communal Kitchens in Eight Provinces," "Memo from the CCP Central Committee on Strengthening the Leadership of the Communal Kitchens," March 18, 1960.

Hu Qiaomu et al. "Report on Resolving the Communal Kitchen Problems at Shaoshan Commune," April 10, 1961. In "Central Committee Transmission of Several Important Documents with Comments by the Chairman."

"Internal Party Communiqué" (from Mao Zedong to Six Levels of Cadres), April 29, 1959.

"Resolution of the CCP Central Committee Regarding Several Issues in the History of Our Party Since the Founding of the PRC," June 27, 1981.

"Resolution on Several Issues Related to the People's Communes," passed by the Sixth Plenum of the Eighth CCP Central Committee on December 10, 1958.

"Urgent Directives from the CCP Central Committee Regarding Current Policy Problems in the Rural People's Communes" (also known as the "Twelve Provisions on Agriculture"), November 3, 1960.

4. OFFICIAL DOCUMENTS: PROVINCIAL GOVERNMENTS

GANSU

CCP Gansu Provincial Committee on Submitting "The Historical Experience and Lessons of Tongwei," July 5, 1965.

"Comrade Wang Feng's Report to the Chairman Regarding the Rural Communal Kitchens and Other Issues," May 9, 1961.

"Inspection Report by the Gansu Provincial Party Committee on Several Issues Relating to the Implementation and Execution of the Spirit of the Northwest Bureau's Lanzhou Conference Over the Last Two Years," adopted by the Fourth Plenary Session of the Third Provincial Party Congress on December 3, 1962.

HEBEI

"CCP Hebei Provincial Committee Briefing on the Edema Situation," December 17, 1960.

"Hebei Provincial Party Committee Authorized Transmission: Comrade Shi Xudong's Views on Handan City's Special Need for Provisions," November 1, 1960.

"Hebei Provincial Party Committee Report Regarding a Vigorous Mass Campaign to Competently Carry Out Food Supply Work and Make Good Livelihood Arrangements," October 18, 1960.

"Hebei Provincial Party Committee Transmission: Report by the Leading Party Group of the Health Department Regarding Immediately Launching a Campaign to Treat and Prevent Disease," August 17, 1961.

"Hebei Provincial Party Committee Transmission: Situation Report of the Leading Party Group of the Provincial Public Security Bureau Regarding Incidents of Food Poisoning in the Province," April 29, 1960.

"Hebei Provincial Party Committee Transmission with Instructions: Report by the

Finance and Trade Department of the Provincial Party Committee Regarding Views on Vigorously Engaging in Mass Campaigns for Rectifying Food Supply Discipline and Strengthening Food Management," September 27, 1960.

"Hebei Provincial Party Committee Transmission with Instructions: Report of the Ba County Party Committee Regarding the Treatment of Edema at Jianchapu Commune," February 2, 1960.

"Hebei Provincial Party Committee Transmission with Instructions: Report of the Neiqiu County Party Committee on Facilitating Arrangements for the People's Livelihood in Zhongxian Administrative District of Longyao Commune," February 10, 1960.

"Report of the CCP Hebei Provincial Committee and the Hebei Provincial People's Committee Regarding the Meeting Called on the 1959 Agricultural Products Purchase and Sale Agreement," March 14, 1959.

JIANGSU

"CCP Jiangsu Provincial Party Committee Transmission with Instructions: Investigation Materials Compiled by the Office of the Provincial Party Committee and Xinghua County on Three Different Types of Production Brigades," October 9, 1960.

"CCP Jiangsu Provincial Party Committee Transmission with Instructions: Nantong County Party Committee's Investigation Report Regarding Food Supply Problems at Shigang People's Commune," March 30, 1959.

JILIN

CCP Jilin Provincial Committee. "Report on Pilot Programs Implementing and Executing the Central Committee's Urgent Directive," December 28, 1960.

———. "Views on Cutting Down the Labor Force, Readusting Arrangements for the Labor Force, and Shrinking the Urban Population to Support the Battlefront of Agricultural Production," December 29, 1960.

"CCP Jilin Provincial Committee and Jilin Provincial People's Committee's Stipulations Regarding Certain Issues in the Life of People in the Countryside," January 7, 1959.

"CCP Jilin Provincial Committee Circular Regarding Some Localities Violating the Central Committee Directive by Repeating the Error of Indiscriminate Transfer of Resources," January 14, 1961.

"CCP Jilin Provincial Committee Directive on Adjusting a Proportion of the Wage System to the Supply System in the Rural People's Communes and Rectifying the Communal Kitchens," June 20, 1959.

"CCP Jilin Provincial Committee Notice on Solving the Problem of Commune Members Farming Individual Plots of Land," June 2, 1959.

"CCP Jilin Provincial Committee Report on Trends in the Thinking of Rural Grassroots Cadres and the Masses During Discussions of the Chairman's Directives," June 11, 1959.

"CCP Jilin Provincial Committee Report Regarding Deployment to Convene a Representative Assembly of Commune Members," May 5, 1959.

"CCP Jilin Provincial Committee Summary of Work to Rectify the Collectives and Settle Accounts," November 9, 1959.

"CCP Jilin Provincial Committee Transmission: Jilin Municipal Party Committee's Report Regarding the Current Edema Situation," January 5, 1961.

"CCP Jilin Provincial Committee Transmission with Instructions: Report by the Leading Party Group of the Provincial People's Procuratorate Regarding Authorized Arrests of Criminals in the Province in 1959," April 4, 1960.

"CCP Jilin Provincial Committee Transmission with Instructions: Report by the Tongyu County Party Committee on Immediately Halting the Mass Emaciation and Death of Livestock," April 27, 1960.

"CCP Jilin Provincial Party Committee Transmission with Instructions: Siping Prefectural Party Committee's Transmission with Instructions of Lishu County Party Committee's 'Notice Regarding Serious Errors of Indiscriminate Transfer of Resources by Heshan Commune While Implementing Policies,'" July 15, 1961.

"CCP Jilin Provincial Committee's Urgent Notice Regarding Promptly Treating Severe Edema," June 26, 1961.

"Notice on the Need to End Suicides in the Villages," February 20, 1960.

"Provincial Party Committee Agreement with the Views of the Provincial Politics and Law Committee Regarding Transferring the Jurisdiction for Authorizing the Arrest of Criminals to the County Party Committee in Areas Resolving the Inadequate Thoroughness of the Democratic Revolution," July 18, 1960.

"Provincial Party Committee Transmission: Jilin Municipal Party Committee's Urgent Notice Regarding Rigorously Curbing the Unauthorized Occupation of Communal Farmland by Enterprises," March 26, 1961.

"Provincial Party Committee Transmission with Instructions: Briefing by the Leading Party Group of the Grain Bureau Regarding the Problem of a Minority of Commune Members Fleeing Yanji County's Badao Commune," June 15, 1960.

"Provincial Party Committee Transmission with Instructions: Exposing False Progressiveness, Uprooting True Backwardness: Jiuzhan People's Commune's Report on Rectifying Work Styles and the Commune," March 18, 1961.

"Provincial Party Committee Transmission with Instructions: Provincial Finance and Trade Department's Report Regarding the Convening of a Conference on Living Arrangements in the Countryside," March 18, 1962.

"Provincial Party Committee Transmission with Instructions: Report by the Tongyu County Party Committee on Rapidly Reversing the Mass Emaciation of Large Livestock," April 19, 1960.

"Provincial Party Committee Transmission with Instructions: Report of the Public Security Bureau Work Group Regarding Violations of Law and Discipline at the Siping Custody and Repatriation Station," December 25, 1961.

"Provincial Party Committee Transmission with Instructions: Suggestions by the Leading Party Groups of the Public Security Bureau and Civil Affairs Bureau on Resolutely Curbing the Free Population Flow," November 13, 1961.

"Report to the Central Committee and Northeast Bureau Regarding the Food Situation and Problems in Living Arrangements," February 11, 1961.

SHANGHAI

"Report by the CCP Shanghai Municipal Committee on the Problems in Fengxian County," May 22, 1959.

"Shanghai Municipal Party Committee's Telephone Report to the Central Committee Regarding the Municipal Party Committee's Enlarged Conference," September 2, 1959.

SICHUAN

"CCP Sichuan Provincial Committee Directive on Combating Right-deviating Thought, Increasing Grain Production While Economizing on Consumption, and Successfully Overcoming the Famine," September 2, 1959.

CCP Sichuan Provincial Committee Office. "Situational Bulletin on the Rural Socialist Education Movement," December 18, 1959.

———. "Situational Bulletin Regarding Carrying Out a Pilot Project for the Socialist Education Campaign Among Factory and Mining Workers," November 28, 1959.

"CCP Sichuan Provincial Committee Transmission with Instructions: Nanchong Prefectural Party Committee's Transmission of the Yingxi Rectification Pilot Project Work Group Situational Report on Carrying out the 1961 'Three Includes and One Award' During the Rectification of Yingxi Commune," March 16, 1961.

"CCP Sichuan Provincial Committee Transmission with Instructions: Situation Report Forwarded by Comrade Yan Hanmin on the Campaign to Combat Right Deviation, Drive Enthusiasm, Increase Grain Production, and Economize on Consumption to Overcome the Famine in Wanxian City's Longbao Commune," September 23, 1959.

YUNNAN

"Provincial Party Committee Directive Regarding Several Issues in the Rural Rectification of Work Styles," August 17, 1957.

"Provincial Party Committee Memo Regarding Three Surveys of Food Supply Arrangements," January 11, 1961.

"Provincial Party Committee Notice Regarding Several Issues in Fumin County's Campaign to Counterattack Reactionary Landlords, Rich Peasants, and Counterrevolutionaries," August 12, 1957.

"Provincial Party Committee Report to the Central Committee Regarding the Struggle Against Right Deviation Launched in Provincial-level Organs," October 28, 1959.

"Yunnan Provincial Party Committee Report Regarding Several Key Experiences in the Counterattack Against Landlords, Rich Peasants, and Counterrevolutionaries," September 12, 1957.

ZHEJIANG

"CCP Zhejiang Provincial Committee Transmission with Instructions: Huangyan County Party Committee's 'Investigative Report Regarding the Thinking in Each Social Class in the Countryside,'" March 12, 1956.

"Provincial Party Committee Transmission: 'The Situation of Eating Without Paying and Planning Grain Consumption in the Satellite Production Team of Dayang People's Commune in Jiande County' and 'The Establishment of a Food Planning and Management System in Fuyang County's Changkou Commune,'" December 29, 1958.

"Provincial Party Committee Transmission: Two Sets of Material From the Provincial Party Committee Office Regarding Food Supply Pressures in Some Areas," May 25, 1959.

"Provincial Party Committee Transmission with Instructions: Report of the Leading Party Group of the Grain Bureau Regarding the First Provincial Grain Conference in 1959," July 1, 1959.

5. SPEECHES AND MEMOS BY CENTRAL LEADERS

"Central Committee Directives Regarding Health Work," drafted for the Central Committee by Mao Zedong, March 16, 1960.

Chairman Mao's Directives upon Hearing the Report of the Hebei Provincial Party Committee, 1961.

"Chairman Mao's Remarks at Xinyang," November 13, 1958.

"Chairman Mao's Speech at the Enlarged Central Committee Work Conference," January 31, 1962.

"Comrade Li Xiannian's Remarks During the Central Committee Telephone Conference," April 19, 1959.

"Comrade Li Xiannian's Remarks on the Evening of September 10 During the Telephone Conference Convened by the Central Committee on Lowering Rural and Urban Grain Ration Standards (record)," September 10, 1960.

"Comrade Liu Shaoqi Inspects the Cities and Villages of Jiangsu," *People's Daily*, September 30, 1958.

Comrade Liu Shaoqi's Speech at the Conference of Provincial and Municipal Party Secretaries (written record), February 1, 1959.

Comrade Liu Shaoqi's Speech at the Party Cadre Conference (written record), September 27, 1958.

"Comrade Peng Zhen's Remarks During the Central Committee Telephone Conference on January 3 (summary)," January 3, 1959.

Comrade Tan Zhenlin's Remarks During the Central Committee Secretariat Telephone Conference on January 3, 1959 (written record by the Sichuan Provincial Party Committee Office).

Comrade Tan Zhenlin's Summing Up at the Wheat Symposium for Ten Provinces and Cities (written record), February 21, 1959.

Comrade Wang Congwu's Speech (on the Xinyang Incident) at the Meeting of the Standing Committee of the Henan Provincial Party Committee, December 6, 1960.

Comrade Xu Zirong's Speech (on the Xinyang Incident) at the Meeting of the Standing Committee of the Henan Provincial Party Committee, December 6, 1960.

Kang Zhuo. "Chairman Mao Arrives at Xushui," *People's Daily*, August 11, 1958.

Li Fuchun. "Report Regarding the 1959 National Economic Plan Draft," April 21, 1959.

———. "Report Regarding the 1960 National Economic Plan Draft," March 31, 1960.

Li Xiannian. "Speech to the Conference of Food and Commerce Bureau Heads," August 26, 1961.

Liao Zhigao to Li Dazhang. "Interposed Remarks at the Symposium of First Secretaries of Central Committee Regional Bureaus and Some Provincial and Municipal Party Secretaries Convened by the Chairman on the Evening of the Twenty-third," December 25, 1960.

"Main Points of Li Xiannian's Remarks at the Preparatory Meeting for the National Conference of Finance and Trade Secretaries," September 10, 1959.

Mao Zedong. "Conversation with Comrades Kapo and Balluku," February 3, 1967.

———. "Interposed Remarks While Hearing Reports at the CCP Central Committee Work Conference," December 30, 1960.

———. "Mao Zedong's Remarks at the Central Committee Working Conference in Beijing," June 12, 1961.

———. "Speech at the Beidaihe Central Committee Work Conference Core Group Meeting," August 9, 1962.

———. "Speech at the Lushan Conference," July 23, 1959.

"Mao Zedong's Interposed Remarks at the Chengdu Conference," March 1958.

"Mao Zedong's Six Speeches at the Chengdu Conference," March 9, 10, 20, 22, 25, 26, 1958.

"Mao Zedong's Speech at the Nanning Conference," January 12, 1958.

"Mao Zedong's Speeches at the Enlarged Politburo Meeting at Beidaihe," August 17, 19, 21, 30, 1958.

"Mao Zedong's Speeches at the [First] Zhengzhou Conference," November 2, 6, 7, 9, 10, 1958.

"Mao Zedong's Speeches at the Second Session of the Eighth National Congress of the CCP," May 8, 17, 18, 20, 23, 1958.

"Mao Zedong's Speeches at the [Second] Zhengzhou Conference," February 27 and 28, March 1 and 5, 1959.

"Mao Zedong's Speeches at the Wuchang Conference," November 21, 22, 1958.

"Record of Chairman Mao's Comments at a Symposium of Party Secretaries of Xinxiang, Luoyang, Xuchang, and Xinyang Prefectures," morning of February 27, 1959.

Record of Comrade Liu Shaoqi's Remarks to Comrades of the Leading Party Group of the All-China Federation of Women, June 14, 1958.

"Record of Remarks by State Statistical Bureau Director Xue Muqiao at the Henan Province Statistical Work Symposium." *Statistical Work*, no. 12 (1958).

(Shaanxi Provincial First Secretary) Comrade Zhang Desheng's Transmission of the Chairman's and Premier's Directives at the Central Committee Conference. (File date illegible, but content indicates late 1960 or early 1961.)

Speeches by Chairman Mao, Premier Zhou, and Deng Xiaoping While on an Inspection Visit in Hebei in 1958.

Speeches by Mao Zedong, Liu Shaoqi, and Deng Xiaoping at the Chengdu Conference (edited record by the Sichuan Provincial Party Committee Office), April 15, 1958.

Speeches by Mao Zedong, Liu Shaoqi, Premier Zhou, and Deng Xiaoping at the CCP Central Committee Work Conference, 1961.

"Summary of Remarks by Comrade Li Xiannian During the Central Committee Secretariat Telephone Conference on October 15, 1959."

"Summary of Remarks by Director Jia Qiyun at the Conference of All Provincial and Municipal Statistical Bureau Heads." Jiangsu provincial archives, series no. 31335, vol. 2125.

Tan Zhenlin. "Launching the Great Food Substitute Mass Movement" (report at the National Food Substitute Conference), November 10, 1960.

Tan Zhenlin and Liao Luyan's Report to the Central Committee and Chairman Mao. "Main Situation, Problems, and Views Regarding Agricultural Production and the Rural People's Communes," November 16, 1958.

Tan Zhenlin's Remarks at the Gansu Province Third Representative Assembly (written record), May 25, 1960.

Tan Zhenlin's Remarks at the Henan Provincial Cadre Conference, July 15, 1958.

Tan Zhenlin's Remarks During the National Telephone Conference, November 2, 1960.

Tan Zhenlin's Speech at the National Conference on Financial and Economic Work, February 12, 1960.

Tao Zhu. "Humen Commune Investigative Report," *People's Daily*, February 25, 1959.

(Vice-minister of Public Security) Xu Zirong. "Statistical Report Regarding Several Key Figures Since the Suppression of Counterrevolutionaries," January 14, 1954.

"The Chairman's Speech at the Conference of Provincial and Municipal Party Secretaries (recorded notes)," afternoon of February 1, 1959.

Xue Muqiao. "How Statistical Work Can Leap Forward." *Statistical Work*, no. 5 (1958).

INDEX

academia, 9–10, 18, 78–79, 119, 251, 254–55

acorn flour, 343

"adjustment, consolidation, replenishment, and enhancement," 433, 499, 503

agriculture, 6, 23, 25, 108, 145–46, 505, 506; Anhui Province, 269–319; Bo County, 295–304; close-planting, 207, 259, 260, 262, 435; collectivization, 156–63; cooperatives, 156–59; deep-plowing, 77, 201–202, 259–60; exaggerated crop-yield claims, 25–37, 74–76, 86, 114, 115, 127, 146, 206, 257–58, 264, 270–71, 296, 306–308, 322–31, 337, 394; false reporting and private withholding, 28–37, 47, 58, 76–77, 86, 127, 134, 149, 207, 211, 227, 309, 322, 334–38, 393, 394; farming implements, 146, 156–57, 161, 167, 203, 241, 306, 316; Fengyang, 270–86; Five Winds, 248–68, 305–10; food crisis, 320–49; Gansu Province, 112–55; Henan Province, 23–86; high-yield myth, 326–31, 496; household farming, 150, 167, 178–80, 188, 207–208, 229–30, 258, 286, 315–19, 337, 341, 398–99, 406, 432, 439–43, 507, 508–10; irrigation projects, 71–74, 77, 78, 80, 92, 113, 119, 146, 275, 284–86, 306, 332, 452; official response to crisis, 431–64; people's communes as foundation of totalitarian system, 156–73; planting patterns and slogans, 146; procurement quotas, 26–37, 76, 82, 113, 115, 126, 146, 227, 306–309, 320–49, 393, 394, 398, 399–406, 447–49; responsibility fields, 286, 314, 315–19, 441–43, 508–10; satellite communes, 73–77, 119, 199–200, 212, 263–64, 295–96, 306–307, 326–30, 496; Sichuan Province, 197–247; state purchasing monopoly, 19, 22, 69, 157, 161, 320–25, 394, 465, 486–87; tax, 6; urban labor sent back to countryside, 443–45; Wuwei, 286–95; Xinyang Incident, 23–68; Yintao Project, 122–25, 146, 154. *See also* collectivization; grain; people's communes; *specific crops*

alfalfa stalks, 115

algae powder, 343

"An'gang Constitution," 265

Anhui Daily, 305, 306

Anhui Province, 15, 16, 23, 94, 113, 181, 183, 184, 216, 255, 269–319, 325, 329, 400–405, 444, 447, 472, 474, 508; Bo County, 295–304; cannibalism, 278–79, 289–90, 302–304, 311; cover-up of crisis in, 310–13; Fengyang, 270–86; Five Winds, 271–72, 305–10; irrigation projects, 284–86; overall situation in, 304–19; population loss, 394, 395, 411, 415; procurement quotas, 270–71, 296, 306–309, 318; public security, 477; rectification measures, 281–84; responsibility fields, 315–19; starvation deaths, 269–319, 394; Wuwei Crisis, 286–95

anti-party cliques, 68–71, 112–20, 294, 391, 508

anti-rightism, 7, 23, 31, 46, 69, 71, 84–85, 92, 162, 325, 376; Anti-Rightist Campaign, 23, 31, 46, 84–85, 92, 112, 162, 392, 487, 494, 499; campaign against right deviation, 68–71, 80, 88, 90–92, 94, 112–22, 131, 147, 148, 161, 172, 184, 224, 227–30, 232–40, 264, 266, 268, 282, 297–98, 338, 353, 360, 388–93, 398, 433, 452, 487; Pan, Yang, Wang Incident, 68–71, 112

Anti-Rightist Campaign. See anti-rightism

An Ziwen, 59, 60, 311, 415, 430

arts, 18, 256–57, 266, 493

"assault on backwardness," 225, 227

backyard furnaces, 78

bad elements, 42, 47, 61, 152, 188, 282, 439, 445, 478, 490; blamed for Xinyang Incident, 61–68, 84, 85; Gansu Province, 112–20

Baiguochong Reservoir, 73

ball bearings, 77

bamboo, 23

Banister, Judith, 417, 420

Banqiao Commune, 278

Bao "Qingtian," 195

barley, 274

beating deaths, 29–32, 149, 216, 261, 289, 336, 510; Fengyang, 282–84; Sichuan, 216, 225–28; Tongwei, 149; Xinyang Incident, 29–37, 47–49, 62

behavioral restraint, invisible system of, 495–96

Beidaihe Conference, 78, 172, 248, 250, 257, 350, 459, 491, 511

Beijing, 12, 184, 339, 342, 351, 356, 399, 401, 402, 414, 434, 460, 461, 514

Beijing Daily, 262

Bengbu, 279, 306–14, 316, 317, 444

big-character posters, 71, 117, 118, 146, 507

"big drought, big harvest," 25–26

Bi Kedan, 82–83

birth rates, 13, 67, 185, 348, 394, 407–30; Anhui Province, 310; Gansu Province, 131, 132; Henan Province, 83–84; research by Chinese scholars, 419–30; research by population experts overseas, 416–19; Sichuan Province, 228, 244–47. *See also* population; *specific provinces*

Bishan County, 213, 215

Biyu Commune, 148

Bo County, 295–304; cannibalism, 302–304; communal kitchens, 297–99; starvation deaths, 300–302

Bo Gu, 350

bones, aged, 347

Bo Yibo, 90, 97, 268

Bozhou, 16

buckwheat, 115, 139

Buddhism, 160

Bumper Harvest Roads, 202

burial, 12, 13, 137, 278, 280, 298, 303–304; alive, 219, 242, 278, 283, 284; mass graves, 13, 14, 41, 43, 44, 242, 301; mourning rites, 278; shallow, 278; tombstones, 12

cabbage, 79

Cadre Privilege Wind, 248, 261, 267, 305

cadres, 8, 21, 23, 80, 89, 98, 105–106, 114, 168–70, 184, 261, 263, 434, 445–47, 458–60, 504; abusive, 21, 24–25, 30–32, 44–45, 47, 49, 73, 149, 159–60, 189–91, 202, 210–11, 252, 261, 281–84, 289, 310, 335–36, 445–47, 473, 482; Anhui Province, 269–319; blamed for food crisis, 61–68, 84, 85, 445–47, 482; communal kitchens, 174–96; death rate, 42; extravagances and corruption, 45, 221–23, 280–81, 299, 309, 445–47, 458–61; Five Winds, 248–68, 305–10; food crisis, 320–49; food penalties, 223–29; Gansu Province, 112–55; Henan Province, 23–86; Lushan Conference, 350–93; Mao and, 397–99, 436–39, 445–47; promotion of, 264–65; Sichuan Province, 197–247; system,

264–65; Tongwei Problem, 137–53; Xianju Incident, 159–60; Xinyang Incident, 24–68

caloric intake, 345–47

Calot, Gérard, 417, 420

Cambodia, 521

Campaign Against Right Deviation. *See* anti-rightism

canal projects, 71–73, 119, 122–25

cannibalism, 14, 40, 41–42, 349; Anhui Province, 278–79, 289–90, 302–304, 311; taboo, 279; Tongwei, 141–44, 147; Xinyang Incident, 41–46, 51

Caodian Commune, 278

Cao Shuji, 84, 246, 311, 395, 427, 430

capital construction, 79, 90–91, 275, 358, 443–44, 452, 505, 506; Henan Province, 77–80; opposition to rash advance, 90–104, 366. *See also specific projects*

capitalism, 33 89, 158, 248, 440

"cartification," 77

cattle, 120, 121, 240

Central Military Commission (CMC), 489–90

Central Plains Commentary, 70

Changchuan Committee, 132

Changhe Commune, 148

Changle County, 398–99

Changshan Commune, 202, 227–28

Changzhou, 445

Chaotic Directives Wind, 248, 253, 258–61, 267, 305, 392, 435

Chayashan Commune, 34–35, 48, 53, 74, 77, 163–65, 169, 366

Chen Bingyin, 163

Chen Boda, 98, 100, 102, 165–66, 193, 364, 378–79, 434, 436, 501, 517; Lushan Conference and, 378–79

Chen Chengyi, 112–13

Chen Duxiu, 350

Chengdu Conference, 73, 87, 98–104, 159, 163, 197–99, 204, 326, 463

Chengguan Commune, 48, 50, 75, 121, 139, 141

Chengjiao Commune, 42

Chen Guangfu, 287

Chen Guodong, 215, 406

Chengxi Commune, 204, 210, 222

Chen Huaitong, 231

Chen Xuemeng, 277

Chen Yi, 98, 382, 509

Chen Yinque, 10

Chen Yizi, 427

Chen Yun, 18, 90, 97–100, 106, 114, 263, 321, 334, 350, 357, 370, 443, 500, 505–508

Chen Zhengren, 361, 378

Chiang Kai-shek, 25, 96, 488, 490

children, 140, 190, 252, 275, 283; beating, 283–84; Blue Baby Syndrome, 346; burial alive, 283; death rate, 42; nurseries, 177; orphans, 42, 43, 49, 134–35, 141, 211, 216, 276, 280, 284, 289, 301, 303; starvation deaths, 29–32, 38–49, 53, 65, 133–53, 209–21, 226, 228, 243, 275–80, 285, 289, 300, 301–302, 312–13, 346

China, map of, vii

China Population: General Introduction, 420–21, 422, 423, 430

China Youth, 78

Chinese Academy of Sciences (CAS), 254–55, 331, 342, 343

Chinese Communist Party (CCP), 7–10, 17–18, 25–26; Anhui Province, 269–319; Central Committee, 50–72, 81–86, 88–111, 115, 126, 138, 150–55, 161, 169, 172, 179, 185–96, 197, 204–209, 236, 239, 248, 258, 267, 293–94, 299, 311–19, 336–42, 350–93, 396, 431–64, 481, 487, 493, 499–522; Central Inspection Commission, 24, 52, 57–68, 313, 415; communal kitchens, 174–96; conference politics, 367, 492; death toll concealed by, 49–68, 290–91, 309–14, 398, 406–408; Five Winds, 248–68, 305–10; food crisis, 320–49; Four Clean-Ups campaign, 513–18; Gansu province, 112–55; Great Famine's impact on, 499–522; investigation of Xinyang

Chinese Communist Party (*cont.*)
Incident, 57–61; Lushan Conference, 350–93; Pan, Yang, Wang Incident, 68–71, 112; party leadership, 487–88; response to food crisis, 431–64; Second Session of the Eighth National Congress, 70, 87, 101, 104–11; Seven Thousand Cadres Conference, 499–505; Sichuan Province, 197; systemic causes of Great Famine, 483–98; system of social control, 478–82; Tenth Plenum of the Eighth CCP Central Committee, 507–12, 519; Three Red Banners, 87–111, 199–204; Tongwei Problem, 137–53; Xinyang Incident, 23–68

Chinese Population Yearbook, 411, 416, 420–21, 422, 423

Chonggang Commune, 468

cities, 19, 339–42, 443–45, 458, 494; food ration for, 339–42, 486; subsidization of, 19; urban labor sent back to countryside, 443–45

civil war, 23, 200

clam shells, 38

clay consumption, 14, 210, 214–15

climate, 452–56

close-planting, 207, 259, 260, 262, 435

Coale, Ansley J., 417, 420, 422

Coercive Commandism Wind, 248, 261, 267, 305, 392

collectivization, 6, 19–22, 113, 145–46, 156–63, 271, 286–87, 306, 320, 341, 432, 434, 438, 441, 465, 486, 496, 510, 511; withdrawals and upheavals, 159–62; Xianju Incident, 159–60. *See also* people's communes

communal kitchens, 20–21, 43, 58, 78, 80, 81, 127, 140, 145, 174–96, 209, 251, 262, 281, 297–99, 308, 332, 357, 365, 374, 398, 406, 433, 451, 452, 497; Bo County, 297–99; closing of, 30–34, 37, 39, 45, 82, 151, 181, 184, 185, 191–96, 230, 286, 292, 293, 296, 297, 299, 315–16, 346, 394, 497; eliminating the family unit, 174–77; families driven to destitution

by, 177–79; grain hoarding, 28–37, 47, 58, 76–77, 127, 134, 149, 207, 334–38, 394; Henan Province, 184–88, 189; investigation groups, 193–96; "mechanization" of, 80; rise and fall of, 179–88; Sichuan Province, 200, 202–203, 208–12, 217, 221, 222, 229, 237; waste, 188–91

commune (term), 164

commune dining halls. *See* communal kitchens

communes. *See* people's communes

communism, 9, 68, 89, 145, 164–65, 249, 387, 431, 484–85, 518; retreat to socialism from, 170–73; Three Red Banners and, 87–111, 199–204; transition to, 145–46, 164–66, 250–54, 358, 432; worldview, 9, 89–90, 94, 519–20

Communist Canal, 72–73

Communist Wind, 79–80, 119, 120–22, 125, 154, 171, 202, 207, 248–54, 266–68, 270, 287, 305, 351, 354, 365, 392, 431, 435, 438, 493; in Anhui, 271–72, 305–10; historical legacy of, 248–54

"Compilation of Questions," 78–79

conference politics, 367, 492

Constitution, 490–92

cooperatives, 101, 156–59, 262, 287, 353, 365

corn, 48, 76, 204, 223, 228, 259, 273, 330; powdered roots, 343; stalks, 38

cotton, 23, 115, 263, 332

counterrevolutionaries, 42, 60–61, 152, 161, 282, 322, 439, 445, 446, 490, 495; blamed for Xinyang Incident, 62–68, 84, 85; Gansu Province, 112–20; rebellions and crime, 468–82; Xu Guohe, Zhang Wanshu clique, 115–20

crime, 465, 473–78

cult of personality, 101–102, 369, 385, 389

Cultural Revolution, 7, 11, 19, 22, 107, 246, 286, 295, 302, 311, 319, 370, 373, 379, 382, 386, 389, 415, 436, 443, 453, 491, 499, 512, 517, 521

culture, 255–57, 266, 493; Exaggeration
    Wind, 255–57
currency, 433–34

Daijang Commune, 287–88
Damiao Commune, 278
Daming County, 157–58
Dangyang County, 251
Danjiangkou Reservoir, 72
Daozuo Commune, 241–42
Daxihe Commune, 285
Daxing Commune, 213, 215
Dayi Commune, 16, 202, 214
deaths. *See* beating deaths; burial;
    executions; natural deaths; *specific
    provinces and communes*; starvation
    deaths; suicide
Dechang County, 322
deep-plowing, 77, 201–202, 259–60
democracy, 22, 485, 490–92
democratic revolution, supplemental
    lessons in, 152–53
Dengfeng County, 255
Deng Liquin, 164, 361, 362
Deng Xiaoping, 70, 98, 104, 110, 114, 115,
    120, 231, 239, 263, 295, 318, 340, 436,
    441, 500, 505, 508–509, 517, 520, 522
Deng Zihui, 158, 250–51, 318–19,
    507–508, 511
Deng Zili, 231
despotism, 484
detainees, 50, 310
Dianjiang County, 210, 471
dictatorship of the proletariat, 21, 485
Ding Shu, 425–26
Dingxi Prefecture, 137–53
disease (term), 217
Dishuidong, 460–61
dissuasion stations, 297, 301, 303
dogs, 40, 141
Dong Biwu, 57, 312
Dong Fu, 246
Dong Jianyi, 137
Dou Minghai, 147–48, 150, 153, 154
drought, 25, 27, 72, 76, 115, 305–306,
    453–56

Du Daozheng, 334
Dujiang Dam, 197–98, 241

Economic News, 308
economy, 22, 23, 486–87; Anhui
    Province, 269–319; collectivization,
    156–63; Five Winds, 248–68,
    305–10; food crisis, 320–49; Lushan
    Conference, 350–93; market, 22;
    official response to crisis, 431–64;
    opposition to rash advance and,
    90–104, 366; Sichuan Province,
    197–247; state purchasing monopoly,
    19, 22, 69, 157, 161, 320–25, 394, 465,
    486–87; systemic causes of Great
    Famine, 483–98; Tenth Plenum of the
    Eighth CCP Central Committee and,
    507–12; Xilou and May Conferences
    on, 505–507
edema, 4, 38, 48, 57, 81, 114, 115, 128, 132,
    135, 136, 192, 193, 210, 215–18, 276,
    281, 296, 297, 312, 322, 347–48, 349,
    394, 448, 460, 463; as "epidemic,"
    216–18; hospitals, 218–21
education, 6–7, 9–10, 18, 78–79, 119,
    251–55, 266; Exaggeration Wind
    and, 255
eggs, 218, 281, 342, 450, 451
egret droppings, 38
"Eight Essential Crops," 146
Eighth National Party Congress, 91–94,
    369, 518; First Session of, 110; Second
    Session of, 70, 87, 101, 104–11
Eighth Plenum of the Eighth CCP
    Central Committee. *See* Lushan
    Conference
electrification, 202, 251, 284
Engels, Friedrich, 88, 102, 164, 165,
    387
ethnic discontent, 465–68
Exaggeration Wind, 98, 99, 200, 205, 207,
    248, 253, 254–58, 264, 267, 305–308,
    327–30, 354, 392, 435; Anhui Province
    and, 305–308; high-yield myth, 327–30
executions, 65, 322
"extraction" duty, 224

family unit, elimination of, 174–77
famine of 1928–30, 13
famine of 1958–62. *See* Great Famine
Fan County, 251, 434
Fanghu Commune, 40, 41
Fanhe Commune, 252–53, 260, 336
Fengdu, 16, 335
Feng Peiran, 25
Fengyang, 16, 270–86; irrigation, 284–86;
    rectification measures, 281–84;
    starvation deaths, 275–80
"Fengyang Flower Drum Song," 269
Feng Yuxiang, 381
feudalism, 484–85
firewood, 298
First Five-Year Plan, 92, 95, 519
First Session of the Eighth National
    Congress, 110
fish, 38, 161, 222, 281, 459, 461, 462
Five-Category Elements, 42, 61, 281–82
"Five Eliminates," 146
Five Winds, 207, 248–68, 270, 276,
    305–10, 315, 392, 394, 436, 452, 482;
    Anhui province and, 271–72, 305–10;
    Cadre Privilege Wind, 261, 267,
    305, 392; Chaotic Directives Wind,
    258–61, 267, 305, 392; Coercive
    Commandism Wind, 248, 261, 267,
    305, 392; Communist Wind, 248–54,
    266–68, 305–10, 392; Exaggeration
    Wind, 254–58, 264, 267, 305–308,
    327–30, 392; irrepressible force of,
    266–68; source of, 261–63
floods, 453–56
food crisis, 320–49; caloric intake,
    345–47; fatal pathologies of starvation,
    347–49; food substitute campaign,
    342–44; grain procurement campaign,
    332–37; Mao and high-yield myth,
    326–31, 496; official response to,
    431–64; state purchasing monopoly,
    320–25, 394, 465, 486–87; urban,
    339–42. *See also* Great Famine; *specific
    foods, communes, and provinces*;
    starvation deaths
Food Ministry, 320–49

food poisoning, 115, 344
food substitutes, 14, 37–39, 115, 139, 147,
    210, 269, 277, 298, 331, 342–44, 346
Four Clean-Ups campaign, 265, 513–18.
    See also Socialist Education Movement
"Four Don't Plants," 146
"four harmful creatures" (*also* "four
    pests"), 72, 73
free markets, 440
Fucheng Commune, 286
Fujian Province, 112, 184, 322, 332–33,
    400, 401–405; population loss, 396,
    413, 415
Fuling County, 219, 228

Gannan, 132–33
Gansu Daily, 136, 504
Gansu Province, 16, 112–55, 179, 184,
    185, 187, 191, 196, 254, 325, 329, 400,
    402, 403, 405, 446, 459, 504; campaign
    against right deviation, 112–22, 131,
    147, 148; cannibalism, 134–35, 137,
    140–44, 147; counterrevolutionaries,
    112–20; death rate, 120, 128–32;
    exaggerated yields, 114, 115, 127, 146;
    Gansu Province, 134–35, 137, 140–44,
    147; handling and repercussions of
    Gansu problem, 153–55; political
    pressure to create lies, 112–15;
    population loss, 394, 395, 412;
    procurement quotas, 113, 115, 126,
    146–49; rebellions and looting, 470–75;
    Sichuan Province, 214; starvation
    deaths, 114, 115, 122, 126–55, 394;
    Tongwei Problem, 137–53; Yintao
    Project, 122–25, 146, 154
Gao De, 35
Gao Gang, 156–57, 294, 387, 388
Gao Yang, 78
garlic, 79
General Line, 87, 101, 184, 197, 233,
    236, 372, 376, 386, 388, 518; birth of,
    104–11. *See also* Great Leap Forward
government and politics, 7–10, 25–26;
    Anhui Province, 269–319; campaign
    against false reporting and private

withholding, 28–68, 76–77, 134, 149, 207, 211, 227, 309, 322, 334–38, 393, 394; communal kitchens and, 174–96; conference politics, 367, 492; death toll concealed, 49–68, 290–91, 309–14, 398, 406–408; Five Winds and, 248–68, 305–10; food crisis, 320–49; Four Clean-Ups campaign, 513–18; Gansu Province, 112–55; Great Famine's impact on, 499–522; Henan Province, 68–86; Lushan Conference, 350–93; opposition to rash advance and, 90–104, 366; Pan, Yang, Wang Incident, 68–71, 112; response to food crisis, 431–64; Seven Thousand Cadres Conference, 499–505; Sichuan Province, 197–247; social stability during Great Famine, 465–82; systemic causes of Great Famine, 483–98; system of social control, 478–82; Tenth Plenum of the Eighth CCP Central Committee, 507–12, 519; Three Red Banners, 87–111, 199–204; Tongwei Problem, 137–53; Xinyang Incident, 23–68. *See also* Chinese Communist Party (CCP)

grain, 6, 16, 20, 23, 72; Anhui Province, 269–319, 400, 401, 403, 405; Bo County, 295–304; caloric intake, 345–47; collectivization and, 156–63; communal kitchens and, 174–96; depots, 473; exaggerated crop-yield claims, 25–37, 74–76, 86, 114, 115, 127, 146, 206, 257–58, 264, 270–71, 296, 306–308, 322–31, 337, 394; exports, 19, 324, 335, 342, 447, 450–51; false reporting and private withholding, 28–37, 47, 58, 76–77, 86, 127, 134, 149, 207, 211, 227, 309, 322, 334–38, 393, 394; Fengyang, 270–86; food crisis, 320–49; Gansu Province, 112–55, 400, 401, 403, 405; Henan Province, 23–86, 400, 401, 403, 405; high-yield myth, 326–31, 496; imports, 335, 341–42, 444; official response to crisis, 431–64; per capita allocation, 399, 404–405;

procurement quotas, 26–37, 76, 82, 113, 115, 126, 146, 227, 306–309, 320–49, 393, 394, 398, 399–406, 447–49; production during the Great Famine, 399–400; rationing system, 20, 168, 179–84, 187, 208, 248, 251, 252, 254, 287, 298–99, 321–22, 435, 451, 478, 479, 486; reserves, 46, 51, 333, 337, 339–42, 368, 449–50; sales to rural areas, 323–24, 399, 402–405, 448–49; Sichuan Province, 197–247, 400, 401, 403, 405; state purchasing monopoly, 19, 22, 69, 157, 161, 320–25, 394, 465, 486–87; theft, 473–76; Tongwei Problem, 137–53; urban food ration, 339–42; waste of, 20, 188–91, 323, 332, 459; Wuwei, 286–95; Xinyang Incident, 23–68; yields, 89, 146, 241, 251, 288, 306–307, 356. *See also* procurement quotas; *specific grains*

grain requisition and sales. *See* state purchasing monopoly

graves. *See* burial

Great Famine, 3, 12–16; Anhui Province, 269–319; Bo County, 295–304; chronology of, xv–xxvi; communal kitchens and, 174–96; Fengyang, 270–86; Five Winds, 248–68, 305–10; food crisis, 320–49; Gansu Province, 112–55; Henan Province, 68–86; impact on Chinese politics, 499–522; lack of large-scale social turmoil, 476–82; Lushan Conference, 350–93; natural disasters, 452–56; official response to crisis, 431–64; population loss, by province, 394–430; population research by Chinese scholars, 419–30; population research by experts overseas, 416–19; public order before and during, 465–76; reasons for disparity in the effects of, 396–406; riots and rebellions, 465–82; Sichuan Province, 197–247; social stability during, 465–82; systemic causes of, 483–98; Three Red Banners, 87–111, 199–204; Tongwei Problem, 137–53;

Great Famine (*cont.*)
   total population loss during, 406–11;
   Wuwei, 286–95; Xinyang Incident,
   23–68, 445, 448. *See also* starvation
   deaths
Great Leap Forward, 7, 12–16, 19, 87;
   Anhui Province, 269–319; birth of,
   104–11; Bo County, 295, 304; communal
   kitchens, 174–96; Fengyang, 270–86;
   Five Winds, 248–68, 305–10; food
   crisis, 320–49; Gansu Province, 112–55;
   Henan Province, 68–86; irrigation
   projects, 71–73, 74, 77, 78, 80, 92, 113,
   119, 146, 275, 284–86, 306, 332, 452;
   lack of large-scale social turmoil,
   476–82; Lushan Conference, 350–93;
   official response to crisis, 431–64;
   population loss, by province, 394–430;
   public order before and during, 465–76;
   riots and rebellions, 465–82; shifting
   form of, 77–80; Sichuan Province,
   197–247; social stability during,
   465–82; Three Red Banners, 87–111,
   199–204; Tongwei Problem, 137–53;
   Wuwei, 286–95; Xinyang Incident,
   23–68. *See also* people's communes
Greene, Felix, *A Curtain of Ignorance*, 15
Guan Feng, 248
Guangdong Province, 161, 162, 184, 325,
   329, 333–34, 400, 401, 403, 405, 472.
   494; population loss, 396, 412
Guangming Daily, 493
Guangshan County, 30–32, 37–39, 44, 46,
   47, 50, 51, 53, 65
Guangxi Province, 184, 400, 401, 403,
   405; population loss, 394, 395, 412
Guangzhou Conference, 164, 316, 509
Guantang Commune, 301, 303
Guantao, 16
Guangxi Province, 322
Gucheng Commune, 299, 300–301
Gucheng Reservoir, 124
guesthouses, 460–61
Guihua Temple Incident, 468
Guizhou Province, 16, 184, 185–86, 254,
   340, 400, 402, 403, 405, 460, 463, 497;
   population loss, 394, 395, 412;
   rebellions and looting, 471–72, 474
Gulin County, 217–18, 224
Guo Moruo, 256
Guo Shuzhi, 34–35
Gushi County, 42, 52, 55, 57, 62, 66, 73
gynecological disorders, 67, 81, 132, 135,
   136, 217, 220, 228, 275, 348, 409

Hai Rui, 353–54
Hangzhou, 192, 460
Han regions, 465
Hayek, Friedrich, *The Road to Serfdom*,
   485
Hebei Province, 157–58, 162, 181, 182,
   184, 185, 188, 189, 249–54, 257, 325,
   330, 340, 399, 401, 402, 404, 405, 447,
   472, 504, 513, 514; population loss,
   396, 413
He Chenghua, 127–28, 153
Hechuan County, 238, 482
Heilongjiang Province, 185, 399, 401,
   403, 404, 444, 494; population loss,
   396, 413
He Long, 98, 356, 361, 363, 380–84
hemp, 301
Henan Daily, 46, 70, 78, 81
Henan Province, 16, 23–28, 101, 155,
   163–65, 169, 175, 184, 216, 251, 255,
   318, 325, 327, 340, 354, 378, 400, 402,
   403, 405, 442, 444, 446, 447, 450; CCP
   investigation of Xinyang Incident,
   57–61; communal kitchens, 184–88,
   189; death rate, 38–47, 83–84; death
   toll concealed, 49–68; grain hoarding
   and false reporting output, 28–37;
   grassroots cadres blamed for Xinyang
   Incident, 61–68, 84, 85; industry,
   77–80; irrigation projects, 71–74, 77,
   78, 80; Pan, Yang, Wang Incident,
   68–71, 112; population loss, 394, 395,
   412; procurement quotas, 26–37, 76,
   82; satellite communes, 73–77;
   starvation deaths, 23–68, 80–86, 394;
   Xinyang Incident, 23–68
Heping Commune, 76, 167

Hetun Commune, 229, 241
high-yield myth, 326–31, 496
Hiroshima, 16
hoarding, 28–37, 47, 76–77, 127, 134, 149, 207, 334–37, 394
Hongguang Commune, 198–200, 203, 222, 247
Hong Kong, 14, 473
Hongmiao Commune, 288
Hongtai Commune, 134, 135
hookworm, 217–18
hospitals, 218–21
"hot-blooded" youth, 263–64
household farming, 150, 167, 178–80, 188, 207–208, 229–30, 258, 286, 315–19, 337, 341, 398–99, 406, 432, 439–43, 507–10
household registration. *See hukou* system
Huaibei irrigation project, 306
Huaibin County, 39–45, 65, 395
Huaidian Commune, 30–34, 48–49
Huailai County, 189
Huangchuan County, 32–37, 42–47, 57, 62
Huang Kecheng, 98, 360, 361, 366, 367, 369, 377, 381, 384, 386, 388, 511
Huang Yongsheng, 381
Huayuankou project, 73
Hubei Province, 23, 46, 101, 125, 162, 184, 251, 267, 354, 400, 401–405, 450, 460, 472, 507; population loss, 396, 413
hukou system, 20
Hunan Province, 184, 191, 322, 345, 352, 355, 400, 402, 403, 436, 460, 461, 472, 497, 502; population loss, 394, 395, 412
Hungarian uprising (1959), 355–56, 519
Hu Qiaomu, 91, 193–95, 360–64, 368, 378–80, 436; Lushan Conference and, 379–80
Hushan Commune, 47
Hu Sheng, 248

illiteracy, 72, 73, 119, 255
Imperial era, 18, 170, 485–86, 495, 509
income differentiation, 157
India, 16, 34, 509
Individual Farming Wind, 510, 511

industrialization, 12, 19, 20, 28, 72, 77–80, 89, 108, 135, 146, 251, 254, 320, 332, 352–53, 394, 398, 434, 443–44, 451–52, 486, 488; Anhui Province, 275; backyard furnaces, 78; Exaggeration Wind, 254, 257, 258; Henan Province, 77–80, 82; opposition to rash advance, 90–104, 366; Sichuan Province, 201–202; Three Red Banners, 89–104; urban labor sent to countryside, 443–45. *See also* iron production; steel production
influenza, 217, 218, 219
Inner Mongolia, 325, 397–404, 414, 459
insects, 115, 344; eating, 344
intellectuals, 10–11, 249, 263, 266, 392, 494, 508–509
International Communist Movement, 519–20
International Congress of Communist and Workers' Parties, 94, 104
invisible system of behavioral restraint, 495–96
iron production, 28, 78, 79, 201, 254, 275, 394, 398, 434; backyard furnaces, 78
irrigation projects, 20, 57, 58, 71–74, 77, 78, 80, 92, 113, 119, 146, 275, 284–86, 306, 332, 452; "cartification," 77; Fengyang, 284–86; wasteful, 71–73; Yintao Project, 122–25, 146, 154

Japan, 11, 16
Jiabiangou, 136–37
Jiangbei County, 215, 219, 232, 239
Jiang Hua, 94
Jiang Qing, 483–84, 515
Jiangsu Province, 161, 184, 260, 325, 331, 400, 401–404, 445, 447, 460; population loss, 395, 412
Jianguo Commune, 333
Jiang Weiqing, 192
Jiangxi Province, 184, 287, 400, 401–405; population loss, 394, 396, 413
Jiang Zhenghua, 419–25, 428
Jia Qiyun, 406
Jichuan Commune, 141, 43

Jilin Province, 185, 259, 325, 339, 399, 401–404, 444, 480; population loss, 394, 396, 413; rebellions and looting, 472, 476–78

Jinggang Mountain, 373

Jing Gennian, 141–42

Jingning County, 114, 130, 254

Jin Hui, 425–26, 430

Jining, 16

Jinmen, 456

Jinsha, 16

Jintang County, 219, 227, 244

Jinya Commune, 179

July 1 Commune, 42

Ju'nan County, 251

Kaicheng Commune, 288

Kang Sheng, 97, 179, 352, 356, 360, 363, 378

Kangxi, Emperor, 197

Kang Youwei, *The Great Harmony*, 170–75, 249, 262

Ke Qingshi, 94, 97, 102, 105–108, 204, 313, 351, 353, 361–64, 379, 386

Khrushchev, Nikita, 361–62, 382, 456, 515; –Mao rivalry, 90, 94, 456, 510, 519–20

Korean War, 90, 519

Kuomintang, 11, 23, 25, 56, 61, 62, 64, 85, 93, 229, 481, 488

labor reform camps, 50, 136–37, 150, 161

landlords, 42, 60–62, 152, 282, 439, 445–47, 478, 490; blamed for Xinyang Incident, 61–68, 84, 85

Land Reform movement, 6, 60, 62, 156–57, 162, 169, 265, 447

Lankao-Shangqiu Sanyizhai People's Great Leap Canal, 73

Lanzhou, 136

Lanzhou Conference, 152, 153

leaf protein, 343

leap forward (term), 108–10

Leinan County, 333

Lenin, Vladimir, 88, 102, 164, 387, 485, 519

Liang Dajun, 112–13

Liang Zhiyuan, 295, 300, 301–303, 430

Liao Bokang, 239–40, 246, 415, 430

Liaoning Province, 185, 252, 260, 336, 339, 340, 399, 401–404; population loss, 396, 412

Li Chengrui, 420, 422

Li Dazhang, 233

Li Fuchun, 90, 97, 108, 318

Li Jian, 57, 313, 314, 415

Lijiang Xiaoliangshan Riot, 466–67

Li Jingquan, 97, 178, 197, 198, 200, 204–11, 218, 223, 229–34, 237, 239, 340, 351, 364, 386, 433, 436, 459

Li Lei, 133–35

Li Li, 54, 55

Li Lisan, 350

lima beans, 223, 228

Limin Commune, 285

Lin Biao, 98, 105, 352, 369, 372, 375–77, 382–85, 502–503; Lushan Conference, 375–77

Linxia, 128, 129, 133–35, 191

Li Qindan, 301

liquor, 463

Li Rui, 353–54, 360–64, 368–69, 378–81, 384, 389

Li Ruiying, 28–29, 51, 55

Li Ruojian, 396

Li Shinong, 113, 305

literature, 170–71, 256, 257, 266, 493

Liufu Commune, 274

Liu Jianxun, 86

Liu Jiemei, 162

Liu Lantao, 58, 387

Liu Mingbang, 44, 52, 55

Liu Shaoqi, 15–16, 19, 58–61, 88–91, 94, 96, 98, 99, 104, 156–57, 164, 175, 177, 189, 249, 250, 261–63, 314, 318, 331, 362, 364, 368–73, 379, 384, 385, 434, 436, 441, 452, 461, 491; Five Winds, 261–63; Four Clean-Ups campaign, 513–18; Lushan Conference, 368–70; –Mao rift, 499–518; Seven Thousand Cadres Conference, 499–505; Tenth Plenum of the Eighth CCP Central Committee, 507–12

Liu Wencai, 30–31

Liu Xiushan, 113, 305

Liu Zongtang, 243; *Discourse on Feudalism*, 484

livestock, 20, 79, 81, 119–22, 141, 145, 146, 152, 160–61, 167, 177, 180, 252, 287–88, 432, 439–40; die-off of, 209–10, 241, 252, 392; slaughtered, 475. *See also specific animals*

Li Wenyao, 45–46

Li Xiannian, 56, 61, 90, 97, 98, 215, 336, 338, 342, 420, 450

Li Xuefeng, 51

Li Zhenggao, 10

Li Zhenhai, 57

Long March, 61, 119, 137–38, 200, 370

Longxi County, 114, 121, 130

Longyang Commune, 142, 143, 149

Longzhong, 122–23

looting, 473–78

Lou Benyao, 163, 164

lower-middle peasants, 157

Lu County, 218, 474–75

Lu Dingyi, 164, 165, 352

Luoding, 16

Luo Longji, 463–64

Luo Ronghuan, 98

Luo Ruiqing, 354, 381, 503

Luoshan County, 38–39

Luoyang, 23

Lushan Conference, 25, 26, 80, 114, 120, 150, 172, 181–84, 187, 204, 208–209, 233–34, 264, 266, 268, 291, 337, 350–93, 431, 477, 496, 503; campaign against right deviation, 389–93; Chen Boda and, 378–79; He Long and other military officers, 380–83; Hu Qiaomu and, 379–80; Lin Biao and, 375–77; Liu Shaoqi and, 368–70; Peng Duhai and, 355–88, 508; standing committee meeting, 384–85; Three Red Banners, 351–54, 370, 377, 388–91; Zhou Enlai and, 370–73; Zhu De and, 373–75

Lushan County, 216, 219

Lu Xianwen, 26–29, 35, 44, 55, 56, 58, 62, 65–68, 82, 85, 163; "The History, Social Origins and Lessons of the Xinyang Incident," 67–68

Lu Xuebin, 294–95

Macheng County, 333

Majia Commune, 242–43

Ma Longshan, 24, 25, 53, 55, 57, 62–65, 85

manure, 72, 241

Mao Zedong, 8, 10, 13, 17–22, 49, 54, 58, 65, 66, 69, 73–74, 80, 81, 86, 88, 138, 145, 152, 165, 233, 247, 263, 265, 269, 457, 483–98; Anhui Province and, 269, 287, 294, 304–19; cadres and, 397–99, 436–49, 445–47; as "Chairman," 355; Chengdu Conference, 98–104, 197–99, 204, 326; collectivization and, 156–63; communal kitchens and, 174–96; cult of personality, 101–102, 369, 385, 389; extravagances and food eaten by, 460–63; fascination with people's communes, 170–73; Five Winds, 248–68, 305–10; food crisis, 320–49; Four Clean-Ups campaign, 513–18; high-yield myth and, 326–31, 496; influence of, 397–99; inner circle, 351–54; –Khrushchev rivalry, 90, 94, 456, 510, 519–20; "Letter to Zhang Wentian," 386; Li Jingquan and, 204–209; –Liu Shaoqi rift, 499–518; Lushan Conference, 181–84, 209, 233, 291, 350–93; military and, 488–90; at Nanning Conference, 95–98; opposition to rash advance and 90–104, 366; Peng Dehuai's letter to, 355–88, 508; response to food crisis, 431–64; Second Session of the Eighth National Congress, 104–11; self-criticism, 437–38; Seven Thousand Cadres Conference, 499–505; systemic causes of Great Famine, 483–98; Tenth Plenum of the Eighth CCP Central Committee, 507–12, 519; Three Red Banners, 87–111; totalitarian ideological control, 492–94; writings of, 107, 108, 286, 386–90, 435–36, 445; Xinyang Incident investigation, 58–61 market economy, 22

Marx, Karl, 88, 102, 164, 249, 387; *The Communist Manifesto*, 249; *Das Kapital*, 107, 463

Marxist fundamentalism, 520–21

May Conference, 506

meat, 48, 280, 281, 304, 340, 450–51, 458–63; claim that Mao went without, 461–63. *See also* cannibalism; cattle; pigs; poultry

meat essence, man-made, 343

media, 11, 15, 18, 46, 70, 74–75, 87, 91, 94, 95, 97, 108–10, 134, 165–66, 176, 183, 199–200, 248–49, 266, 305–308, 325, 327, 435, 438, 465, 493. *See also* propaganda; *specific publications*

Mengjin Commune, 76

Mentai Commune, 273, 274

Mianyang County, 210, 213, 267

Mianzhu Commune, 203, 209

middle peasants, subclasses of, 157, 161

militarization of civilian life, 145, 149, 166, 167, 168–69, 177, 202, 249, 299, 481, 521

military, 17, 119, 137–38, 145, 149, 166–69, 177, 202, 249, 299, 372, 380–83, 456, 481, 482, 488–90

millet, 32, 76, 115

Min County, 114, 130, 132

Ming dynasty, 269, 374

monsoons, 123

mushrooms, 301

Nagasaki, 13, 16

Nanchang Uprising, 380

Nanning Conference, 72, 95–98, 497

Nanyang, 23, 24, 82, 84

National Day, 192, 370

National Food Conference (1953), 321

National People's Congress (NPC), 490–92; Eighth, 70, 87, 101, 104–11

National Program for Agricultural Development, 72

natural deaths, 44, 83, 407–10, 411

natural disasters, 452–56

New Village Movement, 170, 272

Nine Critiques, 520–21

Ningxia Province, 184, 400, 402, 403, 414

Ningxiang County, 177

nuclear weapons, 13, 16, 456–57

oil, 128, 136, 160, 240, 298, 342, 450, 462

"one-finger" formula, 54, 56, 210

"one piece of land to one piece of sky," 73

Pan, Yang, Wang Incident, 23, 24, 68–71, 112

Pan Fusheng, 68–71, 84–85

Paoma Commune, 251–52

Paoziyan Village, 259

peanuts, 5, 274, 332

peanut sprouts, 38

peas, 274

Peasant Daily, 134

penalties, food, 223–29

Peng Dehuai, 18, 79, 90, 98, 138, 182, 187, 233, 264, 266, 352–69, 461, 499; Lushan Conference and letter to Mao, 355–88, 508; reexamination of case against, 508, 511

Peng Zhen, 98, 340, 369, 384, 385, 435, 500, 501

people's communes, 7, 20–22, 87, 101, 145, 156–73, 366, 370, 398; Anhui Province, 269–319; Bo County, 295–304; communal kitchens, 174–96; death rate, 42–43; elimination of family unit, 174–77; exaggerated crop-yield claims, 25–37, 74–76, 86, 114, 115, 127, 146, 206, 257–58, 264, 270–71, 296, 306–308, 322–31, 337, 394; false reporting and private withholding, 28–37, 47, 58, 76–77, 86, 127, 134, 149, 207, 211, 227, 309, 322, 334–38, 393, 394; Fengyang, 270–86; Five Winds, 248–68, 305–10; food crisis, 320–49; food penalties, 223–29; as foundation of totalitarian system, 156–73; Gansu Province, 112–55; Henan Province, 23–86; household farming, 150, 167, 178–80, 188, 207–208, 229–30, 258, 286, 315–19, 337, 341,

398–99, 406, 432, 439–43, 507–10; launching of movement, 163–70; Mao's fascination with, 170–73; military, 145, 149, 167–69, 177, 202, 249, 299, 481, 521; official response to crisis, 431–64; population loss, by province, 394–430; power structure, 121–22, 167–70, 172–73; rationing system, 20, 168, 179–82, 187, 208, 248, 251, 252, 254, 287, 298–99, 321–22, 435, 451, 478, 479, 486; responsibility fields, 286, 314–19, 441–43, 508–10; riots and rebellions, 465–82; satellite, 73–77, 119, 199–200, 212, 263–64, 295–96, 306–307, 326–30, 496; Sichuan Province, 197–247; size, 167; social stability during Great Famine, 465–82; state purchasing monopoly, 19, 22, 69, 157, 161, 320–25, 394, 465, 486–87; systemic causes of Great Famine, 483–98; three-level ownership system, 121–22, 167; Three Red Banners, 87–111, 199–204; Tongwei Problem, 137–53; Wuwei, 286–95; Xinyang Incident, 23–68. *See also* communal kitchens; *specific communes*

People's Daily, 71–78, 91, 94, 95, 97, 108–10, 163, 165, 183, 188, 200, 246, 248, 250, 287, 304, 327, 329, 380, 442, 452, 493

People's Liberation Army (PLA), 119, 137–38, 200, 353, 356, 360, 361, 380, 488–90

People's Republic of China (PRC), establishment of, 17, 58, 87, 98, 266, 490–92

Pi County, 16, 198–200, 243, 244

pigs, 41, 48, 77, 79, 80, 120–22, 141, 192, 207, 208, 230, 240, 271, 306, 321, 330, 439–40, 450; die-off of, 209–10, 241, 252, 392

plow oxen, 240, 324, 392

poetry, 256–57, 291–92, 389, 483

Pohu Commune, 49, 57, 84

politics. *See* Chinese Communist Party (CCP); government and politics

Pol Pot, 521

population, 12–13, 184, 394–430; Anhui Province, 269–319; communal kitchens, 174–96; death rates, by province, 394–430; effect of Great Famine on each province, 411–14; Fengyang, 269–319; Five Winds, 248–68, 305–10; floating, 479–80; Gansu Province, 120, 128–32, 138–39; grain sales to rural areas, 323–24, 399, 402–405; Henan Province, 83–84; influence of Mao on cadres, 397–99; loss, by province, 394–430; official response to crisis, 431–64; per capita allocation of grain and, 399, 404–405; pyramid, 410–11; reasons for disparity in effects of Great Famine, 396–406; research by Chinese scholars, 419–30; research by population experts overseas, 416–19; Sichuan Province, 197–247; social stability during Great Famine, 465–82; systemic causes of Great Famine, 483–98; system of social control, 478–82; Tongwei Problem, 137–53; total loss during Great Famine, 406–11; unnatural deaths based on official figures, 415–16; urban labor sent back to countryside, 443–45. *See also* birth rates; *specific provinces and groups*; starvation deaths

post offices, 1, 49, 51, 128, 290–91

poultry, 20, 141, 177, 180, 203, 222–24, 252, 271, 287–88, 306, 321, 432, 439–40, 451

powdered roots, 343

precipitation anomaly percentages, 453–55

procurement quotas, 26–37, 76, 82, 113, 115, 126, 146, 306–309, 320–49, 393, 394, 398, 399–406, 447–49; Anhui Province, 270–71, 296, 306–309, 318, 401; food crisis, 320–49; Gansu Province, 113, 115, 126, 146–49; Henan Province, 26–37, 76, 82, 402; Sichuan Province, 227, 230–33, 402; Xinyang Incident, 26–37 propaganda, 74–75, 91, 108–10, 165, 180, 183, 199–200, 216–21, 254, 264–66, 325, 461, 481, 492–94, 520; Five Winds, 248–68, 305–10; high-yield myth, 326–30, 496. See also media

Propaganda Department, 91, 110, 165, 180, 183, 216, 254–55, 352, 362, 432

protein deprivation, 343–49

public order and security, 465–82, 510

Pujiang County, 259

pumpkins, 398

punishment, 21, 149, 159; Anhui Province, 269–319; collectivization withdrawals and upheavals, 159–62; for false reporting and private withholding, 28–37, 47, 58, 76–77, 134, 149, 207, 211, 227, 309, 322, 334–38, 393, 394; food crisis, 320–49; food penalties, 223–29; Gansu Province, 112–55; Sichuan Province, 197–247; Tongwei Problem, 137–53; Xinyang Incident, 23–68. See also beating deaths; executions; struggle and criticism sessions

P'u Yi, Emperor, 8

Qian Hanxuan, 290

Qian Qinghuai, 34

Qian Xuesen, 328–29, 337

Qiaogou Commune, 42

Qiao Peihua, The Xinyang Incident, 29–30

Qiezang Commune, 134, 135

Qiliying People's Commune, 166

Qing dynasty, 8, 54, 123

Qinghai Province, 16, 112, 184, 400, 402–405; population loss, 394, 413; rebellions, 470, 477

Qingshui County, 127, 130

Qingxia Commune, 259

Qin Shihuang, 105, 483–84, 492–94

radio, 266, 493

railways, 50, 202, 275; looting, 473–74, 478

rape, 196, 281, 284, 275

rapeseed, 242

rash advance, 90–104, 352, 434; opposition to, 90–104, 352, 366, 432

rationing system, 20, 168, 179–82, 187, 208, 248, 251–54, 287, 298–99, 321–22, 435, 451, 478, 479, 486

rats, 38

recreational construction, 460–61

rectification measures, 153, 204–209, 231–32, 281–84, 285, 350, 391, 431, 433, 439, 442, 445–47

Red Flag, 165–66, 329, 378, 379

Red Flag Canal, 125

refugees, 50, 57, 127, 227, 272, 287, 301, 473, 479–80, 495

relief aid, in Tongwei, 151–53

Renhe Commune, 42

reservoir projects, 72, 73, 119, 122–25, 285

responsibility fields, 286, 314, 315–19, 441–43, 508–10

revisionism, campaign against, 518–21

rice, 4, 5, 203–204, 223, 259, 273, 274, 435; double-cooked, 346; food crisis, 320–49; straw, 38, 347. See also grain

rich peasants, 42, 61, 64, 152, 157, 158, 282, 286, 439, 445, 446, 478, 490

right deviation, struggle against. See anti-rightism

riots and rebellions, 465–82; nipped in the bud, 481–82

Romance of the Kingdoms, The, 8, 377

Rong County, 16, 202, 227, 244

Rooster Mountain, 23, 24, 28, 29; Conference, 54–55

Ruan Dimin, 153

"ruffian movements," 265

salvation fields. See responsibility fields

Sanpisi Commune, 32, 42–43, 52–53

satellite communes, 34, 71, 73–77, 119, 199–200, 212, 263–64, 295–96, 306–307, 326–30, 496

satellites. See Sputniks

sciences, 254–55, 266, 331

scrap metal, 119

Second Five-Year Plan, 91–95, 108, 249

Second Zhengzhou Conference, 171–72, 205, 266

Sen, Amartya, 16

"seven guarantees" rationing system, 168

Seven Thousand Cadres Conference, 153, 314, 452, 499–505, 508, 510

Sha, Yang, Peng anti-party clique, 112

Shaanxi Province, 162, 400, 402–405; population loss, 396, 414

Shandong Province, 16, 112, 166, 184, 185, 216, 251, 311, 315, 325, 340, 378, 400, 401–405, 434, 446, 447, 459–60, 497; population loss, 394, 395, 399, 406, 412, 414, 415

Shangcai County, 62

Shangcheng County, 57, 77

Shanghai, 172, 184, 339, 342, 351, 400, 401, 403, 414, 444, 460, 507

Shanghai Conference, 353–54, 356, 393

Shangli Commune, 288

Shangqiu, 84

Shangxi Province, 144, 184, 185, 325, 340, 399, 401–405; population loss, 394, 396

Shaoshan, 193, 194, 195, 461

Shaowu County, 322

sheep, 79, 120, 121, 122

Shi Shaoju, 65–67

Shi Xiangsheng, 80

Shizhu County, 322

Shizi Commune, 451

Shou'an Commune, 259

Shouzhang County, 251

Shuangliu Commune, 44, 51, 225

Shucha Commune, 304–305

Shu Tong, 378, 433, 435, 459–60

Sichuan Daily, 200

Sichuan Province, 16, 155, 177–78, 181, 184, 197–247, 259, 322, 325, 335, 400, 402–405, 436, 451, 460, 495; birth rate, 244–47; campaign against right deviation, 233–40; cannibalism, 214; communal kitchens, 200, 202–203, 208–12, 217, 221, 222, 229, 237; countercurrent of relief in, 229–33; Eight Stipulations, 205; "epidemic," 216–21; food penalties, 223–29;

industry, 201–202; longest lasting famine in, 209–16; population loss, 394, 395, 397, 411, 415; procurement quotas, 227, 230–33; rebellions and looting, 471, 474–75, 478, 482; rectification measures, 204–209, 231–32; starvations deaths, 197–247, 394; Three Red Banners, 199–204

"Sixty Work Methods," 97

Snow, Edgar, 15

socialism, 9, 33, 34, 60, 158, 174, 248–50, 358, 359, 433; launching of people's commune movement, 163–73; retreat from communism to, 170–73

Socialist Education Movement, 22, 161–62, 232, 282, 319, 391–93, 443, 499, 512, 513, 516

social stability, 465–82, 494–95; integrated social structure, 494–95; looting, 473–76; public security, 476–82; reasons for lack of large-scale social turmoil, 476–82; riots and rebellions, 465–73

songs, 255, 269, 272, 280

Song Wenbin, 199, 200, 206

Song Zhihe, 36

sorghum, 76

Soviet Union, 16, 17, 88–90, 164, 363, 371, 456–58; blamed for Great Famine, 456–58; Chinese relations with, 89–90, 94, 164, 361–62, 372, 456–58, 509, 510, 519–20; communism, 89–90, 94, 164, 253, 361–62, 487, 519–20

soybeans, 32, 218, 273, 274, 462

Sputniks, 25, 74, 164, 199–200, 254–55, 295–96, 306–307, 326–32, 398

Stalin, Joseph, 88, 90, 102, 164, 363–64, 372, 379, 381, 387, 485, 510, 515, 519

starvation, fatal pathologies of, 347–49

starvation deaths, 5, 11, 12–17, 73, 106, 113, 172, 177, 449, 499, 510; Anhui Province, 269–319, 394; Bo County, 295–304; caloric intake, 345–47; communal kitchens, 174–96; concealed by government, 49–68, 290–91, 309–14, 398, 406–408; as "epidemic," 216–21;

starvation deaths (cont.)
Fengyang, 270–86; food crisis, 320–49; Gansu Province, 114, 115, 122, 126–55, 394; Henan Province, 23–68, 80–86, 394; natural disasters, 452–56; official response to crisis, 431–64; population loss, by province, 394–430; research by Chinese scholars, 419–30; research by population experts overseas, 416–19; Sichuan Province, 197–247, 394; stages of 347–49; Tongwei Problem, 137–53, 481; Wuwei, 286–95; Xinyang Incident, 23–68, 82, 84, 85, 445, 448, 450, 481

state purchasing monopoly, 19, 22, 69, 157, 161, 320–25, 394, 465, 486–87

steel production, 12, 20, 28, 78, 79, 82, 85, 89, 94, 108, 201–202, 254, 257, 258, 263, 275, 332, 352–53, 359, 366, 394, 398, 434, 452; backyard furnaces, 78; "big kiln steel-forging," 201

struggle and criticism sessions, 6, 8, 24–25, 34, 61, 71, 107, 147, 149, 158, 162, 282, 288, 330, 386, 478, 511

substitute foods. See food substitutes

sugar, 281

suicide, 32, 37, 38, 79, 82–83, 127, 148, 149, 161, 214, 220, 225–27, 239, 289, 290, 336, 382

Suiping County, 34–35, 39, 74, 75, 163–64, 327, 378

Sun, Chen, Liang anti-party clique, 112–13

Sun Diancai, 112–13

Sun Yatsen, 8, 183, 447

Su Zhenhua, 381

Suzhou, 458–59

sweet potatoes, 27, 45, 77, 189, 203, 204, 210, 230, 232, 262, 271–76, 318, 330, 332, 346, 398

Tanghe County, 82

Tangshan earthquake, 13, 16

Tan Zhenlin, 58, 71, 72, 81, 84, 104, 114, 150, 154, 164, 204, 313, 329, 331, 333, 340, 354, 360, 377; Lushan Conference, 377

Taolin Commune, 33, 37, 38, 45

Taoping Commune, 210, 221, 226

Tao River, 123, 124, 143

Tao Zhu, 56, 85, 86, 97, 100, 102, 329, 334

"taro scrubbing," 225–26

teahouses, 23, 197

temperature productivity (TSPt), 455–56

"ten guarantees" rationing system, 168

Tenth Plenum of the Eighth CCP Central Committee, 507–12, 519

theft, 473–78

Third Five-Year Plan, 89, 249

Three Red Banners, 9, 10, 23, 29, 54, 71, 87–111, 113, 171, 172, 197, 266, 351, 431, 432, 435, 445, 469, 481, 499–510, 518; in Sichuan Province 199–204; Lushan Conference, 351–54, 370, 377, 388–91

"three parts natural disaster and seven parts man-made disaster," 452, 453, 502. See also natural disasters

"three-year natural calamity," 452–54. See also natural disasters

three years of hardship, 11, 131, 461–62, 475. See also natural disasters

Tian Jiaying, 193, 207, 361, 364, 378, 379, 436, 503, 506

Tianjin, 339, 342, 399–402, 414, 497

Tianjin Guesthouse, 460–61

Tianqiao Commune, 290

Tianshui, 132

tiaozi, 243

Tibet, 359, 397, 466

Tiefosi Reservoir, 73

Tito, Josip Broz, 9, 357

tobacco, 273, 274, 276

Tongcheng County, 308

Tongwei County, 114, 128–31, 137–53, 187

Tongwei Problem, 16, 137–53, 481; relief effort, 151–53

totalitarian system, 3, 17–22, 156–73; administrative process, 17–22, 156–73; homogenization of Chinese society under, 18; party leadership, 487–88; people's communes as foundation of, 156–73; systemic causes of Great Famine, 483–98

tree bark, 37–39, 133–34, 147, 298, 346
Tsinghua University, 9–10
Tuqiao Commune, 288
"Twelve Agricultural Provisions," 436–37
Twenty-Three Provisions, 513, 515

United Kingdom, 94
United States, 89, 90, 94, 456, 520
universities, 9–10, 78–79, 119, 251
urban food ration, 339–42, 486
urban labor, sent to countryside, 443–45

vegetable supplements, 346
Verdict-Reversing Wind, 510, 511
"Views on the Appropriate
    Amalgamation of Small-Scale
    Agricultural Cooperatives into Large
    Collectives," 101, 159

Wang Binglin, 29, 53, 75–76
Wang Bingxiang, 150–51, 153
Wang Congwu, 59–60, 64, 313, 314
Wang Dafu, 46, 54, 55
Wang Feng, 196
Wang Guanmei, 513–15
Wang Guohua, 55
Wang Jiaxiang, 509
Wang Jifan, 192
Wang Meisong, 345–48
Wang Ming, 350, 380, 388
Wang Renzhong, 56, 63, 84, 85, 101, 107,
    433
Wang Tingdong, 68–71
Wang Weizhi, 394–95, 406, 416, 428–30
Wang Zhen, 108
Wanle, 177–78
Wanli, 3–5
Wannian, 177–78
Wan Shangjun, 9–10
Wanshu Zhang, 275
War of Resistance, 380
wasted food, 20, 188–91, 323, 332, 459
water conservancy projects, 71–73, 92,
    122–25, 146, 202, 306
"wave-gazing" faction, 103
Wen Dongxian, 192

Wenjiang County, 242, 244
Wen Minsheng, 86
Wen Yiduo, 10
wheat, 49, 72, 123, 160, 175, 202, 204, 223,
    274, 297, 301, 320–21, 330; exaggerated
    crop-yield claims, 74–76; powdered
    roots, 343. See also grain
"white flags," 70, 117, 118, 145, 259
wild herbs, 23, 27, 37, 38, 81, 177, 191, 210,
    224
Wind of Gloom, 510–11
woks, 298
women, 28–29, 51, 59, 65, 66, 141–44, 160,
    202, 281, 417; death rate, 42;
    gynecological disorders, 67, 81, 132,
    135, 136, 217, 220, 228, 275, 348, 409;
    rape, 196, 281, 284, 475; workers, 78,
    258, 275
Women's Federation, 66, 67, 133, 175, 479,
    481
work points, 441
World War II, 13, 16
Wuchang Conference, 355, 379, 434
Wudian Commune, 276–78, 280–84
Wuhan Conference, 102–103
Wu Lengxi, 98, 350, 364, 378, 380
Wuma Commune, 219, 295–96
Wuwei County, 114, 122, 132, 181,
    286–95, 473; crisis, 286–95
Wuxiu County, 251
Wuyi Commune, 223, 232
Wu Zhipu, 48, 55–58, 62, 66–69, 73–86,
    98, 164, 354, 378, 433, 436

Xiangnan Commune, 142
Xiangshan Commune, 287
Xianju County, 159–62
Xianju Incident, 159–60
Xiao County, 310, 313
Xiao Feng, 246
Xiaogang Commune, 189
Xiaogang Village, 286
Xiao Hua, 381, 382
Xiaoxihe Commune, 271–76, 280–83
Xiazhuang Commune, 47
Xichuan County, 82

Xi County, 34, 44–47, 51, 65
Xi Daolong, 114, 144–53
Xilou Conference, 505–507
Xincai County, 46, 53
Xinhua News Agency, 11, 15, 128, 142, 212, 243, 312, 334, 380, 493
Xinjiang Province, 184, 397, 400, 402–403, 414
Xinyang, 16, 23–68, 329
Xinyang Incident, 23–68, 445, 448, 450, 481; beating deaths, 29–37, 47–49; cannibalism, 41–46, 51; CCP Central Committee investigation, 57–61; death rate, 38–47, 53, 58, 59, 64, 445, 448, 450; death toll concealed, 49–68; government cover-up, 49–68; grain hoarding and false reporting on output, 28–37; grassroots cadres blamed for, 61–68, 84, 85; procurement quotas, 26–37; starvation deaths, 23–68, 82, 84, 85, 481
Xiping County, 51, 75, 76
Xipu, 199–200
Xishui, 8, 125, 332
Xi Zhongxun, 57, 124
Xu, Zhang counterrevolutionary clique, 115–20
Xuanwei County, 469
Xuchang, 24, 82, 84
Xu Da, 374
Xue Muqiao, 257–58
Xu Guohe, 115–20
Xushui Commune, 250, 262
Xushui County, 249–54, 330
Xu Xiaorui, 127
Xu Xilan, 25, 65
Xu Zirong, 63–64

Ya'an County, 216, 219, 243
Yahekou project, 72
Yang Jue, 68–71
Yang Shouji, 62, 65, 66
Yang Weiping, 47, 53–56, 67
Yang Xiushen, 3–7, 12
Yang Zhenning, 10
Yan Zhongru, 54

Yao Kuijia, 287, 288, 290–91, 293
Ye Fei, 103
Ye Jianying, 98, 138
Yellow River, 73, 82
Ye Zilong, 431, 497
Yibin County, 220, 221
Yingjing, 16
Yinjian Commune, 279, 283
Yinma Labor Farm, 136
Yintao Project, 122–25, 146, 154
Yongchang Commune, 122
Yongxing Commune, 218–19, 220
You'ai Commune, 200, 244
Youth League, 3–4, 7, 47, 69, 148, 152, 239, 249, 272, 286, 478, 479, 481
Yuanyang, 58–59
Yu County, 78
Yu Dehong, 26, 40, 46, 63
Yu Guangyuan, 255
Yu Keshu, 239
Yumen, 135–36
Yunnan Province, 162, 167, 184, 190, 322, 325, 400, 402–405, 473; population loss, 395, 413; rebellions, 467–73, 477–78
Yu Sang, 58
Yu Wenhai, 41
Yuzhong County, 179–80

Zeng Qingmei, 309–10
Zeng Xisheng, 291, 305–10, 314–19, 433
Zhang Dafa, On the Golden Bridge, 142–44
Zhang Fu (Smithy Zhang), 51–52
Zhang Fuhong, 24–25
Zhang Guotao, 350
Zhang Guozhong, 249
Zhang Jiayi, 234–36
Zhang Kaifan, 113, 183, 184, 290–95, 305
Zhang Lu, 175
Zhang Qingwu, 407
Zhang Shengzhi, 66–67
Zhang Shufan, 25–28, 43–46, 55–58, 63, 330
Zhangshuyi Commune, 127
Zhangtao Commune, 44

Zhang Tiangao, 251–52

Zhang Tixue, 11, 46

Zhang Wanshou, 115–20

Zhang Wentian, 356, 362–67, 373, 382, 386, 388, 511

Zhang Xiruo, 96

Zhang Yihe, 495

Zhang Zhongliang, 112–15, 118, 124–27, 148, 149, 153–55

Zhaopingtai project, 72

Zhao Yushu, 271, 278–79, 280

Zhao Ziyang, 333–34

Zhejiang Daily, 95

Zhejiang Province, 112, 158, 181, 184, 400, 401–404, 441; population loss, 394, 396, 413; Xianju Incident, 159–60

Zhengyang County, 53

Zhengzhou, 58, 73, 171, 251

Zhengzhou Conference, 121, 164, 171–72, 251, 334, 393, 433–35

Zhenning County, 254

Zhenyuan County, 115–20, 470

Zhongpu Commune, 64

Zhou Boping, 406

Zhou Enlai, 18, 59, 60, 76, 85, 90–111, 138, 164, 175, 193, 263, 291, 340–41, 352, 362, 364, 370–73, 384, 406, 436, 445, 457, 458, 461, 470, 500, 501, 505, 506, 509; "leap forward" phrase, 109–10; Lushan Conference, 370–73; opposition to rash advance, 90–104

Zhou Hui, 354, 360, 361, 381, 383–84

Zhou Lin, 340, 463

Zhou Xiaozhou, 103, 182, 193, 352, 354–61, 364, 367, 373, 381–88, 433, 461, 511

Zhou Yi, 216

Zhu De, 98, 114, 124, 362, 373–75, 384, 436, 460

Zhuping County, 255

Zhu Suiping, 35–36

Zhu Yuanzhang, Emperor, 269, 374

Zunyi, 16

Zuowei, 42